The Law of the Single Europe

The Law of the
Single European Market

Unpacking the Premises

Edited by

Catherine Barnard
Trinity College, Cambridge

and

Joanne Scott
Clare College, Cambridge

HART PUBLISHING
OXFORD AND PORTLAND, OREGON
2002

Hart Publishing
Oxford and Portland, Oregon

Published in North America (US and Canada) by
Hart Publishing
c/o International Specialized Book Services
5804 NE Hassalo Street
Portland, Oregon
97213-3644
USA

Distributed in Netherlands, Belgium and Luxembourg by
Intersentia, Churchillaan 108
B2900 Schoten
Antwerpen
Belgium

Hart Publishing is a specialist legal publisher based in Oxford, England. To order
further copies of this book or to request a list of other publications please write to:

Hart Publishing, Salters Boatyard, Folly Bridge, Abingdon Rd, Oxford, OX1 4LB
Telephone: +44(0)1865 245533 Fax: +44(0)1865 794882
email: mail@hartpub.co.uk
WEBSITE: http//:www.hartpub.co.uk

British Library Cataloguing in Publication Data
Data Available

✓ISBN 1–84113–271–3 (hardback)
1–84113–344–2 (paperback)

Typeset by J&L Composition Ltd, Filey, North Yorkshire
Printed and bound in Great Britain by
T J International, Padstow, Cornwall.

Preface

This edited collection explores the legal foundations of the single market project in Europe, and examines the legal concepts and constructs which underpin its operation. With a deadline of 31 December 1992, the single market project should have been a matter of historical rather than current interest. Yet, the four freedoms remain the uncontested heart of the European Community legal order—largely unscathed by the debates on flexibility. The four freedoms are also perhaps the most familiar area of EU law. These very reasons justify reconsideration of the underlying core concepts. These concepts have often been confused rather than clarified by the rapid evolution of the Court of Justice's case law. This confusion is significant not only in conceptual terms, but also in normative terms since the nature of the single market bargain is contested and unclear.

The concepts underpinning the functioning of the single market have important implications for the European legal order, in terms of the relationship between state and market, levels of governance, and judicial and political actors. They also have wider ramifications for the new Member States who see access to the four freedoms as a principal attraction of the EU, and for the World Trade Organization which is increasingly looking to the European Union when developing its own set of premises according to which global trade relations will be managed.

The approach adopted in this collections is a thematic one, with each theme being explored in the context of the different freedoms. The themes covered include discrimination, mutual recognition, market access, pre-emption and harmonization, enforcement, mandatory requirements, flexibility, subsidiarity and proportionality. Separate chapters explore the link between competition law and the single market, the rapidly evolving case law on capital, and the external dimension of the single market. A horizontal analysis of this sort will serve to exemplify the nature of the issues arising, and the sources of underlying confusion

The papers which form the basis of this collection were first presented at a conference in the Faculty of Law, University of Cambridge in April 2001. We are very grateful to all the participants at the seminar for their contribution. We are particularly grateful for the financial support offered by the British Academy and the Centre for European Legal Studies at Cambridge.

Table of Contents

List of Contributors

Albertina Albors-Llorens is a Fellow of Girton College and Lecturer in Law, University of Cambridge.

Kenneth Armstrong is Senior Lecturer in law at Queen Mary, University of London.

George A. Bermann is Beekman Professor of Law, Jean Monnet Professor of European Union Law, and Director, European Legal Studies Center, Columbia University School of Law.

Catherine Barnard is a University Senior Lecturer in law and Fellow of Trinity College, Cambridge University.

Nicholas Bernard is in Law at Queen's University, Belfast.

Paul Craig is Professor of English Law, St. John's College, Oxford.

Marise Cremona is Professor of European Commercial Law and Deputy Director of the Centre for Commercial Law Studies at Queen Mary, University of London.

Gráinne de Búrca is Professor of European Union Law at the European University Institute, Florence.

Simon Deakin is Robert Monks Professor of Corporate Governance University of Cambridge and a Fellow of Peterhouse.

Michael Dougan is a Fellow of Downing College and a Newton Trust Lecturer at the Faculty of Law, University of Cambridge.

Elspeth Guild is Professor of European Migration Law at the University of Nijmegen.

Steve Peers is a Reader in Law at the University of Essex.

Joanne Scott is Reader in European Law, and Fellow of Clare College, Cambridge University.

Stefaan Van den Bogaert is a Researcher at the European University Institute, Florence.

Stephen Weatherill is Jacques Delor Professor of European Community Law and Fellow of Somerville College, University of Oxford.

Table of Cases

EUROPEAN COURT OF HUMAN RIGHTS

WTO

NATIONAL

United States of America

Table of Legislation

EUROPEAN

Treaties

Decisions

Directives

Regulations

Notices

NATIONAL

Netherlands

United Kingdom

United States of America

1

The Evolution of the Single Market

PAUL CRAIG

THIS CHAPTER charts the evolution of the single market from the inception of the Community to the Nice Treaty. It is therefore necessarily concerned with a development across time, and that is the methodology employed. The periods covered are from the Rome Treaty to the Single European Act (SEA), from the SEA to the Treaty on European Union (TEU), and from the TEU to the present. There are two theses in the following analysis.

In descriptive terms, it will be argued that any accurate evaluation of the meaning, content and development of the single market must take account of four factors. These are the primary Treaty articles themselves, Community legislation, the ECJ's jurisprudence and action taken by the Community institutions. All four are of importance for an understanding of the single market, and, as will be seen, they interact in interesting and significant ways.

In normative terms, it will be argued that discussion of the internal market cannot be divorced from matters such as social policy, consumer policy, economic and monetary union, the environment, industrial policy and the like. It is clearly not possible to engage in detailed examination of these areas. They cannot however be excluded from an analysis of the single market since they are of integral importance to the nature of the single market programme.

FROM THE ROME TREATY TO THE SINGLE EUROPEAN ACT

The Rome Treaty: Foundations for a Common Market

The Rome Treaty laid the foundations for economic integration. This was the principal focus of the Treaty, and it was a conscious decision after the failures of the more ambitious attempts at European integration of the mid-1950s.[1]

---

[1] P Craig and G de Burca, *EU Law, Text, Cases and Materials*, 2nd ed (Oxford, Oxford University Press, 1998), Chap. 1.

The particular form of economic integration chosen was a common market. It was therefore more ambitious than other, lesser modes of integration.[2] In a pure free trade area (FTA) tariffs and quotas between the participating states are removed. Each of the states will therefore concentrate on producing those goods in relation to which it has a comparative economic advantage. The states will however retain their own national tariffs as against third countries. This necessarily creates tension, since imports into the FTA will be diverted via the state that has the lowest external tariff, which will thereby gain the advantage attendant upon this trade diversion. This difficulty is removed by a customs union (CU), since external tariffs to third countries are equalised. It will also be common for there to be rules prohibiting discrimination for the CU members in product markets.[3]

The basic distinguishing feature of a common market (CM) is that it will, in addition to the rules found in a customs union, also contain provisions for free movement of factors of production: labour, goods, capital, establishment and services. The economic rationale for this is straightforward. Free movement of factors of production facilitates the optimal allocation of resources in the CM. Unemployment in, for example, Southern Italy means that there is an excess of supply of labour over demand. If there is a labour shortage in, for example, Germany then the value of labour within the CM as a whole will be enhanced if labour is able to move freely from Italy to Germany. There are three other features of the common market as it exists in the EC that are worthy of note.

First, classic theories of economic integration tended to emphasize negative integration, the removal of barriers to trade in terms of tariffs, quotas and the like. It is clear that positive integration was also important even in the original EEC.[4] The paradigm of positive integration is harmonization of banking or corporate law in order to break down non-tariff barriers to trade. Secondly, classic theories of economic integration tended to concentrate on direct barriers to trade imposed by the state itself, as epitomised by tariffs. In addition, the EEC captured non-tariff barriers applied by the state that can prevent the creation of a level playing field, as exemplified by the prohibition on state aids. It reached further still in its focus on the actions of private parties. The EEC's competition policy was designed in part at least to prevent private parties re-creating barriers to trade along national lines, as in the case of cartels which seek to divide the Community market along national lines. Thirdly, it is recognised that while the free play of market forces may be the default position in a common market, there will be certain areas in which state regulation will persist. The reasons for this are varied and contentious. They will be touched on

---

[2] B. Balassa, *The Theory of Economic Integration* (Illinois, Irwin, 1961).

[3] A customs union may, but need not, lead to a net increase in overall economic welfare for the world at large, D Swann, *The Economics of Europe*, 9th ed. (London, Penguin, 2000), Chap. 4.

[4] This may also be so for some other economic groupings, J Pelkmans, *European Integration, Methods and Economic Analysis* (Essex, Longman, 1997), pp. 7–9.

further below.[5] Where such regulation is deemed to be desirable, the rules will often be devised and administered by the Community. The Common Agricultural Policy is the prime example.

The Rome Treaty laid the essential legal foundations for a common market. Articles 23–27[6] provided for a customs union. Customs duties and charges with equivalent effect as between the Member States were prohibited, and a common external tariff in relation to third countries was adopted. Free movement of factors of production were also secured in the original Rome Treaty. Articles 28–31[7] prohibited quantitative restrictions on the free movement of goods. Articles 39–42[8] dealt with free movement of workers, while Articles 43–55[9] provided for freedom of establishment and the provision of services. The Rome Treaty also provided for the passage of directives or regulations to flesh out the bare bones of these Treaty articles. Free movement of capital was dealt with rather differently. The Treaty Articles which now govern this area, Articles 56–60, were introduced by the Treaty on European Union (TEU). Prior to this the relevant articles of the Rome Treaty were a good deal less peremptory than those concerning goods, workers, establishment and services. The states were under an obligation to abolish progressively the restrictions on capital movements, but only to the extent necessary to ensure the proper functioning of the common market.[10] The centrality of capital movements to the macro-economic stability of the Member States' economies lay behind this softer approach. The Treaty articles on free movement were complemented by those dealing with matters such as competition[11] and state aids.[12]

These Treaty provisions laid the foundation for the common market, but they took the form of negative integration: they prohibited discrimination against foreign goods, workers etc. It is clear, as Pelkmans has stated, that negative integration by itself would still fall short of a true common market.[13] Positive integration to harmonize the laws of the Member States was needed in order to ensure a properly functioning common market. The Rome Treaty dealt with this in two ways. There were particular Treaty articles, such as Article 47,[14] which empowered the making of directives for the mutual recognition of qualifications, in order to facilitate freedom of establishment. There was also a general enabling provision in Article 94,[15] which allowed for the making of directives for

---

[5] See below, pp. 5–6.
[6] Previously, Arts. 9, 10, 12, 26, 27.
[7] Previously Arts. 20, 34, 36, 37.
[8] Previously Arts. 48–51.
[9] Previously Arts. 52, 54–61, 63–66.
[10] J Usher, *The Law of Money and Financial Services in the European Community* (Oxford, Oxford University Press, 1994), pp. 14–16.
[11] Arts. 81–82, previously 85–86.
[12] Arts. 87–89, previously 92–94.
[13] Pelkmans, above n. 4, p. 8.
[14] Previously Art. 57.
[15] Previously Art. 100.

the approximation of the laws of the Member States as directly affected the functioning of the common market. This required a unanimous vote in the Council.

Community Legislation: Reinforcing the Ideal of a Common Market

It was always clear that provisions concerning the common market in the Rome Treaty would need to be fleshed out by Community legislation. The general structure of the chapters dealing with free movement was the same. The relevant Treaty articles contained a basic prohibition on national rules which impeded free movement. This was qualified by exceptions on the grounds of public health, security and the like. The scope of application of the Treaty article might also be limited, as in the case of workers, by excluding employment in the public service. Provision was then made for Community legislation which would fill out the interstices of the Treaty articles. This could take the form of regulations or directives, designed to facilitate the attainment of the basic principles contained in the Treaty itself. The Commission lost little time in introducing these key legislative instruments.

They varied in nature. Some of these provisions were designed to lay down *general, substantive guidance as to the ambit and meaning of the basic Treaty articles*. Directive 70/50[16] concerning the free movement of goods provides a good example. It defined in Article 2 the types of discriminatory measures which would be caught by what is now Article 28 EC. In Article 3 it laid the foundation for the application of Article 28 to indistinctly applicable rules, a foundation which was to be built on in the *Cassis de Dijon* case.[17] The 1961 General Programmes for the abolition of restrictions on freedom of establishment[18] and services[19] served a similar function, specifying the types of national provisions which would be regarded as unlawful under the respective Treaty articles.

Other Community legislation established the *substantive rights* which flowed from the principal Treaty articles. Regulation 1612/68 stipulated the duties incumbent on the Member States, such as the prohibition of quotas for foreign nationals. It went further and laid down the rights which foreign workers and their families could enjoy in the host country.

Yet other pieces of Community legislation were of a more *procedural* nature, specifying the applicable administrative rules to govern free movement. Directive 68/360[20] served this function in relation to workers, setting out the

---

[16] [1970] OJ Sp. Ed., I, p. 17.
[17] Case 120/78, *Rewe-Zentrale AG v. Bundesmonopolverwaltung für Branntwein* [1979] ECR 649.
[18] OJ Sp. Ed., 2nd Series, IX, p. 7.
[19] OJ Sp. Ed., 2nd Series, IX, p. 3.
[20] [1968] OJ Sp. Ed., II, p. 485.

detailed rules on residence permits and the like. Directive 73/148 performed the analogous function for establishment and the provision of services.[21]

Legislation was also passed to *limit the discretion* possessed by the Member States. The fact that the free movement Treaty articles contained exceptions allowing Member States to derogate on the grounds of public policy, health, security etc made it especially important to set limits to the meaning of these broad phrases. This prevented Member States taking divergent interpretations of the exceptions and, at the same time, facilitated judicial control. This was the rationale for Directive 64/221.[22] The subject matter meant that there were limits as to how far it was possible to specify the meaning of terms such as public policy or public security. The Directive nonetheless established important points of substantive principle, such as the fact that criminal convictions could not in themselves constitute a reason for refusing entry, and that entry must be based on the personal conduct of the individual. It also enshrined procedural protections, for example, a right to challenge acts of the administration where this was available to a national of that state.

The important legislation discussed thus far was primarily concerned with negative integration. The objective was to flesh out the primary Treaty articles in order to remove barriers to free movement of workers, establishment and the provision of services. The Community also promulgated measures directed towards positive integration, aimed at harmonizing the laws of the Member States through the use of what is now Article 94. There were, however, difficulties with this legislative mechanism. In procedural terms, this Article requires unanimity. In substantive terms, the directives devised by the Commission in the 1970s and early 1980s normally demanded agreement between the states on a detailed measure which was often difficult to attain. The process of securing agreement between nine or twelve states on such provisions was slow and cumbersome. Thus a typical directive passed during this period would define with great specificity what was to be regulated, for example, the packaging and labelling of dangerous substances. There would then be an obligation on the Member State not to place such a substance on the market unless it was properly labelled. The directive would indicate the type of warning which had to be placed on the product, and the national authorities would be obliged to approve appropriate packaging which complied with the directive. The relationship between the procedural and the substantive difficulties is brought out clearly by Pelkmans.[23]

> In the 'old' approach approximation of national economic regulation usually boiled down to extremely detailed lawmaking at the Community level. Partly, this was caused by unanimity—a recalcitrant Member State could insist on any detail. Partly, it reflected a lack of trust among Member States. The degree of decentralization under

---

[21] [1973] OJ L172/14.
[22] [1963–4] OJ Sp. Ed., p. 117. This Dir. also provided guidance as to the meaning of the Treaty.
[23] Pelkmans, above n. 4, p. 38.

the Rome Treaty was still so great that approximation only of the objectives (so as to prevent market failure) would have required an enormous compliance machinery to verify implementation by the Member States. Thus, once the EC did regulate, it regulated all the details too, given insufficient monitoring and very slow and limited compliance machinery.

Technical developments meant, moreover, that the Commission was fighting a losing battle. As fast as it succeeded in securing the passage of a directive to cover one technical problem, so ten more would emerge on the horizon. This was the result of technical innovation combined with the emergence of new types of market, such as that generated by the revolutionary changes in telecommunications or computers.

It was the judicial contribution of the ECJ which radically altered the nature of both negative and positive integration.

The ECJ: Legislative Catalyst, Mutual Recognition and Purposive Interpretation

The doctrines of direct effect and supremacy enunciated by the ECJ were of general importance for Community law, and thus also for those provisions concerned with the single market. That can be taken as read. The discussion will focus on the more particular contributions made by the ECJ to the single market enterprise. In the period between the Rome Treaty and the SEA the ECJ made a number of vital contributions to the creation of a single market. The three most important will be considered here: legislative catalyst, mutual recognition and purposive interpretation of the Treaty articles and Community legislation. These will be considered in turn.

The role of the ECJ as *legislative catalyst*, and the importance of this for the single market, appear clearly in *Reyners*.[24] The ECJ was willing to accord direct effect to Article 43 on freedom of establishment, even though it had not yet been fleshed out by Community legislation in the manner envisaged by the Treaty. The absence of this legislation led a number of governments to argue that Article 43 was therefore not ripe for direct effect. They argued further that it was not for the 'court to exercise a discretionary power reserved to the legislative institutions of the Community and the Member States'.[25] The Court disagreed. It accorded primacy to the prohibition of discrimination within Article 43 itself. The further legislation was perceived as a way of effectuating this goal. The absence of the legislation could not, however, be allowed to impede 'one of the fundamental legal provisions of the Community'.[26] The obligation in Article 43

---

[24] Case 2/74, *Reyners* v. *Belgian State* [1974] ECR 631.
[25] *Ibid.*, para. 7.
[26] *Ibid.*, para. 24.

remained intact even though the directives had not been passed by the end of the transitional period. Indeed, such directives were said to be superfluous 'with regard to implementing the rule on nationality, since this is henceforth sanctioned by the Treaty itself with direct effect'.[27] The ECJ adopted the same approach in relation to services,[28] and the cases are significant for single market integration.[29] The relevant Community legislation had not been promulgated within the requisite period because of the unwillingness of the Member States within the Council to make the necessary compromises to allow it through. This was the period of legislative malaise or sclerosis in which getting things done in the Council operating under the shadow of the veto was especially problematic. The ECJ signalled that it was not willing to allow Article 43 to atrophy. The Court would develop the meaning of Article 43 itself through adjudication should the detailed legislation not be forthcoming. The decision therefore constitutes a prime example of the use of normative supranationalism to overcome the deficiencies of decisional supranationalism:[30] the Court would use the former via direct effect to overcome the deficiencies in the latter through the logjam in the legislative process. Yet it was equally apparent that legislation in these areas would be desirable, since it could give generalised, detailed guidance in a way which adjudication could not. The use made of the decision by the Commission in dealing with the Council will be considered in the following section.

In terms of judicial contribution to the single market pride of place must however go to *mutual recognition* as enunciated in *Cassis de Dijon*.[31] The ECJ held that Article 28 could apply to national rules which did not discriminate against imported products, but which inhibited trade nonetheless because they were different from the trade rules applicable in the country of origin. The presumption was that, once goods had been lawfully marketed in one Member State, they should be admitted into any other state without restriction. This was so unless the state of import could successfully invoke one of the mandatory requirements by way of defence: fiscal supervision, protection of public health, fairness of commercial transactions and the defence of the consumer. The *Cassis de Dijon* judgment therefore encapsulated a principle of mutual recognition: Member States must respect the trade rules of other states and not seek to impose their own rules on goods lawfully marketed in another Member State. There were however limits to this judicially created form of integration. The effect of *Cassis de Dijon* was essentially negative and deregulatory, serving to invalidate trade barriers which could not be justified under one of the mandatory requirements, but it did not ensure that any positive regulations would be

---

[27] *Ibid.*, para. 30.

[28] Case 33/74, *Van Binsbergen* v. *Bestuur van de Bedrijfsvereniging voor de Metaalnijverheid* [1974] ECR 1299.

[29] P Craig, 'Once Upon a Time in the West: Direct Effect and the Federalization of EEC Law' (1992) 12 *OJLS* 453 at 463–7.

[30] J Weiler, 'The Community System: the Dual Character of Supranationalism' (1981) 1 *YBEL* 267.

[31] Above n. 17.

put in place of the national measures which had been struck down. It was vitally important nonetheless. Many restrictions on inter-state trade were of the very kind adjudicated upon in *Cassis de Dijon* itself: differential rules applying as between states relating to the content, or packaging of the goods. The fact that the ECJ in *Cassis de Dijon* held that these rules could not, subject to the mandatory requirements, be used as against goods lawfully marketed in the state of origin, transformed the integration process. It had, as is well known, a profound effect on the Commission's regulatory strategy. This will be considered below. Before doing so we should however consider the other main contribution made by the ECJ to the process of single market integration.

There are numerous examples of the ECJ's *purposive interpretation* of the Treaty and legislation concerning the common market. A small sample can be given here. In the field of customs duties and charges a broad interpretation was accorded to the term 'charges having an equivalent effect',[32] while in the context of taxation the Court gave a similarly wide meaning to discrimination.[33] The same general approach is apparent in relation to the case law on free movement. The Court's jurisprudence evinces its determination to catch discriminatory state action, in whatever form, which impeded the free movement of goods;[34] and we have already seen the importance of the ECJ's contribution via the *Cassis de Dijon* judgment extending the application of Article 28 to indistinctly applicable national rules. In its case law on free movement of workers the ECJ imposed an autonomous meaning of the concept of worker,[35] gave a broad interpretation to that concept,[36] and limited the application of the public service exception in the face of fierce opposition from some Member States.[37] It interpreted the Community legislation based on Article 39 so as to ensure that the procedural requirements as to residence permits and the like did not undermine the right contained in the primary Treaty article.[38] It gave a broad reading to the substantive rights of a worker,[39] and made it clear that it would not tolerate discrimination between foreign workers and those in the host state.[40] The jurisprudence on freedom of establishment was similarly designed to ensure

---

[32] Case 24/68, *Commission v. Italy* [1969] ECR 193; Cases 2 and 3/69, *Social Fonds voor de Diamantarbeiders v. SA Ch. Brachfeld & Sons* [1969] ECR 211.
[33] Case 112/84, *Humblot v. Directeur des Services Fiscaux* [1985] ECR 1367; Case 168/78, *Commission v. France* [1980] ECR 347; Case 170/78, *Commission v. United Kingdom* [1983] ECR 2265.
[34] Case 207/83, *Commission v. United Kingdom* [1985] ECR 1201; Case 45/87, *Commission v. Ireland* [1988] ECR 4929.
[35] Case 75/63, *Hoekstra (nee Unger) v. Bestuur der Bedrijfsvereniging voor Detailhandel en Ambachten* [1964] ECR 177.
[36] Case 53/81, *Levin v. Staatssecretaris van Justitie* [1982] ECR 1035; Case 139/85, *Kempf v. Staatssecretaris van Justitie* [1986] ECR 1741.
[37] Case 149/79, *Commission v. Belgium* [1980] ECR 3881.
[38] Case 48/75, *Royer* [1976] ECR 497; Case 118/75, *Watson and Belmann* [1976] ECR 1185.
[39] Case 32/75, *Fiorini (nee) Cristini v. SNCF* [1975] ECR 1085; Case 63/76, *Inzirillo v. Caisse d'Allocations Familiales de l'Arrondissement de Lyon* [1976] ECR 2057.
[40] Case 65/81, *Reina v. Landscreditbank Baden-Wurttemberg* [1982] ECR 33.

that this key Treaty provision was not undermined by national protectionism. We have already considered the importance of *Reyners*. This was developed by cases which made it clear that national authorities could not simply refuse, without explanation, to allow nationals of another state to practice a trade or profession on the ground that their qualifications were not equivalent to the corresponding national qualification. To the contrary, the ECJ held that national authorities had a positive obligation to facilitate free movement, even where Community legislation providing for the recognition of qualifications had not been passed.[41] Freedom of establishment could moreover avail a national against her own state, at least where harmonizing legislation had been passed.[42] It should be added that the ECJ, not surprisingly, read the exceptions to free movement based on public policy, security, and health, narrowly.[43]

The Commission: Proactive and Reactive

The Commission throughout this period was both proactive and reactive. It was proactive in seeking to promote the passage of the regulations and directives which would breathe life into the bare bones of the Treaty articles. It was the engine room of the Community, and saw its role as the guardian of the Treaties, ensuring wherever possible that the obligations contained therein were fulfilled within the stipulated time. The Commission was also reactive, in the sense of responding to developments taking place both in the wider political forum, and in the ECJ, making the best of these opportunities to further the goals laid down in the Treaty.

We shall be considering the way in which the Commission reacted to the *Cassis de Dijon* decision in the following section. This reactive role of the Commission is also exemplified by the Communication[44] addressed to the Council in response the *Reyners* decision. The Commission began by drawing out the implications of the decision. Article 43 was directly applicable from the end of the transitional period, and hence restrictions on the freedom of establishment based on nationality were no longer maintainable.[45] This meant that the provisions of certain directives previously adopted by the Council, the object of which was to postpone the lifting of restrictions on certain activities, were

[41] Case 71/76, *Thieffry v. Conseil de l'Ordre des Avocats a la Cour de Paris* [1977] ECR 765; Case 222/86, *UNECTEF v. Heylens* [1987] ECR 4097.
[42] Case 115/78, *Knoors v. Secretary of State for Economic Affairs* [1979] ECR 399; Case 246/80, *Broekmeulen v. Huisarts Registratie Commissie* [1981] ECR 2311.
[43] Craig and de Burca, above n. 1, pp. 594–604, 786–800.
[44] *Commission Communication to the Council on the Consequences of the Judgment of the Court of Justice of June 21 1974, in Case 2/74 (Reyners and the Belgian State) on the Proposals for Directives Concerning the Right of Establishment and Freedom to provide Services at Present before the Council*, SEC (74) 4024 final.
[45] *Ibid.*, para. I.1.

without effect. These provisions could not derogate from the unconditional rule laid down in the Treaty Article itself.[46] This was equally true in relation to attempts to delay the implementation until measures designed to co-ordinate mutual recognition of diplomas were in place. These delaying tactics were invalid since they constituted a derogation from the unconditional rule in Article 43 itself.[47] Nor was it necessary to pass directives designed solely to abolish restrictions based on nationality since these had become superfluous in the light of the *Reyners* case.[48] The Council should, however, continue work on directives relating to Article 47[49] and the mutual recognition of diplomas, since these were not affected by the ECJ's judgment.[50] The Commission therefore reinforced the Court's ruling. The application of the principles in Article 43 could not be avoided, because of the inability or unwillingness of Member States to agree on the implementing provisions. If the Member States continued to be tardy then the Court itself, aided by Commission intervention, would fill out the more detailed meaning of the Treaty Article. The resulting norms might not be those which the states themselves would have agreed to had they enacted the legislation themselves. If the states delayed in promulgating these norms in order to ensure that they accorded with their own interests, they might find that they had little say in the rules developed by the Court, in circumstances where this legislation had not materialized from the Council. It would be mistaken to think that the decision in *Reyners*, and the Commission's Communication, suddenly led to a positive surge of legislative activity in this area. It did not. The Council did however pass a Resolution[51] acknowledging the importance of mutual recognition of diplomas and the like. It accepted that directives should resort as little as possible to the prescription of detailed training requirements, that lists of diplomas recognized as equivalent should be drawn up, and that advisory committees should be established. A number of harmonization directives were also passed covering particular economic sectors. In the absence of more general provisions the ECJ continued to develop its jurisprudence in this area, limiting the ability of Member States to refuse entry to the host state where the applicant possessed the relevant qualifications in her home state.[52]

---

[46] *Ibid.*, para. I.2.
[47] *Ibid.*, para. I.2–3.
[48] *Ibid.*, para. II.
[49] Previously Art. 57.
[50] Above n. 44, para. III.
[51] *Council Resolution on the Mutual Recognition of Diplomas, Certificates and Other Evidence of Formal Qualifications*, [1974] OJ C98/1.
[52] See above, ns. 41, 42, and Case 340/89, *Vlassopoulou v. Ministerium für Justiz, Budes-und Europaangelegenheiten Baden-Württemberg* [1991] ECR 2357.

FROM THE SINGLE EUROPEAN ACT TO THE TREATY ON EUROPEAN UNION

The Single European Act

The Passage of the Single European Act

The SEA was of major significance for the single market project. Some view it as an elite bargain, albeit one made with the Commission's influence.[53] Others stress inter-state bargains and employ the language of liberal intergovernmentalism.[54] Space precludes any detailed evaluation of these contending theories.[55] Suffice it to say that I share the general approach advanced by Amstrong and Bulmer who take a broad institutionalist view of this event in the evolution of the EU.[56] On this view, while the Member States were the key players within the European Council, it was the very existence of this body which 'provided an institutional opportunity for the European Commission to make an input into shaping the guidelines of integration'.[57]

It is necessary to say a little about the factual background that led to the passage of the SEA in order to understand its significance.[58] By the early 1980s much still remained to be done notwithstanding the efforts of the Commission and the Court. It was, moreover, this very sense that the Community was falling behind its agenda which generated a feeling of pessimism in the Community in the late 1970s and early 1980s. There seemed to be no ready way in which the Community would ever attain its goals, and the reality of single-market integration appeared to be as far away as ever.

This problem was not lost on the European Council, which, in the early 1980s, considered various techniques for expediting the passage of Community initiatives. The initial 'marker' for internal market reform was laid down at the European Council meeting in Luxembourg in 1981. The initiative received further impetus in 1983 with the creation of a specific Council of Internal Market Ministers, and with the 1983 Stuttgart Declaration which proposed ways of tackling the difficult policy issues. The reform momentum continued at the

[53] W Sandholtz and J Zysman, '1992: Recasting the European Bargain' (1989) 42 *World Politics* 95.
[54] A Moravcsik, 'Negotiating the Single European Act: National Interests and Conventional Statecraft in the European Community' (1991) 45 *International Organization* 19.
[55] For a general analysis of theories of integration, see, P Craig, 'The Nature of the Community: Integration, Democracy and Legitimacy' in P. Craig and G. de Burca (eds.), *The Evolution of EU Law* (Oxford, Oxford University Press, 1999), Chap. 1.
[56] K Armstrong and S Bulmer, *The Governance of the Single European Market* (Manchester, Manchester University Press, 1998), Chap. 1.
[57] *Ibid.*, pp. 18–19.
[58] Lord Cockfield, *The European Union: Creating the Single Market* (Chichester, Chancery Law Publishing, 1994); M Cowles, 'Setting the Agenda for a New Europe: the European Round Table and EC 1992' (1995) 33 *JCMS* 501; D Cameron, 'The 1992 Initiative: Causes and Consequences', in A. Sbagia (ed.), *Euro-politics: Institutions and Policymaking in the 'New' European Community* (Washington, Brookings Institute, 1992), pp. 23–74; Amstrong and Bulmer, above n. 56, pp. 17–22.

Fointainebleau Summit in 1984 where the Commission was asked to prepare a report on the internal market. It was at this meeting that the connection between reform of the internal market, and institutional reform became firmly embedded. Leading industrialists supported the idea of opening up the internal market, as did a number of leading Member States that favoured economic liberalisation. The Commission added its weight to the call for Treaty reform. Jacques Delors took office at the beginning of 1985, and the Commission under his Presidency was eager to find a major goal which would enhance the Community's development.[59] The consensus was to focus on the internal market. Barely a week after taking office Delors went to the European Parliament and announced the Commission's intention to pledge itself to complete the internal market by 1992. In March 1985 the European Council called on the Commission to draw up a detailed programme with a specific timetable for achieving a single market by 1992.

The Commission responded with a White Paper, *Completing the Internal Market*,[60] which was to provide the foundations for the passage of the SEA. The Commission's White Paper set out to establish the 'essential and logical consequences'[61] of accepting the commitment to a single market. The Commission noted that the Community had lost momentum 'partly through recession, partly through a lack of confidence and vision',[62] but it said that the mood had now changed, and that the Commission was ready to take up the challenge.[63] The White Paper focused on the removal of physical, technical and fiscal barriers to trade. The general thrust of the Commission's approach was to move away from the concept of harmonization towards that of mutual recognition and equivalence,[64] by building on the *Cassis de Dijon* jurisprudence. For the future, harmonization would in general only be used in relation to those trade barriers which survived scrutiny under the *Cassis de Dijon* test. This meant that many barriers to trade would fall because of the *Cassis de Dijon* doctrine of mutual recognition. It was only where they survived because the Member State advanced a plausible claim that the trade restriction was necessary on one of the mandatory grounds of public health, fiscal supervision etc, that the Commission would undertake harmonization in order to remove such problems.[65] The Commission's White Paper did not rest content with the enunciation of general strategies. The Annex to the Paper listed 279 legislative measures, together with a timetable for the promulgation of each measure. The object was to complete this legislative process by 31 December 1992. The momentum behind the

---

[59] H Schmitt von Sydow, 'Basic Strategies of the Commission's White Paper' in R Bieber, R Dehousse, J Pinder, J Weiler (eds.), *1992: One European Market?* (Baden-Baden, Nomos, 1988).
[60] COM(85)310, 14 June 1985.
[61] *Ibid.*, para. 3.
[62] *Ibid.*, para. 5.
[63] *Ibid.*, para. 7.
[64] *Ibid.*, para. 13.
[65] *Ibid.*, para. 65.

proposals gathered force with studies of the projected cost savings generated by the completion of the internal market.[66]

The European Council endorsed the White Paper at the Milan Summit in June 1985. Inter-governmental meetings which gave shape to the Single European Act followed. The SEA was signed on 17 February 1986 and entered into force after ratification by Member States on 1 July 1987. The Act contained new procedures designed to facilitate the passage of legislation for completion of the internal market. It should not, however, be thought that there was complete agreement between the major political players. There was not. The Commission pressed for more far-reaching changes than the Member States were willing to accept.

The SEA and Institutional Reform

The SEA introduced a number of changes to the Community's decision-making structure which affected the Council, the EP and the Commission.

In the Council unanimity was replaced by qualified-majority voting in relation to certain Treaty articles, including, in certain respects, those concerned with mutual recognition of diplomas, services, and capital movements.

The most significant institutional change was the creation of the co-operation procedure in Article 252,[67] which for the first time gave the EP a meaningful role in the legislative process.[68] The EP had long been pressing for an enhanced status, over and beyond the mere right to be consulted if and when the Treaty stipulated that this should be so. The attempts by the EP to secure for itself an equal role with the Council in the legislative process were studiously ignored, or sidelined, in the negotiations which led to the SEA. What did emerge in the form of the co-operation procedure was a good deal less than equal status. It did nonetheless transform the Community decision-making process. It made the EP a real player, all the more so given that the co-operation procedure was made applicable to Article 95, the main vehicle for internal market reform. It made it necessary for the Commission to be more astute in managing the enactment of legislation, and changed the overall institutional perception of the EP in the Council and the Commission.[69]

The SEA also formalised the practice of delegation subject to committee oversight. Prior to the SEA, the Council had, for some considerable time,[70]

---

[66] M Emerson, M Aujean, M Catinat, P Goybet, A Jacquemin, *The Economics of 1992, The E.C. Commission's Assessment of the Economic Effects of Completing the Internal Market* (Oxford, Oxford University Press, 1988); P Cecchini, *The European Challenge 1992, The Benefits of a Single Market* (Aldershot, Gower, 1988).

[67] Previously Art. 189c.

[68] See Craig and de Burca, above n. 1, pp. 132–34, for a description of this process.

[69] M Westlake, *The Commission and the Parliament: Partners and Rivals in the European Policy-Making Process* (London, Butterworths, 1994), pp. 37–8.

[70] C Bertram, 'Decision-Making in the EEC: The Management Committee Procedure' (1967–68) 5 *CMLRev*. 246.

conditioned the exercise of power delegated to the Commission on the approval of a committee composed of Member State representatives. The Council was unwilling to delegate power without some institutionalized checks to ensure that Member State interests were properly represented in the detail of the decision-making process. This was all the more so at a time when the Council was wary of the Commission's federalizing tendencies. There was no express warrant for this in the original Treaty. While the ECJ had upheld the constitutional validity of this form of delegation, it was felt that it should be placed on a firmer foundation. This was done through amendment of Article 202.[71] It thereby legitimated, in formal terms at least, what has become known as Comitology. The new approach to harmonization, discussed below,[72] fuelled the growth of committees designed to implement powers which had been conferred on the Commission.[73]

The SEA and Internal Market Reform

Two major legislative innovations were of prime importance for the single market project: Article 14[74] and Article 95.[75] *Article 14* states that:

1. The Community shall adopt measures with the aim of progressively establishing the internal market over a period expiring on 31 December 1992, in accordance with the provisions of this Article and of Articles 15, 26, 47(2), 49, 80, 93 and 95[76] and without prejudice to the other provisions of this Treaty.

2. The internal market shall comprise an area without internal frontiers in which the free movement of goods, persons, services and capital is ensured in accordance with the provisions of the Treaty.

3. The Council, acting by a qualified majority on a proposal from the Commission, shall determine the guidelines and conditions necessary to ensure balanced progress in all the sectors concerned.

The importance of Article 14 was reinforced by Article 3(1)(c). As modified by the Treaty on European Union, it provides that the activities of the Union shall include an internal market characterized by the abolition, as between the Member States, of obstacles to the free movement of goods, persons, services

---

[71] Previously Art. 145.

[72] See below, pp. 23–5.

[73] Dec. 87/373, [1987] OJ L 197/33, *Council Decision Laying Down Procedures for the Exercise of Implementing Powers Conferred on the Commission.* For general discussion, C Joerges and E Vos (eds.), *EU Committees: Social Regulation, Law and Politics* (Oxford, Hart Publishing, 1999); M Andenas and A Turk (eds.), *Delegated Legislation and the Role of Committees in the EC* (The Hague, Kluwer Law International, 2000).

[74] Previously Art. 7a. Prior to the passage of the TEU this was Art. 8a. What was Art. 7 stated that the common market should be progressively established during a transitional period of twelve years. This has been repealed by the Treaty of Amsterdam since it is now otiose.

[75] Previously Art. 100a.

[76] Previously Arts. 7c, 28, 57(2), 59, 84, 99 and 100a.

and capital. Under Article 14(1) the Community is obliged to attain the internal market by the specified date.[77] This obligation is imposed on the Community institutions as such, but the Member States have a duty pursuant to Article 10[78] to co-operate in the endeavour. Article 14(1) indicates the specific provisions of the Treaty which are to be used to achieve the internal market. These provisions were either introduced or amended by the SEA, but Article 14(1) makes it clear that this list is without prejudice to other provisions of the Treaty.[79] Article 14(2) gives a particular meaning to the internal market, which could be defined in a variety of ways.[80] The framers of the SEA chose a two-part formulation: it is to be an area without internal frontiers, in which free movement of goods, persons etc is ensured. The attainment of an area without internal frontiers can be judged by whether any border controls still exist on free movement. Such controls are essentially formal in nature. It is considerably more difficult to determine how freely goods, persons, and capital can move within the Community, even when border controls have been removed.[81] Although the legislative programme outlined in the White Paper has been largely realized, it would be mistaken to assume that attaining the internal market is a once-and-for-all, static objective. It would, as von Sydow, stated, be a tragic illusion to believe that the adoption of these measures would complete the internal market. They are rather the tip of an iceberg of Community action.[82]

The legal effect of Article 14 is an issue of some difficulty. It is clear from a working paper in the negotiations leading to the SEA that the Commission intended Article 14 to have direct effect. The Commission also proposed that if national rules on free movement were not removed by the agreed date, they would automatically be recognized as equivalent. These suggestions 'stunned the participants at the Intergovernmental Conference'.[83] They were too radical for the Member States, and the Commission was forced to modify its suggestions. This it did in an amended working paper submitted to the Conference.[84] The Member States were still concerned at the possibility that the Article could produce legal consequences. They therefore attached a Declaration to the Article which stated that the participants in the IGC expressed their 'firm political

---

[77] Derogations can however be granted to particular states pursuant to Art. 15, previously 7c. See C D Ehlermann, 'The Internal Market Following the Single European Act' (1987) 24 *CMLRev.* 361 at 374.

[78] Previously Art. 5.

[79] This is in part because there are other Treaty provisions, such as Art. 37 (previously 43), which may form the basis for measures designed to secure the internal market. It also serves to ensure that Member States can still make use of provisions such as Article 30 (previously 36), or the mandatory requirements of *Cassis de Dijon*, to justify rules which might hamper intra-Community trade, pending the passage of the requisite Community measures which will render such national rules otiose.

[80] K Armstrong, 'Governance and the Single European Market', *The Evolution of EU Law*, above n. 55, pp. 747–8.

[81] Wyatt and Dashwood's *European Union Law*, 4th ed. (London, Sweet & Maxwell, 2000), p. 502.

[82] Von Sydow, above n. 59, p. 92.

[83] Ehlermann, above n. 77, p. 371.

[84] *Ibid.*, pp. 371–2.

will' to complete the internal market, but that setting the date of December 31st 1992 did not create 'an automatic legal effect'. The possibility that Article 14 will have legal consequences cannot, however, be discounted. It is at the very least necessary to distinguish between the legal effect of the Article *vis-à-vis* the Community itself, and in relation to possible actions against the Member States via direct effect.

The possibility that Article 14 will have legal effects against the Community itself[85] is based in large part on its mandatory wording. The possibility of using Article 232[86] in the event of Commission or Council inaction would depend on whether the criteria for such an action were met.[87] It is necessary that the measures which it is claimed should have been enacted are defined with sufficient specificity for them to be identified individually, and adopted pursuant to Article 233.[88] This will not be so where the relevant institutions possess discretionary power, with consequential policy options, the content of which cannot be identified with precision. The application of this criterion to Article 14 depends, as Wyatt and Dashwood state,[89] upon the nature of the alleged failure to act. It would, for example, be difficult to maintain that the Article 232 criterion was met if the allegation was that the Commission had failed to promote measures designed to ensure the free movement of goods, persons, services, or capital. This is 'too general an objective, and its attainment too fraught with policy choices, to be the subject of proceedings under'[90] Article 232. There may, by way of contrast, be a greater possibility for such an action where the allegation was that the Council had failed to adopt a specific Commission proposal. Even in this instance much would depend upon the nature of the proposal. A damages claim will be even more difficult to prove.[91]

It may also be possible for Article 14 to have legal consequences for the Member States. This could mean that, even if the relevant Community measures had not been enacted, it would still be open to an individual to argue that Member States' rules which constituted a barrier to the completion of the internal market should not be applied if they were incompatible with Article 14 itself. It would have to be shown that Article 14 fulfils the conditions for direct effect, the most problematic of which is that there must be no further action required before the norm can have direct effect. The ECJ has been willing to accord direct effect to certain Treaty Articles, notwithstanding the fact that further action is clearly intended in order to flesh out the Article,[92] but it would,

---

[85] *Ibid.*, p. 372. See also H J Glaesner, 'The Single European Act: Attempt at an Appraisal' (1987) 10 *Fordham Intl. LJ* 446.

[86] Previously Art. 175.

[87] On Art. 232, see Craig & de Burca, above n. 1, pp. 490–494.

[88] Previously Art. 176. Case 13/83, *European Parliament* v. *Council* [1985] ECR 1583.

[89] Above n. 81, pp. 504–505.

[90] *Ibid.*, p. 505.

[91] Case T-113/96, *Edouard Dubois et Fils SA* v. *Council and Commission* [1998] ECR II-125.

[92] Craig, above n. 29.

nonetheless, be bold for the Court to hold that Article 14 is directly effective. This is especially so given that the Article does contemplate further Community action, and given also that, pending such action, national measures that are valid under, for example, *Cassis de Dijon*, will continue to be lawful. Moreover, even though the Declaration may not formally preclude direct effect, it does clearly signal Member State intent in this respect.[93] The recent jurisprudence, discussed below,[94] indicates that while the ECJ has not ruled out the direct effect of Article 14, it will nonetheless be reluctant to find such an effect. The question until now has been of the possibility of direct effect where relevant Community measures to implement the internal market have not been passed. Where, however, they have been promulgated, matters are different. The Community measure adopted might itself have direct effect, and so, too, might Article 14.

The other main innovation in the SEA was *Article 95*, which allowed the passage of harmonization measures by qualified majority, rather than unanimity. Article 95 has proven to be a valuable way to enact harmonizing provisions, and these have the added legitimacy of input from the European Parliament. The ECJ has read the Article broadly, but the *Tobacco* case[95] shows that there are limits in this regard. The broader implications of the case, and the reasoning used therein, will be examined below.[96] The main problem hitherto has been that of boundary disputes between Article 95 and other Treaty articles. Article 95 only operates 'save where otherwise provided in this Treaty'. This means that other, more specific Treaty provisions, such as Articles 37, 44, 47, or 71, should be used for measures designed to attain the internal market where they fall within the subject matter areas of those Articles. Boundary disputes will however normally only arise where a party has good reason to raise the point. In the past this has normally been the European Parliament, which had differing rights to participate in the legislative process, depending on the particular article in the Treaty which was the basis for the enactment. It therefore had a strong interest in ensuring that its legislative rights under Article 95 were not by-passed by the enactment of legislation on the basis of a different Treaty article giving it less extensive rights in the legislative process.[97] The general test propounded by the ECJ for the resolution of such boundary disputes was that regard should be had to the nature, aim, and content of the act in question.[98] Where these factors

---

[93] In Case C-378/97, *Criminal Proceedings against Wijsenbeek* [1999] ECR I-6207, para. 9 the ECJ referred to the Declaration attached to Art. 14 but did not comment on its legal effect. For a discussion of the effect of the declaration prior to this decision see, A Toth, 'The Legal Status of the Declarations Annexed to the Single European Act' (1986) 23 *CMLRev.* 803.

[94] See below, pp. 34–5.

[95] Case C-376/98, *Germany v. European Parliament and Council* [2000] ECR I-8419

[96] See below, pp. 33–4.

[97] See, e.g., Case 68/86, *United Kingdom v. Council* [1988] ECR 855; Case 11/88, *Commission v. Council* [1989] ECR 3799; Case C–151/91, *Commission v. Council* [1993] ECR I–939; Case C–187/93, *European Parliament v. Council* [1994] ECR I–2857.

[98] Case C–300/89, *Commission v. Council* [1991] ECR I–2867; Case C-426/93, *Germany v. Council* [1995] ECR I-3723; Case C-271/94, *European Parliament v. Council* [1996] 2 CMLR 481.

indicated that the measure was concerned with more than one area of the Treaty, then it might be necessary to satisfy the legal requirements of two Treaty articles.[99] The ECJ has, however, also made it clear that this will not be insisted upon where the relevant legal bases under the two articles prescribe procedures which are incompatible. Boundary disputes are less likely to occur after the Treaty of Amsterdam since the legislative procedure applicable for most Treaty articles, including Article 95, is co-decision.

The remainder of Article 95 qualifies the powers given by Article 95(1). These qualifications differ in nature, and their presence in the Treaty was the result of the political negotiations which attended the passage of the SEA. Article 95(2) contains a straightforward exception to Article 95(1), by providing that the latter shall not apply to fiscal provisions, to those relating to the free movement of persons, or to those relating to the rights and interests of employed persons. These areas were felt by the Member States to be particularly sensitive, hence their exclusion from the ambit of Article 95(1). Legislation for these areas will therefore have to be passed either by using Article 94 or a more specific provision of the Treaty where one exists.[100] Article 95(3) instructs the Commission, when passing measures under Article 95(1) relating to health, safety, environmental protection, and consumer protection, to take as a base a high level of protection, taking into account in particular any new development based on scientific facts. Article 95(3) was included to placate countries such as Germany and Denmark, which were concerned that the harmonization measures might not be stringent enough. Member States were also allowed to adopt temporary measures in the event of a sudden and unforeseen danger to health, life, etc.[101]

It was however Article 95(4) which received most critical attention, and was one of the principal defects emphasized by those opposed to the SEA.[102] It allowed a Member State to retain a national provision, even after the passage of a harmonization measure. The state could do so where it deemed that this was necessary on grounds of major needs referred to in Article 30,[103] or relating to protection of the environment or the working environment. The national provision had to be notified to the Commission, which would verify that it was not discriminatory or a disguised restriction on trade. It should however be noted that the Member State concerns which can legitimately trigger Article 95(4) are finite: the matters covered by Article 30, plus the environment and working

[99] Case 165/87, *Commission v. Council* [1988] ECR 5545, [1990] 1 CMLR 457.
[100] For fiscal provisions, see Art. 93 (previously 99), which requires unanimity in the Council and consultation with the EP; for free movement of persons, see Art. 18(2) (previously Art. 8a(2)), which does now impose the Art. 251 procedure in this area, but stipulates that unanimity is none the less required by the Council when using this procedure; for the rights of employed persons, see Arts. 44 and 47 (previously Arts. 54 and 57).
[101] Art. 95(10), previously 100a(5).
[102] P Pescatore, 'Some Critical Remarks on the "Single European Act"' (1987) 24 *CMLRev.* 9.
[103] Previously Article 36.

environment. Other state concerns, such as consumer protection, which can jus-tify national measures under *Cassis de Dijon*[104] pending adequate harmoniza-tion measures, find no place in Article 95(4).[105] It is clear moreover that Article 95(4), being an exception which derogates from the Treaty, will be restrictively construed, and the Commission's powers of scrutiny have been increased by later Treaty amendments. In any event many of the more dramatic fears about the impact of Article 95(4) have not been borne out by state practice. Concerns that Member States would routinely seek to invoke the Article to prevent the application of harmonization measures have proven to be unfounded.[106]

The SEA and the development of Social and Cohesion Policy

Discussion of the SEA tends to concentrate almost exclusively on the provisions concerning reform of the internal market *stricto sensu*. This is too narrow a view. Armstrong and Bulmer are surely correct to point out that the 'SEM/SEA package deal covered a broad range of policy and institutional issues'.[107] The SEA should not therefore be seen as a free-standing, neo-liberal agenda. A num-ber of countervailing measures were introduced. Social policy was strengthened by the introduction of what was at the time Article 118A, designed to encour-age improvements in the health and safety of workers. The aim was to prevent increased competition resulting from the internal market leading to a decline in standards in the working environment.[108] The SEA also saw the introduction of the idea of social dialogue between employers and employees via what was Arti-cle 118B. The inclusion of the new title on economic and social cohesion was equally important. The principle of social and economic cohesion, aimed at reducing the disparities between the regions of the Community, was introduced by Article 158.[109] The Member States were to conduct their own policies so as to attain this end, and the Community's common policies were to be imple-mented taking account of social and economic cohesion. More direct support was to be forthcoming from the Structural Funds.[110] While there was no formal linkage between the single market programme and the broader social policies included in the SEA, it was nonetheless clear that 'some Member States saw the Treaty's cohesion commitments as intrinsic to the new economic bargain of the SEM/SEA'.[111]

---

[104] Above n. 17.
[105] It should not, however, be forgotten that Art. 95(4), by way of contrast to Art. 30 (formerly 36) and the *Cassis de Dijon* mandatory requirements, can be invoked by a state even though a harmonization measure has been passed.
[106] Wyatt and Dashwood, above n. 81, pp. 515–16.
[107] Armstrong and Bulmer, above n. 56, p. 29.
[108] *Ibid.*, p. 27.
[109] Previously Art. 130a.
[110] Art. 159, previously Art. 130b.
[111] Armstrong and Bulmer, above n. 56, p. 28.

Community Legislation: Implementing the Single Market Programme

It is well known that the period after the SEA saw intense legislative activity designed to 'complete' the internal market by 1992. The actual nature of the legislation enacted during this period is less well known. Space precludes any detailed analysis of the legislative output. Some idea as to what was actually being done between 1986 and 1992 is, however, essential for an understanding of the evolution of the single market.

The legislative activity during this period focused, not surprisingly on the removal of the physical, technical and fiscal barriers identified in the Commission's White Paper. Article 95 was the principal, although not the only, Treaty foundation used for the passage of legislation. Directives, as might be expected, were the main legislative instrument, although a number of initiatives were enshrined in regulations. The Commission employed diverse legislative strategies, substantive and procedural, general and particular, to attain its 1992 goal.

The paradigm *substantive* legislation took the form of a directive to approximate the laws of the Member States relating to health and safety and the like. We have seen that the effect of the *Cassis de Dijon* judgment was to foster market integration through the principle of mutual recognition. Goods lawfully marketed in one state could be sold freely in another state, but the latter could rely on the mandatory requirements or Article 30 to justify excluding the goods, in the absence of Community action on the matter. The Commission's response in the post-1986 period was to draft legislation to harmonize the laws of the Member States on health and safety and the like, thereby removing this obstacle to trade. This new approach to harmonization will be examined in detail below. Suffice it to say for the present that it was used in relation to numerous areas. The preference was for legislation which covered a reasonably wide range of subject matter, as exemplified by the directives on construction,[112] product safety,[113] medicinal products,[114] and machinery.[115] Not all directives aspired to this level of generality. A number were akin to the directive relating to the 'external projections forward of the cab's rear panel of motor vehicles of category N'.[116] There was also much substantive Community legislation during this period aimed at removing physical barriers to trade. Customs barriers themselves had of course been abolished long before 1986. There were, however, a

---

[112] Dir. 89/106, [1989] OJ L40/12, *Council Directive on the Approximation of Laws, Regulations and Administrative Provisions of the Member States Relating to Construction Products*.

[113] Dir. 92/59, [1992] OJ L228/24, *Council Directive on General Product Safety*.

[114] Dir. 92/25, [1992] OJ L113/1, *Council Directive on the Wholesale Distribution of Medicinal Products for Human Use*.

[115] Dir. 89/392, [1989] OJ L183/9, *Council Directive on the Approximation of the Laws of the Member States Relating to Machinery*.

[116] Dir. 92/114, [1992] OJ L409/17.

plethora of more particular matters concerning customs duties which were addressed after 1986.[117]

There was also a good deal of *procedurally-oriented* legislation passed to complete the internal market. The paradigm here was the imposition of the obligation to disclose information. This might be to ensure that consumers were in a better position to make a reasoned choice as between products, as exemplified by the directive on transparency of gas and electricity pricing.[118] It might be to aid traders, as in the case of the regulation specifying the information which national customs authorities should supply to traders about the Community customs rules.[119] The provision of information might also be integral to the attainment of a specific Community goal, as in the case of the directive on access to information on the environment.[120]

The third technique used in the post-1986 era was to extend *mutual recognition by legislation*. This was most apparent in the sphere of professional qualifications. Differing rules in the Member States on the qualifications required for the pursuit of a profession can clearly hinder free movement. Prior to 1986 the Community had tackled this problem by sectoral directives aimed at co-ordinating and harmonizing these rules. This was however a slow and difficult process. The approach changed with the passage of Directive 89/48,[121] which encapsulated the principle of mutual recognition. The essential thrust of the provision was that if a Community national wished to take up a regulated profession in any Member State, the competent authorities could not refuse permission on the ground that the qualifications were inadequate, provided that the person had satisfied certain conditions. These were the completion of a three-year higher education course in the Community, plus the necessary training to take up the regulated profession. There were exceptions to this scheme for circumstances where the ground covered in the course taken differed from that of the host state. While the approach of mutual recognition was not unproblematic,[122] it did nonetheless prevent a state from refusing to accept qualifications

---

[117] See, e.g., for one among many, Reg. 1854/89, [1989] OJ L186/1, *Council Regulation on the Entry in the Accounts and Terms of Payment of the Amounts of the Import Duties or Export Duties Resulting from a Customs Debt.*

[118] Dir. 90/377, [1990] OJ L185/16, *Council Directive concerning a Community Procedure to Improve the Transparency of Gas and Electricity Prices Charged to Industrial End-Users.*

[119] Reg. 1715/90, [1990] OJ L160/1, *Council Regulation on the Information provided by the Customs Authorities of the Member States concerning the Classification of Goods in the Customs Nomenclature.*

[120] Dir. 90/13, [1990] L158/56, *Council Directive on the Freedom of Access to Information on the Environment.*

[121] Dir. 89/48, [1989] OJ L19/16, *Council Directive on a General System for the Recognition of Higher-Education Diplomas awarded on Completion of Professional Education and Training of at least Three Years Duration*; Dir. 92/51, [1992] OJ L209/25, *Council Directive on a Second General System for the Recognition of Professional Education and Training to Supplement Directive 89/48/EEC.*

[122] J Pertek, 'Free Movement of Professionals and Recognition of Higher Education Diplomas' (1992) 12 *YBEL* 293.

obtained elsewhere in the Community. The Directive in effect borrowed from *Cassis de Dijon*, by enshrining mutual recognition in legislative form.

The Court: Reaping the Burdens of Success

There are two dominant strands in the case law on the internal market between the SEA and the TEU.

The law on free movement of goods saw the ECJ grapple with the 'burdens of success'. Legal history is replete with instances where legal doctrine created to tackle a particular problem has then developed in ways which the original creators may not have envisioned. Problems of over and under-inclusiveness are endemic to rules, and this is as true of judicially-created doctrine as it is of legislation. The success of mutual recognition as articulated in *Cassis de Dijon* led to the difficulty of deciding on the boundary lines of Article 28. Its application to indistinctly applicable rules was of real importance for the realization of the single market project. This very success led to an ever-increasing number of challenges to national regulatory norms. It was easier to create the *Cassis de Dijon* doctrine than to delimit its scope. Virtually all rules which concern trade, directly or indirectly, could be said to affect the free movement of goods in some way. To treat them as being within Article 28 would however require the defendant to find a mandatory justification. It could also place significant burdens on the national courts, which could be required to apply proportionality to balance variables that were not readily justiciable. The difficulties became readily apparent in the Sunday Trading cases[123] and in *Cinetheque*.[124] Academics struggled to find a meaningful criterion through which to define the application of Article 28, but opinions differed markedly as to what the test should be.[125] Concerns were also voiced that the protective function played by national regulatory rules would be outweighed by the desire to enhance a free market in which standards of consumer protection would be depressed.[126]

The second strand of the jurisprudence during this period saw the ECJ continue to build on the purposive interpretation it had developed prior to the SEA. The same themes are apparent, as exemplified by the case law on freedom of establishment. The ECJ expanded on its rulings in *Reyners*[127] and *Thieffry*.[128] It

---

[123] Case 145/88, *Torfaen BC v. B & Q plc* [1989] ECR 3581.

[124] Cases 60 and 61/84, *Cinetheque SA v. Federation Nationale des Cinemas Francais* [1985] ECR 2605.

[125] E White, 'In Search of the Limits to Article 30 of the EEC Treaty' (1989) 26 *CMLRev*. 235; K Mortelmans, 'Article 30 of the EEC Treaty and Legislation Relating to Market Circumstances: Time to Consider a New Definition' (1991) 28 *CMLRev*. 115; J Steiner, 'Drawing the Line: Uses and Abuses of Article 30 EEC' (1992) 29 *CMLRev*. 749.

[126] S Weatherill and P Beaumont, *EC Law*, 2nd. ed. (London, Penguin, 1995), p. 532.

[127] *Reyners*, above n. 24.

[128] *Thieffry*, above n. 41: national authorities had a positive obligation to facilitate free movement, even where Community legislation providing for the recognition of qualifications had not been passed.

used direct effect to foster the single market by breaking down barriers to free movement. National authorities could not refuse, without explanation, to allow nationals from another Member State to practise their profession on the ground that their qualifications were not equivalent to the corresponding national qualification. The national authorities had to make an objective assessment of the equivalence of the relevant regulations, and this was so even where there was no Community measure providing for equivalence.[129] The difficulties of securing agreement within the Community legislature would not, therefore, be allowed to hinder realization of fundamental Community goals. The ECJ's case law served moreover to lay the foundations for the Community legislature when it did act. The mutual recognition of qualifications laid down in Directive 89/48[130] generalises from the judicial doctrine and enshrines it in legislation.

The Commission and the New Approach to Harmonization

We have already touched on the new approach to harmonization in the preceding discussion. It must now be considered in more detail, since it was crucial to the Commission's post-1986 strategy.

The traditional approach to harmonization was problematic. The directives could be difficult to implement, because of their detail. They could be overregulatory: the result would be a Community-prescribed standard which might be over rigid. They could moreover be inflexible in the face of new technological developments. Pelkmans[131] has summarized the disadvantages of the traditional approach to harmonization. It was time-consuming, and generated excessive uniformity. It failed to develop links between harmonization and standardization, thereby leading to inconsistencies and wastage of time. The process was very slow relative to the increase in national regulation. The problems of certification and testing were often neglected. There were also difficulties with implementation by Member States, and Ministers lacked political interest in the subject.

The Commission recognized these shortcomings. Thus in its proposals to the Council and Parliament for a *New Approach to Technical Harmonization and Standards*,[132] the Commission acknowledged the advances which had been made through the directives which had been passed. However it also accepted that eighteen years' experience had shown the difficulties with such an approach, stemming from attempting to harmonize by means of detailed technical specification. The Commission admitted that the results of harmonization

---

[129] Case 222/86, *UNECTEF*, above n. 41; Case 340/89, *Vlassopoulou v. Ministerium fur Justiz, Budes- und Europaangelegenheiten Baden-Wurttemberg* [1991] ECR 2357.
[130] Dir. 89/48, above n. 121.
[131] J Pelkmans, 'The New Approach to Technical Harmonization and Standardization' (1987) 25 *JCMS* 249, 252–3.
[132] Bull. EC 1–1985.

had been negligible in certain industrial fields. The multiplicity of national technical regulations, and the speed of technological change, was too fast for there to be any realistic hope that the Community, acting through its existing harmonization techniques, could keep pace.

The new approach to harmonization was based on mutual recognition, as derived from *Cassis de Dijon*. A product lawfully manufactured in a Member State should be capable of being bought and sold in any other Member State. Mutual recognition should be the norm. No harmonization measures were required with respect to national measures which would be condemned under the *Cassis de Dijon* reasoning. These national rules would be invalid, unless they came within the mandatory requirements. This strategy was reinforced by Member States' obligation to provide information to the Commission before adopting technical standards.[133] The Commission could then require a delay of six months, in order that possible amendments could be considered, or a delay of one year if the Commission decided to press ahead with a harmonization directive on the issue.

Legislative harmonization was restricted to laying down essential health and safety standards, and European standardization was promoted. The formulation of technical specifications to meet safety etc requirements was delegated to private standardization organs. These technical specifications were not binding as such. The directives promulgated under the new approach to harmonization did however stipulate that governments were obliged to presume that the products manufactured in accordance with the European standards complied with the 'fundamental requirements' stipulated in the directive. Member States had, therefore, to accept goods which conformed to the standard. If they wished to argue that the standard was inadequate then they would have the burden of proof. The bodies principally responsible for standardization are the European Committee for Standardization (CEN), and the European Committee for Technical Standardization (CENELEC). A directive passed pursuant to the new approach laid down in general terms the health and safety requirements which the goods had to meet. The setting of standards was designed both to help manufacturers prove conformity to these essential requirements, and to allow inspection to test for conformity with them. Allowing a manufacturer to show that its goods complied with the essential safety requirements, even if they did not comply with the Community standard, provided flexibility.[134]

The advantages of the new approach to harmonization were considerable. Directives could be drafted more easily since they were less detailed. The excessive 'Euro-uniformity' of the traditional approach was avoided. Safety objectives were stipulated, but there was flexibility on the standards through which this compliance could be achieved. The need for unanimity in voting was

---

[133] Dir. 83/189, [1983] OJ L109/8, *Council Directive laying down a Procedure for the Provision of Information in the Field of Technical Standards and Regulations.*
[134] See, e.g., Dir. 89/392, above n. 115.

circumvented through Article 95. More Community directives could be made, and hence the gap between Community harmonization and the volume of national technical regulations could be reduced. This is not to say that the new approach was problem-free. The adequacy of the funding for standardization bodies, the sufficiency of the bodies able to undertake the certification process, and the representation of consumer interests, have all been causes for concern.[135] The Commission recognised the need for improvements in these areas.[136] Notwithstanding these difficulties the new approach to harmonization allowed progress to be made in this important area.

It would nonetheless be mistaken to assume that the new approach to harmonization was entirely uniform.[137] The Community might regulate the relevant field, albeit in a general way, and thereby pre-empt inconsistent national rules. Whether the harmonization measure was intended to preclude any national measures could itself be a contentious issue.[138] There could be partial regulation which left some issues for national law.[139] Other areas might not be subject to Community regulation at all, because of the difficulty of reaching agreement, or because of lack of time.

The general Community approach shifted towards minimum, rather than total harmonization. Total harmonization entailed exhaustive regulation of the given field, the corollary being the pre-emption of national action in that area. Minimum harmonization enabled Member States to maintain more stringent regulatory standards than those prescribed by Community standards, provided that these were compatible with the Treaty. The Community legislation would set a floor, and the Treaty a ceiling, with Member States being free to pursue their own policies within these boundaries.[140]

The Internal Market: Tensions and Concerns

It would be wrong to assume that the evolution of the internal market between 1986–1992 was unproblematic. A number of independent concerns were voiced. There is nonetheless an underlying connecting theme, which is unsurprising, but

[135] Pelkmans, n. 131 above, pp. 263–5; Armstrong and Bulmer, above n. 56, pp.157–63.
[136] *Commission Green Paper on the Development of Standardization: Action for Faster Technical Integration in Europe*, COM(90) 456 final; *The Broader Use of Standardization in Community Policy*, COM(95) 412 final.
[137] A McGee and S Weatherill, 'The Evolution of the Single Market—Harmonisation or Liberalisation' (1990) 53 MLR 578.
[138] Case 148/78, *Pubblico Ministero v. Ratti* [1979] ECR 1629.
[139] Case 88/79, *Ministère Public v. Grunert* [1980] ECR 1827; Cases C-54 and 74/94, *Criminal Proceedings against Cacchiarelli and Stanghellini* [1995] ECR I-391; Cases C-320, 328–329, 337–339/94, *RTI v. Ministero delle Poste e Telecomunicazione* [1996] ECR I-6471.
[140] S Weatherill, 'Beyond Preemption? Shared Competence and Constitutional Change in the European Community' in D. O' Keefe and P. Twomey (eds.), *Legal Issues of the Maastricht Treaty* (Chichester, Chancery Law Publishing, 1994), Chap. 2; M Dougan, 'Minimum Harmonization and the Internal Market' (2000) 37 CMLRev. 853, 855–6.

important. The transfer of an increasing range of responsibilities from state to Community has meant that many of the traditional debates about the appropriate direction of governmental action have surfaced within the Community. This can be exemplified through three of the concerns found in the literature.

The first was as to whether consumer interests were being sufficiently protected. Some national rules which impede trade are designed to protect consumers. This is recognized in the *Cassis de Dijon* list of mandatory requirements. It is acknowledged also in the Commission's acceptance of the need for harmonization in areas where Member States have legitimate health and safety interests. There were nonetheless worries as to whether the harmonization directives adequately balanced consumer and manufacturing interests. The fear was that business interests would be the dominant force in the standardization bodies, and that social policy would very much take a back seat.[141] These anxieties were addressed in part by the establishment in 1992 of ANEC, the European Association for the Co-ordination of Consumer Representation in Standardisation, a body which is independent of the European standards agencies themselves. There were nonetheless still problems concerning access of ANEC to the CEN technical board, and also to the Commission's own standing committee.[142] It should however be recognised that these concerns are also present when regulations about product safety and the like are made at national level. Tensions, which result from the imbalance in power between consumer and commercial interests, are not created by harmonization measures being passed at Community rather than national level. They are endemic in most Western-style market economies.

A second tension inherent in the single market project is the impact on the weaker economies, that could suffer in the increased competitiveness of more open markets. This point was expressed powerfully by Dehousse,[143] who argued that market integration had to be accompanied by improvements in social and economic cohesion if it was to be politically acceptable. While the SEA contained a commitment to this end it did not give the Community additional means. Fulfilment of the single market project could therefore generate macro-economic and social tensions between rich, poor, and middle-class economies within the Community. We should not however be surprised by this tension. It is present within nation states. A free enterprise, market-driven, national economic policy will not infrequently create regional problems within a particular country. There will be areas in which there is high unemployment, decline of traditional

---

[141] McGee and Weatherill, above n. 137, pp. 585, 595; N Reich, 'Protection of Diffuse Interests in the EEC and the Perspective of Progressively Establishing an Internal Market' (1988) 11 *Jnl. Cons. Policy* 395; J Pelkmans, 'A Grand Design by the Piece? An Appraisal of the Internal Market Strategy', in *1992: One European Market?*, above n. 59, p. 371.

[142] B Farquhar, 'Consumer Representation in Standardisation' (1995) 3 *Consumer Law Jnl.* 56; Armstrong and Bulmer, above n. 56, p. 165.

[143] R Dehousse, 'Completing the Internal Market: Institutional Constraints and Challenges', in *1992: One European Market?*, above n. 59, p. 336.

industries, and relative poverty. There will be calls for regional assistance. Small wonder that a vigorous policy of increased competitiveness throughout the Community will produce similar tensions, albeit on a larger scale.

The third concern relates to the nature of market freedom itself. The meaning of this phrase, the manner in which such freedom is to be attained, and the appropriate limits to free markets, are all matters on which there is considerable disagreement. These are key issues that have divided political parties at national level. The completion of the internal market threw this issue into sharp relief at the Community level. It went beyond the mere removal of technocratic obstacles to trade. It embraced, as Weiler noted,[144] 'a highly politicized choice of ethos, ideology and political culture: the culture of "the market"'. The removal of barriers to free movement was a means to maximize utility, premised on the assumption of formal equality of individuals, in which market efficiency was prized above other competing values.[145] We shall see how far this conception of the single market altered in the last decade of the old millennium.

FROM MAASTRICHT TO NICE VIA AMSTERDAM

The Treaty and the Expansion of Community Competence

This is not the place for any general exegesis on the changes brought about by the Maastricht, Amsterdam and Nice Treaties. It is the provisions concerning the internal market which are apposite here. The very specification of the provisions relevant for the internal market is not however self-evident. It is necessary, as argued at the outset, to recognise that the internal market will be affected not only by changes which pertain directly to, for example, free movement or harmonization, but also by Treaty modifications which qualify the free market foundations of that market.

In *institutional terms* the European Parliament increased its power through the introduction of the co-decision procedure in the Maastricht Treaty, Article 251. This procedure was modified in the Amsterdam Treaty, further strengthening the EP's power. Most community legislation is now made in this way, including harmonization provisions under Article 95. This Article has itself been modified. Whereas Article 95(4) had previously spoken of a state 'applying' national provisions on one of the specified grounds, it is now framed in terms of 'maintaining' such provisions. This implies that a state cannot invoke the Article to justify *new* national provisions that derogate from the harmonization measure, but can only use it to justify the *retention* of existing provisions.[146] The

---

[144] J Weiler, 'The Transformation of Europe' (1991) 100 *Yale LJ* 2403 at 2478.
[145] *Ibid.*, p. 2478.
[146] This view is further reinforced by Art. 95(5) which is framed in terms of the 'introduction' of national provisions based on new scientific evidence.

Member State concerns which can trigger Article 95(5) are also limited: there must be new scientific evidence relating to the environment etc, and there must be a problem which is specific to that state. The Commission's powers of scrutiny have been reinforced by Article 95(6). Prior to the Amsterdam Treaty, Article 100a(4) spoke in terms of the Commission 'confirming' the national provisions. Article 95(6) now speaks of the Commission 'approving or rejecting' them. This shift in emphasis has itself been reinforced by modifications to Article 95(4) made by the Amsterdam Treaty, requiring the state to explain the reasons for maintaining the national provisions.[147] The ECJ has, moreover, confirmed that it can judicially review the invocation of what is now Article 95(4).[148] The process under Article 95 should not, however, be thought of in overly adversarial terms. Articles 95(7) and (8), introduced by the Amsterdam Treaty, are designed to facilitate a negotiated solution to the problem which initially caused the state to invoke Article 95(4) or (5). In addition to the changes to co-decision and harmonization, there was of course the introduction of subsidiarity, which has had an impact on the volume and nature of rules designed to implement the single market.[149]

In *substantive* terms, the provisions on economic and monetary union were the main innovation in the Maastricht Treaty. An important, albeit contested, argument in favour of monetary union was based on the link between the single market and a single currency. This was captured vividly in the Commission's slogan of 'one market, one money'. While it is clearly possible to have a single market without a single currency it was argued that the single market would work better with a single currency than without. This was certainly the Commission's oft-repeated view.[150] A single currency would enable business to save on 'menu costs', in the sense of not having to maintain differential prices for each market, thereby facilitating marketing strategies for the entire Community. Consumers would be able to make direct price comparisons of the same or similar products in different countries. A single currency would, moreover, render it easier than hitherto to develop a single market in banking and financial services. The link between monetary union and the single market was reinforced by the argument that a single currency would protect against the costs associated with large exchange rate movements and competitive devaluation. Such changes in exchange rates can 'distort the single market by unpredictable shifts of advantage between countries unrelated to fundamentals'.[151] These currency fluctuations slow down economic growth by creating business uncertainty, which is not conducive to investment or rational planning.[152] The very existence of wide price differentials caused in part by different currencies, combined with

---

[147] Art. 95(5) contains a similar reasoning requirement.
[148] Case C–41/93, *France v. Commission* [1994] ECR I–1829.
[149] Armstrong and Bulmer, n. 56, above, pp. 292–96.
[150] See, e.g., *Commission's Work Programme for 1998.*
[151] C Johnson, *In with the Euro, Out with the Pound* (London, Penguin, 1996), p. 47.
[152] *The Impact of Currency Fluctuations on the Internal Market*, COM(95) 503 final.

exchange rate changes, serves to fuel attempts by Member States to prevent parallel imports and impede intra-Community trade.

EMU was however not the only area in which there was a link between substantive policies and the internal market. The Maastricht Treaty amended or introduced Community competence in other areas which had an affect on the internal market agenda *stricto sensu*. Thus the original Rome Treaty contained no general reference to consumer protection. The implication was, as Weatherill states, that 'the consumer was expected to be the passive beneficiary of the restructuring of European markets; integration through law was *itself* a form of consumer policy'.[153] It is nonetheless clear that consumer policy is intricately related to the internal market since it is concerned with the protection of societal values, even if this may be at the expense of market integration. While the ECJ's jurisprudence listed consumer protection as one of the mandatory requirements, it was the Maastricht Treaty that introduced a new head of Community competence for consumer policy, Article 153. Community power over social policy was also augmented by the Treaty changes in the 1990s. The development of social policy is far too complex to detail here. Suffice it to say that the original Rome Treaty contained relatively little on this important topic. The original provisions were themselves the result of a compromise between competing French and German visions. The outcome was Article 119, as it then was, which did have substance, and Articles 117 and 118, which were, in Barnard's words, textually broad, but legally shallow.[154] Labour law and social policy were generally perceived to 'lie at the very heart of national sovereignty'.[155] As the Community evolved there was increasing concern that 'the ambitious single market programme would not succeed unless it had the support of the Community citizens',[156] and that this meant increased involvement by the Community in social policy. The 1989 Community Social Charter was followed by the Social Chapter and the Social Policy Protocol attached to the Maastricht Treaty. The willingness of the Labour government to accept these provisions led to their reintegration into the main body of the Amsterdam Treaty, in what are now Articles 136–145. There was also a new title on Employment. The aims of Community social policy are eclectic.[157] They provide for protective measures to ensure that a race to the bottom does not occur after EMU. They help to foster a skilled, productive workforce, by providing the requisite safe working conditions, which can enhance efficiency.[158] The Community social dimension does moreover fit more broadly with the notion of citizenship. It is clear therefore

---

[153] S Weatherill, 'Consumer Policy', in *The Evolution of EU Law*, above n. 55, p. 692. Italics in the original.
[154] C Barnard, 'EC "Social" Policy', in *The Evolution of EU Law*, above n. 55, p. 481.
[155] *Ibid.*, p. 482.
[156] *Ibid.*, p. 483.
[157] *Ibid.*, pp. 506–508.
[158] S Deakin and F Wilkinson, 'Rights vs Efficiency? The Economic Case for Transnational Labour Standards' (1994) 23 *ILJ* 289.

that the evolution of Community social, and consumer policy cannot be ignored when considering the strategy for the internal market *stricto sensu*.

There is moreover a link between many of these areas of new or expanded Community competence, and harmonization. Minimum harmonization was institutionalized[159] in the Treaty provisions dealing with these areas.[160]

Community Legislation: Procedural and Substantive, Hard Law and Soft Law

That the single market project did not come magically to an end in 1992 is borne out by the plethora of legislation enacted thereafter concerning the single market. This is, as in the period between 1986–1992, part procedural and part substantive.

The most important procedural norms were concerned with the provision of information. The obligations on Member States to inform the Commission of proposed technical standards were consolidated and extended to services.[161] This was complemented by an obligation to provide information on national measures derogating from the principle of free movement of goods.[162] There was also, unsurprisingly, a large volume of substantive legislation.[163] Some was concerned with health and safety in relation to goods. Some related to public procurement. Yet other directives were concerned with the environment. Many of these directives contained minimum harmonization clauses.[164] Perhaps the most notable feature of the legislation enacted during this period was the increased emphasis on services. It is legislation relating to banking, investment services, insurance, securities markets, credit institutions and the like which comes increasingly to occupy the attention of the Community legislature. The rationale is not hard to find. It is made clear in the Commission reports

---

[159] Dougan, above n. 140, p. 855.

[160] The environment, Art. 176 in respect of measures adopted under Art. 175; consumer protection, Art. 153(5), in respect of measures adopted under Art. 153(3)(b) and (4); social policy, Art. 137(5), in respect of measures adopted under Art. 137(2) and (3).

[161] Dir. 98/34, [1998] OJ L204/37, *European Parliament and Council Directive Laying Down a Procedure for the Provision of Information in the Field of Technical Standards and Regulations*; Dir. 98/48, [1998] L217/18, extending this to services.

[162] Dec. 3052/95, [1995] OJ L321/1, *Decision of the European Parliament and Council Establishing a Procedure for the Exchange of Information on National Measures Derogating from the Principle of Free Movement of Goods within the Community*.

[163] See, e.g., Dec. 283/1999, [1999] OJ L34/1, *Decision of the European Parliament and of the Council Establishing a General Framework for Community Activities in Favour of Consumers*; Dir. 96/92, [1997] OJ L27/20, *Directive of the European Parliament and the Council Concerning Common Rules for the Internal Market in Electricity*; Reg. 1980/2000, [2000] OJ L237/1, *Regulaton of the European Parliament and of the Council on a Revised Eco-Label Award Scheme*; Dir. 1999/93, [2000] OJ L13/12, *Directive of the European Parliament and of the Council on a Community Framework for Electronic Signatures*; Dir. 2000/31, [2000] OJ L178/1, *Directive of the European Parliament and of the Council on Certain Legal Aspects of Information Society Services, in particular E-Commerce, in the Internal Market*.

[164] Dougan, above n. 140, pp. 855–56.

considered below, and is also manifestly apparent to avid readers of *Single Market News*.[165] In an increasingly service driven economy Community integration in these areas becomes all the more important. It is all the more important and all the more difficult. Many of the relevant national rules will be designed to ensure fiscal supervision, the stability of the banking sector, consumer protection and the like. Community harmonization may therefore be needed if the areas are to be opened up. Moreover, the inherent complexity of, for example, the banking sector, means that it will often be necessary to pass a series of directives over time which gradually increase the degree of integration in the area.

The other feature which becomes more apparent in this period is the increased resort to a balance of legislative and non-legislative measures in order to achieve a given outcome. Now, to be sure, we know that this is always the case to some extent at least. The admixture of formal and informal law is a common feature of any legal order. The difference in the late 1990s is that this feature is positively lauded in the Community, rather than seen as a cause for apology or criticism. Thus the Commission in its *2000 Review of the Internal Market Strategy* includes a neat check list of the legislative and non-legislative measures it intends to take in order to achieve its goals in each of the areas comprising the single market.[166] The same readiness to use the full range of policy instruments is apparent in the Nice European Council. In the implementation of the Social Agenda 'all existing Community instruments bar none must be used: the open method of co-ordination, legislation, the social dialogue, the Structural Funds, the support programmes, the integrated policy approach, analysis and research'.[167]

The ECJ: The Boundaries of Community Competence, and the Effective Exercise of Community Power within those Boundaries

The 1990s have seen a complex body of jurisprudence concerning the internal market. There is little doubt that this case law could be viewed in a variety of ways. It will be argued in this section that there are two dominant strands within this jurisprudence, the first of which is well known, the second of which much less so. The first sees the ECJ refining, and to some extent limiting, the boundaries of Community competence. The second sees the Court, in tandem with the Commission, showing increased concern for the effective exercise of Community power in the areas where it has been held to exist. It will be argued that the latter strand of case law, coupled with Commission action, is ultimately more important for the internal market project than the former.

---

[165] The Newsletter of the Internal Market DG. See, e.g., No. 24, December 2000; No. 25 March 2001.
[166] COM(2000) 257 final.
[167] Nice European Council, 7–9 December 2000, Annex 1, para. 28.

Let us begin nonetheless with the *case law in which the Court has refined and limited the scope of Community competence*. This has been manifest in a number of ways.

The *Keck* decision,[168] in which the ECJ redefined the scope of Article 28, is perhaps the best known example of this. We have already seen the problems caused by the uncertain scope of Article 28 post-*Cassis de Dijon*. The ECJ's response in *Keck* was to rule that selling arrangements did not come within Article 28. This was subject to the proviso that the relevant provisions applied to all affected traders within the national territory, and that they affected in the same manner, in law and fact, the marketing of domestic products and those from other Member States.[169] Where those conditions were fulfilled, selling rules did not by their nature prevent market access, any more than they impeded the access of domestic products. Such rules were therefore outside the scope of Article 28. These criteria have been applied in many subsequent cases.[170] Reaction to the *Keck* decision was not generally favourable. Commentators pointed to the difficulties of defining selling arrangements, and to the fact that restrictions relating to selling could also impede market access.[171] Space precludes discussion of this issue here.[172] What is more apposite for the present discussion is to reveal other instances where the ECJ has limited the scope of Community competence.

In this respect the *Tobacco* judgment is of particular importance.[173] The ECJ struck down a Directive[174] designed to harmonize the law relating to the advertising and sponsorship of tobacco products. The Directive had been passed pursuant to Articles 47, 55 and 95, but most of the argument focused on the applicability of Article 95 itself. The ECJ read Article 95 in the light of Articles

---

[168] Cases C-267 and 268/91, *Criminal Proceedings against Keck and Mithouard* [1993] ECR I-6097.

[169] *Ibid.*, para. 16.

[170] See, e.g., Cases C-69 and 258/93, *Punto Casa SpA v. Sindaco del Commune di Capena* [1994] ECR I-2355; Case C-292/92, *R. Hunermund v. Landesapothekerkammer Baden-Württemburg* [1993] ECR I–6787; Case C-387/93, *Banchero* [1996] 1 CMLR 829; Case C-379/92, *Peralta* [1994] ECR I-3453; Cases C-140–142/94, *Dip SpA v. Commune di Bassano del Grappa* [1995] ECR I-3257; Case 412/93, *Societe d'Importation Edouard Leclerc-Siplec v. TFI Publicite SA* [1995] ECR I-179. The ECJ may characterise certain rules which affect selling in some manner as part of the nature of the product itself, and hence within the ambit of Art. 28, Case C-368/95, *Vereinigte Familiapress Zeitungsverlags- und Vertriebs GmbH v. Heinrich Bauer Verlag* [1997] ECR I-3689.

[171] See, e.g., N Reich, 'The "November Revolution" of the European Court of Justice: *Keck, Meng* and *Audi* Revisited' (1994) 31 *CMLRev.* 459; D Chalmers, 'Repackaging the Internal Market—The Ramifications of the *Keck* Judgment' (1994) 19 *ELRev.* 385; L Gormley, 'Reasoning Renounced? The Remarkable Judgment in *Keck & Mithouard*' (1994) *Euro. Bus. L. Rev.* 63; S Weatherill, 'After *Keck*: Some Thoughts on how to Clarify the Clarification' (1996) 33 *CMLRev.* 885; Case 412/93, above n. 170, paras. 38–45, AG Jacobs. For more recent discussion, see, S Weatherill, 'Recent Case Law Concerning the Free Movement of Goods: Mapping the Frontiers of Market Deregulation' (1999) 36 *CMLRev.* 51; C Barnard, 'Fitting the Remaining Pieces into the Goods and Persons Jigsaw' (2001) 26 *ELRev.* 35.

[172] Craig and de Burca, above n. 1, pp. 617–627; Cases C-34–36/95, *Konsumentombudsmannen (KO) v. De Agostin: (Svenska) Forlag AB and TV-Shop; Sverige AB* [1997] ECR I-3843; Case C-405/98, *Konsumentombudsmannen (KO) v. Gourmet International Products AB (GIP)* [2001] I-1795.

[173] Case C-376/98, *Germany v. European Parliament and Council*, [2000] ECR I-8419.

[174] [1998] OJ L 213/9.

3(1)(c) and 14. It concluded that the measures referred to in Article 95 must be intended to improve the conditions for the establishment and functioning of the internal market. It did not, as argued by the Commission, Council and EP,[175] give any general power of market regulation. This would, said the ECJ, be contrary to the wording of Articles 3(1)(c) and 14, and it would be incompatible with the principle contained in Article 5, that the powers of the Community were limited to those specifically conferred on it.[176] The ECJ held that a measure adopted on the basis of Article 95 must genuinely have as its object the improvement of the conditions for the establishment and functioning of the internal market. If mere disparities between the relevant national rules, and the abstract risk of obstacles to the exercise of fundamental freedoms, or of distortions of competition, could justify the use of Article 95, then judicial review of compliance with the proper legal basis would be rendered 'nugatory'.[177] Any distortion of competition must, moreover, be appreciable. If this were not required then 'the powers of the Community legislature would be practically unlimited'.[178] This was because national laws often imposed different regulatory conditions on activities. These could impact indirectly on the conditions for competition as between undertakings. If the EC could rely on the smallest distortions of competition to justify using Article 95 then this would contradict the principle in Article 5, that the Community only has the powers specifically conferred on it.[179] It followed that the ECJ must therefore verify whether a measure enacted under Article 95 in fact pursued the objectives stated by the Community legislature,[180] and whether the distortion of competition, which the measure purported to eliminate, was appreciable.[181] When viewed in this way the Directive had not been validly made under Article 95.

The *Tobacco* case is important not only in and of itself, but also because of the conceptual and practical connection between the issue raised therein and that in *Keck*. It should be remembered that harmonization through Article 95 was meant to operate primarily where mutual recognition through *Cassis de Dijon*, as limited by *Keck*, could not do the job. Similar concerns pervade the judgments in both *Keck* and *Tobacco*. In both cases the ECJ made it clear that mere disparities between national rules were insufficient to bring either Article 28 or 95 into to play. In both there is an underlying concern as to the limits of the respective Articles. If Article 28 were to be construed too broadly then it would be excessively deregulatory, and destructive of Member State regulatory competence. The same theme is apparent in relation to Article 95. This Article must be limited, said the ECJ, since otherwise any difference in national

---

[175] Case C-376/98, above n. 173, para. 45.
[176] *Ibid.*, para. 83.
[177] *Ibid.*, para. 84.
[178] *Ibid.*, para. 107.
[179] *Ibid.*, para. 107.
[180] *Ibid.*, para. 85.
[181] *Ibid.*, para. 106.

regulations would be used to justify Community intervention, thereby giving the Community almost unbounded positive regulatory competence.

Evidence of the ECJ's desire to refine and limit Community competence is also to be found in other parts of its jurisprudence which are of particular relevance to the internal market project. The Court has, for example, been reluctant to accord direct effect to Article 14. In *Wijsenbeek*[182] the applicant claimed that a Dutch penalty for failure to produce a passport when entering the country was invalid, *inter alia*, for breach of Article 14. He argued that the Article had direct effect from the end of December 1992, with the consequence that the Member States no longer had competence in this field. It could not therefore impose border controls, at least in relation to internal frontiers. The ECJ rejected the argument. It held that in the absence of Community measures requiring Member States to abolish controls of persons at the internal frontiers, Article 14 could not have direct effect notwithstanding the expiry of the December 1992 deadline. Any such obligation presupposed harmonization of the laws of the Member States governing the crossing of the external borders, immigration, the grant of visas, and asylum.[183] A similar reluctance to find that Article 14 has direct effect is also apparent in *Echirolles Distribution*.[184] The applicant argued that Article 14(2) rendered illegal a French law imposing resale price maintenance on books. In an earlier case[185] the ECJ had found the French law to be compatible with the Treaty, but the applicant argued that this had been overtaken by the SEA and the introduction of Article 14. The ECJ disagreed. In a terse judgment it held that while the internal market was one of the objectives of the Treaty, it had to be read in conjunction with other Treaty provisions designed to implement those objectives. Since Articles 28, 30 and 81 had not been amended, the ECJ's interpretation of them in the earlier case could not be called in question.[186]

It would of course be wrong to present the entirety of the Court's case law as restrictive of Community competence. Maduro is surely correct to point out that the story is subtler.[187] It is one in which the Court has shifted the focus of its activism from the free movement of goods to the other freedoms, such as

---

[182]   Above n. 93.

[183]   *Ibid.*, para. 40. Moreover, even if Art. 14 were to be regarded as according Community nationals an unconditional right to move freely within the Community, Member States would still be able to impose passport controls at internal frontiers in order to be able to check whether a person was in fact a Community national, para. 43.

[184]   Case C-9/99, *Echirolles Distribution SA* v. *Association du Dauphine* [2000] ECR I-8207

[185]   Case 229/83, *Leclerc* v. *Au Ble Vert* [1985] ECR 1.

[186]   Case C-9/99, above n. 184, paras. 23–24.

[187]   M Maduro, *We the Court: The European Court of Justice and the European Economic Constitution* (Oxford, Hart Publishing, 1998), pp. 100–102; E Johnson and D O' Keefe, 'From Discrimination to Obstacles to Free Movement: Recent Developments Concerning the Free Movement of Workers 1989–1994' (1994) 31 *CMLRev.* 1313.

establishment, services[188] and persons.[189] The rationale for this shift is that market integration may be less developed in these other areas.

We should however now consider the other, neglected, aspect of the Court's jurisprudence during this period. This is concerned with *ensuring the effective exercise of Community power in the area in which the Community does have competence.* The saga of *Keck* and indeed *Tobacco* is one much beloved by lawyers. It appeals to their natural ability to dissect and analyse judgments in order to decide what are the criteria of Community competence and whether they withstand scrutiny. The issues raised by these cases are important. It is nonetheless easy to lose sight of the wood for the trees. The key issue in *Keck* is the effect of this judgment on the completion of the single market. To be sure we can all conjure up examples where rules relating to selling arrangements might impede market access. The judgment does however contain criteria enabling such rules to be caught, if they are discriminatory in law or fact. Such rules can moreover be characterised as part of the nature of the goods themselves and hence can be brought within Article 28. In any event, heresy though it might be thought to say so, the fact that some selling rules might escape the reach of Article 28 is of minor importance for the completion of the internal market.

It is certainly minor as compared with the effectiveness of Article 28 in those areas to which it does indubitably apply. This issue is barely touched on by lawyers at all.[190] The general assumption is that mutual recognition, the core of *Cassis de Dijon*, works just fine. We accept almost without question the self-executing nature of this proposition: producers of goods which cross borders will be able to rely on mutual recognition to avoid the imposition of national rules relating to product characteristics in the state of import. Matters are not so simple. The Commission produced no internal paper bemoaning the drastic consequences for the internal market of the *Keck* judgment. It did produce a paper testifying to the centrality of mutual recognition as the cornerstone of the internal market order. The Commission's paper on *Mutual Recognition*[191] begins by making clear the importance of mutual recognition for the single market. Mutual recognition is moreover regarded as an example of subsidiarity, in the sense that it avoids the need for the 'systematic creation of rules at Community level' thereby allowing for greater observance of 'local, regional and national traditions'.[192] The paper notes however that mutual recognition does not always operate effectively. A number of proposals are made to improve it in this regard.[193] There is to be increased monitoring of mutual recognition by the

---

[188] Case C-384/93, *Alpine Investments* [1995] ECR I-1141.

[189] Case C-415/93, *Bosman* [1995] ECR I-4921.

[190] See, however, K Mortelmans, 'The Common Market, the Internal Market, and the Single Market: What's in a Market?' (1998) 35 *CMLRev.* 101.

[191] Commission Communication to the European Parliament and the Council, *Mutual Recognition in the Context of the Follow-up to the Action Plan for the Single Market*, 16 June 1999.

[192] *Ibid.*, p. 4.

[193] *Ibid.*, pp. 7–12.

Commission itself. This is to be complemented by measures designed to improve awareness of mutual recognition by producers of goods and services. Member States, who have the primary responsibility for mutual recognition, should deal with requests concerning the application of the principle within a reasonable time. They must also include mutual recognition clauses in national legislation.

It is this latter obligation which provides the link between the Commission strategy and the input from the ECJ. The obligation to insert such clauses derives from the *Foie Gras* case.[194] The case was in many respects just like many others. The French imposed requirements as to the composition of *foie gras*. Why then should the Commission have used its scarce resources to prosecute France under Article 226, in relation to a product that was barely produced elsewhere? The answer is not hard to find. The Commission argued that the French Decree containing the requirements for *foie gras* must also contain a mutual recognition clause in the legislation itself, permitting preparations for *foie gras* which had been lawfully marketed in another Member State to be marketed in France. The ECJ accepted this argument.[195] Henceforth any state which imposes requirements as to product characteristics and the like must also include a mutual recognition clause in the enabling legal instrument.

This may not be the best known of recent cases on free movement, but it is nonetheless important for the effective exercise of Community power in those areas where it does have competence. The central problem with the efficacy of mutual recognition is that will be applied by a range of inspection and control bodies at national level. Their degree of awareness, and understanding, of Community law may vary greatly. The obligation to include mutual recognition clauses within the relevant national legal instrument is one way to alleviate this problem. National bodies will, other things being equal, be more likely to take cognisance of a principle that is expressly laid down in such legislation. The Commission paid testimony to the importance of this by stating that 'it is through such clauses that not only individuals, but also the competent national authorities and the heads of inspection and control bodies become aware of how mutual recognition has to be applied in a given area'.[196]

The Commission, the European Council and the Reconceptualization of the Internal Market

The single market project did not magically come to an end in December 1992. We have already seen the continuing flow of internal market legislation post-1992. This was matched by a number of reports that addressed various aspects

---

[194] Case C-184/96, *Commission v. France* [1998] ECR I-6197.
[195] *Ibid.*, para. 28.
[196] *Mutual Recognition*, above n. 191, p. 11.

of the Community regulatory process. These reports can be broadly divided into groups. In the first, the Commission focused on completion of the internal market in a relatively narrow economic sense. In the second group, the focus shifted. The concern for economic integration *per se* is still evident, but the internal market is consciously conceptualized in a broader, more holistic, manner. Consumer welfare, social policy, environmental policy and the like are all regarded as important facets of the internal market strategy.

There have been *many reports focusing on attainment of the internal market in the economic sense of the term*. In 1993 the Commission produced its strategic programme on *Making the Most of the Internal Market*,[197] in which it reviewed macro-issues such as the completion of the legal framework, and the management and development of the single market. In 1996 the Commission undertook a wide-ranging study on *The Impact and Effectiveness of the Single Market*.[198] The study measured the economic gains from the internal market, in terms of increase in GDP, lower inflation, higher employment etc. It also confirmed areas where further action was required, such as public procurement, tax harmonization, company law, and the transposition of directives. The Commission developed these themes in its *Single Market-Action Plan*,[199] in which it identified four principal strategic goals for the development of the single market. These were: making the rules more effective, dealing with market distortions, removing sectoral obstacles to market integration and delivering a single market for the benefit of all citizens. The Amsterdam European Council officially endorsed these goals in 1997. The 1997 *Action Plan* led to further reports which focused on specific aspects of free movement. In the context of free movement of goods and services attention was given to the principle of mutual recognition.[200] The Commission rightly regarded this as fundamental to the creation of the single market, and its report contained a number of recommendations designed to improve its operation in practice. There have been specific initiatives directed towards services. These have highlighted their importance in the Community economy as a whole, and have underlined the need to ensure that the single market functions effectively in this area.[201] Particular attention has been given to financial services.[202] Much work has been done in the context of free movement of people to improve the provisions on mutual

---

[197] COM(93) 632 final.

[198] COM(96) 520 final.

[199] Communication of the Commission to the European Council, *Action Plan for the Single Market*, SEC(97) 1 final.

[200] Communication from the Commission to the European Parliament and the Council, *Mutual Recognition in the Context of the follow-up to the Action Plan for the Single Market*, 16 June 1999.

[201] *An Internal Market Strategy for Services*, COM(2000) 888.

[202] Commission Communication, *Financial Services – Implementing the Framework for Financial Markets: Action Plan*, COM(1999) 232; *Institutional Arrangements for the Regulation and Supervision of the Financial Sector*, January 2000; *Financial Services Priorities and Progress, Third Report*, COM(2000) 692/2 final.

recognition of professional qualifications, and a new simplified directive has been adopted.[203] This directive was part of the more general Commission initiative designed to consolidate, codify and simplify EU legislation.[204]

A broader conception of the internal market is however also to be found in a number of the major papers emanating from the Commission and the European Council. The internal market is conceptualized in more holistic terms, to include not only economic integration, but also consumer safety, social rights, labour policy, and the environment. This shift did not occur at any single moment. It developed across time. Nonetheless certain important steps in this progression can be identified.

The *1997 Action Plan* is significant in this respect. The fourth strategic target was to deliver a single market for the benefit of all citizens. The Commission's introduction to the *Action Plan* consciously stressed that 'the single market was not simply an economic structure', but included basic standards of health and safety, equal opportunities and labour law measures.[205] This theme was carried over in the *1997 Action Plan* itself. The strategic target of delivering a single market for the benefit of all citizens was particularised through action directed towards, *inter alia*, the protection of social rights, consumer rights, health and the environment, and the right of residence.[206]

The Lisbon European Council constituted another important stage in the reconfiguration of the internal market agenda. The meeting, held in March 2000, focused on employment, economic reform and social cohesion. It set a 'new' strategic goal: the Union was to become 'the most competitive and dynamic knowledge-based economy in the world, capable of sustainable economic growth with more and better jobs and greater social cohesion'.[207] Completion of the internal market was to be one way of achieving this strategy.[208] The modernisation of the European social model through the building of an active welfare state was to be another. This was crucial to ensure that 'the emergence of this new economy does not compound the existing social problems of unemployment, social exclusion and poverty'.[209] This objective was further particularised in terms of better education, an active employment policy,

---

[203] *Professional Qualifications: Commission Welcomes Adoption of Simplification Directive*, 26 February 2001; Dir. 2001/19, [2001] OJ L206/1, *Directive of the European Parliament and of the Council on the General System of the Recognition of Professional Qualifications*.

[204] Commission Communication on *Simpler Legislation for the Internal Market (SLIM): A Pilot Programme*, COM(96) 204 final; *Commission Report on the SLIM Pilot Project*, COM(96) 559 final; Report from the Commission to the European Parliament and the Council, *Results of the Fourth Phase of SLIM*, COM(2000) 56 final; T Burns, 'Better Lawmaking? An Evaluation of Law-making in the European Community' in P Craig and C Harlow (eds.), *Lawmaking in the European Union* (The Hague, Kluwer Law International, 1998), Chap. 21.

[205] *Single Market Action Plan sets Agenda*, 18 June 1997, p. 2.

[206] *Action Plan*, above n. 199, pp. 9–11.

[207] Lisbon European Council, 23–24 March 2000, para. 5.

[208] *Ibid.*, paras. 5, 16–21.

[209] *Ibid.*, para. 24.

modernising social protection and promoting social inclusion.[210] These commitments were reiterated at the Feira European Council.[211] The same theme permeated the Nice European Council.[212] While it was mainly concerned with enlargement, the European Council also considered a 'New Impetus for an Economic and Social Europe'. It approved the European Social Agenda developed by the Commission, which was characterised by the 'indissoluble link between economic performance and social progress'.[213] This link had been forged by the Commission, and endorsed by the European Parliament.[214] A high level of social protection, coupled with services of general interest vital for social cohesion, constituted the common core of values for the Community: economic growth and social cohesion were seen as mutually reinforcing.[215] The Stockholm European Council echoed the same idea. There was 'full agreement that economic reform, employment and social policies were mutually reinforcing',[216] internal market policies should take due account of services of general interest,[217] and a 'dynamic Union should consist of active welfare states'.[218]

The principal Commission reports concerning the internal market in 2000 pick up and develop the ideas articulated by the European Council. Thus the *2000 Review of the Internal Market Strategy*[219] took the strategic remit of the Lisbon European Council as its starting point. The internal market should be made as effective as possible in economic terms, but it must also seek to foster job creation, social cohesion and safety. This is reflected in the detailed list of legislative and non-legislative initiatives appended to the report, many of which deal specifically with issues of consumer health and safety and the like.[220] The same stress on the interconnection between the economic and social aspects of the internal market is to be found in the later report on the *Functioning of Community Product and Capital Markets*.[221] In economic terms, a properly functioning internal market was seen as the key to prosperity for Community citizens. This meant breaking down barriers to trade where they existed, especially in the services sector. In social terms, the internal market was seen as the guarantee of specific rights to safe, high-quality products.[222] The Commission accepted the conclusions of the Internal Market Council of March 2000, that

---

[210] *Ibid.*, paras. 25–34.
[211] Feira European Council, 19–20 June 2000, paras. 19–39, 44–49.
[212] Nice European Council, 7–9 December 2000.
[213] *Ibid.*, para. 15.
[214] *Ibid.*, Annex 1, paras. 8–9.
[215] *Ibid.*, Annex 1, paras. 9, 11.
[216] Stockholm European Council, para. 2.
[217] *Ibid.*, para. 16.
[218] *Ibid.*, para. 25.
[219] COM(2000) 257 final.
[220] *Ibid.*, pp. 15–17.
[221] *Economic Reform: Report on the Functioning of Community Capital and Product Markets*, COM(2000) 881 final.
[222] *Ibid.*, pp. 3–4.

high levels of consumer protection and consumer confidence were needed for a well-functioning internal market.[223] It acknowledged also that environmental concerns required a 'reinforced, symbiotic integration of environmental policy and economic reforms inside the Internal Market'.[224] The updated Commission Communication on *Services of General Interest*[225] consciously drew on the conclusions of the Lisbon and Feira European Councils, and stressed the economic and social aspects of such services.

CONCLUSION

The single market has evolved since the inception of the Community and continues to do so. The Treaty articles, secondary Community legislation, the ECJ and CFI, and the Community institutions have all been important in this development. It is, moreover, readily apparent that they have interacted with each other. The Community institutions have drawn on judicial doctrine to shape legislative and administrative priorities. The judiciary has been cognisant of legislative and administrative difficulties with the single market, and has fashioned legal doctrine to alleviate these problems. Community legislation has fleshed out the bare bones of the Treaty articles, to make the single market a more concrete reality in specific areas, and the ECJ has read this legislation, and the enabling Treaty articles, in a purposive manner. Treaty amendments reflect changing perceptions as to the nature of the Community order, with increased attention being given to social concerns. These changes have been affected by, and continue to affect, deliberations in the European Council. A plethora of factors, the precise configuration of which can vary, will affect the implementation and application of Community legislation.[226]

The terms used to describe the subject reflect these contributions to its realisation. The language of the common market has a primarily economic focus, that of the single market has been principally used within political discourse, while the phrase internal market is that most commonly found within Community legislation and judicial decisions. The interpretation of these terms is moreover malleable. The inclusion of broader social, environmental and consumer concerns has been achieved by reconceptualizing the previously understood notion of the single/internal market. This should not surprise us, since the development of the single market is itself indicative of the changing nature of the Community order.

---

[223] *Ibid.*, p. 5.
[224] *Ibid.*, p. 5.
[225] *Services of General Interest in Europe*, COM(2000) 580 final. These are services that public authorities decide should be provided even though ordinary market forces may not do so, para. 14.
[226] M Smith, 'In Pursuit of Selective Liberalization: Single Market Competition and its Limits' (2001) 8 *JEPP* 519.

2

Pre-emption, Harmonisation and the Distribution of Competence to Regulate the Internal Market

STEPHEN WEATHERILL

INTRODUCTION

T HIS CHAPTER EXAMINES the impact exerted by Community law
on the competence of public authorities in the Member States to regulate
commercial activity which is carried out on their territory. This may typically cover the regulation both of commercial parties established on home territory that are active in the wider cross-border market and also of actors based
elsewhere that direct their commercial strategy at the market of the regulating
State. The chapter explains how the distribution of competence between public
authorities under EC law is powerfully driven by the objective of establishing a
single market. Integrative objectives cannot be achieved if EC law operates on an
assumption of regulatory autonomy enjoyed by all participating States. This
requires examination, first, against the background of the relevant provisions of
the EC Treaty, most prominently those dealing with free movement, and, secondly, in the context of secondary legislation which typically spells out more
fully, though not exhaustively, how the powers and responsibilities of State
authorities shall be distributed. It will be demonstrated that the dominant legislative preference is for a system of 'home State control', according to which harmonised rules of proper regulatory conduct are agreed at Community level but
enforced at national level and pursuant to which it is assumed that 'home States'
will subject firms based on their territory to the agreed Community rules while
'host States', in which target consumers of the firm are based, are excluded from
actively applying not only domestic rules, but even in some circumstances the
agreed Community rules. The host State's competence is pre-empted; the home
State is expected to perform the job of supervision. But in so far as a 'home State'
is asked to apply rules against its (corporate) citizens in favour of citizens of 'host
States' one may assume that the very basis of representative democracy will militate against effective enforcement. Incentives to cheat are plain, but how, then, is

the regulatory bargain underpinning the making of a market for Europe to be safeguarded?

A system has been skilfully created according to which the Community's extensive rule-making capacity is supported by implementation and enforcement mechanisms that depend not on a discrete Community bureaucracy but instead on the administrative and legal infrastructure already existing within the Member States. National bodies are supposed to become also *Community* bodies. The chapter argues that, notwithstanding the vitality of litigation employing EC law as a corrective against defaulting States, the risk of an enforcement deficit inherent in the division of competence between home States and host States is serious. This perception, that the pattern designed to manage and stabilise the internal market is built on constitutionally shaky foundations, leads to an insistence that an inquiry into the home State/ host State model must interrogate the dilemma of emerging transnational governance in Europe which assumes the *economic* viability of constructing a single market against a *political* background of multiple sources of legislative authority. And yet the conclusions drawn from examination of this remarkable experiment are optimistic. It is contended that the process represents a constructive re-shaping of political power within the European Union.

PRIMARY COMMUNITY LAW AND THE FUNCTIONS OF THE HOME
STATE AND THE HOST STATE.

Most of the case law arising under the Treaty provisions governing free movement of goods and services concerns situations in which a trader based in one State finds access to the market of another State impeded by public measures taken in that other State. This is the classic case in which conformity with the rules of the 'home State' is insufficient to allow penetration of the market of the 'host State' where the regulatory regime is different. It is the domain of *Cassis de Dijon*[1]. Infrequently cases have arisen in which the impediment is not to imports but instead to exports; where the 'home State' finds its rules under attack for their restrictive effect on the export strategy of traders wishing to reach a 'host State'. Comparable issues arise in such circumstances, although the Court is significantly less receptive to attacks against rules impeding exports than it is to challenge to impediments to imports[2]. However, this paper focuses on the paradigm case, that of a trader in State *x*, the home State, challenging restrictive rules in the market it wishes to enter, that of State *y*, the host State.

---

[1]   Case 120/78 *Rewe Zentrale* v *Bundesmonopolverwaltung fur Branntwein* [1979] ECR 649.
[2]   Case 15/79 *Groenveld* [1979] ECR 3409; cf Case C-384/93 *Alpine Investments* [1995] ECR I-1141.

The development of a qualified principle of home State control

The Court insists that home State supervision 'is not a principle laid down by the Treaty'[3]. Indeed, it is important to appreciate that neither a principle of absolute host State control nor one asserting absolute home State control is capable of securing the objectives of European economic integration as set out in the Treaty. A rule of absolute host State control, depriving traders of any right to operate in new markets without adapting themselves fully to local market conditions, would subvert the very notion of competitive market restructuring and the realisation of economies of scale. A rule of absolute home State control, stripping away any role for regulation of economic activities on their territories by public bodies in so far as the relevant commercial party is based in another Member State and acting in conformity with the rules applicable there, finds no support in the Treaty. Such a model of ferocious inter-State regulatory competition is opposed by the presence of provisions such as Articles 30 and 55 EC and is more generally inconsistent with the very existence in the Treaty of a power to harmonise divergent national laws, a process which is itself required to take into account interests other than simple market-opening[4]. The constitutional collision between home State and host State control needs to be managed in a more sophisticated manner than the selection of an absolute rule at either end of the spectrum. Consequently the framework idea of a split in competence between the home State and the host State has come to play a vigorous role in the shaping of the Treaty provisions governing free movement of goods and services. It has formed the basis for the European Court's bold jurisprudence which has converted the Treaty rules into a subtle, flexible and intrusive set of instruments for advancing market integration while seeking to take account of legitimate national interests in regulatory protection.

The bare bones of the relevant Treaty provisions provide no hint of this voyage of discovery. Article 28 EC provides gnomically for a prohibition against 'quantitative restrictions on imports and all measures having equivalent effect', but it has been radically re-cast by the Court into a formula for determining the remarkably *limited* circumstances in which a 'host State' is entitled to apply its rules in a way that will exclude imported goods (or, under the authority of Article 49 EC, services) from its market or make difficult their access to it. In *Cassis de Dijon*[5] the Court first articulated clearly how and why national regulatory autonomy would be subjected to the requirements of Community law in so far as the exercise of such autonomy damaged product market integration[6]. The

---

[3]   Case C-233/94 *Germany v Parliament and Council* [1997] ECR I-2405, para. 64.
[4]   See in particular Art 95(3); in different vein, Art 95(4) *et seq*; and more generally the Treaty's *Querschnittsklausel*, Articles 6, 152(1), 153(2).
[5]   Note 1 above.
[6]   The roots of *Cassis* lie in Case 8/74 *Dassonville* [1974] ECR 837 and Case 33/74 *Van Binsbergen* [1974] ECR 1299 but the language used in *Cassis* is novel and it deserves its iconic status.

blackcurrant liqueur, Cassis de Dijon, was made and freely available in France but could not be sold in Germany *not* because of any rule forbidding the availability to consumers of non-German products *but rather* simply because German mandatory specifications governing the product were different from, and stricter than, those prevailing in France. The problem was inter-State regulatory diversity; the effect was the exclusion of a French product from the German market. The Court, invited to interpret the meaning of Article 28 in such circumstances, provided an enduring formula according to which to assess whether Germany, as the host State, may prevent a product conforming to the rules of the home State, *in casu* France, from reaching its domestic market.

It began by insisting on the primacy of host State control in the absence of common Community rules. 'It is for the Member States to regulate all matters relating to the production and marketing of alcohol and alcoholic beverages on their own territory'. But this initial concession to the host State is deceptive. The Court proceeded to qualify this statement and to subject the permissible application of host State rules to a significant threshold requirement. It added that

> 'Obstacles to movement in the Community resulting from disparities between the national laws in question must be accepted in so far as those provisions may be recognised as being necessary in order to satisfy mandatory requirements'.

The host State is therefore permitted to apply its rules only on condition that they carry a sufficient justification in the public interest to prevail over the interest in the integration of markets. The Court added that these 'mandatory requirements', a most inelegant phrase better rendered as 'compelling interests' or simply as 'the public interest'[7], which may be advanced as counterweights to the interest in securing trade integration included 'in particular the effectiveness of fiscal supervision, the protection of public health, the fairness of commercial transactions and the defence of the consumer.' Moreover, in accordance with the principle that inter-State trade restrictions are treated as exceptional, the burden is on the regulating State to make that case in support of its rules. The core of the *Cassis* ruling therefore concludes by turning on its head the initial embrace of host State control. The Court stated that

> 'There is therefore no valid reason why, provided they have been lawfully produced and marketed in one of the Member States, alcoholic beverages should not be introduced into any other Member State; the sale of such products may not be subject to a legal prohibition on the marketing of beverages with an alcohol content lower than the limit set by the national rules'.

---

[7] On the question of mis-translation, S Weatherill and P Beaumont, *EU Law*, 3rd ed (London Penguin Books, 1999) p575, n35. For fuller inquiry into their nature, see Scott chapter 10 in this volume.

Home State control applies as a form of (judicially applied) non-absolute principle of mutual recognition. It prevails in the absence of a sufficiently compelling basis for host State control.

This approach to the distribution of competences between home and host States in the quest to construct an integrated market covering the territory of all the Member States of the Union does not go so far as to dictate that *either* one State *or* the other but never both shall be permitted to regulate a particular product or service sector. The space allowed to a host State to justify its rules means that it is at least possible that dual regulation will occur. But these circumstances are limited by the rules of the Treaty, boldly interpreted by the Court. Dual regulation will frequently be impermissible, as in *Cassis de Dijon* itself where there was no adequate reason demonstrated by Germany for subjecting a product that had already met French standards to its own different standards. The result should be the release of wider consumer choice and intensified competition as products and services originating in other Member States but previously suppressed on export markets by local measures of market regulation become more readily available. This shift from (national) public regulation to private autonomy in the market is central to expectations of properly-functioning common markets. It is a form of 'negative integration', in the sense that integration of markets is achieved by eliminating obstructive national rules without replacing them with European-level public regulation, but it is the rules of the *host* State that are targeted.

Since *Cassis de Dijon* the Court has refined its formula and amended some of the detailed language, but it has remained remarkably faithful to the core approach found in the judgment. In fact, the principal subsequent changes in the flow of the mainstream of free movement case law have not concerned the Court's ruling in *Cassis de Dijon* itself but rather later perversions of it. The *Keck* ruling[8] finally addressed the problem that even matters of purely local market regulation, lacking any connection with the quest to integrate markets, had been swept within the embrace of Article 28 and consequently had required justification, but *Keck* was not an assault on the essence of *Cassis de Dijon* but rather a retreat from its more enthusiastic though ill-advised extensions, among which the most striking was the Court's pair of *Sunday Trading* cases[9]. In fact, within the analytical framework favoured by this chapter, *Keck* could be read as an attempt by the Court to strip out from this area of the law instances where there is no need to pursue a host State/home State analytical framework because in fact the matter can be left for regulation by the host State without any damage being inflicted on trade in imports[10]. So whereas the question of

---

[8] Cases C-267 and C-268/91 [1993] ECR I-6097.

[9] Case 145/88 *Torfaen BC* v *B&Q plc* [1989] ECR 765, Case C-169/91 *Stoke-on-Trent and Norwich City Councils* v *B & Q plc* [1992] ECR I-6635.

[10] Cf Barnard and Deakin chapter 8 and De Burca chapter 7 in this volume; N Bernard, 'La libre circulation des marchandises, des personnes et des services dans le Traite CE sous l'angle de la competence', (1998) 34 *CDE* 11.

exactly what must be shown of a measure of trade regulation before the rule-maker falls under an obligation to justify it according to standards recognised by Community law has proved awkward in recent years, the (logically subsequent) question of the circumstances in which a (demonstrated) trade barrier may be treated as justified is still today addressed by the Court in a manner which reveals no material distinction from that elaborated over twenty years ago in *Cassis de Dijon*. And, *Keck* or no *Keck*, the type of fact pattern at stake in *Cassis de Dijon*, in which a product marketed lawfully in one Member State was excluded from the market of another by divergent local technical specifications, would still today fall for resolution in the same way—the regulator would have to justify its choices[11].

Assessing the deregulatory implications of the case law

The Court's case law is widely and correctly regarded as providing a strong emphasis in favour of deregulation within the Community, but it does not assert an unqualified suppression of host State control. The bulk of the case law in this area has served as helpful illustration of the operation of the principle of non-absolute mutual recognition, according to which the host State may demonstrate justification for the assertion of regulatory needs which are sufficient to prevail over less stringent home State rules even where this impedes cross-border trade in goods and services. Trade-restrictive regulatory diversity is not excluded; equally, depression to the lowest common denominator of regulatory protection among the Member States is not inevitable. The Court asserts that 'the fact that one Member State imposes less strict rules than another Member State does not mean that the latter's rules are disproportionate and hence incompatible with Community law'[12]. A regulating State may set tougher standards than its competitors provided they are underpinned by a justification recognised by Community law. In *Alpine Investments*[13], a relatively unusual case because the challenged rules were those of a home State accused of restricting export trade, the Court agreed that a desire to maintain the high reputation of the quality of the financial services in the Netherlands was a sufficient reason for the imposition of stricter standards than those applied to similar traders in other States such as the United Kingdom. In the field of goods a similar acknowledgement that States may legitimately differ in their assessment of risk may be identified in *Eyssen*[14]. The Dutch authorities were sufficiently anxious

---

[11] See eg classic *Cassis de Dijon* cases such as Case C-315/92 *Clinique* [1994] ECR I-317, Case C-470/93 *Mars* [1995] ECR I-1923, Case C-220/98 *Estee Lauder Cosmetics* [2000] ECR I-117.
[12] Eg Case C-3/95 *Reisebüro Broede* [1996] ECR I-6511.
[13] Case C-384/93 note 2 above.
[14] Case 53/80 [1981] ECR 409. Similarly, Case C-473/98 *Kemikalieinspektionen* v *Toolex Alpha AB* [2000] ECR I-5681.

about the danger to human health presented by the use of a particular type of preservative in cheese that they introduced a ban. Other less cautious Member States were prepared to allow such additives. The Dutch ban impeded trade in cheeses manufactured in more permissive States, but the Court accepted that regulatory attitudes could legitimately vary in such circumstances and did not find the Netherlands to have acted unlawfully even though they had intervened in the market more vigorously than the norm elsewhere. The leeway afforded to heavier regulators may encompass respect for divergent assessment of the same risk, as in *Eyssen*, or it may cover a case where local conditions dictate that the threat is peculiarly sensitive. In *Estee Lauder Cosmetics*[15] the Court accepted that in deciding whether a commercial practice forbidden under national rules is 'misleading'—and its suppression therefore potentially justified despite the damage inflicted on cross-border trade—'it is necessary to take into account the presumed expectations of an average consumer who is reasonably well informed and reasonably observant and circumspect'. This suggests a Community-wide benchmark but the Court added that 'social, cultural or linguistic factors' may justify special local anxiety about particular practices tolerated elsewhere. A degree of local regulatory diversity is envisaged in the application of the Treaty provisions on free movement[16].

Nevertheless it is transparently true that most cases before the European Court are decided in a manner unfavourable to host State regulators with the result that trade integration is advanced and local regulatory preferences are suppressed. *Cassis de Dijon* itself is such a decision. So too is the famous *Beer Purity* case[17], in which it was ruled that strict German rules governing the permissible ingredients of *Bier* unlawfully restricted the commercial opportunities in Germany of producers brewing elsewhere according to different recipes and traditions. The result was *not* that production according to traditional German methods was no longer viable, but rather that such production would be—at long last—vulnerable to out-of-State competition. Consumer choice would expand. There is a strong deregulatory impetus in this case law, infused by a preference for the private autonomy of traders and consumers in the market over public regulation[18].

In another of the disproportionately high number of cases in these realms that have reached the Court from Germany, *Mars*[19], the Court simply refused to lend credence to the German submission that a restriction on marketing techniques favoured by Mars elsewhere in Europe was properly suppressed in

---

[15] Case C-220/98 note 11 above.

[16] See further S Weatherill, 'Recent case law Concerning the Free Movement of Goods: Mapping the Frontiers of Market Deregulation' (1999) 36 *CMLRev* 51.

[17] Case 178/84 [1987] ECR 1227.

[18] Cf E-J Mestmaecker, 'On the Legitimacy of European Law' (1994) 58 *RabelsZ* 615 and more generally W Sauter, *Competition Law and Industrial Policy in the EU* (Oxford, Oxford University Press, 1997).

[19] Case C-470/93 note 11 above.

Germany because of the risk that consumers would be confused. It curtly observed that the reasonably circumspect consumer would not be duped and made it plain that the host State's rules contravened EC law of free movement. In the services sector, the *Tourist Guide* cases provide an equally powerful glimpse of the assumption that consumers are in general better served by deregulation and cross-border competition than by exclusionary local regulatory practices. The Court observed that competition between tour operators would ensure the hiring of competent guides and that accordingly a State licensing regime governing access to the profession could not be justified[20]. Consumers could take care of themselves adequately without the need for such public intervention.

The constitutional dimension of the law of free movement

In so far as host State regulators typically 'lose', one may choose to assume that this apparent imbalance in outcome is attributable to a 'pro-trade' bias embedded in the very structure of Community law itself or, more institutionally specifically, as one located in or exacerbated by the Court's approach. Such a criticism would depict a Court too reluctant to acknowledge the value of regulatory diversity, even eccentricity, and prone to obliterate the nuances of local cultural colour as a result of its addiction to the shift of power away from (national) public actors to the market. A specific manifestation of this bias could be taken to reside in the burden of proof in questions of justification, which rests on the national regulator not the cross-border trader. Such accusations would be hard to refute, for value judgements of a necessarily imprecise nature are at stake. At a detailed level one might cite cases concerning the collision between free trade and local regulatory preferences in which the Court has been visibly cautious in setting out the order of priority. *Vereinigte Familiapress Zeitungsverlags- und vertriebs GmbH* v. *Heinrich Bauer Verlag*[21] confirmed that the original list of 'mandatory requirements'—more helpfully, the broader notion of the 'public interest'—was not closed, thereby allowing the Court flexibility in renovating the interests it would take into account in adjudicating on the collision between trade integration and local (host State) regulatory autonomy. Austrian rules prohibited the inclusion of prize crossword puzzles in magazines and newspapers. This restricted trade in press products manufactured in Germany where such schemes were permitted. The European Court accepted that in principle it was open to Austria to justify these rules as methods for protecting small publishers from fierce and potentially fatal competition from large publishers able to attract a readership by the lure of large prizes. The

---

[20] Case C-154/89 *Commission* v *France* [1991] ECR I-659.
[21] Case C-368/95 [1997] ECR I-3689.

Court accepted that '[m]aintenance of press diversity may constitute an over-riding requirement justifying a restriction on the free movement of goods'. It added that such diversity helps to safeguard freedom of expression, as protected by Article 10 of the European Convention on Human Rights, which forms part of the pattern of rights protection guaranteed under the Community legal order[22]. However, the Court also noted that the values of fundamental rights would also properly be invoked by German traders, able to argue that the Austrian rule interfered with their (non-absolute) rights to freedom of expression[23].The Court preferred to leave the acutely difficult task of adjudicating whether the law challenged in the case should be treated as compatible with EC law to the referring Austrian court. One might legitimately wonder just how it could or should weigh these competing interests, but for present purposes the key point is that the Court is in principle prepared to assess the validity of the host State's regulatory choices in an evolving context which is open to permeation by factors of considerable social and political breadth[24].

But, beyond 'case-crunching', there is another more fundamental objection to a critique that portrays the European Court as too deeply wrapped in the enticing embrace of deregulated markets. Would one not expect most cases to be decided in favour of cross-border trade? After all, the development of European market integration confronts the dead wood of centuries of regulatory tradition in all the Member States. The whole point of the exercise is regulatory renovation, and a bonfire of red-tape on the pyre of Article 28 constitutes the anticipated, even necessary, method. From this perspective, the European Court is frequently asked to deal with the collision between, on the one hand, the making of a market for Europe and, on the other, national rules introduced for once sound reasons that have generations ago lost their purpose mixed together with other national rules cherished by national producers as convenient means for insulating themselves from the threat of out-of-State competition. So, rather than being biased in favour of trade, the Court is in fact engaged in weeding out unrepresentative and outdated manifestations of national-level decision-making that are hostile to and inappropriate in an integrating European market of the type to which the Member States have committed themselves under the EC Treaty. Appreciation of a more overt constitutional dimension is of fundamental importance to a full grasp of the nature of the process of adjudication under the law of free movement[25]. Host State control, to the exclusion of the home State's preferences, would mean imports would always be required to

---

[22] And see now Art 11 Charter of Fundamental Rights of the EU, agreed at Nice in December 2000.
[23] The Court cited its landmark ruling on this point in Case C-260/89 *ERT* [1991] ECR I-2925; and that of the ECHR in *Informationsverein Lentia v Austria* A No 276 (1993).
[24] *Cf* eg Case C-275/92 *Schindler* [1994] ECR I-1039; Case C-124/97 *Markku Juhani Laara* [1999] ECR I-6067.
[25] See in particular the groundbreaking work of M Poiares Maduro, *We, the Court* (Oxford, Hart Publishing, 1998).

satisfy local market rules before gaining access. This model might be taken as reflection of a pure notion of State sovereignty; or, in a more sophisticated though still inadequate perspective, as a means of connecting the accountability of the regulating authority to the parties most directly affected by trade on the territory for which the regulating authority is responsible. But such a 'pure' host state model obstructs the realisation of economies of scale, damages the pursuit of transfrontier economic restructuring and, at a deeper level, tends to oppose the very dynamic inherent in the process of European integration. Moreover, it typically involves the exclusion of out-of-state trading interests from the rule-making process and the neglect of in-state consumer interests. That is, the connection between competence to regulate and responsibility to those affected is inadequately captured by a model which rests on assumptions of (host) State control in a European market which transcends the State. So the free movement case law 'forces' host States to justify their choices in the light of the impact on affected constituencies who are not otherwise (adequately) represented in domestic local political processes but who, most vividly in the case of traders with a direct commercial stake in achieving European market re-structuring, are able to rely on EC law in litigation before national courts in order to jolt national regulatory tradition. Accordingly one could persuasively characterise many of the cases discussed above as representing the European Court's attempts to employ EC trade law (where necessary and appropriate[26]) to feed in out-of-state trading interests and in-state consumer interests to (national) systems for producing regulation which are otherwise over-representative of the interest group comprising in-state traders.

So the rules successfully challenged in cases such as *Cassis de Dijon* and *Tourist Guides* reflected national protection of local suppliers which was not at all advantageous to local consumers or traders based in other Member States, and the application of the rules of free movement served to correct the malfunction of national political processes which were not attuned to the opportunities presented by the broader sweep of market integration in Europe. Moreover, although the desirable scope of the spillover of free movement law into national social policy choices is a (properly) contested matter[27], there is potential in the application of a comparable analysis to the Treaty rules on State Aids and State Monopolies which have also frequently been relied on by private litigants to shake up often long-standing and cosily anti-competitive domestic public sector arrangements[28]. In this sense, EC trade law, by imposing on national political processes an obligation to respect the interests of 'foreign'

---

[26] *Cf* the '*Keck* debate', note 10 above.

[27] Eg M Poiares Maduro, 'Europe's Social Self: "The Sickness unto Death"', in J Shaw (ed), *Social Law and Policy in an Evolving EU*, (Oxford, Hart Publishing, 2001).

[28] Articles 87–89 and 86 EC respectively. See e.g. on aid Case C-354/90 *Fédération National de Commerce Extérieur des Produits et al v France* [1991] ECR I-5505, on monopolies Case C-41/90 *Hoefner and Elsner v Macrotron* [1991] ECR I-1979. See generally M. Smith, 'In pursuit of selective liberalization: single market competition and its limits' (2001) 8 *JEPP* 519.

actors, reflects and seeks to address the problems caused by the gap between the growth of a European market and the absence of European political institutions equipped with a general regulatory competence[29]. The home State/host State model for distributing competences in the construction and management of the internal market under primary EC law is, at one level, an exercise in deregulation but, in addition, it asserts unexpectedly direct intervention in orthodox assumptions about responsibility and affected constituencies in national political decision-making.

PATTERNS OF HARMONISATION AND THE FUNCTIONS OF THE HOME STATE AND THE HOST STATE

The implication of the analysis set out in the preceding section is that the Treaty provisions on free movement can be worked hard in pursuit of European market deregulation under a model of home State control. This Court-driven deregulatory cutting edge to the law of free movement bites independently of any legislative intervention to establish common *Community* rules of market regulation. In fact, the vigorous application of the Treaty provisions on free movement as tools of 'negative integration' greatly diminishes the need to rely on 'positive' integration introduced by the Community's legislature to complete the market-building process by establishing harmonised rules for trade. But there remains a role for legislative harmonisation, albeit that it is confined to the exceptional circumstances when dual regulation is permitted under primary law —when a sufficiently strong reason has been advanced to justify the continuing application of host State measures notwithstanding their restrictive effect on inter-State trade.

On the simplest model of legislative harmonisation, diverse national rules are eliminated in favour of a single Community rule. The harmonised rule promotes trade integration by virtue of its uniform EC-wide application while also transplanting to European level the imperative of respect for the variety of interests that have stimulated (different forms of) regulatory intervention over time in the Member States. Here, then, there is a vertical re-distribution of competence, from State-level to the Community as rule-maker. In the context of the legislative harmonisation programme, that core bargain struck between the long-standing culture of local regulatory competence and the broader quest for cross-border integration can be re-shaped within the political process, where the necessary weighing of competing values may be thought to belong more comfortably than in the judicial setting discussed above.

As far as particular instruments of secondary legislation are concerned (at least) four (not unconnected) questions arise. First, what is the scope of

---

[29] An absence forcibly confirmed by the Court in C-376/98 *Germany v Parliament and Council* [2000] ECR I-8419, *Tobacco Advertising*, examined further below.

coverage of the secondary legislation (below p 52)? Second, within that scope, what is the content of that regime—what is the *quality* of the harmonised standard (p 52 and 56 below)? Third, within the scope of that agreed 're-regulatory' regime, what is the intended effect of the secondary legislation on residual host State competence? Does any remain or is it 'pre-empted' by the EC's intervention (below p 58)? Fourth, and raising some distinct issues, how are the common rules to be enforced? In particular if the home State fails to secure compliance with the agreed re-regulatory standards, can the host State withdraw the right of market access to the home State's traders (below p 63)?

In each case, the role of the European Court in interpreting the constitutional impact of the secondary legislation and in interpreting the substance of the protective rules will be highly significant, given that controversial issues may not be adequately dealt with in the text of the legislative measure.

What is the scope of coverage of the secondary legislation?

Beyond the scope of the secondary legislation there is no pre-emption and normal rules of primary Community law apply. This is a question of interpretation. Undoubtedly it is a difficult question at the technical level and the Court will frequently find itself asked to decide a point that has, wittingly or otherwise, been left unresolved in the text of the adopted measure. In such circumstances the Court may be forced into a decision that will be significant at the margins in fixing the reach of the Community instrument, but is unlikely to carry real constitutional weight. So in *Kemikalieinspektionen* v *Toolex Alpha AB* the Court, asked to consider the reach of Community secondary legislation, decided that the measures harmonised only rules governing the labelling and packaging of trichloroethylene and that accordingly Member States remained free to regulate the industrial use of the substance, subject only to the demands of Article 30 EC.[30]

The content of the re-regulatory regime

Legislative harmonisation is, like judicial harmonisation, deregulatory in the sense that, on the simplest model, fifteen diverse (national) rules are reduced to one (Community) rule in order to establish a common rule as the platform for a common market. But legislative harmonisation is also 're-regulatory'. If the task were merely to set a common rule, its content would be of no concern. All that would matter would be that it should apply in common. But this is not merely a deregulatory enterprise. The Community has to make a choice about

---

[30] Case C-473/98 n 14 above.

the level at which that uniform rule shall be pitched. It must 're-regulate'. In fact, since harmonisation is an attempt to provide a 'Europeanised' framework within which to cope with the complex pattern of diverse regulatory choices made over time within the Member States, and given that, moreover, the 'Community' is not at all an entity wholly divorced from the anxieties of its Member States, it is inevitable that close attention will be paid to the quality of the chosen standard, whether it lie in the field of labour market regulation, environmental protection or private law. Harmonisation, as a vertical re-distribution of competence from Member States to the Community, is more than merely a technical process of eliminating trade barriers, as is made plain by the aspiration to high standards set out in Article 95(3) EC, a rather flimsy provision but today buttressed by the Treaty's *Querschnittsklausel* on the integration of environmental, health and consumer concerns into other common policies including, no doubt, market-making[31]. In fact legislative harmonisation provides a classic example of the way in which trade integration 'spills over' to confront and infuse ever more complex areas of regulatory policy. So the single market programme has generated a much more extensive pattern of (re-) regulation of economic activity undertaken at European level than might have been appreciated from its deceptively bland and politically astute non-committal billing as a value-free exercise in improving competitiveness[32].

The principal focus of this chapter is on the constitutional questions surrounding the distribution of competences in the project to construct the internal market. This is an issue that arises only after the content of the EC regime has been agreed. It would therefore be possible to skip discussion of how the re-regulatory bargain is brokered and to limit analysis to what occurs thereafter, in allocating competences to home and host States. But such neglect of the profoundly sensitive nature of the negotiation of a harmonised Community rule would in turn lead to a gross under-appreciation of how delicate are the subsequent questions of fixing the scope of respective competences (below p 58) and of then determining what shall be the consequences of violation of the harmonised rules (below p 63). Accordingly an introductory account, albeit brief, is required in order to demonstrate the formidably complex range of interests which influence the shaping of the deceptively banal notion of a 'common rule for a common market'.

In determining the content of the harmonised rule, the Community legislature could fix on a model of absolute host State control, to the exclusion of the home State's preferences, which would mean imports would always be required

---

[31] Cf note 4 above.

[32] Cf M Egan, *Constructing a European Market* (Oxford, Oxford University Press, 2001); K Armstrong and S Bulmer, *The Governance of the Single European Market* (Manchester, Manchester University Press, 1998); K Armstrong, *Regulation, Deregulation, Re-regulation* (London, Kogan Page, 2000); already far-sighted at an early date was R Bieber et al (eds), *1992: One European Market* (Baden-Baden, Nomos, 1988). Also central to this picture is 'comitology'; eg C Joerges and E Vos, (eds) *EU Committees: Social Regulation, Law and Politics* (Oxford, Hart Publishing, 1999).

to satisfy local market rules. It has already been explained above in association with the shaping of the law under the Treaty that such an unqualified model would fundamentally contradict the assumptions of the integrative project. It is all the more plain that legislative harmonisation cannot privilege host State control in such an absolute manner. Trading freedom would be maximized were the other extreme, a rule of *home* State control, to prevail, that is, were host State competence to interfere with imports wholly excluded under a regime which insists that conformity with home State requirements is a passport to access to the EU-wide market. But this has not been adopted as an generally applicable unqualified rule in Europe either. Although the Commission was attracted by automatic mutual recognition of divergent national technical standards as the rule governing the internal market after 1992, the Member States were prepared to introduce in the Single European Act only a more cautious regime of recognition by Council decision. And even this was left unused and then deleted by the Treaty of Amsterdam[33]. In orthodox *communautaire* discourse such a model of absolute home State control is perceived as conducive to a race to the bottom in regulatory protection. The suspicion is that national authorities would be driven by a regime which allows firms based on one State's territory to supply the entire market freed of the obligation to comply with local (host State) rules to respond by reducing burdens on business in order to attract or at least to retain footloose firms. A 'pure' regime of home State control is perceived to maximise incentives to slash and burn regulatory protection which will ignite a conflagration spreading from State to State in Europe.

This chapter can devote only one superficial paragraph to insisting that the rationales that have led to such political distaste for absolute home State control deserve fuller interrogation[34]. Such a model is typically characterised as creating distortion of competition within the Community, for costs incurred by economic operators vary State by State according to the chosen legal regime, and yet, on another level, it *generates* competition—between States as regulators. Further in this vein, one may suspect that the elimination of regulatory diversity in favour of common Community standards may be a strategy preferred by high-cost States seeking to suppress the competitive advantage of low-cost States able to attract 'consumers' of regulation to their territory[35]. Such scepticism about harmonisation may also be driven by anxieties about the competitiveness of Community industry in global markets should its regulatory

---

[33] It was Art 100b EC. See C Ehlermann, 'The Internal Market following the Single European Act', (1987) 24 *CMLRev* 361, 399–402.

[34] See, much more fully, D Esty and D Geradin, (eds) *Regulatory Competition and Economic Integration* (Oxford, Oxford University Press, 2001); also Deakin and Barnard chapter 8 in this volume.

[35] The Court may change the environment. Where it extends the reach of trading freedoms under its interpretation of primary law, affected States may be provoked into seeking 're-balancing' via legislative action. For instance the context in which postal services were the subject of liberalisation was altered by the ruling in Case C-320/91 *Corbeau* [1993] ECR I-2533; the 'post-*Centros*' debate (Case C-212/97 [1999] ECR I-1459) in company law is intriguing in this vein.

system be locked into a rigid single framework which, once fixed, is notoriously hard to alter[36]. I should emphasise that I do not make these comments in order to sign up to a model of uninhibited regulatory competition within the EC based on a system based on 'pure' home State control of economic operators, but rather I suggest that more attention should be paid to identifying rationales for the introduction of common rules as part of the host State/home State bargain than is found in bland invocation of the notion of 'distorted' competition. There *are* other possible rationales for European harmonisation, for example rooted in the advantages in global markets of competing 'upwards' in standards-setting in order to acquire a reputation for high quality[37], and in improving productivity and increasing inward investment by judicious labour market regulation [38]. Beyond the normative, I suspect that in the economic and political conditions prevailing in modern Western Europe countries it is in most sectors highly improbable that a race to the bottom in regulatory protection is likely to occur. There is little evidence that electoral or economic advantage can be gained through such tactics. One may doubt that firms are truly sufficiently mobile to make competitive deregulation worthwhile; or, at least, one may doubt it is politically attractive to pursue the magnitude of the deregulation required to lure them to be so[39]. If scepticism about the empirical evidence is well-founded[40], that too invites a need to find rationales for Community rules that go beyond 'pure' home State control that are more sophisticated than mere prevention of the race to the bottom.

Currently, however, it seems that the rhetorical political power of the fear of the race to the bottom remains strong enough to deter pursuit of 'pure' home State control (and perhaps, for other, better reasons, it *should* so deter it). The inevitable outcome is a harmonised regime designed to open up cross-border trade within which evolved anxieties expressed over time in different ways in different Member States will be the subject of Community-wide regulation under a compromise—a 're-regulatory' bargain. So whereas primary Community law, interpreted by the Court, involves a division of competence between home and host States, secondary legislation elaborated by the political institutions

---

[36] Cf famously F Scharpf, 'The Joint-Decision Trap: Lessons from German Federalism and European Integration' (1988) 66 *Public Administration* 239. For scepticism about the enduring nature of blockages see G Peters, 'Escaping the Joint-Decision Trap: Repetition and Sectoral Politics in the EU' (1997) 20 *West European Politics* 22.

[37] An influential starting-point is M Porter, *The Competitive Advantage of Nations* (Baisingstoke, Macmillan, new ed, 1998).

[38] Eg on the case for transnational labour standards see S Deakin, 'Labour Law as Market Regulation' in P Davies et al (eds), *EC Labour Law: Principles and Perspectives* (Oxford, Oxford University Press, 1996).

[39] In sector-specific contexts, see C Barnard, 'Social dumping and the race to the bottom: some lessons for the European Union from Delaware?' (2000) 25 *ELRev* 57; M Faure, 'Regulating Competition vs Harmonization in EU Environmental Law' in D Esty and D Geradin (eds) n 34 above; J Wouters, 'European Company Law: *Quo Vadis?*' (2000) 31 *CMLRev* 257.

[40] Contrast the possibility of a race downwards in active enforcement of EC rules once agreed, considered in pp 67–69 below.

involves attention to the distribution of competences among Member States and the Community itself in the cause of promoting market integration. And here too absolute choices for either home or host State control are unappealing.

Compromise and the re-regulatory bargain

The question, then, is the *intensity* of regulation under the 're-regulatory bargain'. This bargain involves the setting of common Community standards which are designed to take care of the interests of both the 'home' State and the 'host' State. Both parties would share an interest in a common European regime of regulation. The interests of the home State might appear to be in unobstructed trade for 'its' firms, so that its chief ambition would be to secure that the common regime be pitched at a level that will result in those firms incurring few or no compliance costs. The interests of the host State might be seen to be directed at ensuring that the common regime, within which interests that were previously protected by national rules tending to inhibit trade are now protected by European-level rules, is not likely to prejudice the interests of, for example, consumers or environmental protection. The host State will be less sensitive to cost implications.

Of course that model is grossly superficial. The interests at stake in the propulsion of an EC initiative cannot be simply separated out as 'home State = integration', 'host State = re-regulation'. The notion of the 'State' requires disaggregation, for different components of a State's apparatus, split sectorally or split geographically, for example, may have very different preferences, which are also susceptible to alteration over time. Moreover these are not necessarily interests of States at all, but rather of discrete interest groups with varying levels of influence on national political processes. And both public and private constituencies may use action on the EC plane to acquire what cannot be readily extracted locally[41], although the resources at their disposal to exert effective influence at transnational level will plainly vary[42]. A demand-led examination of Community 're-regulation', encompassing both public and private actors, is required to understand the full picture[43].

---

[41] The literature on this multi-faceted phenomenon is vast and growing; see eg J Hunt, 'Success at Last? The amendment of the Acquired Rights Directive' 24 *ELRev* 215 (1999); J Fairbrass and A Jordan, 'Protecting biodiversity in the EU; national barriers and European opportunities?' (2001) 2001 *JEPP* 499.

[42] Eg A Heritier, 'Policy-making by subterfuge' (1997) 4 *JEPP* 171; M Pollack, 'Representing diffuse interests in EC policy-making', (1997) 4 *JEPP* 572; also J Greenwood and M Aspinwall, *Collective Action in the European Union* (London, Routledge, 1998).

[43] For a survey of the extensive literature, see S Hix, *The Political System of the European Union*, (Basingstoke, Macmillan, 1999), Ch 8. These issues plainly transcend the EU case; see eg Special Issue: Governance and International Standards Setting (2001) 8/3 *JEPP*; G Bermann, M Herdegen and P Lindseth, *Transatlantic Regulatory Co-operation* (Oxford, Oxford University Press, 2001); Esty and Geradin, n 34 above.

For example, one may surmise that a first-best option for traders might be common Community rules imposing a rule of no-regulation, but a second-best (and better than simply leaving the matter for regulation under primary Community law) option might be common Community rules imposing regulatory burdens. That is, the fact of having common rules agreed at Community level and applied by the home State according to which integration may reliably proceed serves as the vital lure even if those rules may impose regulatory costs (and even if those costs exceed those currently applied within the trader's national system). So, for example, the banking sector has been integrated under conditions which guarantee conformity with certain protective standards governing, for example, deposit guarantees set out at Community level, albeit enforced by home States[44], plus a concession that host States may be able to act in defence of the 'general good'[45]. Among rejected models was unconditional respect for home State regulatory choices, which would have been an implausibly extreme political deal in the heavily regulated European business landscape[46]. Against such backgrounds solutions are bartered through the Community process, reflecting the plurality of affected interests under the 're-regulatory' model, and, incidentally, appreciation of diverse demand patterns illuminates just why associating the subsidiarity slogan with the mothballing of the supply-side of the market for regulation is hopelessly superficial.

So we might expect that the EC will inevitably develop a model somewhere between the extremes of absolute host State and absolute home State control, as it struggles to satisfy a diverse batch of interest groups. The nature of the compromise, in relation to both the content of the regime and the distribution of competences, will be affected by a regime of voting that varies by sector and over time and by the ebb and flow of political fashion. A further expectation would be that secondary legislation adopted under the harmonisation programme is likely to apply a common regime which is closer to the home State model than the host State model. This is because the home State control model is more likely to deliver effective market integration and because home states are physically in a better position to exercise effective direct control over suppliers. Other areas of Community activity that lie more remote from the market-building process such as environmental protection may be expected to be less wedded to a model which minimises or even excludes dual regulation. A more detailed examination is now called for.

---

[44] Directive 89/646 OJ 1989 L386 and Directive 94/19 OJ 1994 L135/5. The validity of Dir 94/19 was unsuccessfully challenged in Case C-233/94 note 3 above.
[45] Arts 19(4), 21(5), 21(11) Dir 89/646.
[46] See more fully E Avgouleas, 'The Harmonisation of Rules of Conduct in EU Financial Markets' (2000) 6 *ELJ* 72.

What is the intended effect of the secondary legislation on residual national (host State) competence?

This chapter's dominant concern is with constitutional questions surrounding decisions about the distribution of competences driven by the objective of constructing the internal market. The Treaty supplies no general rule governing the effect of legislative harmonisation, nor has one been elaborated by the European Court or by the legislature.

It is possible to discover examples of secondary legislation putting in place a model of home State control, under which host State competence to regulate in the field occupied by the Directive is entirely excluded or 'pre-empted' in pursuit of the creation of conditions akin to an internal market, albeit that the home State is not left free to choose how to regulate 'its' firms (if at all), but rather there is an agreed Community content to the rules which the home State is required to enforce. For example, in *Commission* v. *UK.*, the 'Dim Dip' case[47], the UK required that all new vehicles carry dim-dip lights, a specification which was not listed in Directive 76/756. This excluded cars made in other States not equipped with such lights. Directive 76/756 was held exhaustive as regards the lighting devices which might be made compulsory for motor vehicles. The UK could not regulate the matter given the comprehensive coverage of the Directive. The Court, faced with submissions by the UK that the dim dip mechanism improved road safety, refused even to consider the merits of the matter. The adoption of EC legislation had put an end to the competence of the host State unilaterally to invoke such concerns and its only route to regulatory reform would be to persuade its partners of the need to amend the Community rules themselves[48]. In this way the perceived need to establish Community-wide groundrules is reflected in a mandatory regime that all States are required to implement. And then products are free to circulate throughout the entire territory of the EC and cannot be subjected to further requirements imposed by a host State concerning their composition, unless, exceptionally, the EC measure explicitly permits this[49]. This clear, straightforward transfer of power from national to Community level is vital to the building of a cross-border market. Pre-emption of national competence secures a basis for commercial confidence in the legal rules of the internal market game.

Despite the importance of the model exemplified by 'Dim Dip' in market-building, it is plain that it is improbable that the sensitivity of the process of 're-regulation', which, as the previous sub-section illustrates, has multiple impacts

---

[47] Case 60/86 [1988] ECR 3921.

[48] See similarly eg Case 148/78 *Ratti* [1979] ECR 1629; Case 190/87 *Moormann* [1988] ECR 4689; Case C-83/92 *Pierrel* [1993] ECR I-6419.

[49] In fact De Búrca has uncovered a surprisingly high number of specific exemptions allowed to individual or small groups of States under harmonisation Directives; 'Differentiation within the Core: the Case of the Common Market', in G De Búrca and J Scott (eds), *Constitutional Change in the EU: from uniformity to flexibility?* (Oxford, Hart Publishing, 2000).

in society, will be allowed to cause consistent exclusion of host State competence across the whole field of the Community's regulatory endeavours. The tension of geographical and functional expansion in the EU brings with it inevitable difficulties in maintaining the normative appeal of the slogan 'one size fits all'. That is apparent in the disinclination of States to accept the notion of 'classic pre-emption' as a generally applicable rule governing the impact of Community legislative activity on residual national competence. As Norbert Reich accurately predicted, '[T]he more competences the Community is acquiring, the less exclusive will be its jurisdiction'[50].

A specific example is found in the technique of minimum harmonisation. Articles 176, 137 and 153 EC, governing competence to legislate in the fields of environmental protection, social policy and consumer protection respectively, stipulate that national measures that are stricter than the agreed Community standard are permitted, provided they are compatible with the Treaty. Such a measure establishes a common EC-wide rule, but as a minimum only, as a floor above which Member States may introduce stricter rules up to the ceiling set by the Treaty itself, in particular by the rules of free movement. But what role can or should the minimum formula play in the field of harmonisation designed to serve the end of market integration? Articles 94 and 95 (ex 100 and 100a) are bare of explicit reference to the impact on national competence of measures adopted thereunder, save only for inclusion of the managed and strictly limited derogation foreseen by Articles 95(4) *et seq*[51]. One may assume that the minimum formula is appropriate in the fields of environmental, social and consumer protection because the dominant purpose of the relevant Treaty provisions is to pursue the objectives of those policies and not explicitly to integrate markets, whereas, by contrast, one might choose to argue that Articles 94 and 95, as foundation stones of market building, should always pre-empt national competence to act in the occupied field. The Court's interpretation of Directive 76/756 in 'Dim Dip' follows this resolutely pro-integrative line, but legislative practice across the large number of relevant measures adopted under the name of harmonisation by the Community is not consistent.

There are individual Directives formally adopted as measures of harmonisation designed to advance the building of an integrated market which contain a minimum clause. This is common in the batch of measures harmonising the legal protection of the economic interests of consumers. Directive 85/577 governing 'Doorstep Selling' provides an example. In *Buet*[52] a French decision to ban doorstep selling of certain materials was not treated as pre-empted by the

---

[50] 'Competition between Legal Orders: A New Paradigm of EC Law' (1992), 29 *CMLRev* 861, 895.
[51] The Court confirmed that a narrow interpretation should be placed on these provisions in Case C-41/93 *France v Commission* [1994] ECR I-1829 and in Case C-319/97 *Antoine Kortas* judgment of 1 June 1999 (although the detailed significance of *Kortas* is much reduced by the amendments made by the Amsterdam Treaty, see Art 95(6)). On Commission practice, see eg Dec 2001/571 OJ 2001 L202/46 (Germany).
[52] Case 382/87 [1989] ECR 1235.

existence of the Directive which governs exactly that marketing practice and which requires only that the consumer be given a seven-day cooling off period after concluding such a contract. The Court took the view that because the Directive, though adopted under Article 100, provides explicitly for Member States to apply measures more favourable to the consumer, stricter rules were allowed even where they obstructed imported goods, provided only that they were justified (which the Court thought they could be, given their function of protecting vulnerable consumers). One might ask how market-building under Article 100 could rationally permit such fragmentation. The correct answer *at the political level* would be that Directive 85/577 in fact had little to do with market-building and was instead an instance of the Council borrowing Article 100 in order to express its unanimous political preference for the development of a legislative programme of consumer protection at a time when the Treaty conferred no relevant competence in that field. Much the same explanation applies to the presence of a minimum formula in environmental legislation adopted under Article 100 in the years before 1987 when Community legislative competence in that field was consecrated by the Single European Act[53]. But read *formally*, it seemed that Directive 85/577 demonstrated that even harmonisation under the core internal market provisions of Articles 94 and 95 (ex 100 and 100a) may incorporate scope for persisting market division, in so far as residual competence vested in a host State could be exercised in a manner that would restrict trade yet remain lawful according to the *Cassis de Dijon* formula[54].

However, our understanding of the law on this point appears now to be radically changed by the Court's ruling in *Tobacco Advertising*, (more properly known as *Germany v Parliament and Council*)[55]. This decision poses general questions about the nature and purpose of the harmonisation programme. It reveals the readiness of the Court to quarrel with the views of the majority in Council on the reach of the Treaty by insisting that a tighter connection between 're-regulation' and the building of an internal market must be demonstrated than has been (occasional) past legislative practice. But, of more direct relevance to this chapter, the decision also has a detailed impact on the separation of legal bases in the Treaty with reference to the pre-emptive effect of secondary legislation adopted under them. We may imagine two forms of minimum harmonisation, differing according to whether market access is allowed to out-of-state goods conforming with the minimum Community rule but not the host State's chosen stricter rule. If such market access is allowed, the value of the regime of minimum harmonisation to the regulating State is plainly

---

[53] For an account see Weatherill and Beaumont n 7 above pp1036–49.

[54] Just as the Directive itself appears to have little do with market-building, so one might also question whether, post-*Keck* (n 8 above), national rules such as those addressed in *Buet* would be treated as exerting a sufficient impact on cross-border trade even to require justification. But this does not defeat the larger point made in the text about the difficulty of aligning such a minimum clause with the objectives of harmonisation.

[55] Case C-376/98 [2000] ECR I-8419.

diminished, for its goals may be undermined by non-conforming imports which cannot be excluded. But if market access is denied under such a minimum model, integration is damaged. This is, in the first instance, a preference for prioritising home State control and in the latter a preference for prioritising host State control. Or, put another way, the former accelerates a type of inter-State regulatory competition that increases the probability that the minimum rule will in practice become also a maximum rule, while a 'race to the top' seems dependent on the latter model, that is, on the *absence* of a market access presumption in favour of goods from a low-regulating State targeted at a high-regulating State. Denying market access is necessary to ensure the low-regulator has an incentive to emulate the high-regulator[56].

The assumption underpinning *Buet* seems to be that harmonisation legislation may employ the latter model, that is, that stricter rules above the minimum may be applied to imports as well as to domestic goods, provided they are justified under Article 28's *Cassis de Dijon* formula. But *Tobacco Advertising* appears to insist that a harmonisation measure must ensure access to the market of conforming imported goods, and confines the application of stricter rules to domestic goods alone. The Court criticised Directive 98/43 on the advertising of tobacco products because it

> contains no provision ensuring the free movement of products which conform to its provisions, in contrast to other Directives allowing Member States to adopt stricter measures for the protection of a general interest[57].

This, among other findings, deprived the Directive of a valid basis under Articles 57(2), 66 and 100a (now Articles 47(2), 55 and 95). So, it seems, only one type of minimum harmonisation is permitted via Article 95 EC; that which favours home State control, albeit that the home State must apply (as a minimum) the agreed Community rules. A systematic search of the legislation and case law would surpass the ambition of this chapter, but this decision may affect the validity, or at least the proper interpretation, of adopted Directives containing the minimum formula but lacking an explicit 'market access' clause in favour of conforming (imported) goods. It would seem to mean that a case such as *Buet* should be decided on the basis that the minimum clause in the Directive allows the introduction of stricter rules provided they apply only to domestic practices[58]. The application of stricter rules against imports is constitutionally

---

[56] D Vogel, 'Trading up and governing across: transnational governance and environmental protection', (1997) 4 *JEPP* 556 shows how the introduction of stricter product-related environmental standards in California has generated copying elsewhere so as to facilitate penetration of the large Californian market—but this can succeed only where such rules are *lawful* trade barriers; cf, in the European context, the importance of the Court's role in shaping the scope of the Treaty rules on free movement, n 35 above. See also Deakin and Barnard chapter 8 in this volume.
[57] Para. 104 of the ruling.
[58] Cf on minimum rules and *export* trade Case C-1/96 *Ex parte Compassion in World Farming* [1998] ECR I-1251, examined by G Van Calster (2000) 25 *ELRev* 335.

pre-empted and, as in *Dim Dip*, there is no question of weighing up the advantages and disadvantages of the national measure. In so far as a measure of harmonisation must unavoidably be interpreted on its terms as permitting the application of stricter rules also to imports it is presumably not valid and must seek its legal base elsewhere in the Treaty.

Tobacco Advertising, by appearing to exclude the possibility of a Directive adopted as a measure of harmonisation permitting stricter national rules to be applied against imports, except via the managed procedure found in Article 95(4) *et seq*, insists on a pro-integrative model, but one that is not conducive to regulatory experimentation by States above the minimum norm. However, as a general observation, the imposition of standards that are minimum in character reflects appreciation that the Community's functional and geographic expansion has drawn into its purview a range of interests that cannot adequately be served by a one-dimensional insistence on its law as a means for facilitating trade integration through the suppression of national competence. Articles 176, 137 and 153, the Treaty provisions governing environmental, social and consumer protection respectively, are not directed at the integration of markets, and so, one may conclude, the failure to establish a uniform regime, in so far as individual States may 'opt upwards' by virtue of the minimum clause, is tolerable. More fully, this may be taken to represent confirmation that integration and uniformity are inapt as paramount guiding values in such realms and that space should be preserved for diverse local preference and for regulatory experimentation[59]. In the increasingly wide range of areas of Community activity that lie beyond the framework for building an internal market, the Community typically does not occupy the field entirely, to the exclusion of Member State choice, but rather both rule-makers remain active in the field and, one may hope, can learn from each other[60]. This perspective argues for allowing only a narrow reach to the classic pre-emptive effect of Community intervention. Analogous anxiety to accompany expansion in the Community's competence with more permissive definition of the consequence for national competence of its exercise is at the heart of recently introduced Treaty provisions which explicitly place certain forms of action off limits the Community. So the Community has lately acquired competence to act in the field of public health, but although it

---

[59] Cf S Weatherill, 'Flexibility or Fragmentation: Trends in European Integration' in J Usher (ed), *The State of the European Union* (Harlow, Longman, 2000); M Dougan, 'Minimum Harmonisation and the Internal Market' 37 *CMLRev* 853 (2000). More broadly, B Rosamond, *Theories of European Integration* (Basingstoke, Macmillan, 2000). On associated maturation of the academic discipline, see J Shaw, 'European Union Legal Studies in Crisis? Towards a New Dynamic' (1996) 16 *OxJLS* 231; J Hunt and J Shaw, 'European Legal Studies: Then and Now' in D Hayton (ed), *Law's Future(s)* (Oxford, Hart Publishing, 2000).

[60] Eg the Commission reports that a 4-year concession made on accession allowing Austria, Finland and Sweden to apply stricter environmental and health standards generated a review that led to the adoption of higher EU-wide standards in a number of relevant areas, COM (98) 745. See generally, D Chalmers, 'Inhabitants in the field of EC environmental law' in P Craig and G De Búrca (eds), *The Evolution of EU Law* (Oxford, Oxford University Press, 1999).

may adopt incentive measures, harmonisation of laws is explicitly excluded by Article 152(4)[61]. The same is true of cultural policy under Article 151(5). Moreover both provisions, along with Article 153 governing consumer protection, emphasise the Community's role in *supporting* and *supplementing* Member State action, an audible whisper of subsidiarity. At times of Treaty revision States have embraced a formal expansion of competence and agreed the exercise of powers to be subjected ever more frequently to qualified majority voting; but, as a type of compensatory bargain, the States have asserted other methods for clinging to control over paths to be taken by the Community[62]. This is 'preemption'—the constitutional re-distribution of competence between the Member States and the Community—seen in its full and increasingly sensitive context. More broadly still, there are close associations between scepticism about the value or even the sheer feasibility of securing uniformity in the wider sweep of Community activity and the developing 'flexibility debate' within which authority in the wider framework of the Union is increasingly layered[63].

QUESTIONS OF ENFORCEMENT AND THE FUNCTIONS OF THE HOME STATE AND THE HOST STATE

Consequences of breaking the re-regulatory bargain

It has been explained that an inevitably complex and frequently ill-defined 're-regulatory' bargain is typically struck in the adoption of secondary legislation. The purpose of this section is to investigate examples of the distribution of competence between home and host States but, in particular, to consider how it is envisaged that misapplication of the agreed rules should be tackled. Particular illumination may be obtained from a situation in which a re-regulatory standard is not enforced by the home State and is therefore not complied with by a commercial party based in the home State but active in the host State. Of course, the home State could be the subject of enforcement proceedings initiated by the Commission or by another Member State and in principle could also be challenged by a private party relying on Community law. But, if the re-regulatory bargain has been broken by the home State's failure to apply the rules, is the host State able to respond by withdrawing the right of market access to non-conforming goods or services?

---

[61] This proviso was a major reason for the legislature's (unsuccessful) attempt to fit harmonisation of tobacco advertising rules under Article 95 (ex 100a), Case C-376/98 n 55 above.

[62] Cf A Dashwood, 'States in the European Union' (1998) 23 *ELRev* 201, examining 'conservatory' *vs* 'constitutionalising' elements.

[63] See essays collected in De Búrca and Scott (eds) n 49 above, with copious bibliographic references. Use of ever more novel instruments, reflecting these tensions, persists; cf D Hodson and I Maher, 'The Open Method as a new mode of governance' (2001) 39 *JCMS* 719.

In some circumstances this is possible. Imagine a host State is seeking to refuse market access to a product which is missing an element required by the Community regime rather than (as in *Dim Dip*[64]) seeking to impose an additional element unforeseen by the Directive. Even where the Directive has in principle pre-empted host State regulatory competence, the product may be lawfully excluded because it is not made in such a way as to fall within the scope of the regime.

However, it appears that both the Court and the legislature are attracted by the prospect of confining the simple equation between breach of re-regulatory bargain and retaliatory denial of market access to cases involving direct non-compliance with rules governing product composition.

The Court was asked to consider the matter in circumstances where a relevant Directive had *not* specified the consequences of non-conformity in *R v MAFF, ex parte Hedley Lomas (Ireland) Ltd*[65]. The fact pattern is atypical; the alleged infraction was by a host State to which a home State declined to permit export. But the model is of general instructive value. The British authorities had systematically refused to issue licences for the export to Spain of live animals because of anxieties about practices in Spanish slaughterhouses falling short of those imposed by Directive 74/577. The Court found the UK to have violated Article 34 (now 29) EC. The UK's allegation that Spain was in breach of the Directive provided no possible justification. The Court stated that the absence of provisions in the Directive harmonising procedures for monitoring compliance, on which the UK had relied, simply meant that Member States were obliged under Articles 5 and 189 (now 10 and 249) to 'to take all measures necessary to guarantee the application and effectiveness of Community law'. It added that 'Member States must rely on trust in each other to carry out inspections on their respective territories'.

This is *not* incompatible with the principle that non-conforming goods may be excluded. The issue in *Hedley Lomas* was different. The goods were not the problem. Rather, their treatment was the subject of an alleged infraction of EC law. This could not be addressed by obstructing cross-border movement. But the decision demonstrates a deep suspicion about permitting a response to (alleged) mis-application of Community re-regulation which takes the form of trade restriction. The Court's long-standing view that orthodox international law remedies of retortion are excluded from EC law by the existence of the Treaty's relatively sophisticated system of enforcement[66] here caused it to embrace a solution based on occupation of the field achieved by Community legislative intervention and an expectation of implementation by all Member States on

---

[64] Note 47 above.
[65] Case C-5/94 [1996] ECR I-2553.
[66] Eg Cases 90/63 and 91/63 *Commission v Luxembourg and Belgium* [1964] ECR 625; and, subsequent to *Lomas*, Case C-11/95 *Commission v Belgium* [1996] ECR I-4115.

their own territory, subject to a supervisory system built around alliance between national and European courts.

Some Directives provide more fully for the consequences should there be non-compliance with the re-regulatory rules by the State charged by Community law with the responsibility for their enforcement. Here too one may observe a strong desire to confine retaliation in the shape of denial of market access even in admitted instances of violation of the protective standards agreed within the re-regulatory bargain.

Directive 89/552 (as amended by Directive 97/36), the 'Television without Frontiers' Directive, provides a helpful illustration[67]. This provides in Article 2a(1) that

> Member States shall ensure freedom of reception and shall not restrict retransmissions on their territory of television broadcasts from other Member States for reasons which fall within the fields coordinated by this Directive.

This is an assertion of a basic principle of home State control (though 'home' for these purposes has been contested in litigation[68]). That control shall include the application of the agreed Community standards. The re-regulatory bargain, according to which anxieties which previously prompted a plurality of market-fragmenting national restrictions on broadcasting freedom are now addressed by common Community rules, is set out in Articles 10–21 of the Directive. These govern the conduct of 'Television advertising, sponsorship and teleshopping'. It is provided that 'All forms of television advertising and teleshopping for cigarettes and other tobacco products shall be prohibited'; television advertising for alcoholic beverages must comply with defined criteria. Although the primary constitutional purpose of these restrictions on commercial freedom is the making of a transfrontier market in this sector[69], Article 3(2) of the Directive makes plain that these are nevertheless duties of 're-regulation' imposed on home States, in return for which host States have surrendered the competence to set stricter rules *and*, importantly, host States are also able to act directly in cases of violation of the agreed rules *only in exceptional circumstances*. The Directive provides that broadcasting services may be suspended by the receiving State even where that duty of regulation imposed on the home State has been violated *only* provided specific substantive and procedural criteria are satisfied. These exceptional circumstances are set out in Article 2a(2) and arise in the event of a breach of Article 22 relating to impairment of 'the physical, mental or moral development of minors' and/or Article 22a forbidding broadcasts

---

[67] Dir 89/552 OJ 1989 L298, amended by Dir 97/36 OJ 1997 L202. Other sectors that would repay more systematic examination include Banking under Dirs 89/646 and 94/19 n 44 above and e-commerce under Dir 2000/31 OJ 2000 L178.

[68] Eg Case C-222/94 *Commission v UK* [1996] ECR I-4025. But Dir 97/36 has amended the relevant provisions in Art 2, see C A Jones, 'Television without Frontiers' (1999–2000) 19 *YEL* 299.

[69] In para 98 of the judgment in Case C-376/98 n 55 above the Court goes out of its way to confirm the validity of use of the harmonisation legal base to adopt this restriction.

containing 'any incitement to hatred on grounds of race, sex, religion or nationality'. But the power to suspend services is available only where the infringement is manifest, serious and grave, there must have been at least two prior infringements in the preceding twelve months and the receiving State must have engaged in consultation of a defined type with broadcaster, Commission and transmitting State[70].

The elimination of multiple regulation of traders is central to achieving an integrated market. The Commission has confirmed that it

> would particularly stress the increased importance of a correct application of the so-called home country control principle (according to which broadcasters are subject only to the law of the country in which they have their principal place of business) in an audiovisual environment which—thanks to the proliferation of broadcasting capacities due to digital technology—favours the growth of transnational services[71].

The Directive accordingly contains a strong impetus towards freedom of transmission and market restructuring by limiting the power of the host State and relying heavily on the principle of home State control, even where the re-regulatory bargain enshrined in the Community measure has been broken by the home State. Market access is to be maintained in all but extreme cases and any infraction of the home State duty to regulate is to be addressed by the legal methods recognised by Community law, involving both European Court and national courts, and not by direct action against the broadcaster[72].

The constitutional dimension of enforcement

The constitutional dimension that underpins the attempt to redistribute regulatory functions between the Member States in pursuit of a viable structure of European market integration that is not supported by nor predicated on the existence of a European State, examined above in connection with primary law, merits re-injection at this point. The truly remarkable pattern of 'indirect rule', according to which rule-making is located at transnational level but the overwhelming majority of implementation and enforcement activity is allocated to and embedded within established national structures of law and administration, lies at the heart of the nature of the beast that is the European

---

[70] The Commission's 3rd report on the application of Dir 89/552, covering mid-1997 to end-2000, reports only one instance, COM (01) 09, p 12.
[71] 2nd report on the Dir's application, COM (97) 523; the 3rd Report n 70 above claims growth in cross-border activity in the sector.
[72] Case C-14/96 *Paul Denuit* [1996] ECR I-4115; cf the Court's distinction between action under the Dir against a broadcaster and (the greater scope for) action against an advertiser in Joined Cases C-34/95, C-35/95 and C-36/95 *Konsummentombudsmannen* v *De Agostini Forlag* [1997] ECR I-3843.

Community[73]. The 'indirect rule' pattern is fundamental to the EC's character-isation as a bureaucracy which, judged by the size of its own staff and direct expenditure, is simply tiny. In this sense the European Community's primary *modus operandi* is not at all to replace national political processes but rather to require adaptation of existing national systems in order to induce recognition of the salience of un- or under- represented interests that are associated with the process of market integration and deeper inter-State co-ordination. There is a (developing) European market, but there is to be no replacement European State. The gap is bridged by widening the horizons of political, administrative and legal actors within the Member States. It will be recalled that the qualified home State/host State model developed by the Court under Articles 28 and 49 can persua-sively be taken as a method for subjecting national political processes that under-represent interests in market integration to a control that reflects the affected constituencies. So *Cassis de Dijon* subverts host State autonomy and demands that trade-restrictive rules be justified given their prejudicial impact in the con-text of an integrating, inter-State market (above pp 48–51). The 're-regulatory bargain' under secondary legislation can be approached in a similar fashion. Interests that over time have prompted regulation of the market in host States have not been entirely swept aside (though this may sometimes occur); rather, the fact that their expression collided with the process of European market building has caused them to be absorbed into the EC legal order and, under this model of vertical re-distribution of competence, it is now necessary to look (albeit not necessarily exclusively) to Community level—the governing Directive—for the location of the protective rule. Consider a trader in home State X supplying consumers in host State Y. Interested parties in the host State no longer expect enforcement by 'their' authorities, those of State Y. Rather home State X, implementing the Directive under the model of 'indirect rule' foreseen by Articles 10 and 249 EC, is responsible. So home State X has, via the EC's 're-regulation', become obliged to work as a law enforcement agency on behalf of consumers in host State Y. A home State acts on behalf of all Community citizens not simply its own[74].

But why would home States act in this way? Especially (but not only) where the traders based in the home State are politically influential and where damage done by failure to police compliance with EC Directives would largely be felt by citizens in host States, it is not obvious that there are incentives for home States to act effectively to enforce the 're-regulatory bargain'. Quite the reverse. The domestic political mandate is not at all tied to the interests of out-of-State consumers. The EC intervention is based on the construction of a European

[73] T Daintith (ed), *Implementing EC Law in the UK: Structures for Indirect Rule* (Chichester, Deventer, Wiley, 1995). Cf J Vervaele (ed), *Administrative Law Application and Enforcement of Community Law in the Netherlands* (The Hague, Kluwer, 1994); J Vervaele et al (eds), *Compliance and Enforcement of EC Law* (The Hague, Kluwer, 1999).

[74] This is made explicit in recital 22 to Directive 2000/31 n 67 above.

market but associated rule-enforcement is tied to the reality of State systems which are apt to generate decisions (about law enforcement as well as law making) that reflect the interests able directly to influence State political processes; and those are narrower than those envisaged at EC level as affected by market-building achieved by the adoption of secondary legislation. The model of home State enforcement on behalf of parties in the host State runs directly counter to the basics of national-level representative democracy.

This constitutional dimension therefore suggests that there are severe problems in expecting public authorities in the Member States to represent faithfully the interests that the re-regulatory bargain struck through the Community political process assumes they should absorb. Why enforce rules that will damage home-based firms and advantage out-of-state consumers?[75] This suggests that one might predict a degree of regulatory competition between States not in rule-setting (when harmonisation is accepted, for some of the reasons set out above at p 56) associated with the rhetoric of suppressing a race to the bottom and/or with private parties demanding common rules as a trustworthy foundation for a common market) but rather subsequently in rule-enforcement. Home State control may in principle constitute a more efficient market-building device than host State control, but there are problems associated with the plausibility of home State respect for the foundational rules of the European re-regulatory bargain that are directly connected to the ambitiously dexterous constitutional sleight of hand that treats *national* agencies, anchored to a political chain of State-focused responsibility and accountability, as responsible for the enforcement of *Community* rules governing the European market.

This identifies 'indirect rule' as both strong and weak. It is strong in that it harnesses established national legal and bureaucratic systems to the fulfilment of the Community's mission, allowing the Community to operate as a remarkably lean administration[76] while also tending to sweeten the potentially alienating 'foreign' flavour of EC rules by embedding them within everyday local practice. It is weak for the same reason; these are *national* bodies on which such heavy reliance is being placed and, under a perspective that admits minimum deviousness, their heterogenous architecture may simply be unsuitable for the absorption and application of EC-derived rules or, in a context of more injurious delinquency, those national bodies may be induced into deliberate cost-cutting lax enforcement[77]. Given that resource constraints dictate that research into the respect paid to those rules in everyday administrative and

[75] To adhere to the example of broadcasting, see complaints of systematic violation of Dir 89/552's advertising rules recorded in the 3rd Report, note 70 above, p 11. Cf the factual background to Case C-14/96, note 72 above, and other cases examined by Jones n 68 above.

[76] A 'regulatory State' in Majone's phrase, G. Majone, *Regulating Europe* (London, Routledge, 1996). Raising normative questions, see C Joerges, 'Der Philosoph als wahrer Rechtslehrer' (1999) 5 *ELJ* 147.

[77] On the breadth of reasons for non-compliance, see P Van den Bossche, 'In search of remedies for non-compliance: the Experience of the EC', (1996) 3 *Maastricht Journal* 371.

judicial practice in the Member States tends to be sector-specific or even Directive-specific and confined to a small pool of Member States, one becomes readily suspicious that an understanding of 'European law' that focuses on the wording of the Treaty, legislative texts and decisions handed down in Luxembourg may be remote from the diversity of practice among the Member States. The fear is that the current (largely inevitable) 'Don't ask, don't tell' attitude to the quality of implementation of EC rules in the Member States[78], a calculated insouciance likely to prove even more alluring on enlargement, may breed a credibility gap filled only by rumour of laxity elsewhere. This will tend to generate a corrosive spiral of inter-State competitive under-implementation.

Problems and possibilities in improving compliance control

How would poor compliance with EC rules be supervised? Litigation is, once again, the obvious control mechanism, which can illuminatingly be analysed as EC law's method for ensuring that 'indirect rulers', national actors charged with the legal responsibility to apply EC law in favour of affected parties beyond those dominant nationally, do not shirk their task as a result of pressures consequent on their location within national political milieux and their absence of direct political accountability to 'European market interests'. Properly is EC law's deep penetration into national systems regarded as the principal feature which distinguishes it from orthodox international law and, indeed, the relative difficulty of evading obligations once undertaken at EC level combined with the increasing possibilities that such obligations may be imposed by qualified majority vote operate as major factors in explaining the recent sharpening of State sensitivity to the definition of the reach of EC competence[79]. EC law has teeth and their incisive effect renders credible the commitments undertaken on a reciprocal basis by all the Member States. In connection with the Treaty rules on free movement, it has been shown above that litigation driven by interested economic actors has played a vigorous role in securing adaptation of national regulatory cultures. So the EC rules, deployed as weapons before national courts, bruise the complacency of host states tempted to resist imports which do nothing for the market opportunities of firms based on their territory. And all States are equally subject to this pressure. So, equally at the level of secondary legislation, we might assume that violation of the re-regulatory bargain by a home State, whether deliberate or not, will be the subject of a litigious response that will re-direct defaulting national practice back to the European straight and narrow.

---

[78] M Shapiro, p29 in Vervaele (1999) n 73 above.
[79] Cf generally 'flexibility', n 63 above.

That may happen. But, as I have argued more fully elsewhere[80], there are reasons to be cautious about the value of litigation generally in securing the stabilisation of the internal market; and, in particular, there are reasons to be anxious that the likelihood of litigation serving to restrain violation of the obligation to regulate markets effectively in accordance with Community Directives is much lower than the likelihood of litigation aimed at opening up markets in line with the Treaty provisions governing free movement. Litigation as a strategy is important but its contribution to fostering reliable adherence to the rules of EC law is likely to be *ad hoc* and *ex post facto*. In particular, litigation is more likely to play a prominent role in securing the enforcement of 'negative law', where violations are relatively clear-cut, tend to hurt identifiable individual traders and concern affected parties commercially enthusiastic to pursue their complaint, than it is in the context of 'positive law'. This is EC law's 'implementation imbalance'. Violations of the rules of market re-regulation are often hard to detect, both because the very obligation of effective enforcement is itself disturbingly imprecise[81] and because enduring respect for the continuing obligation to enforce Community rules is exceedingly difficult to monitor[82]. States are tempted to exhibit 'creative compliance' with Community rules. This susceptibility is especially alluring given that willing litigants are rarer. Most rules of market re-regulation affect diffuse interests—consumers, proponents of environmental protection—and individual litigants are unlikely to possess a sufficient incentive to pursue the defaulting State. At a more jurisprudentially fundamental level they are less likely than thwarted cross-border traders to be able to show violation of a *right* that is granted to the individual under Community law. In any legal order, the orthodox theoretical assumption in such circumstances would be that collective action would be required. The Commission plays this role in the Community system, but its resources are limited and its intervention is typically slow and on occasion disrupted by politicking. Some national systems may permit or promote collective intervention[83], but this varies

---

[80] S Weatherill, 'Reflections on EC law's "implementation imbalance" in the light of the ruling in Hedley Lomas' in L Krämer, H-W Micklitz and K Tonner (eds), *Law and Diffuse Interests in the European Legal Order* (Baden-Baden, VIEW/ Nomos, 1997); S Weatherill, 'Addressing problems of Imbalanced Implementation in EC Law: Remedies in an Institutional Perspective', C Kilpatrick, T Novitz and P Skidmore (eds), *The Future of Remedies in Europe* (Oxford, Hart Publishing, 2000).

[81] When, for example, does allocation of a small budget to an enforcement agency breach Articles 10 and 249 EC rather than merely reflect fiscal prudence in the allocation of scarce public resources?

[82] The Commission's famous internal market 'League Tables' and 'Scoreboards', available via http://europa.eu.int, refer only to data on transposition of Directives on paper. They tell us nothing about practical and enduring fidelity to Community rules. Nor could the Commission be expected to accumulate such data.

[83] Cf C Barnard, 'A European Litigation Strategy: the Case of the EOC' in J Shaw and G More, *New Legal Dynamics of European Union* (Oxford, Oxford University Press, 1995); C Hilson, 'Community Rights in Environmental Law: Rhetoric or Reality' in J Holder (ed), *The Impact of EC Environmental Law in the UK* (Chichester, Wiley, 1997). See generally H W Micklitz and N Reich (eds), *Public Interest Litigation before European Courts* (Baden-Baden, Nomos, 1996), dealing not only with the Community judicature.

State by State and Community rules are largely lacking[84]. So, seen from the perspective of a State body pondering whether to yield to pressure from local interests to slacken its commitment to the costly enforcement of EC rules, occasional neglect of rules governing, say, water quality or animal welfare is a violation that is qualitatively distinct from restrictions imposed on the import of manufactured goods. In summary, litigation can be, first, no more than a single component of a more broadly-based strategy for securing a viable internal market and, second, it is especially vulnerable to criticism for its patchy effect in the field of positive rather than negative law.

Of the first element of this criticism at least the Commission is perfectly well aware. It continues to rest a heavy emphasis on litigation as a tool of market management but it has wisely concluded that it must develop more pervasive methods for stabilising the internal market than the essentially *ad hoc, ex post facto* route taken by it and by private litigants through the courts. In summary[85], the Commission has busily aimed to devise a web of arrangements designed to improve and intensify co-operation in the management of the internal market, both vertically, between itself and interested public and private parties in the Member States, and horizontally, between different actors at national level. This strategy embraces obligations to notify the Commission of national initiatives that may interfere with cross-border trade, thereby to facilitate Commission supervision, exhortation to States to publicise contact addresses at which dissatisfaction with practice may be directed and frequent soft law encouragement to improve the quality of national supervision and sanctions. The Commission also hopes that periodic publication of 'League Tables' and 'Scoreboards' will induce better rates of compliance without the need for more formal approaches to defaulting States.

Techniques devoted to improving transparency in the management of the market are fundamentally aimed at generating *confidence* in the viability of the internal market among both traders and consumers[86]. The Commission is trying to achieve a great deal here, and it bears the risk that straining to do more than it is able may damage its reputation. It has probably already paid such a price in recent years. But it deserves credit for seeking imaginative schemes for improving compliance with EC law in a political environment which firmly locks it into the model of 'indirect rule'[87]. The inclusion of an insistence on

---

[84] For a small step see the Consumer Injunctions Directive, Dir 98/27 OJ 1998 L166/51; and see proposals on standing in the White Paper on Environmental Liability, COM (00) 66.

[85] For more detail see K Mortelmans, 'The Common Market, the Internal Market and the single market, What's in a Market?' (1998) 35 *CMLRev* 101; S Weatherill, 'New Strategies for Managing the EC's Internal Market', in M Freeman (ed), *Current Legal Problems* (Oxford, Oxford University Press, Vol 53, 2000); K Armstrong, 'Governance and the Single European Market' in Craig and De Burca n 60 above.

[86] Eg Commission report on the Consumer Action Plan, COM (01) 486, esp p11.

[87] The tightness of the grip may be gauged by proposals in the competition field, the area most prominently 'Europeanised' at the level of rule-enforcement, to *surrender* exclusive Commission

improving the application of EC rules at national level in the Commission's White Paper on Governance, published in the summer of 2001, confirms that this is no mere technical matter[88]. It goes to the heart of sustaining a viable system for governing the Union built on horizontal and vertical co-operation between actors at different levels rather than on any desire to make a State at European level[89]. In general the Commission's quest to create a culture of compliance, within which political opprobrium is brought to bear on those who decline to play the EC game, is worthwhile. And, to ensure that anxieties expressed above about mis-application of rules by Member States are not presented in disproportionately gloomy terms, it is plain that in many instances EC law *is* applied more-or-less faithfully and that it *does* cause intriguing local constitutional adaptation[90].

CONCLUSION

The principal purpose of this chapter has been to expose the constitutional implications of the building of an internal market in the European Union under a system which assumes the dominance of national legal and administrative institutions in the implementation and enforcement of rules agreed at transnational level. It has shown that Community law operates by injecting into national practice an obligation to respect interests in the making of a transnational economy. Competence distribution between home and host States is central to understanding the techniques used both under the Treaty and under secondary legislation to pursue the quest to minimise inefficient dual regulation.

A concluding assessment invites a choice of emphasis. One might focus on the dark side of internal market building, which could involve condemnation of the Court for its perceived imbalanced application of the rules of free movement combined with anxiety that the re-regulatory bargain struck in the adoption of secondary legislation is, to some extent in content but much more so in its practical application, more vigorously targeted on effective protection of trading freedoms rather than interests in effective regulation. This perspective would hold that market freedoms may no longer be adequately constrained by national public authorities, because of the deep impact of free movement law, while the

competence over the Art 81(3) power to exempt, thereby releasing (possibly diverse) national level application; OJ 1999 C132, White Paper on Modernization.

[88] COM (01) 428 pp 25–26. Similarly, Green Paper on EU Consumer Protection, COM (01) 531, pp 16–19.

[89] Cf more generally F Snyder, 'Governing Economic Globalisation: Global Legal Pluralism and European Law' (1999) 5 *ELJ* 334; and for a positive account in the context of 'comitology' n 32 above, see C Joerges and J Neyer, 'From Intergovernmental Bargaining to Deliberative Political Processes: the Constitutionalisation of Comitology' (1997) 3 *ELJ* 273.

[90] Cf on 'indirect rule' note 73 above.

Community is unable to step in to plug the gap. This would generate the accusation that the pattern of distribution of competence between home and host States under EC primary and secondary law has privileged private market power at the expense of public intervention.

My basic objection to such a critique is the mistaken assumption that, were it not for the meddling EC, the challenge of transnational economic growth would be cheerfully met by States acting unilaterally or according to conventional forms of intergovernmental co-operation. I choose instead to place a more positive interpretation on this sketch of the evolution of the internal market, preferring to treat it as symptomatic of a more subtle yet fundamentally constructive alteration in political assumptions. What has occurred is constitutionally rather remarkable. The daring attempt to make a European market without investing any significant resources in the creation of European-level enforcement agencies is opposed by basic principles of representative democracy which remain rooted at State level. State actors have been placed in a context in which they are expected to address and promote the interests of parties with no access or only limited access to national political processes. As explained, this is true under the Treaty rules governing free movement (especially p 48 above) and it is true under the relevant instruments of secondary legislation (especially p 66 above). The inefficiencies and inequities that flow from the exercise of State regulatory autonomy are addressed under the home State/ host State model which has been used imaginatively to achieve a vertical and horizontal re-distribution of competence to exercise public functions in order to promote the achievement of the EC's objectives. In this sense membership of the European Union and subjection to its law generates an adaptation of national legal and political orders which reflects the reality of the impact of transnational economic, political and social activity. EC law makes no assumption of the need for a new State at European level. It is not blindly driving political structures to 'chase' the market, rather it seeks to respond by re-shaping the perspectives of States within a politically more open-textured regime. So 'constitutionalism' in the EC represents a remarkably subtle and multi-faceted process through which to cope with the need to mould systems of governance that will allow Europeans to co-operate constructively without having to make impossible choices *between* national *or* European political authority. The internal market is being built according to a vertical and horizontal distribution of competences and not through the imposition of alienating hierarchies.

3

Proportionality and Subsidiarity

GEORGE A. BERMANN

INTRODUCTION

T
HIS CHAPTER IS ABOUT proportionality and, very subsidiarily, about subsidiarity. As far as proportionality is concerned, I deal with it in this chapter both as a standard for determining the appropriateness of proposed legislation and as a standard for determining the validity of legislative measures, that is to say, both as a political and a legal doctrine. But I do so only with respect to *Community*, and not *national*, measures.

It is well-known, of course, that the proportionality principle has a vital role to play in determining the appropriateness and validity of *national* measures.[1] Indeed a comparison is frequently drawn between the manner in which the Court of Justice approaches the proportionality of Community measures, on the one hand, and the proportionality of national measures, on the other. It is commonly said that the Court has traditionally employed, consciously or unconsciously, a stricter test (or at least a stricter degree of scrutiny) in the application of proportionality where a Member State measure is concerned than where a Community measure is concerned. But there are indications that this may be changing, with the differences becoming less pronounced.

That proportionality review of Community and Member State measures might diverge should not, however, come as a complete surprise. As applied to Community measures, the principle of proportionality is a means of ensuring that the political branches of the Community respect fundamental notions of rationality in their determination of the measures to be taken in furtherance of legitimate Community objectives. The interest that proportionality, as employed in this context, seeks to protect is essentially an interest in rationality. To be sure, appeals to rationality are in turn likely to be made in an effort to

---

[1] For a recent study of the Court's application of the proportionality principle to national measures, see Jan H. Jans, 'Proportionality Revisited' , (2000) 27 *Legal Issues of European Integration* 239.

protect other interests, interests that invalidation of a measure on disproportionality grounds may be thought to advance. These interests include, notably,
(a) autonomy interests (i.e. the interest in not being regulated or in being regulated more favorably),[2] (b) local interests (i.e. the interest in having matters regulated, if regulated at all, at a sub-Community level, and (c) substantive
interests other than, and potentially in conflict with, the substantive interests
that the Community measure in question was seeking to advance. Indeed, a
legal challenge against a Community measure is unlikely to be brought at all (at
least not at the instance of a private litigant) unless the complaining party has
or perceives an ulterior interest that invalidation of the Community measure
would advance. But this identification of interests goes primarily to the question
of incentives, or motivations, for raising the principle of proportionality, rather
than to the nature of the proportionality inquiry as such.

By contrast, when the principle of proportionality is applied to national
measures, this traditionally follows from a prior determination, explicit or
implicit, that such measures potentially threaten a fundamental principle or
value of Community law. Historically, that principle often took the form of one
of the four freedoms. This is precisely what was meant by subjecting to proportionality analysis any national measure that got 'caught' by one or more of
the treaty provisions whose purpose is to promote the free movement of goods,
persons, services or capital, and thereby advance market integration and the
internal market. By contrast, Community measures do not need to be 'caught,'
prior to their subjection to the principle of proportionality. More recently, we
are finding that the Community measure may be predicated, not on one of the
four freedoms (or other aspect of the internal market), but rather on a substantive policy that has been brought within the Community sphere—such as environmental or consumer protection, or social policy—and for the promotion of
which the Treaty expressly gives the Community legislative powers independent
of the completion of the internal market.

I am therefore not surprised at the occasional disparity in the Court's
deployment of the principle, according to whether Community or national
measures are its target. I recognize, of course, that there is also a case to be
made for predicting the opposite pattern. When the Court examines a *Community* measure by reference to proportionality, it is advancing the rule of law and
accountability at the Community level—a level of which it itself is a part. By
contrast, deployment of proportionality against *national* measures inevitably
raises issues, or at least concerns, of federalism. A national measure subject to
proportionality review under Community law is presumably a measure that, by
reason of subject matter, falls within Member State competence. Nonetheless
the Court is presuming to decide whether the Member State can justify that

---

[2]   Takis Tridimas, 'Proportionality in Community Law: Searching for the Appropriate Standard of
Scrutiny' in E. Ellis (ed.) *The Principle of Proportionality in the Laws of Europe* (Oxford, Hart
Publishing, 1999), 65.

measure when examined from the point of view of its collateral effects on the internal market. This may explain the reported increase in deference being shown by the Court in its proportionality review of national measures.

The fact remains, however, that while application of a Community law principle of proportionality to national measures unquestionably implicates federalism (and while that fact, taken alone, might militate in favor of a more deferential use of proportionality), its application to such measures is propelled by the assumption that market integration and the internal market—core Community values—are actually or potentially, directly or indirectly, somehow in the balance. Community measures do not come under proportionality scrutiny with quite that prior assumption.[3]

Because I believe that the differences in the practice of proportionality review by the Court of Justice can be understood in this way, I propose to keep proportionality's two domains separate and to focus here on application of the proportionality principle to *Community* measures.[4]

I have two further independent, and quite different, reasons for maintaining a focus on Community measures. First, as mentioned, I mean also to examine in this chapter the principle of subsidiarity. Subsidiarity, as understood within the Community legal order, chiefly expresses limitations on the exercise of the Community's, not the Member States', legislative powers. It is true that if the conditions for the exercise of Community legislative power expressed by the subsidiarity principle are not met, then legislative action should be taken, if at all, at the Member State level or lower. But subsidiarity in itself has nothing further to say about the substance or tenor of the legislation that Member States may or may not then adopt. To the extent that subsidiarity raises legislative justification questions, it raises them exclusively about *Community* measures.

Second, I wish to bring some recent American jurisprudential experience to bear on the proportionality question. It is interesting to observe that, while American constitutional law has long had a chapter that resembles, in its concerns, the principle of proportionality as applied to *national* measures (I refer essentially to the 'dormant' or 'negative' commerce clause), this case law has seen rather little evolution in recent years. It is fair to say that when State measures are examined under the dormant commerce clause, the question asked is

---

[3] Advocate-General Francis Jacobs has taken a broadly similar view. See Francis G. Jacobs, 'Recent Developments in the Principle of Proportionality in European Community Law,' in *The Principle of Proportionality in the Laws of Europe* above n. 2, 1, 21 (1999). See also Tridimas, above note 2, pp 66–67.

[4] Occasionally, the Court, while sustaining a *Community* measure as proportionate, proceeds to invalidate (or cause to be invalidated) a *national* measure that was enacted to implement it. See for example, *Wachauf* v. *Germany*, Case 5/88, [1989] ECR 2609. Unlike the usual case involving a national measures, where the claim is that the measures does not meet the standards for justifying an exception to or derogation from a directly effective treaty provision or an overriding Community policy, here the national measure will (or at least should) be assessed as an instrument which actually purports to implement Community law; Gráinne de Búrca, 'The Principle of Proportionality and its Application in EC Law,' (1993)13 *Yearbook of European Law* 105, 125.

still whether the State measure (assuming it not to be discriminatory on its face) places unreasonable burdens on interstate commerce, and that the scrutiny applied by the courts in answering that question is still rather far from 'strict.'

There has, on the other hand, been an unanticipated revival of the chapter or chapters of American constitutional law that resemble the principle of proportionality as applied to *Community* measures. One branch of this revival takes the form of enforcing stricter limits on the scope of 'interstate commerce' as a justification for the enactment of federal legislation. The United States Supreme Court has taken recently to asking of federal legislation a question it had not asked for over fifty years, namely whether a federal statute under scrutiny was sufficiently linked to problems of interstate commerce to justify Congress' reliance on the interstate commerce clause in its adoption.[5]

More interesting for present purposes, however, is a newer jurisprudential branch related not to Congress' use of the commerce clause as a basis for the enactment of federal legislation, but rather to Congress' use of the 14th Amendment, which among other things prohibits denials of due process and equal protection of the law at the hands of State officials. The Amendment concludes with a section 5, authorizing Congress to enact positive legislation to 'enforce' the substantive purposes of the Fourteenth Amendment. It is on this basis that Congress has enacted much of the federal civil rights, equal rights and non-discrimination legislation that is currently on the books. As of late, the Supreme Court has initiated a review of Congressional justification for resorting to section 5 in the adoption of such legislation, and has as a result struck down several major pieces of federal 14th Amendment-based legislation in just the past few years. What makes this recent federalism development so interesting for present purposes is that the Court has expressly embraced a principle of 'proportionality'—using that very term—in determining whether the 14th Amendment furnishes an adequate constitutional basis for the legislation in question. I propose to examine this nascent proportionality jurisprudence in light of the better established Court of Justice jurisprudence on proportionality-based judicial review.

WHAT DOES A PROPORTIONALITY INQUIRY ENTAIL?

I turn first to proportionality as a limitation on Community lawmaking. The Court's enforcement of the notion of proportionality, if not the concept of proportionality itself, tells us that the inquiry potentially entails a succession of distinctive inquiries.

---

[5] See notes 64–69 below and accompanying text.

Justiciability

The first of these inquiries may be described as a kind of threshold question into proportionality's justiciability. Justiciability may in turn be confronted either in general or in specific terms. Put in general terms—'may courts entertain a proportionality inquiry?'—the question has effectively been answered in the affirmative in the Community law system. Proportionality is a matter that parties may raise in challenging Community legislation, whether in a direct challenge to the legality of such a measure in a Community court (assuming standing in such a court) or by way of preliminary reference from a national court (assuming that the challenger has standing in a national court and that the validity of a Community measure is relevant to the outcome of that proceeding). In other words, in the Community law system, as in so many national law systems, proportionality figures conspicuously among the doctrinal weapons in the general arsenal of weapons that may be leveled at the legality of a legislative measure.[6]

The Court of Justice has clearly situated proportionality among the general principles of law (derived principally from the constitutional traditions of the Member States) that are binding on the Community institutions.[7] Accordingly, proportionality is, at least as a general proposition, a fully justiciable principle. The Maastricht Treaty's introduction of the principle into the Treaty Establishing the European Community[8] certainly did nothing to lessen this impression; nor did the attention that the principle received in a special Protocol to the Treaty of Amsterdam.[9]

While proportionality is a claim that may as a *general* matter be advanced in these situations, the inquiry might possibly, by way of exception, be foreclosed in the case of certain *specific* measures as to which the Court finds itself

---

[6]   See Tridimas, above note 2, p 66.

[7]   Case 11/70, *Internationale Handelsgesellschaft* v. *Einfuhr- und Vorratstelle fur Getreide und Futtermittel*, [1970] ECR 1125; Case 4/73, *Nold* v. *Commission*, [1974] ECR 491.

[8]   EC Treaty, art. 5: 'Any action by the Community shall not go beyond what is necessary to achieve the objectives of this Treaty.'

[9]   As concerns proportionality in particular, the Protocol requires the Community to do the following: (1) legislate 'only to the extent necessary,' (2) legislate in as simple terms as possible, consistent with achieving its objectives, and (3) favour directives to regulations, as well as framework directives to detailed measures (para. 6). The Commission in particular is called upon specifically to take duly into account the need for any burden, whether financial or administrative, falling upon the Community, national governments, local authorities, economic operators and citizens, to be minimized and proportionate to the objective to be achieved (para. 9). The following paragraph shows that, like the principle of subsidiarity more directly, the principle of proportionality may, in particular, favour Member State freedom of action: (7) Regarding the nature and extent of Community action, Community measures should leave as much scope for national decision as possible, consistent with securing the aim of the measure and observing the requirements of the Treaty. While respecting Community law, care should be taken to respect well established national arrangements and the organization and working of Member States' legal systems. Where appropriate, and subject to the need for proper enforcement, Community measures should provide Member States with alternative ways to achieve the objectives of the measures.

ill-equipped to conduct such an inquiry.[10] This would chiefly be due to the Court's conviction that it lacks sufficient knowledge or experience in a certain field to apply the usual proportionality criteria or because it feels that the assessments in the field made by the political branches of government at the Community level should not be reviewed by courts but should instead be left, unreviewed, in the hands of those coordinate branches. It is interesting that, while courts in national systems have occasionally ruled that a given measure should be shielded from general proportionality review due to the basically 'political' character of the matter, the Court of Justice has yet to do so.

The Meaning of Proportionality

Assuming a proportionality inquiry in the courts is not off-limits, either generally or specifically, we arrive at the question of the terms in which it is clothed. It is widely agreed that, at its most general, an assessment of proportionality requires an inquiry into the relationship between a particular objective, on the one hand, and the means used to attain or promote it, on the other. But the question then arises in what terms the requirement of 'reasonableness' is to be described. At least three distinct formulations may be imagined.

First, and most simply, it is possible to ask merely whether the relationship between legislative means and ends is facially reasonable, by which I mean that it is not implausible in logic and/or experience. This is sometimes referred to, in US parlance, as the 'rational relation' test, because it essentially asks whether a reasonable person might conclude that the means selected is a suitable one for purposes of achieving the objective in view. The inquiry is not in principle a deeply searching inquiry and, not surprisingly, few Community measures have fallen victim to it.[11]

However, it is also possible to put the matter much more sharply, by inquiring into whether the means that has been proposed, or actually chosen, is in any relevant respect 'excessive' for purposes of achieving the objective to which we may assume it to be rationally related. Inquiring more specifically into 'excessiveness' opens at least a second and third definitional possibility.

By way of a second proportionality inquiry, one may ask whether the relationship between means and ends is tightly rational in the sense that the benefits of the measure, stated in terms of its objective, outweigh the costs of the measure, stated in terms of that same objective. For obvious reasons, a challenger is likely to invoke, as against the benefits of the measure, its costs measured not only in terms of the stated objective, but in terms of *all* the legally protected

---

[10] Gráinne de Búrca deals chiefly with the prospect of non-justiciability of the principle of proportionality in specific contexts; de Búrca, above note 4, pp 107–10.

[11] An exceptional example might be *Crispoltoni v. Fattoria Autonoma Tabacchi di Citta di Castello*, Case C-368/89 [1991] ECR I-3695.

interests that may be directly or indirectly affected. As de Búrca puts it, '[m]ost of the cases involving proportionality concern a challenge to a particular measure [to the effect that] some legally recognized interest or right has been unacceptably infringed.'[12]

A third and no less searching inquiry would be to ask whether a measure is excessive in the sense of being 'unnecessary' because its objective could have been satisfactorily achieved through a means imposing fewer net costs. Alongside the basic reasonableness inquiry and the cost-benefit analysis, this inquiry has become a common, if not standard, feature of the proportionality assessment.[13] Americans tend to call this a 'least drastic means' inquiry.

Some, and occasionally all, of these inquiries figure into the Court's assessments in the proportionality cases that have come its way.[14] They are all part of the German administrative law concept of proportionality,[15] upon which the Court of Justice and European Community law commentators appear to have drawn. Moreover, they are not mutually exclusive. In principle, courts may require that measures satisfy all three conceptions of proportionality cumulatively.

'Excessive' Proportionality Claims

For proportionality to carry any more than this three-fold baggage would, it seems to me, be excessive in itself. De Búrca raises, and largely rejects, the prospect of courts pushing their proportionality inquiry still further by asking whether a measure entails an expenditure of resources that is 'excessive' in relation to other, different legitimate objectives to which those resources could be harnessed. While all the other inquiries that I have previously formulated are ones that both political decision-makers and judicial-reviewers can legitimately ask under the banner of proportionality, this is a question that entails a direct prioritization among competing public policy objectives. It is accordingly appropriate for the political decision-makers, and only the political decision-makers, to be asking and answering it.

With the possible exception of the basic rationality inquiry, each of the above three questions entails the performance of a balance. But what is balanced

---

[12] de Búrca, above note 4.

[13] The inquiry is typified by rulings of the Court of Justice to the effect that States may not impose marketing prohibitions where labeling requirements will adequately serve the public health or safety interest in view. See, for example, *Commission* v. *Germany* (German beer), Case 178/84, [1987] ECR 1227.

[14] Jacobs, above note 3, at 2 ('As the cases . . . demonstrate, the Court does not always articulate the principle in the full manner advocated by German theorists'). For a good example of a 'cost/benefit' inquiry by the Court of Justice, see *Commission* v. *Denmark* (Beverage containers), Case 302/86, [1988] ECR 4607.

[15] See Jürgen Schwarze, *European Administrative Law* (London, Sweet & Maxwell, 1992) 687 (1992), discussing the German notion of *Verhaltnismassigkeit*.

against what differs according to the proportionality question that is being asked. A cost-benefit analysis basically entails a balance between a measure's advantages and disadvantages. A 'least drastic means' inquiry basically entails a comparison among means: are they reasonably equally effective and, if so, among them which entails the fewest restrictions on other values? By contrast, the final inquiry, which, like de Búrca, I believe pushes proportionality beyond its own limits, would not compare the benefits and costs of means, or compare means themselves, but would instead compare the importance of competing or potentially competing objectives.

Degrees of Scrutiny

Even if courts refrain from conducting the latter inquiry, the fact remains that proportionality—particularly its second and third branches—may lead them into making the same determination that the political branches will already have made, and into making it in precisely the same terms. To the extent that this occurs, judicial review of proportionality raises serious separation of powers questions, and more fundamental questions of legitimacy and accountability. 'Substitution of judgment' (meaning displacement of political by legal assessments) is the phrase commonly used to capture these risks.

So far as we can tell, the Court of Justice, like many national courts that deploy the proportionality doctrine, basically deals with this problem by adjusting the proportionality inquiry in terms of 'level of scrutiny'—although the Court may not, and indeed does not, always say so. At one extreme, it is quite possible for a court to assess for itself, independently and *de novo*, the elements that enter into the various branches of the proportionality assessment. But it is equally possible for the Court to give the assessments that the political branches made on those matters a strong presumption of correctness, overruling one or more of them only when persuaded that they are manifestly unreasonable. And it is possible, of course, for a court to show varying degrees of deference lying between these two extremes.

It has been convincingly shown that the Court of Justice, when assessing the proportionality of Community measures, tends to accord at least some degree of deference to the political branches. In the *Fedesa* case,[16] for example, the Court ultimately found that the challengers failed to show that the institutions, in adopting a hormone ban, had chosen a 'manifestly' unsuitable means, a means whose costs 'manifestly' outweighed its benefits, or a means that was 'manifestly' not the least drastic among the means that were available. Overall, de Búrca concludes 'that the Court of Justice is protective of the institutions'

[16] *R. v. Minister for Agriculture, Fisheries and Food, ex parte Fedesa*, Case C- 331/88, [1990] ECR I-4023 (ban on hormones not inappropriate means of protecting public health and alleviating consumer anxiety, the financial loss not being disproportionate).

policy-making and discretionary decision-making power and that it does not readily intervene on the ground of disproportionality, except where the adverse impact on the applicant appears particularly severe or unfair.'[17] This is particularly apt to be the case under circumstances of scientific uncertainty or, more generally, complexity.[18]

The Court was perhaps most expansive on this point in its *Working-Time Directive* judgment.[19] After laying down the elements of proportionality in fairly conventional style, the Court continued:

> As to judicial review of those conditions, however, the Council must be allowed a wide discretion in an area which, as here, involves the legislature in making social policy choices and requires it to carry out complex assessments. Judicial review of the exercise of that discretion must therefore be limited to examining whether it has been vitiated by manifest error or misuse of powers, or whether the institution concerned has manifestly exceeded the limits of its discretion.

As de Búrca,[20] Jacobs[21] and others[22] have speculated, a good many different factors go into determining the precise degree of deference paid to the political judgment of the institutions and, more generally, the manner in which the proportionality principle is applied. These factors include the breadth of the grant of authority under the treaty or legislation, the importance of the public interest sought to be achieved, the degree of urgency, the extent to which assessments require technical expertise unavailable to courts (or, on the contrary, entail determinations to which courts bring special competence), the scale and duration of the measure, the seriousness of the hardship or adverse impact on private interests, the specificity of the interests affected, and the extent to which the measure raises 'equal treatment' or other fundamental 'constitutional' or other legal problems.[23]

Let us, for example, consider the question whether the Court's level of scrutiny of a Community measure should depend on whether proportionality is raised, on the one hand, by a private party claiming that the measure causes disproportionate harm or loss to the individual or, on the other hand, by a Member State asserting excessive administrative burdens and loss of national or local

---

[17] See, for example, *Schrader v. Hauptzollamt Gronau*, Case 265/87, [1989] ECR 2237; *Bozetti v. Invernizzi*, Case 179/84, [1985] ECR 2301; *Stolting v. Hauptzollamt Hamburg-Jonas*, Case 59/83, [1979] ECR 713; *Biovilac v. EEC*, Case 59/83, [1984] ECR 4057.

[18] See, for example, *Safety Hi-Tech Srl v. S & T Srl*, Case C-284/95, [1998] ECR I-4301.

[19] *United Kingdom v. Council*, Case C-84/94, [1996] ECR I-5755. To the same effect, see also *Germany v. Parliament and Council*, Case C-233/94, [1997] ECR I-2405; *Germany v. Council*, Case C-426/93, [1995] ECR I-3723 (Statistical registers); *Germany v. Council* (Bananas), Case C-280/93, [1994] ECR I-4973.

[20] See note 4 above.

[21] According to Jacobs (above note 3, p 3) the case law 'allows for a more or less exacting standard of judicial review depending on the character and context of the measure under review.'

[22] See, for example, Tridimas, above note 2, pp 68–69.

[23] de Búrca, above note 4. For a similar conclusion regarding the Court's use of the proportionality principle vis-à-vis national measures, see Jans, above note 1, pp 263–64.

policymaking autonomy. It seems to me eminently sensible that, all things being equal, the Court should take a closer look at a claim of individual harm as compared to the claim of Member State harm.[24] Though individual Member States rarely have a legislative veto any longer, they nevertheless play a central role (and may in any event be heard) in the Community's legislative processes. Unlike the proportionality claims of private parties, there is ample opportunity for their proportionality-based arguments to be accommodated in the fashioning of Community policy.[25]

Considerations such as these may explain why the Court does in fact occasionally take a 'hard look' at a Community measure, annulling it as in violation of the principle of proportionality. De Búrca's survey of the cases shows a not insignificant number of cases not only in agriculture[26] and trade,[27] but also in areas of harmonization of domestic laws, in which proportionality challenges have succeeded. Admittedly, a number of these cases entailed systems of forfeitures or sanctions,[28] or involved measures having an adverse impact on a very small number of traders, but not all of them do. This is consistent with Emiliou's findings,[29] as well as with those of Jacobs who has reviewed them on the basis of the Court's very recent judgments.[30]

No one who has seriously studied the proportionality cases involving Community measures seems very comfortable drawing general conclusions on the basis of which firm predictions may be drawn—either as to the terms in which and the level of scrutiny with which the Court will apply the proportionality principle in any given case or as to the probable outcome.[31] Tridimas expresses

---

[24] See generally Nicholas Emiliou, *The Principle of Proportionality in European Law: A Comparative Study* (London, Kluwer Law International, 1996).

[25] On the other hand, it must be recognized that non-privileged applicants are more likely to be given standing to question the proportionality of Community law measures where they participated in the procedure leading to the adoption of that measure.

[26] *Bela-Muhle Josef Bergmann KG v. Grows-Farm GmbH & Co., KG*, Case 114/76, [1977] ECR 1211; *Granaria*, Case 116/76, [1977] ECR 1247; *Olmuhle and Becher*, Joined Cases 119–120/76, [1977] ECR 1269); *Crispoltoni I*, Case C-368/89, [1991] ECR I-3695.

[27] *The Queen v. Customs and Excise, ex parte National Dried Fruit Trade Association*, Case 77/86, [1988] ECR 757.

[28] *Atalanta Amsterdam BV v. Produktschap Voor Vee en Vlees*, Case 240/78, [1979] ECR 2137; *Maas*, Case 21/85, [1986] ECR 3537; *Buitoni*, Case 122/78, [1979] ECR 677; *The Queen ex parte E.D.&F. Man (Sugar) Ltd. v. IBAP*, Case 181/84, [1985] ECR 2889.

[29] *Emiliou*, above note 24.

[30] Jacobs, above note 3, pp 5–8. Jacobs cites in particular two judgments concerning the legality of Commission regulations levying a charge on imports of preserved mushrooms. *Hupeden v. Hauptzollamt Hamburg-Jonas*, Case C-295/94, [1996] ECR I-3375; *Pietsch v. Hauptzollamt Hamburg-Waltershof*, Case C-296/94, [1996] ECR I-3409. For earlier cases raising similar issues in the same sector, see *Werner Faust*, Case C-24/90, [1991] ECR I-4905; *Wunsche*, Cases C-25–26/90, [1991] ECR I-4939, 4961. But see *Binder v. Hauptzollamt, Stuttgart-West*, Case C-205/94, [1996] ECR I-2871.

[31] Jacobs (above note 3, p 8) is quite explicit:
'From the above brief survey of recent cases, it is difficult to draw any general conclusions about the standard of review. That may be a difficulty inherent in any analysis, simply because the context varies greatly from one case to another, the type of issue addressed also varies, and much will depend on the nature of the evidence and the level of argument addressed to the Court.'

the apparent consensus in remarking that 'far from dictating a uniform test, proportionality is a flexible principle which is used in different contexts to protect different interests and entails varying degrees of judicial scrutiny. It is by its nature flexible and open-textured.'[32] Emiliou tends to agree.[33]

It is difficult to argue with this assessment from a descriptive point of view. It is also difficult to argue with it from a prescriptive point of view either. Judicial resources are precious, particularly in the Community, where they are concentrated in a remarkably small set of judicial hands. Moreover, proportionality, by its very nature, conjures—more than any other general principle of law deployed by the Court—a revisiting of the legislative merits, thus raising serious separation of powers (hence, legitimacy) concerns. Even though we may arrive (as we largely have) at a consistent and doctrinally coherent statement of the proportionality principle, the Community courts need the freedom to intensify or relax the level of scrutiny with which they enforce that principle as the cases come along. In point of fact, they will act in this fashion, whether we acknowledge their right to do so or not. And no one, in my judgment, has marshaled a strong case that their doing so has caused any substantial harm or injustice.

SUBSIDIARITY

If proportionality occupies a central place in judicial review of Community legislation, indications thus far are that subsidiarity does not. This is not, in my judgement, due to the non-justiciability of the subsidiarity principle. Certainly the Court has said nothing to suggest its non-justiciability, far from it; nor have the Community institutions or the Member States. Indeed the Amsterdam Treaty's Protocol on the Application of the Principle of Subsidiarity and Proportionality suggests the contrary.[34]

But justiciability notwithstanding, it is noteworthy that only in two cases thus far has the Court of Justice more or less confronted the principle of subsidiarity in the context of challenges to the validity of Community measures.[35] In accordance with many predictions, including the author's own, the Court appears to be avoiding the 'merits,' so to speak, of the subsidiarity question; by the 'merits,' I mean the question whether the subsidiarity-based preconditions

---

[32] Tridimas, above note 2, p 76.

[33] Emiliou, above note 24, p 171 ('[T]he requirements of proportionality cannot be precisely formulated or even exhaustively defined. They necessarily depend on the type of case.')

[34] Paragraph 13 of the Protocol states: 'Compliance with the principle of subsidiarity shall be reviewed in accordance with the rules laid down by the Treaty.'

[35] See notes 39–41 below and accompanying text.

for the exercise of the Community's legislative authority in areas of concurrent competence are met.

There are a range of available techniques for avoiding the subsidiarity question, and they differ widely. It may be held, as the Court of First Instance has done, that the principle of subsidiarity may not be leveled at Community measures adopted prior to the entry into force of the amendments introduced by the Maastricht Treaty. This seems eminently reasonable.[36]

More questionable is the suggestion that since the principle of subsidiarity has no application in areas of exclusive Community competence, it does not apply to the question of the validity of harmonization directives adopted at the Community level—the theory being that only the Community, and not the Member States, has competence to 'harmonize' Member State law. This is a questionable proposition because what really matters is not whether Member States share in the Community's competence to *harmonize* laws in a given regulatory field, but rather whether they have reserved competence to *legislate* at least to some extent within that field. In most areas subject to Community law harmonization, the Member States have done exactly that. To treat a field as subject to exclusive Community competence merely because, while the Member States may admittedly *legislate* in the field, they cannot *harmonize* in the field, is to free the Community from the precise 'discipline' to which the principle of subsidiarity meant to subject it. Indeed the very validity of a harmonization/legislation distinction is subject to question. In *United Kingdom* v. *Council (Working time directive)*,[37] a case which is dealt with more fully below,[38] the Court assumed the principle of subsidiarity to be applicable, even though the underlying treaty provision clearly contemplated harmonization (albeit without that precise term being used).

A more principled way to cabin the principle of subsidiarity as a judicial tool is to 'proceduralize' it, in the sense of requiring the institutions to make a reasoned 'finding' that the conditions permitting Community action in fields of concurrent competence are met. The judgments thus far rendered by the Court of Justice are consistent with the notion that subsidiarity, as a judicial instrument, will be fundamentally procedural in nature. But those judgments give us little reason to believe that, even as a procedural requirement, subsidiarity is going to be taken very seriously. On the contrary, the indications that we have suggest that quite perfunctory 'findings' may quite easily pass muster.

Germany v. *Parliament and Council (deposit guarantee schemes)*[39] was a challenge to a Community directive requiring the creation by the Member States of deposit guarantee systems. Germany complained, among other things, that

---

[36] A possible exception would be in the field of environmental protection, inasmuch the subsidiarity principle was introduced in that field by the Single European Act, effective 1987.
[37] Case C-84/94, [1996] ECR I-5755.
[38] See note 41 below.
[39] Case C-233/94, [1997] ECR I-2405.

the Council and Parliament had failed to comply with the requirement of reasons laid down in the Treaty, and more particularly failed to give its reasons for concluding that the principle of subsidiarity justified adoption of the directive. The Court's treatment of that claim, which is now well known,[40] suggested that it would suffice for the institutions to reach and state a 'subsidiarity' conclusion and that it was not necessary that they recite detailed, much less convincing, evidence in support of that conclusion. *United Kingdom* v. *Council (Working time directive)*[41] reinforces this impression as does *Netherlands* v *Parliament*.[41a] It must be recognized, however, that for reasons best known to them, neither Germany nor the United Kingdom (nor the Netherlands) had challenged the 'merits' of the subsidiarity issue, focusing instead on issues of presentation.

The possibility cannot be excluded that the day will come when the Court eventually rules that a finding that the conditions for the exercise of the Community's legislative authority in areas of concurrent competence, as laid down in the subsidiarity principle, are not satisfied. The *Tobacco advertising* case put an end to suggestions that the Court would *never* find a harmonization measure so insufficiently related to the functioning of the internal market as to render it essentially *ultra vires*. In my judgment, the Court should leave open the possibility (however remote it may be) of a like invalidation of a Community measure on subsidiarity grounds—if only as a healthy reminder to the institutions that they should genuinely take subsidiarity considerations into

---

[40]   The Court stated:

> 26. In this case, we observe that in the directive's second recital, the Parliament and Council concluded that 'there was reason to worry about the situation that might arise in the event of unavailability of the deposits of a credit establishment having branches in other Member States,' and that it was indispensable that a minimum harmonized level of deposit protection be guaranteed, wherever the deposits happen to be located within the Community. These recitals show that the Community legislature considered that the purpose of the measure could—on account of the dimensions of the action that was contemplated—be better achieved at the Community level . . ..

> 27. Moreover . . . the Parliament and Council observe that the action taken by the Member States pursuant to an earlier Commission recommendation had not served to achieve completely the results that had been desired. Thus, the Community legislature concluded that the purpose of its action could not satisfactorily be achieved by the Member States.

> 28. From these recitals, it follows that the Parliament and Council, in any event, had specified the reasons for which they considered that their action was in conformity with the principle of subsidiarity, and therefore they complied with the requirement of reasons . . ... It cannot be required, in this regard, that the principle be expressly mentioned.

[41]   Case C-84/94, [1996] ECR I-5755. The Court (para. 47) stated:

> Once the Council has found that it is necessary to improve the existing level of protection as regards the health and safety of workers and to harmonize the conditions in this area while maintaining the improvements made, achievement of that objective through the imposition of minimum requirements necessarily presupposes Community-wide action, which otherwise, as in this case, leaves the enactment of the detailed implementing provisions required largely to the Member States.

[41a]   Case C-377/98 *Netherlands* v *European Parliament and Council* (biotechnology), judgment of 9 October 2001. The Court stated:

account in the course of the Community legislative process. As a judicial instrument within the European Community, the subsidiarity principle should probably not be expected to deliver a great deal more than that.

The Member States have certainly done what they can to reinforce the 'procedural' message. The guidelines adopted by the European Council at Edinburgh in 1992 and, more recently, the Amsterdam Treaty's Protocol on the Application of the Principle of Subsidiarity and Proportionality[42] clearly sound that note.

> 31. It should be borne in mind that, under the second paragraph of Article 3b of the EC Treaty, in areas which do not fall within its exclusive competence, the Community is to take action only if and insofar as the objectives of the proposed action cannot be sufficiently achieved by the Member States and can therefore, by reason of the scale or effects of the proposed action, be better achieved by the Community.
>
> 32. The objective pursued by the Directive, to ensure smooth operation of the internal market by preventing or eliminating differences between the legislation and practice of the various Member States in the area of the protection of biotechnological inventions, could not be achieved by action taken by the Member States alone. As the scope of that protection has immediate effects on trade, and, accordingly, on intra-Community trade, it is clear that, given the scale and effects of the proposed action, the objective in question could be better achieved by the Community.
>
> 33. Compliance with the principle of subsidiarity is necessarily implicit in the fifth, sixth and seventh recitals of the preamble to the Directive, which state that, in the absence of action at Community level, the development of the laws and practices of the different Member States impedes the proper functioning of the internal market. It thus appears that the Directive states sufficient reasons on that point.

[42]   The Protocol provides in pertinent part:

> (1) In exercising the powers conferred on it, each institution shall ensure that the principle of subsidiarity is complied with . . ..
>
> (4) For any proposed Community legislation, the reasons on which it is based shall be stated with a view to justifying that it complies with the principles of subsidiarity and proportionality; the reasons for concluding that a Community objective can be better achieved by the Community must be substantiated by qualitative, and wherever possible, quantitative indicators.
>
> . . .
>
> (9) Without prejudice to its right of initiative, the Commission should:
>
> . . . consult widely before proposing legislation and, wherever appropriate, publish consultation documents;
>
> justify the relevance of its proposals with regard to the principle of subsidiarity; whenever necessary, the explanatory memorandum accompanying a proposal will give details in this respect . . ..
>
> . . .
>
> submit an annual report to the European Council, the Council and the European Parliament on the application of [the subsidiarity principle] . . ..
>
> (11) While fully observing the procedures applicable, the European Parliament, as an integral part of the overall examination of Commission proposals, consider their consistency with [the subsidiarity principle]. This concerns the original Commission proposal as well as amendments which the European Parliament and the Council envisage making to the proposal.
>
> (12) In the course of the procedures referred to in [the treaty articles governing the legislative process], the European Parliament shall be informed of the Council's position on the application of [the subsidiarity principle], by way of a statement of the reasons which led the Council to adopt its common position. The Council shall inform the European Parliament of the reasons on the basis of which all or part of a Commission proposal is deemed to be inconsistent with [the subsidiarity principle].

PROPORTIONALITY (AND SUBSIDIARITY)
IN SUPREME COURT CASE-LAW

In sum, notwithstanding the Court of Justice's considerable prudence in its exercise, the principle of proportionality strikes me as far the more potent judicial instrument for controlling the output of the Community legislative process. Recent developments in the U.S. Supreme Court's constitutional jurisprudence, in my judgement, lend substantial support to this belief. As indicated at the outset, I refer chiefly to the largely unexpected emergence of a 'proportionality' doctrine in the Court's jurisprudence under the 14th Amendment, but I will also examine, by reference to the Court's Interstate Commerce Clause review of federal legislation the 'subsidiarity' aspects of its recent case law.

Proportionality and Congress' Exercise of Power to Enforce the 14th Amendment

The 14th Amendment to the U.S. Constitution provides, in pertinent part:

> 1. . . . No State . . . shall make or enforce any law which shall abridge the privileges or immunities of citizens of the United States; nor shall any State deprive any person of life, liberty, or property, without due process of law; nor deny to any person within its jurisdiction the equal protection of the laws.
>
> . . .
>
> 5. . . . The Congress shall have power to enforce, by appropriate legislation, the provisions of this article.

Over the last forty years, Congress has predicated the enactment of numerous pieces of federal social justice legislation on section 5 of the 14th Amendment as appropriate means of enforcing the substantive provisions of the 14th Amendment, and more particularly its 'due process' and 'equal protection' clauses.

The relevance of the 14th Amendment to subsidiarity and proportionality basically lies in the following. The 14th Amendment was added to the US Constitution, following the American Civil War, precisely in order to ensure that the American states (and persons acting under the authority of the States) would be required to respect the principles of due process and equal protection which, by that time, were already binding on the federal government (and persons acting under its authority) by virtue of the 5th Amendment dating back to 1791. One might have expected that the Supreme Court would directly deploy proportionality-like principles in its policing of State and local government measures under the 14th Amendment.

At the same time, however, section 5 of the 14th Amendment also created a new constitutional basis for positive federal legislative action, by specifically enabling Congress to enact legislation where required to ensure that the States, when acting within their own proper constitutional sphere, did not infringe the federal constitutional principles of equal protection and due process. In light of this potentially vast grant of new federal legislative powers, one might have expected the Court to introduce proportionality- and subsidiarity-like principles as limits on their use.

Despite the 14th Amendment's long history, Congress' reliance on it as a basis for federal legislation targeting the States has only recently come under serious scrutiny by the Supreme Court. It is true that most of the federal statutes that have been challenged present the peculiarity of creating federal judicial causes of action, thereby creating specific difficulties so far as their application to the States is concerned. This particular problem arises from the fact that, according to the 11th Amendment of the Constitution, as judicially construed, no State may be sued in federal court without its consent. It would appear then that, while Congress may be entitled under various provisions of the Constitution to enact legislation creating judicial remedies, it may not—consistent with the 11th Amendment—constitutionally provide for their application to the States themselves. The Supreme Court has resoundingly acted on this belief, invalidating federal legislation under the Interstate Commerce Clause insofar as that legislation sought to subject States to suit in federal court.[43] The Court has subsequently ruled that, although the 11th Amendment itself refers only to the States' immunity from suit in *federal* court, a broader (largely unwritten) constitutional principle of state sovereign immunity prevents Congress from subjecting the States to suit without their consent in their own *state* courts as well.[44]

At the same time, however, the Court has acknowledged that Congress may, through appropriate legislation based on the 14th Amendment, 'abrogate' the 11th Amendment bar.[45] (Parenthetically, the notion that Congress may avoid the effect of one constitutional amendment by the mere adoption of legislation pursuant to another—albeit subsequent—constitutional amendment strikes me and others as peculiar, to put it mildly. The real reason for the Court's taking this position must be that otherwise certain landmark civil rights legislation targeting the States—such as the Voting Rights Act of 1965—would be rendered invalid.)

At the time that the Court first made this pronouncement about the use of the 14th Amendment to overcome 11th Amendment immunity, it was not thought that the courts would look very deeply into the question of the 'appropriateness' of that legislation as a tool for enforcing the guarantees of due process and equal protection against the States. But a majority of the Supreme Court has

---

[43] *Seminole Tribe of Florida v. Florida*, 517 U.S. 44 (1996).
[44] *Alden v. Maine*, 527 U.S. 706 (1999). The Court of Justice's *Francovich* jurisprudence certainly provides a lively contrast.
[45] *Fitzpatrick v. Bitzer*, 427 U.S. 445 (1976).

clearly indicated that this is precisely what is to be done. Moreover, the majority has placed the notion of proportionality (as well as 'congruence') at the analytic center of this inquiry. In every case that the Supreme Court has recently
decided under this analysis, a slim majority of the Court has voted to strike
down the federal legislation in question as unconstitutional, giving as its reason
for doing so Congress' failure to make a proportional and congruent use of the
14th Amendment's enforcement clause.

Thus, in *Kimel v. Florida Board of Regents*,[46] a majority of the Court concluded that the federal Age Discrimination in Employment Act of 1967
(ADEA)[47] did not validly abrogate the States' 11th Amendment immunity
because 'the substantive requirements that the ADEA imposes on state and local
governments are disproportionate to any unconstitutional conduct that could
conceivably be targeted by the Act.' The Court so held on the strength of its
prior rulings that classifications according to age are, for various reasons, not
constitutionally 'suspect' as are classifications by race or gender. Since discrimination on account of age is subject only to a 'rational basis' test of constitutional review, the Court considered the likelihood of state violations of the
equal protection rights of older persons to be insufficient to justify the remedial
legislation in question. In other words, the statute (which broadly prohibited all
discrimination on account of age, subject to certain exceptions) was found to
prohibit a substantially broader range of conduct than was likely to be held
unconstitutional under 'rational basis' standards. It was, to that extent, judged
excessive.

When the Court turned to the ADEA's legislative record, it found that Congress' extension of the ADEA to the States 'was an unwarranted response to a
perhaps inconsequential problem,' since 'Congress never identified any pattern
of age discrimination by the States, much less any discrimination whatsoever
that rose to the level of constitutional violation.' Indeed, '[t]he evidence com-
piled . . . to demonstrate such attention by Congress to age discrimination by
the State falls well short of the mark.'[48] In sum, 'Congress had virtually no
reason to believe that state and local governments were unconstitutionally discriminating against their employees on the basis of age.' 'Although that lack of
support is not determinative of the section 5 inquiry, Congress' failure to
uncover any significant pattern of unconstitutional discrimination here confirms that Congress had no reason to believe that broad prophylactic legislation
was necessary in the field.'[49]

---

[46] 528 U.S. 62 (2000).
[47] 29 U.S.C. secs. 621 et seq.
[48] 528 U.S. p 89.
[49] Id. p 91.

More recently, in *Board of Trustees of the University of Alabama* v. *Garrett*,[50] a majority of the Court found the Americans with Disabilities Act (ADA)[51] to be an invalid attempt by Congress to abrogate the States' 11th Amendment immunity. The Court concluded that Congress had made only general findings and had cited merely 'anecdotal' incidents of employment discrimination on the part of the States against the disabled. In the absence of an identifiable history and pattern of unconstitutional conduct, the legislation could not be said to be appropriate.

But the Court went further. It found that even if a sufficient pattern had been shown, the rights and remedies granted by the ADA were not 'congruent and proportional' to the targeted violation. The Court reasoned as follows:

[W]hereas it would be entirely rational (and therefore constitutional) for a state employer to conserve scarce resources by hiring employees who are able to use existing facilities, the ADA requires employers to 'make existing facilities used by employees readily accessible to and usable by individuals with disabilities.' The ADA does except employers from the 'reasonable accommodation' requirement where the employer 'can demonstrate that the accommodation would impose an undue hardship on the operation of the business of such covered entity.' However, even with this exception, the accommodation duty far exceeds what is constitutionally required in that it makes unlawful a range of alternate responses that would be reasonable but would fall short of imposing an 'undue burden' upon the employer. The Act also makes it the employer's duty to prove that it would suffer such a burden, instead of requiring (as the Constitution does) that the complaining party negate reasonable bases for the employer's decision . . ..

. . .

Congressional enactment of the ADA represents its judgment that there should be a 'comprehensive national mandate for the elimination of discrimination against individuals with disabilities.' Congress is the final authority as to desirable public policy, but in order to authorize private individuals to recover money damages against the States, there must be a pattern of discrimination by the States which violates the 14th Amendment, and the remedy imposed by Congress must be congruent and proportional to the targeted violation. Those requirements are not met here . . ..

The Court's majority has similarly scrutinized federal legislation purporting to enforce the 14th Amendment's guarantee of due process, as distinct from equal protection. In *Florida Prepaid Postsecondary Education Expense Board* v. *College Savings Bank*,[52] the majority ruled that the federal Patent and Plant Variety Protection Remedy Clarification Act,[53] which subjected States to patent infringement suits, was not appropriate legislation under section 5 of the 14th

---

[50] 531 U.S. 356 (2001).
[51] 42 U.S.C. secs. 12111–17.
[52] 527 U.S. 627 (1999).
[53] 35 U.S.C. secs. 271(h), 296(a).

Amendment and was thus incapable of abrogating the States' 11th Amendment immunity. The Court reasoned that Congress had failed to identify a pattern of patent infringement by the States, 'let alone a pattern of constitutional violations.'[54] Because the majority thought it unlikely that many of the acts of patent infringement addressed by the statute could be considered as unconstitutional, it found the statute to be 'out of proportion' in scope to its supposed remedial or preventive objectives. 'Congress appears to have enacted this legislation in response to a handful of instances of state patent infringement that do not necessarily violate the Constitution.'[55] The statute's 'indiscriminate' scope offended the principle that the means chosen by Congress must be proportional to Congress' legitimate aims.

Although the 14th Amendment issue may appear to have grown out of the 11th Amendment cases, that is not the case. There is no reason to suppose that proportionality attacks cannot be mounted against 14th Amendment-based laws that do *not* create causes of action in federal court against the States, thus triggering 11th Amendment questions. In fact in its very first 'proportionality and congruence' cases under the 14th Amendment, Congress had not sought, as such, to subject the States to suit in federal court.

In *City of Boerne v. Flores*,[56] the Court applied the 'congruence and proportionality' standard to hold that the Religious Freedom Restoration Act of 1993 (RFRA)[57] was an inappropriate use of the 14th Amendment. The RFRA, whose purpose Congress identified as supporting freedom of exercise of religion as guaranteed by the 1st Amendment,[58] prohibited government from 'substantially burdening' a person's exercise of religion, even if the burden results from an otherwise valid rule of general applicability, unless the government can demonstrate that the burden being imposed '(1) is in furtherance of a compelling governmental interest; and (2) is the least restrictive means of furthering that compelling governmental interest.' The statute created no cause of action as such, much less a cause of action against the States in federal court.

In *City of Boerne*, a church invoked the RFRA in support of its challenge to a local government decision denying it, on historic preservation grounds, a building permit to enlarge its physical premises. The case gave the Court an opportunity to examine the adequacy of the RFRA's legislative basis in the 14th Amendment. While admitting that Congress, in seeking to deter or remedy constitutional violations, may prohibit conduct that is not itself unconstitutional, a majority of the Court concluded that the legislative record contained insufficient (and, in the Court's view, mostly 'anecdotal') evidence of the

---

[54] 527 U.S. p 640.

[55] Id. pp 645–46.

[56] 521 U.S. 507 (1997).

[57] 42 U.S.C. secs. 2000bb et seq.

[58] The 14th Amendment's due process clause has been interpreted as, among other things, subjecting the States to the obligation to respect the 1st Amendment.

94   *George A. Bermann*

unconstitutional conduct that the RFRA appeared to target. More important, the majority concluded that the RFRA was 'so out of proportion to a supposed remedial or preventive object that it cannot be understood as responsive to, or designed to prevent, unconstitutional behavior.'[59]

The majority deemed the statute disproportionate in large part because, rather than 'enforce' the 14th Amendment, the statute sought to 'define' its scope and indeed to enlarge its substantive meaning:

> . . . RFRA cannot be considered remedial, preventive legislation, if those terms are to have any meaning. RFRA is so out of proportion to a supposed remedial or preventive object that it cannot be understood as responsive to, or designed to prevent, unconstitutional behavior. It appears instead to attempt a substantive change in constitutional protections. Preventive measures prohibiting certain types of laws may be appropriate when there is reason to believe that many of the laws affected by the congressional enactment have a significant likelihood of being unconstitutional . . ..
>
> RFRA is not so confined. Sweeping coverage ensures its intrusions at every level of government, displacing laws and prohibiting official actions of almost every description and regardless of subject matter . . ..
>
> The stringent test RFRA demands of state laws reflects a lack of proportionality or congruence between the means adopted and the legitimate end to be achieved. If an objector can show a substantial burden on his free exercise, the State must demonstrate a compelling governmental interest and show that the law is the least restrictive means of furthering its interests . . .. Requiring a State to demonstrate a compelling interest and show that the law is the least restrictive means of achieving that interest is the most demanding test known to constitutional law . . .. Even assuming RFRA would be interpreted in effect to mandate some lesser test . . .. the statute nevertheless would require searching judicial inquiry of state law with the attendant likelihood of invalidation. This is a considerable congressional intrusion into the States' traditional prerogatives . . ..[60]

The majority supported its conclusion by invoking the separation of powers principle; it argued that in seeking to define the scope and meaning of the 14th Amendment, Congress had sought to decide future cases and controversies, and that such a function was the province of the judiciary.

The reasoning set forth in *City of Boerne* is doubly ironic. In the first place, the majority invoked and employed the principle of proportionality against Congress in order to prohibit Congress from, in effect, itself imposing the principle of proportionality (in the form of a requirement of 'least drastic means' in burdening the free exercise of religion) upon state and local governments. Moreover, in condemning the legislation as in violation of the principle of the

[59] 521 U.S. p 532.
[60] 521 U.S. pp 532–34.

separation of powers, the Court itself appears to have committed a far more serious violation of that principle.

More recently, a majority of the Court, in the case of *United States v. Morrison*,[61] struck down the Violence Against Women Act of 1994,[62] a statute which provided a federal civil remedy for victims of gender-motivated violence. The suit arose out of a civil claim by a university student rape victim against her rapists and against a Virginia state university for its inadequate response to that incident. A majority once again invalidated the statute for its lack of 'congruence and proportionality between the injury to be prevented or remedied and the means adopted to that end.' Its stated reasons for so concluding were that (a) the 14th Amendment does not justify the enactment of legislation creating causes of action arising out of essentially private conduct or providing a remedy essentially directed at private parties, and (b) in any event the record did not demonstrate that the problem of discrimination against victims of gender-motivated crimes exists in all or even most of the States.

With respect to the first branch of its reasoning, the majority appears to have assumed (without explanation) that it is disproportionate and incongruent to attack state violations of equal protection by creating a civil remedy against private parties. Nor did the majority explain why a 'state action' dimension was missing insofar as allegations against the state of Virginia were concerned. (The congressional record of the legislation sought to document pervasive bias against victims of gender-motivated violence in state justice systems—and consequently a denial of equal protection of the laws—through stereotypes about women, excessive attention to the behavior and credibility of victims, insufficient investigation and prosecution of claims of violence, and too lenient punishment of those convicted.) With respect to the second branch of its reasoning, the majority broke new ground by suggesting that an otherwise valid federal enactment would be 'incongruent' if it addressed at the federal level a problem that exists only in some, and not all, the States.

The *City of Boerne* and *Morrison* cases show the Supreme Court's readiness to review federal legislation enacted under the 14th Amendment from a proportionality perspective even when 11th Amendment immunity is not an issue. The RFRA did not create a cause of action at all, while the Violence Against Women Act was challenged chiefly as a basis for lawsuits against private persons rather than against States. The result in both cases was invalidation of the legislation, essentially on grounds of proportionality as understood by the Court. Clearly, the proportionality doctrine's scope of application is fully as broad as Congress' power to enforce the substantive provisions of the 14th Amendment.

The 14th Amendment proportionality cases are especially interesting because it has been understood and accepted that Congress' powers under section 5 of

---

[61] 529 U.S. 598 (2000).
[62] 42 U.S.C. sec. 13981(b).

the 14th Amendment are not confined to enacting legislation that merely 'parrots' the wording of the 14th Amendment. On the contrary, its power 'includes the authority both to remedy and to deter violations of rights guaranteed thereunder by prohibiting a somewhat broader swath of conduct, including that which is not itself forbidden by the Amendment's text.'[63] If this is so, the proportionality inquiry gives the courts the opportunity to determine on a case by case basis just how much more broadly than section 1 of the 14th Amendment Congress is permitted to 'sweep' when exercising its legislative enforcement powers under section 5 of the Amendment.

In their reasoning and their results, the recent cases show how dramatically the workings of the proportionality doctrine in this context can reduce Congress' scope of legislative discretion. From a more explicitly comparative point of view, they show that the notion of proportionality lends itself to still further and more far-reaching analytic uses than those of which the Court of Justice has thus far availed itself. True, one could argue that the Supreme Court majority, by condemning excessive federal legislation, is doing nothing more in the recent cases than imposing on Congress a 'least restrictive means' requirement. But the fact is that the cases do something quite a bit different than comparing what Congress has done with what Congress might less restrictively have done in meeting a legitimate objective. They question whether Congress was right in coming to the conclusion that anything by way of enforcement of the 14th Amendment needed to be done at all.

In some sense—indeed precisely because they call into question the *necessity* for federal legislative intervention—the Supreme Court's recent proportionality cases more closely resemble a *subsidiarity* than a *proportionality* inquiry, as those terms are used in European Community law. But this is not quite the case either. The subsidiarity principle in Community law invites a determination as to whether the States are capable of effectively addressing an acknowledged problem and whether federal intervention is called for in arriving at a solution. The Supreme Court's recent 14th Amendment jurisprudence asks and answers (mainly in the negative) the question whether there is a demonstrable problem to begin with.

Subsidiarity and the Limits on the Interstate Commerce Clause

At first glance, the principle of subsidiarity also appears to have recently made an important appearance in U.S. Supreme Court jurisprudence. As is well known, a majority of the Court ruled in *United States* v. *Lopez*[64] that Congress could not constitutionally enact the Gun-Free School Zones Act of 1990[65] on

---

[63] *Kimel*, above note 46.
[64] 514 U.S. 549 (1995).
[65] 18 U.S.C. sec. 922(q)(1)(A).

the basis of the Interstate Commerce Clause of the Constitution, because Congress had failed, in enacting the legislation, to find the requisite impact on interstate commerce. Following *Lopez*, some commentators maintained that the Court had predicated its ruling less on the absence of an effect on interstate commerce than on the absence of *findings* of such an effect, thus leaving open the question whether, when Congress makes such findings, the Court will consider itself free to 'look behind' them and examine their credibility. My own reading of *Lopez* is that the Court has reserved for the courts the right to decide whether interstate commerce is genuinely implicated, although the precise criteria for making that determination remain somewhat elusive.

This conclusion is borne out by the case of *United States* v. *Morrison*, which, as noted above,[66] invalidated the Violence Against Women Act of 1994. The statute was sought to be justified as an enactment based not only on section 5 of the 14th Amendment, but also on the Interstate Commerce Clause, but the latter justification failed as well. In *Morrison*, a majority of the Court read *Lopez*, at least in part, as holding quite simply that, regardless of what Congress might or might not have found, 'the link between gun possession and a substantial effect on interstate commerce was attenuated.' *Morrison* is explicit on this point:

> In contrast with the lack of congressional findings that we faced in *Lopez*, [the Violence Against Women Act] *is* supported by numerous findings [by Congress] regarding the serious impact that gender-motivated violence has on victims and their families. But the existence of congressional findings is not sufficient, by itself, to sustain the constitutionality of Commerce Clause legislation.[67]

The majority was unimpressed by the argument that conduct not itself coming within interstate commerce comes within the Interstate Commerce Clause based 'solely on that conduct's aggregate effect on interstate commerce.' It expressed instead the fear that, if the Court adopted that approach, Congress' use of the commerce clause 'could completely obliterate the Constitution's distinction between national and local authority.'[68]

In an important sense, the recent Interstate Commerce Clause cases and the subsidiarity principle show a strong kinship. Both reflect, and mean to address, basic federalism concerns, and more particularly concerns about the allocation of regulatory authority among the levels of government. But there is nevertheless a fundamental difference. Neither in *Lopez* nor in *Morrison* did the Court

---

[66] See notes 61–62 above and accompanying text.

[67] The Court then quoted Chief Justice Rehnquist's concurrence in *Lopez* to the effect that '[s]imply because Congress may conclude that a particular activity substantially affects interstate commerce does not necessarily make it so. Rather, whether particular operations affect interstate commerce sufficiently to come under the constitutional power of Congress to regulate them is ultimately a judicial rather than a legislative question, and can be settled finally only by this Court.'

[68] The Court, while stopping short of laying down a categorical rule to this effect, also expressed doubt that 'non-economic' activity could be a proper subject of regulation under the Interstate Commerce Clause.

decide that federal legislation was *unnecessary*, in the sense that the States were shown to be capable of dealing effectively with the problem at hand. Rather, the Court found that federal legislation was *unauthorized* because interstate commerce was simply not meaningfully implicated. In *Lopez*, it will be recalled, the majority emphasized that interstate commerce, like the Interstate Commerce Clause, has 'outer limits.' Properly viewed, these cases find their closest analogue, not in the subsidiarity principle, but in the Court of Justice's recent *Tobacco advertising* judgment and the considerations on which that judgment rests.[69]

CONCLUSION

In truth, despite their kinship with subsidiarity as instruments of federalism, the Supreme Court's recent interstate commerce cases contain a good deal more *proportionality* than *subsidiarity* thinking. Forcefully evoking the 'means-ends' reasoning that is characteristic of proportionality, they address the strength of the rational relationship between what Congress has set out to accomplish and how it has gone about doing so. Viewed in combination with the 14th Amendment cases canvassed earlier (in which proportionality of course appears by its very name), these cases show the Court subjecting the 'means-ends' conclusions arrived at by Congress to what can best be described as severely strict scrutiny.

The Supreme Court thus appears to have reserved its sharpest proportionality critiques for federal legislation when and insofar as that legislation addresses legal domains traditionally reserved to the States. A majority of the Court has, in effect, made *proportionality* into a powerful and distinctive instrument for the protection of U.S. *federalism*. As noted, it has gone so far in the name of proportionality as to condemn Congress' own attempt to impose respect for proportionality on the States. Interestingly, the Court has not administered that level of scrutiny to federal legislation when challenged in any constitutional respects other than federalism, except perhaps where constitutionally protected individual rights are concerned. This of course only reflects the current Supreme Court majority's constitutional preoccupation with safeguarding the autonomy and prerogatives of the States.

The comparative lessons to be drawn are therefore not simple. In at least one respect, the US experience reflects a marked difference from the European experience. More specifically, federal legislation seems to be coming under much stronger federal proportionality review than the review traditionally applied to state legislation under the 14th Amendment (or, for the matter, the dormant commerce clause), particularly where the federal measure in question is challenged on federalism grounds. This finding of course in turn reflects the current

---

[69] *Germany v. Parliament and Council (Tobacco advertising)*, Case C-376/98, [2000] ECR I-8419.

Supreme Court majority's preoccupation with state sovereignty. To the extent that the European Court of Justice is more committed to market integration than to state sovereignty, its apparently stricter proportionality review of Member State as compared to European Union measures is not surprising.

On the other hand, the American cases tend to reinforce the impression from European Court of Justice case law that, as between proportionality and subsidiarity, the former is potentially by far the more potent instrument of judicial intervention. True, the Court of Justice has, by all accounts, exhibited considerable prudence up to now in subjecting Community measures to proportionality review. But the U.S. Supreme Court's recent adventures in proportionality doctrine demonstrate the extraordinary potential of that doctrine, in the hands of a judiciary so minded, for curbing the exercise of 'federal' legislative power—a potential that, it seems to me, the Court of Justice has not even begun to exploit, if it ever will. At the same time, these adventures reveal the considerable risks to which a powerfully robust judicial doctrine of proportionality can expose a legal system's traditional and basic understandings about the separation of powers.

4

Flexibility in the European Single Market

NICK BERNARD*

INTRODUCTION

FLEXIBILITY, IN THE sense of differentiated integration,[1] has gradually emerged over the last decade as a feature of a new constitutional orthodoxy in the European Union. The Treaty of Amsterdam represented, in this respect, a decisive shift. For the editors of the Common Market Law Review, flexibility is the '*leitmotiv* that sounds persistently throughout the [Amsterdam] Treaty'.[2] It is not that flexibility constituted an entirely new phenomenon. As Tuytschaever points out, 'differentiation has been part of the Community legal order from the very outset'.[3] Even in the sacrosanct core internal market, multiple examples could be found of derogations, different timescales for implementation or other forms of differentiation resulting from the wide discretion sometimes left to Member States in the implementation of Community rules.[4] What was significant about Amsterdam was that flexibility was no longer seen as an *ad hoc* pragmatic answer to the difficulty of reaching agreement on common rules, but as a central element of the institutional and constitutional architecture of the EU.[5]

Some might see in the single market the last bastion of resistance to the ascendancy of this new orthodoxy. After all, internal market rhetoric, with its

---

* A precursor of this chapter was presented at a workshop on the European Single Market at the University of Cambridge, 27–28 April 2001. I am grateful to the participants, and Jo Shaw in particular, for their comments. The usual disclaimer applies.
[1] For elaboration on the meaning and manifestations of differentiated integration, see F. Tuytschaever, *Differentiation in European Union Law*, (Oxford, Hart Publishing, 1999).
[2] Editorial, 'The Treaty of Amsterdam: Neither a Bang nor a Whimper', (1997) 34 *CMLRev.* 767, p. 768.
[3] Tuytschaever, above n. 1, p 7.
[4] Cf. G. de Búrca, 'Differentiation within the "Core"? The Case of the Internal Market', in G. de Búrca, and J. Scott, (eds), *Constitutional Change in the EU: From Uniformity to Flexibility?*, (Oxford, Hart Publishing) 2000, p. 133.
[5] On the constitutional significance of flexibility, see J. Shaw, 'Relating Constitutionalism and Flexibility in the European Union', in de Búrca, and Scott, above note 4, p. 337.

insistence on the removal of 'distortions' of competition and equalisation of the conditions of competition and the fundamental (economic) rights of all (market) citizens in the Community-wide single market, points towards uniformity rather than diversity and flexibility. While exceptions to the paradigm of uniformity might be tolerated, they would still be perceived as exceptional and anomalous. This understanding of the single market as a space of uniformity is neatly captured in this extract from the Opinion of Advocate General Tesauro in the *Titanium Dioxide* case:[6]

> I do not see how it is possible to achieve a genuinely single, integrated market without eliminating divergences between national legislation which, by having a differing impact on production costs, prevents the development of competition on the basis of real equality within the Community.

If there is room for flexibility in such a framework, it is for a different kind of flexibility. It is the flexibility of markets, and of economic agents, freed from (excessive) regulatory shackles to innovate and adapt to changing market circumstances. One particular dimension of this kind of flexibility has always been at the heart of the single market. It is the stated purpose of European market integration to remove rigidities that partition the single market along national lines and to ensure the free circulation of goods, services, persons and capital throughout the European internal market.

It might be tempting to regard flexibility in the first sense of flexible integration as antinomic to flexibility in the second sense of flexible market regulation. In this view, flexible integration leaves the door open to the imposition by Member States of rigidities in the market place. Their relationship, however, is more complex. To start with, disparities between the laws of the Member States do not necessarily result in obstacles to trade. The whole point of mutual recognition is to allow for flexible integration, leaving market regulation in the hands of the Member States while at the same time preventing the use of that competence in a way that would partition the market. Many have expressed doubts, however, that a system of mutual recognition can work in the EU. The first half of this chapter will explore the difficulties that have been experienced in the application of the principle of mutual recognition since *Cassis de Dijon*.[7]

Flexible market regulation cannot be reduced to the removal of obstacles to movement across the single market and there is no reason to assume *a priori* that the adoption of uniform rules at Community level will necessarily result in a more flexible regulatory framework. EU regulation can be just as rigid as national regulation. Economic and Monetary Union has pushed the issue of flexible regulation to the top of the single market agenda. The second half of

---

[6] Case C-300/89 *Commission v Council* [1991] ECR I-2867.
[7] Case 120/78 *Rewe-Zentrale AG v Bundesmonopolverwaltung für Branntwein* [1979] ECR 649.

this chapter will investigate the way in which the theme of flexible markets and flexible regulation have reshaped single market policies.

FLEXIBLE INTEGRATION

The enthusiasm sometimes expressed by the Commission for the principle of subsidiarity [8] may have less to do with a strong belief in the values that underpin it than with making virtue out of necessity. This is especially true in the context of the single market where many reports, after extolling the virtues of subsidiarity, then go on to stress the obstacles created by national regulation or administrative practices. This necessity is first a political necessity, as reflected in the predilection of Member States for the instrument of the directive rather than the regulation for internal market measures. It is also a practical necessity. The 'indirect rule'[9] system which underlies the functioning of the EC makes enforcement a matter primarily for the Member States. At the level of rulemaking, it is also plain that the Community legislative and administrative apparatus could not cope with the sheer volume of legislation needed for market regulation without at least partial reliance on national regulation. The attraction of mutual recognition as an alternative to centralised Community regulation is, in this context, obvious.

Beyond political and practical necessity, there are in principle a number of advantages to a decentralised approach to European market governance. From the perspective of democratic legitimation, the primary mode of legitimation of EU economic governance remains based on output, notwithstanding some initiatives designed to give additional input to the views of citizens in the shaping of internal market policy. However, if democracy is government not just for the people but also by the people, input legitimation is also required and the input legitimacy of legislation adopted at national or local level is likely to be higher than that adopted at Community level. Apart from issues of democratic legitimation and from the perspective of regulatory innovation, 15 systems of regulation give more potential scope for more experimentation and mutual learning than a single centralised one.

Mutual recognition and the Court of Justice

The judgment of the Court in *Cassis de Dijon*[10] was influential in the development of mutual recognition as a core principle of organisation of the

---

[8] See, for instance, the *Better Lawmaking* annual reports.
[9] Cf. T. Daintith (ed.), *Implementing EC law in the United Kingdom : structures for indirect rule*, (Chichester, Wiley, 1995).
[10] Case 120/78 *Rewe-Zentrale AG* v *Bundesmonopolverwaltung für Branntwein* [1979] ECR 649.

single market, under which goods lawfully produced and marketed in one of the Member States should in principle be allowed entry to the market of all other Member States.[11]. The Commission's communication on the case makes this plain.[12] The Court's own case law is, however, more ambiguous.

Mutual recognition or functional parallelism?

Weiler points out that the Court 'preaches the rhetoric of mutual recognition . . . but practices functional parallelism'.[13] The point is well illustrated by contrasting the *UHT Milk* and *Woodworking Machines* cases.[14] Whereas the Court is ready to find a duty on Member States to recognise regulations and controls enacted and carried out in other Member States that provide equivalent guarantees to their own rules and controls (*UHT Milk*), the duty stops at recognising rules enacted under a different regulatory philosophy and not directly functionally equivalent to their own (*Woodworking Machines*). 'True' mutual recognition would require going one step further and recognising not just different ways of satisfying the regulatory objectives of the host state but also accepting the regulatory choices of the home state themselves.

   In truth, the picture is more mixed. For one thing, functional parallelism is only an apt description for these cases where a Member State can argue that it has a reasonable case for taking measures for a particular objective of public interest and the issue then becomes whether the guarantees provided by home state legislation and control are sufficient. In that sense, mutual recognition remains accepted as the starting point, mandatory requirements (and functional parallelism) constituting the exception to the principle. Secondly, although the Court justifies its results on the basis of functional equivalence, by 'demonstrating' that there exist alternative means less restrictive of trade to satisfy the legitimate objective invoked by the host state, there is in reality rarely true functional parallelism. To take Weiler's own example drawn from *Cassis de Dijon*, labelling will not prevent some consumers from being misled as to the alcohol contents of a liqueur that does not correspond to their traditional expectations: 'some cannot read, others do not read'.[15] To that extent, under the cover of functional parallelism, there may in fact lie *de facto* mutual recognition.

---

[11] Cf. *Cassis de Dijon*, at paragraph 14.

[12] Communication from the Commission concerning the consequences of the judgment given by the Court of Justice on 20 February 1979 in case 120/78 ('*Cassis de Dijon*'), OJ 1980 C256/2.

[13] J. H. H. Weiler, 'The Constitution of the Common Market Place: Text and Context in the Evolution of the Free Movement of Goods', in P. Craig and G. De Búrca (eds.), The Evolution of EU Law, (Oxford, Oxford University Press, 1999), 349, pp. 366–367.

[14] Case 124/81 *Commission v UK (UHT Milk)* [1983] ECR 203 and case 188/84 *Commission v France (Woodworking Machines)* [1986] ECR 419 respectively.

[15] Above note 13, p. 368.

This, however, assumes that the Court of Justice is willing to accept the logic of mutual recognition and therefore uphold the legitimacy of control by the home state. The principle of mutual recognition is not a free-for-all where traders can challenge any rules imposed by either the country of origin or destination of the goods. As the Commission states in its *First Report on the Application of the Principle of Mutual Recognition in Products and Services Markets*,[16] the function of the principle is to allow entry to the markets of other Member States for products which are 'in conformity with the regulations and with the fair and traditional production processes of the exporting country, and marketed within that country'.[17] In other words, the principle of mutual recognition is a mechanism of allocation of regulatory competence to the country of origin ('home country control principle'), designed to avoid goods being subject to a dual burden of regulation by home and host country.[18] There cannot be mutual recognition if there is nothing to 'mutually recognise'.

Mutual recognition and the free movement of goods

The Court would seem to accept the mutual recognition logic in the free movement of goods. Thus, while it subjects control by the host state to justification, it does not do so, under the *Groenveld* jurisprudence,[19] in relation to the home state. Some commentators see this as a sign of incoherence in the case law of the Court. However, it is better seen as the logical consequence of a mutual recognition approach. Similarly, and contrary to appearances, the judgment of the Court in *Keck*,[20] far from constituting an exception to mutual recognition, can in fact be seen as a reflection of that principle. Just like *Cassis-Groenveld*, *Keck* operates a mechanism of allocation of regulatory competence. This time, however, instead of allocating competence to the Member State where the goods are manufactured, competence is allocated to the country where the goods are sold.[21] Moreover, in so far as *Keck*-like rules target the sales process by traders in the state where the goods are sold, it does not constitute a departure from the home country control principle of the *Cassis-Groenveld*

---

[16] SEC (1999) 1106.

[17] *Ibid*, p. 3.

[18] Cf. N. Bernard, 'La libre circulation des marchandises, des personnes et des services dans le Traité CE sous l'angle de la compétence', (1998) 34 *Cahiers de droit européen* 11.

[19] Case 15/79 *Groenveld* [1979] ECR 3409.

[20] Joined cases C-267&268/91 *Keck and Mithouard* [1993] ECR I-6097.

[21] The corollary is that assumption of jurisdiction for *Keck*-like rules ('selling arrangements') by the state of manufacture would constitute a breach of Article 29. Admittedly, this is not made explicit in *Keck* but it seems beyond doubt that any attempt by the state where goods are produced to regulate where and when those goods are to be sold in another Member State would constitute a breach of Article 29, which would have to be justified by mandatory requirements. See, in this respect, the Opinion of Advocate General Jacobs in case C-384/93 *Alpine Investments v Minister van Financiën* [1995] ECR I-1141, paragraph 55.

case law. It just happens that, in this case, the home country of the trader whose activities are regulated is the country where the goods are sold rather than produced.[22]

Mutual recognition and the free movement of workers, freedom of establishment and freedom to provide services

In the field of services, establishment and the free movement of workers, on the other hand, reconciliation of the case law of the Court with the mutual recognition principle encounters some difficulties. One could mention the *Bosman* case,[23] but I would like to focus on the *Alpine Investments* case,[24] in the context of freedom to provide services, as a particularly clear manifestation of the departure of the Court from the principle.

In *Alpine Investments*, the Court held that a ban on 'cold-calling'[25] imposed by the Dutch finance minister on providers of certain financial services established in the Netherlands was capable of constituting a restriction on the freedom to provide services and, as such, was subject to a requirement of justification on grounds of imperative reasons of public interest. If that was not enough, the Court even went further by specifying that protection of consumers in other Member States was not in principle the concern of the Dutch authorities. As a consequence, protecting consumers in other Member States could not in itself constitute a legitimate interest worthy of protection by the Court. The ground on which the Court nevertheless upheld the ban was the need to 'maintain the good reputation of the national financial sector' and thereby ensure the smooth functioning of Dutch financial markets.[26] One would have thought that protecting the reputation of a sector of the national economy looked suspiciously like an economic justification. It is hard to understand why the prevention of industrial dispute in a sector of the national economy is regarded by the Court as an economic ground of justification which is not acceptable under Articles 28–30 EC[27] but protection of the reputation of a

---

[22] It is important to distinguish the trader whose activity is being targeted by the rule, and the trader to whom it is formally addressed. Thus, requirements relating to product characteristics typically consist of bans on the marketing of products not conforming to the requirements. Even though it is therefore the seller to whom the rules are formally addressed, it is nevertheless the manufacturer whose activity is targeted by the rule. For further discussion, see N, Bernard, Legal Aspects of Multi-level Governance, (London, the Hague, Kluwer Law International, (forthcoming)), 36 et seq.

[23] Case C-415/93 *URBSFA and others* v *Bosman* [1995] ECR I-4921.

[24] Above, note 21.

[25] Viz. offering goods or service for sale over the telephone without prior solicitation or agreement of the person to whom the goods or services are being offered.

[26] See paragraphs 42–44 of the judgment.

[27] See case C-398/95 *Syndesmos ton en Elladi Touristikon kai Taxidiotikon Grafeion* v *Ypourgos Ergasias* [1997] ECR I-3091.

sector of the national economy is regarded as an acceptable ground under Article 49 EC.

It would seem that the Court completely lost sight of the 'big picture' in *Alpine Investments* and applied legal concepts such as obstacle to the provisions of services and justification mechanically without any regard to the structure of regulation in a single market based on mutual recognition. It surely cannot be right that Member States cannot take into account the interests of consumers in other Member States when regulating traders established on their territory. This would mean that traders can engage in all sorts of fraudulent activities and dubious commercial practices as long as their victims are residents of other Member States. If the same approach were adopted in relation to goods, it would mean that, in the absence of harmonisation, a Member State could not impose any safety requirements on exported goods and would be under a duty to allow unsafe goods to be exported. Far from assisting in the removal of barriers to trade, the approach taken by the Court in *Alpine Investments* is in fact detrimental to free movement by making host country control essential in the absence of harmonisation. Moreover, as *Alpine Investments* itself shows, host country control may be an ineffective way of ensuring compliance with regulatory requirements when the supplier of services is established in another Member State. Clearly, control of remote methods of sales promotion, using the telephone or other means such as the internet, can usually only be effective when undertaken by the state in which the supplier is established. If the logic of *Alpine Investments* were followed to its conclusion, it would require the establishment of Alpine Investments in all Member States in which it markets its products, so as to enable the authorities of the host country to exercise effective control. In its *First Report on mutual recognition*, the Commission noted that

> In the services sector, the difficulties [in the application of the principle of mutual recognition] are related to rules which are designed to protect the consumer, a goal which is praiseworthy in itself, but which is often associated with a perception that this can only be fully accomplished by means of checks in the country of destination.[28]

As *Alpine Investments* shows, this is a perception which is also shared, albeit implicitly, by the Court of Justice. *Alpine Investments* should stand as a reminder that mechanical application of the rules on free movement without consideration of their underlying purpose is not always the best way to achieve market integration but can, on the contrary, occasionally be harmful to this objective.

---

[28] Above note 16, p. 7.

CAN MUTUAL RECOGNITION WORK?

Mutual recognition and administrative discretion

According to Weiler, mutual recognition in *Cassis de Dijon* was 'a colossal market failure', the main reason for this failure being that 'one cannot plan, produce and market product lines hoping that eventually a court decision will vindicate a claim of mutual recognition or functional parallelism'.[29]

Whether mutual recognition should be considered a success or a failure depends on the expectations that one places in it. If mutual recognition was expected to be a panacea capable of removing all barriers to trade, it was bound to be a dismal failure. However, this would have been an unrealistic expectation of what could reasonably be achieved through the operation of the principle. Where the regulatory stakes are high[30] and the differentials in regulatory policies between the Member States substantial, mutual recognition is unlikely to work. This is not so much, as is sometimes suggested, because of the danger of a 'race to the bottom' between the Member States, where each Member State outdoes the other in loosening the regulatory environment on firms established on its territory so as to provide them with a competitive advantage.[31] Empirical evidence of a genuine problem of this kind is patently lacking. There is a more immediate and direct reason for the rejection of mutual recognition when issues such as the safety of goods or the protection of consumers of financial services are at stake. Member States do not trust the regulatory standards of the other Member States and are simply not ready to give access to their market to potentially unsafe goods. The problem is thus one of direct externalities rather than indirect economic externalities.

In principle this should not preclude recourse to mutual recognition in those areas where the differentials between the regulatory policies of the Member States are not so great, or have been diminished through minimum harmonisation,[32] and where the regulatory issues do not assume such a high profile. This should be regarded as the proper area in which mutual recognition can work and it is in this field that its successes and failures should be assessed. In this context, Weiler's statement may be somewhat over-emphatic. Some empirical studies tend to convey a more balanced picture of the success or failure of the mutual recognition strategy. Thus, the study carried out as the background to

---

[29] Above note 13, p 368.

[30] When, for instance, they involve issues of health and safety or, particularly in relation to services, consumer protection.

[31] In labour markets, the preferred terminology is that of 'social dumping' but we are talking of the same phenomenon.

[32] There is therefore no absolute opposition between harmonisation and mutual recognition. They can work in tandem, as is typically the case in relation to financial services, where basic harmonisation is achieved through Community legislation and the home country control/mutual recognition principle then takes over.

the Commission's Communication on the *Impact and Effectiveness of the Single Market* suggests that, 'the mutual recognition principle works without problem for many non-contentious products (e.g. steel, water pipe fittings)' even though substantial obstacles persist in other areas.[33] Similarly, in its *First Report on the Application of the Principle of Mutual Recognition in Products and Services Markets*,[34] the Commission also attributes to mutual recognition a large part of the three-fold increase of the proportion of intra-Community trade in total Member States' external trade. The 'tip of the iceberg (the refusals) must not be allowed to distract attention from the submerged part (the very large number of cases where mutual recognition is applied without any difficulty)'.[35]

Yet, even in areas where mutual recognition could be conceived as an acceptable solution, its lack of automaticity remains an important obstacle to its smooth operation. Since there are areas in which substantial policy differentials persist and where, therefore, Member States should be allowed to proceed on the basis on functional parallelism rather than mutual recognition, the test applied by the courts across the board has to allow for functional parallelism and, therefore, the possibility of invoking mandatory requirements. Mutual recognition claims must as a result be assessed on a case-by-case basis rather than through operation of an automatic principle. Operation of mutual recognition is therefore dependent in practice on the exercise of their discretion by regulatory authorities of the Member States. This can be the case even where the mutual recognition principle is supported by Community legislation. For instance, directives on the so-called 'mutual recognition' of diplomas,[36] still follow a functional parallelism logic, in so far as they allow the host state to impose compensatory measures, such as aptitude tests or a period of traineeship, when there is a 'substantial' difference between the training acquired in another Member State and that required in the host state.[37] An individual decision of equivalence is therefore still needed. The Commission noted in its *First Report on Mutual Recognition* that application of the mutual recognition principle 'is less often hindered by the formal content of the legislation itself than by the practical decisions made by the authorities that are in direct contact with citizens or economic operators'.[38] Such administrative practices may well be caught by the rules on free movement.[39] However, identifying and proving the

---

[33] Cf. EC Commission, *The single market review: Dismantling of barriers. Technical barriers to trade*, Luxembourg: EUR-OP, 1996.

[34] Above note 16, p. 5.

[35] *Ibid.* p. 3.

[36] Directives 89/48/EEC (OJ 1989 L260/22), 92/51/EEC (OJ 1992 L209/25) and 1999/42/EC (OJ 1999 L201/77). Note, however, in Article 4 of the latter, the automatic recognition awarded to those who have exercised the professional activity concerned for a certain period of time.

[37] This is also the approach taken by the Court on the basis of the free movement provisions in the Treaty: see Cf. cases 340/89 *Vlassopoulou* [1991] ECR 2357.

[38] Above note 16, p. 7.

[39] Cf. Case 21/84 *Commission* v *France (postal franking machines)* [1985] ECR 1356.

existence of such practices is bound to be problematic. It is in this context that Weiler's argument has all its weight. Even though the Commission 'encourages economic operators not to abandon their claims to the rights, which are theirs under the application of mutual recognition',[40] it often entails less risks and is more cost effective to give up and conform to the standards of the host state than wait for a hypothetical positive outcome to litigation.

Effective operation of the mutual recognition principle cannot rely exclusively on private enforcement through the courts. An active policy of identification of problems in the operation of the principle and the machinery to solve them is necessary.

Information gathering

A noticeable development in internal market management is the proliferation of notification procedures designed *inter alia* to identify problems in the operation of single market rules.[41] Two mechanisms are of primary interest here. At the rule-making level, Directive 98/34[42] requires the Member States to notify new national technical regulations and standards. At the implementation level, Decision 3052/95[43] places Member States under a duty to communicate information on measures that they take to prohibit or remove access to its market for certain goods.

In the first two years of operation of Decision 3052/95 in 1997 and 1998, the Commission received notification of only 102 measures and ten Member States did not notify anything at all.[44] It is manifest that there is under-reporting on a vast scale. The Commission attributes this in part to the time needed to 'break in' the new system, drawing a comparison with the time it took to put in place the system of notification of new national standards and technical regulations.[45] While there is undoubtedly some truth in that, it should be borne in mind that Decision 3052/95 will typically have to be implemented lower down the administrative chain within the Member States by officials with little awareness of Community law. It is therefore likely that, without substantial information and training action, under-reporting is likely to persist for some considerable time.

[40] *Ibid*, p. 8.
[41] In addition to Decision 3052/95 and Directive 98/34 referred to below, one should add the 'rapid intervention mechanism' in Regulation 2679/98/EC, OJ L 337/8 and notification obligations normally included in 'new approach' directives.
[42] Directive 98/34/EC laying down a procedure for the provision of information in the field of technical standards and regulations, OJ 1998 L204/37.
[43] Decision 2052/95/EC establishing a procedure for the exchange of information on national measures derogating from the principle of the free movement of goods within the Community.OJ 1995 L321/1.
[44] See EC Commission, *Report on the implementation of Decision 2052/95/EC in 1997 and 1998*, COM (2000) 194 Final, p. 21.
[45] *Ibid.* p. 15.

Directive 98/34 puts the Commission (and the other Member States) in a position to make comments on a proposed new technical regulation by a Member State and identify potential hindrances to trade. With reference to mutual recognition, the Commission's policy has been to insist on the insertion of mutual recognition clauses in technical regulations adopted by the Member States.

The Commission has found support for this policy in the judgment of the Court of Justice in the *Foie Gras* case.[46] The Court found France in breach of its obligations under Article 30 of the EC Treaty[47] for failing to include such a clause in a decree regulating the use of various trade descriptions relating to products based on *foie gras*. *Foie gras* seemed an unlikely candidate for the Commission to pick up a fight on mutual recognition clauses. It is a typically French product and production outside France is marginal. Whatever production there is outside France conforms to French trade description practices and no other Member State has legislated on the issue. Thus, unlike, for instance, the trade description 'beer' which is known and used in different Member States with different brewing practices, French trade descriptions are the *de facto* Community, indeed worldwide, conceptual norms for *foie gras* based products. Secondly, the consumer protection case for a mandatory system of trade descriptions is stronger than for many other food products. Price and quality differentials between the various trade descriptions are significant.[48] French consumers are generally familiar with the main descriptions as quality indicators but unfamiliar with the underlying contents and production methods to which those trade descriptions relate. Listing ingredients and describing production processes on the label is thus not a realistic alternative from a consumer protection point of view. Given these circumstances, the likelihood of consumers being misled by stepping outside the trade description system is relatively high.[49] The Advocate General had found that the non-inclusion of a mutual recognition clause in the French legislation on *Foie Gras* did not constitute an infringement of Article 30 of the EC Treaty. The Court, however, considered that the affixing of informational labels would be sufficient for consumer protection purposes and that the mandatory trade description system without mutual recognition clause constituted a breach of Article 30.

The judgment is unlikely to have any noticeable effect on intra-Community trade in *foie gras* based products. It is a pure statement of principle. Its significance lies in the upholding by the Court of the Commission's practice of requiring mutual recognition clauses. If the Court is ready to require a mutual recognition clause in such a weak case as *foie gras* based products, it is likely to

---

[46] Case C-184/96 *Commission v France* [1998] ECR I-6197
[47] Now Article 28 EC.
[48] Thus, whole *foie gras* is typically twice the price of block of *foie gras* and several times the price of other *foie gras* based products.
[49] Indeed, the likelihood of the consumer being *intentionally* misled by using trade description reserved for higher quality products to market lower quality products is high.

uphold such a requirement in relation to other products. The advantage of a mutual recognition clause is that it alerts traders to the possibility of benefiting from free movement through mutual recognition rather than having to apply standards and technical regulations of the host state.

Co-operation and problem-solving

Directive 98/34 provides for the setting up of an advisory Standing Committee consisting of representatives of the Member States with the possible assistance of technical experts. The Committee's remit is not limited to discussion of the drafts notified under Directive 98/34 but may also serve as a forum for discussions, exchanges of views and search for solutions in relation to problems on the implementation of single market rules. In particular, problems identified through the Decision 3052/95 mechanism may be discussed in the Committee.

A particularly difficult problem for the operationalisation of the mutual recognition principle in certain sectors or in relation to certain goods is that there may exist strong expectations on the part of users and consumers that products and services will conform to standards to which they are used in the national context. Overcoming such problems requires a more intense level of co-operation further down the chain. Thus, agreements between testing and certification bodies may be necessary so that tests and procedures are mutually recognised and enjoy a comparable level of confidence. Testing and certifications bodies, however, have little incentives to conclude agreements, since their income from testing fees diminishes when such agreements are concluded and double testing eliminated. It is also doubtful that a Member State could be in breach of its obligations under the Treaty for failing to take steps to ensure the conclusion of such agreements. A case could be made on the basis of Article 10 EC and the so-called *Strawberries* judgment[50] that Member States are under a positive duty to take steps to prevent or remove obstacles to free movement, whatever the cause of those obstacles. However, the extent of that duty is not clear. There clearly must be limits to the duty imposed by Article 10. Thus, a poor transport infrastructure undoubtedly creates an obstacle to the movement of goods. However, it is unlikely, short of a deliberate policy to downgrade transport routes of importance to intra-Community trade, that a Member State would be in breach of its obligations under Article 10 and 28 EC for not providing a sufficiently good transport infrastructure.

A similar problem can occur in the field of services. The absence of regulatory barriers in the UK to the provision of services by travel agents established in other Member States will be of little help if British consumers are reluctant to buy a flight or holiday package from a firm which is not a member of the

---

[50] Case C-265/95 *Commission v France* [1997] ECR I-6959.

Association of British Travel Agents and does not hold an ATOL licence.[51] It is notable, in this respect, that the impossibility for the (now defunct) Dublin-located French internet bank First-e to join the British Banking Ombudsman scheme, notwithstanding the presence of 50 000 account holders in the UK, was highly publicised in consumer protection programmes in the UK. While consumers could benefit from the protection of the French scheme, this provided only limited re-assurance and the bank decided to set up its own independent adjudication scheme in an effort to overcome the problem of lack of consumer confidence.

The problem is particularly acute in the case of financial services, which can easily be provided remotely (notably through the internet) and where consumer confidence is an important element. For the Commission, the solution lies in ensuring a uniform minimum level of protection throughout the EU coupled with a policy of information of the consumer. The uniform minimum level of protection can be realised through minimum harmonisation[52] but softer approaches are also possible. Thus, in relation to alternative consumer dispute resolution mechanisms, the Commission issued a Recommendation on the principles to be followed by bodies with responsibilities for out-of-court settlement of consumer disputes.[53] A Memorandum of Understanding was also reached with the main national bodies involved in out-of-court settlements in the financial sector, concerning cross-border consumer disputes.[54] Under the provisions of the memorandum, consumers can obtain from the relevant body in their home state information on the competent scheme to handle any dispute they might have with a provider of financial services in another Member State. The system envisaged in the memorandum is premised on the notion that, provided dispute settlement bodies abide by the standards of behaviour defined in the Commission Recommendation and the consumer is provided with enough information on the scheme, the consumer will be happy to deal with a scheme in another Member State. This seems extremely optimistic. It is plain that it is much easier for consumers to deal with local schemes, not least as there is no guarantee that the remote scheme will be able to handle complaints in a

---

[51] Air Travel Organisers Licensing (ATOL) is a statutory guarantee scheme run by the British Civil Aviation Authority to protect consumers against the risk of insolvency of firms offering flight and package holidays.

[52] This would be the policy followed in the case of guarantee schemes for deposits held by credit institutions, of which Directive 94/19 on deposit-guarantee schemes OJ 1994 L135/5 constitutes a first step. On the unsuccessful challenge by Germany to the validity of this Directive, see case C-233/94 *Germany v Parliament and Council* [1997] ECR I-2405.

[53] Commission Recommendation 98/257/EC OJ 1998 L115/31. The Recommendation covers issues of independence, transparency, adversarial nature, legality, representation and whether decisions should be binding on the parties. The Commission has also issued another Recommendation, concerning consensual resolution of consumer disputes: Recommendation 2001/310/EC on the principles for out-of-court bodies involved in the consensual resolution of consumer disputes, OJ 2001 L109/56.

[54] The text of the memorandum is available from the Commission's Internal Market website:http://www.europa.eu.int/comm/internal_market/en/finances/consumer/adr.htm.

language easily understood by the consumer.[55] To that extent, there is still a significant disincentive for consumers to contract with out-of-state suppliers and this may hinder the development of cross-border e-commerce. It should be stated, however, that the memorandum envisages dispute resolution by the local scheme of the consumer provided the financial services supplier has accepted the jurisdiction of the latter.[56] Statutory schemes, however, may well be unable to provide for such voluntary jurisdiction.[57] When consumer confidence is a major concern, mutual recognition has to be backed up with substantial co-operation going beyond national bodies acting as letter-boxes for corresponding authorities in other Member States.

Despite its apparent simplicity, the mutual recognition principle can thus be institutionally very demanding. It cannot therefore constitute a general solution to the problems of market integration in the EU. On the other hand, the very demands that it places on the system of regulation have some attractive features. It requires authorities in the Member States to co-operate towards the finding of solutions to regulatory problems. It tends to promote a more informed and fine-tuned form of decision-making oriented towards mutual learning and, to that extent, it promises a higher quality of regulation than harmonisation from high above may be capable of delivering. This, however, assumes that significant resources are directed towards it. In a climate of budgetary restraint, mutual recognition may be unable to deliver its promises.

FLEXIBLE MARKETS

The *Internal Market Strategy*[58] for 2000–2004, adopted by the Commission in 1999, signals a departure in internal market policy. According to the Commission, it 'has been conceived to reflect the characteristics of a more mature Internal Market'.[59] As further explained in the 2000 Review of the Strategy,[60] 'the Internal Market has already changed the face of the European economy'. What needs to be done now is to create a 'regulatory and institutional framework which stimulates innovation, investment and economic efficiency'

[55] There is ambiguity in the memorandum on the question of the language. Point 7 of the memorandum specifies that the consumer may elect to deal with the competent scheme in the language of his contract with the financial services supplier pr the language in which (s)he normally dealt with the latter. On the other hand, point 8 specifies that the parties to the memorandum will provide information to the Commission regarding the languages in which they can handle enquiries, deal with complaints and issue decisions, suggesting that there is no assumption that the remote scheme will in fact be able to handle enquiries along the terms of Point 7. If that is the case, there may be issues of translation and of who bears the costs of translation as between the scheme itself, the consumer and the supplier.
[56] See point 6.3 (c) of the memorandum.
[57] Cf the First-e example mentioned above.
[58] COM(1999) 624 Final.
[59] *Ibid*. p. 1.
[60] COM(2000) 257 Final.

and 'create—and adapt to—new business opportunities'.[61] The 2001 Review of the Strategy [62] sends the same message. While emphasising the need not to forget the 'nuts and bolts' of the single market, such as mutual recognition and standardisation,[63] it nevertheless places this in the context of the need, 'in an era of breathtaking change', for an internal market

> that is flexible and adaptable, free of unnecessary regulations and red tape, and which continues to be a catalyst for our prosperity. An Internal Market that empowers our businesses and citizens as much as it serves their needs.[64]

Table 1: Evolution of Strategic Objectives between the Action Plan for the Single Market (1997) and the Strategy for Europe's Internal Market

Action Plan	*Strategy*
Making the single market rules more effective	Improve the quality of life of citizens
Dealing with key market distortions	Enhance the efficiency of Community product and capital markets
Removing sectoral obstacles to market integration	Improve the business environment
Delivering a single market for the benefit of all citizens	Exploit the achievements of the internal market in a changing world

Thus, single market policies are no longer primarily focused on market integration *per se* but on the functioning of that market within the context of a wider economic policy. A comparison between the strategic targets in the 1997 *Action Plan for the Single Market*[65] and the strategic objectives of the 1999 *Internal Market Strategy* is quite revealing of this evolution (Cf. Table 1).

Methodologically, the Strategy is very much in line with the 1997 Action Plan. It follows the pattern of broad strategic objectives and shorter-term target actions to be completed within the next 18 months. At the level of detailed contents of the actions to be completed, there is also a good deal of continuity with the Action Plan and, beyond it, the 1985 White Paper on *Completing the Internal Market*.[66] The broad context and general orientation, however, has changed. Market opening and market integration are still very much present[67]

---

[61] *Ibid*, p. 2.
[62] COM(2001)198 Final.
[63] *Ibid*. p.6.
[64] *Ibid*, p. 2.
[65] CSE (1997) 1.
[66] COM (1985) 310 Final.
[67] Thus, further liberalisation in the field of postal services, gas and electricity or integration of financial services markets in the Strategy can be seen as a direct continuation of the 1992 programme.

there but they are not what gives the Strategy its coherence and general thrust. Micro-economic reform oriented towards making markets more 'flexible' is the overarching purpose behind the Strategy. This change of direction owes much to Economic and Monetary Union.

The impact of EMU

Economic and Monetary Union has had a profound impact on internal market policy-making in two ways. Firstly, it has put into place the conditions for the emergence of a Community economic policy, within which single market policies become subsumed. It has therefore affected the structure of single market policy-making. Secondly, it is not just *any* Community economic policy that EMU has brought about. EMU has locked European economic policy within a particular neo-liberal approach which, at the micro-economic level, translates into a strong emphasis on flexible markets.

As regards the structural aspect, the development of a Community economic policy has been made necessary by the requirement of co-ordination of the economic policies of the Member States. In purely formal legal terms, economic co-ordination is not new. In its original 1957 version, the EEC Treaty already required Member States to co-ordinate their economic policies.[68] However, what was in 1957 little more than an exhortation has become post 1992 in the run-up towards monetary union a necessity. The institutional framework for economic co-ordination has thus been strengthened by the establishment of a system of multi-lateral surveillance based on a regular review of compliance of Member States with Broad Economic Policy Guidelines issued by the Council on a basis of a Commission recommendation and after review by the European Council.[69]

The linkage between single market policies and economic co-ordination between the Member States is explicit in the *Internal Market Strategy* itself, which refers to the implementation by the Member States of the Broad Economic Policy Guidelines in the context of the 'Cardiff process'.[70] Thus, the 2000 revision of the Strategy states that

> since the Broad Economic Policy Guidelines (BEPG) play a central role in the co-ordination of economic policies between the Member States, the recommendations in

---

[68] Article 105(1) EEC required that 'in order to facilitate achievement of the objectives set out in Article 104, Member States shall coordinate their economic policies. They shall for this purpose provide for cooperation between their appropriate administrative departments and between their central banks. The Commission shall submit to the Council recommendations on how to achieve such cooperation.' Articles 103 and 107 EEC also required the Member States to regard their conjunctural and exchange rates policies as a 'matter of common concern'.

[69] See Article 99 EC for the details of the procedure.

[70] The Cardiff process refers to the approach to structural reforms in product and capital markets agreed at the Cardiff European Council in June 1998.

the BEPG on product and capital market reform form an integral part of the Internal Market Strategy.[71]

Policy integration, both horizontal as between EC policy areas and vertical as between national and Community policies, was further strengthened by the 'Lisbon Process'. The Lisbon European Council in March 2000 set up a comprehensive framework for an economic and social policy aimed at achieving the ambitious strategic goal of becoming within the next decade 'the most competitive and dynamic knowledge-based economy in the world, capable of sustainable economic growth with more and better jobs and greater social cohesion'. One cannot overstate the impact of Lisbon on the *Internal Market Strategy*. The priority target actions in the 2000 and 2001 review of the Strategy were drawn from the conclusions of the Lisbon European Council and its consolidatory follow-up at the Stockholm European Council in March 2001.

The other impact of EMU concerns the substantive values informing economic policy and, therefore, single market policies. The institutionalisation of EMU on the basis of the paradigm of 'sound' public finances and price stability,[72] notably through the establishment of an independent central bank and the hedging of national fiscal policies through the Stability and Growth Pact,[73] has spawned an economic discourse centred on 'modernisation' and reform designed to promote flexibility in the economy notably through a more 'enterprise-friendly' regulatory environment.

Flexibility and de-regulation

The Commission is keen to reassure us that flexibility does not mean a lowering of standards or a threat to social values but rather a safer way to secure these values in a context of globalisation and international competition. Flexibility is not about de-regulation but about better regulation. Thus, in the 2001 review of the *Internal Market Strategy*, the Commission states that 'nobody is, of course, arguing against regulation as such. Or indeed in favour of a lowering of standards.' The problem is that 'some aspects of rule-making do not work well . . . Some of our laws, at national and European level, have become too

---

[71] See the 2000 Review of the Strategy, above note 60, p. 3. See also the 1999 version of the Strategy, above note 58, p. 8 and the 2001 Review, above note 62, p. 24.

[72] Cf. K. Dyson, *Elusive Union—The Process of Economic and Monetary Union in Europe*, (London; Longman, 1999). On the overarching importance of price stability in EU monetary policy, see Art 105(1) EC.

[73] Council Regulation Regulation 1466/97/EC on the strengthening of the surveillance of budgetary positions and the surveillance and coordination of economic policies, OJ 1997 L209/1 and Council Regulation 1467/97/EC on speeding up and clarifying the implementation of the excessive deficit procedure, OJ 1997 L 209/6 form, together with the Resolution of the European Council on the Stability and Growth Pact, OJ 1997 C236/1, the 'Stability and Growth Pact'.

complicated and contain excessive detail.'[74] Of course, all depends on how 'working well' is defined and what kind of 'innovation' one wishes to promote. Thus, not everybody would necessarily share the Commission's vision of two-tier pay systems, under which new employees are hired at lower salaries than existing ones as a praiseworthy 'innovative solution' to labour costs management.[75]

Notwithstanding the Commission's protestation that this does not mean a lowering of standards, it is difficult to avoid the conclusion that there is an inherent tension between flexibility in this sense and the pursuit of regulatory objectives other than facilitation of trade. Among the magic tricks at the disposal of the Commission to transform a lowering of standards into a better way to address the regulatory problem, the principle of proportionality is particularly effective. Thus, in its proposal for a Regulation on sales promotions in the internal market,[76] the Commission does not propose to impose a ban on making participation in promotional games subject to purchase because this would be 'disproportionate'. According to the Commission, given the odds of winning such contests, the idea that a consumer might be swayed to buy the product solely by the contest is 'untenable'. All that consumer protection requires is that the winnings/odds ration is easy to calculate thanks to appropriate transparency provisions.[77] This consumer is a familiar figure, who appears every now and then in the caselaw of the Court of Justice. It is a rational, calculating and informed individual, who always reads product labels attentively and takes purchasing decisions after careful weighting of the pros and cons. It is this very person that makes national lotteries a fundamentally non-viable economic proposition, since the idea that such a consumer would purchase a lottery ticket given the odds of winning is 'untenable'!

Techniques of flexible market governance

The Lisbon European Council called for the setting up by 2001 of 'a strategy for further coordinated action to simplify the regulatory environment including the performance of public administration, at both national and Community level'.[78] In March 2001, the Commission produced for the Stockholm European Council an *Interim Report on Improving and Simplifying the Regulatory Environment*,[79] identifying weaknesses in current processes and proposing a

---

[74] Above note 62, p. 11.
[75] Cf. Commission Communication on the *European airline industry: From Single Market to World-wide Challenge*, COM (1999) 182 Final.
[76] COM (2001) 546 Final.
[77] *Ibid.* pp. 12 and 14.
[78] Point 17, fifth indent of the Presidency conclusions.
[79] COM (2001) 130 Final.

number of solutions to overcome them. Broadly speaking, the Commission's ideas on reforming the regulatory process can be regrouped under three topics: (i) improving the production and flows of information; (ii) searching for alternatives to the standard legislative procedure and (iii) ensuring a greater involvement of citizens and business interests in the decision-making process.

As regards (i), the Commission proposes to intensify and systematize prior consultation of interested parties, in particular through the internet, and to conduct qualitative and quantitative impact analyses.[80] At the other end of the legislative chain, the effects of Community regulation should regularly be appraised to decide whether it should be adapted to changing circumstances.[81] In areas subject to rapid technological, organizational or market change, the Commission would propose to introduce in the legislation a deadline for re-examination of the act or a 'sunset clause'.[82] Thirdly, better access to information on Community law, notably through the use of the new technologies should be ensured.[83]

As regards (ii), the Commission suggests using self-regulation[84] or co-regulation [85] where appropriate and also making more use of delegated powers to the Commission. This would allow for simpler 'framework' legislative acts, which could be adopted more quickly. The Commission also recommends maximizing the use of existing procedures speeding up the adoption process, such as systematic and early qualified majority voting in the Council and agreements between the institutions so as to wrap things up at first reading. In relation to (iii), consultation and evaluation procedures should include stakeholders.

None of this is radically new, as the examples mentioned in the footnotes indicate. It is rather an inventory of the 'reservoir of policy solutions'[86] previously developed in various contexts. Thus, the Report is more significant as the expression of the more systematic, self-conscious exercise in thinking about the regulatory environment and the regulatory process than in the specific solutions it puts forward.

[80] For a pilot project on this, see the Commission communication on the Business Test Panel, COM (1998) 197 final.

[81] This is a frequent requirement in directives. See, for instance, Article 23 of the Postal Services Directive: Parliament and Council Directive 97/67/EC on common rules for the development of the internal market of Community postal services and the improvement of quality of service, OJ 1997 L15/14.

[82] The Postal Services Directive (*ibid.*) cumulates both options: see Articles 7(3) (review) and 27 (sunset clause).

[83] Cf. the EUR-Lex, Dialogue with Citizens and Dialogue with Business websites on http://europa.eu.int.

[84] Cf. Commission Recommendation 89/542/EEC for the labelling of detergents and cleaning products OJ 1989 L291/55 (voluntary agreement between representative bodies and the Commission).

[85] Cf. the role of standardisation bodies in 'new approach' directives.

[86] Cf. K. Armstrong, 'Governance and the Single European Market' in P. Craig and G. de Búrca, above note 13, 745, p. 784.

These solutions may or may not work in delivering a more adaptable regulatory framework. To take the example of 'co-regulation' under the new approach to technical harmonisation, standardization bodies *may* be more efficient at producing standards and updating them than the Community legislator. The experience acquired until now is mixed. The Comité Européen de Normalisation (CEN) has had difficulties keeping up with the volume of standards required to be adopted for the new approach to succeed, let alone update the standards. In some areas, progress has been painfully slow.[87] In principle, the absence or inadequacy of standards is not an absolute bar for new approach directives to function, since compliance with standards is optional. Manufacturers are free to demonstrate by other means that their products comply with a directive even though they do not comply with a standard implementing the directive.[88] However, this tailor-made approval route is more lengthy and costly. The timely publication of standards is crucial for the sound operation of the new approach.

It is clear from the Report that the drive towards a more responsive, adaptable and simpler regulatory *framework* does not mean a simpler regulatory *process*. If we take the 'Community method' of co-decision by Council and European Parliament on the basis of a Commission proposal as our point of reference, the Report presents a picture of a more complex and diversified regulatory *process* involving a wider range of actors.

The production of regulatory knowledge is an important aspect of the framework put forward in the Report. Participation of stakeholders should be seen in this light. It has less to do with a concern over the participation of the citizenry in the production of norms as a matter of democratic principle than with the feeding of their experience and knowledge in to the regulatory process. Systematic reviews of legislation at regular intervals and sunset clauses are also a reflection of the concern over generating and updating regulatory knowledge on an on-going basis through monitoring and testing.

The Report, which is focused on EU regulatory processes, does not deal with the issue of the flexibility of *national* regulatory frameworks.[89] This, however, is addressed in the context of the 'Cardiff process' and the Broad Economic

---

[87] Thus, in relation to construction products, less than 10% of mandated harmonised standards have been adopted: See Commission, Internal Market Score Board No 9, November 2001, p. 16.

[88] The effect of approved harmonised standards is to give a presumption of conformity to the Directive.

[89] The one exception is the issue of implementation of Community law. While the Report does not go into much detail, it is worth noting on page 8 the preference expressed for regulations over directives 'in appropriate cases, and more especially when it comes to the adoption of detailed technical norms requiring uniform application in the Member States'. The Commission's White Paper on Governance (COM (2001) 428 Final) goes even further in advocating the use of regulation as a matter of course for the completion of the internal market. This seems to fly in the fact of the protocol on the application of the principles of subsidiarity and proportionality annexed to the EC Treaty by the Treaty of Amsterdam. The protocol specifically states that 'other things being equal, directives should be preferred to regulations'.

Policy Guidelines. The Cardiff process is based on the open method of co-ordination.[90] The Lisbon European Council describes the open method as the 'means of spreading best practice and achieving greater convergence towards the main EU goals' and as a means to 'help Member States to progressively develop their own policies'.[91] For Hodson and Maher, the open method constitutes a 'radicalization' of subsidiarity.[92] The open method relies on 'soft' guidelines, non-observance of which does not give rise to any formal sanction. The guidelines are country-specific. The underlying idea is that, while the overall objective of reform towards more a more flexible market environment is shared by all the Member States, the appropriate course of action depends on the particular characteristics of each Member State. Thus, the guidelines are broadly oriented in the same direction but leave much leeway for individualisation to the circumstances of each Member State. In order to enable comparisons and the sharing of experience, the method relies on benchmarking. Periodic monitoring and evaluation allow for mutual learning and peer review. Thus, enhancing the capital of regulatory knowledge lies at the heart of the open method.

CONCLUSION

In some ways, single market policy has followed the general trend towards flexible integration. Certainly, we no longer understand the single market as requiring systematic harmonization of all market rules. The Commission is also keen to reaffirm the importance of mutual recognition as one of the cornerstones of the single market. However, the distinction between national and EU level of decision-making has become increasingly blurred. As we have seen above, mutual recognition cannot be equated with a repatriation of autonomous decision-making at national level. The successful operation of the principle requires a significant degree of co-ordination and co-operation between national authorities in the Member States. Secondly, and more importantly, under the sound public finance paradigm of EMU, there has been a significant convergence of regulatory values which removes much of the edge on debates about the appropriate locus of decision-making. EMU has had a direct and immediate impact on the powers of the Member States in monetary and fiscal policy; this has not been the case in relation to market regulation. It has not induced in itself significant new transfers of competence to the EU level nor is there any marked tightening of the freedom of action left to the Member States by EU market legislation. What has been changed by EMU, however, is the conceptual frame and system of values that

---

[90] The term itself was adopted at the Lisbon European Council but it is based on earlier initiatives, one of which is the Cardiff process on the reform of product and capital markets.
[91] Presidency Conclusions of the Lisbon European Council, at paragraph 37.
[92] D. Hodson and I. Maher, 'The Open Method as a New Mode of Governance: The Case of Soft Economic Policy Co-ordination', (2001) 39 *Journal of Common Market Studies* 719, p. 728.

informs market regulation. The sound money and sound finance paradigm of EMU has promoted the development of a political discourse privileging deregulation and flexible markets. It would be excessive to attribute this exclusively to EMU. Other factors, such as globalisation and evolving economic patterns in the light of rapid technological change, have also played a role.[93] EMU, however, has certainly been a strong catalyst in entrenching this discourse in EU and national political elites. Formally, Member States enjoy a significant amount of freedom in regulating markets. However, there is an expectation that this freedom will be exercised within a specific conceptual frame. The value of local decision-making has less to do with adaptation to local values and desires than with ensuring the most effective way of carrying forward the agenda of 'modernisation' and restructuring of markets induced by EMU.

The same could be said of participation of citizens in decision-making. In its third *Report on the functioning of Community products and capital markets*[94] the Commission stated that economic reform was giving citizens an 'increasingly leading role' in EU governance. This increasingly leading role, however, manifests itself in the growth, 'as developing economic reforms cut into the number and dimension of economic activities protected from competition, ... [of] the number of opportunities open to private initiative in the new European economy'. Thus, the citizen is constructed purely as an economic agent and 'participation in EU governance' is participation in the market. Even in the context of consultation processes, it is clear from the *Interim Report on Improving and Simplifying the Regulatory Environment*[95] that it is as economic agents that 'citizens' are being involved in the decision-making process.

The point is not that the pursuit of the objective of more flexible regulatory frameworks is necessarily wrong but rather that both the mechanisms of participation of 'citizens' and the open method of co-ordination constitute a densification of governance which have a disenfranchising effect on citizens. Participation in EU market governance is premised on the acceptance of the neoliberal conceptual frame of modernization, restructuring and flexible markets. It may be that this is the best policy to follow in a context of globalisation. This, however, should be a decision for citizens to make.

[93] Cf. K. Dyson, 'EMU as Europeanization: Convergence, Diversity and Contingency' (2000) 38 *Journal of Common Market Studies* 645, p. 649.
[94] COM (2000) 881 Final.
[95] Above note 79.

5

Horizontality: The Court Attacks?

STEFAAN VAN DEN BOGAERT *

INTRODUCTION

FOR MANY YEARS, the European Court of Justice maintained a strict line between the Community rules on competition, which are addressed to undertakings, and the rules on free movement, which were held to apply to measures of Member States.[1] After it had become clear that this dichotomy engendered lacunae in the application of Community law, the Court started a process of closing the gaps, which led to the competition rules being applied— under certain circumstances—to Member States' behaviour[2] and, correspondingly, to the free movement rules being construed as imposing obligations on private parties.[3]

It is the latter issue, commonly referred to as the *horizontal direct effect*[4] of the fundamental freedoms, which shall be addressed in this chapter. The immediate cause of renewed interest in the principle of horizontal direct effect of the fundamental freedoms is to be traced back to a recent decision of the Court of Justice on the matter, in which it eschewed once more using the sibylline language that had gradually become its trademark and delivered a judgment clearly bearing marks reminiscent of some of the great judgments in the early days of the Court. With one big uncompromising sweep, the Court's statements in the

---

* Researcher at the European University Institute, Florence. An earlier version of this chapter was presented at a workshop in Cambridge on 27–28 April 2000 on 'The Legal Foundations of the Single market: Unpacking the Premises'. I would like to thank all participants to the workshop and in particular Jeff Kenner, Graínne de Búrca and Catherine Barnard for their critical and valuable comments. All remaining inaccuracies and errors are of course entirely my responsibility.

[1] See e.g. Joined Cases 177 and 178/82 *Criminal proceedings against Van de Haar and Kaveka de Meern* [1984] ECR 1797.

[2] See line of cases starting with Case 13/77 *GB-INNO-BM v ATAB* [1977] ECR 2115, para. 28–29.

[3] D. Waelbroeck, 'Les rapports entre les règles sur la libre circulation des marchandises et les règles de concurrence applicables aux entreprises dans la CEE', in F. Capotorti et al., *Liber Amicorum Pierre Pescatore: Du droit international au droit de l'intégration* (Baden-Baden, Nomos, 1987) 781, called this development the 'privatisation' of free movement and the 'publicisation' of competition.

[4] For some critical comment with regard to the use of this terminology, see Baquero Cruz, *The Economic Constitutional Law of the European Community: between Competition and Free Movement*, Florence, EUI-thesis [2000] 213–217.

case of *Angonese*[5] resuscitated the whole debate on the question of whether private parties (be it individuals, private associations, corporations, etc.) are, and if indeed so, to what extent, bound by the Treaty provisions on freedom of movement.

The structure of the chapter will be the following: in the first part, the evolution of the relevant case law of the Court of Justice with regard to the different fundamental freedoms will be outlined. The second part will consist of a critical evaluation of the reasons which have led the Court to accept horizontal direct effect of Article 39 EC, and of a balancing of the different arguments expressed in favour of and against horizontal direct effect of the free movement provisions. In the third and final part, a tentative attempt will be made to anticipate the future approach of the Court concerning this matter.

RELEVANT CASE LAW OF THE EUROPEAN COURT OF JUSTICE

Free Movement of Workers, Establishment and Services

In many of the cases concerning this particular matter, the Court of Justice has dealt with Articles 39, 43 and 49 EC at the same time. For the purposes of this chapter, they will therefore be handled together.

Walrave: collective measures

The first case in which the European Court of Justice was asked to deal with the issue of horizontal direct effect was *Walrave and Koch* v *International Cycling Union* (hereinafter referred to as the 'UCI')[6]. The Court had to decide whether the rule of the UCI relating to medium-distance world cycling championships behind motorcycles, according to which the pacemaker had to be of the same nationality as the stayer, was compatible with Articles 12, 39 and 49 EC. Walrave and Koch, two Dutch nationals who were generally considered by the UCI itself to be amongst the best pacemakers in the world, and who used to participate in these races as pacemakers for stayers of other nationalities, in particular Belgians and Germans, because of a paucity of top-class Dutch stayers at the material time,[7] regarded this provision of the rules of the UCI as discriminatory.

It was undisputed in the proceedings that the UCI, being an association of national bodies concerned with cycling as a sport, was a private association. The Court of Justice firstly pointed out that it had been alleged that the prohibitions of any discrimination on grounds of nationality, laid down in

[5] Case C-281/98 *Roman Angonese* v *Cassa di Risparmio di Bolzano* [2000] ECR I-4139.
[6] Case 36/74 *Walrave and Koch* v *Union Cycliste Internationale* [1974] ECR 1405.
[7] Warner AG in Case 36/74 *Walrave and Koch* v *Union Cycliste Internationale* [1974] ECR 1423.

Articles 12, 39 and 49 EC, 'refer only to restrictions which have their origins in acts of an authority and not to those resulting from legal acts of persons or associations who do not come under public law.'[8] Subsequently, however, it refuted this allegation and held that the prohibition of discrimination 'does not only apply to the action of public authorities but extends likewise to rules of any other nature aimed at regulating in a collective manner gainful employment and the provision of services.'[9]

The Court based this decision upon three grounds: firstly, it stipulated that the

> abolition as between Member States of obstacles to freedom of movement for persons and to freedom to provide services, which are fundamental objectives of the Community contained in Article 3(c) of the Treaty, would be compromised if the abolition of barriers of national origin could be neutralised by obstacles resulting from the exercise of their legal autonomy by associations or organisations which do not come under public law.[10]

This can be described as the *effet utile* argument. Secondly, it said that since

> working conditions in the various Member States are governed sometimes by means of provisions laid down by law or regulation and sometimes by agreements and other acts concluded or adopted by private persons, to limit the prohibitions in question to acts of a public authority would risk creating inequality in their application.[11]

This could be referred to as the *uniform application* argument. Thirdly, it emphasised the general nature of the terms of the relevant Treaty provisions, not distinguishing between the source of the restrictions to be abolished and extending to rules and agreements which do not emanate from public authorities.[12] This will be called the *general wording* argument.

At this point, two provisional observations deserve to be made in this respect. Firstly, the Court has unequivocally stipulated that the scope of application of the Community provisions on free movement of workers and freedom to provide services does not cover only actions of public authorities, but extends also to rules of any other nature insofar as these measures regulate the subject matter concerned in a *collective manner*.[13] Hence, to that extent public and private regulation are put on the same footing by the Court of Justice. This decision therefore undoubtedly constitutes a significant development in the jurisprudence of the Court in Luxembourg. However, it is submitted that one should not overestimate its importance either: the private party involved in the proceedings, the International Cycling Union, is an association with a

---

[8] *Walrave*, para. 15.
[9] *Walrave*, para. 17.
[10] *Walrave*, para. 18.
[11] *Walrave*, para. 19.
[12] *Walrave*, para. 20–21.
[13] This decision has been confirmed in Case 13/76 *Donà v Mantero* [1976] ECR 1333, para. 17.

quasi-government status, as it acts as the ultimate regulatory body within its field of competence and performs State-like functions.[14] Arguably, at this stage of the Court's case law on the matter, only this kind of private party seems to be subject to free movement scrutiny. Secondly, it also needs to be emphasised that the case turned on a measure which clearly discriminated between Community nationals on grounds of nationality.

Haug-Adrion: full horizontal direct effect?

It was in *Haug-Adrion*[15] that the Court of Justice hinted for the first time that it just might be prepared to go beyond *Walrave* and extend the applicability of the Community provisions on freedom of movement of workers and services to private parties. The case concerned the compatibility with Articles 12, 39 and 49 EC of an insurance scheme under which no-claims bonuses were not granted to owners of vehicles bearing customs registration plates. In its judgment, it omitted all reference to collective measures, and held instead that the Treaty provisions in question

> are intended to eliminate *all measures* (emphasis added) which, in the fields of free movement of workers and freedom to provide services, treat a national of another Member State more severely or place him in a situation less advantageous, from a legal or factual point of view, than that of one of the Member State's own nationals in the same circumstances.[16]

This general statement had the potential of opening up a wide array of private measures to challenge. However, somewhat surprisingly, at the time the whole issue was not really taken up any further in the legal doctrine, presumably because the standardised contract terms at stake in the particular case could be considered as comparable to collective agreements[17], or possibly because the Court reached the conclusion that the measure concerned was not discriminatory and thus not contrary to the Treaty provisions invoked.[18]

Bosman: beyond discrimination

Subsequently, in the seminal *Bosman* case[19], the Court of Justice, in true 'procession of Echternach style', first appeared to retreat one step from its previous findings before finally taking several steps forward. At stake was the

---

[14] The same could be said about the Italian Football Federation in *Donà*.

[15] Case 251/83 *Haug-Adrion v Frankfurter Versicherungs-AG* [1984] ECR I-4277.

[16] *Haug-Adrion*, para. 14.

[17] Roth, 'Drittwirkung der Grundfreiheiten', in Due/Lutter/Schwarze (eds.), *Festschrift für Ulrich Everling*, Vol. 2, (Baden-Baden, Nomos, 1995), 1239.

[18] *Haug-Adrion*, para. 18.

[19] Case C-415/93 *Union Royale Belge des Sociétés de Football Association ASLB v Jean-Marc Bosman* [1995] ECR I-4921.

compatibility with Articles 39, 81 and 82 EC of the nationality clauses emanating from the representative football federations FIFA and UEFA, two private associations governed by Swiss law, and the so-called football transfer rules—according to which a professional football player was not free to move to a new club without the payment of a transfer fee, even if his contract with his previous club of affiliation had expired.

First of all, the Court returned to the reasoning already adopted in *Walrave* and repeated once more that not only action of public authorities, but also rules of any other nature aimed at regulating gainful employment in a collective manner fell under the scope of Article 39 EC.[20] After this matter had been settled, the Court made a giant leap forward: whereas in its previous case law it had only submitted discriminatory rules of private associations to the test of compliance with the free movement provisions, it now brought genuinely non-discriminatory private measures under direct free movement scrutiny. Indeed, the Court ruled that even though the transfer rules in question did not discriminate on grounds of nationality, they still directly affected players' access to the employment market and were thus capable of impeding the freedom of movement of workers.[21] And the Court didn't leave it at that. When UEFA objected that the Court's interpretation made Article 39 of the Treaty 'more restrictive in relation to individuals than in relation to Member States, which are alone in being able to rely on limitations justified on grounds of public policy, public security or public health'[22], the Court rejected this argument for being based on a false premise, and ruled in an unequivocal way in paragraph 86 that 'there is nothing to preclude individuals from relying on justifications on grounds of public policy, public security or public health. Neither the scope nor the content of those grounds of justification is in any way affected by the public or private nature of the rules in question.'[23]

Again, it is worth pausing briefly to make some comments on the case law of the Court. Firstly, the decision in *Bosman* represents the first occasion on which the Court has held the Treaty provisions on freedom of movement of workers to be applicable in a dispute between two private parties concerning a truly non-discriminatory measure. This will almost automatically entail a significant increase in the number of cases coming under the Court's scrutiny.[24] Secondly,

---

[20] *Bosman*, para. 82–84.

[21] *Bosman*, para. 103.

[22] *Bosman*, para. 85.

[23] See also Case C-350/96 *Clean Car Autoservice v Landeshauptmann von Wien* [1998] ECR I-2521, para. 24.

[24] In two other sports cases, the Court neatly proceeded along the path it had previously chosen in *Bosman*, albeit with a different outcome: see Case C-176/96 *Jyri Lehtonen and Castors Canada Dry Namur-Braine v Fédération Royale Belge des Sociétés de Basketball* [2000] ECR I-2681, para. 49 on workers; Joined Cases C-51/96 and C-191/97 *Christelle Deliège v Ligue Francophone de Judo et Disciplines ASBL and Others* [2000] ECR I-2549, para. 64 on services. For further information, see e.g. S. Van den Bogaert, 'The Court of Justice on the Tatami: Ippon, Wazari or Koka' (2000) 25 *European Law Review* 554–563.

after *Bosman* it was still not unequivocally clear whether Article 39 EC applied to all private measures or, rather, only to collective regulations. Presumably, the Court's remarkable statement in paragraph 86 of the judgment can be used to shed some light on this issue. The Court's express ruling that *private individuals* can rely on grounds of public policy, public security or public health to justify private measures appears to convey implicitly but nevertheless inevitably the message that the Court is inclined towards the former option. This statement was wider than it strictly had to be, for at the time, only measures regulating employment or the provision of services in *a collective manner* were caught by the free movement provisions. An alert observer would have realised what was about to happen.

Angonese: horizontal direct effect

Ultimately, it would take the Court five more years to provide explicit confirmation about horizontal direct effect. The Court formulated its views on this specific matter against the background of the case of *Angonese*[25]. Angonese, an Italian national whose mother tongue is German and who is resident in the province of Bolzano, applied to take part in a competition for a post with a private bank in Bolzano. One of the conditions for entry to the competition was possession of a certificate of bilingualism (in Italian and German), which used to be required in Bolzano for access to a managerial career in the public service. The specific certificate was issued by the local public authorities after an examination which was held only in that province. Angonese is perfectly bilingual, but he was not in possession of that specific certificate. On that basis he was denied admission to the competition. Although acknowledging the right of the bank to select its future staff from persons who are perfectly bilingual, Angonese considered the requirement to have and to produce the certificate unlawful and contrary to the principle of freedom of movement for workers.

In its judgment, the Court of Justice initially trod on well-known territory, reaffirming the *Walrave* principle that the prohibition of discrimination based on nationality applies not only to public regulations but also to private rules aimed at regulating in a collective manner gainful employment and the provision of services. It also embraced exactly the same line of reasoning, based on the arguments of the general wording of Article 39, the requirement of effectiveness and the necessity of uniform application of the principle of non-discrimination.[26] Subsequently, however, the Court introduced a new element into the debate, originating from its decision in the second *Defrenne* case[27]. In that case, the Court had ruled that

---

[25] Case C-281/98 *Roman Angonese v Cassa di Risparmio di Bolzano* [2000] ECR I-4139.
[26] *Angonese*, para. 30-33.
[27] Case 43/75 *Gabrielle Defrenne v Sabena* [1976] ECR 455.

the fact that certain provisions of the Treaty are formally addressed to the Member States does not prevent rights from being conferred at the same time on any individual who has an interest in compliance with the obligations thus laid down.[28]

And accordingly it had held, in relation to a provision of the Treaty which was mandatory in nature (Article 141 on equal pay for men and women), that 'the prohibition of discrimination applied equally to all agreements intended to regulate paid labour collectively, as well as to contracts between individuals.'[29] On the basis of these statements, the Court construed a bridge with Article 39 EC in the present case, emphasising that

> such considerations must, *a fortiori*, be applicable to Article 39 of the Treaty, which lays down a fundamental freedom and which constitutes a specific application of the general prohibition of discrimination contained in Article 12 of the EC Treaty. In that respect, like Article 141 of the EC Treaty, it is designed to ensure that there is no discrimination on the labour market.[30]

This enabled the Court to continue: 'Consequently, the prohibition of discrimination on grounds of nationality laid down in Article 39 of the Treaty must be regarded as applying to private persons as well.'[31]

Again, it is important to make two observations. Firstly, for the time being, the Court has rendered only Article 39 EC applicable to private parties. Secondly, the specific obligation to obtain the certificate of bilingualism which was held to infringe Article 39 EC was indirectly discriminatory. What the impact of these two elements may be for further case law of the Court on horizontal direct effect, will be outlined in part four of the chapter.

Free Movement of Goods

The case law of the European Court of Justice with regard to horizontal direct effect in the field of the free movement of goods has developed in a completely different way. Contrary to its jurisprudence on the free movement of persons and services, in which the Court appears to have gradually moved towards a recognition of the applicability of the relevant Treaty provisions in disputes between private parties (or is still moving in this direction), the Court has consistently refuted this possibility in the field of the free movement of goods, albeit after an approach which seemed initially receptive.

[28] *Defrenne*, para. 31.
[29] *Defrenne*, para. 39; *Angonese*, para. 34.
[30] *Angonese*, para. 35.
[31] *Angonese*, para. 36.

Dansk Supermarked: horizontal direct effect?

An early case in which the Court was asked to express its views on the issue of the applicability of Article 28 EC to private parties was *Dansk Supermarked*[32]. Imerco, a Danish company, had placed an order in the United Kingdom for a china service bearing the words 'Imerco fiftieth anniversary', with the purpose of selling this exclusively to its members. It was agreed that the manufacturer could market some substandard pieces in the United Kingdom, provided that these are not exported to Denmark. Nevertheless, Dansk Supermarked obtained some of the china in the UK and offered it for sale in Denmark at a price below that charged for the original pieces sold by Imerco. The Court of Justice was seized with the question whether the Treaty provisions precluded the application of the Danish laws on copyright, trademarks and marketing.

In a truly remarkable statement, the Court observed that

> it is impossible in any circumstances for agreements between individuals to derogate from the mandatory provision of the Treaty on the free movement of goods. It follows that an agreement involving a prohibition on the importation into a Member State of goods lawfully marketed in another Member State may not be relied upon or taken into consideration in order to classify the marketing of such goods as an improper or unfair commercial practice.[33]

Quite understandably, this decision received a lot of attention in the legal literature.[34] Many commentators concluded on the basis of this judgment that the application of Article 28 EC was not limited to the Member States and that it did indeed produce horizontal effects between private parties.[35] As Steindorff put it, 'it is hardly possible to state more clearly that the freedom of movement of goods laid down in Article 30 [28] EC is also binding to private parties'.[36] However, despite the unequivocal language of the Court in *Dansk Supermarked*, doubts have arisen about the validity of its statements in this case, for a number of reasons.[37] First of all, it has been advocated that what was at stake in this case was not so much the agreement between the two undertakings, but rather the compatibility of the applicable Danish legislation with the provisions of the Treaty. The Court pronounced its decision with regard to the application and the understanding or interpretation of the applicable national

---

[32] Case 58/80 *Dansk Supermarked* v *Imerco* [1981] ECR 181.

[33] *Dansk Supermarked*, para. 17.

[34] P. Pescatore, 'Aspects judiciaires de l'acquis communautaire', [1981] *Revue Trimesterielle de Droit Européen* 617, at 630.

[35] See for example M. Maresceau, 'De toepasbaarheid van het europese recht door de nationale rechterlijke instanties', [1982] *Tijdschrift voor Privaatrecht* 41, at 60; D. Waelbroeck, 'Les rapports entre les règles sur la libre circulation des marchandises et les règles de concurrence applicables aux entreprises dans la CEE', in F. Capotorti et al., *Liber Amicorum Pierre Pescatore: Du droit international au droit de l'intégration* (Baden-Baden, Nomos, 1987) 781, at 785; Schroeder, *Sport und Europäische Integration*, (München, VVF, 1989) at 128.

[36] Steindorff, *EG-Vertrag und Privatrecht*, (Baden-Baden, Nomos 1996) at 282.

[37] See for example Roth, above, n.17, pp 1235–1237.

law.[38] According to Marenco, the Court simply wanted to exclude the possibility that the parties would circumvent the application of the national law by an agreement between them.[39] As Baquero has emphasised, it was therefore not really necessary to deal with the agreement that was not binding upon Dansk Supermarked.[40] Furthermore, this chamber judgment has not been mentioned in subsequent case law. One could therefore wonder whether it is still good law.

Intellectual property cases: separate line of cases

Apart from *Dansk Supermarked*, only a series of intellectual property cases could possibly be invoked to support the assertion that private parties are bound by the Treaty provisions on free movement of goods, but it is submitted that these cases should be regarded as a separate line of case law which cannot be taken to imply that Article 28 EC is applicable to private parties.[41] It is suggested that cases concerning intellectual property rights are not relevant for our discussion because of the territorial nature of these rights.[42] In every one of these cases, even though the parties involved in the dispute may be private, it is always the specific national legislation conferring rights marked by territoriality which is considered to be incompatible with Community law. In the case of *Deutsche Grammophon*[43], the Court formulated this argument as follows:

> it would be in conflict with the [free movement of goods] for a manufacturer of sound recordings to exercise the exclusive right to distribute the protected articles, conferred upon him by the legislation of a Member State, in such a way as to prohibit the sale in that State of products placed on the market solely because such distribution did not occur within the territory of the first Member State.[44]

Van de Haar & Co.: dichotomy between Articles 28 and 81–82 EC

In the rest of its case law on the free movement of goods, the Court of Justice has no longer shown any inclination towards an acceptance of the concept of horizontal direct effect of Article 28 EC. On the contrary, on a couple of

---

[38] Jaensch, *Die unmittelbare Drittwirkung der Grundfreiheiten, Untersuchung der Verpflichtung von Privatpersonen durch Art. 30, 48, 52, 59, 73b EGV*, (Baden-Baden, Nomos 1997) p 60; Kluth, 'Die Bindung privater Wirtschaftsteilnehmer an die Grundfreiheiten des EG-Vertrags', (1997) 122 *Archiv des öffentlichen Rechts* 557–582.

[39] Waelbroeck, above, n.3 at 785.

[40] Baquero Cruz, above, n.4 at 225–226. See also Capotorti AG *in Dansk Supermarked*, para. 4.

[41] Quinn & MacGowan, 'Could Article 30 Impose Obligations on Individuals?' (1987) *European Law Review* 172–175.

[42] See for example, P Oliver, *Free Movement of Goods in the European Community*, 3rd edn (London, Sweet & Maxwell, 1996) at 59.

[43] Case 78/70 *Deutsche Grammophon Gesellschaft v Metro-SB-Großmärkte* [1971] ECR 487, para. 13.

[44] See also Case 119/75 *Terrapin v Terranova* [1976] ECR 1039; or Case C-200/96 *Metronome Musik v Music Point Hokamp* [1998] ECR I-1953, para. 14.

occasions, such as in the case of *Van de Haar*[45], concerning sales of tobacco products to persons other than resellers at prices lower than those appearing on the excise labels, the Court emphasised that it is important to bear in mind the exact context in which the provisions of the Treaty are situated. It then distinguished explicitly between the competition rules and the rules on the free movement of goods, thus clearly suggesting that private parties are not directly bound by Article 28 EC.[46] In the subsequent case of *Vlaamse Reisbureau's*[47], concerning Dutch legislation on trade practices for travel agents and agreements between tour operators and travel agents, the Court was even more outspoken when it stipulated explicitly that 'since Articles 28 and 29 of the Treaty concern only public measures and not the conduct of undertakings, it is only the compatibility with those articles of national provisions of the kind at issue in the main proceedings that need be examined.'[48] This has remained the consistent position of the Court of Justice on the particular issue.[49]

Summary

After *Angonese* the case law on free movement of persons can be summarised as follows: the situation is reasonably straightforward as far as the free movement of *workers* is concerned, as the Court of Justice has unequivocally stated that Article 39 EC is horizontally directly effective. The question remains whether only discriminatory conduct of private parties is covered by Article 39 or whether non-discriminatory private measures are also covered by Article 39 EC.

As far as the freedom of *establishment* and the freedom to provide *services* are concerned, the situation has not fully crystallised yet. In the case of *van Ameyde*[50], the Court of Justice had a rare occasion to deal with the issue of horizontal direct effect specifically in the context of Article 43 EC. The Court held that it was 'not relevant whether a discrimination originated in measures of a public authority', as it was sufficient that 'it results from the rules of whatever kind which seek to govern collectively the carrying out of the business in question.'[51] At the time, this decision fitted squarely within the overall approach adopted by the Court in the field of free movement of workers. However, since then, the matter has not really been raised. In the

---

[45] Joined Cases 177 and 178/82 *Criminal proceedings against Van de Haar and Kaveka de Meern* [1984] ECR 1797.
[46] *Van de Haar*, para. 11–12.
[47] Case 311/85 *Vereniging van Vlaamse Reisbureau's v Sociale Dienst van de Plaatselijke en Gewestelijke Overheidsdiensten* [1987] ECR 3821.
[48] *Vlaamse Reisbureau's*, para. 30.
[49] See Case 65/86 *Bayer AG und Maschinenfabrik Hennecke GmbH v Süllhofer* [1988] ECR 5249, para. 11.
[50] Case 90/76 *S.r.l. Ufficio van Ameyde v S.r.l. Ufficio Centrale Italiano di Assistenza Assicurativa Automobilista in Circolazione Internazionale* [1977] ECR 1091.
[51] *van Ameyde*, para. 28.

field of services, the last decision of the Court on the matter dates back to *Deliège*, in which it held Article 49 EC to be applicable to rules of a private nature aimed at regulating the provision of services in a collective manner, even though these rules are indistinctly applicable. Basically, the Court stopped one step short of conferring on the free movement of services exactly the same horizontal direct effect as it had given to the provisions on free movement of workers. Whether this current and somewhat unbalanced situation amounts to a mere coincidental and temporary imperfect congruence between workers, on the one hand, and establishment and services, on the other hand, or rather reflects the boundaries of possible parallelism, emphasising the differences between these three sets of rules, still remains to be seen.[52] In this respect, it should not be forgotten that these final steps, taken by the Court in *Bosman* and *Angonese* in the field of workers, involved a substantial extension of the scope of application of the free movement provisions, respectively entailing that Article 39 EC covers genuinely non-discriminatory measures restricting access to the employment markets of Member States and purely individual private conduct. As already indicated, it is still uncertain whether these two extensions may be combined with each other. Be that as it may, it cannot be ruled out that the Court does not want to go that far within the domains of establishment and services. But then, by the same token, it may equally well be that the Court is simply waiting for an appropriate occasion to bring its case law on establishment and services into line with that on workers. After all, the facts of *Angonese* clearly fell solely within the scope of Article 39 EC.

In the field of the free movement of *goods*, the Court has not left much room for doubt anymore, but here the Court has reached the opposite conclusion, for Article 28 EC does not seem to be applicable to private parties. Admittedly, the Court's statements in *Dansk Supermarked* which explicitly pointed in the other direction have never been officially overruled, but for the reasons outlined above, it can seriously be doubted whether it is still necessary to attach any particular weight to this judgment. Moreover, the cases on intellectual property rights may indeed convey the impression that Article 28 EC is applied in a dispute between private parties, but it is submitted they are somewhat misleading in this respect, as it is in fact the relevant national legislation granting these rights which is tested for its compliance with the free movement rules, rather than private acts or agreements.

---

[52] See e.g. Daniele, 'Non-Discriminatory Restrictions to the Free Movement of Persons', (1997) 22 *European Law Review* 191–200; Friedbacher, 'Motive Unmasked: The European Court of Justice, the Free Movement of Goods and the Search for Legitimacy', (1996) 2 *European Law Journal*, 226–250.

EVALUATION OF HORIZONTAL DIRECT EFFECT

As we have seen, private parties are bound by the prohibition of discrimination on grounds of nationality as set down in Article 39 EC. If the decision of the Court did not come entirely as a surprise, as the Court had already slightly lifted the veil on its future intentions previously, when stating that there was 'nothing to preclude *individuals* from relying on justifications on grounds of public policy, public security or public health'[53], then the principled, unequivocal terms in which the Court couched its judgment in some way did. Clearly, the Court has not left much room for speculation any more. Whether one likes it or not, horizontal direct effect is there, and at least for the moment, it is there to stay.

In this part of the chapter, the principle of horizontal direct effect as pronounced by the Court will be subjected to a critical evaluation, and it will be determined whether it satisfactorily passes the test. Firstly, a closer look will be taken at the arguments which were brought forward by the Court to under-pin its decision to render the Treaty provisions on free movement of workers applicable to private parties. Secondly, arguments adduced for and against hor-izontal direct effect of the fundamental freedoms will be examined and balanced in order to find out whether this principle deserves a legitimate place within the European construct.

Ratio decidendi of horizontal direct effect

As already mentioned in the second part, the Court of Justice has advanced four different arguments to support the thesis concerning horizontal direct effect of the free movement provisions.

General wording of the relevant Treaty provisions

Firstly, the Court points out that the Treaty provisions on the fundamental free-doms are drafted in general terms. They are not specifically addressed to the Member States and therefore do not, as such, stand in the way of horizontal direct effect being attributed to them. Indeed, Article 39 EC simply speaks of the 'abolition of any discrimination based on nationality', while Articles 43 and 49 EC are limited to generally prohibiting restrictions on the freedom of estab-lishment or the freedom to provide services. Only Article 28 EC, stipulating that 'quantitative restrictions on imports and all measures having equivalent effect shall be prohibited between Member States', could be said to apply probably only to public acts, but the subsequent change in the *Dassonville*–formula[54] in

---

[53] *Bosman*, para. 86.
[54] Case 8/74 *Procureur du Roi v Dassonville* [1974] ECR 837.

Keck[55] has cast doubt upon that interpretation: in *Dassonville*, the Court dealt with 'all trading rules enacted by the Member States'[56], whereas in *Keck*, it simply referred to 'any measure which is capable of directly or indirectly, actually or potentially, hindering intra-Community trade'.[57] Consequently, the specific wording of the Treaty provisions does not exclude that private acts are covered under their scope.[58]

Conversely, it is also true that the Treaty does not explicitly confirm or require that the free movement provisions bind individuals either, whereas within the ambit of the competition rules for example, it is specifically stated that they are addressed to private undertakings. And in the case of *van Gend en Loos* [59], the Court had outlined that within the new legal order of international law which the Community constitutes, the obligations imposed on individuals had to be spelled out 'in a clearly defined way'.[60]

Moreover, it seems to appear from the legal context in which the fundamental freedoms were originally embedded that they were not aimed at private measures. Advocate General Lenz noted that despite the general wording of Article 28 EC, 'a comparison with the wording of, for example, Articles 31 and 32 shows that the measures in question must be ones taken by the Member States.' The same could be said about other Treaty provisions, such as for example the former Articles 50, 53, 62, 64 or 65. However, in this respect it should be acknowledged that the legal framework of the free movement provisions has somewhat changed, as the Treaty of Amsterdam has repealed some provisions which were used as authority for the proposition that the free movement rules were addressed to Member States. According to Article 10 of the Amsterdam Treaty, the deletions cannot affect the *acquis communautaire*, but in principle there seems to be nothing to prevent changes in the interpretation of the free movement provisions from occurring.[61]

Effet utile

Secondly, the Court insisted that the abolition, as between Member States, of obstacles to freedom of movement would be compromised if the abolition of State barriers could be neutralised by the creation or resurrection of obstacles resulting from the exercise of legal autonomy by associations or organisations not governed by public law. This would seriously endanger the Community's

---

[55] Joined Cases C-267&268/91 *Criminal Proceedings* v *Keck and Mithouard* [1993] ECR I-608.
[56] *Dassonville*, para. 5.
[57] *Keck and Mithouard*, para. 11.
[58] See also Roth, above, n.17, at 1241.
[59] Case 26/62 NV *Algemene Transporten Expeditie Onderneming van Gend en Loos* v *Nederlandse Administratie der Belastingen* [1963] ECR 1.
[60] *van Gend en Loos*, at 12; Preedy, *Private Regulations and the Fundamental Freedoms of the EC Treaty*, European University Institute [1999] pp 26–27.
[61] For a concurrent opinion, see Baquero Cruz, above, n.4 pp 247–8.

Internal Market project characterised by the abolition, as between Member States, of obstacles to the free movement of goods, persons, services and capital.[62] It is abundantly clear that the most effective way to remove all barriers to free movement and to fully realise a true internal market, an area without internal frontiers[63], is to apply the free movement rules also to private parties. Indeed, to borrow from Pescatore

> the purpose of any legal rule [. . .] is to achieve some practical aim and it would be running counter to its essential purpose if one handled it in such a way as to render it practically meaningless. Effectiveness is the very soul of legal rules.[64]

However legitimate it may be to pursue the greatest possible effectiveness of the free movement provisions and thus to promote integration within the Community, it is important to bear in mind that the argument of the *effet utile* is not an end in itself, but rather a means to an end. And regardless of what Macchiavelli may have said, within the Community the end does not always justify the means. The European Union to which the Member States have surrendered part of their sovereignty is the result of fundamental ideological, political, economic and social choices made by the Member States. It represents an underlying commitment to a particular version of the 'market' and the 'state'. Were the Court to pursue the effectiveness of the free movement provisions at all costs within this particular framework, this would inevitably lead to an unwarranted intrusion into the private sphere and would risk entailing problems concerning the division of competencies, as will be demonstrated below. Therefore, it is necessary to treat the effet utile argument with caution.[65] It should come into the picture only if the horizontal direct effect of the free movement provisions can also be explained on other grounds.[66]

Uniform application

Thirdly, the Court argued that limiting the application of the prohibition of discrimination to acts of a public authority risks impairing the principle of uniform application of Community law, and therefore the proper functioning

---

[62] Article 3(1)(c) EC.

[63] Article 14 EC.

[64] P. Pescatore, 'The Doctrine of "Direct Effect": An Infant Disease of Community Law', (1983) *European Law Review* 155, p 177.

[65] Dänzer-Vanotti, 'Der Europäische Gerichtshof zwischen Rechtsprechung und Rechtsetzung', in Due/Lutter/Schwarze (eds.), *Festschrift für Ulrich Everling*, Vol. 1, (Baden-Baden, Nomos, 1995) 205–21.

[66] Körber, 'Innerstaatliche Anwendung und Drittwirkung der Grundfreiheiten?—Anmerkung zum Urteil des EUGH vom 6.6.2000, Roma Angonese/Cassa di Risparmio di Bolzano SpA, Rs. C-218/98-' *EuropaRecht* 6 (2000), at 948 considers the reasoning of the Court with regard to this argument as an example of *petitio principii*: the Court proceeds from the assumption that private parties are bound by the fundamental freedoms, but if private acts do not fall within the scope of the free movement provisions, the effectiveness of the freedoms in this respect cannot be questioned. And it still remains to be seen whether private parties are bound by the free movement provisions.

of the internal market, since working conditions in the different Member States are sometimes governed by provisions laid down by law or regulation and sometimes by agreements or acts concluded by private persons. In *Simmenthal*[67], the Court had already made it clear that

> rules of Community law must be fully and uniformly applied in all the Member States from the date of their entry into force and for as long as they continue in force. Those provisions are therefore a direct source of rights and duties for all those affected thereby, whether Member States or individuals, who are parties to legal relationships under Community law.

Evidently, the free movement provisions should not be applied differently according to the status of privatisation or nationalisation within the respective Member States. This also points in the direction of catching private parties under the free movement umbrella.

In this respect, it is worth pointing out that in his opinion in *Faccini Dori*, Advocate General Lenz was fully supportive of these arguments, albeit within the context of possibly granting horizontal direct effect to directives:

> It is unsatisfactory that individuals should be subject to different rules, depending on whether they have comparable legal relations with a body connected with the State or with a private individual. Secondly, it is contrary to the requirements of an internal market for individuals to be subject to different laws in the various Member States even though harmonising measures have been adopted by the Community.[68]

However, the observations which were previously made with regard to the argument of *effet utile* can be repeated here and should function as a kind of *caveat*: in the current state of affairs within the European Union, submitting all measures, regardless of whether they are public or of any other nature, to the scrutiny of the Court of Justice in order to guarantee the principle of uniform application of Community law, would be unacceptable from the point of view of private autonomy and would be liable to infringe the principle of division of competencies, both between the EU and the Member States and as between the legislature and the judiciary.

---

[67] Case 92/78 *Simmenthal SpA v Commission* [1979] ECR 777.

[68] Lenz AG in Case C-91/92 *Faccini Dori v Recreb* [1994] ECR I-3340. Similarly in favour of horizontal direct effect of directives, Jacobs AG in Case C-316/93 *Vaneetveld* [1994] ECR I-769; Van Gerven AG in Case C-271/91 *Marshall v Southampton and South West Hampshire Area Health Authority* [1993] ECR I-4387. However, up until now, as is commonly known, the Court has consistently rejected this proposition: see e.g. G. Betlem, 'Medium Hard Law—Still No Horizontal Direct Effect of European Community Directives After *Faccini Dori*', (1995) *Columbia Journal of European Law* 469–96.

Analogy with Article 141 EC

The final argument advanced by the Court to underpin its conclusion on horizontal direct effect of Article 39 EC was the perceived parallelism between Articles 39 and 141 EC on equal pay. In *Defrenne II*, the Court had stated that even though the provision concerned was formally addressed to the Member States, that did not prevent rights from being conferred at the same time on an individual who has an interest in compliance with the obligations laid down in that provision. According to the Court, the prohibition of discrimination applied equally to all agreements intended to regulate paid labour collectively, as well as to contracts between individuals. And if that was true in the context of Article 141, *a fortiori* it had to be true in the free movement sphere. Some parallels can indeed be drawn between Article 39 and Article 141: both are mandatory in nature, they both contain a prohibition of discrimination, and, importantly, both are, at least partly, inspired by underlying social motives.

However, in spite of all these analogies, this line of argumentation of the Court does not entirely convince. Firstly, as Jaensch argues, Articles 39 and 141 are conceptualised differently in the framework of the Treaty.[69] Article 141 EC imposes upon Member States the obligation to ensure that the principle of equal pay for male and female workers for equal work or work of equal value is applied. The principle of equal pay must thus be transposed by the Member States into their national legislation. As far as the principle of free movement of workers is concerned, by contrast, no further implementation into the national legal order is required. Secondly, the circumstances which have led the Court in *Defrenne II* to attribute horizontal direct effect to Article 141 EC were somewhat peculiar:[70] originally, it was foreseen that the principle of equal pay was to be implemented in the legal orders of all Member States by the end of 1961. Yet by the end of 1975, not all Member States had acted accordingly. In order to set an example, discipline the Member States and the Community institutions and to force them to comply with the obligations imposed in the Treaty, the Court held Article 141 to be horizontally directly effective, implying that it could be directly invoked in proceedings against private employers before the national court. The Court reached this conclusion in spite of the fact that the Treaty provision was explicitly addressed to Member States. It therefore had to make use of a *contra legem* interpretation which it has, for example, up until now always refused to apply in the context of directives.[71] In the light of this, it is not completely clear whether it is really appropriate to draw upon analogies with Article 141 to render Article 39 applicable to private parties.

[69] Jaensch, above, n.38 pp 66–7.
[70] Jaensch, above, n.38 p 67–8; Körber, above, n.66 p 949.
[71] See for example Lenz, Tynes and Young, 'Horizontal What? Back to Basics' (2000) 25 *European Law Review* 509–22.

The advantages and disadvantages of finding the fundamental freedoms horizontally directly effective

The decision of the Court of Justice to interpret Article 39 EC so as to impose obligations on private parties will engender both beneficial and adverse effects. In this section, both the potentially positive and negative consequences will be examined in order to discern in which direction the balance ultimately lies.

Arguments in favour of horizontal direct effect

The attribution of horizontal direct effect to Article 39 EC will undoubtedly increase the effectiveness of the principle of free movement of workers and mark a next stage in the still ongoing integration process towards the realisation of the internal market. The principle of horizontal direct effect may prove to be extremely functional in the abolition of the remaining obstacles to freedom of movement that had previously escaped the Court's scrutiny.[72] Furthermore, from a more social point of view, the fact that now individual private acts can also be held to infringe the provisions on free movement of workers offers the Community migrant workers protection against discrimination on grounds of nationality at another level, namely in the private sphere, in which the great majority of workers are employed, whereas this protection was previously restricted to collective measures in the public or the quasi-government sphere.[73] Another element which might be advanced in favour of horizontal direct effect is the fact that it constitutes, at least at first sight, a rather simple and straight-forward solution to the problem identified. Potential alternatives risk complicating the matter and often lead to the same final outcome anyway. At that point, they risk becoming just surrogates, *ersatz* for the real thing.[74]

Arguments against

Several objections exist against the Court's decision to catch private measures under the Community rules of free movement. Firstly, the applicability of the free movement provisions to private parties will inevitably interfere with the specific doctrinal relationship between the free movement rules and the competition rules as laid down in the framework of the Treaty. This is especially true as far as the free movement of goods is concerned, since a significant part of the field of free movement of workers falls outside the scope of the competition

---

[72] Schaefer, *Die unmittelbare Wirkung des Verbots der nichttarifären Handelshemnisse (Art. 30 EWGV) in den Rechtsbeziehungen zwischen Privaten*, (Frankfurt am Main, 1987).
[73] Lane and Nic Shuibhne, 'Case C-281/98, *Roman Angonese v Cassa di Risparmio di Bolzano SpA*, Judgment of 6 June 2000, not yet reported', (2000) 37 *Common Market Law Review* 1237, p 1244.
[74] Cf. the plea of Van Gerven AG in *Marshall* for horizontal direct effect of directives.

rules.[75] It has been argued that if the Court were to decide that the provisions on free movement of goods also bound private behaviour, this would have serious repercussions: it would throw the entire relationship between Articles 28 and Articles 81 and 82 EC , and thus the entire functioning of the scheme of the Treaty, into turmoil.[76] Advocate General Capotorti highlighted in his opinion in the case of *Van Tiggele* that 'there is an important distinction between Articles 28 and 29 on the one hand and Articles 81 and 82 on the other, not only with regard to those subject to the prohibition but also with regard to the nature of the behaviour which is prohibited'.[77] Public measures restricting trade between Member States are by their very nature incompatible with the free movement of goods precisely because of the impediment they cause to intra-Community trade, whereas agreements between private undertakings only infringe the competition rules if they, apart from having a detrimental effect on trade between Member States, also have the object or effect of restricting competition. The explanation for this stricter regime under Article 28 EC lies in the fact that public measures which adversely affect inter-state trade are implicitly considered to have a more automatic, negative effect on trade than the anti-competitive behaviour of private undertakings.[78] In addition, the scope of application of the competition rules is further limited by the following factors[79]: firstly, Articles 81 and 82 EC only apply to private undertakings, and thus not to all private parties; secondly, they catch only certain types of private behaviour (agreements, decisions or concerted practices or abuses of a dominant position); and thirdly, following the *de minimis* rule,[80] the competition rules only come into play when the restriction of competition has been appreciable. The sphere of application of Article 28 EC does not contain any such limitations. All this inevitably means that were Article 28 EC to be interpreted by the Court of Justice so as to be applicable to private parties without any further due, it would have a much broader scope than Articles 81 and 82 and practically render them redundant. And this, of course, can not be the intention of the Court.

Secondly, it is alleged that horizontal direct effect of the fundamental freedoms disturbs the delicate balance of division of competencies between the European Union and its constituent Member States and thus creates an issue of subsidiarity.[81] According to Article 5 EC:

---

[75] See e.g. Case C-67/96 *Albany International* v *Stichting Bedrijfspensioenfonds Textielindustrie* [1999] ECR I-5751; Baquero Cruz, above, n.4 pp 255–6.
[76] Quinn and MacGowan, above n. 41.
[77] Capotorti AG in Case 82/77 *Openbaar Ministerie* v *Van Tiggele* [1978] ECR 25, at 42.
[78] Quinn and MacGowan, op.cit., n.73 pp 167–70.
[79] R. Whish, Competition Law, (Butterworths, London, 1993).
[80] Commission Notice on Agreements of Minor Importance [1986] OJ C231/2, as amended by [1994] OJ C368/20.
[81] Preedy, above, n.60, pp 67–71.

The Community shall act within the limits of the powers conferred upon it by this Treaty and of the objectives assigned to it therein.

In areas which do not fall within its exclusive competence, the Community shall take action, in accordance with the principle of subsidiarity, only if and insofar as the objectives of the proposed action cannot be sufficiently achieved by the Member States and can therefore, by reason of the scale or effects of the proposed action, be better achieved by the Community.

Any action by the Community shall not go beyond what is necessary to achieve the objectives of this Treaty.

By granting horizontal direct effect to the freedom of movement of workers, the Court has extended the competence of the Community deeply into the sphere of private law, which has traditionally belonged to the preserve of the Member States. Kluth has argued that the application of the free movement rules to private conduct would put into question the limits between the power of the State and private autonomy, involving an important degree of socialisation of private law, and causing the end of the private law society and the departure from the liberal concept of the single market as a fundamental pillar of the Community.[82]

This is a rather dramatic statement, prompting the need to look at things in perspective. Private autonomy is not absolute. There is always auto-regulation from within the market and the mandatory provisions of the applicable national legislation which have to be complied with. In addition, private parties also have to bear in mind the possible application of the Community competition rules. It would thus be an inaccurate representation of the situation to state that private parties were operating in a complete legal vacuum from a Community point of view before the Court decided to declare the free movement provisions to be horizontally directly effective. However, in this respect it must be acknowledged that the application of the free movement rules potentially has a much more pervasive impact on the private sphere than the application of the competition rules, as they appear from *Angonese* to apply to all individuals and not only to undertakings, do not require a *de minimis* threshold to be passed and require only an effect on inter-state trade to trigger their application. Evidently, it is extremely unlikely that the Member States will let this happen. To some extent, it might be reassuring that the Court is sending out some signals of its willingness and determination to limit the scope of application of the free movement provisions, distinguishing between product characteristics and selling arrangements within the sphere of goods[83] and attempting to introduce a similar threshold to the field of the other free movement provisions.[84]

---

[82] Kluth, above, n.38 p 557.

[83] See *Keck* and subsequent cases, e.g. Case C-292/92 *Hunermund* v *Landesapothekerkammer Württemberg* [1993] ECR I-6787.

[84] See e.g. Fennelly AG in Case C-190/98 *Graf* v *Filzmoser Maschinenbau GmbH* [2000] ECR I-493.

Thirdly, the Court seems to have disregarded the traditional principle of separation of powers between legislature and judiciary as established by Montesquieu in *De l'esprit des lois*. Legislative action would have been appropriate and even required to extend the Community's competence further into the private sphere. The Community possesses the necessary tools to achieve this objective. In this respect, it suffices to refer to Treaty provisions such as Article 94, 95 or 308 EC. The Community has already promulgated legislative acts regulating some particular aspects of the private sphere, such as, for example, a directive on unfair contract terms in consumer contracts.[85] However, instead of this preferred course of action, the intervention of the Court more or less confronted the Member States with an accomplished fact.

In an attempt to counter or at least attenuate the force of this argument, one may ask the question whether the fact that the Court fulfils this special role of driving force of the integration process is not precisely one of the unique features of this so-called new legal order?[86] Besides, in comparison to the doctrines of direct effect and supremacy, which were also constructs of judicial activism and which could really be considered as giant leaps for Community-kind, the recognition of horizontal direct effect of Treaty provisions seems to be only a small step for the Court. Furthermore, in the period of the so-called Luxembourg compromise, the whole weight of the integration process and the future of the Community more or less rested on the shoulders of the Court. This changed with the Single European Act and the breakthrough of qualified majority voting, but the new 'eurosclerosis' detected at the Intergovernmental Conferences in Amsterdam and Nice may have prompted the Court to take up its leading role again.

Fourthly, closely linked to the previous point is the argument that the Court has delivered a serious blow to the principle of legal certainty.[87] It may still seem feasible to try to abolish private measures which somehow discriminate on grounds of nationality, but removing all private measures which are non-discriminatory but nevertheless restrict freedom of movement seems to be an endless task. The situation is further complicated by the fact that the precise content and scope of the concept of 'restriction' has not been fully determined yet. The Court will inevitably have to deal with all suspect private rules and behaviour on a case-by-case basis and will have to engage in an examination of all arguments advanced for justification purposes.

Finally, a fifth objection against the attribution of horizontal direct effect to the Treaty provisions on free movement has to do with the issue of justification. As the Court has held, there is nothing to preclude individuals relying on grounds of public policy, public security and public health to justify private

---

[85] Council Directive 93/13/EEC of 5 April 1993 on unfair terms in consumer contracts [1993] OJ L95/29.

[86] Admittedly, this is a highly contentious proposition.

[87] Körber, above, n.66, pp 946–7.

measures which are considered as an obstacle to the freedom of movement. However, this solution seems to be unworkable in practice.[88] It is submitted that private parties have only individual interests, they pursue private aims, their motivations and objectives are generally of a non-altruistic nature.[89] These particular grounds of justification are therefore clearly meant to be invoked solely by Member States.

Conclusion

Even though all four arguments on which the Court of Justice based its decision to render Article 39 EC horizontally directly effective have a certain intrinsic value and all contribute in some way to the cause, the Court's reasoning does not entirely convince and gives the impression of being incomplete.[90] Furthermore, however legitimate and important the Court's intentions and objections may have been when declaring Article 39 EC applicable to private parties, the fact is that this operation does not only produce beneficial effects. There are downsides to it as well, and they are many, and they are serious. Serious consideration should be given to the question whether horizontal direct effect constitutes the appropriate answer to the problem of the perceived gaps in the application of Community law. If the Court is of the opinion that the price to pay is not too high and decides to pursue the idea of horizontal direct effect within the fields of the fundamental freedoms, it is to be hoped that it does so cautiously.

FUTURE DEVELOPMENTS ?

The rather broad sketch of the question of whether private parties are bound by the Treaty provisions on freedom of movement in part two demonstrates that this issue is still far from being completely settled. Despite several judgments from the Court of Justice, many questions surrounding the problem of horizontal direct effect still remained unanswered. When dealing with each of these issues in this part, the observations made in part three will be borne in mind.

---

[88] O'Keeffe and Osborne, 'The European Court Scores a Goal', (1996) *International Journal of Comparative Labour Law and Industrial Relations*, 125–6.
[89] Streinz & Leible, 'Die unmittelbare Drittwirkung der Grundfreiheiten—Überlegungen aus Anlass von EuGH, EuZW 2000, 468, Angonese', (2000) 15 *EuZW* 459, p 461.
[90] For a concurrent opinion, see Lane and Nic Shuibhne, above, n.71, p 1244.

Horizontal direct effect of Article 39 EC: beyond discrimination?

The first issue which needs to be tackled is to what extent Article 39 EC is horizontally directly effective. In *Bosman*, the Court extended the scope of application of the provisions on free movement of workers to non-discriminatory measures which restrict access to the labour market of other Member States, but the transfer rules in question were not individual rules, but rules which were meant to regulate gainful employment in a collective manner. Subsequently, in *Angonese*, the Court simply stipulated that the prohibition of discrimination on grounds of nationality is applicable to private persons as well, omitting every reference to the concept of 'restriction'. As such, there is nothing objectionable about this statement, because the requirement of possession of the specific certificate, unilaterally imposed by the private undertaking in question, constitutes a clear example of an indirectly discriminatory measure.[91]

Acceptable though the Court's approach may be, it inevitably prompts the question whether only discriminatory individual rules are covered under Article 39 EC, or alternatively, whether its scope extends also to genuinely non-discriminatory individual measures? There seems to be uncertainty about this in the legal literature. One commentator has already observed that the Court's judgment is limited to the discriminatory rules, therefore not being relevant for non-discriminatory restrictions.[92] Another somewhat more cautiously limited himself to stating that the *Bosman* decision of prohibiting also genuinely non-discriminatory restrictions to the free movement of workers was not reiterated in this case.[93] On the basis of the evolution from an initial discrimination-based analysis to a wider, more general prohibition of restrictions which seems to have characterised the case law of the Court of Justice with regard to the different fundamental freedoms[94], it could certainly be advocated that the Court will extend its forthright stance on the horizontal direct effect of Article 39 EC to truly non-discriminatory obstacles. In addition, this argument gains further weight thanks to the Court's statement in *Bosman* to the effect that individuals

---

[91] *Angonese*, para. 45.
[92] Baquero Cruz, above, n.4, p 234.
[93] Körber, above, n.66, pp 949–50.
[94] This development did not occur simultaneously in the different free movements, but initiated within the framework of goods and was subsequently followed for services until the trend was concluded within the provisions on workers and establishment. For goods, see Case 8/74 *Procureur du Roi v Dassonville* [1974] ECR 837; Case 120/78 *Rewe-Zentrale AG v Bundesmonopolverwaltung für Branntwein* [1979] ECR 649; Joined Cases C-267&268/91 *Criminal Proceedings v Keck and Mithouard* [1993] ECR I-608. For services, see Case C-76/90 *Säger v Dennemeyer* [1991] ECR I-4221; Case C-288/89 *Stichting Collective Antennevoorziening Gouda & Others v Commissariaat voor de Media* [1991] ECR I-4035. For workers and establishment, Case C-19/92 *Kraus v Land Baden-Württemberg* [1993] ECR I-1663; Case C-415/93 *Union Royale Belge des Sociétés de Football Association ASLB v Jean-Marc Bosman* [1995] ECR I-4921.

could rely on grounds of public policy, public security or public health to justify the—in casu non-discriminatory—rules.

On the other hand, in this respect it might also be interesting to look at the particular reasoning which brought the Court to the conclusion that the prohibition of discrimination on grounds of nationality laid down in Article 39 EC applies to private parties. When the Court in its previous case law on this issue originally held that the scope of Article 39 EC covered not only public acts, but also private acts insofar as they were aimed at regulating labour in a collective manner, and later on in *Bosman* added genuinely non-discriminatory measures to the category of measures to be examined upon compliance with the provisions on free movement of workers, it invariably grounded its decisions upon the same three arguments, namely the general wording of Article 39 EC, the need for a uniform application of the Treaty and the requirement of the *effet utile* of the Treaty. Now, when the Court in *Angonese* decided to attribute full horizontal direct effect to Article 39 EC, it added a new, fourth argument to its reasoning, based upon an analogy between Article 141 EC and Article 39 EC. This at least conveys the impression that this last argument has been decisive in the attribution of horizontal direct effect to the freedom of movement of workers. In this respect, it is important to stress that the principles on equal pay contained in Article 141 EC are based on a prohibition of discrimination on grounds of sex, and do not go beyond discrimination. Originally, in *Defrenne*, the Court limited the horizontal direct effect of Article 141 EC to instances of 'direct and overt' discrimination.[95] Since the Court's decision in *Jenkins*[96], indirectly discriminatory private conduct is also scrutinised under Article 141 EC. It is submitted that if the horizontal direct effect of Article 141 EC is limited to discriminatory measures, and if the Court has invoked the analogy between Article 141 and Article 39 EC to declare that individual private conduct is caught by Article 39, then logically the horizontal direct effect of Article 39 EC should be limited to discriminatory rules or conduct as well.[97] In the current constellation, characterised by strong suspicion about the concept of horizontal direct effect for the reasons outlined above, the latter option seems to be preferable, at least for the time being.

---

[95] *Defrenne II*, para. 18 and 40; see also Case 129/79 *Macarthys Ltd.* v *Smith* [1980] ECR 1275, para. 14–15.

[96] Case 96/80 *Jenkins v Kingsgate (Clothing Productions) Ltd.* [1981] ECR 911, para. 9-14; see also Case 170/84 *Bilka Kaufhaus GmbH* v *Weber von Hartz* [1986] ECR 1607; or Case 171/88 *Rinner-Kühn v FWW Spezial-Gebäudereinigung GmbH* [1989] ECR 2743.

[97] In this respect, it must be observed that the Court's recent case law on positive action within the social field could possibly be invoked to undermine this line of argumentation, as it could be interpreted as somehow going beyond discrimination. In Case C-450/93 *Kalanke v Freie Hansestadt Bremen* [1995] ECR I-3051, para. 18, the Court held that Article 2(4) of Directive 76/207/EEC is 'specifically and exclusively designed to allow measures which, although discriminatory in appearance, are in fact intended to eliminate or reduce actual instances of inequality which may exist in the reality of social life.' See also Case C-409/95 *Marschall v Land Nordrhein-Westfalen* [1997] ECR I-6363.

Transposition to other freedoms?

A second issue which needs to be addressed is whether the Court's decision to recognise the horizontal direct effect of Article 39 EC can and/or will be transposed to the respective fields of application of the other free movement provisions.

One author is of the opinion, firstly, that the Court's decision will be implemented also within the scope of the freedom to provide services, but secondly, could not state with certainty whether the same would happen within the ambit of the freedom of establishment, and thirdly, rejected outright the possibility of acceptance of this declaration within the field of the free movement of goods.[98] Another scholar contends that the *Angonese* decision is limited to the field of workers and is, in principle, not relevant for the other freedoms. The free movement of workers is different: failing to make this distinction would risk assimilating workers to commodities under Community law. Baquero Cruz asserts that the Court considers 'discriminating against workers as graver than discriminating against goods or services, economic activities where private forms of discrimination naturally fall under the competition rules—with its "appreciable effects' threshold."[99] In his opinion, if the Court had really been in favour of the so-called convergence of the free movement rules, it would have solved the case by applying Article 7(4) of Regulation 1612/68.[100] This solution 'would have preserved a single personal scope for all the economic freedoms as a matter of Community constitutional law. The special personal scope for the workers provision would have been considered a matter of secondary or statutory law.'[101] The fact that the Court did not do so demonstrates that the Court prefers to ensure an enhanced protection for workers as a matter of constitutional law.

It should be emphasised that the question of the possible transposition of the specific principle proclaimed by the Court in *Angonese* to the other fundamental freedoms is inextricably linked to the debate about the convergence of the free movement provisions. In the opinion of Advocate General Lenz, the convergence of economic freedoms in European Community law is objectively necessary. The four fundamental freedoms of the common market are not only based on a common foundation, they also form a unity, and the same criteria should be applied as far as possible in dealing with them. According to the Advocate General, 'for example, there is no sensible reason discernible why free movement of goods ought to be better protected than free movement of persons, since both are of fundamental importance for the internal market.'[102]

---

[98]   Körber, above, n.66, 950.
[99]   Baquero Cruz, above, n.4, p 235.
[100]   Regulation 1612/68 [1968] OJ L 257/2, [1968] OJ Special Edition 475.
[101]   Baquero Cruz, above, n.4, p 235.
[102]   Lenz AG in *Bosman*, para. 200; see also Mattera, 'La libre circulation des travailleurs à l' intérieur de la Communauté européenne' (1993) 4 *Revue du Marché Unique Européen* 68.

It seems unmistakably true[103] that the Court of Justice has endeavoured to establish a uniform approach to the free movement rules,[104] even though this tendency is still not unanimously accepted in the legal literature.[105] First of all, all fundamental freedoms have been granted direct effect by the Court,[106] although that was not always self-evident.[107] Furthermore, the Court has also broadened the scope of all freedoms from prohibitions of discrimination on grounds of nationality towards prohibitions of obstacles to the freedoms and generalised the mandatory requirements justification within the field of goods to all other freedoms ('objective justifications in the general interest'). Finally, even the infamous *Keck* decision does not seem to be able to put a spoke in the wheel of convergence, in the light of the valuable recent attempts to elaborate a new common standard for all free movement provisions.[108]

Freedom to provide services and freedom of establishment

In the light of all this, the odds are that the Court will extend the *Angonese* principle that private conduct is caught by Article 39 EC to the provisions on the freedom to provide services.[109] Already in *Walrave*, Advocate General Warner opined that the Articles 39 and 49 EC were 'in every material aspect parallel'.[110] And the Court subsequently confirmed that the activities referred to in Article 49 'are not to be distinguished by their nature from those in Article 39, but only by the fact that they are performed outside the ties of a contract of employment.'[111] According to the Court, 'this single distinction cannot justify a

---

[103] This approach of the Court has nevertheless not been applauded unequivocally: see L. Daniele 'Non-Discriminatory Restrictions to the Free Movement of Persons', (1997) 22 *European law Review* 191–200.

[104] See e.g. Behrens, 'Die Konvergenz der wirtschaftlichen Freiheiten im europäischen Gemeinschaftsrecht', (1992) 27 *EuropaRecht* 145; Mortelmans, 'Excepties bij non-tarifaire belemmeringen: assimilatie in het nieuwe EG-verdrag?' (1997) *Sociaal-Economische Wetgeving* 182; M. Maduro, *We The Court* (Oxford, Hart, 1998) 101.

[105] Hatzopoulos, 'Recent Developments of the Case Law of the ECJ in the Field of Services', (2000) 37 *Common Market Law Review* 65; or Martin, 'Discriminations, entraves et raisons impérieuses dans le Traité: trois concepts en quête d'identité', (1998) *Cahiers de droit européen* 261.

[106] Goods: Case 74/76 *Iannelli & Volpi SpA* v *Ditta Paolo Meroni* [1977] ECR 557; Workers: Case 167/73 *Commission* v *France* [1974] ECR 359; Establishment: Case 2/74 *Reyners* v *Belgium* [1974] ECR 631; Services: Case 33/74 *van Binsbergen* v *Bestuur van de Bedrijfsvereniging voor de Metaalnijverheid* [1974] ECR 1299.

[107] Craig, 'Once Upon a Time in the West: Direct Effect and the Federalization of EEC Law', (1992) 12 *Oxford Journal of Legal Studies* 453.

[108] See especially Jacobs AG in Case C-412/93 *Leclerc-Siplec* v *TF1 Publicité* [1995] ECR I-179; Case C-190/98 *Graf* v *Filzmoser Maschinenbau GmbH* [2000] ECR I-493; Weatherill, 'After Keck: Some thoughts on how to clarify the clarification' (1996) 33 *Common Market Law Review*, at 885; Barnard, 'Fitting the remaining pieces into the goods and persons jigsaw?' (2001) 26 *European Law Review* 52–59.

[109] Delannay, 'Observations sur l'affaire "Union Cycliste Internationale"', (1976) *Cahiers de droit européen* 209, pp 217–23.

[110] Warner AG in *Walrave*, p 1425.

[111] *Walrave*, para. 23.

more restrictive interpretation of the scope of the freedom to be ensured.'[112] Besides, it is suggested that the decisive reason for considering the rules on free movement of workers applicable to individuals, namely the perceived analogy between Articles 39 and 141 EC, can be transposed without too many difficulties to the domain of services, as Article 49 EC is equally mandatory in nature, also lays down a fundamental freedom and constitutes a specific application of the general prohibition of discrimination contained in Article 12 EC. Another argument which could be adduced to support the assertion that the Court might be prepared to extend its case law on the applicability of Article 39 EC to the field of services lies in the existence of Regulation 1612/68[113]. This instrument of secondary legislation was specifically intended to further implement some of the principles laid down in the Treaty provisions on free movement of workers. Article 7(4) of Regulation 1612/68 stipulates that

> any clause of a collective or individual agreement or of any other collective regulation concerning eligibility for employment, employment, remuneration and other conditions of work or dismissal shall be null and void in so far as it lays down or authorises discriminatory conditions in respect of workers who are nationals of the other Member States.

It cannot seriously be disputed that this clause can be applied to private employers. It could therefore be considered as introducing horizontal direct effect within the field of free movement of workers 'through the back door'. In the preliminary ruling in the case of *Angonese*, the referring national judge had asked the Court of Justice to examine the compatibility of the requirement to obtain that specific certificate of bilingualism with Article 7(4) of Regulation 1612/68. The Court concluded that this provision was not infringed and proceeded to examine the question submitted solely in relation to Article 39 EC.[114] As such, there does not seem to be anything inherently wrong with the Court's decision. The Court adopted a rather strict—maybe even unnecessarily strict—interpretation of Article 7(4). However, even though the contested clause requiring possession of the certificate may, strictly speaking, not be part of a collective or individual agreement or of any other collective regulation, as required by Article 7(4), it does undoubtedly concern eligibility for employment and moreover, it is indirectly discriminatory. It seems that a simple, straightforward teleological interpretation would have sufficed to include within its material scope of application the unilateral conditions (which in effect take the form of 'standard clauses') imposed by a private undertaking in order to apply for a post.[115] The outcome of the case would have been the same, and the Court

---

[112] *Walrave*, para. 24.

[113] Regulation EEC 1612/68 of the Council of 15 October 1968 on freedom of movement for workers within the Community, OJ Sp.Ed. [1968] L257/2, p. 475.

[114] *Angonese*, para. 23–27.

[115] See for a concurrent opinion, Körber, above., n.66, p 934.

would have avoided exposing itself to the harsh criticism which is undoubtedly awaiting it now from commentators opposed to the idea of rendering the Treaty provisions on the fundamental freedoms applicable to private persons. If the Court of Justice had applied the Regulation to the circumstances of the case, it would have avoided the issue of horizontal direct effect of Article 39 EC. Equally the question about possible horizontal direct effect of Article 49 EC would not have arisen, as Regulation 1612/68 does not apply to services.[116] It is submitted that the Court, by choosing the hard way and solving this case under the heading of Article 39 EC, while it would have been perfectly feasible to come to a solution on the basis of Article 7 of the Regulation, has—deliberately?—left the door ajar for a transposition of its decision to the field of services. Rather than weakening the convergence between the fundamental freedoms, the Court's approach therefore seems to allow it to be reinforced.

It can be argued that this whole argumentation, *mutatis mutandis*, also holds true for Article 43 EC, concerning the principle of freedom of establishment. Articles 39 and 43 EC are clearly based on the same conception, requiring equal treatment of persons who have exercised their right of free movement and are settled in a Member State. The distinguishing feature between them is whether the persons concerned are working as employees or as self-employed.[117] In *van Binsbergen*, Advocate General Mayras stressed that the general principle of equal treatment on grounds of nationality in Article 12 EC lay behind the Treaty Articles on workers, establishment and services alike.[118] The field of establishment may actually be at least as appropriate to adopt the perceived parallelism between Articles 39 and 141 EC as the field of services, given that the social objectives, inherent in Article 141 EC, seem to have always received a prominent place in the former, whereas in the latter, the promotion of the mobility of the services and the idea of the creation of the internal market were often predominant,[119] just as in the sphere of the free movement of goods.[120]

Free movement of goods

However, notwithstanding the general trend towards convergence of the fundamental freedoms, one can still perceive some differences in the Court's approach in respect of the free movement of goods provisions which are independent of the fact that the Court may not yet have had the opportunity to extend its case law in one field to the spheres of other freedoms, and which can be explained by

---

[116] See also Preedy, above, n.60, p 18.
[117] See Case C-107/94 *Asscher v Staatssecretaris van Financiën* [1996] ECR I-3089.
[118] Mayras AG in *van Binsbergen*.
[119] Warner AG in Case 52/79 *Procureur du Roi v Debauve* [1980] ECR 833, at 872; Craig & de Búrca, *EU Law: Text, Cases and Materials*, (Oxford, Oxford University Press, 1998), p 729.
[120] See Gulmann AG in Case C-275/92 *HM Customs and Excise v Schindler* [1994] ECR 1039, p 1059.

the simple fact that the freedoms to a certain extent have characteristic features distinguishing them from one other.[121] To name but the obvious, persons, regardless of whether they be employed workers, self-employed established in given Member State or self-employed service providers, are different from and have a greater intrinsic value than goods. Correspondingly, they deserve to receive protection in accordance with their status. It is clear that a significant part—not to say the biggest part—of all professional activities are carried out in the private sphere. The Court had therefore good reasons to hold that the Treaty provisions imposed obligations upon public authorities and private parties alike. A contrary decision would have deprived these Articles of much of their practical relevance.[122] On the other hand, the scope of application of Article 28 EC varies considerably from those of the Articles 39, 43 and 49 EC. It is mostly concerned with measures emanating from the public authorities of the Member States. Consequently, there are no similar compelling reasons to render Article 28 EC applicable to private parties. This is not to say that it is impossible to interpret Article 28 EC so as to impose obligations on private parties. Rather, it is advocated that it would seem more appropriate not to do so, especially in the light of the perceived negative effects, outlined above. Therefore, in order to abolish private measures which are liable to infringe Article 28 EC, one should keep relying in the first place on the specific set of rules which are concerned with the activities of private parties, the competition rules.

Furthermore, Article 10(1) imposes upon the Member States the obligation to take all appropriate measures to ensure fulfilment of the obligations arising out of the Treaty or resulting from action taken by the institutions of the Community and to facilitate the achievement of the Community's tasks. It is submitted that if a Member State fails to live up to these obligations, for example under Article 28 EC, the Commission may take action under Article 226 EC and bring the matter before the Court of Justice.[123] This appears to be an important additional instrument to fill the gaps in the application of Community law. The case of *Commission v France*[124] serves to illustrate this point. The factual circumstances of the case were the following: for more than a decade, the Commission had received many complaints concerning the passivity of the French authorities in the face of violent acts committed by private individuals and by protest movements of French farmers directed against agricultural products from other Member States. The Commission submitted that France had failed to fulfil its

---

[121] See e.g. K. Mortelmans, 'Towards convergence in the application of the rules on free movement and on competition?', (2001) 38 *Common Market Law Review* 613, at 617–619; D. O'Keeffe and J. Bavasso, 'Four freedoms, one market and national competence: In search of a dividing line' in *Liber Amicorum in Honour of Lord Slynn of Hadley*, (The Hague, Kluwer Law International, 2000).

[122] Quinn and MacGowan, above, n.41, p 165.

[123] Case 231/83 *Cullet v Centre Leclerc* [1985] ECR 305.

[124] Case C-265/95 *Commission v France* [1997] ECR I-6959.

obligations under the common organisation of the markets in agricultural products and Article 28 EC, in conjunction with Article 10 EC.

In his opinion, Advocate General Lenz paved the way for the Court. He submitted that 'there can be no doubt in this case that the conduct of private individuals in question would constitute an infringement of the principle of the free movement of goods if it could be attributed to the French Republic.'[125] He concluded that the present case clearly showed that the free movement of goods could also be jeopardized by actions committed by private individuals and considered it therefore necessary, 'for the protection of the practical effectiveness of Article 28, to infer from the Treaty a duty for Member States to combat such actions by private individuals. Such a duty is, of course, an obligation to act, that is, an obligation arising from the first paragraph of Article 10.'[126]

The Court accepted the open invitation. It solemnly declared that

> as an indispensable instrument for the realisation of a market without internal frontiers, Article 28 therefore does not prohibit solely measures emanating from the State which, in themselves, create restrictions on trade between Member States. It also applies where a Member State abstains from adopting the measures required in order to deal with obstacles to the free movement of goods which are not caused by the State. The fact that a Member State abstains from taking action or, as the case may be, fails to adopt adequate measures to prevent obstacles to the free movement of goods that are created, in particular, by actions by private individuals on its territory aimed at products originating in other Member States is just as likely to obstruct intra-Community trade as is a positive act. Article 28 therefore requires the Member States not merely themselves to abstain from adopting measures or engaging in conduct liable to constitute an obstacle to trade but also, when read with Article 10 of the Treaty, to take all necessary and appropriate measures to ensure that that fundamental freedom is respected on their territory.[127]

The Court of Justice readily admitted that the Member States retain exclusive competence as regards the maintenance of public order and the safeguarding of public security, and that they unquestionably enjoy a margin of discretion in determining what measures are most appropriate to eliminate barriers to the importation of products in a given situation. However, the Court concluded that ultimately it falls to the Court to assess 'whether the Member State concerned has adopted appropriate measures for ensuring the free movement of goods.'[128] Ultimately, the usefulness of this solution will depend on how much

---

[125] Lenz AG in Case C-265/95 *Commission v France* [1997] ECR I-6959, at 6969; see also Fennelly AG in Case C-52/95 *Commission v France* [1995] ECR I-4443, p 4455.

[126] Lenz AG, at 6979. This particular interpretation was, in his opinion, implicitly present in the Court's judgment in Case C-16/94 *Dubois and Général Cargo Services* [1995] ECR I-2421.

[127] *Commission v France*, para. 30–32.

[128] *Commission v France*, para. 35.

discretion the Court is willing to grant the Member States and how much control it will exert over the 'appropriateness' of the acts of Member States.[129]

Recently the Council adopted—on the basis of Article 308 EC—a Regulation establishing a mechanism in order to remove obstacles to the free movement of goods caused by action or inaction on behalf of the Member States.[130] The Commission is empowered to notify a Member State when it considers that an obstacle is occurring in a Member State, requesting the Member State to take all necessary and proportionate measures to remove the obstacle. Subsequently, the Member State has five days to inform the Commission of the steps it has taken or intends to take to abolish the obstacle.[131] If the Member State fails to comply with the Commission's decision, the Commission may immediately bring the matter before the Court of Justice.

The scope of application of the Regulation may be limited to the free movement of goods and it may not be that simple to satisfy the conditions for application of the mechanism,[132] so its practical relevance may still be limited, but still, the initiative appears to be promising, as it seems to meet some of the objections against horizontal direct effect of the free movement provisions (no breach of the separation of powers, more legal certainty, etc.). If it turns out to be effective, it might very well serve as a model for the other freedoms, to complement the principle of horizontal direct effect or even, who knows, to substitute it. Interesting decisions of the Court are undoubtedly awaiting us.

---

[129] Muylle, 'Angry Farmers and Passive Policemen: Private Conduct and the Free Movement of Goods', (1998) 23 *European Law Review* 469–474.
[130] Council Regulation 2679/98 of 7 December 1998 on the functioning of the internal market in relation to the free movement of goods among the Member States, [1998] OJ L337/8.
[131] Article 5 Regulation 2679/98.
[132] See e.g. the restrictive definition of an 'obstacle' in Article 2.

6

Enforcing the Single Market: The Judicial Harmonisation of National Remedies and Procedural Rules

MICHAEL DOUGAN*

INTRODUCTION

WRITING IN 1989, Bronckers queried whether, balancing the ambitious legislative programme required to invigorate the process of economic integration against the existing mechanisms for enforcing Community law before the domestic courts, 'trade and industry' stood a chance against the Member States. He concluded that some concession of procedural autonomy was the price the Member States must pay for building their Single Market.[1]

The pioneering spirit of the Single European Act may since have faltered, but the problems posed by decentralised enforcement vex yet more intensely than before. Indeed, Community intervention in the domestic systems of remedies and procedural rules invites critical analysis along two complementary axes. The first is the imperative of effectiveness—demanding an adequate standard of enforcement for Treaty norms within each Member State. In this regard, the Court of Justice continues its struggle to define the Member State's margin of discretion to regulate or restrict the exercise of Community rights through the national courts. This struggle has provided inexhaustible fuel for an effervescence of academic discourse: assessing the unstable and often inconsistent meaning of 'effective judicial protection'; querying its relationship with competing Member State interests in (say) legal certainty and the fair administration of justice; pondering

* This chapter is based on doctoral research supported by the Arts and Humanities Research Board. I am grateful to participants at the Single Market Workshop, in particular to Imelda Maher, for their comments and suggestions.
[1] M Bronckers, 'Private Enforcement of 1992: Do Trade and Industry Stand a Chance Against the Member States?' (1989) 26 *CMLRev* 513.

its implications for wider debates about (for example) the constitutional limits of judicial activism.[2]

The second axis, which has by comparison provoked a less vigorous and less varied response, is the imperative of uniformity—demanding normative equality of treatment between the Member States (without necessarily implying any particular level of treatment, so long as it is the same across the entire Community). This chapter will explore two competing conceptual models of the imperative of uniformity, and their respective implications for ongoing debate about the decentralised enforcement of Treaty norms: the traditional 'integration through law' approach; and an alternative 'sectoral' interpretation. These models will then act as critical perspectives through which to assess the developing caselaw and, in particular, changing judicial understandings of the Community's interest in harmonising national remedies and procedural rules.

TWO COMPETING CONCEPTUAL MODELS OF THE COMMUNITY'S ENFORCEMENT DEFICIT

Integration Through Law and the Enforcement Deficit Debate

Academic discourse on the 'problem' of national remedies and procedures has traditionally been dominated by a particular conceptual approach to the study of Community law. This approach can conveniently be referred to as 'integration through law'. It asserts that the basic purpose of the Community is to promote an 'ever-closer union among the peoples of Europe'; the concomitant function of the Treaty legal order is to consolidate this process of convergence by creating a uniform body of binding norms, guaranteed to be applied effectively across the Member States.

The primary justification for an 'integration through law' approach to EC legal studies is economic, related to the creation of a Single Market based on the principles of free movement and equalised conditions of competition. The success of the Single Market requires that the relevant Treaty rules and Community legislation be formulated and applied, not only effectively within each Member State (so as to prevent free movement being reduced in practice to mere paper guarantees), but also uniformly as between the various Member States (so as to minimise the persistence of unfair competitive advantages in the European market-place). However, such economic considerations are now supplemented by what might be termed a welfare perspective. Community competence has expanded dramatically, so as to embrace not only issues which impinge directly upon the operation of the Single Market, but also important aspects of social policy—ranging from public health and environmental protection to consumer

---

[2] For a comprehensive survey: A Ward, *Judicial Review and the Rights of Private Parties in EC Law* (Oxford, OUP, 2000) Chs. 2–4.

rights and labour solidarity, and culminating in the inauguration of 'citizenship of the European Union'. The further the Community pursues welfare policies which are increasingly removed and autonomous from the traditional dynamics of the Single Market, the more difficult it becomes to argue the case for an effective and uniform supranational legal order by reference to the essentially economic logic of free movement and undistorted competition. But the growth of such welfare-orientated policy sectors provides 'integration through law' with an alternative or additional justification for effectiveness and uniformity in the application of Treaty rules, i.e. as essential components in a contemporary process of European integration which rightly consists in the creation of a common body of social rights enjoyed by all the citizens of the Union.[3]

Direct effect and supremacy are the central pillars of the legal order developed by the Court of Justice with a view to securing the effective and uniform application of Community law across the Member States, and thus of realising the Treaty's multifarious objectives in the economic and social spheres.[4] These principles are not unproblematic even in themselves: consider (for example) the Court's much-maligned approach to horizontal direct effect for directives,[5] and the intermittent resistance demonstrated by certain national judges to the full logic of supremacy.[6] But even assuming that a provision of Community law has direct effect and the domestic courts are prepared to enforce it in preference to contradictory national rules, this may not in itself be sufficient to satisfy the underlying demands of either effectiveness or uniformity. In particular, it is possible that the sanctions and procedures available for the decentralised enforcement of Community norms may be inadequate within any given Member State, or simply different from those available in other jurisdictions. From the standpoint of the Single Market, such a situation disrupts the operation of fundamental policies such as free movement for goods and persons, and distorts competitive conditions as between Community undertakings. This is particularly true as regards those sectors of Treaty activity which remain dominated by the objectives of economic integration (for example: competition policy and state aids).[7] Viewed from a welfare-based perspective, the same situation undermines the standards of protection individuals are supposed to enjoy under Community law, and contradicts the principle of equal treatment between

---

[3] Eg: AG La Pergola in Cases C-4–5/95 *Stöber and Pereira* [1997] ECR I-511; AG Léger in Case C-214/94 *Boukhalfa* [1996] ECR I-2253; AG Jacobs in Case C-274/96 *Bickel and Franz* [1998] ECR I-7637.

[4] Case 26/62 *van Gend en Loos* [1963] ECR 1; Case 6/64 *Flaminio Costa v. ENEL* [1964] ECR 585.

[5] Eg: M Dougan, 'The "Disguised" Vertical Direct Effect of Directives?' [2000] *CLJ* 586 and [2001] *CLJ* 253.

[6] Eg: N Reich, 'Judge-made "Europe à la carte": Some Remarks on Recent Conflicts between European and German Constitutional Law Provoked by the Banana Litigation' (1996) 7 *EJIL* 103; C Tams, 'German Constitutional Court Bows to Europe' [2001] *CLJ* 256.

[7] Eg: M Storme (ed.), *Approximation of Judiciary Law in the European Union* (Dordrecht, Nijhoff, 1994). Cf. Council Resolution on the effective uniform application of Community law and on the penalties applicable for breaches of Community law in the Internal Market [1995] OJ C188/1.

citizens of the Union. This is particularly true as regards those sectors of Treaty activity which pursue increasingly autonomous social objectives (for example: environmental, consumer and employee protection).[8]

Proceeding from those basic assumptions about the nature of European integration and concomitant role of the Treaty legal order which characterise an 'integration through law' perspective, it is thus possible to demonstrate that the Community suffers from an 'enforcement deficit', brought on by its reliance on the fragmented systems of judicial protection presently offered by the Member States.[9] The necessary cure is prescribed with admirable logic: if national remedies and procedures undermine the effectiveness and uniformity of Community law, Community law must render national remedies and procedures more effective and uniform. A substantial body of academic opinion therefore argues that the only way genuinely to overcome the difficulties posed by the enforcement deficit is to harmonise the present panoply of national remedial and procedural provisions so as to conform to a common Community-wide standard.[10] This ideal of a 'unified system of judicial protection' has provided those who reason from an 'integration through law' perspective with a workable conceptual yardstick against which to assess the Community's legislative and judicial efforts to address the enforcement deficit— and, more often than not, to find those efforts sadly lacking.

The underlying essentials of this 'integration through law' analysis have been accepted as orthodox not only by its adherents, but also by its detractors. For example, certain commentators have questioned the manner in which the (admittedly valid) Community goal of effectiveness interacts with competing interests operating at the level of each Member State, such as the need to protect legal certainty in administrative or contractual relationships, as embodied in the imposition of limitation periods for the commencement of proceedings.[11]

---

[8] Eg: E Szyszczak, 'Making Europe More Relevant To Its Citizens: Effective Judicial Process' (1996) 21 *ELRev* 351 and 'Building a European Constitutional Order: Prospects for a General Non-Discrimination Standard' in A Dashwood and S O'Leary (eds.), *The Principle of Equal Treatment in EC Law* (London, Sweet & Maxwell, 1997).

[9] Eg: J Bridge, 'Procedural Aspects of the Enforcement of European Community Law through the Legal Systems of the Member States' (1984) 9 *ELRev* 28; M P Chiti, 'Towards a Unified Judicial Protection in Europe?' (1997) 9 *European Review of Public Law* 553. Note the more nuanced (though still essentially integrationist) analysis of W van Gerven, 'Of Rights, Remedies and Procedures' (2000) 37 *CMLRev* 501.

[10] Eg: D Curtin, 'Directives: The Effectiveness of Judicial Protection of Individual Rights' (1990) 27 *CMLRev* 709; G de Búrca, 'Giving Effect to European Community Directives' (1992) 55 *MLR* 215; A P Tash, 'Remedies for European Community Law Claims in Member State Courts: Toward a European Standard' (1993) 31 *Columbia Journal of Transnational Law* 377; I Sebba, 'The Doctrine of Direct Effect: A Malignant Disease of Community Law' 1995/2 *LIEI* 35; C Himsworth, 'Things Fall Apart: The Harmonisation of Community Judicial Procedural Protection Revisited' (1997) 22 *ELRev* 291; E Deards, 'Curiouser and Curiouser? The Development of Member State Liability in the Court of Justice' (1997) 3 *EPL* 117.

[11] Eg: M Hoskins, 'Tilting the Balance: Supremacy and National Procedural Rules' (1996) 21 *ELRev* 365; A Biondi, 'The European Court of Justice and Certain National Procedural Limitations: Not Such a Tough Relationship' (1999) 36 *CMLRev* 1271. Cf. concerns that Community intervention challenges national cultural identity: C Harlow, '*Francovich* and the Problem of the Disobedient State' (1996) 2 *ELJ* 199.

Other commentators have queried how far the creation of a 'unified system of judicial protection' would in fact serve the (admittedly valid) objective of increasing the uniform application of Community law. After all, the daily administration of any harmonised system of judicial protection would still lie in the hands of national authorities; the latter would retain broad discretion as regards matters such as prosecution policy and the assessment of damages.[12] Moreover, empirical research suggests that there are marked national and regional variations as regards important aspects of rule-enforcement, such as the willingness of individuals and undertakings to have recourse to litigation as a means of dispute settlement.[13]

This chapter will seek to construct a more fundamental critique, by challenging the internal assumptions which support the initial 'integration through law' analysis and thus structure the subsequent enforcement deficit debate. The problem with the argument that uniformity provides a sufficient rationale for Community intervention in the national systems of judicial protection lies in its unwavering faith in the belief that the vocation of the Treaty project is to promote a continuous process of supranational convergence. It will be argued that this interpretation has failed to keep pace with wider trends in the Treaty's political and legal evolution. In particular, the imperative of uniformity is under direct challenge from within the Community order itself by the increasingly common phenomenon of 'regulatory differentiation'.

Differentiation as Both a Symptom and a Cause of Constitutional Change

The underlying weakness of 'integration through law' lies in its skewed vision of the Community's historical development. In particular, its analysis focuses almost entirely on the expansionist aspect of the Treaty system. This expansion can be rationalised along four main axes: 1) horizontal—the growth of the Community's power to regulate different sectors of activity, beginning with the Common Market, spreading to important aspects of social policy and now touching upon issues such as citizenship and human rights; 2) vertical—the expansion of the Community's competence relative to that of the Member States within any given sector of activity, based around the principles of direct effect for Community rules within the domestic legal orders, their supremacy over competing provisions of national law, and the possibility that Community legislation pre-empts entirely the competence of each Member State to regulate in respect of that subject-matter for the future; 3) institutional—the expansion of the Community's competence to adopt legislation through supranational

---

[12] Eg: C Harding, 'Member State Enforcement of European Community Measures: The Chimera of 'Effective' Enforcement' (1997) 4 *MJ* 5. Cf. Case C-326/88 *Hansen* [1990] ECR I-2911.
[13] Eg: S Deakin and F Wilkinson, 'Contract Law and the Economics of Inter-Organisational Trust' in C Lane and R Bachmann (eds.), *Trust Within and Between Organisations* (Oxford, OUP, 1998).

rather than intergovernmental decision-making procedures, such as the spread of co-decision between Council and European Parliament, and of majority rather than unanimous voting within Council itself; 4) geographical—from the original six Member States, to the current fifteen, and a possible future group of twenty-five or even thirty nations.

Such expansion both demonstrates and reinforces the 'integration through law' conviction that the Community's vocation is to create an ever-closer degree of economic and/or political European union. From this ever-closer union springs the desire to build a level playing-field, on which all economic actors can operate under equal competitive conditions, and/or all beneficiaries of Community norms can enjoy the same levels of social and welfare rights. This in turn fuels the argument for harmonising divergent national regulatory regimes so as to conform as closely as possible to a single uniform standard set by the Community institutions, and justifies a critical interpretation of everything from the lack of horizontal direct effect for directives, to tolerance of the fair-weather commitment to supremacy shown by certain domestic judges, to reliance on fragmented systems of national remedies and procedural rules.

However, expansion represents only one of two essential tenets in the evolution of the Community legal order. It has been convincingly argued that the Member States accepted not only the benefits but also the burdens of the original Treaty of Rome because they were in a position to control the day-to-day running of the Community system: for example, through unanimity in a Council which dominated the legislative process. The Member States remain prepared to accept the economic and political advantages yielded by their Treaty membership even despite the process of aggrandisement identified above, but only on condition that the system retains safeguards to accommodate their own national interests where these do not coincide with the common Community goal. Thus, the Community's recent history has been characterised not only by a continuing process of Treaty expansion, but also and as a result by a counter-process which attempts to define more clearly the limits to the Community's powers in their relationship with pre-existing national competencies, and to accommodate those Member States which wish to retain a greater degree of control over their own policy-making prerogatives.[14]

This analysis draws heavily on what political scientists might label a 'neo-realist' model for explaining the dynamics of Community development. By stressing the predominant role played within the Treaty system by the Member States, and presuming that the latter act in pursuit of their individual national preferences as much as for the sake of some collective vision of a shared

---

[14] J Weiler, 'The Community System: the Dual Character of Supranationalism' (1981) 1 *YBEL* 267; J Weiler and U Haltern, 'Constitutional or International? The Foundations of the Community Legal Order and the Question of Judicial Kompetenz-Kompetenz' in A-M Slaughter, A Stone Sweet and J Weiler (eds.), *The European Court and National Courts: Doctrine and Jurisprudence* (Oxford, Hart Publishing, 1998).

political destiny, European union is therefore interpreted as a system of 'state bargains', albeit of a relatively complex and stable nature.[15] The convenience of such an analysis lies in the fact that it offers a linear explanation of why and how one finds regulatory differentiation within the Community legal order: certain Member States no longer feel their national interests to be compatible with a strategy of continuous integration; they therefore use their position at the centre of the Treaty system to resist undesirable levels of uniformity, and instead to promote forms of diversity more accommodating of their own needs. Regulatory differentiation is thus interpreted as a pragmatic attempt to resolve the tensions generated by the Community's simultaneous pressure for continuing expansion and counter-pressure for delimitation or contraction.[16]

As a result, the idea of a normative level playing-field in either an economic or a socio-political sense is difficult to defend as a general characteristic of the contemporary Community legal order. The mere fact of Community involvement in a given sphere of activity does not mean that the regulatory regime established to achieve its objectives will consist of uniform norms, nor that uniformity is its ultimate goal. Indeed, it is possible to identify a sliding scale of Community and national competence to construct regulatory frameworks capable of furthering substantive Treaty policy objectives.

On the one hand, it is perfectly plausible to describe the Community rules implementing competition policy as 'uniform'. The Treaty eschews any formal influence by the Member States over the substantive policy objectives pursued under Articles 81 and 82 EC, and thereby excludes almost entirely the phenomenon of regulatory differentiation from the sphere of interest occupied by Community law. For example, the threshold requirements which activate Community supervision over various types of market conduct, and the justifications which might exempt abusive agreements and practices from being annulled, are defined entirely by the Treaty itself.[17] Moreover, the possible parallel application of Community and domestic competition rules to conduct which affects inter-State trade is strictly controlled so as to maximise the uniform application of the Treaty. Thus, national law may not prejudice the full operation of Articles

---

[15] Though neo-realism has been heavily criticised, eg: R Dehousse and G Majone, 'The Institutional Dynamics of European Integration: From the Single Act to the Maastricht Treaty' in S Martin (ed.), *The Construction of Europe* (Dordrecht, Kluwer, 1994). Multi-level governance is currently more in vogue, eg: M Jachtenfuchs, 'Theoretical perspectives on European Governance' (1995) 1 *ELJ* 115; G Marks, L Hooghe and K Blank, 'European Integration from the 1980s: State-Centric v. Multi-Level Governance' (1996) 34 *JCMS* 341; P Craig, 'The Nature of the Community: Integration, Democracy, and Legitimacy' in P Craig and G de Búrca (eds.), *The Evolution of EU Law* (Oxford, OUP, 1999). Consider also the influence of regulatory competition theorists, eg: D Esty and D Geradin (eds.), *Regulatory Competition and Economic Integration: Comparative Perspectives* (Oxford, OUP, 2001).

[16] M Dougan, 'Minimum Harmonisation and the Internal Market' (2000) 37 *CMLRev* 853.

[17] As interpreted by the CFI / ECJ and supplemented by secondary measures adopted by the Commission, eg: Vertical Restraints Regulation 2790/1999 [1999] OJ L336/21. Further: A Albors Llorens chapter 12 in this volume.

81 and 82 by purporting, for example, to validate an agreement which the Commission has judged to be void, or to invalidate a practice which has been granted block or individual exemption under the Treaty.[18]

On the other hand, it seems difficult to describe Community action on the environment, consumers or social matters (let alone on education or culture) as being particularly 'uniform' when, even as regards the territory occupied by the Treaty, the Member States enjoy significant influence over the scope and content of substantive policy. Such influence is facilitated, in particular, by the use of minimum harmonisation clauses, allowing the Member States to construct higher standards of welfare protection than those envisaged by the Community itself;[19] and the frequent grant of derogations, permitting the Member States to fall below the regulatory standards agreed by the Community as a whole.[20] This web of mixed responsibility and regulatory diversity has been complicated still further by the use of individually negotiated opt-outs permitting Member States to derogate not only from the specific provisions of a particular legislative act, but also from entire sectors of Community activity.[21] Moreover, the Treaty of Amsterdam sought to harness this ad hoc system of 'flexibility' by introducing the principle of Closer Cooperation, authorising the pursuit of 'variable geometry' within the framework of the Treaties (albeit subject to certain substantive and institutional restrictions).[22]

Against this background, 'integration through law' presents a preconceived constitutional model of the Treaty and its legal system which has become increasingly untenable. A more appropriate response would be to accept the reality of a political and legal shift in the outlook of the Community: European union is as much about managing our respective differences as it is about promoting uniformity, and Community law has an equally valid role in forwarding both these aims. Indeed, one might justly argue that differentiation is fast attaining the status of a central organisational principle within the Treaty

---

[18] Case 14/68 *Walt Wilhelm* [1969] ECR 1. However, the Commission's draft Regulation on the Implementation of Articles 81 and 82 COM(2000) 582 Final provides for the mutually exclusive application of Community and domestic competition rules. Cf. R Walz, 'Rethinking *Walt Wilhelm*, Or the Supremacy of Community Competition Law Over National Law' (1996) 21 *ELRev* 449; R Wesseling, 'Subsidiarity in Community Antitrust Law: Setting the Right Agenda' (1997) 22 *ELRev* 35.

[19] Further: M Dougan, 'Minimum Harmonisation and the Internal Market' (2000) 37 *CMLRev* 853. Also: S Weatherill chapter 2 in this volume.

[20] Eg: Product Liability Directive 85/374/EEC [1985] OJ L210/29; Working Time Directive 93/104/EC [1993] OJ L307/18; Acquired Rights Directive 77/187/EEC [1977] OJ L61/26.

[21] Further: F Tuytschaever, *Differentiation in European Union Law* (Oxford, Hart Publishing, 1999).

[22] Further: G Edwards and E Philippart, *Flexibility and the Treaty of Amsterdam: Europe's New Byzantium?*, CELS Occasional Paper Number 3 (Cambridge, CELS, 1997). The Treaty of Nice would loosen considerably the conditions for Enhanced Cooperation within the First Pillar, eg, by deleting the existing national veto over Council authorisation.

system.[23] This interpretation generates further implications of its own. In particular, it suggests the need to undertake a process of doctrinal reconsideration and adaptation, the goal of which should be to update our conceptual understandings of the Community legal order, through the re-evaluation of certain longheld assumptions which unduly emphasise the Treaty's integrative mission and consequent need for normative uniformity, and have therefore fallen out of step with the Community's recent pattern of development.[24]

This argument is reinforced by the principles of subsidiarity and proportionality enshrined in Article 5 EC, which clearly impose an institutional and intellectual obligation to think more carefully about the ambit of Community activities, and of the legal rules which serve to support them.[25] By questioning the need for and nature of collective action, particularly as regards its impact on the pre-existing competencies of the Member State, subsidiarity and proportionality contemplate the existence of alternative national or regional levels of substantive policy formulation, and thus encourage the construction of diverse regulatory frameworks within the Treaty system. In particular, the Protocol introduced at Amsterdam directs that '[t]he Community shall legislate only to the extent necessary', and that Community action should be 'restricted or discontinued where it is no longer justified'.[26]

A Sectoral Interpretation of the Community's Enforcement Deficit

Differentiation must be understood both as a symptom of fundamental restructuring within the European Union, and also as a cause of constitutional revision within the Community legal order itself, whereby it is incumbent upon both the responsible institutional actors and interested academic commentators to reconsider those aspects of the relationship between Community and domestic law which no longer reflect the underlying character of the Treaty system by reason of their undue emphasis on the imperative of uniformity, and thereby of their demands for an unnecessarily intrusive quantity and quality of Community regulatory action. This process of doctrinal reconsideration and adaptation should extend to the supposedly fundamental Community concerns which continue to structure debate about the nature of the enforcement deficit.

---

[23] Further: G de Búrca and J Scott (eds.), *Constitutional Change in the EU: From Uniformity to Flexibility?* (Oxford, Hart Publishing, 2000). Contrast, eg: D Curtin, 'The Constitutional Structure of the Union: A Europe of Bits and Pieces' (1993) 30 *CMLRev* 17.

[24] Further: J Shaw, 'European Union Legal Studies in Crisis? Towards a New Dynamic' (1996) 16 *OJLS* 231.

[25] Cf. N Reich, 'The "November Revolution" of the European Court of Justice: *Keck, Meng* and *Audi* Revisited' (1994) 31 *CMLRev* 459; G de Búrca, 'The Principle of Subsidiarity and the Court of Justice as an Institutional Actor' (1998) 36 *JCMS* 217.

[26] Paras. 6 and 3 Protocol. Cf. G Bermann chapter 3 in this volume.

The most obvious implication of differentiation for the policy framework surrounding the Community's enforcement deficit is that uniformity (whether understood from an economic and/or socio-political perspective) is neither a general principle nor a primary goal of the Community legal order, and can no longer be portrayed as a blanket justification for pursuing the maximum possible degree of harmonisation. Thus, there is no sound conceptual rationale for some grand scheme to create a unified system of judicial protection in Europe. This is not to say that the imperative of uniformity has become redundant. The point is rather that the Community has evolved into a more complex entity than 'integration through law' permits, characterised by varying degrees of integration and differentiation across different policy fields. As such, uniformity is now possessed of only relative merit, and the policy framework surrounding the debate about national remedies and procedures should display greater sensitivity towards this fact. It is therefore suggested that uniformity should be interpreted at a 'sectoral' level—selectively matching the required level of remedial-procedural harmonisation to the actual degree of substantive approximation achieved within any given policy area, and therefore to the variegated nature of the Community's current programme for supranational integration.

In some sectors—generally those closely connected to the functioning of the Internal Market—the Community does continue to insist on the creation and maintenance of a high degree of substantive uniformity. The example given above was the competition regime under Articles 81 and 82 EC, which is essential to the goal of market integration and the creation of a genuine level playing-field among economic operators. In this situation, one concedes that the goal of uniformity lying at the heart of Community regulation is threatened by significant variations in the relevant legal frameworks subsisting at national level, and that this applies as much to remedial as to substantive rules. In principle, Community legislation harmonising the procedures available for decentralised enforcement might therefore seem entirely appropriate. This is particularly true in the light of the Commission's 1999 White Paper and 2000 draft Regulation, which would encourage greater decentralised enforcement of competition law, in particular, by abolishing both the notification procedure and the Commission's monopoly over the grant of Article 81(3) individual exemptions.[27] The White Paper/draft Regulation recognise that this modernisation process might pose risks to the uniformity of competition law, and thus propose mechanisms to ensure greater coherency within the enforcement network, for example, whereby the initiation of proceedings by the Commission would extinguish the competence of the domestic competition authorities in respect of the same matter. However, the tension between encouraging increased decentralisation of enforcement while still maintaining uniformity of

---

[27] White Paper on the Modernisation of the Rules Implementing Articles 81 and 82 of the EC Treaty [1999] OJ C132/1; Proposal for a Council Regulation on the Implementation of Articles 81 and 82 COM(2000) 582 Final.

substantive policy refocuses attention on the case for some sectoral harmonisation of domestic remedies and procedures—an issue not addressed by the White Paper/draft Regulation but which surely warrants more serious consideration.[28]

By contrast, in other sectors it seems more difficult to argue that normative uniformity constitutes an absolute or even significant objective of the Treaty's regulatory activities. As regards welfare-orientated fields such as environmental, consumer and employee protection, the interaction between Community and national authorities (for example, through the use of minimum harmonisation) means that substantive policy will differ from Member State to Member State—both tolerating and legitimising cross-border variations in the compliance costs actually suffered by different groups of economic undertaking, and in the levels of protection actually enjoyed by different categories of Union citizen. In turn, this makes it much more difficult to identify a single Community substantive regime the uniformity of which is necessarily undermined by the lack of a harmonised Community remedial regime applicable to decentralised enforcement before the national courts. And if the Treaty has no real or at least immediate ambition to establish a completely uniform substantive regime in fields such as environmental, consumer or employment policy, why should the Community nevertheless nurture a real or immediate concern to establish a completely uniform set of remedial and procedural provisions? Indeed, for the Community to insist that these partially harmonised rights be accompanied by highly harmonised standards of judicial protection would represent Treaty action going further than is necessary to achieve its own objectives and, as such, an infringement of the principles of subsidiarity and proportionality set out in Article 5 EC.

However, this sectoral model presents certain problems. First, how does one actually define a 'sector' for the purposes of examining the extent of the Community's interest in substantive uniformity, and therefore of the appropriate need for remedial harmonisation? There is an undoubted convenience in dividing the Community's policymaking and legislative activities into manageable conceptual compartments such as 'competition policy', 'environmental protection' or 'consumer policy'. However, the reality is much more complicated than such a scheme admits: the idea of a discrete field of Community policy which can be marked off from all others by clearly ascertainable boundaries is in many respects unsustainable; postulating the appropriate level of abstraction at which any sort of sectoral analysis should take place is therefore an innately

---

[28] Cf. S Kon and A Maxwell, 'Enforcement in National Courts of the EC and New UK Competition Rules: Obstacles to Effective Enforcement' [1998] *ECLR* 443; M Todino, 'Modernisation From the Perspective of National Competition Authorities: Impact of the Reform on Decentralised Application of EC Competition Law' [2000] *ECLR* 348; F Louis, 'Les conséquences pratiques de la réforme envisagée par le Livre Blanc de la Commission' [2001] *CDE* 218.

troublesome task. Nowhere is this problem more acutely illustrated than in the case of the 'Single Market'.

For example, application of the primary Treaty provisions on free movement requires the ECJ to balance the demands of greater market integration (by dismantling divergent national rules which hinder cross-border trade) against the need for continuing market regulation (by respecting domestic legislation which performs a socially useful function), and thus to articulate both the welfare goals recognised as worthwhile under the Treaty and their value relative to the efficient operation of the Internal Market—including environmental, consumer and employee protection.[29] This complex intertwining of apparently sectoral Treaty objectives is further illustrated by recent developments on free movement for persons. The ECJ appears to have accepted that Article 18 EC creates a right to move and reside freely across the Member States for Union citizens, irrespective of their economic status and therefore of their contribution to the process of market integration.[30] Together with the introduction of Title IV on Visas, Asylum and Immigration, and the commitment to creating an area of freedom, justice and security,[31] this confirms that the *acquis communautaire* on free movement for persons must now be located within a broader policy framework than the Internal Market alone. Even competition policy—a Treaty competence with Common Market credentials par excellence—finds itself increasingly expected to renegotiate its own turf with competing social policy concerns, as in recent caselaw excluding the application of Article 81 to collective agreements between management and labour which seek to create high levels of employment protection, and thus to advance the welfare objectives set out in Article 2 EC.[32]

Moreover, as regards secondary legislation, it will be recalled that many of the Community's welfare-orientated competencies originally developed as offshoots from the Common Market. This was so in terms of both their rationale (as the logical extension of a process of economic integration which sought to minimise discrepancies of regulatory burden), and their legal basis (as harmonisation measures adopted under Articles 94 and 95 EC). A significant number of Community acts which we have grown accustomed to think of as

---

[29] Eg: Case 120/78 *'Cassis de Dijon'* [1979] ECR 649; Case 178/84 *Commission v. Germany* [1987] ECR 1227; Case 302/86 *Commission v. Denmark* [1988] ECR 4607; Cases C-369 and 376/96 *Arblade and Leloup* [1999] ECR I-8453. In particular: Case C-2/90 *Commission v. Belgium* [1992] ECR I-4431; Case C-379/98 *PreussenElektra* (Judgment of 13 March 2001).

[30] Eg: Case C-85/96 *María Martínez Sala* [1998] ECR I-2691; Case C-274/96 *Bickel and Franz* [1998] ECR I-7637; Case C-356/98 *Kaba* [2000] ECR I-2623; Case C-357/98 *Yiadom* [2000] ECR I-9265; Case C-135/99 *Elsen* (Judgment of 23 November 2000); Case C-184/99 *Grzelczyk* (Judgment of 20 September 2001). Cf. Case C-413/99 *Baumbast* (Opinion of 05 July 2001; Judgment pending; Commission Proposal for a Directive on the rights of citizens of the Union and their family members to move and reside freely within the territory of the Member States COM(2001) 257 Final.

[31] Art. 61 EC.

[32] Eg: Case C-67/96 *Albany International* [1999] ECR I-5751; Cases C-115–117/97 *Brentjens' Handelsonderneming* [1999] ECR I-6025.

'environmental', 'consumer' or 'social' legislation were therefore introduced to pursue economic as well as welfare objectives, and cannot be easily assigned to one policy sphere or another. It is true that the old 'flanking policies' have now been granted autonomous legal bases of their own within the Treaty.[33] However, this apparent separation of policy sectors is more a matter of form than of substance. Many Community initiatives still pursue not only a welfare but also some economic goal, such as potentially to straddle more than one legal basis; and the guidelines developed by the Court of Justice mean that the dividing line between formal Treaty sectors may well be difficult to draw in practice.[34] The problem is exacerbated by the fact that the Community is expressly required to pursue high standards of protection for interests such as the environment, consumers and public health not only through their own autonomous legal bases, but also by integrating these objectives into all other initiatives pursued under authority of the Treaty.[35] This legal framework perhaps explains how, for example, Community consumer policy continues to rely chiefly on the Internal Market legislative competencies provided under Articles 94 and 95 EC, despite the opportunities for regulatory action available under the designated Treaty title on Consumer Policy.[36]

In short: the idea of a 'sectoral approach' to the enforcement deficit debate relies on certain assumptions which do not necessarily reflect the reality of the Community's complex and dynamic regulatory agenda. As a result, it seems hard to imagine how a coherent policy of matching remedial to substantive harmonisation on a sectoral basis could be maintained in practice. While (at one extreme) the quest for uniformity in fields such as environmental, consumer and social protection seems more illusory than real, and (at the other extreme) the weight of the enforcement deficit falls on soundly market-orientated policy concerns such as competition law and state aids, the intractable problems raised by any attempt to map out the fluid boundaries of the wider Internal Market mean that it is difficult to ascertain what level of substantive uniformity this tentative sector pursues, and therefore what degree of remedial harmonisation it deserves. At the very least, it seems clear that such uniformity is not so absolute as stereotyped assumptions about free movement and equalised competitive conditions would appear to suggest, given the intimate interweaving of social welfare concerns (and consequent pressure for differentiated regulatory techniques) into the economic fabric of the market integration process.[37]

---

[33] Eg: Title XIX on environmental policy; Title XIV on consumer policy; Title XI on social policy.
[34] Eg: Case C-155/91 *Commission* v. *Council (Waste Directive)* [1993] ECR I-939. Also: Case C-376/98 *Germany* v. *Parliament and Council* [2000] ECR I-8419. Cf. Case C-300/89 *Commission* v. *Council (Titanium Dioxide)* [1991] ECR I-2867.
[35] Eg: Arts. 6, 153(2) and 152(1) EC. Also: Art. 95(3) EC.
[36] Further: J Stuyck, 'European Consumer Law After the Treaty of Amsterdam: Consumer Policy In or Beyond the Internal Market?' (2000) 37 *CMLRev* 367.
[37] Cf. G de Búrca, 'Differentiation Within the Core: The Case of the Common Market' in G de Búrca and J Scott (eds.), *Constitutional Change in the EU: From Uniformity to Flexibility?* (Oxford, Hart Publishing, 2000).

The second problem posed by our sectoral model relates to the imperative of effectiveness. After all, updating our understanding of the imperative of uniformity, so as to redefine the Treaty's legitimate interest in harmonising the procedural infrastructure of decentralised enforcement, does not detract from the continuing need for effectiveness in the enforcement of all Community rules, and thus for a minimum level of Treaty supervision over national remedies. The fact remains that every Community measure pursues some identifiable objective (whether in protecting free movement and fair competition within the Single Market, or in advancing the collective and individual welfare rights of Union citizens), the attainment of which may be imperilled by, and must therefore be protected against, inadequate or positively obstructionist implementation mechanisms provided by the Member States. This is true regardless of the discretion left to the domestic authorities to assist in the normative elaboration of the policy objectives in question. Moreover, it follows that our sectoral analysis cannot purport to offer a panacea for the complex issues thrown up by the decentralised enforcement of Community norms—such as the perennially controversial task of striking an appropriate balance between the Treaty interest in guaranteeing minimum standards of judicial protection, and competing domestic concerns over the prejudicial impact of Community intervention on (for example) the need for legal certainty and fair administration of justice.

Such problems highlight not only the advantages but also the very real limits of any sectoral approach to analysis and resolution of the Community's enforcement deficit. In fact, the utility of the sectoral model depends largely on the purpose to which it is put and, in particular, on the institutional actor to whose activities it is applied. Clearly, a sectoral understanding of the problem posed by national remedies and procedures does not easily translate into a manifesto for detailed policy development, such as could be taken up by a legislature and used as a blueprint for concrete change. But this should not detract from the relevance of the sectoral approach viewed primarily as a conceptual model, i.e. as a way of rethinking the policy framework surrounding the enforcement deficit, and of challenging the outdated 'integration through law' analysis which has traditionally dominated academic debate over the matter. In particular, our sectoral model can be applied in the manner of a critical conceptual tool by which to analyse the ECJ's approach to Community control over national procedures. How far does the caselaw reflect, exceed or frustrate the Community's legitimate interest in harmonising the remedial conditions applicable to the decentralised enforcement of its own norms?

UNIFORMITY AND DIFFERENTIATION IN
THE COURT OF JUSTICE'S CASELAW

The ECJ rarely articulates its approach to the imperative of uniformity explicitly. Ascertaining the nature of changing judicial attitudes towards the enforcement deficit becomes an exercise in conceptual tectonics: by mapping the shifting contours of the normative landscape, one begins to understand something of the underlying policy forces which have shaped it. For these purposes, it is possible to identify three main historical periods in the caselaw: an early period of extensive deference to national autonomy; a middle period of increasing Community remedial competence; and the most recent period, in which the Court attempts to strike some more acceptable balance between its previous extremes.

Early Period: Extensive Deference to National Autonomy

The early period of the ECJ caselaw embodied a loose-knit strategy of 'negative harmonisation' which paid more than mere lip-service to the presumption of domestic autonomy in the provision of remedies and procedural rules to govern the exercise of Treaty rights. For example, the Court in *Rewe/Comet* held that domestic limitation periods may apply in Community cases, provided they are reasonable in duration.[38] In *Russo*, the availability of compensatory damages in respect of losses suffered through a Member State's breach of its Community obligations fell to be determined by domestic law.[39] Similarly, the Court in *Roquette Frères* decided that the Member States were entitled to apply their own rules regarding the payment of interest, its rate and the date from which it should be calculated.[40] The principles of equivalence and effectiveness justified only limited Community intervention where the Member State transgressed the generous boundaries of domestic discretion appointed by the Court, for example, by refusing to countenance the reimbursement of unlawfully levied charges.[41]

This approach might seem to suggest that the ECJ devoted little conceptual importance to the quest for uniformity of enforcement as between the Member States. Indeed, on several occasions the Court asserted that divergent systems of remedies and procedural rules, provided they complied with the basic requirements of equivalence and effectiveness, could not be said to distort competition

---

[38] Case 33/76 *Rewe-Zentralfinanz v. Landwirtschaftskammer für das Saarland* [1976] ECR 1989; Case 45/76 *Comet* [1976] ECR 2043.
[39] Case 60/75 *Russo* [1976] ECR 45. Also: Case 101/78 *Granaria* [1979] ECR 623.
[40] Case 26/74 *Roquette Frères* [1976] ECR 677. Also: Case 6/60 *Humblet* [1960] ECR 559.
[41] Case 177/78 *McCarren* [1979] ECR 2161. Cf. Case 158/80 *Rewe-Handelsgesellschaft Nord v. Hauptzollamt Kiel* [1981] ECR 1805.

within the Common Market.[42] However, other dicta suggest that the Court was aware of the problems posed by inequality of treatment under the fragmented domestic systems of judicial protection, but was equally mindful of its own institutional limitations and preferred to leave the necessary task of harmonisation to the legislature.[43]

In either case, the preponderance of academic opinion asserts that the Court's response was inadequate. Throughout the 1970s and early 1980s, the Treaty order was still dominated by the quest to create a Common Market based on free movement for economic factors such as goods and services, and on equalised conditions of competition as between undertakings operating within the Community market. Moreover, the forms of normative differentiation recognised under Treaty law were of a relatively limited nature: minimum harmonisation was common in secondary legislation, but had not yet been 'institutionalised' within the Treaty text itself; derogations were also widespread, but the sort of wholesale opt-outs from entire policy sectors found at Maastricht, and the more generalised principle of Closer Cooperation introduced at Amsterdam, belonged to the entirely transformed political landscape of the future. Uniformity might thus appear to have constituted a genuine aspiration of Community policy, and in turn to have provided a legitimate template for Community intervention in the domestic systems of legal protection. The Court could hardly have been faulted for pursuing on the remedial plane the sort of approximation sought after at a substantive level. The fact that it failed to do so seems a valid criticism of this particular era in the caselaw.

Middle Period: Increasing Community Remedial Competence

By contrast, the Court's middle period jurisprudence was dominated by increasing levels of Community remedial competence. For example, *Emmott* held that, even if a domestic limitation period was reasonable in the *Rewe/Comet* sense, it must nevertheless be set aside where the Member State failed correctly to implement a Community directive within its prescribed deadline.[44] In *Factortame*, the Court decided that the national courts must be able to offer interim protection to claimants seeking to assert their Community rights by judicial process, even if such relief is not ordinarily available under domestic rules.[45] Similarly, and without reference to its ruling in *Russo*, the Court in *Francovich* held that individuals must be able to obtain compensation for losses suffered through a

---

[42] Eg: Case 811/79 *Ariete* [1980] ECR 2545; Case 826/79 *MIRECO* [1980] ECR 2559.
[43] Eg: Case 265/78 *Ferwerda* [1980] ECR 617; Cases 66 and 127–8/79 *Salumi* [1980] ECR 1237; Case 130/79 *Express Dairy Foods* [1980] ECR 1887; Case 54/81 *Fromme* [1982] ECR 1449; Cases 205–215/82 *Deutsche Milchkontor* [1983] ECR 2633.
[44] Case C-208/90 *Emmott* [1991] ECR I-4269.
[45] Case C-213/89 *Factortame* [1990] ECR I-2433.

breach of their Community rights perpetrated by the Member State, under conditions prescribed by the ECJ itself.[46] *Marshall II* perhaps went furthest of all: the victim of a discriminatory dismissal contrary to the provisions of the Equal Treatment Directive must be able to obtain full compensation for her losses; notwithstanding the judgment in *Roquette Frères*, such reparation must include the payment of interest to represent losses suffered through the effluxion of time.[47] Indeed, the early 1990s saw the birth of widespread academic expectations that the Court had embarked upon a strategy of 'positive harmonisation'—promoting a single Community-level code of remedies and procedural rules for the indirect enforcement of Treaty norms which would replace the various pre-existing domestic systems.[48]

Viewed from an 'integration through law' perspective, this prospect seemed no more than a faithful reflection of the growing maturity of the Treaty legal order itself. After all, the later 1980s and early 1990s witnessed a period of significant expansion in the scope and intensity of Community power. Consider: first, the consolidation by the Court of its own system of decentralised enforcement (based upon a generalised acceptance by the Member States and domestic judiciaries of the doctrines of direct effect and supremacy); secondly, the drive to realise the full economic ambitions of the Single Market (initiated by the judgment in *Cassis de Dijon*, and continued by both the Commission's New Approach to Technical Harmonisation and the institutional amendments introduced by the Single European Act to facilitate the process of economic integration); and thirdly, the gathering pace of Community competence to regulate ever-wider fields of social welfare for the ordinary citizen (consumer protection, social policy, environmental protection, public health, education and culture). Taken together, these developments all seemed naturally to justify the Court's apparent policy of increasing Community control over domestic remedies and procedures, i.e. so as finally to achieve the sort of uniform application for Treaty norms which the Community's established economic and growing social ambitions demanded, but which the fledgling mechanisms of decentralised enforcement had thus far proved unable to deliver.

However, when viewed from the alternative perspective developed above, the roots of this middle period caselaw were in fact feeding from shallow soil. Indeed, with the benefit of hindsight, one can discern how this new and robust jurisprudence was incapable of sustaining its own conceptual momentum. It will be recalled that the Community's recent history consists essentially of two inter-related strands: not only expansion (along horizontal, vertical, institutional and geographical axes); but also, and in large part in consequence,

---

[46] Cases C-6 and 9/90 *Francovich* [1991] ECR I-5357.
[47] Case C-271/91 *Marshall II* [1993] ECR I-4367.
[48] Eg: D Curtin and K Mortelmans, 'Application and Enforcement of Community Law by the Member States: Actors in Search of a Third Generation Script' in D Curtin and T Heukels (eds.), *Institutional Dynamics of European Integration* (Dordrecht, Nijhoff, 1994).

contraction (or at least the urge to define more clearly the limits of Treaty power, and its relationship to the competing claims of divergent national policies). The consistent and continuing growth of Community power may well have injected fresh impetus into the Court's assertion of remedial competence relative to that of the Member States; but it also unleashed that array of socio-political tensions whose practical resolution lay in the steady spread of differentiated regulatory techniques within the Treaty legal order. Such normative diversity has in turn undermined the very imperative of uniformity upon which any notion of a unified system of judicial protection depends.

Thus, by concentrating almost exclusively on the strand of expansion and neglecting the strand of contraction, an 'integration through law' perspective seeks to portray the Court's middle period caselaw as a desirable, even necessary, step on the path towards full-scale remedial harmonisation. But this task appears increasingly misguided, the more its intellectual foundations are undermined by the tide of regulatory differentiation sweeping through much of the Community legal order, and by the elevation of 'flexibility' to the status of a central constitutional principle within the Treaty itself. Indeed, current trends towards normative diversity have attained such extent and depth that the sort of general drive towards the positive harmonisation of national remedies and procedural rules suggested by the Court's middle period caselaw and championed by many of the commentators appears increasingly to embody an over-inflated definition of the Community's interest in the imperative of uniformity, and thus an unduly intrusive conception of the Court's mandate to pursue the approximation of the domestic systems of judicial protection.

Current Caselaw: Negative Harmonisation Reaffirmed

However, the ECJ itself has since moved on to forge a new normative framework. The main characteristic of the most recent caselaw consists in a definite retreat away from the idea of positive harmonisation, and back towards the more orthodox pattern of negative approximation, whereby Community law usually acts as an incomplete rather than exhaustive template for the approximation of the Member States' pre-existing systems of judicial protection. In particular, the Court tends to prescribe only the minimum guarantees expected under the Treaty, leaving significant scope for national autonomy to elaborate more favourable standards of remedies and procedures for the enforcement by individual citizens of their Community rights.

Consider, by way of illustration, the caselaw on the right to reparation. With the benefit of hindsight, it is now clear that the primary purpose of the *Francovich* jurisprudence is the furtherance of specific judicial policy objectives relating to the legal accountability of the national authorities. The Court clearly felt that domestic laws offering total or partial immunity from liability in respect of the exercise of public power in general, and legislative prerogatives in particular, were unacceptable within the hierarchical constitutional system established by the Treaty, and strove to establish minimum guarantees of accountability so as to vindicate both the rule of Community law and the individual's rights. But while *Francovich* affirms the need for the effective judicial protection of the citizen and ensures that this imperative extends to cover the actions of all public authorities, it neither imposes uniform substantive conditions for the attribution of liability, nor necessarily requires recognition of some 'Community action for damages'.[49]

For example, the existence of a 'direct causal link' between breach and loss is to be determined according to national law (subject to residual Community surveillance via the principles of equivalence and effectiveness).[50] In any case, the Court's threefold criteria for the imposition of liability to make reparation remain minimum standards only—the Member State may choose to make reparation easier to obtain.[51] As regards the reparation itself, compensatory damages are not the only possible form of relief: the Member State may decide retrospectively to apply the relevant Community rules to the claimant, subject only to a supplementary damages action in respect of consequential losses.[52] The heads of recoverable loss are themselves to be determined, in principle, by domestic law—though the ECJ has held, for example, that compensation for lost profits and interest representing damage suffered through the effluxion of time cannot be ruled out completely.[53] The procedures applicable to a *Francovich* action for reparation are also determined, in principle, by national law: this is true (say) of rules establishing time-limits for commencing proceedings,[54] restricting the admissibility of evidence,[55] imposing a requirement to exhaust alternative remedies,[56] and identifying the body against which any claim for reparation must be brought.[57] As a result, the ability of individuals to obtain reparation in respect of a breach of their Treaty rights will still differ

---

[49] Further: M Dougan, 'The *Francovich* Right to Reparation: Reshaping the Contours of Community Remedial Competence' (2000) 6 *EPL* 103.

[50] Cases C-46 and 48/93 *Brasserie du Pêcheur* [1996] ECR I-1029. Further: F Smith and L Woods, 'Causation in *Francovich*: The Neglected Problem' (1997) 46 *ICLQ* 925. Cf. Case C-319/96 *Brinkmann* [1998] ECR I-5255; Case C-140/97 *Rechberger* [1999] ECR I-3499; T Tridimas, 'Liability for Breach of Community Law: Growing Up and Mellowing Down?' (2001) 38 *CMLRev* 301.

[51] Cases C-46 and 48/93 *Brasserie du Pêcheur* [1996] ECR I-1029.

[52] Cases C-94–5/95 *Bonifaci* [1997] ECR I-3969; Case C-373/95 *Maso* [1997] ECR I-4051; Case C-131/97 *Carbonari* [1999] ECR I-1103; Case C-371/97 *Gozza* [2000] ECR I-7881.

[53] Cases C-46 and 48/93 *Brasserie du Pêcheur* [1996] ECR I-1029; Cases C-397 and 410/98 *Metallgesellschaft* (Judgment of 08 March 2001). Cf. AG Jacobs in Case C-150/99 *Stockholm Lindöpark* (Judgment of 18 January 2001), para. 81 Opinion of 26 September 2000.

[54] Case C-261/95 *Palmisani* [1997] ECR I-4025.

[55] Case C-228/98 *Dounias* [2000] ECR I-577.

[56] Cases C-46 and 48/93 *Brasserie du Pêcheur* [1996] ECR I-1029; though note the limits established in Cases C-397 and 410/98 *Metallgesellschaft* (Judgment of 08 March 2001).

[57] Case C-302/97 *Konle* [1999] ECR I-3099; Case C-424/97 *Haim II* [2000] ECR I-5123; Case C-118/00 *Larsy II* (Judgment of 28 June 2001).

from Member State to Member State, depending on both the substantive and remedial conditions for liability recognised within each separate jurisdiction.

The current general trend for Community law to prescribe incomplete and merely minimum standards of judicial protection, within and beyond which the Member States remain free to construct an independent and potentially divergent framework of remedies and procedural rules, attracts the disapproval of those who reason from an 'integration through law' perspective: the ECJ appears to have sacrificed vital Treaty interests in constructing an effective and uniform system of legal protection, in the face of political pressure from disgruntled Member States intent on holding the Community's natural development hostage to their own parochial interests.

But when viewed through the alternative paradigm suggested above, a different picture emerges. By refusing to pursue the logic of positive harmonisation suggested by its middle period caselaw, the Court of Justice seems implicitly to have rejected an 'integration through law' analysis of the compelling need to centralise the normative framework of legal protection available for the domestic enforcement of Community law. By reaffirming in its place a preference for mere negative harmonisation, the stance currently adopted by the Court appears instead to coincide with an understanding of the increasingly limited quality of uniformity such as is postulated by our alternative sectoral model. This interpretation is reinforced by the Court's newfound enthusiasm for the requirement of equivalence, as evidenced in recent cases such as *Levez* and *Preston*.[58] After all, equivalence seeks to promote equality of treatment only as regards the remedies available within one particular Member State, and does nothing to address or reduce the differing levels of judicial protection applied across the various Member States. By injecting fresh impetus into the principle of equivalence as a vehicle for Community intervention in the domestic judicial systems, the Court seems implicitly to recognise and even legitimise the Community's current state of remedial fragmentation.

Furthermore, this strategy of mere negative harmonisation for national remedies and procedural rules seems well-suited to that category of sectors indeed characterised by only incomplete and minimum levels of substantive approximation: for example, environmental, consumer and social policy. It may also be appropriate for the Single Market itself, insofar as the goals of free movement and equalised competitive conditions have become indelibly marked by the trend towards regulatory differentiation carried into the Treaty heartland via those welfare elements inherent in the process of economic integration.

---

[58] Case C-326/96 *Levez* [1998] ECR I-7835; Case C-78/98 *Preston* [2000] ECR I-3201.

Current Caselaw: Positive Harmonisation On a Sectoral Model?

However, one would anticipate that, insofar as the ECJ was truly sensitive to some sectoral understanding of the imperative of uniformity, its general acceptance of mere negative approximation for the domestic standards of judicial protection would be supplemented by the pursuit of more positive harmonisation, in respect of those areas of Treaty (and especially Single Market) activity which remain characterised by a relatively centralised framework of substantive norms. In this regard, consider first the Court's caselaw on the recovery of unlawful state aids.

In *Deutsche Milchkontor*, the Court imposed on national authorities a general obligation to recover Community monies wrongly paid to their recipient. For these purposes, ordinary domestic procedural rules apply, provided they do not have the effect of rendering recovery practically impossible, and that the interests of the Community are taken fully into consideration. In particular, national rules may take account of the need for legal certainty by requiring recovery proceedings to be commenced within prescribed limitation periods.[59] In principle, the same approach applies to the recovery of state aids found by the Commission to have been granted in breach of Articles 87 and 88 EC.[60] But in *Alcan II*, the ECJ adapted its principles to meet the specific characteristics of the state aids sector.[61] Where the national authorities seek recovery of aid found by the Commission to have been granted contrary to Articles 87–88, the recipient cannot rely on the expiry of domestic time-limits (even those of reasonable duration) to resist repayment. Treaty regulation of state aids is characterised by a mandatory system of notification to and verification by the Commission, with the operation of which it is presumed any diligent businessman will be aware. In particular, when aid is found to be incompatible with Community law, the role of the national authorities is merely to give effect to the Commission's decision. Since the national authorities thus lack any discretion in the matter, recipients of unlawful aid cannot claim to be in a position of legal uncertainty after the Commission has adopted a decision requiring recovery. Such recovery cannot therefore be precluded on the grounds that the national authorities have permitted the expiry of domestic limitation periods.[62]

Alcan II departs from the template of negative harmonisation provided for by *Deutsche Milchkontor*, and creates instead a uniform approach to the limitation periods which must be applied by national courts in state aid cases, at least

---

[59] Cases 205–215/82 *Deutsche Milchkontor* [1983] ECR 2633. More recently, eg: Case C-366/95 *Steff-Houlberg* [1998] ECR I-2661; Case C-132/95 *Jensen and Korn* [1998] ECR I-2975.
[60] Eg: Case 94/87 *Commission v. Germany* [1989] ECR 175; Case C-142/87 *Belgium v. Commission* [1990] ECR I-959. Cf. Case C-390/98 *Banks v. Coal Authority* (Judgment of 20 September 2001).
[61] Case C-24/95 *Alcan II* [1997] ECR I-1591.
[62] Also: Case C-5/89 *Commission v. Germany* [1990] ECR I-3437. Cf. Art. 14 Regulation 659/99 [1999] OJ L83/1; A Sinnaeve and P-J Slot, 'The New Regulation on State Aid Procedures' (1999) 36 *CMLRev* 1153.

where the Commission has adopted a decision finding aid incompatible with the Treaty and ordering its recovery.[63] Moreover, this highly centralised level of procedural harmonisation was expressly justified by reference to the corresponding degree of substantive centralisation achieved under the Treaty, whereby the state aids regime is promulgated and applied by the Community institutions, with only very limited scope for any independent exercise of Member State discretion. Other judgments reinforce this perception that state aids has been identified by the Court as a distinct sector ripe for a distinct solution to the problems posed by decentralised enforcement, for example: by ruling out the ability of undertakings to rely on any defence of passing on;[64] and by asserting Community competence to both require and detail the payment of interest, over and above recovery of the principal sum.[65] Similarly, Advocate General Cosmas in *France* v. *Ladbrokes and Commission* argued that the Community should define for itself the conditions for application of the defence of legitimate expectations: this would ratify de jure the extensive intrusion into national remedial autonomy which already exists de facto post-*Alcan II*; it would also better reflect the allocation of competencies between the Community and domestic authorities as regards the substantive regulation of state aids.[66]

The caselaw on the recovery of state aids therefore provides clear support for the sort of sectoral model proposed above. However, a useful contrast might well be drawn with the ECJ's approach to the domestic enforcement of competition policy. Centralised supervision does not play so prominent a role in the enforcement of Articles 81 and 82 as it does under Articles 87 and 88.[67] Indeed, the 1999 White Paper / 2000 draft Regulation envisage that, with the abolition of both notification and the Commission's monopoly over the grant of individual exemptions, this distinction between the two regimes will become even more marked.[68] Nevertheless, competition policy shares with state aids certain common features: a crucial role in the functioning of an Internal Market based on

---

[63] The position remains unclear as regards situations where simple lack of due notification generates a procedural incompatibility under Art. 88(3) EC, which may then be raised before the domestic courts to challenge the validity of the relevant aid: Case C-354/90 'French Salmon' [1991] ECR I-5505; Case C-39/94 SFEI v. La Poste [1996] ECR I-3547. Cf. H-J Priess, 'Recovery of Illegal State Aid: An Overview of Recent Developments in the Case Law' (1996) 33 CMLRev 69.

[64] Case C-5/89 Commission v. Germany [1990] ECR I-3437; Case C-24/95 Alcan II [1997] ECR I-1591; Case C-298/96 Oelmühle Hamburg [1998] ECR I-4767. Cf. Cases 205–215/82 Deutsche Milchkontor [1983] ECR 2633; Case 199/82 San Giorgio [1983] ECR 3595; Cases C-192–218/95 Comateb [1997] ECR I-165; Cases C-441–442/98 Mikhailidis [2000] ECR I-7145.

[65] Case T-459/93 Siemens [1995] ECR II-1675 (upheld by the ECJ on other grounds in Case C-278/95P [1997] ECR I-2507). Cf. Case 54/81 Fromme [1982] ECR 1449.

[66] Case C-83/98P France v. Ladbroke Racing and Commission [2000] ECR I-3271.

[67] Contrast the limited direct effect of state aids rules (Case 78/76 Steinike und Weinlig [1977] ECR 595; Case C-354/90 'French Salmon' [1991] ECR I-5505) with the more widespread direct effect of competition rules (Case 127/73 BRT v. SABAM [1974] ECR 51; Art. 9(1) Regulation 17/62 [1959–1962] OJ Special English Edition p. 87).

[68] Though greater decentralisation is also on the agenda for Arts. 87–88: M Ross, 'State Aids and National Courts: Definitions and Other Problems—A Case of Premature Emancipation?' (2000) 37 CMLRev 401.

fair and equal conditions of competition; and therefore the pursuit of a high degree of substantive uniformity, with little scope for the Member States independently to construct differentiated normative regimes. For this reason, it was argued above that the Community has a genuine interest in approximating the remedies and procedural rules applicable to the decentralised enforcement of its substantive competition policy.

Such considerations notwithstanding, the ECJ's approach here has been decidedly laissez faire: the ordinary presumption of national autonomy applies to the decentralised enforcement of Articles 81 and 82; subject to ad hoc negative harmonisation through the principles of equivalence and effectiveness.[69] So, claimants will enjoy basic guarantees such as the right of access to judicial redress, and entitlement to seek interim relief.[70] But there is little indication that the Court is prepared to construct any more comprehensive framework of Community-prescribed procedural law. For example, the ECJ in *Otto* v. *Postbank* rejected an argument that the principles of judicial protection applicable to the decentralised enforcement of Articles 81 and 82 should be developed in tandem with the standards required of the Commission itself within the context of centralised enforcement.[71] In particular, there was no reason why the privilege against self-incrimination which applies to Commission investigations under Regulation 17 should extend to civil proceedings before the domestic courts.[72]

The dispute in *Courage* v. *Crehan* provided the ECJ with an opportunity to revisit its previous caselaw, taking into account the changing legal environment generated by the Commission's modernisation programme.[73] The case concerned a rule of English law prohibiting the parties to an unlawful contract from seeking damages inter se—thus preventing a publican from obtaining financial compensation in respect of losses allegedly suffered under a beer tie agreement prohibited by Article 81 EC. There is support for the argument that the *Francovich* action for damages should extend beyond acts of the state to the conduct of individuals;[74] and that the uniform application of Community competition law justifies harmonising the substantive conditions under which private parties must make reparation.[75] However, the Court's approach in *Courage* v. *Crehan* is more complex. Article 81 is a fundamental safeguard for the proper

---

[69] Eg: Case C-242/95 *GT-Link* [1997] ECR I-4449; Case C-126/97 *EcoSwiss* v. *Benetton* [1999] ECR I-3055; Case C-340/99 *TNT Traco* v. *Poste Italiane* (Judgment of 17 May 2001). Also: Cases 46/87 and 227/88 *Hoechst* [1989] ECR 2859; Case C-67/91 *'Spanish Banks'* [1992] ECR I-4785.

[70] Case 222/84 *Johnston* v. *Chief Constable of the RUC* [1986] ECR 1651; Case C-213/89 *Factortame* [1990] ECR I-2433.

[71] Case C-60/92 *Otto* v. *Postbank* [1993] ECR I-5683. Cf. Case T-353/94 *Postbank* v. *Commission* [1996] ECR II-921; C S Kerse (1997) 34 *CMLRev* 1481.

[72] Cf. Case 374/87 *Orkem* [1989] ECR 3283.

[73] Case C-453/99 *Courage* v. *Crehan* (Opinion of 22 March 2001; Judgment of 20 September 2001).

[74] Eg: AG van Gerven in Case C-128/92 *Banks* v. *British Coal Corporation* [1994] ECR I-1209.

[75] Eg: L Hiljemark, 'Enforcement of EC Competition Law in National Courts: The Perspective of Judicial Protection' (1997) 17 *YBEL* 83.

operation of the Single Market, and its effective enforcement would be endangered without the availability in principle of compensation for losses suffered through an anti-competitive agreement. So, the Member State cannot impose an absolute bar on one party to the unlawful contract seeking compensation from the other. On the one hand, the Member State is entitled to restrict the availability of compensation, for example, where the parties negotiated the contract from an equal bargaining position, and compensation would permit the claimant to benefit from his/her own wrongdoing. On the other hand, the Member State cannot rule out compensation where the claimant occupied a position of relative weakness in concluding the contract, and therefore cannot be held responsible to any significant degree for its anti-competitive terms or effects.

The full implications of the judgment in *Courage* are difficult to decipher. The Court gave no indication that it intends to develop some general principle of private liability to pay compensation in respect of breaches of the Treaty for which the individual can be held responsible, based on the relatively sophisticated template of the *Francovich* action for reparation against public authorities.[76] However, at least as regards Article 81, the Court has introduced a more intrusive qualification to the general presumption of Member State autonomy in determining which remedy is the most appropriate adequately to redress the consequences of a private party's delinquency under Community law—insisting that damages should be available in principle, and offering guidance as to the circumstances in which they should be paid in practice.[77] To this extent, *Courage* appears to reinforce the Court's previous suggestion in *EcoSwiss v. Benetton*, that the central role performed by competition law within the Single Market justifies a certain level of special treatment as regards the problems posed by decentralised enforcement.[78] However, it is also possible that the Court's reasoning, based on the imperative of effectiveness rather than that of uniformity, will eventually extend beyond Article 81 to cover private liability as regards other Community policies—whether they relate directly to the Internal Market (Article 82 certainly, but perhaps also the free movement of persons); or pursue more autonomous yet equally fundamental welfare objectives (such as consumer or employee protection).

For now, the overall position concerning competition policy suggests that the ECJ's continued attempts to address the enforcement deficit remain difficult to explain by reference to our sectoral model alone. It is possible that this apparent conceptual diffidence may in fact be explained by the Court's complex institutional position. Both the practical limitations of lawmaking through the

---

[76] Further: R Whish, *Competition Law* 4th edn. (London, Butterworths, 2001) Ch. 8.
[77] Contrast with the choice of remedy offered to the Member State under the Equal Treatment Directive: Case C-271/91 *Marshall II* [1993] ECR I-4367.
[78] Case C-126/97 *EcoSwiss v. Benetton* [1999] ECR I-3055.

piecemeal process of litigation,[79] and the issues of constitutional legitimacy raised by the Treaty legislature's increasing willingness to address the threats allegedly posed by domestic remedies and procedures,[80] have led many commentators to query whether any process of remedial harmonisation would not better be entrusted to the political institutions.[81] Indeed, several Advocates General and the Court itself have recently suggested that, whilst uniformity may remain a valid objective of Treaty regulation, responsibility for drawing up any more advanced plans for Community intervention in national procedural law lies with the Commission, Council and Parliament.[82] So, perhaps the current caselaw should be interpreted as a manifestation, not of some lack of judicial enthusiasm for the imperative of uniformity even where this appears justified at a sectoral level, but of the Court's renewed awareness of its own institutional constraints.

On the other hand, the Community legislature's efforts in the sphere of the enforcement deficit remain relatively limited, leaving significant regulatory gaps within which judicial creativity might still enjoy some credible freedom of manoeuvre.[83] For example, Advocate General Cosmas in *France* v. *Ladbroke Racing and Commission* believed that, in the continuing absence of legislative intervention, the Court would be justified in pursuing for itself the Community-level harmonisation of remedies and procedural rules required to ensure the fair and equal application of Articles 87 and 88 EC as regards the domestic recovery of unlawful state aids.[84] Similarly, the Commission's refusal to endorse proposals for harmonising the domestic standards of judicial protection within the context of its current programme for greater decentralised enforcement of Articles 81 and 82 EC might be interpreted as an invitation to legitimate judicial

---

[79] Eg: F Snyder, 'The Effectiveness of European Community Law: Institutions, Processes, Tools and Techniques' (1993) 56 *MLR* 19; G Mancini, 'Crosscurrents and the tide at the European Court of Justice' (1995) 4 *IJEL* 120.

[80] Eg: Public Procurement Directives 89/665/EEC [1989] OJ L395/33 and 92/13/EEC [1992] OJ L76/14; Return of Cultural Objects Directive 93/7/EEC [1993] OJ L74/74; Protection of Financial Interests Regulation 2988/95 [1995] OJ L312/1; Burden of Proof Directive 97/80/EC [1998] OJ L14/6; Consumer Injunctions Directive 98/27/EC [1998] OJ L166/51; Sale of Consumer Goods Directive 99/44/EC [1999] OJ L171/12. Cf. Art. 65 EC (introduced at Amsterdam).

[81] Eg: J Steiner, 'The Limits of State Liability for Breach of European Community Law' (1998) 4 *EPL* 69; R Craufurd Smith, 'Remedies for Breaches of EU Law in National Courts: Legal Variation and Selection' in P Craig and G de Búrca (eds.), *The Evolution of EU Law* (Oxford, OUP, 1999); C Harlow, 'A Common European Law of Remedies?' in C Kilpatrick, T Novitz and P Skidmore (eds.), *The Future of Remedies in Europe* (Oxford, Hart Publishing, 2000).

[82] Eg: Case C-290/91 *Johannes Peter* [1993] ECR I-2981; Case C-132/95 *Jensen and Korn* [1998] ECR I-2975; Case C-298/96 *Oelmühle Hamburg* [1998] ECR I-4767; Case C-231/96 *Edis* [1998] ECR I-4951; Case C-260/96 *Spac* [1998] ECR I-4997; Cases C-279–281/96 *Ansaldo Energia* [1998] ECR I-5025; Case C-228/96 *Aprile* [1998] ECR I-7141; Case C-343/96 *Dilexport* [1999] ECR I-579.

[83] Cf. the ECJ's observations on the scope of its own judicial function in Cases C-46 and 48/93 *Brasserie du Pêcheur* [1996] ECR I-1029, paras. 24–27.

[84] AG Cosmas in Case C-83/98P *France* v. *Ladbroke Racing and Commission* [2000] ECR I-3271.

action.[85] Yet, whereas in the situation of state aids the Court feels sufficiently secure of its own mandate to embark upon an ambitious campaign of remedial centralisation, in the context of competition policy it remains wedded to the minimalist strategy of ad hoc negative harmonisation.[86] Thus, concerns about lawmaking through litigation, or the relationship between judiciary and legislature, cannot in themselves offer an entirely convincing explanation for the current caselaw. It is tempting to conclude that the Court approaches the enforcement deficit without any clear, or at least coherent, understanding of the appropriate role to be performed by the imperative of uniformity—particularly when viewed from a sectoral perspective.[87]

SUMMARY

Luxembourg continues to deliver a volatile body of caselaw on domestic remedies and procedural rules, which in turn reveals an underlying sense of uncertainty about the appropriate allocation of competence in the decentralised enforcement of Treaty norms as between the Community and its Member States. This chapter sought to address one aspect of the surrounding policy framework: the role performed by the imperative of uniformity; and in particular, the insights which recent scholarship on differentiation and flexibility might usefully share with research on the enforcement deficit debate. Three conclusions seem pertinent.

First, the most recent phase in the ECJ's jurisprudence rejects implicitly the pressure for greater remedial harmonisation exerted by a traditional 'integration through law' analysis, and flirts instead with the challenges of doctrinal reconsideration stimulated by the rise of regulatory differentiation within the Community legal order—reflecting a more limited sympathy with the imperative of uniformity such as forms the basic conceptual premises of an alternative 'sectoral' model.

Secondly, viewed from this sectoral perspective, the general trend of mere negative approximation which has dominated the recent caselaw provides an

---

[85] Part 3 of the Explanatory Memorandum accompanying the draft Regulation COM(2000) 582 Final. Cf. Part 8.2 of the Commission's Summary of Observations on the White Paper (29 February 2000).

[86] Subject, of course, to future clarification and exploration of the reasoning in *Courage* v. *Crehan*.

[87] An interpretation reinforced by Case C-58/95 *Gallotti* [1996] ECR I-4345: AG Fennelly observed that Waste Directive 91/156/EEC [1991] OJ L78/32 was adopted under Art. 175 EC on environmental policy, was thus subject to the minimum harmonisation facility in Art. 176, and in turn demanded only minimum standards of Community intervention in the Member State's remedial competence; whereas the ECJ hinted that the same limited degree of procedural harmonisation would apply even if the measure had been adopted under Art. 95 EC with a view to equalising conditions of economic competition within the Internal Market. Other examples of (limited) uniformity-differentiation discourse in the remedies caselaw: Case C-336/94 *Dafeki* [1997] ECR I-6761; Case C-125/97 *Regeling* [1998] ECR I-4493.

adequate standard for Community intervention in the domestic systems of judicial protection, on grounds of securing the uniform application of Treaty norms, in respect of sectors such as environmental, consumer and social policy. It is arguable that this general trend is also appropriate for related aspects of the Internal Market. The ideal of free movement across a regulatory level playing-field has been compromised by the Treaty's commitment to pursue higher standards of social protection within the process of economic integration itself, and thus by the Treaty's need to furnish a legal infrastructure capable of accommodating differences in the capacity and willingness of the various Member States to agree a common welfare agenda. Against such a background, some degree of diversity in the mechanisms available for decentralised enforcement cannot be described as inherently incompatible with the contemporary process of Community market-building.

Thirdly, it is nevertheless possible to identity certain sectors of Community policy, intimately related to the functioning of the Single Market, which remain relatively untouched by the process of regulatory differentiation and may thus claim a legitimate interest in attaining some more advanced state of remedial harmonisation, so as to safeguard the goal of normative uniformity still being pursued at a substantive level. In this regard, the caselaw on state aids suggests that the ECJ is sometimes prepared to recognise and address this problem. However, the caselaw on the domestic enforcement of Treaty competition policy demonstrates that the Court's approach is not entirely consistent, creating a genuine 'enforcement deficit' through undesirable inequalities in the standards of judicial protection available to economic undertakings operating on the Community market which remains to be resolved by future judicial or legislative intervention.

7

Unpacking the Concept of Discrimination in EC and International Trade law

GRÁINNE DE BÚRCA

INTRODUCTION

T
HE NOTION OF DISCRIMINATION has always been fundamental to international trade law, constituting one of the principal conceptual tools for identifying impermissible trade restrictions. It continues to be a key, albeit increasingly complex and widening concept in world trade law, where its centrality amongst the norms of the WTO system is unquestioned.[1]

It will be argued in this chapter that whereas the origins of international trade law indicate that its primary goal was to eliminate national protectionism, and not to promote international regulatory convergence or harmonization, even this basic notion of protectionism is a potentially slippery one capable of expansion and indeterminacy in practice. The principle of non-discrimination was developed in order to further this primary goal, as a means of helping to identify protectionist measures, but the discrimination concept is also a complex and expansive one. While the EU is now clearly a far more closely integrated regional system in which the goal of anti-protectionism was from the outset accompanied by a strong programme of market integration and harmonisation, buttressed in recent years by an ambitious project of political and constitutional integration, a look at the WTO system indicates that many of the same legal developments—albeit that they happened much more quickly, explicitly and intensively within the European system—are becoming apparent in that context. The expansion and blurring of the notions of protectionism and discrimination on the one hand, and the move towards norms of indirect discrimination and 'unnecessary' barriers, as well as the increasing complexity of the notion of direct discrimination (through the subtleties of determining 'like'

[1] See T. Cottier and P. Mavroidis, (eds) *Regulatory Barriers and the Principle of Non-Discrimination in World Trade Law* (Ann Arbor, University of Michigan Press, 2000).

products) are all to be seen occurring in the context of the provisions of the WTO agreements. The balance between a strong market culture and the regulatory space to pursue other policy goals is clearly shaped in important part by these foundational concepts—in other words, by the breadth of the basic prohibition on trade barriers—and in part by the nature and scope of the possibility for justifying such barriers.[2]

A common misapprehension is to assume that these concepts—protectionism, discrimination, market access etc—have relatively fixed or stable meanings, and that the pattern or strength of trade liberalisation depends on which of them is the animating principle underlying the legal norms. On the contrary, consideration of the development of the EC internal market and of the GATT/WTO system over time suggests that the concepts themselves are eminently fluid and that their construction is capable of changing as the economic and political context in which they are being interpreted alters. The EU and the WTO, in their different ways, are highly dynamic entities and their norms are in a process of ongoing articulation and development. This is partly through a process of contestation before the courts and dispute settlement bodies of the two entities, and partly through the relationship between law and politics—or more narrowly, the balance between negative and positive integration—within the respective systems.[3] Further, the deeper policy questions concerning the relationship between market and society, which are mediated by the balancing of trade liberalisation norms and 'domestic' (which in the WTO context includes also 'EU') regulatory autonomy, cannot be avoided by the choice of concept to underpin the system. That balance is implicit in and will emerge in the construction of whatever fundamental concept is chosen—whether protectionism, discrimination, market access or some other—although the balancing process used is likely to vary depending on these. Many factors including the types of values and non-economic norms which can be brought into the balance, the degree of importance to be given to the trade liberalisation aim and where the weight of presumption will lie, will vary in accordance with the nature and structure of the basic concept chosen to constitute the trade liberalisation norm. Ultimately, however, the underlying and fundamental policy questions can never be entirely avoided, but can only be structured differently, because the very act of elevating free trade norms—whether by 'constitutionalising' them as in the European context, or by vastly strengthening and privileging them as under the reformed WTO system—necessarily forces some version of that choice onto all communities which participate in the system.

[2] See chapter 10 by Joanne Scott in this volume.
[3] For different views of this relationship see A. Von Bogdandy, 'Law and Politics in the WTO: Strategies to Cope with a Deficient Relationship' (2001) 5 *Max Planck Yearbook of United Nations Law*, and R. Howse and K. Nicolaidis 'Legitimacy and Global Governance: Why Constitutionalizing the WTO is a Step too Far,' in P. Sauve and A. Subramanian (eds.) *Equity, Efficiency and Legitimacy: The Multilateral Trading System at the Millennium* (Brookings Institution, Washington, D.C., 2001).

THE RELEVANCE OF THE DISCRIMINATION CONCEPT IN
THE EC INTERNAL MARKET

In the EU, in which many of the trade rules were initially inspired by the GATT, both the meaning and usage of the term discrimination remains rather confused, despite years of case law and of academic commentary on the subject. Some years ago Nick Bernard argued (before the *Bosman*[4] ruling, but after *Alpine Investments*[5] and *Schindler*[6] cases had been decided) that discrimination remains a concept at the heart of the EC's internal market,[7] the concept which is called upon most to distinguish between legitimate and illegitimate market regulation. Others, including more recently Catherine Barnard, have argued rather the opposite, suggesting that substantial hindrance of market access is gradually emerging as, and should be comprehensively recognised by the ECJ as, the key to the internal market freedoms.[8] Another line of argument proposed by Chris Hilson perceives a role both for discrimination and for market access principles in different areas of EC trade and free movement.[9]

Certainly, it could not plausibly be argued that market access has now entirely replaced discrimination as the operative EC internal market principle,[10] although it may be true that much of the conceptual work of the core discrimination principle in identifying impermissible trade barriers was done in the earlier years of the Community's existence.[11] Within a system which is now as closely integrated in political as well as economic terms as the EU, the main

---

[4] Case C–415/93, *Union Royale Belge des Sociétés de Football Association and others* v. *Bosman* [1995] ECR I–4921.

[5] Case C–384/93 *Alpine Investments* v. *Minister van Financiën* [1995] ECR I–1141.

[6] Case C–275/92, *Customs and Excise* v. *Schindler* [1994] ECR I–1039.

[7] N. Bernard 'Discrimination and Free Movement in EC Law' [1996] *ICLQ* 82. Accordingly, in his view, the EC internal market can be characterised as a decentralised system promoting regulatory pluralism.

[8] C. Barnard 'Fitting the Remaining Pieces into the Goods and Persons Jigsaw' (2001) 26 ELRev 35. See also S. Weatherill 'After Keck: Some Thoughts on how to Clarify the Clarification' (1996) 33 *CMLRev* 885.

[9] C. Hilson 'Discrimination in Community Free Movement Law' (1999) 24 *ELRev* 445. See also L.Daniele 'Non-discriminatory Restrictions on the Free Movement of Persons' (1997) 22 *ELRev.* 191.

[10] For two recent cases in which the discriminatory nature or otherwise of particular restrictions were extensively debated, see case C–17/00, *François De Coster and Collège des bourgmestre et échevins de Watermael-Boitsfort*, judgment of 29 November 2001 in which the ECJ discussed whether a Belgian tax on satellite dishes was discriminatory or not, and ultimately concluded that it did indirectly (and unjustifiably) discriminate against non-Belgian-based operators; and case C–493/99 *Commission* v *Germany*, 25 October 2001 concerning whether national legislation on labour arrangements for construction companies constituted a discriminatory measure or otherwise restricted the freedom of establishment of non-German companies.

[11] In the external trade policy of the EC, however, the non-discrimination principle is not observed in the same way as it is in the internal market domain. See, for a full discussion of this, and of the tension between the Most Favoured Nation principle on the one hand and the EC's preferential trade agreements on the other, M. Cremona 'Neutrality or Discrimination? The WTO, the EU and External Trade' in G de Búrca and J. Scott, (eds,) *The EU and the WTO: Legal and Constitutional Aspects* (Oxford Hart, 2001) p. 151, and her chapter in this volume (14) describing the other principles which underpin the EU's 'external market' policy.

obstacles to inter-state trade which are perceived as remaining tend not to be identified by the fact that they discriminate, but rather by their more generally trade-restrictive effects. Besides, apart from the four freedoms, the rules on internal taxation in Article 90 EC are still clearly governed by the non-discrimination principle, and customs duties, which are prohibited under Article 25, by their nature imply the existence of discrimination against foreign products. And even if the situation with regard to customs duties is not wholly as clear as it once was, given that internal regional customs duties which apply to domestic as well as to foreign goods are also caught by the Treaty prohibition,[12] differential treatment remains a key factor in identifying impermissible pecuniary charges. Further, the existence of discrimination remains relevant to the kind of justification which can legitimately be offered by a state to explain a trade restriction.[13] Nonetheless, in the field of free movement of goods, persons and services in particular, it is fair to say that while the early years of development of this area of law may have focused on more *direct* forms of discrimination, followed by several decades of jurisprudential and legal debate over more *indirect* kinds of discrimination and over the notion of indistinctly applicable measures, some of the 'cutting-edge' questions now centre around which kinds of non-discriminatory regulation are caught by the Treaty's free movement rules.[14]

This, of course, is very much a state-of-the-art picture, and as Paul Craig's chapter in this volume demonstrates, the EC's common or internal market has actually been in a process of development over the years and has undergone continuous change. Where a clearer discrimination criterion was highly relevant at the outset, its importance in detecting suspect market barriers within the EC has reduced with the gradual removal of the most obvious trade restrictive measures. It has reduced in accordance with the density of positive regulatory legislation adopted at EU level following the single market programme, and the years of the mutual recognition strategy which have reduced the likelihood of differing domestic standards in many fields which caused differential burdens for imported and domestic products. In other words, if we are seeking to understand the shifting role of discrimination in the constitution of the Community's internal market, it would be highly artificial to consider only the framework 'negative integration' rules—the Treaty provisions which establish the internal market—and their interpretation over the years by the Court of Justice. In the first place, those rules are qualified and contextualised by the adoption of a

---

[12] C-363/93 *Lancry* [1994] ECR I-3957. See P. Oliver 'Some Further Reflections on the scope of Articles 28–30 EC' (1999) *CMLRev* 183.

[13] See the cases cited at footnote 34 below, and more generally the chapter by J. Scott in this volume. (10)

[14] See recently S. Weatherill 'Recent Case Law concerning the Free Movement of Goods: Mapping the Frontiers of Market Deregulation' (1999) 36 *CMLRev* 51 : 'Whereas the battleground in Article 30 cases pre-*Keck* was justification, it has now shifted to the previously scarcely contested terrain on which it must be asked whether a sufficient impact on cross-border trade has been shown'.

dense regulatory programme at European level and by the very existence in the Treaty of legislative competences and autonomous EU norms in other fields such as social, environment, consumer and health policy. And secondly, the very meaning of the negative integration Treaty provisions is far from fixed, and their construction and interpretation by the ECJ has changed in the light of the intensifying integrated market. In other words, the Treaty provisions on the internal market, however fundamental they may be considered to be in their status as European economic constitutional norms, are not fixed in their meaning. Without any amendment to their terms, the interpretation of these provisions has clearly changed over the years in response to the changing market context within which they have been construed. The judicial move from construing Articles 39 (ex 48) , 43 (ex 52) and 49 (ex 59) as going beyond discrimination to cover genuinely even-handed non-discriminatory restrictions, for example, occurred in the context of a more closely integrated internal market with a higher number of regulatory standards and a more developed mutual recognition system.

Discrimination also remains very much a key concept in the WTO system, which continues to develop as a trading system of increasing power and significance. And while there may well be lessons for the WTO to learn from the EU's internal market history—even if the parallels between the two systems are limited and the likelihood of their growing significantly closer in nature remains distant—there is another dimension of greater relevance for the EU. That is the fact that since the European Community is a WTO member which is subject, on behalf of its member states, to the trade rules of the WTO agreements, the EC's own regulatory measures fall to be scrutinised by reference to the discrimination concept and other related norms, to see whether they are compatible with those requirements. The question of the WTO-compatibility of EU measures has had a high profile in recent years—for example in relation to the controversies concerning beef hormones, genetically modified organisms and bananas—despite the uncertainty which for long has surrounded the legal status of WTO norms within the EU legal order, and despite the conclusion of the direct effect debate by the European court's case law.[15]

Finally, the shift away from the centrality of discrimination as an explanatory concept in the development of the EC internal market and the increased emphasis on market access should not lead to the symbolic importance of the former being overlooked. A revisiting of the policy considerations and the normative assumptions underlying the non-discrimination and the market-access rules respectively brings to the surface the fundamental questions about the role of trade liberalisation, and about the type of economy and society which are shaped by the privileging of particular trade norms.

---

[15] See in particular cases C-149/96, *Portugal v. Council* [1999] ECR I-8395, T-18/99, *Cordis Obst und Gemüse Großhandel GmbH v Commission* [2001] ECR I-913 and Case T-2/99, *T Port GmbH & Co v. Council* [2001] ECR I-2093.

THE ORIGINS OF THE DISCRIMINATION CONCEPT IN
INTERNATIONAL TRADE LAW

The concept of non-discrimination which has developed in more recent times has a clear ethical dimension—the general notion of justice as equality being one which is increasingly widely accepted not only in modern political theory but also in the practices of social and political life.[16] In the context of EC internal market norms, if we consider the application of the non-discrimination principle to the free movement of persons, it seems plausible to posit a relationship with other instances of EU non-discrimination law such as the anti-racism directives, which have a deeper normative justification.[17] However, given the origins of international trade liberalisation, it would be a mistake—despite the trend in some current literature which seek to defend a 'human rights' basis for the development of international trade norms[18]—to place too much emphasis on the ethical dimension of equal treatment in this respect. It is undeniable that the arguments for trade liberalisation, both political and economic, have been largely instrumental. According to Jackson, the economic arguments for the non-discrimination principle in international trade, (and more specifically for the most-favoured nation dimension of that principle) were threefold: first as being likely to minimise distortions in the principles which motivate economic institutions (eg companies being required to buy products from afar despite the heavy transportataion requirements because of higher tariffs imposed on neighbouring country products); secondly as being linked more generally to a policy of freeing trade from as much governmental interference as possible, and thirdly as minimizing transaction costs (e.g. the origin of goods question becomes less relevant for customs officials).[19] In terms of political arguments for the non-discrimination principle, he lists the avoidance of trade cliques which could cause rancour between countries, the stabilisation of the economic environment and the reduction of international tensions. All of these are functional, instrumental arguments for non-discrimination in trade. Classical trade theory maintains that even unilateral trade liberalization enhances national welfare over a protectionist policy, and reciprocal trade liberalisation through the non-discrimination principle has certainly consolidated its position

---

[16] See most recently R. Dworkin *Sovereign Virtue: The Theory and Practice of Equality* (Cambridge, Mass., Harvard UP, 2000).

[17] See e.g. Directive 2000/43/EC of 29 June 2000 implementing the principle of equal treatment between persons irrespective of racial or ethnic origin. OJ [2000] L180/22.

[18] See E-U. Petersmann 'The WTO Constitution and Human Rights' (2000) 3 Journal of International Economic Law 19, and 'How to Constitutionalize International Law and Foreign Policy for the Benefit of Civil Society?' (1998) 20 *Mich. J. Int'l L.*, 7. For a thorough critique of the notion of a 'human right' to trade, see S. Peers 'Fundamental Right or Political Whim? WTO Law and the European Court of Justice' in *The EU and the WTO: Legal and Constitutional Aspects* (De Búrca and Scott (eds)Hart, 2001).

[19] J. H. Jackson, *The Jurisprudence of GATT and the WTO* (Cambridge, CUP, 2000), Chapter 5 'Equality and Discrimination in International Economic Law – the GATT' 57.

in the second half of this century in the international domain with the advent of the GATT and the WTO.[20]

Protectionism, essentially, is the protection of national production against competition from foreign trade. The non-discrimination principle in the field of trade was designed specifically to prohibit protectionism. At this stage, it could be argued that to shift from the language of discrimination to the language of protectionism is merely to move the definitional problem into a potentially narrower band. In the context of trade, a discriminatory measure can be defined as one which draws a distinction between two similar groups to the disadvantage of one (direct discrimination), or which results in disadvantageous treatment for one group over the other (indirect discrimination). A protectionist measure, on the other hand, can be defined as one which is designed to shield domestic trade from the effects of foreign trade for no reason other than to protect the domestic trade. Discrimination—even if confined to direct discrimination—is thus a broader category since a distinction could deliberately be drawn between imports and domestic products in a way which disadvantages imports, but for a reason other than to protect domestic production. At the same time the category of discrimination *includes* protectionism, since a measure cannot be designed to protect the domestic market against the effects of foreign trade without either drawing a distinction to the disadvantage of foreign products or resulting in disadvantageous treatment to them. Thus protectionist measures are the sub-category of discriminatory measures which are most suspect under international trade law. It is difficult to articulate a legally (even if ethically or economically) acceptable justification for a clearly protectionist measure.[21] And if an additional reason is put forward for a measure which appears to be designed to protect domestic production (as for example, the rather strained national security justification put forward by Ireland in the *Campus Oil* case[22]), then the conclusion would be that it is discriminatory but not necessarily protectionist because it is not designed to shield domestic effects from foreign trade *for no reason other than* to protect domestic trade. Trade liberalisation, and the norms of international trade law, were based essentially on the principle of eradicating protectionism and ensuring equal treatment of foreign and domestic products. They were not necessarily aimed, despite some disagreement in the

---

[20] See generally M. Trebilcock and R. Howse, *The Regulation of International Trade* 2nd edn (London Routledge, 1999), Chap. 1.

[21] The GATT, for example, provides in Article XIX an emergency safeguard clause to allow for protectionism in the event of serious injury being threatened to domestic producers.

[22] See case 72/83 *Campus Oil and Others* [1984] ECR 2727. There the impugned domestic measure was allegedly designed to protect domestic oil refining processes for another reason, i.e. that of ensuring the continuation of essential national services through oil supplies in the event of a strike. See also more recently case C-398/98, *Commission v Greece*, 25 October 2001, in which the court ruled that a law which discriminated in favour of Greek oil refineries by making the transfer of a storage obligation conditional upon the purchase of petroleum products from refineries established in Greece, could not be justified on purely economic grounds, and there were less restrictive ways of addressing public security concerns.

GATT/WTO literature on this point, at promoting trade per se or at eradicating *any* form of national regulatory barrier. They were intended essentially to eliminate protectionism but not to interfere more extensively in other domestic regulatory choices.

A SLIPPERY SPECTRUM: PROTECTIONISM—DIRECT DISCRIMINATION—INDIRECT DISCRIMINATION—MARKET ACCESS

The core function of the 'non-discrimination' principle as it originated in international trade law could therefore be said to be to help in identifying those measures or rules which are protectionist. Discrimination—whether direct or indirect—will generally provide *evidence* of protectionism. Yet if the category of protectionist measures were as limited as the preceding paragraph suggests, and were confined only to those measures designed specifically to protect against foreign trade, international trade rules would affect relatively few national measures. A very substantial degree of domestic regulatory autonomy would remain. The reality, however, is somewhat different. The concept of protectionism is in reality hardly less contested or blurred than that of discrimination, as can be seen even in the use of terms such as '*de facto* protectionism', or 'protectionist effects'.[23] In other words, once we move away from the idea of deliberate, intentional protectionism—or even once attention focuses on how such intentional protectionism might be proven where it is not clearly acknowledged or explicit on the face of a measure—we move into the realm of having to assess the discriminatory effects of a measure and to contemplate the likely authenticity of any other regulatory purpose, apart from domestic protectionism, which is claimed.[24] Thus not only does it become difficult to identify a protectionist measure, which is not something that will necessarily be readily evident on the face of a measure, but the question of regulatory purpose becomes relevant. In other words, the need to balance the alleged purpose of the measure against its apparently disparate impact on foreign trade will not necessarily be avoided by choosing a prohibition which covers 'protectionist' measures only.

The argument that international trade law, unlike within a closely integrated regional trade system like the EU, aims mainly at eradicating protectionism in international trade and operates by means of relatively uncontroversial anti-discrimination rules, becomes rather more strained as soon as we look beyond the labels of 'protectionism' and 'discrimination' to examine what these

---

[23] See for a discussion in the US context, Don Regan 'The Supreme Court and State Protectionism: Making Sense of the Dormant Commerce Clause' (1986) 84 *Michigan Law Review* 1091.
[24] See M. Maduro 'Reforming the Market or the State? Article 30 and the European Constitution: Economic Freedom and Political Rights' (1997) 3 *ELJ* 55, and more generally *We, the Court* (Oxford, Hart Publishing 1998).

concepts mean in practice. Once we move beyond very readily identifiable protectionism (say, of the kind represented by a quantitative restriction proper)
there is no clear rule which can, of itself, distinguish a legitimate from an illegitimate trade-restrictive measure. The non-discrimination concept operates
only as part of a set of evidentiary guides to determining whether a measure is
to be qualified as impermissibly protectionist or not. And beyond the clearest
kinds of protectionism, we move very quickly onto a spectrum of regulatory
measures whose legitimacy and compatibility (whether with EC or WTO law)
involves some consideration of the regulatory purposes of the measure, and will
necessitate some kind of balancing between these other purposes and its trade
restrictive effects. At one end of this spectrum lie deliberately protectionist rules
only, and at the other end lie any rules which hinder trade. In between, broadly
speaking, lies a range of directly discriminatory rules and rules which are not
on their face discriminatory but which have indirectly discriminatory effects.
Within the EU, the picture has gradually changed over the years but by now the
'constitutionalized' trade norms of the EC Treaty cover virtually the whole
spectrum, so that probably only quite a small section covering insubstantial barriers to trade between states remains untouched and truly within a sphere of
national regulatory autonomy. Within the WTO—to whose rules the EC is subject—the position is less clear and while the trade liberalisation norms are certainly narrower in coverage, the WTO like the EU is by no means a static system
and is in the process of continual development, in part through the actions of
its dispute settlement bodies. Protectionist and directly discriminatory trade
restrictions are clearly caught by various provisions of the WTO Agreements,
and other non-discriminatory forms of trade restriction are now caught by the
Agreements on Technical Barriers to Trade (TBT), and on Sanitary and
Phytosanitary Measures (SPS).

Another, finer intermediate distinction has recently been drawn between non-
nationality-based regulatory classifications which represent 'de facto discrimination', and non-nationality-based regulatory classifications which represent an
innocuous disparate impact on trade, and are unrelated to protectionism.[25] This
seems rather difficult to apply as a test or distinction given that both measures
are non-nationality based and therefore non-discriminatory on their face, and
both have a disparate impact on imports as opposed to domestic products.
Without actually developing some means of detecting a hidden intention or
motive, it seems difficult to distinguish protectionist from non-protectionist
measures on this standard.[26] It might of course be possible to develop an

[25] R. Howse and E Tuerk 'The WTO Impact on Internal Regulations: A Case Study of the
Canada—EC Asbestos Dispute' in G. de Búrca and J. Scott (eds) *The EU and the WTO: Legal and
Constitutional Aspects* (Oxford, Hart Publishing, 2001) p. 283.
[26] A similar question is posed by Joanne Scott in her chapter in relation to situations where the
'mandatory requirements' apparently cannot be used to justify facially neutral or 'indistinctly applicable' measures, because the Court of Justice seems to presume the existence of a form of hidden
deliberate discrimination.

effects-based test, either a *de minimis* kind of limit, or a classification of some measures as being 'too uncertain and indirect' to be capable of amounting to de facto discrimination (e.g. a standard of the kind seen in some of the Article 28 EC case law on planning regulations for superstores). But it is difficult to imagine how 'innocuous' as opposed to 'protectionist' indirect discrimination could readily be identified unless there is some means of detecting a deliberate intention to discriminate, or unless an effects-based standard is used as a substitute.

It has been argued that the discrimination requirement in Articles III (the national treatment principle) and XI (prohibiting quantitative restrictions proper, not measures of equivalent effect) prevents the WTO dispute settlement bodies from becoming 'a kind of routine reviewing court for ordinary domestic regulations, placing undue limits on non-protectionist, regulatory processes'.[27] However, this account of the trade-liberalisation principles of the GATT/WTO as being narrowly drawn and therefore not becoming a tool for such routine or excessive regulatory review, is challenged not only by the fact that provisions of the TBT and SPS agreements now prohibit forms of non-discriminatory barrier to trade, but also by the increasing subtlety of the determination of 'like products' under the national treatment principle of Article III. These latter features inevitably reduce the desired clarity and boundedness of the 'discrimination' concept and make it less likely that the need to weigh the aims of domestic regulatory choices against free trade can be avoided. Howse and Tuerk, for example, argue that the WTO agreements are primarily about preventing 'cheating' and they perceive the advent of the TBT and SPS agreements as ways of ensuring transparency and consistency 'that provides trading partners with assurances that protectionism is not embedded at some deep level in the regulatory process itself'.[28]

There are some fairly difficult distinctions here, however, which are not resolved by using strong terminology such as 'cheating' to refer to protectionist measures, in particular since it is normally difficult to identify deliberate protectionism on the face of a measure. There is an understandable tendency amongst certain commentators to understate the potential of the WTO system and even its current scope, by emphasising the centrality of the discrimination principle, and arguing that market access and market integration are in no way objectives of the system and that the Members retain substantial regulatory autonomy.[29] The reality however is that it is a changing, expanding and powerful trading system, and that the regulatory autonomy of members is increasingly being affected in various ways by the provisions of the WTO agreements. The very considerable differences between the political and institutional contexts of the EU and the WTO do not mean that we cannot predict that the

---

[27] R. Howse and E. Tuerk, footnote 25 above, at p 285.
[28] *Ibid.* See also M. Trebilcock and R. Howse, *The Regulation of International Trade*, 2nd edn (London Routledge, 1999) Chap 2.
[29] See for example, A. Von Bogdandy, above note 3.

WTO system will push states towards greater regulatory convergence, albeit without the kind of market-correcting institutions which exist within the EU.[30] An attempt to define the non-discrimination principle as a narrow anti-protectionist tool will not, given the fluidity of these various trade-liberalisation concepts and their expansive tendency, suffice to prevent some version of the scrutiny of national regulatory choices and erosion of domestic regulatory autonomy that has taken place for many years at EU level. Rather than denying the dynamic and expansive nature of the system, its powerful (and indeed dangerous) potential should arguably be recognised and confronted. Rather than attempting definitional restriction by asserting that discrimination is a narrow concept, the excessive privileging of free trade norms over domestic regulatory choices should be challenged instead in more direct ways, for example by arguing for a stronger status, institutionally and normatively, for other values such as those which animate the 'exceptions' in Article XX.

THE BALANCING OF VALUES: AT THE DEFINITIONAL STAGE OR THE JUSTIFICATORY STAGE?

To come back to the point made at the beginning of this chapter, the nature of the socio-economic space governed by the relationship between market-liberalising rules and regulatory autonomy is defined not only by the scope and confines of the trade liberalisation norm chosen, (whether that be phrased as an anti-protectionist, an anti-direct discrimination, anti direct-and-indirect discrimination or an anti-market hindrance rule), but also by the notion of justification which is permitted. As demonstrated in Joanne Scott's chapter, the nature and scope of the grounds of justification may vary depending on the kind of trade-restrictive measure in question—usually, depending on whether the measure is directly discriminatory or not—and within the EC internal market this unfortunately remains an area of some confusion. However, the list of exceptions within the GATT, GATS, TBT and SPS agreements, as well as the listed exceptions within the EC Treaties and the broader notion of mandatory requirements, bring the balancing of values more explicitly to the surface than the concepts of protectionism or discrimination in themselves do. Whereas the task of determining whether a measure is protectionist or discriminatory very often entails a scrutiny of the effects of the measure and its alleged regulatory purpose, the scrutiny at this initial stage tends to be less explicit and to focus

---

[30] On the development of mutual recognition in the international trading context, see K. Nicolaïdis, 'Exploring a New Paradigm for Trade Diplomacy: The US-EU Mutual Recognition Agreements,' in *Proceedings of the European Union Community Association, World Conference*, (Office of Publications of the EC, Brussels, 1997) and 'Non-Discriminatory Mutual Recognition: An Oxymoron in the new WTO Lexicon?' in T. Cottier and P. Mavroidis, (eds) above, note 1, at p 267.

more on effects.[31] At the stage of justification of a measure which has been held to breach one of the free market norms, the balancing of interests tends to be more structured and more intensive—depending in particular on how the proportionality principle comes into play[32]—it generally entails a shift in the burden of proof on to the regulating state, and normally allows for fuller articulation of the policy choices at issue.

Yet, as also mentioned above, this kind of balancing also takes place, albeit in a less explicit or in a more circumscribed way, at the stage of considering whether discrimination or protectionism exists. The determination of whether or not a tax measure is discriminatory or protectionist under Article 90 of the EC Treaty, for example, regularly involves the Court of Justice examining the likeness of products (very often alcoholic products!), or the declared aim of a particular tax classification; and under Article 25 the question whether a charge is a discriminatory one equivalent to a customs duty has often been answered only after considering and rejecting various other suggested regulatory purposes for the charge. Further, as demonstrated by the Walloon waste case,[33] to determine whether or not a regulation discriminates against imported goods under Article 28 may require—as with the assessment of similar products under Article 90—consideration of the notion of 'likeness', which brings with it regulatory purposes and characteristics other than the physical properties of a product.[34] This fact has been particularly well illustrated recently in the WTO context by the Asbestos ruling of the Appellate Body, in which some of the implications of the early Tuna/Dolphin panel reports have been reversed.[35] In the Tuna/Dolphin cases,[36] the GATT panels took the view that regulations governing the taking of dolphins incidental to the taking of tuna could not affect tuna as a product. This conclusion suggested that dolphin-unfriendly tuna was no different as a product from dolphin-friendly tuna and that the process by which tuna were caught was not relevant for the purposes of trade regulation.

---

[31] For a recent illustration of the difficult analytical distinction between indirectly discriminatory and non-discriminatory environmental measures, and also for a fairly detailed attempt to balance the potentially discriminatory effects of a fuel tax against its legitimate environmental goals, see AG Jacobs in Case C-451/99 *Cura Anlagen GmbH* v *Auto Service Leasing GmbH (ASL)*, opinion of 25 September 2001

[32] See G. de Búrca 'The Principle of Proportionality and its Application in EC Law' (1993) 13 *YBEL* 105.

[33] Case 2/90 *Commission v. Belgium* [1992] ECR I-4431

[34] See however the difference in the respective approaches of the Advocate General and the Court in the 'green electricity' case C-379/98, *PreussenElektra AG v Schhleswag AG, in the presence of Windpark Reußenköge III GmbH and Land Schleswig-Holstein* [2001] ECR I-2099. AG Jacobs found the reasoning in the earlier Walloon Waste case to be flawed, whereas the ECJ avoided pronouncing on that issue and found the restriction in question—without discussing whether or not it was discriminatory—to be justified on environmental grounds. See also Case C-389/96, *Aher-Waggon GmbH v Bundesrepublik Deutschland* [1998] ECR I-4473.

[35] EC—Measures Affecting Asbestos and Asbestos-containing Products, WT/DS135/AB/R 12 March 2001

[36] 30 ILM (1992) 1598 (Tuna/Dolphin I), 33 ILM (1994) 839 (Tuna/Dolphin II).

In the recent Asbestos ruling, however, not only did the Appellate Body look beyond the physical properties and end-uses of a product to determine whether it was 'like' another product for the purposes of determining discrimination, but it went on, in reversing the ruling of the Panel below, to consider consumer preferences as an important factor in the determination of likeness.[37] To quote directly from the Appellate Body's ruling: 'evidence about the extent to which products can serve the same end-uses, and the extent to which consumers are— or would be—willing to choose one product instead of another to perform those end-uses, is highly relevant evidence in assessing the "likeness" of those products'. Although this remains, according to the panel, a question of economic competitive relationships and substitutability,[38] the ruling certainly opens the possibility that, for example, tuna-unfriendly dolphin could be shown to be 'unlike' tuna-friendly dolphin if consumer preferences to that effect could be demonstrated. Further, the Appellate Body ruled that the existence of a health risk could also be considered within the context of determining likeness, and not only as part of the justification stage of reasoning. Thus, the regulatory aim of the French measure restricting the import of products containing chyrostile asbestos—which was clearly the protection of public health and safety— became relevant at the stage of identifying whether discrimination existed, since discrimination would not be held to exist if the differential treatment related to products which were unalike.

Apart from the less overt nature of the weighing of regulatory choices which is likely to take place at the definitional stage, rather than at the stage of justification where the competing values at stake are explicitly articulated, it is also the case that the evidential burden may vary. Thus, once discrimination or a sufficiently restrictive effect on trade has been shown, the burden shifts to the defendant to show that there was an adequate justification for the measure and that it was proportionate and necessary, whereas the initial onus of demonstrating a breach lies on the complainant to make out a case of discrimination. Undoubtedly by 'constitutionalising' the negative internal market norms, as has been done in the EU context, trade liberalisation has been presumptively elevated over other values so that a clear (and in many instances compelling) case has to be made out for the justifiability of other regulatory goals which might restrict trade.

---

[37] For the earlier 'aims and effects' test for determining likeness which had been adopted by panels, and which was later rejected by the Appellate Body, see R. Hudec 'GATT Constraints on National Regulation: Requiem for an "Aim and Effects" Test', (1998) 32 *The International Lawyer* 623. See also the chapters by R. Hudec '"Like Product: The Differences in Meaning in GATT Articles I and III" and P. Mavroidis '"Like Products": Some Thoughts at the Positive and Normative Level' in T. Cottier and P.Mavroidis (eds), above note 1, pp 101 and 125.

[38] See the interesting 'concurring opinion' on the point by one member of the Appellate Body in para 153 of the Report.

CONCLUSION

Crucially, it must be recognised that the choice to elevate and enshrine trade liberalising norms within strong institutional, supranational or international systems like the EU and the WTO carries with it the inevitable consequence that other social and political choices will be constrained in significant ways. The particular concept which is selected to underpin the fundamental trade liberalisation rule, whether anti-protectionism, non-discrimination, market access or another, will to some extent (and in conjunction with the nature of the 'justification' stage) shape the way in which the different values—market freedom versus other social, political and environmental choices—are balanced and what the accommodation between them is to be. The key point being made in this chapter is that engagement in that process of balance is unavoidable once a clear trade liberalisation norm is legally and institutionally privileged within a system like the EC or the WTO, and that it is very important to allow for an explicit and open articulation of the different values at stake.

Further, even if the most restrictive point on the conceptual spectrum is chosen to locate the fundamental trade liberalisation norm—i.e. a clear anti-protectionism rule—the lessons of the EU and of GATT/WTO demonstrate that these concepts are not static but that they tend to evolve and change in the context of the economic and political system in which they function. This occurs both in response to the activities of states or of economic agents who lobby for the free trade norms to be challenged or enforced,[39] to the judicial or dispute resolution bodies which define and construe those norms in particular circumstances, and in response to the relationship between legal and political processes within the particular system. In other words, although the market framework established by the WTO is very different from the internal market of the EC with its more developed political processes and much higher degree of positive integration, it is nonetheless true that the norms of the WTO have created incentives and impulses towards the development of international

---

[39] Far more rarely do non-economic actors have the opportunity to influence the development of trade liberalisation norms. In the EU, the standing rules for direct actions before the ECJ are very strict, rights of intervention under the statute of the Court are very limited, and the preliminary reference mechanism depends on both the existence of standing before a domestic tribunal and the willingness of a national court to refer. The Trade Barriers Regulation in the EU, like the 1974 Trade Act in the US, gives economic operators a role in the initiation of disputes. In the WTO context, however, hopes raised by the apparent willingness of the Appellate Body in the Shrimp/Turtle case WT/DS58/AB/R, 12 October 1998 to consider accepting amicus curiae briefs were disappointed again by the rejection of all of the submissions received from public interest as well as economic organisations in the more recent Asbestos case, WT/DS135/AB/R 12 March 2001. See P. Mavroidis 'Amicus Curiae Briefs. Before The WTO: Much Ado About Nothing' Jean Monnet Working Paper 2/2001, http://www.jeanmonnetprogram.org/papers/papers01.html.

standardisation processes and international regulatory convergence more generally.[40]

While the EC internal market may have moved beyond discrimination as the primary trade liberalisation concept, and have embraced a more interventionist market-access approach, the relationship between the various concepts is a shifting one and the distinction between them far more fluid than some of the discussions on discrimination may suggest. On the one hand, the notion of discrimination—even direct discrimination—certainly remains relevant to the EC's internal market, not only because of provisions such as Articles 25 and 90 and the more limited kinds of justification apparently available for discriminatory measures under Article 30, but also because as a polity which is subject to the rules of the WTO, the EU's regulatory measures fall to be examined for compatibility with the non-discrimination principle embodied in several of its norms.[41] But on the other hand, the argument that the WTO trade liberalisation system is clearly distinct from that of the EU's internal market because it is primarily based on the non-discrimination principle is deprived of some of its explanatory force and relevance by a number of factors. These include, firstly, the fact that the determination of whether discrimination exists has become a subtle and multi-faceted one in which regulatory purpose of a measure may be considered in the assessment of 'likeness'; secondly, the fact that prohibitions on forms of non-discriminatory trade restriction are now to be found in the provisions of other WTO Agreements, and finally, because the concept of discrimination has become an ever more complex, expansive and fluid notion which does not serve so easily to confine the scope and strength of the trade-liberalisation norm which it purports to delimit.

---

[40] See note 30 above.

[41] See G. de Búrca and J. Scott 'The Impact of WTO on EU Decision-making' in G. de Búrca and J. Scott (eds) *The EU and the WTO: Legal and Constitutional Issues* (Oxford, Hart Publishing, 2001), p 1.

8

Market Access and Regulatory Competition

CATHERINE BARNARD AND SIMON DEAKIN*

INTRODUCTION

I T SEEMS THAT THE EC RULES on freedom of movement for goods and persons show some signs of converging around a principle of 'market access'.[1] According to this principle, national legal measures which have the effect of either *preventing or seriously hindering* access to the home market (or a relevant part of it) from another Member State would either be *per se* illegal or would have to be justified by a version of the 'rule of reason'. It has been argued that by displacing the confused and fragmented case-law which has emerged when applying the non-discrimination principle, a market access test would not only introduce greater doctrinal coherence into a currently confused area of law; but it could also create a space for more effective regulatory competition within the EC.

The purpose of this paper is to examine in more detail the relationship between the proposed market access principle and the concept of regulatory competition. We argue that a move to market access would be helpful in clarifying the issues at stake over regulatory competition. At the same time we question whether an *unqualified* market access principle would achieve the benefits which regulatory competition is meant to bring about. On the contrary, unless the emerging economic jurisprudence of the Court addresses legitimate concerns about the effects of the market access principle on Member State autonomy, the market access test will struggle to gain acceptance.

Our focus on regulatory competition may need some justification. The stated aim of the EC rules on free movement is not regulatory competition, but market integration.[2] In so far as they promote market access, the free movement rules also have the effect of protecting what can be seen as fundamental rights in the

---

* Trinity College and Peterhouse, Cambridge respectively. We should like to thank Tammy Hervey for her comments as discussant.
[1] C Barnard, 'Fitting the Remaining Pieces into the Goods and Persons Jigsaw?' (2001) 26 *ELRev* 35.
[2] See, e.g. Article 14 EC.

economic sphere. The debate over regulatory competition, by contrast, is concerned with arrangements for rule-making and the division of powers between state-level bodies and transnational entities, an apparently separate set of issues.

On closer inspection, however, it becomes clear that market access and regulatory competition are two sides of the same coin. Within a federal constitutional framework (or in a transnational entity such as the EC), mobility of economic resources is one of the first preconditions for the emergence of a market in legal rules. When courts review laws of Member States against criteria of how far such laws obstruct, or promote, economic mobility, they are necessarily defining the scope and nature of regulatory competition. Their approach to market access will therefore have profound implications for the nature of the law-making process and for the content of legal rules in a variety of substantive areas, as well as for the division of powers, and the doctrines of preemption and subsidiarity. Given the importance of the issues at stake, it would be preferable if these considerations were to be more clearly articulated by the courts as part of a market access test. This would engender a more meaningful debate on the effects of free movement jurisprudence and its relationship to other areas of EC policy making, including harmonising Directives and other forms of policy intervention such as the open method of coordination (OMC). As part of this debate, it should be possible to set more coherent limits to the market access principle than has hitherto been the case.

In developing this argument we outline in the next section the theoretical foundation of regulatory competition, the so-called pure theory of decentralised law-making, and draw out its legal implications. We then move on in the third section to a closer examination of the predominant conception of regulatory competition in practice, which we refer to as the model of 'competitive federalism', and examine its implications for the market-access test. We find that decisions which make adequate sense when expressed in the customary doctrinal language of free movement and market integration often appear inconsistent when seen through the lens of competitive federalism. In the fourth section we argue that much of the difficulty stems from problems with the idea of 'competitive federalism', and we consider alternative approaches, both in respect of legislation and judicial intervention, which acknowledge space for diversity in rule-making between the Member States. The final section is a conclusion.

REGULATORY COMPETITION: THEORETICAL UNDERPINNINGS

The term 'regulatory competition' refers to a process whereby legal rules are selected (and de-selected) through competition between decentralised, rule-making entities (which could be nation states or other units such as regions or localities). Three justifications are normally given for regulatory competition: firstly, it allows the content of rules to be matched more effectively to the preferences or *wants* of the consumers of laws (citizens and others affected); secondly, it promotes diversity and experimentation in the search for effective legal solutions; and thirdly, by providing mechanisms for preferences to be expressed and alternative solutions compared, it promotes the flow of information on effective law making.

In Tiebout's influential formalisation of this idea,[3] the mechanism through which competition operates is mobility of persons and resources across jurisdictional boundaries. In his 'pure theory' of fiscal federalism, local authorities compete to attract residents by offering packages of services in return for levying taxes at differential rates. Consumers with homogenous wants then 'cluster' in particular localities. The effect is to match local preferences to particular levels of service provision, thereby maximising the satisfaction of wants while maintaining diversity and promoting information flows between jurisdictions.

Tiebout's model can be applied to laws since they, like public services, have the character of what economists refer to as indivisible public goods, that is to say, they cannot easily be priced individually because of issues of non-excludability. Hence collective consumption is more cost-efficient. Laws, then, are seen as products which jurisdictions *supply* through their law-making activities, in response to the *demands* of consumers of the laws, that is, individuals, companies and other affected parties. If supply and demand can be brought into equilibrium, then, in the terminology of welfare economics, *static* or *allocative* efficiency will be maximised. This is another way of saying that the wants or preferences of the various parties will have been satisfied to the greatest possible extent.

At the heart of this conception of regulatory competition is decentralisation. The process cannot work unless effective rule-making authority is exercised by entities operating at a devolved or local level. It is argued that a centralised or 'monopoly' regulator would, by contrast, behave like any other monopoly; contrary to the normal laws of supply and demand, the price of the product goes up while the quantity supplied diminishes, so driving a wedge (a 'social cost') between an optimal economic outcome and what actually occurs. To avoid this outcome implies conferring law-making powers on lower-level units, subject only to the principle that there must be some level below which further decentralisation becomes infeasible because of diseconomies of scale.

Perhaps the best known case of regulatory competition is the so-called Delaware effect in US corporations law. Over 40% of New York stock-exchange-listed companies, and over 50% of Fortune 500 companies, are incorporated in Delaware. Some commentators have argued that Delaware's success in attracting such a high level of company incorporations has been achieved by lowering

---

[3] C Tiebout, 'A pure theory of local expenditure' (1956) 64/5 *Journal of Political Economy* 416.

standards.[4] As Cary has famously argued,[5] when coining the term 'race to the bottom' about Delaware, the state has gained its pre-eminence in the corporate charter market due to its ability to attract incorporations favourable to managers at the expense of shareholders. He claimed that corporate standards were deteriorating, particularly in respect of fiduciary duties, leading to the rights of shareholders *vis-à-vis* management being watered down to 'a thin gruel'.[6] As part of this process, Delaware, 'a pygmy among the 50 states prescribes, interprets, and indeed denigrates national corporate policy as an incentive to encourage incorporation within its borders, thereby increasing its revenue'.[7] To counter this, Cary proposed the enactment of a Federal Corporate Uniformity Act, allowing companies to incorporate in the jurisdiction of their own choosing but removing much of the incentive to organise in Delaware or its rival states.[8]

Although some EC company lawyers have supported harmonisation precisely in order to avoid a Delaware style 'race to the bottom',[9] the idea that Delaware law represents a lowest common denominator has been challenged by accounts which argue that any attempt by managers to downgrade shareholder interests would, over time, lead to a hostile response by the capital markets. Managers therefore have an incentive to incorporate under the law of a state which favours shareholder interests since '[s]tates that enact laws that are harmful to investors will cause entrepreneurs to incorporate elsewhere'.[10] If this is the case, 'Delaware attracts incorporations not because its laws are lax, but because they are efficient'.[11] Thus, some commentators argue that Delaware has so perfected the art of matching its laws to the demands of the users of those laws that it has won the race to the top.[12] In general, while the claim that Delaware company

---

[4] For further details, see C Barnard 'Social Dumping Revisited: Lessons from Delaware' (2000) 25 *ELRev* 57 and C Barnard, 'Regulating Competitive Federalism, in the European Union? The Case of EU Social Policy' in J Shaw (ed), *Social Law and Policy in an Evolving European Union*, (Oxford, Hart, 2000).

[5] W Cary, 'Federalism and Corporate Law: Reflections Upon Delaware' (1974) 83 *Yale Law Journal* 663, 669.

[6] Ibid 666.

[7] Cary, above, n.5, 701.

[8] Ibid, 701.

[9] C Schmitthoff, 'The future of the European company law scene', in C. Schmitthoff (ed.) *The Harmonisation of European Company Law* (London: UKNCCL, 1973), 9.

[10] *Amanda Acquisition Corp. v. Universal Foods Corp.* 877 F.2d 496 (1989), per Easterbrook J., cited in D Charny, 'Competition among Jurisdictions in Formulating Corporate Law Rules: An American perspective on the "Race to the Bottom" in the European Communities', (1991) 32 *Harvard International Law Journal* 422, 431–2, also in S Wheeler (ed.) *A Reader on the Law of the Business Enterprise* (Oxford, OUP, 1994). See also F Easterbrook and D Fischel, 'The corporate contract' (1989) 89 *Columbia Law Review* 1416.

[11] Charny, above n.10.

[12] See, for example, R Winter, 'State Law, Shareholder Protection and the Theory of Corporation' (1977) 6 *J.Leg.Stud.* 251; D Fischel, 'The "race to the bottom" revisited: Reflections on recent developments in Delaware's Corporation Law' (1982) *Northwestern University Law Review* 913, 916 and 920. See also F Easterbrook 'The Economics of Federalism'(1983) 26 *Journal of Law and Economics* 23, 28 and F Easterbrook and D Fischel, 'Voting in Corporate Law' (1983) 26 *J.L.&Ec.*395.

law is efficient remains much disputed,[13] it is generally agreed that regulatory competition need not, necessarily, imply a degradation of standards.[14]

In terms of the legal framework required, the pure theory envisaged by Tiebout is clearly opposed to harmonising measures which aim to impose uniform laws on local jurisdictional entities. These laws would simply obstruct the spontaneous movement to equilibrium of the forces of supply and demand. However, it is less often noticed that the pure theory is ambivalent with regard to centralised judicial review of national-level regulation. This is because, in a *perfectly* competitive market for legal rules, it would be enough for the courts formally to guarantee the right of free movement on the part of the consumers of laws. In the somewhat unrealistic world imagined by the pure theory, the correct response to a legislature which, for example, banned the advertising of alcohol (as in *GIP*[15]), or which insisted on applying its own minimum wage legislation to foreign workers on its territory (as in *Rush Portuguesa*[16]), would be for the factors of production to decide whether or not to quit that state for one which provided a more appropriate regulatory regime. Hence voters who were unhappy with a state's alcohol advertising ban would exit to what they regarded as a more congenial legal regime, while labour-only subcontractors would shun a country which applied its labour standards in an over-rigid way.

Taking the process back one stage, such laws could be avoided in the first place in so far as their negative effects imposed a potential cost on legislators in the jurisdictions adopting them. If such laws reduced the wealth of the citizens of the country concerned, legislators would, it is presumed, have an incentive to avoid adopting them (this would be the case if the well-being of the legislators was linked to the well-being of the country in some way). On the other hand, it might well be the case that citizens (and legislators acting on their behalf) prefer to pay the price for having high standards in areas of product safety and social policy. They may prefer, in other words, to trade off a part of national wealth in return for social redistribution or environmental protection. If this is the case, there is nothing in the pure theory to say that they should not have the right to do so. A federal judicial body should no more prevent the exercise of local-level sovereignty by striking down such laws, than a federal legislature should seek to occupy the field at their expense.

As we have seen, in the world of the pure theory, freedom of movement is *assumed* for the purpose of setting up the formal economic model. The model does not aim to explain the institutional underpinnings of mobility (such as the

---

[13] L Bebchuck and A Ferrell, 'Federalism and takeover law: the race to protect managers from takeovers' (1999) 99 *Columbia Law Review* 1168.

[14] See generally the essays in D Esty and D Geradin (eds.) *Regulatory Competition and Economic Integration: Comparative Perspectives* (Oxford, OUP, 2001).

[15] Case C-405/98 *Konsumentombudsmannen (KO)* v *Gourmet International Products AB (GIP)*, judgment of 8 March 2001.

[16] Case C-113/89 *Rush Portuguesa Ltd* v. *Office Nationale d'Immigration* [1990] ECR I-1417.

mechanics of the principle of non-discrimination, and the (federal) legislation to facilitate free movement). Instead, the model is aimed at showing that, *given* an effective threat of exit, spontaneous forces would operate in such a way as to discipline states against enacting laws which set an inappropriately high (or low) level of regulation. The model can, however, be used as a benchmark against which to judge institutional measures aimed at instituting regulatory competition. Since, in the 'real' world, mobility of persons and of non-human economic resources is self-evidently more limited than it is in the world of pure theory, two prerequisites for making exit effective may be identified: legal guarantees of freedom of movement for persons and resources, and application of the principle of mutual recognition.[17] In addition, it is accepted that some unwanted side effects of competition ('externalities' or spill-over effects of various kinds) may arise, thereby giving rise to an efficiency-related argument for some harmonisation, although there is in general a presumption against federal intervention and in favour of allowing rules to emerge through the competitive process. Thus the task of analysis, in this approach, becomes that of identifying how far the 'real world' departs from the pure theory, and using legal mechanisms to realign the two.[18] This is the approach to regulatory competition which is generally characterised as *competitive federalism*.

COMPETITIVE FEDERALISM AND MARKET ACCESS IN THE EU

The Logic of Competitive Federalism in the EU

The logic of competitive federalism appears to lend support to a strong, substantive version of market access[19] and to a wide principle of mutual recognition. Legal guarantees of mobility for persons and resources would maximise the disciplinary effects of exit. Hence, a strong version of market access should in principle apply to the right of free movement of persons and to the right of freedom of establishment and to supply services. However, this alone is not sufficient. Even with strong legal guarantees of free movement, linguistic, cultural and other practical 'barriers' to movement on the part of people and organisations could be expected to persist, at least in the context of the EU (by comparison to the culturally more homogenous USA). Nevertheless, migration may still have a powerful effect. It may be sufficient for a few, 'marginal' consumers to make (or be prepared to make) the move in order for a disciplinary effect to arise. Another possibility is 'selective regulatory migration'. This occurs where persons are free to adopt the laws of a particular Member State for selected

---

[17] Mutual recognition is considered further in Kenneth Armstrong's chapter in this volume.
[18] R Van den Bergh, 'The Subsidiarity Principle in European Community Law: Some Insights from Law and Economics' (1994) 1 *Maastricht Journal of European and Comparative Law* 337.
[19] This terminology is explained in detail below in the next sub-section.

purposes. In essence the Delaware effect is an illustration of this—an enterprise can choose to be bound by just one aspect of Delaware law (its corporations law)[20] while remaining subject to the laws of other member states in relation, for example, to employment law or product liability.

In practice, regulatory competition within the EC does not rest on migration alone. Given the practical barriers to free movement within the EC, in general, it is easier (or, less costly) for goods to move to persons rather than the other way round: therefore, free movement of goods acts as a proxy for free movement of persons. Thus the *Cassis de Dijon* principle,[21] by requiring the receiving or 'host state' to open its markets to goods legitimately produced in any other Member State (the 'home state'), provides a vital additional mechanism for subjecting laws to the forces of regulatory competition. This is the essence of 'mutual recognition'. Consumers in the host state now have a choice of goods produced under different regulatory regimes. Competition between *goods* produced under different legal systems means, in effect, that the *laws* of those systems are thrown into competition with each other too.

Nevertheless, if applied without any qualification, there is the danger that mutual recognition would lead to a race to the bottom, and to a deregulation of standards.[22] If State A, with high standards, is obliged to admit goods from State B with low standards, State A could well be forced to lower its standards to enable its national industries to compete with imported goods on its own domestic market and also on foreign markets. Proponents of deregulation might argue that this result is desirable, since it represents a spontaneous outcome driven by the operation of a market for legal rules. However, in a situation where the process was triggered by judicial intervention, the argument for spontaneity is a weak one. Furthermore, such a race risks leading ultimately to uniformity at the bottom. Thus, as we shall see, a strong market access test undermines the possibility for diversity at national level which is considered one of the strengths of competitive federalism.

The danger of a race to the bottom is acknowledged within EC law on free movement. One restraint on race to the bottom is the principle of reverse discrimination. State A can insist that its own manufacturers produce goods to the higher standards for the domestic market while being obliged to admit State B's goods made to a lower standard. Consumers then have the choice to purchase the cheaper, inferior quality goods or the more expensive, superior quality goods.[23]

---

[20] Due to the application of the doctrine of the state of incorporation doctrine.

[21] Case 120/78 *Rewe Zentrale v. Bundesmonopolverwaltung fur Branntwein* ('*Cassis de Dijon*') [1979] ECR 649.

[22] For a discussion of this problem in respect of food, see O Brouwer, 'Free Movement of Foodstuffs and Quality Requirements: Has the Commission got it Wrong?' (1988) 25 *CMLRev* 237, 248–252.

[23] This is the basis for the TV without Frontiers Directive 89/552 OJ [1989] L 298/23 as amended by Directive 97/36 OJ [1997] L202/60. This issue is considered in detail in M Dougan, 'Minimum Harmonisation and the Internal Market' (2000) 37 *CMLRev* 845, 867.

Stronger protection against a race to the bottom is derived from the presence of justifying factors for state-level laws, such as the derogations provided for in the Treaty and the 'mandatory requirements' discussed in *Cassis de Dijon* and the subsequent case-law.[24] The mandatory requirements idea, and its equivalents in the cases of freedom of movement of workers and services and freedom of establishment, allow Member States themselves to set a 'floor' to the competitive process, subject, however, to the need to satisfy a 'rule of reason' test combined with the concept of proportionality. The mandatory requirements principle allows a degree of autonomy in national law-making to be preserved and sets some ground rules for regulatory competition, without the need to resort to centralised standard-setting through harmonisation. However, the success of this approach depends on how, in practice, the principle is interpreted and applied. If it is applied too strongly, Member States will use mandatory requirements as a cover for laws protecting local interests against competition. If it is interpreted too loosely, a court-induced race to the bottom may still ensue.

How far, then, do the current EC rules on free movement match up to the logic of competitive federalism? In practice, two issues must be resolved. The first relates to the notion of 'access to the market'. Is access to be understood in a formal sense or a substantive sense? The second issue concerns justifications and derogations. We ask how far will the Court allow a Member State to take advantage of a justifying factor, and how stringently it will review the national measure in question by reference to the proportionality test. We now turn to a more detailed examination of these questions, beginning with the concept of market access.

Formal v. substantive access to the market

Tests for determining access to the market can be either formal or substantive. By formal market access, we mean a test which asks whether the formal conditions of entry and exit are met. If any such formal barriers exist they must be removed. Thus, according to the formal market access approach it is sufficient that the goods be allowed onto the foreign market, irrespective of how difficult it is in practice for those goods actually to be sold once they have gained access to that market. By contrast, the substantive sense of the notion of market access focuses on these very practical difficulties experienced once the goods have penetrated the market, and requires that these too be eliminated. To give an example, the formal approach to market access would require a German rule banning the importation of French Cassis into Germany to be struck down. The substantive approach would require not only formal access of French Cassis to

---

[24] See further chapter 10 in this volume by Joanne Scott.

the market (the removal of the import ban) but also, potentially, the elimination of any quality requirements that the French Cassis would have to comply with.

We suggest that it is possible to detect in the Court of Justice's jurisprudence, albeit not clearly articulated, a spectrum of possibilities between these two senses of the test.

Category 1: substantive access required, discrimination irrelevant

At one end of the spectrum there are cases in which the Court favours a strong version of market access, according to which all goods and persons should have substantive, and not simply formal, access to the markets in other Member States. Any national regulation which impedes market access is contrary to the Treaty. This version of market access does not depend on showing any form of discrimination. As Advocate General Jacobs said in *Leclerc*:[25]

> a test of discrimination . . . seems inappropriate. The central concern of the Treaty provisions on the free movement of goods is to prevent unjustified obstacles to trade between Member States. If an obstacle to inter-state trade exists, it cannot cease to exist simply because an identical obstacle affects domestic trade.[26]

With this substantive approach, the emphasis is on direct and substantial hindrance to market access.

This approach can be seen particularly clearly in the cases of *Bosman*[27] and *Alpine Investments*.[28] When considering the rules concerning transfer fees in *Bosman*, the Court said:

> It is sufficient to note that, although the rules in issue in the main proceedings apply also to transfers between clubs belonging to different national associations within the same Member State and are similar to those governing transfers between clubs belonging to the same national association, *they still directly affect players' access to the employment market in other Member States and are thus capable of impeding freedom of movement for workers*. (emphasis added).

In *Alpine*, a case concerning a ban on cold calling in the financial services industry, the Court, having noted that the measure was non-discriminatory, said the national measure '*directly affects access to the markets in services in the other Member States* and is thus capable of hindering intra-Community trade in

---

[25] Case C-412/93 *Leclerc-Siplec* v. *TF1 Publicité* [1995] ECR I-179.
[26] Para.39. See also AG Lenz in Case C-391/92 *Commission* v. *Greece* [1995] ECR I-1621, para.14 'Article 30 [new Article 28] goes beyond a mere prohibition of discrimination . . . The aim of Article 30 continues to be to prohibit such measures in order to establish and maintain an internal market'.
[27] Case C-415/93 *Bosman* v *ASBL* [1995] ECR I-4921.
[28] Case C-384/93 *Alpine Investments* v *Minister van Financiën* [1995] ECR I-1141.

services' (emphasis added).[29] Similarly, in *Schindler*[30] the Court ruled that while a ban on holding national lotteries was non-discriminatory,[31] foreign service providers were denied access to a new market from which they could gain new customers. In all three cases, the burden of demonstrating the existence of a justifying factor then passed to the defendant, usually the Member State.

Centros[32] can also be understood as a case in which the Court struck down a rule on the grounds that it *substantively* impeded market access. Here, a Danish company registrar refused to register a branch of Centros Ltd., a company incorporated in the UK, so as to enable it to carry on business in Denmark. At first sight, this looks like a clear case of *formal* access being denied, the access being that of Centros Ltd. to the Danish market. What was really at stake, though, was the access of Mr. and Mrs. Bryde, the founders of Centros Ltd., to incorporation procedures of UK company law. The Brydes incorporated Centros Ltd. in England for the purpose of avoiding the Danish law relating to minimum capital requirements for privately-held companies. Apparently they never intended that Centros Ltd. would trade in the UK. This was the reason given by the company registrar for his decision; to allow Centros Ltd. to trade in Denmark would be to condone an abuse of Danish company legislation.

In finding that the registrar's decision contravened the principle of freedom of establishment under Article 43 (subject to the possibility of justification), the Court assumed that a *substantive* barrier to the exercise by Mr. and Mrs. Bryde of the right to incorporate their business in the UK was sufficient for it to intervene. Thus, this was not a case of a formal barrier to access. The Brydes were not formally prevented from incorporating Centros Ltd. in the UK. It was simply that the decision to deny them the right to trade through Centros Ltd. in Denmark removed the (substantive) benefit of doing so. Nor was *Centros* a case in which a test of non-discrimination was applied. *Centros*, then, is not the equivalent for freedom of establishment of the *Cassis de Dijon* test of mutual recognition in respect of free movement of goods; it goes beyond *Cassis de Dijon* by adopting a test of market access which is at the category one, extreme end of the approaches adopted by the Court.

The substantive approach to market access guarantees maximum exit, or at least the threat of exit, which provides one of the conditions for the operation of competitive federalism. At the same time, the substantive approach is potentially the most damaging for maintaining national diversity (and the processes of national, democratic law-making)[33] since it requires the removal of the

---

[29] Para.38. It then went on to hold that the national measure could be justified under 'imperative reasons of the public interest' such as 'maintaining the good reputation of the national financial sector' and that the ban on cold-calling was proportionate.

[30] Case C-275/92 *Customs & Excise v. Schindler* [1994] ECR 1039.

[31] Para.53.

[32] *Centros v. Erhvers- og Selskabsstyrelsen* [1999] ECR-I 1459

[33] For a consideration of the US literature on this issue, see L Tribe, *American Constitutional Law*, vol.1, (New York, Foundation Press, 2000), 1052.

national measure which impedes market access. Perhaps for this reason, it is often coupled with a generous approach to the definition of justifying factors, as we shall see in more detail below.[34]

Category 2: substantive access and a discrimination test, with a presumption of hindrance to market access

One step down from category 1 are cases where the Court applies the discrimination test and assumes that if there has been discrimination (direct or indirect) then there has been a hindrance of market access which needs to be justified. This category covers the majority of (older) cases decided on free movement of goods and persons.[35] In the context of goods, the requirement of market access underpins the *Dassonville*[36] formula which defines measures having equivalent effect. The Court said:

> All trading rules enacted by Member States which are capable of hindering, directly or indirectly, actually or potentially, intra-Community trade are to be considered as measures having an effect equivalent to quantitative restrictions.

The point is reinforced in *Rau*.[37] Once the Court had identified that the national restriction (*in casu* that margarine should be packed in cubed-shaped containers) was an indistinctly applicable measure having equivalent effect, it said:

> Although the requirement that a particular form of packaging must also be used for imported products is not an absolute barrier to the importation into the Member State concerned of products originating in other Member States, nevertheless it is of such a nature as to render the marketing of those products more difficult or more expensive either by barring them from certain channels of distribution or owing to the additional costs brought about by the necessity to package the products in question in special packs which comply with the requirements in force on the market of their destination.[38]

It then considered whether the restriction could be justified.

Thus, these cases concern measures which are *per se* illegal: there is a presumption that the national measure constitutes a barrier to market access.[39] Underpinning these cases is a strong sense of mutual recognition: that goods

---

[34] See pp 213–218.
[35] For references see Barnard, above n.1 pp 36–37.
[36] Case 8/74 *Procureur du Roi* v. *Dassonville* [1974] ECR 837, para.5.
[37] Case 261/81 *Walter Rau* v. *De Smedt* [1982] ECR 3961.
[38] Para.13.
[39] See AG Jacobs in Case C-412/93 *Leclerc* [1995] ECR I-179, para.44 where he said that where a national measure 'prohibits the sale of goods lawfully placed on the market in another Member State (as in *Cassis de Dijon*), it may be presumed to have a substantial impact on access to the market, since the goods are either denied access altogether or can gain access only after being modified in some way; the need to modify goods is itself a substantial barrier to market access'.

(qualifications, services) produced in one Member State are capable of being sold in another Member State. While beneficial for encouraging regulatory competition, these cases again can have negative implications for national autonomy and for the preservation of state-level regulations, threatening a race to the bottom. Moreover, where discrimination is present, unlike in category 1 (above), the Court tends to take a stricter line on justification, particularly in the fields of goods, workers and establishment.[40]

Category 3: a discrimination test, but no presumption of hindrance to market access

A further step down are cases in which the Court presumes that there is no hindrance to market access unless discrimination can be shown. This approach can be seen in respect of *discriminatory* selling arrangements. In *De Agostini*[41] the Court considered a Swedish ban on television advertising directed at children under 12 and a ban on misleading commercials for skincare products. It said that 'it cannot be excluded that an outright ban, applying in one Member State, of a type of promotion for a product which is lawfully sold there might have a greater impact on products from other Member States' (paragraph 42). It continued that while the efficacy of various types of promotion was a question of fact to be determined by the national court, 'it is to be noted that in its observations De Agostini stated that television advertising was the only effective form of sales promotion enabling it to penetrate the Swedish market since it had no other advertising methods for reaching children and their parents'.[42] The Court continued that if such an unequal burden in law or fact was found then the national restriction was caught by Article 28 and the burden shifted to the Member State to justify it under principles similar to those in *Cassis de Dijon*.

Again, in *GIP*,[43] the Court said that a ban on advertising (this time of alcoholic drinks) was 'liable to impede access to the market by products from other Member States more than it impedes access to domestic products, with which consumers are instantly more familiar'.[44] It was therefore caught by Article 28. It was for the national court to decide whether the public health derogation contained in Article 30 could be 'ensured by measures having less effect on intra-Community trade'.

De Agostini and *GIP*[45] suggest that in the case of discriminatory selling arrangements there is a presumption that there is no hindrance of access to the

---

[40] See further pp 213–218.
[41] Joined Cases C-34-36/95 *Konsumentombudsmannen* v *De Agostini* [1997] ECR I-3843.
[42] Para.43.
[43] Case C-405/98 *Konsumentombudsmannen (KO)* v *Gourmet International Products AB (GIP)*, judgment of 8 March 2001.
[44] Para.21.
[45] See also Case C-254/98 *Schutzverband gegen unlauteren Wettbewerb* v. *TK-Heimdienst Sass GmbH*, judgment of 13 January 2000, considered below.

market[46] and the national regulation should be allowed to stand (a *per se* legal approach).[47] The trader will then need to work hard to rebut this presumption, possibly by producing actual statistical or other evidence (as in *De Agostini*),[48] to show that there has been an impact on his access to the market.

Thus, according to this (category three) approach, in order to preserve national diversity of regulatory standards, the market access test should mean that only discriminatory restrictions, namely directly or indirectly discriminatory measures (those having a different burden in law and fact or the same burden in law and different burden in fact), should be prohibited unless saved by a derogation or a mandatory requirement. Non-discriminatory measures (those having an equal burden in law and in fact) which do not hinder access to the market (see category 4 below), by contrast, should not be subject to the review of the Court.

One drawback of this approach is that litigants will increasingly argue for a broad construction of the concept of indirect discrimination to ensure that the contested national measure is in principle caught by the Treaty and subject to review by the Court. This had already begun to happen in the pre-*Keck* Sunday trading cases where B&Q argued that the ban on Sunday trading had a greater impact in fact on foreign goods since more foreign goods than domestic goods were sold on Sundays.[49]

Category 4: formal access test

At the other end of the spectrum are cases in which the Court applies a weak form of the market access test—what we term formal market access—without even getting to the stage of considering justifying factors. *Keck*[50] and *Graf*[51] provide examples of this approach. In *Keck*[52] the Court ruled that

---

[46] See AG Fennelly in Case C-190/98 *Graf* v. *Filzmozer Maschinenbau GmbH* [2000] ECR I-493, para.19 'It is legitimate for the Court to develop presumptions about the market effects of different broadly defined categories of rules, provided that, in concrete cases, the validity of the presumption may be tested against the underlying criterion of market access, rather than automatically being taken as being sufficient in itself to dispose of the case.'

[47] See K Armstrong, 'Regulating the free movement of goods' in J Shaw and G More (eds) *New Legal Dynamics of European Union*, (Oxford, Clarendon, 1996).

[48] As the Court said in Joined Cases C-34-36/95 *De Agostini* [1997] ECR I-3843, 'an outright ban', applying in one Member State, on advertising certain products which are lawfully sold there would fall within Article 30 (new Article 28), if it could be shown to have a 'greater impact on products from other Member States' (para.42).

[49] See, e.g. Case 145/88 *Torfaen BC* v *B&Q* [1989] ECR 765 discussed in C Barnard, 'Sunday Trading: A Drama in Five Acts', (1994) 57 *MLR* 449.

[50] Joined Cases C-267/91 and C-268/91 *Keck and Mithouard* [1993] ECR I-6097.

[51] Case C-190/98 *Graf* v. *Filzmozer Maschinenbau GmbH* [2000] ECR I-493.

[52] Joined Cases C-267/91 and C-268/91 *Keck and Mithouard* [1993] ECR I-6097. For comments on this case, see *inter alia* Roth, 'Comment' (1994) 31 *CMLRev*. 845; CELS Treaty project (1997) 22 *ELRev*. 447–452; D Chalmers, 'Repackaging the internal market: the ramifications of the *Keck* judgment' (1994) 19 *ELRev* 385; L Gormley, 'Reasoning renounced? The remarkable judgment in

non-discriminatory restrictions on 'certain selling arrangements' did not breach Article 28 provided the conditions laid down in paragraph 16 were satisfied.[53] The Court said, in paragraph 17, that such measures were not 'by nature such as to prevent their [foreign goods'] access to the market or to impede access any more than it impedes the access of domestic products'.[54] A major difficulty with this ruling is both the extreme formalism involved in singling out the special category of 'selling arrangements'[55] and the assertion in paragraph 17 that certain selling arrangements did not prevent access to the market: certain non-discriminatory selling arrangements, such as a total ban on the sale of a particular product such as cigarettes, pornography, alcohol or illegal drugs,[56] *can* be viewed as preventing access to the market. Nevertheless, the Court has applied the ruling with enthusiasm.[57]

Graf concerned a German national who had worked for his Austrian employer for four years when he terminated his contract in order to take up employment in Germany. Under Austrian law, a worker who had worked for the same employer for more than three years was entitled to compensation when his employment came to an end, subject to a proviso to the effect that the right would be forfeited if the employment was terminated on the worker's own initiative (ie if the worker resigned, as opposed to being dismissed). Graf argued that the proviso contravened Article 39 because it constituted an obstacle to the free movement of workers. The Court disagreed. It said that the Austrian law was genuinely non-discriminatory and that:

> . . . it was not such as to preclude or deter a worker from ending his contract of employment in order to take a job with another employer, because the entitlement to compensation on termination of employment is not dependent on the worker's choosing whether or not to stay with his current employer but on a future and hypothetical event, namely the subsequent termination of his contract without such termination being at his own initiative or attributable to him.

Keck and Mithouard [1994] *EurBusLRev* 63; M Poiares Maduro, '*Keck*: the end? Or just the end of the beginning?' (1994) *Irish J of Eur Law* 33 and 'Reforming the Market or the State? Article 30 and the European Constitution: Economic Freedom and Political Rights' (1997) 3 *ELJ* 55.

[53] Para.16 provides: 'However, contrary to what has previously been decided, the application to products from other Member States of national provisions restricting or prohibiting certain selling arrangements is not such as to hinder, directly or indirectly, actually or potentially, trade between Member States within the meaning of the *Dassonville* judgment (. . .) provided that those provisions apply to all affected traders operating within the national territory and provided that they affect in the same manner, in law and in fact, the marketing of domestic products and those from other Member States.'

[54] Para.17.

[55] See Barnard, above, n.1.

[56] Cf Case 34/79 *Henn and Darby* [1979] ECR 3795 concerned a total ban on the *importation* (as opposed to the sale) of products (*in casu* pornographic literature). This was found to be a quantitative restriction on imports within the meaning of Article 30 (new Art.28).

[57] See, e.g. Case C-292/92 *Hünermund* [1993] ECR I-6787; Case C-412/93 *Leclerc-Siplec v. TF1 Publicité* [1995] ECR I-179.

Such an event is *too uncertain and indirect* a possibility for legislation to be capable of being regarded as *liable to hinder* free movement for workers where it does not attach to termination of a contract of employment by the worker himself the same consequence as it attaches to termination which was not at his initiative or is not attributable to him. . . [58]

From these cases it can be seen that the goods in *Keck* had formal access to the French market; and the worker in *Graf* had formal access both to the German and Austrian labour markets. What the individuals were complaining about was more substantive impediments to their market access. In both cases such complaints fell on deaf ears. Hence in neither case could the applicants challenge the substance of the national legislation in question.

In *Graf*, the distinction between formal and substantive notions of access is made particularly clear in the Opinion of Advocate General Fennelly. He noted that, in *Bosman*, the Court had applied a test of whether 'provisions . . . preclude or deter a national of a Member State from leaving his country of origin in order to exercise his right to freedom of movement', and that in *Gebhard*[59] the Court had talked of 'national measures liable to hinder or make less attractive the exercise of fundamental freedoms guaranteed by the Treaty'. He, nevertheless, argued that these tests related 'solely to the sorts of formal conditions of access to the employment market which were at issue in those . . . cases'. He favoured a test under which

> neutral national rules could only be deemed to constitute material barriers to market access, if it were established that they had actual effects on market actors akin to exclusion from the market. As in the case of rules regarding selling arrangements in the case of goods, there can be no presumption that neutral national commercial regulations, or those governing pay scales, social protection and other matters of concern to workers, have this effect.

As we have seen, the Court in *Graf*, relying on a number of pre-*Keck* cases, identified certain effects which were 'too uncertain and indirect' to hinder free movement of persons. Thus, the national employment legislation in question did not fall under the scrutiny of EC law and national diversity was maintained. One aspect of *Graf* is that the rule in question was regarded as applying in a non-discriminatory manner. In *Keck*, also, the Court identified

[58] Paras. 24–25. Emphasis added. For another example of a case concerning absence of hindrance of market access, or, to be precise where the hindrance to market access is inherent in the structure of the market itself, see Joined Cases C-51/96 and C-191/97 *Deliège* v *Asbl Ligue Francophone de Judo*, judgment of 11 April 2000, para.64 'although selection rules like those at issue in the main proceedings inevitably have the effect of limiting the number of participants in a tournament, such a limitation is inherent in the conduct of an international high-level sports event, which necessarily involves certain selection rules or criteria being adopted. Such rules may not therefore in themselves be regarded as constituting a restriction on the freedom to provide services prohibited by Article 59 [Article 49] of the Treaty'.
[59] Case C-55/94 *Gebhard* v *Consiglio dell'Ordine degli Avvocati e Procuratori di Milano* [1995] ECR I-4165 (establishment of German lawyer in Italy wishing to use the name *avvocato*).

non-discriminatory certain selling arrangements as another area which would never be subject to review. As Advocate General Tesauro noted in *Hünermund*,[60] the purpose of the Community rules in respect of the free movement of goods was to liberalise *inter-state* trade and not to encourage the unhindered pursuit of commerce in the individual Member States. In these cases, then, the Court accepted that provided formal access to the market was permitted, it would not review other measures which might (more substantively) hinder market access.

What marks out *Graf* and *Keck* as cases in which a test of formal market access was appropriate? We have already noted the unsatisfactory aspects of the 'selling arrangements' concept used in *Keck*. In *Graf*, as we have seen, the Court concluded that any negative effect of the rule being challenged was too 'uncertain and indirect', a formula which itself does little to dispel uncertainty. The Court argued that since it was uncertain that Graf would have received compensation upon the termination of employment in any event, for him to lose it by resigning his job to take up an employment in another Member State could not be said to be a sufficient deterrent to freedom of movement. This prompts the question of what the Court would have decided had it been clearer that Graf would otherwise have qualified for compensation. A rule which was discriminatory or which was non-discriminatory but substantially hindered access to the market would have been subjected to closer scrutiny.

However, what more clearly sets *Graf* aside from decisions such as *Centros* is that Graf was claiming, in effect, for a kind of levelling up of labour standards. The logic of his claim was that the standards of employment protection operating under the Austrian law on termination of employment should be *raised* in such a way as to make it easier for workers to exercise rights of entry and exit. If this principle had been accepted, an inverted form of mutual recognition would have been established, under which Member States would have been required to come up to the standards of the most protective jurisdiction in relation to the treatment of migrant workers. It is not surprising that the Court, faced with the invitation to initiate a forced 'race to the top', declined to do so, stressing instead the autonomy of Member States in the labour law field. However, the resulting stress on formal access as the relevant test stands in stark contrast to the emphasis, in *Centros*, on ensuring that the substantive freedom of movement was protected.

In comparing *Centros* and *Graf*, it is difficult to avoid the conclusion that the Court was content to accept a test of substantive market access when it came to striking down national level regulation, only to revert to a test of formal access when it would have had the effect of requiring Member States to level up to a higher degree of social protection. Hence the difficulty with

---

[60] See AG Tesauro's opinion in Case C-292/92 *Hünermund* [1993] ECR I-6787 which seems to have influenced the Court more in *Keck* than that of AG Van Gerven, the Advocate General in *Keck*.

an open-ended, substantive market access test is that, in the words of Advocate General Fennelly, it will be 'exploited as a means of challenging any national rules whose effect is simply to limit commercial freedom'.[61] By contrast, a more restrictive, formal access test has the merit of protecting national legislative autonomy: goods have access to the French market but they cannot be resold at a loss and workers can work in Austria and Germany but they cannot challenge the validity of national employment legislation under EC law.

To sum up the argument so far: the crucial determinants of a market access test are whether access is defined formally or substantively, and whether discrimination between nationals of the host state and those of other Member States is required for the Court's intervention to be triggered. Across the range of free movement cases, we find surprisingly little consistency in the approach of the Court; its decisions range all the way from those in which a substantive access test is coupled with the absence of a discrimination requirement, to those in which a formal access test is adopted. These cases may be explained in part by historical accident and their place in the development of a complex jurisprudence by the Court of Justice. Nevertheless, such explanations do not help with clarity. This uncertainty is compounded when we look more closely at the Court's approach to the application of justifying factors.

Justifying factors

As we have seen, if a substantive market access test is adopted (categories one to three), the focus shifts to justification. In effect, while there is a presumption in favour of market access, this can be rebutted by the Member State demonstrating an overriding national or pubic interest. This was of course the essence of the decision in *Cassis de Dijon*. Having established the principle of mutual recognition, the Court said:

> Obstacles to movement in the Community resulting from disparities between the national laws relating to the marketing of the products in question must be accepted in so far as those provisions may be recognised as being necessary in order to satisfy mandatory requirements relating in particular to the effectiveness of fiscal supervision, the protection of public health, the fairness of commercial transactions and the defence of the consumer.[62]

---

[61] Case C-190/98 *Graf* [2000] ECR I-493, Opinion, at para 32.
[62] Para.8. In addition the Court has recognised the following mandatory requirements: Case 155/80 *Oebel* [1981] ECR 3409 (protection of the working environment); Case 60/84 *Cinethèque* [1985] ECR 2605 (cinema as form of cultural expression); Case 145/88 *Torfaen Borough Council v. B & Q* [1989] ECR 3851 (protection of national or regional socio-cultural characteristics); Case C-368/95 *Vereinigte Familiapress Zeitungsverlags- und vertriebs GmbH ('Familiapress') v Heinrich Bauer Verlag* [1997] ECR I-3689 (maintenance of the plurality of the press); Case 302/86 *Commission v.*

In the context of services, the Court has adopted a similar approach. In *Gouda*[63] the Court said that national restrictions come

> within the scope of Article 59 [new Article 49] if the application of the national legislation to foreign persons providing services is not justified by overriding reasons relating to the public interest or if the requirements embodied in that legislation are already satisfied by the rules imposed on those persons in the Member States in which they are established.[64]

The Court has recognised a much longer and fuller list of justifications in the context of workers and services[65] than in goods[66] and is more lenient in their application in respect of the more sensitive types of services.[67] For example, in *Schindler*[68] the Court had to consider the UK's justifications on a ban on holding national lotteries. The UK pointed to its concerns about preventing crime and avoiding stimulating the gambling sector with damaging social consequences—all this at a time when the National Lotteries Act 1993 had been passed, a fact the Court had noted.[69] Nevertheless, the Court accepted these arguments at face value. It said:

Denmark [1988] ECR 4607 and Case C-389/96 *Aher-Waggon GmbH v. Germany* [1998] ECR I-4473; Case C-120/95 *Decker v Caisse de Maladie des Employés Privés* [1998] ECR I-1831 (preventing the risk of seriously undermining the financial balance of the social security system).

[63] Case C-288/89 *Stichting Collectieve Antennevoorziening Gouda v Commissariaat voor de Media* [1991] ECR I-4007.

[64] Paras.12–13.

[65] See e.g., Case C-288/89 *Gouda* [1991] ECR I-4007 citing professional rules intended to protect the recipients of a service—Cases 110/78 and 111/78 *Van Wesemael* [1979] ECR 35; protection of intellectual property—Case 62/79 *Coditel* [1980] ECR 881; protection of workers—Case 279/80 *Webb* [1981] ECR 3305; consumer protection—Case C-180/89 *Commission v Italy (Tourist Guides)* [1991] ECR I-709, Joined Cases C-34/95, C-35/95 and C-36/95 *De Agostini* [1997] ECR I-I-3843; conservation of the national historic and artistic heritage—Case C-180/89 *Commission v Italy*; turning to account the archaeological, historical and artistic heritage of a country and the widest possible dissemination of knowledge of the artistic and cultural heritage of a country—Case C-154/89 *Commission v France* [1991] ECR I-659, Case C-198/89 *Commission v Greece* [1991] ECR I-727, Case C-23/93 *TV10* [1994] ECR I-4795. In addition, the Court has recognised the need to safeguard the reputation of the Netherlands financial markets and to protect the investing public—Case C-384/93 *Alpine Investments* [1995] ECR I-1141; preventing gambling and avoiding the lottery from becoming the source of private profit—Case C-275/92 *Schindler* [1994] ECR 1039; avoiding the risk of crime or fraud—Case C-275/92 *Schindler* [1994] ECR 1039; avoiding the risk of incitement to spend, with damaging individual and social consequences—Case C-275/92 *Schindler* [1994] ECR 1039; requirements of road safety—Case C-55/93 *Van Schaik* [1994] ECR I-4837; the social protection of workers in the construction industry—Case C-272/94 *Guiot* [1996] ECR I-1905 and Joined Case C-369/96 *Criminal Proceedings against Arblade* [1999] ECR I-8453; and the protection of creditors of a company against the risk of insolvency—Case C-212/97 *Centros v. Erhvers- og Selskabsstyrelsen* [1999] ECR-I 1459, at para.34. See also V. Hatzopoulos, 'Recent Developments of the Case Law of the ECJ in the Field of Services' (2000) 37 *CMLRev* 43, 77.

[66] Case 120/78 *Rewe Zentrale v. Bundesmonopolverwaltung fur Branntwein ('Cassis de Dijon')* [1979] ECR 649.

[67] See C Hilson, 'Discrimination in Community Free Movement Law' (1999) 24 *ELRev* 445, 461.

[68] Case C-275/92 *Schindler* [1994] ECR I-1039, para.61.

[69] See, eg, para.51.

Those particular factors justify national authorities having a sufficient degree of latitude to determine what is required to protect the players and, more generally, in the light of the specific social and cultural features of each Member State, to maintain order in society, as regards the manner in which lotteries are operated, the size of the stakes, and the allocation of the profits they yield. In those circumstances, it is for them to assess not only whether it is necessary to restrict the activities of lotteries but also whether they should be prohibited, provided that those restrictions are not discriminatory.[70]

In goods, by contrast, the Court usually gives short shrift to arguments based on the national need to ensure consumer protection or public health. It either finds that there is no such interest or, despite the fact that the case involves a preliminary reference, that the interest can be protected in a more proportionate manner.[71] Thus, in *Heimdienst*[72] the Court considered national legislation under which bakers, butchers and grocers could

> make sales on rounds in a given administrative district, such as an Austrian Verwaltungsbezirk, only if they also trade from a permanent establishment in that administrative district or an adjacent municipality where they offer for sale the same goods as they do on rounds.

Having noted that the measure concerned a certain selling arrangement, the Court said that the national rule 'in fact impedes access to the market of the Member State of importation for products from other Member States more than it impedes access for domestic products'[73] and thus breached Article 28. It then considered whether the national legislation could be justified under *Cassis de Dijon*-type mandatory requirements such as the need 'to avoid deterioration in the conditions under which goods are supplied at short distance in relatively isolated areas of a Member State'. On the facts it found that the objective could be obtained by measures that had effects less restrictive of intra-Community trade such as by rules on refrigerating equipment in the vehicles used.

In respect of workers, the Court has also taken a restrictive approach to justification. For example, in *Bosman* the Court recognised that non-discriminatory measures could be objectively justified but adopted a rigorous

---

[70] In Case C-124/97 *Läärä* [1999] ECR I-6067, para.36 the Court added that 'the mere fact that a Member State has opted for a system of protection which differs from that adopted by another Member State cannot affect the assessment of the need for, and proportionality of, the provisions enacted to that end. Those provisions must be assessed solely by reference to the objectives pursued by the national authorities of the Member State concerned and the level of protection which they are intended to provide'. This is a departure from the 'majoritarianism' identified by M Poiares Maduro, *We, the Court* (Oxford, Hart, 1998), 72 which has characterised many of the decisions on goods.

[71] Generally labelling is the most proportionate solution: e.g Case 286/86 *Minstère Public v Deserbais* [1988] ECR 4907; Case C-358/95 *Tommaso Morellato v Unità sanitaria locale (USL) n. 11 di Pordenone* [1997] ECR I-1431.

[72] Case C-254/98 *Schutzverband gegen unlauteren Wettbewerb v. TK-Heimdienst Sass GmbH* [2000] ECR I-151.

[73] Para.[54]. Emphasis added.

approach to the various justifications put forward by the football associations. For example, the football associations argued that in view of the considerable social importance of sporting activities, particularly football, in the Community, the aims of maintaining a balance between the clubs by preserving a certain degree of equality and uncertainty as to results and of encouraging the recruitment and training of young players had to be accepted as legitimate. However, the Court, while recognizing that some form of regulation was legitimate, supported Bosman's contention that the application of the transfer rules was not an adequate means of maintaining financial and competitive balance in the world of football. Those rules neither precluded the richest clubs from securing the services of the best players nor prevented the availability of financial resources from being a decisive factor in competitive sport, thus considerably altering the balance between clubs.[74]

The Court is also rigorous in its approach to justification in respect of establishment. In *Centros*, the Court, having found that the case fell within the freedom of establishment principle, then went on to consider whether the Danish government could show that the refusal to register the branch was justifiable in the circumstances. The Danish government argued that the registrar's action was intended to maintain Danish law's minimum capital requirement for the formation of private companies. The purpose of this law was:

> first, to reinforce the financial soundness of those companies in order to protect public creditors against the risk of seeing the public debts owing to them become irrecoverable since, unlike private creditors, they cannot secure these debts by means of guarantees and, second, and more generally, to protect all creditors, public and private, by anticipating the risk of fraudulent bankruptcy due to the insolvency of companies whose initial capitalisation was inadequate.[75]

The Court ruled that the justification offered was inadequate since, in the first place, 'the practice in question is not such as to attain the objective of protecting creditors which it purports to pursue since, if the company concerned had conducted business in the United Kingdom, its branch would have been registered in Denmark, even though Danish creditors might have been equally exposed to risk'.[76] In other words, the registrar's decision failed the proportionality test since it was inconsistent—the vital factor in his refusal was, it seems, the failure of the company to trade in the UK, but this was immaterial to the protection of creditors since they would have been no better off if the company had previously traded and, as a result, had been able to get its branch registered in Denmark.[77]

---

[74] Para.218.

[75] *Centros*, para. 32.

[76] Ibid., para. 35.

[77] For criticism of this aspect of the Court's reasoning in *Centros*, see S Deakin, 'Two types of regulatory competition: competitive federalism versus reflexive harmonisation. A law and economics perspective on *Centros*' (1999) 2 *Cambridge Yearbook of European Legal Studies* (Oxford, Hart Publishing, 2000) 231.

There is a paradox in the Court's approach to justifications. The theory of competitive federalism places emphasis on the need for persons to gain unrestricted access to other national markets to ensure that competition between legal systems functions effectively. According to the model, this would suggest a substantive approach to market access combined with restricted use of the justifications by the Member States. As we have seen, however, this might produce the most damaging effects on the diversity of national laws. Given the low numbers of people taking advantage of the free movement rules, for the reasons outlined above, this model (substantive approach to market access and restricted use of justifications) might be a price worth paying to ensure the successful functioning of regulatory competition. The approach adopted by the Court in the context of free movement of workers and establishment could be justified by this kind of logic. By contrast, since goods are more mobile than persons, there is less of a need for a substantive approach to market access in relation to free movement of goods and greater scope for a more lenient approach to the use of justifications by the Member States to preserve national regulatory diversity. However, as we have seen, the Court's case law tends towards the opposite result: it adopts a *restrictive* approach to the use of the justifications by the Member States in the context of *goods*,[78] while allowing the Member States considerable *latitude* in raising public interest requirements in the context of *services*. This difference in approach might be explained on political rather than economic grounds. It is often difficult for the receiving state to control the activities of a temporary service provider. On the other hand, in the case of certain non-discriminatory selling arrangements the Court has identified an area in which national regulatory autonomy is preserved and protected entirely from judicial review. Although the precise reasoning used to do this in the *Keck* case has been much criticised, the approach taken by the Court makes sense according to the logic of regulatory competition which we have just outlined.

Nevertheless, when a substantive test of market access is coupled with a restrictive reading of justifying factors, as in *Centros, Heimdienst* or *Bosman*, the likely result is a strong push from the Court in the direction of deregulation. While it is possible to construct an argument for deregulation within the EU,[79] it is also possible to put the opposite point of view, in favour of the maintenance

---

[78] Even where the Court accepts that there is a public interest at stake the Court will apply the principle of mutual recognition: Case 272/80 *Frans-Nederlandse Maatschappij voor Biolgishche Producten* [1981] ECR 3277. See also Case C-292/94 *Criminal Proceedings against Brandsma* [1996] ECR I-2159 the Court said that while the host state is entitled to require the product to undergo a fresh examination (a system of double checks), the host state authorities are not entitled unnecessarily to require technical or chemical analyses or laboratory tests where those analyses or tests have already been carried out in another Member State and their results are available to the host state authorities. The Court also applies this approach to the freedom to provide services: the host state can impose additional requirements on the migrant service provider only where the host state's national interest is not already protected from the state of establishment Case C-288/89 *Gouda* [1991] ECR I-4007.

[79] See M Streit and W Mussler 'The Economic Constitution of the European Community: from "Rome" to "Maastricht"' (1995) 1 *ELJ* 5.

of high regulatory standards;[80] either way, the case should be argued on its merits and not dressed up in the language of market integration. This is one difficulty with the model of competitive federalism, but it is not the only one. Competitive federalism threatens to induce not so much a race to the top or to the bottom, but *a race to uniformity* which will undermine the benefits, in terms of diversity and experimentation, which regulatory competition is intended to capture, without guaranteeing that the result will necessarily be efficient.

This, above all, is the lesson of Delaware. It is extremely difficult to judge whether or not the substance of Delaware law is more or less efficient than feasible alternatives. What is clear, however, is that the success of Delaware has spawned numerous imitators, and that a high degree of uniformity in the law of the individual states has resulted from the state competition to attract incorporations. This is in contrast to the diversity which continues to characterise European company law systems.[81] The paradox of competitive federalism, at least in its stronger forms, it that it undermines the possibility for diversity and hence for experimentation which is said to be one of the advantages of a market for legal rules over a system based on harmonisation of standards. It may be that, if diversity is to be preserved, limits must be placed on the market access principle. But this need not imply the end of regulatory competition, as the next section shows.

REFLEXIVE HARMONISATION AND EXPERIMENTALISM: A MEANS TO BALANCE MARKET INTEGRATION AND NATIONAL DIVERSITY IN THE EU?

The model of competitive federalism is one in which efficient rules are 'selected' through the mechanism of competition between states to attract and retain the factors of production. As we have seen, the conditions under which this market can be said to work perfectly are extremely exacting, and legal intervention is needed to bring about 'second-best' solutions. But while promoting market access, these legal interventions do, in their turn, threaten to undermine one of the other essential conditions for a market in legal rules, namely the possibility of diversity at state level. It is in this context that rules limiting market access may be desirable, at least in the sense of restricting the scope allowed to concepts of substantive market access. Thus, there is a role for the *courts* in ensuring that there is a space in which experimentation can occur. We consider this below. Equally important are regulatory or other legislative mechanisms

---

[80] S Deakin and F Wilkinson, 'Rights versus Efficiency? The Economic Case for Transnational Labour Standards' (1994) 23 *ILJ* 289.

[81] See S. Deakin, 'Regulatory Competition versus Harmonisation in European Company Law' in D Esty and D Geradin (eds.) *Regulatory Competition and Economic Integration: Comparative Perspectives* (Oxford, OUP, 2000).

which aim to preserve spaces for experimentation in rule-making, and which promote regulatory learning through the exchange of information between different jurisdictional levels. This approach, which elsewhere we have termed 'reflexive harmonisation',[82] can be seen operating in several contexts within the EU, most notably in the debate over the harmonisation of labour and company law and in the recent emergence of the 'open method of coordination' (OMC) as a technique of regulation in economic and social policy. We will briefly examine the way reflexive harmonisation works.

A number of economic justifications may be offered for harmonising legislation in the fields of labour and company law.[83] A case can be made for company legislation to establish a core of uniform rules which, because of network externality effects, may save on the transaction costs of company formation and thereby promote cross-border capital mobility. In respect of employment protection, justifications range from the defensive goal of avoiding 'social dumping' to the more proactive goal of promoting the efficient use of labour by ruling out low-productivity strategies of firms engaged in regulatory arbitrage between systems.[84] Directives of this kind have a complex relationship to regulatory competition. They mostly set basic or minimum standards as a 'floor of rights' which Member States must not derogate from, but upon which they may improve by setting superior standards.[85] These interventions, then, can be thought of as implicitly encouraging a 'race to the top', while ruling out less socially desirable forms of competitive federalism. They encourage a process by which rules are selected not on the basis of the threat of exit by the factors of production, but through mutual learning by states: legislators may observe and emulate practices in jurisdictions to which they are closely related by trade and by institutional connections.

In this context, it is not inaccurate to speak of 'reflexive harmonisation' by analogy to the idea of reflexive law.[86] The essence of reflexive law is the acknowledgement that regulatory interventions are most likely to be successful when they seek to achieve their ends not by direct prescription, but by inducing 'second-order effects' on the part of social actors. In other words, this approach aims to 'couple' external regulation with self-regulatory processes. Reflexive law therefore has a *procedural orientation*. What this means, in the context of economic regulation, is that the preferred mode of intervention is for the law to underpin and encourage autonomous processes of adjustment, in particular by

---

[82] See S Deakin, ibid.; S Deakin and C Barnard, 'In Search of Coherence: Social Policy, the Single Market and Fundamental Rights' (2000) 31 *Industrial Relations Journal* 331.

[83] D Charny, 'Competition among Jurisdictions in Corporate Law Rules: an American Perspective on the "Race to the Bottom" in the European Communities', in S Wheeler (ed.) *A Reader on the Law of the Business Enterprise* (Oxford, Oxford University Press, 1994) 365–402.

[84] See generally Barnard, above, n.4 and Deakin and Wilkinson, above, n.80.

[85] Ibid.

[86] See generally, G Teubner, *Law as an Autopoietic System* (Oxford, Blackwell, 1993); R Rogowski and T Wilthagen (eds.) *Reflexive Labour Law* (Deventer, Kluwer, 1994).

supporting mechanisms of group representation and participation, rather than to intervene by imposing particular distributive outcomes. This type of approach finds a concrete manifestation in legislation which seeks, in various ways, to devolve or confer rule-making powers to self-regulatory processes. Examples are laws which allow collective bargaining by trade unions and employers to make qualified exceptions to limits on working time or similar labour standards,[87] or which confer statutory authority on the rules drawn up by professional associations for the conduct of financial transactions.[88]

A procedural orientation also implies an important difference in the way in which the law responds to market failures or externalities from the way in which it is normally represented in the law and economics literature. Reflexive regulation does not seek to 'perfect' the market, in the sense of reproducing the outcome which parties would have arrived at in the absence of transaction costs (the so-called 'hypothetical bargaining' standard). This is partly because it is understood that information problems facing courts and legislatures make the process of identifying an 'optimal' bargaining solution extremely hazardous. It is also because of a perception that the essence of competition is that it is a process of discovery or adaptation, rather than the achievement of optimal states or distributions.

In the context we are considering here, this implies a particular role for the transnational harmonisation of laws. The purpose of harmonisation would not be to substitute for state-level regulation; hence, the transnational standard would not operate to 'occupy the field' in the manner of a 'monopoly regulator', but instead to promote diverse, local-level approaches to regulatory problems by creating a space for autonomous solutions to emerge when, because of market failures, they would not otherwise do so. This may involve what some regard as a restriction of competition, in the sense of ruling out certain options which could be associated with a 'race to the bottom', while leaving others open. As we have seen, this is a familiar technique in labour law, where directives mostly set basic labour standards as a 'floor of rights', allowing member states to improve on these provisions but, on the whole, preventing 'downwards' derogations. Reflexive harmonisation operates to induce individual states to enter into a 'race to the top' when they would have otherwise have an incentive do nothing (the 'reverse free rider' effect) or to compete on the basis of the withdrawal of protective standards (the 'race to the bottom'). This is done by giving states a number of options for implementation as well as by allowing for the possibility that existing, self-regulatory mechanisms can be used to comply with EU-wide standards. In these ways, far from suppressing regulatory innovation, harmonisation aims to stimulate it.

---

[87] See Deakin and Wilkinson, above n.80.
[88] See J Black, *Rules and Regulators* (Oxford, Clarendon Press, 1998).

Another form of reflexive harmonisation can be seen in the use of OMC. OMC involves

> fixing guidelines for the Union, establishing quantitative and qualitative indicators and benchmarks as a means of comparing best practice, translating these European guidelines into national and regional policies by setting specific targets, and periodic monitoring, evaluation and peer review organised as 'mutual learning processes'.[89]

Thus, the OMC process is explicitly about experimentation and learning. OMC has already been tried and tested in the policies supporting EMU and then spilled over in to the Luxembourg employment strategy where guidelines are set which are then reflected in national action plans. OMC now peppers the Lisbon strategy. For example, in the context of modernising the European social model, targets are set (raising the employment rate from an average of 61% today to as close as possible to 70% by 2010),[90] benchmarking is used (on giving higher priority to lifelong learning and improved childcare provision),[91] and comparing best practice is encouraged (Member States are to exchange experiences and best practices on improving social protection and to gain a better understanding of social exclusion).[92]

In the context of free movement of goods and persons the Commission's communication on immigration[93] provides an illustration as to how OMC might function in the internal market. The Commission suggests that OMC might complement the Community legislation by providing a framework for reviewing the Member States' implementation. The Communication provides the example of admission of migrants.[94] It suggests that national measures will be adopted taking account of the criteria laid down in the Directive, including the number of migrants to be admitted and the duration of residence permits. The Commission believes that it would then be helpful to discuss such national implementation to 'evaluate their efficacity and identify practice which might be useful in other national situations'.[95]

So far we have discussed different types of *regulation* which may assist in the process of decentralised learning and experimentation in a federal or quasi federal structure. Where does this leave the Court of Justice? Dorf and Sabel, writing primarily in the context of the US constitutional law,[96] suggest that

---

[89] Presidency Conclusions, Lisbon European Council, 23 and 24 March 2000, para.37.
[90] Presidency Conclusions, Lisbon European Council, 23 and 24 March 2000, para.30. It also envisages that the number of women in employment be increased from an average of 51% today to more than 60% by 2010).
[91] Ibid, para.29.
[92] Ibid, paras.31 and 33.
[93] Commission Communication on an open method of coordination for the community immigration policy COM(2001) 387 final.
[94] Ibid, 6.
[95] Ibid.
[96] M Dorf and C Sabel, 'A Constitution of Democratic Experimentalism' (1998) 98 *Colum.L.Rev* 267.

the courts are the institutions in which existing conceptions of constitutional democracy appear to flow seamlessly into experimentalism. . . . Experimentalist courts, like the traditional courts of constitutional democracy, function by a form of direct deliberation: citizens, as individuals or groups, speaking with the authority of their own experience, can demand that the government give reasons for its actions.[97]

Thus, 'by insisting that actors respect the central experimentalist condition of declaring goals and measuring results, the courts can declare and defend inchoate rights without pretending to anticipate the manifold consequences of the finding'.[98] In practical terms this means, according to Dorf and Sabel, that the court judges the parties' abilities to gather, summarise, and use information by their ability to learn from their mistakes while drawing on the efforts of others in their situation to do likewise.[99] For the European Court of Justice and the national courts hearing a free movement of goods and persons case this might mean working on the presumption of access to the market (of at least the category one or two type) but being prepared to acknowledge the existence of mandatory requirements. The Court would then give the defendant Member State the chance to explain why that access should be restricted, based not only on its own local experience, but also by reference to alternatives practised in other Member States. It would also have to explain why the national restriction was particularly suited to the conditions prevailing in that Member State. The individual complainant, on the other hand, would seek to enlarge the circle of comparisons to include responses from other Member States which would help favour the complainant's cause.[100] The defendants would then present reasons based in their own experience for disallowing those comparisons.[101] As Dorf and Sabel point out, 'to be convincing they [the defendants] will have to show that these reasons are consistent not only with the other reasons they give for their actions, but also with those actions (and responses to the reactions they provoke) themselves'.[102] Dorf and Sabel conclude:

In this to and fro, it is the primary actors that define the range of alternatives to be considered in an evaluation of the appropriateness of ends to means, further publicizing the variety of possibilities in the process; and in deciding whether due consideration has been given to these alternatives, the court refers to standards of care and attentiveness—the ability to learn and learn to learn—that emerge from the practice of the relevant parties themselves.[103]

Some of this dialogue already occurs in developing mandatory requirements and in assessing the proportionality of the Member States' action in respect of

[97] 388.
[98] 389.
[99] 400.
[100] Ibid.
[101] 401.
[102] Ibid.
[103] Ibid.

these mandatory requirements. However, as we have seen,[104] this review can vary considerably in its intensity.[105] The experimentalist approach places far greater emphasis on comparison and learning from the actions of others. In this way, the court acts in part as a coordinator of information and, when adjudicating, precipitates primary social actors to devise solutions.[106] Dorf and Sabel cite the example of *Bosman* where the Court, having recognized that the football associations could legitimately impose some form of regulation, left it up to the associations themselves to determine precisely what regulation, merely laying down the benchmark that revenue sharing could achieve the objective of competitiveness. A similar approach can be found in *Heimdienst* where the Court left it up to the Member State to find a way of ensuring the hygiene of foodstuffs being delivered to isolated areas of the state, while suggesting that rules on refrigerating equipment might be appropriate. This method of adjudication, which is particularly appropriate in the context of Article 234 rulings characterised by a division of functions between the European Court of Justice and the national courts, seeks to maintain national diversity while at the same time perturbing the national systems which is the precondition for effective regulatory learning.

CONCLUSIONS

In this chapter we have reviewed part of the free movement jurisprudence of the Court through the lens of a law and economics analysis, with a view to considering how far it discloses a coherent approach to the question of regulatory competition. Viewing the Court's rulings through an *ex post* set of analytical classifications might strike some as unusual. The justification for doing so is two fold. Firstly, while regulatory competition may not be the aim of the Court's interventions, it is certainly one of its most significant effects. Secondly, law and economics analysis of this kind is widely used to understand the workings of market integration rules in other federal or transnational jurisdictions, in particular the United States, where argument has raged over the benefits of the market for legal rules in areas such as corporations law. When these techniques are applied to the free movement case law of the Court, we see a surprising lack of consistency. The Court veers between an approach, in cases such as *Centros*, which combines a strong substantive market access test, to one, in cases such as

---

[104] See section 3.3.
[105] See, e.g. G De Búrca, 'The Principle of Proportionality and its Application in EC Law', (1993) 13 *YBEL* 105, 111. Schwarze calls proportionality 'an extremely variable principle of review' (J Schwarze, *European Administrative Law* (London, Sweet & Maxwell, 1992), 864. But see FG Jacobs: 'Recent Developments in the Principle of Proportionality in EC Law' in E Ellis (ed), *The Principle of Proportionality in the Laws of Europe*, (Oxford, Hart Publishing, 1999) and 'Public Law—the Impact of Europe' [1999] *PL* 232.
[106] Dorf and Sabel, above, n.96.

Keck, which would limit the Court's intervention to situations in which formal access is barred or there is clear evidence of discrimination against non home-state nationals. From the point of view of regulatory competition, it is beside the point to argue that one case arises under the law governing establishment and the other is concerned with goods, since the effects are largely the same in both cases. At the very least, we would expect the Court to offer some explanation of the divergence in approach in this and other cases, but none has been forthcoming.

In addition to inconsistency, the Court's approach risks the worst of both worlds: a race to uniformity, which is also a race to the bottom in the sense of leading to the degradation of standards of market regulation. Because the market access principle is not clearly articulated as such, the importance of this process for the debate over the substance of economic and social policy in the EC is being obscured. The case for a more explicit consideration of these questions is further reinforced by the emergence of clear alternatives to court-led deregulation, in the form of reflexive harmonisation and novel regulatory techniques such as the open method of coordination and, as far as the Court itself is concerned, experimentalism. The need for all parties, including the Court, to articulate more clearly what they are doing and why[107] can only serve to strengthen regulatory competition while at the same time going some way to preserving national autonomy.

---

[107] See also the emphasis on dialogue and participation in the Commission's Governance White Paper COM(2001)428, esp. 15: 'Civil society increasingly sees Europe as offering a good platform to change policy orientations and society. This offers a real potential to broaden the debate on Europe's role. It is a chance to get citizens more actively involved in achieving the Union's objectives and to offer them a structured channel for feedback, criticism and protest.'

9

Mutual Recognition

KENNETH A. ARMSTRONG*

INTRODUCTION

THE CONCEPT OF MUTUAL RECOGNITION is familiar to most students of European Union (EU) law. This familiarity may be due to its promiscuity within EU law, appearing not only across the freedoms of the Single Market, but also in its application to external trade and more recently within the context of EC Treaty Title IV's creation of an area of 'freedom, security and justice'. The principal concern of this paper is the role played by mutual recognition within the Single Market and, given the theme of this collection of essays, Part I of this contribution attempt to unpack the concept of mutual recognition. This unpacking involves distinguishing mutual recognition from, and comparing mutual recognition with, other models that seek to reconcile market integration with market regulation. The process of unpacking also requires us to consider the different modalities through which mutual recognition operates and the different legal mechanisms that mandate or encourage mutual recognition. Part II focuses specifically on mutual recognition in the context of the recognition of the qualifications and work history of EU nationals seeking to work in other Member States. This case study provides a useful means of repacking the premises unpacked in Part I.

Before we commence 'unpacking' mutual recognition it is worth considering mutual recognition's relationship to the broader policy evolution that takes us from the original concept of a 'Common Market' to the modern concept of the 'Single Market'. After all, the relevance of the principle of mutual recognition to the original conception of a 'Common Market' was anything but apparent in the EEC Treaty with only the briefest of mentions of the principle in respect of the recognition of professional qualifications (Article 57 EEC) and the mutual recognition of companies and legal persons (Article 220 EEC). Particularly as regards mutual recognition of qualifications, Article 57 EEC envisaged mutual

* The author would like to thank the editors for their patience and my colleagues Marise Cremona and Claire Kilpatrick for their advice. Thanks are also due to Paul Beaumont for his extremely helpful comments on an earlier draft. All errors and omissions are, unfortunately, my own.

recognition as an *outcome* of an EEC *legislative* process. This image of mutual recognition seems somewhat at odds with our contemporary image of the role of mutual recognition within the Single Market, namely as an alternative to EU legislative action operating primarily at the level of national administrations. It is clear that to understand the relationship between mutual recognition and the Single Market, we need first to unpack the more general policy evolution of the Single Market itself.

Instead of offering a wholly chronological account of policy evolution, we can instead think of three dimensions of policy evolution. The first dimension refers to the placing of limits upon the regulatory autonomy of Member States. One of the key functions of the Treaty rules on free movement within the Single Market is to police and structure the exercise of Member States' regulatory powers to ensure that unjustifiable barriers to free movement do not emerge. The concept of mutual recognition has an obvious role to play in this regard by seeking to prevent the replication of equivalent regulatory processes that have already been carried out in other Member States each and every time a good or service seeks to obtain cross-border market access. This dimension of mutual recognition is well-known and usually depicted as flowing from the ruling of the European Court of Justice (ECJ) in its infamous *Cassis de Dijon* judgment.[1] Our present interest lies in the extent to which mutual recognition and the decision in *Cassis de Dijon* were bundled together by the European Commission in a Communication issued in 1980.[2] In its Communication, the Commission concluded that:

> The principles deduced by the Court imply that a member-State may not in principle prohibit the sale in its territory of a product lawfully produced and marketed in another member-State even if that product is produced according to technical or quality requirements which differ from those imposed on its domestic products.

This interpretation leads to a construction of mutual recognition as more or less synonymous with home state control and, in any event, operating along a dimension concerned with placing limitations on the ability of Member States to exercise their regulatory powers. As Alter and Meunier-Aitsahalia note, not surprisingly, this interpretation did not go unchallenged by the Member States themselves.[3] However, the strong emphasis upon market access and restricting national regulatory autonomy continues on in the Commission's 1985 White Paper on *Completing the Internal Market*. It noted that: 'Following the rulings of the Court of Justice, both the European Parliament and the Dooge Committee have stressed the principle that goods lawfully marketed in one

---

[1]   Case 120/78, *Rewe-Zentrale AG v. Bundesmonopolverwaltung für Branntwein* (*Cassis de Dijon*) [1979] ECR 649.

[2]   See Commission Communication OJ C256, (3.10.80), p. 2 and its academic interpretation by Karen Alter and Sophie Meunier-Aitsahalia, 'Judicial Politics in the European Community: European Integration and the Pathbreaking Cassis de Dijon Decision' (1994) 26(4) *Comparative Political Studies* 535.

[3]   Ibid.

Member State must be allowed free entry into other Member States'.[4] This strongly free movement approach is also exemplified in the White Paper's belief that: 'Any purchaser, be he wholesaler, retailer or the final consumer, should have the right to choose his supplier in any part of the Community without restriction'.[5] We explore this dimension of mutual recognition more fully in Part I but for the moment it is enough to note the political deployment of the concept of mutual recognition and the ECJ's decision in *Cassis de Dijon* to provide a legal and normative foundation for the drive to complete an internal market free from barriers to trade arising from the exercise of Member States' regulatory powers.

A second dimension of the mutual recognition principle can also be discerned in the Commission's Communication on *Cassis de Dijon*, namely, as a means of determining when legislative harmonisation by the Community might be required. Harmonisation would not be required where mutual recognition might operate, while conversely, harmonisation would be necessary as regards barriers to trade caused by national measures which would survive scrutiny under the free movement rules. This aspect of mutual recognition is usually seen as the basis for the launch in 1985 of the 'New Approach' to technical harmonisation based on a division of labour between EU and national levels (as well as a division of labour between legislative harmonisation and European standards-setting). In other words, EU legislative action would be necessary only to harmonise the 'essential requirements' of products, with Member States mutually recognising any additional national technical requirements. It is this dimension—the relationship between national and Community levels of action—that has become of greater importance in the post-1992 world of the Single Market, subsidiarity and ideas of shared responsibility between different levels of government.[6] Post-1992, the Commission adopted a Communication on mutual recognition as a follow-up to its 'Action Plan for the Single Market'.[7] The language is somewhat different from that of the 1985 White Paper in the sense that the value of mutual recognition is seen to lie in the fact that: 'It allows free movement of goods and services without the need for harmonisation of national legislation at Community level'.[8] In this second dimension, mutual recognition becomes closely associated with the placing of normative restrictions on *Community* action whereas the first dimension is concerned to place limits upon the sphere of Member State action.

The concept of mutual recognition is now part and parcel of the Single Market lexicon operating along the two dimensions identified. To this two

---

[4] European Commission, *Completing the Internal Market*, COM(85)310 final, para. 77.
[5] Ibid.
[6] See *Better Lawmaking 1998: a shared responsibility*, COM(98) 715 final.
[7] *Action Plan for the Single Market*, SEC(97) 1 final; Commission Communication, *Mutual recognition in the context of the follow-up to the Action Plan for the Single Market*, June 1999.
[8] Ibid, p. 3.

dimensional picture we need to add a third. As the EU Single Market has evolved it has had to look outwards as well as inwards and the concept of mutual recognition also operates along this third external dimension. Mutual recognition has an important role to play in the context of the World Trade Organisation (WTO) Agreements, particularly in terms of the removal of technical barriers to trade arising at the level of conformity assessment and certification. Mutual recognition is also significant in the context of trade with future accession states. And, as we shall see in Part II, insofar as EU nationals acquire qualifications and work experience outside of the EU, there is a need to consider the application of mutual recognition beyond the internal world of the Single Market.

Perhaps because of the multiple dimensions and contexts in which mutual recognition might be invoked, the significance of mutual recognition as a strategy for reconciling market access with enduring regulatory control has been repeated in all the major EU policy documents concerning the Single Market.[9] And yet at the same time, there often appears to be a dissatisfaction with the ability of mutual recognition to deliver on its promise. This highlights a gulf between, on the one hand an uncritical or immodest tendency to invoke the concept of mutual recognition as a multi-purpose strategy for removing barriers to free movement, and on the other hand the more specific and, therefore, limited conditions for its successful application. Like many faiths, it is easier to believe in as a general credo than it is to practice on a day-to-day basis and as we unpack and repack the mutual recognition concept, the difficulties associated with the concept will become apparent.

PART I – 'UNPACKING'

Three 'Ideal-Types' for Ensuring Market Access and Market Regulation

Our discussion of mutual recognition requires to be situated against the backdrop of competing models for the integration and regulation of the European market namely, home state control, harmonisation of laws, and host state control. These models are sketched below and correspond to the models used by Maduro in his work on the 'European Economic Constitution'.[10] Each model is deliberately presented in pure form to indicate its analytical value.

---

[9] In addition to those previously referred to, we can also note the Commission's 1999 Communication, *The Internal Market Strategy* COM(1999) 624 final.

[10] This paper shares Maduro's concern to consider the deployment of different models of market integration/regulation from a perspective that is sensitive to issues of constitutional legitimacy. As will be explained further below, I depart from Maduro's model in suggesting that there are good reasons not to treat 'home state control' as being synonymous with a principle of 'mutual recognition'. See M. Maduro, *We The Court: The European Court* of Justice and the European Economic Constitution (Oxford, Hart Publishing, 1998), especially Chapter 4.

The first approach to combining market access with enduring regulatory control is to insist on 'host' state control in that market access is to be permitted provided there is regulatory compliance with the substantive and procedural rules of the state in which market access is sought. However, and in order to facilitate market access, host country control can be made subject to a basic non-discrimination requirement, namely equality of treatment with host state nationals. But apart from this right to equality of treatment with host state nationals, market access is premised upon full compliance with the laws of the host state.[11] As such, the market remains segmented with goods, services etc. requiring to comply with multiple sets of regulations whenever they seek cross-border market access: the principle of equal treatment is not enough to secure market access across a single market but rather conditions market access to *each* of the markets of the constituent states.

A second approach is to insist upon 'home' state control.[12] In this approach, provided there is compliance with the substantive and procedural regulatory requirements of the home state (or state in which market access is first sought), thereafter, market access to other markets ought to be permitted. This approach attempts to combine the benefits of free trade with enduring regulatory control through the home state of the good, service, person. As will be evident, a pure model of home state control gives rise to a market in which each good or service only complies with one set of regulatory controls (the home state), but within the market as a whole, different goods and services will have complied with different home state controls.

A third model seeks to ensure access to a single market through the elimination of diverse national regulatory requirements and the creation of a single set of harmonised regulatory requirements.[13] In this way, compliance with harmonised rules is sufficient to ensure access to the market of any of the constituent states. There is a clear attempt to use the national market model to create a transnational single market governed by its own rules.

We can transfer these models directly to the context of the EU with the adoption of one or other model providing a normative map for the role of EU law, the institutions of the EU and for the conceptualisation of the nature of European economic integration. Starting with host state control, market access premised on compliance with the regulatory requirements of the host state implies the on-going centrality of the Member States in the regulation of their own markets. Nonetheless, such controls ought to be tempered through the principle of non-discrimination which underpins the operation of the Treaties (Article 14 EC). In this way, EU law and the courts of the EU and Member States

---

[11] In Maduro's terminology, this is a 'decentralised model' implying that it relies not on the harmonisation of laws at the EU level but instead in enduring host state control subject only to the non-discrimination principle, ibid.

[12] The 'competitive model' to use Maduro's terminology, ibid.

[13] The 'centralised model' in Maduro's terminology, ibid.

can be utilised to police the application of the non-discrimination principle. However, markets will remain segmented on national lines indicating that host state control—even tempered by a non-discrimination principle—is insufficient on its own to integrate individual Member States' markets into a Single European Market. By contrast, a home state approach takes the idea of market access to a Single European Market as its normative foundation, but with enduring regulatory control through compliance with home state regulatory requirements. In this way, the function of EU law ought to be positively to require Member States to grant market access where goods and services comply with the rules of the home state, and negatively, to restrict attempts by host states to impose further regulatory controls. In institutional terms—like the host state approach—it is courts which perform tasks of policing market access. However, the role of the courts under the home state approach also involves courts in making substantive judgements about the mechanisms and levels of market regulation.

The approach which places the harmonisation of diverse rules at the centre of its strategy evidently places the burden of responsibility on the EU legislative organs with EU law (in the sense of regulations, directives, decisions) forming the legal framework for a Single European Market. It is clear that such an approach has connotations of political integration which the other two models do not, in the sense, that what comes with it are issues of how best to secure democratic legitimation through the transfer of norm production away from the structures of Member States to the legislative structure of the EU.

As Maduro notes in his study of these different models, the choice of any given model has both normative and institutional implications. It is with this need to consider both the normative and institutional dimensions of any given strategy that we can turn directly to considering mutual regulation.

Mutual Recognition

The principle of mutual recognition seeks to manage market access under conditions of regulatory pluralism by negotiating between the application of home and host state regulatory controls. Mutual recognition requires that the regulatory history of a product, service or worker acquired in the home state cannot be ignored when it comes to considering what legitimate regulatory controls may be applied in the host state. But as is apparent, it is difficult to offer a generalised and abstract definition of mutual recognition divorced from the legal context in which it is operationalised. Below, two different legal instantiations of mutual recognition are suggested. Mutual recognition acts as a regulatory process norm in the sense that, in procedural terms, the regulatory space occupied by host state regulators is structured by the need to have regard to, and take into account, the regulatory history of a product etc. acquired in the home state. Mutual recognition also acts more directly as a substantive limitation on host state regulators in that the regulatory space occupied by host state regulators is also structured by the requirements under EU law that any measures taken by them are both necessary and proportionate to the pursuit of regulatory goals recognised by EU law.

In the following sections, the procedural and substantive dimensions of mutual recognition are unpacked. Attention then turns to unpacking the relationship between mutual recognition, the decision in *Cassis de Dijon* and free movement. It is argued that this relationship has been misconceived by many in that *Cassis de Dijon* is frequently depicted as both an example of a mutual recognition analysis and as mandating home state control: *ergo* mutual recognition is synonymous with home state control. A somewhat different interpretation of *Cassis de Dijon* is offered here. Thereafter some examples of the application of mutual recognition within the free movement case-law are examined. This is followed by a consideration of the institutional context for the application of mutual recognition and the different types of rules which may be the subject of mutual recognition.

(a) Mutual Recognition as a Regulatory Process Norm

As a regulatory process norm, mutual recognition goes beyond the simple requirement on host state regulators not to discriminate on grounds of nationality. It requires, in addition, that national regulators be 'other-regarding' in the sense that they must, within their own domestic processes, *recognise* and give meaning to information about the regulatory history of a product, service, worker even if that information is sourced outside of the host state i.e. it comes from the regulatory controls imposed in, or recognised by, another state. It extends the principle of non-discrimination by requiring host state regulators to look beyond the national form of the regulatory controls and to consider the potential equivalence of their function. This approach has the virtue of recognising the respective authority of both home and host state regulators, but seeks to mediate their relationship by searching for equivalencies between home and host state regulatory requirements, thereby preventing the duplication of regulatory processes which, under a pure host state control model, would often restrict market access.

Applied in the context of the EU, mutual recognition ought to provide a balance between the respective regulatory prerogatives of Member States and a balance between the role of the Member States as regulators and the role of EU institutions and EU law in requiring that Member States give meaning to the EU regulatory history of products etc. It encourages a Europeanisation of regulation not through the adoption and enforcement of harmonised European norms (a vertical Europeanisation) but instead through requiring an openness to the other regulatory systems of Member States (a horizontal

Europeanisation). This Europeanisation applies not only to the administrative level of government, but also to the legislative branches in the sense that legislative drafting ought not to foreclose acceptance of products etc. complying with 'equivalent' standards. One can also think of a Europeanisation of national courts in that they may be called upon to police the recognition activities of the administrative branches of government. Not surprisingly, the genesis for this Europeanisation of the national systems and for mutual recognition acting as a regulatory process norm can be found in Article 10 (ex 5) EC Treaty.

If the virtue of mutual recognition as a regulatory process norm lies in its encouragement of a Europeanisation of the domestic process of government, then one vice is that host state regulators may have little knowledge or experience of the regulatory traditions of other states necessary in order to engage in comparisons of home and host state regulatory requirements. However, it may not be enough simply to 'find out' what laws exist in another states. There is a deeper question of the 'transplantability' of the laws of one state to another for the purposes of determining equivalencies. As Teubner suggests, law is structurally coupled to the social systems in which it operates.[14] The binding arrangements forged between law and social systems in one state may be quite different in another. This suggests limits to the ability of domestic regulators to reach beyond their domestic systems to comprehend and accept as equivalent the regulatory structures of other states. Ultimately, there is always the danger that if it is left to the host state to give recognition to the regulatory history of a product etc. it may engage in covert protectionism.

Whatever the potential vices of mutual recognition as a regulatory process norm, much of its vitality can be seen in its structuring of national institutional processes. It encourages a Europeanisation of such processes, but without the transfer of regulatory activities away from national systems.

(b) Mutual Recognition as a Substantive Restriction on Regulatory Autonomy

In terms of EU law, the requirement to be 'other-regarding' does not rest simply at the level of a process requirement. The regulatory space occupied by domestic regulators is more substantively structured through the application of the specific Treaty rules on free movement. More specifically, where a Member State seeks to impose its own domestic controls on a product already lawfully placed on the market in another Member State, in addition to the need for such controls to pursue a legitimate regulatory goal, the action must be necessary to obtain that goal and be proportionate. The concept of mutual recognition can be deployed to undermine the argument that host state controls are necessary

---

[14] G. Teubner, 'Legal Irritants: Good Faith in British Law or How Unifying Law Ends up in New Divergences' (1998) 61(1) *Modern Law Review* 11.

or proportionate because functionally equivalent controls have been carried out when market access was obtained in the home state.

In this way, we shift from an analysis of mutual recognition as a process norm within the context of Article 10 EC Treaty to an analysis of mutual recognition within the substantive Treaty rules on free movement. Given the enforceability of such substantive rules both within the national legal systems (under conditions of the direct effect of Treaty rules) and before the ECJ itself (whether through referral of legal issues to the ECJ under Article 234 EC or because the Commission brings infringement proceedings under Article 226 EC), courts take on a more substantive role in market regulation than that implied by a process-norm approach.

It is important to be clear on what mutual recognition adds to substantive review under the free movement rules. Member States may fail to produce a convincing case for the application of national measures restricting free movement for reasons other than violation of the principle of mutual recognition. The principle of mutual recognition is invoked only where the Member State is seeking to impose controls that are functionally equivalent to those which have already been met in the Member State in which the product or service has already been lawfully granted market access.

(c) Substantive Review: Mutual Recognition and the decision in Cassis

For many the following passage from the judgment of the ECJ in *Cassis de Dijon* is the essence of the application of mutual recognition: '[T]here is . . . no valid reason why, provided that they have been lawfully produced and marketed in one of the Member States, alcoholic beverages should not be introduced into any other Member State'.[15] *Cassis de Dijon* is, thereby, depicted as mandating home state control; as being an example of mutual recognition in operation; and, therefore, mutual recognition and home state control become synonymous.[16] I want to suggest that this is at best misleading and at worst a mistaken interpretation of the relationship between *Cassis de Dijon* and mutual recognition.

Given that the idea of free movement within a Single Market is such a core principle, not surprisingly there is a strong presumption in favour of free circulation once goods have lawfully been placed on the market of a Member State. As such, attempts by Member States to impose further controls when cross-border market access is sought will be met with some skepticism. In more legal terms, the thrust of free movement jurisprudence from *Dassonville*

---

[15] *Cassis de Dijon*, above n.1.

[16] As Alter and Meunier-Aitsahalia note in their analysis of *Cassis de Dijon*, the European Commission, in its Interpretative Communication on the *Cassis de Dijon* judgment, strongly emphasised the home country control principle, while minimising the 'mandatory requirements' exception to the free movement principle: above, n. 2.

onwards—at least prior to *Keck*—was in favour of a widening of the net of national measures which might be considered to create obstacles to market access, combined with close scrutiny of the attempts by Member States to justify retention of national controls. But far from mandating a model of home state control, the judgment in *Cassis de Dijon* created further regulatory space for host state controls through its creation of the mandatory requirements exception. To be sure, this regulatory space for host state regulators would be rigorously policed by EU and national courts. As Weatherill notes in his contribution to this volume, the outcome of the judicial analysis would often result in the host state being unable to insist upon the application of its own controls. But analytically, the judicial analysis shifts to the issue of the justification offered by the host state for the application of its rules, rather than merely mandating the application of home state rules. Thus, in *Cassis de Dijon*, the result was that the German authorities had provided no good reason for invoking host state controls *and for that reason* goods lawfully placed on the market in another Member State should be permitted market access. But it would be quite wrong to confuse the outcome of an analysis with the analysis itself. In other words, the correct analysis is one based on the enduring regulatory responsibility of host state regulators 'in the absence of harmonisation' rather than one premised on a pure model of home state control. What mutual recognition does is to provide one means of policing the application of host state controls.

If, then, *Cassis de Dijon* is misleadingly considered to be analytically based on home state control, what then of its relationship to mutual recognition? By far the most important mistake made by interpreters of *Cassis de Dijon* is that there is a failure to distinguish between different processes which might produce the same outcome. The *Cassis de Dijon* 'mutual recognition' paragraph comes after an assessment by the ECJ of the plausibility of the German government's claims to invoke mandatory requirements for the protection of the consumer and public health. The Court concluded that a rule requiring a minimum alcohol content whose effect was to prevent the marketing of *Cassis de Dijon* was either unnecessary or disproportionate to its aim. It is not, however, an example of the ECJ looking for substantive functional equivalencies between home and host state rules by engaging in a comparative exercise and then concluding that the duplication of equivalent rules was unnecessary and disproportionate. Indeed, there was no substantive equivalence between the rules of the home and the host state, hence the trade barrier. Rather, the necessity and proportionality of the German rule was assessed simply by examining the rule on its own and considering whether the Member State had succeeded in justifying its regulatory approach. There is, therefore, a world of a difference between the ECJ concluding that host state controls are unnecessary because there has already been compliance with functionally equivalent controls in the home state (mutual recognition), and the ECJ—for other reasons—concluding that the host state has failed to give a sufficiently plausible, necessary or proportionate justification for departing from free movement rules and, therefore, market access on the basis of compliance with home state controls should be permitted. While both processes may result in an outcome of market access based on home state controls the processes being described are not the same and ought not to be conflated.

The re-interpretation of *Cassis de Dijon* offered here is intended to give a much clearer and parsimonious role for the principle of mutual recognition in free movement analysis. Mutual recognition is but one means of policing attempts by a host state to insist upon the application of its controls rather than being synonymous with a model of the economic constitution and of free movement premised upon home state controls. It is precisely because of the lack of such parsimony and a failure clearly to delineate the boundaries of its application that one can make sense of the paradox noted in the introduction that the concept of mutual recognition is simultaneously held up as a cornerstone of the Single Market and yet there is widespread disappointment with its non-application. Having misunderstood its nature we both expect too much of the concept and are disappointed when it appears not to deliver. The conclusion to be reached is that mutual recognition has an important—albeit limited—role to play in the assessment of the necessity and proportionality of host state measures. In order to operate, it requires a comparison of home and host state measures in order to determine whether there is functional equivalence.

(d) Operationalising Mutual Recognition within the Free Movement Rules

If the decision in *Cassis de Dijon* appears to have been misinterpreted, we should, nonetheless, consider the extent to which mutual recognition *is* operationalised as part of the analysis of the necessity and proportionality of Member States' justifications for derogating from free movement rules. This is not the place to rehearse the corpus of ECJ jurisprudence on free movement. The following is largely illustrative rather than comprehensive and we focus on the issues of consumer protection and protection of health in respect of free movement of goods and freedom to provide services. It is important to keep in mind that we are concerned not with the necessity or proportionality of measures in isolation, but only where it is alleged that equivalent measures have been applied in the home state and for that reason further measures in the host state are not necessary or are disproportionate.

A good case to compare with *Cassis de Dijon* is the decision in *Fietje*.[17] Dutch law required alcoholic products that fell within the scope of domestic legislation to bear the term 'likeur'. This would require products imported from other Member States to have their labels altered. While the ECJ accepted that the measure pursued a goal of consumer protection, it made it clear that the host

---

[17] Case 27/80, *Criminal Proceedings against Anton Adriaan Fietje* [1980] ECR 3839.

state could not apply its laws on consumer protection to imported products where at least the same information as that required by the host state has been provided by the labeling requirements of the home state and where it was just as capable of being understood by consumers in the host state. It fell to the national court to determine whether in fact equivalent information to consumers was ensured by compliance with home state rules. What is noteworthy is that in this case, unlike that of *Cassis de Dijon*, there was an issue of whether compliance with home state controls was enough to ensure equivalent regulatory protection.

Where questions are referred from national courts under Article 234 EC, in principle, it falls to the national courts to determine the equivalence of home and host state rules, although the ECJ may be tempted to decide the issue itself or give a clear 'steer' to the national court. Under infringement proceedings brought by the Commission under Article 226 EC, the ECJ itself is left to consider the issues of necessity and proportionality. The *Commission v. Ireland (Precious Metals)* case is a good example of mutual recognition in operation as a substantive restriction on Member States regulatory powers.[18] It concerned requirements in Ireland to affix hallmarks to precious metals imported into Ireland even through such metals already bore national hallmarks. Clearly this had an impact on intra-Community trade and the issue fell to be determined whether the Irish requirements could be justified as affording protection to the consumer. The ECJ accepted the Commission's argument that the Irish measures could not be justified where the information conveyed by the hallmarks of the home state were equivalent in content to those required under Irish law and were intelligible to Irish consumers.

Consumer protection as regards service provision creates dilemmas for EU law. On the one hand, an important aspect of Treaty rules on the freedom to provide services is that services can be provided in a Member State without the necessity for the service provider to establish in that state. Moreover, as the ECJ identified in *Centros*:[19]

> The right to form a company in accordance with the law of a Member State and to set up branches in other Member States is inherent in the exercise, in a single market, of the freedom of establishment guaranteed by the Treaty.

As such, establishment in a Member State which best suits the regulatory requirements of a company combined with an ability to offer services in another Member State is of the essence of a Single Market. But on the other hand, compliance with laws applicable to companies established in the host state may be necessary to ensure effective protection of the consumer. There is a fear that by establishing outside of the host state, the service provider may escape these regulatory controls. However, the ECJ has observed that national

---

[18] Case C-30/99, *Commission v. Ireland (Precious Metals)* [2001] ECR I-4619.
[19] Case C-212/97, *Centros Ltd. v. Erhervs- og Selskabhysstyrelsen* [1999] ECR I-1459.

rules which require the service provider to establish within the territory of the host state negate the very purpose of the Treaty rules on freedom to provide services and, to this extent, there is a strong presumption in favour of home state control.[20] However, it has also been observed in the context of insurance services that restrictions on the freedom to provide services are compatible with EU law insofar as the rules of the state of establishment are not adequate in order to achieve the necessary level of protection. In this way, national rules applicable to insurance companies established in Germany relating to insurance reserves and other conditions of insurance were also applicable to service providers established outside of Germany. As regards authorisations to conduct business, while the host state could require the authorisation of a service provider, the ECJ stipulated that controls , '. . . may not duplicate equivalent statutory conditions which have already been satisfied in the State in which the undertaking is established'. The Court required the supervisory authority in the host state to take account of the supervisions and verifications already carried out. In other words, there was a substantive limitation on host regulators not to duplicate equivalent controls, but it is left to the host regulators to exercise their supervisory functions having regard to and taking into account regulatory processes already carried out in the home state (mutual recognition as a process norm).

As the Commission has noted in its biennial mutual recognition reports, in the area of financial services there are good reasons relating to the protection of the consumer that will often serve to justify the application of host state controls.[21] As a consequence, a certain degree of harmonisation and co-ordination through the adoption of EU legislation is often required to facilitate service provision and to facilitate the operation of mutual recognition.

In a reversal of the usual situation in which the 'host' state seeks to impose controls on the service provider to protect consumers in the host state, in *Alpine Investments* the issue was whether the 'home' state could impose controls on a service provider established in that state for the protection of consumers in the host state.[22] Alpine Investments contended that such controls were not required because the recipient of services could be adequately protected by controls imposed in the host state. However, the ECJ itself decided that the home state was best placed to control the activities of the company and did not leave open the issue of whether the host state controls were equivalent. Significantly, the ECJ decided the issue itself rather than leaving it to the national court to determine.

It is evident that the ECJ seems to create a significant space for Member States to apply their regulatory controls for the protection of the consumer as regards the provision of financial services, while in respect of goods, the ECJ

---

[20] E.g. see Case C-154/89, *Commission v. France (Tour Guides)* [1991] ECR I-659.

[21] The Commission's first biennial report *On the Application of the Principle of Mutual Recognition in Product and Services Markets*, p. 24.

[22] Case C-384/93, *Alpine Investments v. Minister van Financien* [1995] ECR I-1141.

tends to cut down that regulatory space by assuming that the average consumer can be protected by the provision of equivalent information to that required in the host state. However, in cases where the Court has had to consider measures put in place by national authorities for the protection of health, the ECJ has, while noting that national authorities must act proportionately, left open the door to the application of domestic authorisation procedures even if a good has already been authorised to be placed on the market in another Member State. The Court has repeated that in the absence of harmonisation, it is for the Member State to regulate for risk. Nonetheless, the ECJ does require the application of mutual recognition as a regulatory process norm in the sense of requiring national authorities to have regard to the regulatory history of a product. In *Brandsma*[23], a shopowner was prosecuted for selling an anti-algae product used to clean wall and floor tiles. The product was supplied to Dutch and Belgium companies and the product had been authorised for use by the Dutch authorities but had not been authorised by the Belgian authorities, hence the prosecution. The Court, citing the public interest in protection of health, concluded that the subjection of the product to a further authorisation procedure was not prohibited by Community law. In *Harpegnies*[24], the ECJ again held that a Member State was not prohibited from subjecting a biocidal product to an authorisation procedure in the importing state even though the product had already been authorised in another Member State. However, the national authorities were required to take into account the regulatory history of the product:

> As the Court has previously held (see Case 272/80 *Frans-Nederlandse Maatschappij voor Biologische Producten* [1981] ECR 3277, paragraph 14), whilst a Member State is free to require a biocidal product which has already received approval in another Member State to undergo a fresh procedure of examination and approval, the authorities of the Member States are nevertheless required to assist in bringing about a relaxation of the controls existing in intra-Community trade and to take account of technical or chemical analyses or laboratory tests which have already been carried out in another Member State (see Brandsma, paragraph 12).

Albeit a somewhat crude hypothesis, it is arguable that where the ECJ sees there to be an uncertain risk to consumer or health protection, it is less likely itself to wield mutual recognition as a substantive prohibition on Member States' action and more likely to leave matters to the national courts and the national authorities to determine, while insisting on the application of mutual recognition as a regulatory process norm requiring Member States to 'take account of' the regulatory history of a product or service.

As these cases illustrate, it is simply not acceptable to treat mutual recognition as synonymous with home control if by that we mean that it is

---

[23] Case C-293/94, *Criminal Proceedings Against Brandsma* [1996] ECR I-3159.
[24] Case C-400/96, *Criminal Proceedings Against Harpegnies* [1998] ECR I-1512.

enough for a product or service to be provided in the home state for it to be given EU-wide free circulation. It ignores the regulatory space provided to Member States to seek to justify the exercise of their regulatory powers and it fails to explain how the principle of mutual recognition structures that regulatory space. Mutual recognition must, therefore, be seen as one technique for policing host state controls by requiring not only the application of a basic non-discrimination principle, but also by acting both as a regulatory process norm and as a substantive limitation on Member States' action.

(e) The Institutional Context of Mutual Recognition

With the exception of examples of the ECJ itself applying mutual recognition as a substantive limitation on national regulatory autonomy, for the most part, mutual recognition is to be operationalised within the institutional contexts of the Member States. Given that national courts are also responsible for the application of the free movement rules, the national courts also become an institutional context for the use of mutual recognition as a substantive limitation on the regulatory powers of domestic regulators. However, national courts also have responsibilities derived from Article 10 (ex 5) EC to ensure the application of mutual recognition as a regulatory process norm when it comes to reviewing the legality of administrative action within the scope of EU law.

As some of the examples in the previous section illustrated, the ECJ reminds national administrations that they too are responsible for the application of the mutual recognition principle by taking into account the regulatory history of a product, service etc. As Temple Lang notes, national administrations are themselves within the gaze of Article 10 (ex 5) EC[25]. In areas where there are likely to be repeat requests for recognition of regulatory histories e.g. in the area of recognition of professional qualifications, the administration may adopt standard operating procedures to routinise the recognition process. However, in other areas the administration may have difficulties in responding to requests for recognition. As the Commission has noted, significant barriers to the application of the principle of mutual recognition arise at the administrative level e.g. allocating organisational responsibility for handling the request for recognition; the unwillingness of individual administrators to take responsibility for permitting market access on the basis of mutual recognition; and the wide discretion which administrators may possess.[26]

The extent to which the principle of mutual recognition must be taken into account by national legislatures can be considered in the light of the decision of

[25] See J. Temple Lang, 'The Duties of National Authorities under Community Constitutional Law' (1998) 23 *European Law Review* 109.
[26] The Commission's first biennial report *On the Application of the Principle of Mutual Recognition in Product and Services Markets.*

the ECJ in the *Foie Gras* case.[27] In an Article 226 EC action brought by the Commission, the ECJ held that France violated Article 30 (now 28) EC Treaty when it drafted a law reserving certain trade descriptions for products possessing certain qualities, but did not include a 'mutual recognition' clause to accept products onto the market that complied with the rules of the home state. Leaving aside the issue of whether this case is truly about mutual recognition (there were no equivalent rules in other Member States governing the use of foie gras as a base for food preparations), what is interesting is the idea that legislatures must also be 'other-regarding' when legislating and ensure that products complying with equivalent rules or standards to that of the host state should be permitted market access.[28]

(f) The Types of Rules That May be Recognised

The regulatory controls which may be imposed by a regulator are of different types. Particularly in terms of product regulation one can think of the substantive regulatory requirements which products must comply with (e.g. essential requirements relating to product size, composition, packaging in order to fulfil regulatory goals of consumer protection), as well as procedural requirements relating to the conformity assessment procedures that a product must satisfy (i.e. ensuring that a product meets substantive requirements) and ultimately procedural requirements that attest to the correct application of the conformity assessment procedures. Differences in regulatory requirements at each of these three stages of the regulatory process can create barriers to trade between states, each of which may be tackled through mutual recognition. Although it is tempting to consider that substantive rules will necessarily be the hardest to recognise, precisely because regulatory processes are, again to use Teubner's words, 'structurally coupled' processes, even the recognition of test results applying the same or materially identical substantive norms may prove difficult because of the social context of recognition.

Passive and Active Mutual Recognition

We have already introduced a basic distinction between mutual recognition as a process norm and mutual recognition as a substantive limitation on regulatory autonomy. Another distinction can be made between 'passive' and 'active' mutual recognition. By passive mutual recognition I mean that the host state is

[27] Case C-184/96, *Commission v. France (Foie Gras)* [1998] ECR I-6197.
[28] The context of this case was that the draft of the relevant French law had been notified to the Commission as a technical regulation under Directive 83/189/EEC. The point of this procedure is to allow the Commission and other Member States to request amendments to draft regulations which might otherwise create illegitimate barriers to trade.

effectively only executing regulatory controls that have already been carried out in another state. Recognition in this sense tends to operate at the level of symbolic forms rather than direct comparisons of functions. In other words, albeit that forms such as judgments, qualifications or certificates are the formal symbols of functional processes, the mere existence of the form is enough to provoke the national authority into executing it and giving it practical legal effect. The national authority does not look behind or investigate the nature of the regulatory process carried out outside of the host state, nor does it attempt to 'domesticate' the regulatory history of a good, service or person. It is instead compelled merely to give practical and legal effect to a regulatory process which has already been carried out in another state.

When and why does passive mutual recognition come about? This form of mutual recognition has importance in the judicial field in terms of the recognition of foreign judgments. The essence of passive mutual recognition is that consequent upon prior agreement to recognise one another's court judgments, one state will recognise and allow execution of the foreign judgment. There is no attempt to translate the legal process of the other state into an equivalent legal process of the state of execution. Rather, the 'host' state passively executes the legal form of the judgment.

Similarly, there may be an agreement that other types of certificate or test result or qualification are to be regarded as equivalent to those of the host state and consequent upon that agreement, the host state is obliged to give legal execution to the foreign documentary evidence. This has application in the context of the Single European Market in terms of recognition of test results indicating compliance with substantive rules of product regulation, as well as in areas such as the recognition of professional qualifications. What is significant about passive mutual recognition is that the active work of recognising equivalence has already been carried out elsewhere e.g. through the adoption of EU legislation which requires different national qualifications to be treated as equivalent, or the adoption of an agreement between states to permit mutual recognition of judgments. Passive mutual recognition operates in the host state as the outcome of a regulatory process that must normally be preceded by some form of specific transnational agreement authorising passive mutual recognition. In this way, although this may look like home state control, the obvious difference is that passive mutual recognition does require some prior transnational agreement whether in harmonisation of substantive norms or to require different national certificates/qualifications etc. to be treated as equivalent or simply to obligate legal execution in the host state.

By contrast, 'active' mutual recognition occurs where national regulators are obliged to seek out functional equivalencies between the regulatory processes mandated by the host state and those which have already been carried out in respect of the person, good or service in some other jurisdiction. This active process of mutual recognition requires the domestification of the foreign regulatory process through its translation into some equivalent national regulatory requirement either in whole or in part (i.e. where the home country controls are but one input into a broader bureaucratic administrative/regulatory process). Of its nature, this form of active mutual recognition tends to be individualised in that for any given person, good or service, the national administration must attempt to make sense of what regulatory requirements have already been met and what further controls may legitimately be applied. To be sure, the actual process of active recognition may become routinised and simplified through standard operating procedures and bureaucratic routines, but, nonetheless, the nature of the exercise is still one of having to reach an individual administrative/regulatory decision as to whether to permit free movement.

Whereas passive mutual recognition arises as an obligation to give legal effect to a completed regulatory process in the past, active mutual recognition requires the incorporation of the regulatory history of a product etc. into a contemporaneous regulatory process in the host state. And whereas passive mutual recognition—under the conditions upon which it can be operationalised—gives rise to a guaranteed result, active mutual recognition does not guarantee a specific result. The search for functional equivalence may result in the conclusion that the regulatory requirements of the host state differ markedly from home state regulatory controls and market access will be denied. Or the degree of equivalence may only result in the disapplication of certain of the host state's controls. Or mutual recognition may give rise to market access without further compliance with host state rules.

Limiting Harmonisation Through Mutual Recognition

Thus far we have concentrated upon one dimension of mutual recognition, namely its relationship to the respective application of home/host state controls by Member States. The second dimension of mutual recognition rests with its relationship to harmonisation at the EU level. Students of EU law are familiar with the idea that in the 1980s the Commission adopted a New Approach based on harmonisation of essential requirements while utilising mutual recognition to deal with residual barriers to trade. Of course, what is curious about this story is that it indicates precisely the need for on-going harmonisation where there are wide divergences between the substantive rules of the Member States. The work of 'actively' seeking equivalencies becomes the work of the EU legislative institutions in producing such equivalencies through harmonisation (which in the field of product regulation is also linked to European processes for harmonising technical standards).[29] All of which suggests that the issue is

---

[29] See K. Armstrong and S. Bulmer, *The Governance of the Single European Market*, Chap. 6 (Manchester, Manchester UP, 1998).

usually less a question of the choice between EU harmonisation and national regulation, but rather an issue of the appropriate mix.

Nonetheless, it is evident that insofar as mutual recognition can be operationalised to structure domestic regulatory processes, this has key advantages over the management of an EU legislative framework which may require continual adaptation to deal with changing circumstances and technical progress. Active mutual recognition by the national administrations may be more responsive to changes than an EU legislative response. The difficulty, however, is that a legislative approach which attempts to create clear rights of market access premised upon compliance with harmonised substantive norms is intended to produce a legally secure entitlement. By contrast, active mutual recognition does not give rise to a certain outcome and the result of non-recognition may be time-consuming and costly legal challenges. Thus, we are simply faced with a dilemma rather than a clear choice between mutual recognition and legislative harmonisation. We return to these themes in Part II when considering the legislative approach to the mutual recognition of professional qualifications.

Mutual Recognition as Regulatory Competition or Heterarchical Learning

As Maduro's careful analysis of the European 'economic constitution' illustrates, the choice of model by which to market integrate/regulate is bound up with certain normative ideas. As well as potentially limiting resort to EU harmonisation and, thereby, contributing towards the realisation of subsidiarity in EU governance, a different normative claim that is often made for mutual recognition relates to the control which it may exercise over the activities of national public authorities. That is to say, mutual recognition may be considered to stimulate a competition among rules and a competition among regulators, thereby producing a competitive process of regulatory adjustment and limiting the possibility for 'regulatory failure'.[30] As Majone puts it: '. . . the great merit of the principle is that it replaces centralized by decentralized decision making, in the spirit of the subsidiarity principle, and thus makes possible competition among different regulatory approaches'.[31]

Much of the discussion of the relationship between mutual recognition and competition among rules rests on an assumption that mutual recognition is synonymous with home state control. In other words, it is assumed that if home state control creates a competition among regulators, then so too will mutual recognition. If, however, we are correct in our belief that mutual recognition is

---

[30] See Barnard and Deakin's contribution to this volume. See also Maduro's 'competitive model', above n. 10 and Sun and Pelkmans ,'Regulatory Competition in the Single Market', (1995) 33(1) *Journal of Common Market Studies* 67.

[31] G. Majone, 'Mutual Recognition in Federal Type Systems', EUI Working Paper SPS No 93/1, p. 11.

not synonymous with a model of home state control then that assumption simply no longer holds true. Rather, the space for regulatory competition will be a function of the space for successfully invoking mutual recognition as a technique of market access. By necessity this requires that the difference between home and host state rules not be so great as to prevent mutual recognition's application. This implies a narrow band of potential competition between regulators precisely because if the difference is too great, mutual recognition will not operate and market access will be denied. Thus, the magnitude of competition among rules is likely to be somewhat limited. Indeed, and as Majone himself recognises, the space for mutual recognition and competition may in reality be limited to residual regulatory elements that are not the subject of some prior harmonisation of 'essential requirements'.[32]

Whatever the merits of linking mutual recognition and ideas of competition among rules, I want to suggest an alternative vision of mutual recognition that sees it more as a process for learning between regulators. Where mutual recognition operates in its 'active' form as defined above, national authorities need to make sense of the regulatory history of a good or service or worker within their own domestic regulatory processes. This simple exposure of one regulatory system to that of another may stimulate a bureaucratic learning process as to how other systems regulate. To be sure, bureaucracies may be resistant to learning and instead may tend towards routinised acceptance/rejection of the good etc. onto the national market. Nonetheless, mutual recognition opens up, and may be dependent upon, the possibilities for national regulators to share information, to develop mutual trust[33] and indeed knowledge about the market and its risks. Indeed, it may be necessary to establish transnational structures in order to facilitate processes of information sharing, knowledge generation and mutual trust in order for mutual recognition to be operationalised.

One reason why we may overemphasise regulatory competition and underemphasise regulatory learning may rest upon a fairly basic point about how we think about regulation. As Ladeur notes, much of our thinking about regulation draws upon a model which understands regulation as the application of abstract rules to specific fact patterns.[34] In this way, regulation stands outside and beyond that which is to be regulated lest the public purpose of regulation be tainted or subverted to the particularistic purposes and desires of those to be regulated. Law, as an instrument of regulation, maintains its rationality of generality through its external relationship to its object. Ladeur challenges this model in his recognition that regulatory processes are creative of knowledge

---

[32] Ibid.

[33] As Majone highlights, the absence of trust between national regulators makes it much less likely that mutual recognition can be operationalised, ibid.

[34] See Ladeur, 'Towards a Legal Concept of the Network in European Standard-Setting' in Joerges and Vos (eds.), *EU Committees: Social Regulation, Law and Politics* (Oxford, Hart Publishing: 1999).

both about the object of regulation and about the regulatory function itself. Importantly, Ladeur stresses the role of both public regulators and private market participants in regulatory processes which, under conditions of complexity, are regarded as experimental. While much of the application of the principle of mutual recognition may be routinised, there is scope for thinking of mutual recognition as a more dynamic network concept orientated towards creating channels for the flow of fragments of data and information, especially where regulators seek to apply norms and standards designed to regulate risks in situations which are not necessarily identical from one Member State to another. In other words, where the regulatory treatment of a problem has not yet bedded down into some standard operating procedure because the issue is new in that Member State, information about the regulatory history of products provides the basis for heterarchical learning between and across regulators.

Whether as a mechanism for generating knowledge and information about risks and regulation, or more straightforwardly as a means of providing regulators with knowledge about regulatory structures and processes in other Member States, mutual recognition may have a more significant role in generating regulatory learning than as an engine of regulatory competition.

The Meaning of 'Mutual'

The application of the adjective 'mutual' may simply amplify and reinforce the idea that there are two (or more) regulatory processes (home and host state) that need to be reconciled one to the other. In other words, it is simply restating an empirical observation. The term 'mutual' may have a more normative connotation insofar as it implies 'reciprocity'. However, it is one thing to talk of the reciprocity of the obligation to recognise, it is another to assume that this reciprocity produces a symmetry of economic consequences across the Member States (equality of outcome).

The Member States of the EU are not economically homogenous. The removal of barriers to trade through mutual recognition creates positive trade possibilities for states with efficient production, while less efficiently producing states face the prospect of domestic production being displaced by competition. Moreover, different Member States are likely to be exposed to competition from imports through mutual recognition to different degrees. Brenton, Sheehy and Vancauteren suggest that in areas where mutual recognition can be used to remove technical barriers to trade, this affects 32% of intra-EU imports from Ireland, just over 24% of imports from the UK, almost 18% of imports from Italy, but as little as 5% from Finland.[35] And as regards the future

---

[35] P. Brenton, J. Sheehy, M. Vancauteren, 'Technical Barriers to Trade in the European Union: Importance for Accession Countries' (2001) 39(2) *Journal of Common Market Studies* 265.

accession states of central and eastern Europe, they suggest that almost 50% of EU imports from Romania, 36 % from Lithuania, but only 14% from Estonia may be subject to market access based on mutual recognition. As Brenton, Sheehy and Vancauteren suggest, the economic adjustment for new Member States and the competitive advantages/disadvantages for such states differs across states and across sectors. They note that, 'Mutual recognition sectors such as knitting and clothing industries, are particularly important in EU imports from the Balkan countries and Lithuania whilst they comprise a relatively small share of imports from the Czech Republic and Slovenia'.[36]

It is an inevitable feature of a Single European Market that a certain amount of economic adjustment is part and parcel of membership of the European club. Some states will win and some will lose and it is not enough to justify departure from the fundamental rules of the club that in certain sectors a Member State will suffer negative economic consequences. Nonetheless, it is evident that existing Member States may see a comparative value in market liberalisation through the resort to a legislative process that they can seek to influence compared to the potentially negative consequences of self-interested economic actors seeking to take advantage of the principle of mutual recognition. Member States may seek to use negotiations over harmonisation instruments to minimise short-term effects of free movement (e.g. by negotiating implementation periods which will allow negative consequences to be delayed or to allow economic adaptation or restructuring) or to negotiate compensatory side-payments. By contrast, mutual recognition may have the consequence of facilitating free movement but without any cushioning effect on the national economy. For new states, the economic adjustment may need to be cushioned through negotiations of Structural Funds.

The Obligation to Mutually Recognise

We have noted a number of different applications of the concept of mutual recognition, but here a more systematic approach is adopted. It is noteworthy that mutual recognition is neither confined to its application within the EU, nor it is application solely a matter of legal obligation.

(a) Obligations Arising Under the EC Treaty

The EC Treaty itself does not explicitly impose a general duty to engage in mutual recognition. However, as has been noted, the obligation can be said to follow from the duty of sincere co-operation falling on national authorities under Article 10 (ex 5) EC as well as arising as part of the free movement

---

[36] Ibid, p. 274.

analysis under the EC Treaty. But beyond these implied impositions of the obligation, the Treaty only uses the language of mutual recognition in two instances. Article 47 (ex 57) EC identifies the use of mutual recognition to facilitate freedom of establishment for the self-employed through recognition of 'diplomas, certificates and other evidence of formal qualifications'. Nonetheless, it is through the Council adopting directives that mutual recognition is to be achieved rather than a general duty being placed on national authorities to engage in active mutual recognition. The second instance in which the Treaty speaks of mutual recognition is in Article 293 (ex 220) EC which states that Member States shall enter into negotiations with one another to ensure the mutual recognition of companies and firms. This somewhat esoteric provision was included to create the means for the application of conflict of law rules by first establishing that a company established in one Member State could be recognised as such in another Member State.[37] It is noteworthy that Article 220 EEC envisaged an 'intergovernmental' measure to provide for mutual recognition and indeed in 1968 the then six Member States signed a 'Convention' on the mutual recognition of companies and legal persons.

(b) Obligations under International Agreements

It is apparent that as regards free movement between EU Member States, the obligation to apply the principle of mutual recognition is not dependent upon an express obligation contained within the Treaty. In the context of international agreements to which the Member States and/or the EU are parties, mutual recognition may be self-consciously adopted as an express obligation to facilitate trade between states. As Nicolaidis notes, the use of bilateral or plurilateral 'Mutual Recognition Agreements' (MRAs) is envisaged under the Agreement on Technical Barriers to Trade (TBT) and the General Agreement on Trade in Services (GATS) within the auspices of the WTO.[38] But as Joseph Weiler has noted, the concept of mutual recognition may also have application as a more substantive limitation on state autonomy within the context of GATT rules. He suggests that insofar as mutual recognition operates within EU law as part of the necessity and proportionality analysis under the free movement rules, then similarly it may have application for the interpretation of the doctrine of 'necessity' in respect of Article XX of the GATT.[39]

---

[37] See B. Goldman, 'The Convention Between the Member States of the European Economic Community on the Mutual Recognition of Companies and Legal Persons' [1968/9] 6 *Common Market Law Review* 104.

[38] K. Nicolaidis, 'Mutual Recognition of Regulatory Regimes: Some Lessons and Prospects', Jean Monnet Working Paper 7/97: http://www.jeanmonnetprogram.org.

[39] J.H.H. Weiler, 'The Constitution of the Common Market Place: Text and Context in the Evolution of the Free Movement of Goods' in P.P. Craig and G. de Búrca (eds.), *The Evolution of EU Law* (Oxford, Oxford University Press, 1999).

MRAs are, nonetheless, of importance in the promotion of trade between the EU and non-Member States.[40] In these contexts, the issue lies less with the active mutual recognition of substantive regulatory requirements and more at the level of the passive mutual recognition of conformity assessment certificates. Moreover, under the MRAs entered into between the EU and the United States, Australia and Canada, manufacturers in the EU can have their products tested within the EU for conformity with the substantive regulatory norms of these non-Member States, with passive mutual recognition operating at the level of the importing states' recognition of the testing and certification procedures carried out within the EU[41]. In other words, the state of import is not seeking to recognise the substantive norms of another state as being equivalent to its own, rather, it is only recognising the testing and certification procedures (in compliance with its own substantive norms) which have been carried out in the EU (and vice versa). In this way, one source of technical barrier to trade—recognition of testing and certification—can be eliminated.[42]

MRAs also operate in the context of Association Agreements between the EU and non-Member States and also in the context of agreements between the EU and future Accession States. While these follow the principles which apply to external trade policy more generally, however, one important difference is that mutual recognition of testing and certification is based around common EU substantive norms. Protocols to be annexed to the Europe Agreements (PECAs) were concluded with Hungary and the Czech Republic on Conformity Assessment and Acceptance of Industrial Products in July 2000 and approved by way of Council Decisions in 2001.[43] The PECAs do, however also provide, in the absence of harmonised Community rules, for the mutual recognition of industrial products moving to and from the EU on normal free movement principles. In summary, as regards the obligation to engage in mutual recognition arising from the Europe Agreements and PECAs, it is clear that the specific obligation to mutually recognise is inextricably linked with the more general obligations associated with signing up to the *acquis communautaire* and future membership of the EU.

(c) Obligations Arising Under Substantive EU Legislation

Mutual recognition obligations can be imposed as specific requirements of substantive EU legislation. Space precludes a detailed analysis of Single

---

[40] Indeed, the Council Resolved in 1999 to invite the Commission to develop guiding principles for the management of MRAs and a draft model agreement—OJ C190 (7.7.1999) p. 2.

[41] See Commission Communication, *Community External Trade Policy in the Field of Standards and Conformity Assessment*.

[42] For more detailed analysis of MRAs see Nicolaidis above n. 38.

[43] COM (2000) 741 final and Council Decision 2001/365/EC (Czech Republic) and Council Decision 2001/366/EC (Hungary), OJ L135 (17.5.2001) p1 and p. 35.

Market legislation but it is noteworthy that the very fact that legislation has been adopted may highlight that mutual recognition is operating against a background of prior harmonisation of substantive norms. Consider, for example, Directive 2000/12/EC on credit institutions.[44] If one simply reads the Recitals we find numerous references to the principle of mutual recognition. In reality there is not a lot of active mutual recognition in the substantive provisions of the Directive but rather passive mutual recognition of authorisations to carry out the business of credit institutions. Authorisation is based on home state control, but the home state must comply with the substantive requirements of the Directive and the host state can take measures where it believes the provisions of the Directive are not being complied with. This highlights that although the language of mutual recognition may be used in a Directive, there may in reality be very little active mutual recognition going on.

As was noted above, the introduction of the New Approach to technical harmonisation can be interpreted as creating a residual sphere for the operation of mutual recognition beyond the sphere of harmonised essential requirements. But of course, insofar as New Approach directives themselves create choices, for example, as to the mode of conformity assessment, then it follows that there is an obligation on states to recognise different types of conformity assessment within directives themselves. In this way, under Directive 1999/5/EC, telecoms equipment legitimately carrying the 'CE' mark must be permitted market access not merely because this signifies conformity to harmonised essential requirements but also because it signifies compliance with conformity assessment procedures (of which manufacturers have a choice).[45]

Perhaps the most significant area of substantive legislation on mutual recognition is in respect of the recognition of professional qualifications. In Part II, this area is adopted as a case study to illustrate the different modalities of mutual recognition highlighted in this chapter.

Although it falls outside the scope of an analysis of the Single Market, it is also worth noting the resort to the language and techniques of mutual recognition in what is now termed the area of 'freedom, security and justice' under Title IV EC Treaty. The Council has adopted a Directive on the mutual recognition of decisions on the expulsion of third country nationals.[46] It aims 'to make possible the recognition of an expulsion decision issued by a competent authority in one Member State . . . against a third country national present within the territory of another Member State' (Article 1). However, the recognition is not automatic and any decision to expel is to be determined according to the legislation of the enforcing state and with due respect for the protection of human rights. Also in the field of Title IV, the existence of a

---

[44] OJ L126 (26.5.2000) p. 1.
[45] OJ L91 (7.4.1999), p. 10: See Article 10 in respect of conformity assessment.
[46] Council Directive 2001/40/EC, OJ L149 (2.6.2001), p. 34.

Council Regulation on jurisdiction and the recognition and enforcement of judgments in civil and commercial matters can be noted.[47]

(d) 'Voluntary' Mutual Recognition

It is worth bearing in mind that mutual recognition can operate without it being clearly a matter of legal obligation. One of the key functions of the European Organisation for Testing and Certification (EOTC) is to seek to promote the mutual recognition of product conformity assessment results in areas not harmonised by EC directives. Part-funded by the Commission, the EOTC provides support to industry in the development of agreement groups to support voluntary mutual recognition. Eight agreement groups have been established.

Voluntary mutual recognition can also arise in the shadow of legislation. For example, Directive 91/414/EEC provides a system for the authorisation of the use of plant protection products (e.g. some chemical agent). There is an obligation to mutually recognise authorisations which conform to certain Uniform Principles laid down in the Directive. The Uniform Principles do not apply to applications for an extension of an authorisation for minor uses. However, a Guidance Document has been drawn up by the Commission[48] to give advice to the national designated authorities as to how they might treat an application for an extension of an authorisation for minor use in such a way that mutual recognition of authorisations for minor use can occur. This approach has links with the discussion above concerning mutual recognition as a heterarchical system for learning. Through the use of information about the regulatory history of a product gleaned from the regulatory activities of other authorities, national authorities are encouraged to incorporate such information into their own regulatory determinations in order to consider whether to grant an extension for minor use. As the Guidance document notes, the costs of seeking an authorisation are large compared to the extension for minor use, resulting—in the absence of mutual recognition—in an illegal trade in unauthorised pesticides.

(e) Decision 3052/95/EC – Notification of Non-Application of 'Mutual Recognition'

Article 100b of the EC Treaty (now repealed) was introduced by the Single European Act and required the Commission to draw up an inventory of national measures which might fall within the scope of approximation under Article 100a (now 95) EC but which had not yet been harmonised. The intention was to consider whether groups of national measures could be made subject to

---

[47] Council Regulation EC 44/2001, OJ L12 (16.1.2001), p. 1.

[48] Commission of the EU, *Guidance Documents on Voluntary Mutual Recognition of Minor Use Authorizations*, (Brussels, 10/10/2000).

Community proposals requiring that such measures be treated as equivalent (mandated mutual recognition). However, having carried out this task, the Commission concluded that 'the Commission does not see the need for any specific measures for the recognition of equivalence at Community level'.[49] Instead, the 'firm body of case-law' of the ECJ requiring the application of the principle of mutual recognition could instead be relied upon, but backed up by an obligation to notify the Commission 'where a Member State makes an exception . . . [to the principle of free movement] . . . to satisfy a mandatory requirement or on grounds listed in Article 36 [now 30]'. The Commission drew an analogy with the notification obligation under then Directive 83/189/EEC (now Directive 98/34/EC)[50] and considered that a similar instrument might be adopted for areas not covered by that notification obligation or any other similar notification requirement. This notification system was set up by Decision 3052/95/EC, coming into force on 1 January 1997.[51] Although the Decision does not place an obligation to engage in mutual recognition, it is considered by the Commission to be a technique for managing the non-application of the principle.

Member States must notify to the Commission within 45 days any measures which derogate from the principle of free movement by:

Imposing a general ban on goods,

Refusing to allow goods to be placed on the market,

Requiring the modification of the model or type of product concerned,

Withdrawing the product from the market.

The Decision does not establish what is to follow from notification, although the Commission's 2000 Report on the implementation of the Decision appears to identify four scenarios:[52]

1. notification concerns a temporary measure concerning a specific product—no specific follow-up is required as it usually concerns product defects rather than substantive differences in the laws between states;

2. the notification highlights substantive differences which cannot be removed by mutual recognition—this may require harmonisation measures at EU level;

3. the notification is irrelevant in the sense of either not being needed or being the subject of a more specific notification obligation—either no action is required or the notification is referred to the appropriate Commission service;

---

[49] Commission Communication, *Management of the Mutual Recognition of National Rules After 1992*, COM(93) 669 final
[50] Directive 98/34 EC, OJ L204 (21.7.98), p. 37.
[51] Decision 3052/95/EC establishing a procedure for the exchange of information on national measures derogating from the principle of the free movement of goods within the Community: OJ L321 (30.12.1995) p. 1.
[52] Commission Report on the implementation of Decision 3052/95/CE in 1997 and 1998: COM(2000) 194 final.

4. the notification indicates a breach of Treaty provisions—the Commission must consider whether to launch infringement proceedings under Article 226 EC.

The Commission has received few notifications under the Decision (34 in 1996, 69 in 1998 and 26 in 1999), 90% of which come from three states (France, Germany and Greece)[53]. 10 states have not notified any measures under the Decisions. Part of the problem lies in delineating the Decision's sphere of operation compared to other notification measures (including the invocation of 'safeguard clauses' under particular directives).

However, another reason why it has proved difficult to delineate the Decision's sphere of application lies in the very ambiguity as to the purpose of the Decision. The difficulty lies in the tendency to shift from describing the Decision as applying to derogations from the principle of free movement, and, describing the Decision as applying to non-applications of the principle of mutual recognition. The first interpretation is clearly much broader than the latter. Not all derogations from free movement arise because the Member State has failed to apply the principle of mutual recognition (see the discussion of mutual recognition, *Cassis de Dijon* and free movement above). Yet the Commission's 2000 Report on the Decision continually switches between these different languages. This problem returns us to the theme noted above of a tendency to conflate mutual recognition with home state control. That is to say the Commission tends to see a failure to permit the marketing of a product lawfully marketed in another Member State as *per se* a breach of the mutual recognition principle without considering why the Member State has prevented market access. From the perspective of Member States, it is not clear whether notification is required only in such circumstances that mutual recognition cannot be applied, or in any instance where it decides to invoke mandatory requirements. Not surprisingly, the first few years of the Decision have not produced the results the Commission might wish.

PART II – 'RE-PACKING'

Working in the European Union: Recognising Qualifications and Experience

In Part I, the premises underlying the operation of the principle of mutual recognition were 'unpacked'. In this Part of the paper, those premises are 're-packed' in the specific context of the free movement of persons seeking to work in another Member State. It is not just goods and services that have a 'regulatory history' to which meaning ought to be attached whenever the good or service is offered across borders. Workers—whether employed or self-employed—can also be said to carry with them a certain regulatory history,

[53] Source, Single Market Scoreboard.

particularly in the sense of obtaining experience, specialisations or qualifications which may be necessary either to have access to the market or which condition their status and/or salary within the market. Indeed, it is noteworthy that unlike the fields of goods or services, the original EEC Treaty, in its chapter on 'Establishment' gave formal expression to the application of the principle of mutual recognition through Article 57 EEC (now Article 47 EC Treaty) which empowered the Council to 'issue directives for the mutual recognition of diplomas, certificates and other evidence of formal qualifications'. How then, has mutual recognition been applied both in respect of the self-employed (in particular, 'the professions') and the employed?

The Adoption of the 'Sectoral' Directives

The formal process of mutual recognition of qualifications through the adoption of directives under Article 57(1) EEC (now Article 47(1) EC) was but one strategy to facilitate free movement standing alongside the *liberalisation* of national rules (i.e. the removal of restrictions including discrimination based on nationality) and the *co-ordination* of national rules (i.e. the establishment of certain minimum common requirements across the Member States), again to be achieved through the adoption of directives under Article 57(2) (now 47(2)). In 1962 a General Programme was adopted by the Council to provide for the progressive implementation of the freedom of establishment (at the latest by the end of the transitional period) and for the adoption of transitional measures pending completion of the Programme.[54]

As regards mutual recognition itself, Title V of the Programme provided that when considering the liberalisation and co-ordination of rules on establishment it should be examined whether this should be 'preceded, accompanied or followed by the mutual recognition of diplomas, certificates and other evidence of formal qualifications'. Title V also specified that pending this formal mutual recognition, transitional arrangements could apply including the necessity to produce certificates establishing that an activity had been lawfully carried out in the country of origin.

That the EEC Treaty empowered the Community to adopt legislation providing for mutual recognition reveals little about how the Council ought to act. The General Programme was not specific on whether mutual recognition should precede or follow liberalisation and co-ordination. Therefore, we need to look to institutional practice. However, by the end of the transitional period, there was no institutional practice to examine. It was not until the mid-1970s that the first mutual recognition directives were adopted in respect of doctors,

---

[54] General Programme for the abolition of restrictions on freedom of establishment (Official Journal 15.1.62), OJ Special Edition, 1974, p. 7.

general nurses, dental practitioners and vets, extending in the 1980s to include midwives, architects, pharmacists and hairdressers[55]. It should be noted that the institutional practice was not to limit the scope of mutual recognition merely to the field of establishment but also to extend it to the fields of workers and services[56] with appropriate references in the directives' recitals to the relevant provisions in the Treaty governing workers and services, with additional Treaty support by reference to Article 235 EEC (now 308 EC).

The practice that was adopted for the 'sectoral directives' of the 1970s and early 1980s was to adopt two directives, one co-ordinating national systems by establishing minimum substantive requirements of education and training within the national systems, and one providing for the mutual recognition of the qualifications thereby obtained in the national system and specified within the directive.[57] While it was clear from the case-law of the ECJ in cases such as *Reyners*[58] that the specific Community law requirement of non-discrimination on grounds of nationality was contained in directly effective Treaty provisions and did not require the adoption of directives after the expiry of the transitional period, conversely, there still appeared to be a central role for legislation both as regards the substantive co-ordination of rules on professional qualification and as regards the mutual recognition of qualifications awarded by the national systems.

This legislative approach to mutual recognition has both virtues and vices. Its principal virtue lies in the observation that national systems with diverse standards and procedures for qualification and training may be unlikely to spontaneously and actively recognise the qualifications presented by a person who has obtained such qualification in another Member State. It is not enough to explain this in terms of pure nationalistic protectionism. Rather, we live in a world which orders certain sorts of activities through processes of education, examination and training. More particularly these processes becomed systematised and institutionalised through organisational structures that we call 'the professions'. Beyond the purely technical elements of competency, there is also a sense in which professionals are socialised through national processes of education, examination and training such that the ability to recognise someone as a member of a profession cannot easily be separated from the national processes and structures through which the professional is socialised.

The dual approach of the Community legislature, when considered in light of the foregoing, begins to make sense. Mutual recognition of a qualification (which is but the symbol of different national processes for professional

---

[55] For further details see F. Burrows, *Free Movement in European Community Law*, (Oxford, Clarendon Press,1987), pp. 202–5.

[56] Ibid, pp. 202–3.

[57] The exception is the Architect's Directive which requires the mutual recognition of qualifications but without prior coordination of the requirements of education and training.

[58] Case 2/74, *Reyners v. Belgium* [1974] ECR 631.

qualification) would be unlikely to occur without there also being some mutual co-ordination of national qualification processes through agreement on certain minimum requirements of education and training. By establishing certain common requirements and by then requiring—through directives—the mutual recognition of the qualifications obtained, freedom of movement might thereby be facilitated. Once this 'active' process of recognition had occurred through the legislative process, it would then fall to the national authorities (and where necessary the courts) to engage in a more 'passive' mode of recognition through granting the individual rights under Community law, consequent upon the production of the relevant qualification (in this sense national authorites are simply 'executing' the foreign qualification). Clearly, once persons can bring themselves within the directives, they obtain the direct benefit of free movement as of legal right.

Not surprisingly, however, the adoption of a legislative approach is not without its difficulties and the adoption of directives by the Council proved to be a difficult and time-consuming task. Indeed, the Commission's 1985 White Paper on *Completing the Internal Market* noted that, 'In the field of rights of establishment for the self-employed, little progress has been made, the main reason being the complexities involved in the endeavour to harmonize professional qualifications'.[59] As Watson notes:

> The reasons for the tardiness in the implementation of Article 57 are numerous. An obvious explanation is the complexity of the subject matter. The harmonization and co-ordination of the laws of the Member States in relation to professional and technical qualifications is a mammoth task. Apart from the diversity in the nature and content of programmes of study leading to such qualifications, one is faced with the difficulty of persuading a Member State that the training offered by the academic and professional institutions of another Member State is at least as good if not better than that available within its own territory.[60]

Herein lies a tension. On the one hand, detailed substantive harmonisation and co-ordination may result in more legally secure outcomes, but, on the other hand, there is also the risk that legislation becomes too prescriptive and ossifies national education and training systems. For example, if the harmonisation is geared towards the processes of education and training it may make it difficult to move towards a more outcome-oriented system of professional qualification. That the Council was aware of the problem of over-specifying the level of co-ordination is apparent from the Council Resolution of 6 June 1974.[61] In recognising that 'Directives should be so drawn up that they do not impede

[59] Commission, *Completing the Internal Market*, COM (1985) 310 final, p.25.
[60] See Watson, 'Freedom of Establishment and Freedom to Provide Services: Some Recent Developments', (1983) 20 *Common Market Law Review* 767.
[61] Council Resolution of 6 June 1974 on the mutual recognition of diplomas, certificates and other evidence of formal qualifications which emphasises the close relationship between education policies and the free movement of the 'liberal professions': OJ C98, (20.8.1974), p.1.

efforts towards educational reform in the Member States of the Community', the Council called for future work on mutual recognition to be guided by the desire for a 'flexible and qualitative approach', suggesting that 'directives on the mutual recognition of professional qualifications and on the coordination of the conditions of access to the professions should resort as little as possible to the prescription of detailed training requirements'.

However, to adopt a lighter touch approach runs the risk of producing legislation that simply creates a superficial harmonisation that masks crucial differences between national systems for the education and training of professionals. As a consequence, national administrations may have little faith in the legal regime and barriers to movement may re-emerge.

We shall return to more recent adaptations of these sectoral directives below. For the moment, we can summarise the early approach as involving a high involvement of EC legislative institutions in co-ordinating national education and training requirements and in legislating for mutual recognition, rather than the focus of EC law's attention being the structuring of national administrative processes of active recognition. However, the adoption of legislation was slow and there was an awareness that the development of legally secure modes of recognition might come at the price of stifling new methods of education and training.

The Development of Active Mutual Recognition in the National Systems

As we have already noted, the ECJ had found the principle of non-discrimination on grounds of nationality contained within the Treaty rules on free movement to be directly effective and did not require the promulgation of directives in order to be given effect. Nonetheless, this still left open the issue of whether qualifications obtained by EC nationals in one Member State ought to be recognised in the other Member States in the absence of directives. The case-law of the ECJ in this area is well known but can be summarised briefly.[62] In *Thieffry*[63], a Belgian national was refused admission to the French bar because he did not possess the relevant French qualification, but instead a Belgian law degree. However, the Université de Paris I had recognised the Belgian qualification as equivalent to the French qualification required by the Paris bar. In its ruling on a preliminary reference from the French court, the ECJ ruled that the mere absence of EC directives in the area did not prevent an EC national from enjoying the benefit of free movement where this can be secured through the laws of the Member States or through the practices of the public service or

[62] For fuller discussion see Craig and de Búrca, *EU Law Text, Cases and Materials*, 2nd edition, (Oxford, Oxford UP, 1998), pp. 733–44; Weatherill and Beaumont, *EU Law*, 3rd edition (London, Penguin, 1999), Chapter 19.
[63] Case 71/76, *Thieffry v. Conseil de l'Ordre des Avocats à la Cour de Paris* [1977] ECR 765.

professional bodies. In other words, and looking to Article 5 EEC (what is now Article 10 EC) the Court concluded that national authorities were themselves under a duty to ensure free movement especially where, as here, the French university had recognised the Belgian degree as equivalent. Thus, merely to state that the individual did not possess the relevant French qualification amounted to an unjustified restriction on the freedom of establishment, and instead, the French authorities were required, to the fullest extent possible, to give recognition to the Belgian qualification.

Weatherill and Beaumont rightly note the significance of the Court's resort to Article 5 (now 10) in this context, as providing a 'potentially important instrument in deepening the market integrative thrust' of the Treaty rules on establishment and services.[64] As Temple Lang has noted, while we are more familiar with the idea of national courts acting as Community courts, the idea that national authorities are also subject to duties under Article 5 is less familiar but no less important.[65] To adopt the language used in this paper, Article 5 (now 10) can be seen as legally mandating 'active' mutual recognition on the part of national authorities as a regulatory-process norm. In addition, as Temple Lang and Weatherill and Beaumont identify, other process norms were extended by the ECJ thereby facilitating judicial review within the national legal system to test the legality of a refusal to recognise a foreign qualification in cases such as *Heylens*[66]. *Heylens*, concerned with the Treaty provisions on the free movement of workers, not only required that the assessment of, 'the equivalence of the foreign diploma must be effected exclusively in the light of the level of knowledge and qualifications which its holder can be assumed to possess in the light of that diploma', but also, that where recognition was refused, the individual be given a judicial remedy through which to challenge the decision (combined with an obligation to provide reasons for the refusal to recognise the qualification).

The ECJ's ruling in *Vlassopoulou*[67] gives a very clear example of the requirements now placed on national authorities to give meaning not only to the qualification history, but also the work history, of an EU national seeking access to a profession in another Member State. Thus, the Court required the national authorities to consider whether legal qualifications obtained in the home state were evidence of the equivalent knowledge and experience required by the host state. Even where the qualifications were not directly equivalent, the national authorities had to consider whether knowledge acquired in the host state by way of a course of study or practical experience were sufficient to prove possession of knowledge not evidenced by formal qualifications. Further, where national

---

[64] Above, n. 62, p. 694.
[65] Above. n. 25.
[66] Case 222/86, *UNECTEF v. Heylens* [1987] ECR 4097.
[67] Case 340/89, *Vlassopoulou v. Ministerium für Justiz Bundes- und Europangelegenheiten Baden-Württemberg* [1991] ECR 2357.

requirements permitted entry to a profession only after a period of training, the national authorities had to consider whether professional experience in the home or host state could be considered to satisfy those requirements. And again, access to judicial proceedings to challenge the legality of decision taken by a national authority was considered by the Court to be a procedural requirement.

More difficult for the Court has been the question of the recognition of qualifications obtained by EU nationals outside the EU. The fact that a Member State does recognise such a qualification as equivalent to its own qualification was held by the ECJ not to give rise to an obligation on another Member State also to recognise the qualification.[68] As a consequence, in *Salamone Haim*, an Italian national with a Turkish dentistry qualification could not automatically escape the requirements under German law to undergo a two year training period (even though his qualification had been recognised in Belgium and he had worked there for eight years), whereas possession of an EU qualification would have resulted in a maximum six month training requirement.[69] However, the ECJ did not end its analysis at this point. Looking beyond the automatic 'passive' recognition issue, it stated that the national authorities were, nonetheless, and in light of *Vlassopoulou*, not permitted to refuse the applicant's appointment on the grounds of non-completion of the two-year training period without considering to what extent the experience acquired in another Member State was equivalent to that required by the training period.

The issue of whether a Member State is obliged to recognise a non-EU qualification obtained by an EU national and recognised by another EU state came back to the ECJ in *Hocsman*.[70] What is significant about this case is the attempt by some Member States to restrict the approach adopted in *Vlassopoulou* to cases where no relevant directive had been adopted in the area at issue. They argued that where in fact a directive had been adopted to provide for mutual recognition of qualifications, the directive must be considered to occupy the field and prevent reliance on general Treaty norms requiring active mutual recognition by the national authorities. However, the ECJ rejected this argument and repeated its conclusion in *Vlassopoulou* that the national authorities

> must take into consideration all the diplomas, certificates and other evidence of formal qualifications of the person concerned and his relevant experience, by comparing the specialised knowledge and abilities certified by those diplomas and that experience with the knowledge and experience required by the national rules.

Thus, the obligation to engage in active mutual recognition appears to fill the space that is left by restrictions in the scope for automatic recognition of a

---

[68] Case C-154/93, *Tawil-Albertini* [1994] ECR I-425.
[69] Case C-319/92, *Salamone Haim v. Kassenzahnärztliche Vereinigung Nordrhein* [1994] ECR I-425.
[70] Case C-238/98, *Hugo Fernando Hocsman v. Ministre de l'Emploi et de la Solidarité* [2000] ECR I-6623.

qualification under a particular directive.[70a] This is significant precisely because qualifications obtained outside of the EU will not be covered by sectoral mutual recognition directives within the EU and will not benefit from automatic 'passive' recognition. Instead, the strategy adopted by the ECJ is to require national authorities actively to consider what meaning to attach to such non-EU qualifications.

The General Systems Directives

Extending the scope of mutual recognition of qualifications beyond that of the sectoral directives was part of the package of measures that formed the Commission's 1985 White Paper on *Completing the Internal Market*. The Commission noted that the European Council, at its Fountainbleau meeting in June 1984, had called 'for the creation of a general system for the mutual recognition of university degrees', and indicated its intention to come forward with a framework directive which would not seek to harmonise the content of university degrees but would simply provide for their mutual recognition. Thus the proposal for what became the 1989 General System Directive was part of the 1985 White Paper proposals for action to complete the internal market. Directive 89/48/EEC[71] applies to regulated professionals not covered by the sectoral directives. It applies only to professionals who have completed post-secondary education of at least three years together with any additional training period as may be required for the lawful carrying out of that profession. A Member State may not refuse to authorise an EU national to take up a profession on the basis that he or she does not possess the national qualification. Rather, the national authorities must actively assess the equivalence of qualifications possessed by the EU national. The host authorities must also recognise the level of professional experience acquired by an EU national where the host state imposes a longer period of education and training than that to which the EU national has conformed in the home state. Where, however, there are substantial differences between the matters covered by way of education and training, the host state may require the EU national to undergo an adaptation period or aptitude test in the host state.

Whereas the sectoral directives provide an applicant with a right to establish in another Member State on production of the equivalent qualification to that required by the host state, under the General System Directive, the ability to establish in the host state is dependent upon a process of active recognition in the host state. For the applicant, there is uncertainty as to whether qualifications

---

[70a] The idea that active mutual recognition by national administrations takes over where passive automatic recognition under a directive is not possible is confirmed in respect of the Architects Directive in Case C-31/00, *Conseil National de l'Ordre des Architectes* v. *Dreessen* judgment of the ECJ, 22 January 2002.

[71] OJ 1989 L19/16.

will be treated as equivalent and whether an adaptation period or aptitude test will be required. As Pertek notes, it is rare that the education and training in Member States will have precisely the same content and, therefore, the utility of the General System depends to a great extent on the ability and willingness of national authorities to determine the functional equivalence of qualifications.[72] The General System Directive, therefore, imposes certain procedural safeguards for the applicant by way of completion of the recognition process 'as soon as possible'; the communication of the results of the process by way of a reasoned decision of the competent authority; and, remedies (including remedies before a court or tribunal) shall also be made available (Article 8(2) Directive 89/48). In addition to this, the Directive provides for the creation of a Coordinators Group to facilitate the implementation of the Directive. By bringing together representatives of Member States each having the task of ensuring the uniform application of the Directive, the Directive seeks to provide a mechanism for the exchange of information and the building of mutual trust on which active mutual recognition depends. The Coordinators Group has published a *Code of Conduct* to facilitate implementation of the General Systems approach, indicating both best practice and unacceptable practice.

As well as proposing the 1989 Directive as part of the internal market programme, the Commission also committed itself to assess the functioning of the system to be set up under this directive by the end of 1991. In 1992, the General Systems approach was developed through the adoption of a directive covering the recognition of education and training falling outside the scope of the 1989 directive (particularly non-tertiary level diplomas and certificates).[73] This directive also lays down a more precise time frame for the processing of applications, namely four months from the presentation of all the documents required (Article 12(2)). The 1989 and 1992 Directives have been amended by Directive 2001/19/EC.[74] *Inter alia* the Directive extends the obligation on national authorities to take into account relevant professional experience when considering whether an adaptation period or an aptitude test is required in the event of there being substantial differences in the content of education and training. This follows the approach of the ECJ in *Vlassopoulou*.

There is a sense in which the objective of the General Systems Directives, namely the extension of mutual recognition beyond the sectoral directives, appears to have been overtaken by the jurisprudence of the ECJ in cases such as *Vlassopoulou*. Or perhaps a better way of putting it is that the Directives can now be read as the specific expression of more general legal principles. That is not to say that the Directives are irrelevant. Indeed, they give more specific expression to the obligations on national authorities, as well as establishing an

[72] See J. Pertek, 'Free Movement of Professionals and Recognition of Higher-Education Diplomas' (1992)12 *Yearbook of European Law* 293, p. 314.
[73] OJ L209 (24.7.1992), p. 25 (as amended).
[74] Directive 2001/19/EC, OJ L206, (31.7.2001), p.1.

institutional apparatus—the Coordinators Group—to facilitate its functioning. The more fundamental question is whether the approach adopted by the ECJ and under the General Systems Directives (active mutual recognition by national authorities under the supervisory gaze of EU law) is preferable to the sectoral approach which has hitherto underpinned the legislative approach to mutual recognition.

Extending the Legal Framework—Lawyers

While a Directive on lawyers' services had been adopted in 1977, it was not until 1998 that a Directive was adopted providing for the establishment of lawyers in a Member State other than that in which the qualification was obtained.[75] The Directive allows a lawyer, practising under her home state title, to carry out the same professional activities as a lawyer practising under the host state professional designation. That principle is qualified in respect of certain activities which the Directive permits Member States to exclude from lawyers practising under their home state titles, and in respect of activities which can only be carried out in conjunction with a lawyer of the host state. The Directive also provides for the mutual recognition of qualifications for the purposes of seeking admission to the legal profession of the host state on the same basis as applies under the 1989 General Systems Directive. As regards adaptation periods or aptitude tests, where the host state lays down an adaptation period not exceeding three years or requires an aptitude test, a lawyer with at least three years experience of practise in the law of the host state is to be admitted to the profession without completing an adaptation period or aptitude test. Lesser experience of the law of the host state does not preclude admission without completion of an adaptation period or aptitude test, in that the host state must also take into account additional factors.

Following adoption of the Directive, Luxembourg brought legal proceedings under Article 230 EC Treaty seeking the annulment of the Directive.[76] It argued that the scope of Article 52 EC (now 43) is limited to the application of the non-discrimination principle by requiring that the migrant worker be given equality of treatment with nationals of the host state. By allowing migrant lawyers to work without possessing the qualification required by nationals of the host state, the Directive discriminated between migrant workers and host state workers by creating reverse discrimination. Further it suggested that while services could be provided without compliance with the laws applicable to persons established in the host state, the same could not be said of the freedom of establishment where the Treaty merely required equality of treatment with

---

[75] Directive 98/5/EC, OJ L77, (14.3.1998), p. 36.
[76] Case C-168/98, *Grand Duchy of Luxembourg v. EP and Council* [2000] ECR I-9131.

the host national. The Court side-steps the issue of whether the freedom of establishment is based on host country control, subject only to a non-discrimination requirement, by concluding that the host state lawyer and the migrant lawyer do not enjoy exactly the same privileges and, therefore, their positions are not comparable and no discrimination could be said to arise. Luxembourg also suggested that the Directive was not in the interests of consumers nor the administration of justice, but the Court concluded that the EU legislature had not overstepped the limits of its discretion in balancing the interests of free movement and consumer protection. Additional arguments were also dismissed.

What is interesting about this litigation is the manner in which Luxembourg sought to argue for a model of host state control conditional solely upon a mere non-discrimination requirement. It is evident that the thrust of judicial and legislative policy in this area goes beyond mere non-discrimination to allow for the operation of mutual recognition as both a process norm and substantive limitation structuring the regulatory space of host state regulators.

Adapting the Legal Framework

The legal framework outlined above, in particular, the legislative framework of the sectoral directives and the General Systems Directives, has been the subject of changes and pressures for change throughout the 1990s and the turn of the millennium. In the following sections, these adaptations are highlighted.

(a) Legislative Review post-1992: Subsidiarity and 'SLIM'

In the 1990s the chill winds of subsidiarity and concerns as to the competitiveness of economic agents within the European internal market blew through the corridors of the Commission. The Commission responded with a number of initiatives which had an impact on policy in the area of mutual recognition of qualifications. The first response was a system of legislative review designed to simplify the existing legal framework.[77] The Commission took the opportunity to repeal out-dated directives, to consolidate legislation and to simplify legislation. Directive 1999/42/EC[78] was adopted to apply the general philosophy of the 1989 and 1992 directives to the professional activities previously covered by a number of old transitional directives. However, the process of legislative review set up by the Commission to respond to the principle of subsidiarity was not guided by any clear philosophy or even methodology as to the appropriateness of Community legislative intervention and as such the repeal of a number of

[77] See I. Maher, 'Legislative Review by the EC Commission: revision without zeal' in J. Shaw and G. More (eds.), *New Legal Dynamics of European Union* (Oxford, Clarendon Press, 1995).
[78] OJ L201 (31.7.1999), p. 77.

out-dated directives and the extension of the 1989 and 1992 regimes is hardly sensational. There was no dramatic change in policy.

A further response was the Simpler Legislation for the Internal Market Initiative (SLIM) launched in May 1996.[79] The SLIM methodology is for small teams of national experts to conduct reviews of the operation of legislation in specified areas and to come forward with proposals for simplification. One of the areas chosen for the pilot project was the mutual recognition of diplomas and the attempt to simplify the legislative framework in this area has resulted in significant adaptations to that framework. In some ways, the selection of this area was obvious. The sectoral directives had been amended on numerous occasions to up-date the lists of qualifications. The directive on doctors, dating from 1975, had already been consolidated in 1993 in light of the amendments which had been made to the original text. As we note below, the SLIM review has produced some important adaptations to the legislative framework.

(b) The Role of Sectoral Co-ordination

The sectoral approach based on a (vertical) coordination of education and training requirements coupled with legislated mutual recognition of specified qualifications was out of step not only with the specific approach of the General Systems Directives, but also out of synch with more general trends in EU legislative policy towards a more horizontal approach and less detailed pre-scription of regulatory requirements in EU directives. However, the report of the SLIM team recommended retention of the existing sectoral approach for those areas in which the Community had already adopted directives co-ordinating the national rules on education and training.[80] It considered that the values of the system were 'greater legal certainty for the migrant, ease of operation for national authorities and the fact that the sectoral approach assured employers of a predictable outcome to recognition requests made by job-seekers'. It also thought it unlikely that the necessary majority could be found in the Council to undo the harmonisation work and return full control to national systems. While the SLIM team believed that for national administra-tions the coordinated approach was easy to apply it did recognise that this did create problems 'up-stream' in that the responsibility for seeking equivalences was then left to European legislators in the Commission, Council and EP. However, the SLIM team did not completely reject the possibility of applying the General System to the sectors covered by harmonised directives and recommended a further review. In May 2001, the Commission commenced a

---

[79] COM(96) 204 final; for analysis of the SLIM initiative see K. Armstrong, 'Governance and the Single European Market' in Craig and de Búrca (eds.), *The Evolution of EU Law* (Oxford, Oxford UP, 1999), esp. pp. 756–67.
[80] *Report for the SLIM Exercise on the Mutual Recognition of Diplomas*, Brussels, 22 October 1996. See also COM (1996) 559 final.

consultation exercise (to be completed in September 2001) on 'The Future Regime for Professional Recognition'. In a sense the search is on for a solution to professional recognition somewhere between the sectoral approach with its guaranteed outcomes (but more rigid legal framework) and the General Systems approach with its flexible application (but more uncertain legal outcomes).

(c) Sectoral Advisory Committees

A different, but equally enduring, problem of the sectoral framework has been the role of the sectoral advisory committees established to keep the provisions for education and training under review. The committees are composed of up to forty-five representatives nominated from the professions, teaching establishments and competent national regulatory authorities. In the medical sphere, a Committee of Senior Officials on Public Health was also established to monitor the operation of the directives.[81] The function of these committees was not to act as 'comitology' committees under the Comitology Decision[82] and, instead, changes to the sectoral directives (whether changes to the minimum standards of education and training, or indeed to the lists of qualifications to be given recognition) required the legislative institutions to agree on changes to the directives themselves. Thus, the function of the advisory committees was largely to foster mutual trust between national authorities and to provide for the articulation of the interests of national authorities at the EU level. However, from the perspective of the Commission, the sectoral advisory committees had begun to take on the characteristics of expensive EU-funded lobbyists and it looked to the SLIM team to propose recommendations for reforms to the advisory committee system under the sectoral directives.

The SLIM team found a varied response from those it consulted. The professions, not surprisingly, saw a continued role for the committees but the views from the Member States were mixed. However, there was broad agreement that the advisory committees delivered intangible benefits through the development of mutual trust and personal contacts which facilitated application of the directives and encouraged more general European-wide improvements to education and training standards. In its recommendations the SLIM team sought a re-examination of the composition of the advisory committees, the streamlining of their working methods and better liaison between the advisory committees and the relevant Senior Officials' Committee. As a consequence, the Commission proposed a Council Decision repealing the Decisions establishing the sectoral advisory committees and proposing a streamlined approach to the establishment of new committees with a smaller composition (one representative per Member State), longer term of office (six years instead

---

[81] Directive 75/365/EEC, OJ L167, (30.6.1975), p. 19.
[82] Council Decision 1999/468/EC, OJ L184 (17.7.1999), p.23.

of three) and with a more focused remit being to give the Commission an opinion on matters relating to free movement within the respective professions.[83]

(d) The Nature of Sectoral Co-ordination

In terms of the content of the coordinated requirements of education and training, as we have already discussed, there is a tension between over-specification of requirements (leading to an ossification of educational training and practice) and an under-specification (resulting in superficial harmonisation). That these dilemmas are real rather than theoretical as can be seen in a Memorandum prepared by the British General Medical Council for a meeting of the House of Commons Select Committee on Health in April 2000.[84] While recognising the strengths of the sectoral directives in conferring automatic recognition of certain qualifications, the GMC identified as a weakness of the Doctors Directive that it 'specifically refrains from determining educational standards other than by setting minimum durations for training', and that there were real differences between Member States in terms of the degrees to which graduates possessed both theoretical training and clinical experience. More generally the GMC expressed concerns that the Directive was oriented more towards the specification of education and training *processes* rather than on learning *objectives* and *outcomes*. The position of the SLIM team was that a more outcome-oriented approach was required and that 'the formulation of the minimum requirements should be re-examined with a view to moving to competency-based criteria which places more weight on the outcome of education and training than its content'. The team 'believed that such an approach would carry the additional advantage of diminishing the need for constant updating and would allow sufficient flexibility for Member States to adapt the core requirements to their particular needs'.

(e) Up-dating the Sectoral Directives

A more immediate consequence of the SLIM initiative relates to the mechanisms for up-dating the qualifications given automatic recognition under the directives. Directive 2001/19/EC, as well as amending the General Systems Directives, also amends the sectoral directives. The lists of qualifications to be given automatic recognition are removed from the body of the sectoral directives and instead placed in annexes to the directives which will be up-dated through a simplified mechanism of notification to the Commission. The Commission will publish up-dated lists in the *Official Journal*. This is not a

---

[83] COM(99) 177 final.
[84] GMC Memorandum given in evidence to the House of Commons Select Committee on Health: HC 299i, Session 1999–2000.

comitology procedure. Indeed, whereas the adoption of Directive 97/50/EC[85] had given the Committee of Senior Officials on Public Health a 'comitology' role to update the list of recognised qualifications and designated specialisations under the Doctor's Directive[86], the 2001 Directive repeals this mechanism and merely provides that where the Commission acts under the Directive it is to be assisted by the Committee.

(f) Recognition of non-EU qualifications obtained by EU nationals

Directive 2001/19/EC provides for the situation where a Community national has obtained qualifications which are not listed in the sectoral directives because they have been obtained outside the EU. We have already noted that the ECJ in its *Salomone Haim* and subsequent rulings, while not obliging national authorities automatically to recognise non-EU qualifications even if recognised in another Member State, nonetheless, requires the national authorities to take into account the qualifications and relevant professional experience of the EU national. The 2001 Directive amends each of the sectoral directives to provide that:

> Member States shall examine diplomas, certificates and other evidence of formal qualifications in the field covered by this Directive obtained by the holder outside the European Union in cases where those diplomas, certificates and other evidence of formal qualifications have been recognised in a Member State, as well as of training undergone and/or professional experience gained in a Member State. The Member State shall give its decision within three months of the date on which the applicant submits his application together with full supporting documentation.

Summary

It is evident that the legislative framework surrounding the mutual recognition of qualifications is subject to pressures along all three of the axis noted in the Introduction. That is to say, the extension of the General Systems approach reflects a desire to encourage active mutual recognition by the host state and, in that sense, reflects on-going changes to the relationship between home and host state regulation. At the same time, the debate over the continued relevance of the sectoral approach, together with more general concerns to simplify the EU legislative framework, highlights that it is not enough simply to toll the bell of mutual recognition as if that ineluctably leads to the conclusion that EU legislation is no longer necessary. Rather, the issue is, as ever, one of the balance

---

[85] Directive 97/50/EC, OJ L291, 24.10.97, p. 35.
[86] Directive 93/16/EC, OJ L165, 7.7.93, p.1. This Directive consolidated the many amendments which had previously been made to the original Doctor's Directive which dates back to 1975.

and relationship between, on the one hand, EU legislation and, on the other, active and passive mutual recognition. Finally, and looking beyond the EU, the regime is having to adapt to the need to make sense of the movement of EU nationals beyond the territory of the Member States. The rulings of the ECJ and their recognition within Directive 2001/19/EC are an important reminder that the Single Market has an external as well as an internal dimension.

CONCLUSIONS

The principle of mutual recognition operates along three dimensions: structuring the exercise of national regulatory powers; structuring the relationship between national and EU regulatory initiatives; and, facilitating free movement into and out of the Single Market. It has two types of instantiation with EU law. It can take the form of a regulatory process norm or take the form of a substantive limitation on the exercise of national regulatory powers. In its substantive form, mutual recognition operates as one means of policing host state controls beyond a mere non-discrimination principle. It is not, however, synonymous with a model of home state control even if the application of home state controls is the *outcome* of the mutual recognition analysis. Analytically, mutual recognition is oriented towards the activities of the host state. Mutual recognition performs the parsimonious role of restricting the application of host state controls by reason only of the application of regulatory controls in the home state that are functionally equivalent to those required by the host state. It is not concerned with other reasons for the non-application of host state controls.

Mutual recognition has two principal modalities. In its passive mode, it provides for the execution of symbolic forms produced outside the host state, without assimilating such forms within domestic regulatory processes. In its active mode, recognition involves a domestification of the regulatory history of a product, service or worker within an active host state regulatory process.

These are the principal elements of mutual recognition which, once unpacked, become the analytical tools which can then be re-packed in particular areas of the Single Market. As has been illustrated in the context of the movement of migrant workers and professionals, these elements come together to form a legal framework which changes over time. But even though the framework changes, what endures is the premises which underpin the operation of the principle of mutual recognition within the Single Market.

10

Mandatory or Imperative Requirements in the EU and the WTO

JOANNE SCOTT*

INTRODUCTION

OBSTACLES TO MOVEMENT within the Community resulting from disparities between the national laws relating to the marketing of the products in question must be accepted in so far as those provisions may be recognised as being necessary in order to satisfy mandatory requirements relating in particular to the effectiveness of fiscal supervision, the protection of public health, the fairness of commercial transactions and the defence of the consumer.[1] The concept of 'mandatory' or 'imperative' requirements (otherwise known as overriding reasons relating to the public interest) was introduced by the European Court to soften the blow associated with its expansive reading of the Treaty provisions which seek to ensure respect for the fundamental freedoms. This concept—referred to here as mandatory requirements for the sake of ease of reference—offers the Court a flexible tool to balance the sometimes competing interests of market integration and market regulation; and complements the explicit Treaty based derogations, such as Article 30 EC (ex Article 36 EU). The flexibility inherent in the concept of mandatory requirements derives from the indicative nature of the list of public interest grounds representing mandatory requirements recognised by Community law. This list has expanded over the years and it does seem that the Court has been reluctant to refuse to recognise mandatory requirements put forth by the Member States. Thus, of the public interest reasons submitted by Member States only those of an administrative or economic nature have not been recognized by the Court. This willingness to sanction the existence of mandatory requirements is, however, not matched by a willingness to accept national measures as being necessary to satisfy them. The principle of proportionality—including a least

* I would like to thank Catherine Barnard, Gráinne de Búrca, Eleanor Spaventa and the other workshop participants for their useful comments on this chapter.
[1] Case 120/78 *Rewe-Zentrale AG v. Bundesmonopolverwaltung fur Branntwein* ('*Cassis de Dijon*') [1979] ECR 649, para. 8.

restrictive means test—has been strictly applied to prevent abuse of this flexible instrument.[2]

SCOPE OF APPLICATION

It is well established in the case law of the European Court that the scope of application of mandatory requirements is narrower than that of Article 30 EC (ex Article 36 EC). In particular the Court has stated, on numerous occasions, that mandatory requirements apply only in respect of measures which are not discriminatory, and which apply 'without distinction' to domestic and imported products. Two issues arise in the light of this observation. First is the issue of whether the case law of the Court might not, as some have claimed, be evolving in such a way as to negate the importance of this distinction. It has been suggested that the idea that mandatory requirements may not be invoked in respect of discriminatory measures has been diluted, or even reversed, by the recent case law of the Court. There are those who support this development as both descriptively accurate and normatively attractive. Second, having regard to the traditional case law of the Court it is not entirely clear to what extent mandatory requirements may be invoked in the case of measures which, though nationality neutral on their face, discriminate in fact against imports; that is to say, which discriminate indirectly. These two issues will be considered in turn.[3]

The Evolving Case Law of the Court

Even those who support an extension of the application of mandatory requirements to the realm of discriminatory measures have tended to acknowledge that the Court's case law is equivocal in this respect. Thus, Peter Oliver argues that 'some further prevarication within its ranks on this issue' is to be anticipated,

---

[2] For a discussion of the proportionality principle see the chapter by George Bermann in this volume.

[3] A third issue relating to scope of application arises in the question of the territorial scope of application of mandatory requirements. This is illustrated by *Alpine Investments* (Case C-384/93, [1995] ECR I-1141) where the consumer protection defence was not accepted as applicable by the Court in view of the fact that the consumers which the export restriction sought to protect were those outside of the territory of the regulating state. This seems increasingly perverse in the area of consumer protection as the Community moves towards a common citizenship. It is the case that secondary legislation sometimes restricts the right of a Member State to take steps to protect a given interest outside of their own territory. See, for example, the veal calves directive at issue in *Compassion in World Farming* (Case C-1/96, [1998] ECR I-1251). More generally in the environmental sphere the European Court has gone out of its way to avoid addressing the territorial connection. See especially *Gourmetterie van den Burg* (Case C-169/98, [1990 ECR I-21430, and R. Howse and E. Tuerk, in G. de Búrca and J. Scott (eds) *The EU and the WTO: Legal and Constitutional Issues* (Oxford, Hart Publishing, 2001), for a discussion of this issue in the context of the WTO.

this notwithstanding the fact that the Court appears 'to have reversed its traditional position, albeit tacitly in *De Agostini*'.[4] There must be some doubt, however, as to whether Oliver would adopt the same tentative position today, in the wake of more recent case law of the Court.

Significant, as a starting point, in terms of the assertion of a change of approach on the part of the Court is its decision in *De Agostini*.[5] Here the Court, grappling with the parameters of the *Keck*[6] concept of a selling arrangement, observed that an outright ban on advertising aimed at children less than 12 years of age, and at misleading advertising, is not covered by Article 30 EC unless it is shown that it does not affect in the same way in law, and in fact the marketing, of national products and products from other Member States. It goes on to observe that in the event that it does not affect all products in the same way, it is for the national court to determine whether the ban maybe justified. Significantly in this respect the Court highlights not only the Article 30 EC exceptions, but observes further that:

> Further, according to settled case-law, fair trading and the protection of consumers in general are overriding requirements of general public importance which may justify obstacles to the free movement of goods.[7]

The implication here, according to Oliver at least, is that a discriminatory *Keck*-style selling arrangement may be justified through recourse to mandatory requirements. In fact the statement is more equivocal than this. The Court does not distinguish here between measures which are discriminatory in law (direct discrimination) and those which discriminate in fact (indirect discrimination). Thus we should be aware that read literally as applying mandatory requirements to this category of measures the statement would imply an extension to both directly and indirectly discriminatory measures. The Court goes on to look at the restriction to freedom to provide services implied by the advertising ban at hand. The Court points out that a restriction may result from the application of national rules to persons providing services who are established in another Member State, and who have thus already been obliged to satisfy the requirements of their domestic legislation. (dual burden discourse). The Court goes on to observe that it is for the national court to determine whether those provisions are necessary to meet overriding requirements of general public importance etc., the clear implication being that the mandatory requirements defence is available in such a case. This may be read, as in Oliver, to justify the fact of a radical rethinking by Court. It may equally, however, be read as

---

[4] 'Some Further Reflections on the Scope of Articles 28–30 (ex 30–26) EC' (1999) 36 *CMLRev.* 783, p. 805. See C-34–36/95 *De Agostini* [1997] ECR I-3843.
[5] Ibid.
[6] Joined cases C-267 & 268/91, [1993] ECR I-6097.
[7] Above n.4, para. 46

supporting the more modest proposition that mandatory requirements may be invoked in the case of measures which are indirectly discriminatory (see below).

Decker[8] is also cited by Oliver as evidence in support of this trend. This case concerned the reimbursement of the costs of spectacles by a particular fund. The Fund informed the party concerned, Mrs Decker, that it would not refund the costs as her spectacles had been purchased abroad without its prior authorization. The European Court, in applying established rules on the free movement of goods, categorised these rules as a barrier to free movement, 'since they encourage insured persons to purchase those products in Luxembourg rather than in other Member States, and are thus liable to curb the import of spectacles assembled in those States'.[9] While not accepting that aims of a purely economic nature can justify a barrier to trade, 'it cannot be excluded that the risk of seriously undermining the financial balance of the social security system may constitute an overriding reason in the general interest capable of justifying a barrier of that kind'.[10] While the Court did not accept that this applied in this case, there being no evidence that reimbursement at a flat rate of the cost of spectacles purchased in other Member States would have an effect on the financing or balance of the social security system, there appears to be no doubt that the Court accepted that the mandatory requirements defence could, in principle at least, apply in this case. This is, of course, potentially significant given that the requirement of prior authorization applied only in the case of spectacles purchased abroad and hence this measure appears to be discriminatory, and directly discriminatory at that.

Additional cases may be cited in support of the proposition than mandatory requirements may be invoked in the case of discriminatory measures. Each is environmental in nature. The first, *Dusseldorp*,[11] concerned the movement of waste in the EU, and specifically the exportation from the Netherlands to Germany of two loads of oil filters and related waste. Obstacles were imposed on exports according to Long Term Plan for the Disposal of Dangerous Waste. This provided that export is permitted only if there is insufficient capacity for processing a given type of waste in the Netherlands, unless that export makes it impossible to carry out disposal of an at least equivalent level in the Netherlands. The Dutch government sought to justify the terms of the Dutch long term plan (apparently contrary to Article 29 EC) on the basis of an imperative requirement relating to the protection of the environment. Its arguments were somewhat convoluted in that it suggested that the measures in question were necessary to enable the company concerned to operate in a profitable manner with sufficient material of which to dispose and to ensure it a sufficient supply of oil filters for use as fuel.

---

[8] Case C-177/88 *Nicolas Decker* v. *Caisse de Maladie des Employés Privés* [1990] ECR I-3941.
[9] Above n. 4, para. 36.
[10] Ibid, para. 39.
[11] Case C-203/96 *Chemische Afralsteffen Dusseldorp BV and Others* v. *Minister van Volkshuisvesting, Ruimtelijke Ordening en Milieubeheer* [1998] ECR I-4075.

In the absence of a sufficient supply the company would be obliged to use a less environmentally friendly fuel or to obtain other fuels which are equally friendly to the environment but involve additional costs. The response of the Court is somewhat equivocal. It provides that:

> Even if the national measure in question could be justified by reasons relating to the protection of the environment, it is sufficient to point out that the arguments put forward by the Netherlands government, concerning the profitability of the national undertaking AVR Chemie and the costs incurred by it, are of an economic nature. The Court has held that aims of a purely economic nature cannot justify barriers to the fundamental principle of the free movement of goods.[12]

One can only assume that the judgment is deliberately elliptical, in view of the explicit consideration which AG Jacobs accorded to this issue in his opinion in this case.

One 'celebrated' case in which the Court's reasoning as regards findings of discrimination is not wholly convincing is the *Walloon Waste* case.[13] This concerned a waste import ban instituted by one Belgian region. The Court concluded that this ban was not discriminatory, and hence, in so far as it related to non hazardous waste in respect of which there was not pre-emptory Community legislation, regarded it as susceptible to justification by virtue of a mandatory requirements defence. The Court's reasoning is somewhat contrived. Viewed through the lens of the Community law principle that environmental damage should as a priority be rectified at source, waste produced in one Member State should not be regarded as 'like' waste produced in any other. If the products are not 'alike' any difference in treatment does not in fact amount to discrimination.

It is notable that many, indeed most, of the cases which lend force to the argument that mandatory requirements may be invoked to justify discriminatory restrictions on the movement of goods concern environmental protection.[14] And it is in respect of environmental protection that the Court has taken its most definitive step in this respect in the recent case of *PreussenElektra*.[15] Here the Court was confronted with the legality of a German measure requiring that all electricity supply undertakings which operate a general supply network are obliged to purchase all of the renewable electricity produced within their area of supply. This covered only power produced in Germany and hence gave rise to direct discrimination on grounds of nationality. This notwithstanding, the Court concluded that the measure was not incompatible with Article 30, and did so on the basis that it was:

---

[12] Ibid, para. 44.

[13] Case 2/92 *Commission v. Belgium*, Case C-2/90 [1992] ECR I-4431.

[14] Other cases cited to support this proposition include Case C-389/96 *Aher-Waggon v. Germany* [1998] ECR I-4473, also concerned with protection of the environment in the form of achieving a reduction in noise pollution.

[15] *PreussenElektra AG v Schleswag AG, in the presence of Windpark ReussenKöge III GmbH and Land Schleswig-Holstein* Case C-379/98 [2001] ECR I-2099.

useful for protecting the environment in so far as it contributes to the reduction in emissions of greenhouse gases which are amongst the main causes of climate change which the European Community and its Member States have pledged to combat.[16]

The policy behind the measure was 'also' the Court observed, 'designed to protect the health and life of humans, animals and plants'.[17] The wording of the Court leaves us in little doubt that this is a supplementary justification and there is no suggestion in the judgment that this supplementary justification was crucial to the outcome of the case. Unlike the Advocate General the Court did not explicitly address the issue of the scope of application of mandatory requirements vis-à-vis discriminatory measures.

It is interesting that in *PreussenElektra*, the Court refers to the environmental integration obligation (now in Article 6 EC). This provides that environmental protection requirements must be integrated into the definition and implementation of other Community policies.[18] It introduces its reference to this with the word 'moreover'. Once again this language would appear to imply that this constitutes an additional argument rather than a core, or indispensable, argument. It does, nevertheless, at least raise the possibility that the legal status of the mandatory requirements relating to environmental protection may be different than that of other mandatory requirements, due to the specific status of environmental protection requirements, arising by virtue of the integration obligation. This issue is by no means clear.

Outside the area of goods, in the area of services, there does appear to be one case at least in which the Court has accepted that mandatory/imperative requirements may be invoked in the case of a measure which is directly discriminatory. In *Commission* v. *Netherlands*[19] the rule in question appeared to discriminate directly in favour of a national service provider. All national broadcasting bodies established in the Netherlands were obliged to use exclusively or to some extent the technical resources provided by a national undertaking. As the Court thus acknowledged, these broadcasters were thus precluded from using the services of undertakings established in other Member States. This, the Court added, generates a protective effect for the benefit of the service undertaking established in the national territory, and to that extent disadvantages undertakings of the same kind established in other Member States. While the Court does not address the Dutch government's arguments that the restrictive effects of the measure affect undertakings established in the

---

[16] Ibid, para. 73.
[17] Ibid, para 75.
[18] Ibid, para. 76.
[19] Case C-353/89 [1991] ECR I-4069. This contrasts with the more recent case *Peter Svensson et Lara Gustavsson* v *Ministre du Logement et de l'Urbanisme* (Case C-484/93 [1995] ECR I-2471, where the measure in question appeared to be directly discriminatory in that in order to obtain the benefit in question the lending institution had to be established (either as agency or branch) in Luxembourg. The Court thus deemed that the imperative requirements defence was not available in the circumstances of the case.

Netherlands and other Member States to the same extent, it does note that it is not necessary for all undertakings established in one Member State to be advantaged in comparison with foreign undertakings and that it is sufficient for the purpose of the application of the Treaty provisions on services for the system in question to benefit a national provider of services. This element of (direct?) discrimination notwithstanding, the Court seems to accept that, in principle at least, the measure is susceptible to justification by virtue of cultural policy considerations constituting an overriding requirement relating to the general interest.

Mandatory Requirements and Indirectly Discriminatory Measures

If then there is some confusion as regards the direction in which the Court's case law is evolving as regards the relationship between mandatory requirements and discrimination generally there is, just below the surface, considerable ambiguity in the case law as a whole as to the possibility of relying on mandatory requirements to justify measures which are indirectly discriminatory.

As a starting point it is necessary to observe that the language deployed by the European Court is not conclusive in respect of this question. While it talks consistently of measures which apply *without distinction* to imported and domestic goods as being susceptible to justification by way of the mandatory requirements route, it does not elucidate clearly what this means. While, somewhat less frequently, it talks instead of measures which do not discriminate, or which apply without discrimination, it continues to beg the indirect discrimination question.

Nonetheless a number of cases militate in the direction of a conclusion that mandatory requirements may be invoked even in the case of measures which though facially origin neutral, operate factually to the prejudice of imported goods or services. Weatherill and Beaumont, who would disagree with this conclusion (at least in the case of goods) would nonetheless accept that in *Prantl*[20] the Court applied the mandatory requirements doctrine to a measure which was indirectly discriminatory (Weatherill and Beaumont talk of it being distinctly applicable).[21] Weatherill and Beaumont observe simply that on this occasion the Court 'erred' in allowing consumer protection arguments to be advanced in the case of such a measure.[22] This occasional error hypothesis, though attractive, is perhaps in itself insufficient having regard to the case law of the Court more generally. *Prantl* it seems, does not stand alone. Three categories of cases emerge from the Court's jurisprudence which may be taken,

[20] Case 16/83 *Criminal Proceedings against Karl Prand* [1984] ECR 1299.
[21] S. Weatherill and P. Beaumont *EU Law* 3rd edn (London, Penguin 1999).
[22] Ibid, p. 577.

more or less strongly, to imply that mandatory requirements do in fact apply in the case of measures which are indirectly discriminatory.

A first category of cases concerns measures which are acknowledged to impose a dual burden on imported goods. They are thus indirectly discriminatory according to the dual burden logic. Thus, for example, in *Raisin Germany*[23] a rule regarding bottle shapes was held to be such to make it more difficult or costly for importers to market their products in Germany as they would be obliged to bottle their product for that specific market in bottles which were different from those which they use in their country of origin.

A second category of cases is the more clear cut. Alongside *Prantl*, in the area of goods (see below for the case law in respect of the other freedoms), there does appear to be additional case law to support the proposition that mandatory requirements may be applied in the case of measures which are indirectly discriminatory. Thus, for example, in *Italian Vinegar*[24] the Court, acknowledging the tendency of the rule to favour national goods, observed:

> . . .even if the system established by the Italian legislation applies to national and imported products alike, its effects are still protective in nature. It has been drafted in such a way that it allows only wine-vinegar to enter Italy, closing the frontier to all other categories of vinegar of agricultural origin. It therefore favours a typically national product and to the same extent puts various categories of national vinegars produced in the other Member States at a disadvantage.[25]

Similarly, in *Rau*,[26] the national rule in question concerning the packaging of margarine, was acknowledged by the Court to exert a protective effect. This was evidenced by the fact that 'despite prices appreciably higher than those in some other Member States there is practically no margarine of foreign origin to be found on the Belgian market'.[27] This does seem to imply clearly that the contested rule hit harder in the case of imported goods. Nonetheless, as with *Italian Vinegar*, it was accepted that mandatory requirements could in principle be invoked.

In *Cullet*[28] it was accepted that the national state system of price control may have an effect equivalent to a quantitative restriction where prices are

> fixed at a level such that imported products are placed a disadvantage compared to identical domestic products, either because they cannot profitably be marketed on the conditions laid down or because the competitive advantage conferred by lower prices is cancelled out.[29]

---

[23] Case 179/89, *Commission v. Germany* [1986] ECR 3879.
[24] Case 193/80 *Commission v. Italy* [1981] ECR 3019.
[25] Ibid, para. 20.
[26] Case 261/81 *Walter Rau v. Lebensmittelelwerke v. De Smedt* PVBA [1982] ECR 2961.
[27] Ibid, para. 14.
[28] Case 231/93 *Henri Cullet and Others v. Centre Leclerc Toulouse and Others* [1985] ECR 0305.
[29] Ibid, para. 23.

Thus though 'applicable to domestic products and imported products alike' the measure could fall within Article 30, but also be susceptible to justification by virtue of mandatory requirements, where it operated to the specific detriment of imported goods.

The third category of cases, and the least convincing in a sense, consists of those cases—and there are many—in which it might as a matter of fact have been possible to argue that the contested measure was indirectly discriminatory, and yet mandatory requirements were accepted as applying. Thus in *Miro*[30] or in *German Beer*[31] it would not have been difficult to adduce evidence that the national compositional rules were such as to favour traditionally produced domestic products. It was not that the rules were inherently more difficult to satisfy on the part of the importers but merely that practice had evolved in the regulating Member State in the light of the rules and hence today domestic products were as a matter of fact produced in compliance with the rules. This category of cases is interesting. It is, in itself, notable that the concept of (indirect) discrimination did not feature as a conceptual tool to assist in the analysis of the legitimacy of the measures in question. Had a finding of indirect discrimination been such to preclude any possibility of reliance on mandatory requirements, this absence of any focus upon it would represent a surprising oversight on the part of the advocates in the case.

One possible line of explanation is that favoured by Weatherill and Beaumont whereby indirectly discriminatory measures, though not susceptible in his view to justification by way of mandatory requirements, may be 'objectively justified' in the same manner as indirect discrimination may be in other areas of Community law; notably sex discrimination law. If objective justification operates as the functional equivalent of mandatory requirements for measures which are indirectly discriminatory, then the consequences associated with a finding of indirect discrimination will diminish, perhaps to vanishing point. This is an issue to which we will return below.

If the above offers some support for the proposition that mandatory requirements may be invoked even in the case of measures which are indirectly discriminatory, some cases arising in the area of goods operate to cast doubt upon this proposition. Perhaps the leading case in this respect is that of *Commission v. UK (Souvenirs)*.[32] Here the UK rule requiring goods carry origin marks was found to be applicable without distinction in form only and hence not susceptible to justification by way of a mandatory requirements defence. Similarly, in *Groep*,[33] the Court emphasized that there was nothing in the contested national

---

[30] Case 182/84, [1985] ECR 3731.

[31] Case 178/84, *Commission v. Germany* [1987] ECR 1227.

[32] Case 207/83, *Commission v. United Kingdom of Great Britain and Northern Ireland* [1985] ECR 1201.

[33] Case 6/81 *BV Industrie Diensten Groep v. JA Beele Handelmaatschappij BV* [1982] ECR 707.

practice to suggest that it applied in a manner adapted to the specific needs of national products thereby placing imported products at a disadvantage, and hence that the practice concerned applied without distinction to national and imported products.[34] Thus again the Court examined effect in addition to form in assessing the availability of a mandatory requirements defence. Examination of whether the measure was such to apply 'without distinction' led the Court to analyse impact as well as form.[35]

One final case in the area of goods which is puzzling in this respect is that of *Leclerc*.[36] Here the Court finds that the only justification available in the context of the two aspects of the rule in question took the form of Article 36 EC (now Article 30 EC). It did so on the following basis:

> . . . it must be noted that national legislation which requires traders to abide by specific retail prices and discourages the marketing of imported products can be justified solely on the grounds set out in Article 36.[37]

It reached this same conclusion regarding both parts of the contested rule. Whereas the first part was found by the Court to create 'separate rules' for imported books, rather than merely assimilating the rules applying to imported books to those applying to domestic books, it is possible to conceive of it as discriminatory in nature, and indeed as directly discriminatory in nature. In this sense the conclusion of the Court as regards mandatory requirements is not surprising in this respect. However, the second part of the rule was found not to make a distinction between domestic and imported books. Certainly it was found to discourage the marketing of re-imported books by preventing the importer from passing on any price advantage, but in that the rule is indistinguishable from that in *Cullet* discussed above, and more generally in terms of its discouraging effects from most, if not all, of the national measures deemed to fall *prima facie* within the scope of Article 30. Read literally *Leclerc* would imply that any national law which discourages imports may not be justified on the basis of mandatory requirements.

Confusion reigns. It may be helpful to have regard to the attitude of the Court in respect of the other freedoms. It is notable at the outset to observe that Weatherill and Beaumont, in talking about 'public-interest arguments' that can be used to justify restrictions on the right of establishment conclude that these may be used only where 'the rules do not discriminate *directly* on grounds of nationality' (emphasis added).[38] They go on to acknowledge that requirements

---

[34] Ibid, para. 8

[35] See also Joined Cases 60 and 61/84 *Cinetheque SA and Others* [1985] ECR 2605s, where the Court places emphasis upon the fact that the rule in question did not have the purpose of regulating trading patterns, and that its effect was not such to favour national production. Nonetheless here the 'without distinction' analysis seems to be separate from the analysis of (the absence of) discriminatory effect.

[36] Case 229/83 *Leclerc and others v. SARL 'A Vert' and Others* [1985] ECR 229/83.

[37] Ibid, para. 29.

[38] Above n. 21, p. 682.

relating to residence and establishment are 'in a sense indirectly discriminatory on grounds of nationality' but nonetheless may be justified by overriding concerns in the public interest.[39] And indeed it does seem relatively clearer outside the area of goods that measures which are indirectly discriminatory may nonetheless be justified on the basis of such imperative requirements/overriding public interests. This though the language deployed by the Court is the same as in the area of goods with talk of rules which are applicable without distinction or which are non discriminatory. It is interesting in this respect to observe that one author writing on the secondary establishment of companies notes, like Weatherill and Beaumont, that

> [w]here the impugned measure is applicable without distinction to nationals and non-nationals but discriminatory in effect, it may none the less be lawful if it is justified by imperative reasons of public interest and suitable and necessary for attaining the aim pursued.[40]

In illustrating the availability of the mandatory requirements defence in the case of measures which discriminate indirectly, *Bachmann* provides a useful example.[41] This case concerned the deductability from taxable income of certain contributions relating to the insurance of individuals, deductability being contingent upon the contributions being payble in the regulating state, in this case Belgium. The Court analysed the rules from the perspective of both Article 39 (ex Article 49) and Article 43 (ex Article 52). In respect of persons the Court's judgment is not at all equivocal as regards the issue at hand here. It notes quite simply that there is a risk that the provisions in question may opearate to the particular detriment of those workers (who have carried on an occupation in one Member State and who are subsequently employed, or seek employment, in another Member State) who are, as a general rule, nationals of other Member States. In this respect there appears to be little doubt as to the indirectly discriminatory nature of the rule at hand, or at least its propensity to give rise to discrimination of this kind. Nonetheless, the Court went on to consider whether the rules at hand could be justified in the public interest, and in particular by virtue of the need to ensure the cohesion of the tax system of the Member State concerned. Note that the Court talks about the need to achieve

---

[39] See, however, Case 182/83 *Fearon & Co. Ltd.* v. *Irish Land Commission* [1984] ECR 3677 where the European Court held that a residence requirement requiring those concerned to live or near the land could be imposed on those established in Ireland where it was imposed within the framework of legislation concerning the ownership of rural land which is intended to achieve the objectives set on on its own nationals and those of the other Member States and is applied to them equally. A residence requirement of this kind was found not in fact amount to discrimination which might be found to offend against Article 52 of the Treaty (para. 10). In this sense it should not be automatically assumed that establishment/residence requirements will inevitably operate in a discriminatory manner.

[40] V. Edwards, 'Secondary Establishment of Companies—the Case Law of the Court of Justice' (1998) 18 YEL 221, p. 252.

[41] Case C-204/90 *Hanns-Martin Bachmann* v. *Belgian State* [1992] ECR I-249.

the objective of protecting the public interest, and does not refer to the familiar language of either objective justification or mandatory/imperative requirements. As regards services the rule in question took the form of a requirement that the insurer be established in the Member State in question as a condition of the eligibility of the insured person to benefit from certain tax deductions. In this respect the Court held that this constitutes a restriction on freedom to provide services, but did not allude to whether the restriction was discriminatory in nature. However, as noted above requirements relating to establishment and/or residence are by their nature likely to discriminate in fact against non-nationals.[42] It went on to observe that the requirement of establishment is compatible with the treaty rules on services where it constitutes a condition which is indispensable to the achievement of the public-interest objective pursued; in this case, once again, cohesion of the tax system.

Nonetheless it would be a mistake here, outside the area of goods, to suggest that the case law is all one way. Important in this respect is the *Spanish Films* case.[43] Here a link had been established between the granting of licences for dubbing films from third countries, and the filming and distribution of Spanish films. While on its face applicable without reference to nationality, that rule was held by the Court to have the effect of protecting undertakings producing Spanish films, and of placing undertakings of the same type established in other Member States at a disadvantage. 'Since the producers of films from other Member States are thus deprived of the advantage granted to the producers of Spanish films, that restriction is of a discriminatory nature'.[44] As such that rule, which is not applicable without distinction, may be justified only by reference to the explicit Treaty based exception in Article 46.

In *Futura*[45] the Court recognized that one part of the contested measure 'specifically affects companies or firms having their seat in another Member State',[46] by virtue of the fact that

> if such a company or firm wishes to carry forward losses incurred by its branch, it must keep, in addition to its own accounts which must comply with the tax accounting rules applicable in the Member State in which it has its seat, separate accounts for its branch's activities complying with the tax accounting rules applicable in the State in which its branch is established.

Though the measure was held to affect 'specifically' companies or firms having their seat in another Member State, the Court accepted that it was susceptible

---

[42] For an explicit recognition of this see: C-175/88 *Biehl* [1990] ECR I-1779, which recognizes the discriminatory consequences associated with a residence requirement but nonetheless did not at the outset preclude the possibility of justifying the measure in the general interest.
[43] Case C-17/92 *Federacio de Distribuidores Cinematograficos v. Estado Espanol e Union de Productores de Cine y Television* [1993] ECR I-2239.
[44] Ibid, para. 15.
[45] Case C-250/95 *Futura Participations SA and Singer v. Administration des Contributions* [1997] ECR I-2471
[46] Ibid, para. 26.

to justification by virtue of reasons of public interest, such as the need to be able to ascertain the amount of taxable income in that Member State. It seems from the judgment that the rule in question placed non-resident tax payers wishing to carry losses forward in the same position as resident tax payers who would incur comparable obligations to keep accounts complying with the rules of the state. Thus to the extent that the rule gives rise to discrimination, it does so on the basis of the dual burden logic discussed above. That is to say, as the Court observes in the quotation above, non resident tax payers incur by virtue of this obligation a burden of keeping a second set of accounts, complying with the rules of a second legal system. In this way they are especially disadvantaged.

More generally the companies cases, including *Futura*,[47] are interesting from the perspective of the discussion here, principally because it is not entirely clear what discrimination on grounds of nationality means in the case of legal persons. While, as argued above, there is relative clarity in the proposition that measures which discriminate directly may be justified only on the basis of the Treaty, whereas those which discriminate indirectly may also be susceptible to justification on the basis of the mandatory requirements defence,[48] there is considerable uncertainty as to what constitutes direct discrimination in the context of the secondary establishment of companies. This is in part because the nationality of a company is a legal fiction and depends upon the way in which that fiction is written up by the Member State in question. Bonds of nationality may mean different things in different Member States, according to the company law theory (real seat or place of incorporation) favoured by that state. Thus, whereas the tendency of the Court has been to equate the seat of a company with its nationality—though the case law is not entirely consistent and is confusing—and hence discrimination on this basis has tended to be regarded as direct, discrimination on the basis of fiscal residence has been viewed as indirect and hence susceptible to justification on the basis of mandatory requirements. This has been criticized by Edwards who argues that differences in treatment predicated upon the location of the seat of a company should be equated to differences in treatment based on residence in the case of natural persons, and hence viewed as instances of indirect rather than direct discrimination. Where 'the impugned legislation distinguished according to whether a company was incorporated in the form of a national company' Edwards accepts that it is proper that this be conceived as direct discrimination and hence that the mandatory requirements defence be excluded.[49]

---

[47] See generally Edwards above n. 40.
[48] For the exclusion of mandatory requirements in the case of direct discrimination see, for example, Case 79/85 *Segers* [1986] ECR 2375, Case C-1/93 *Halliburton* [1994] ECR I-1137, and Case C-212/97 *Centros* [1999] ECR I-1459.
[49] Above n. 40, p. 247.

Objective Justification

There are cases in which the Court's approach appears to have more in common with the concept of objective justification than with that of mandatory/ imperative requirements. And certainly for Weatherill & Beaumont, at least in the area of goods, it is through recourse to this concept that indirectly discriminatory measures may be justified albeit, as they acknowledge it has rarely been invoked by the Court. They cite one specific case in support of this proposition, *Gebroeders*.[50] In certain respects this seems to be a surprising example, not least because it is concerned with Member State compliance with a public procurement directive and not the Treaty, but also because the criteria for selecting between tenders are regarded as acceptable by the Court where they are objective, and where they have no discriminatory effects on tenderers from other Member States, be these direct or indirect in nature.

Also interesting from the perspective of justifying indirect discrimination is *Haug-Adrion*.[51] Here the Court was faced with a measure which precluded the granting of no-claims bonuses on insurance contracts to owners of vehicles bearing customs plates. The applicants argued that this was discriminatory in that a refusal to grant the bonus 'mainly concerned nationals of Member States other than the Federal Republic of Germany or persons who did not reside in the Federal Republic of Germany'.[52] Instead of simply acknowledging this and going on to ask whether the resulting indirect discrimination could be justified, the Court rejected this argument on the basis that the conditions applicable 'in no way take into account the nationality or the place of residence of the insured person; they are based exclusively on objective actuarial factors and on the objective criterion of registration under customs plates.'[53] On this basis the Court determined the prohibition on discrimination did not preclude such a measure. The reasoning is not entirely clear, in particular there is some doubt as to whether the Court is basing its findings on the fact that there is no discrimination, because the distinction in question was based on objective criteria and differences and so the situations were not comparable and hence a difference in treatment did not amount to discrimination, or by virtue of its acceptance of the fact that the indirect discrimination involved was susceptible to objective justification.[54]

[50] Case 31/87 *Gebroeders Beentjes BV v. State of Netherlands* [1988] ECR 4635.
[51] Case 251/83 *Haug-Adrion v. Frankfurter Versicherungs-AG* [1984] ECR 4277.
[52] Ibid, para. 15.
[53] Ibid, para. 16. In this the Court appears to have been influenced by the fact that the individual contesting the measure was actually a national of Germany who had bought a car in Germany but who wanted to export it to the Member State in which he resides.
[54] See also Case 238/82 *Duphar BV and Others v. The Netherlands* [1984] ECR 523. Here the Court provides that for the measure in question to be in conformity with the Treaty (Article 28 EC) the choice of medical preparations to be excluded from the Dutch list must be free of any discrimination against imported products. Thus they must be drawn up in accordance with objective and

It might be possible to argue that objective justification plays a rather different role in the context of free movement as opposed to, for example, sex discrimination. Looking at these cases, and others,[55] it might be argued that objective justification plays a role in determining whether the products or services, for example, represent like products or services, and hence whether differential treatment amounts to discrimination. If there are objective reasons which distinguish the products concerned then different treatment does not amount to discrimination. This issue of the meaning of 'like' products is one which has received considerable attention within the framework of the WTO, most recently in the *Asbestos* ruling.[56] This understanding of objective justification as operating as a means of assessing whether there is discrimination, rather than whether the indirect discrimination may be justified, gains some support from the taxation case law. Here differences in treatment are regarded as discriminatory where there is no objective difference which is such to objectively justify the difference. Thus in assessing whether there is discrimination it is necessary to first determine whether those being compared are truly in comparable situations.[57]

Thus it is not entirely clear at what state objective differences enter the equation. On occasion, as Weatherill and Beaumont argue, they appear to play a role which is comparable to that played by mandatory requirements. On these occasions objective justification is operating to legitimate indirect discrimination. At other times, and perhaps more commonly, objective differences are not cited as a means of justifying indirect discrimination, but rather as a means of explaining why what might look like discrimination does not in fact amount to discrimination because the objects of comparison are not comparable, due to the existence of objective differences between them. In this way objective justification operates prior to any finding of discrimination and ultimately to preclude a finding of discrimination. Weatherill and Beaumont frame their discussion of objective justification in an ambiguous manner. '[I]f it can be shown that there are objectively justifiable reasons for the rules in question unconnected with nationality, then the rules will be considered lawful'.[58] This does not tell us whether lawfulness is predicated upon an absence of

---

verifiable criteria without reference to the origin of the products. Thus again the objective justification is not such to sanction indirect discrimination but rather able to operate only where there is no discrimination, direct or indirect. Hence though the language used in this case, and in *Haug-Adrion* (supra n. 53), is resonant of that of objective justification which is familiar from the area of sex discrimination, it may well be that the concept deployed is actually quite distinct.

[55] E.g. C-311/97 *Royal Bank of Scotland* [1999] ECR I-2651.
[56] *European Communities—Measures Affecting Asbestos and Asbestos-Containing Products* WT/DS/135/R, panel report 18 September 2000; Appellate Body Report WT/DS135/AB/R, 12 March 2001.
[57] See, for example, ibid, Case C-279/93 *Schumacker* [1995] ECR I-225, and Case C-107/94 *Asscher* [1996] ECR I-3089.
[58] Above n. 21 at 517.

discrimination, or a justification of indirect discrimination. At any rate Weatherill and Beaumont accept that both objective justification and mandatory requirements reflect 'the same idea that a state is entitled to demonstrate a justification for a rule that tends to protect a national market, provided that reason is not tainted by nationality discrimination'.[59]

Assessment

A long time coming, the assessment of this case law may nonetheless be brief. Two observations flow from it. First, there is considerable confusion and contradiction in the case law of the Court as regards the scope of application of the mandatory requirements doctrine. In addition, there remains some uncertainty as to how this doctrine relates to the concept of objective justification of indirect discrimination.

Second, discussion of the case law emphasizes a basic but important point. The concept of discrimination is a legal construct and its implications depend upon the choice of premises to underpin it. In particular the existence of discrimination depends upon how the idea of 'like' products is conceived and applied. This is susceptible to manipulation according to a range of factors. This is clear on the basis of the recent *Asbestos*[60] ruling of the WTO Appellate Body where the AB overturned the findings of the panel as regards the 'likeness' of the products. Particularly significant in this respect was the conclusion of the AB that likeness may depend, *inter alia* on non economic social considerations such as, for example, the implications of the products concerned for human health. Famously too in *Tuna/Dolphin* the issue of like products was at the heart of the dispute, with the question arising as to whether products harvested in a different way should be considered 'alike' where differences in production or harvesting are not finally reflected in differences in the products themselves. Experience in the GATT/WTO teaches us that determination of which products may legitimately be compared in order to determine the existence of discriminatory treatment is intensely political and not a straightforward objective process. In the EU this conclusion is supported by the *Walloon Waste* case, a

---

[59] Above n. 21 p. 518. It is worth noting that Craig and de Burca have put forward an argument in respect of this discussion which seems to have some merit. They argue that measures which are indirectly discriminatory are susceptible to justification by virtue of mandatory requirements other than where these are purposively (intentionally) discriminatory. According to some understandings of sex discrimination law, there is some normative merit to this argument. Michael Rubenstein, for example, in the context of a discussion of equal pay for equal work, notes that the concept of intentional indirect discrimination simply does not make sense. If the intention is to discriminate then by definition the discrimination is by reference to sex (or nationality) and not some other objective factor and hence the discrimination is direct. Whatever the normative merits of this thesis, it seems clear that it would serve, at a descriptive level, to explain only some of the cases discussed above, and often it would be a question of assessment rather than clear fact as to which.
[60] See the discussion below at pp. 288.

case which illustrates how the concept of like products may be manipulated in order to avoid the constraints on the scope of application of mandatory requirements.

If the concept of discrimination is a legal construct, the premises of which are by no means fixed, so too the distinction between direct and indirect discrimination. As is clear from the area of goods, it is inherent in the nature of regulation that domestic goods will more often satisfy domestic regulatory regimes than imported goods. Domestic practices will have evolved in the light of home state regulation. Thus, very often as a matter of fact, fewer imported products will comply with domestic regulation than domestic goods. It is not necessarily that it is more difficult for them to do so (other than in terms of the dual burden discourse) but rather simply that they will not do so because practices in that state have evolved in the light of different rules. Does this (a *German Beer* type scenario) constitute indirect discrimination and if so on what basis? Is the dual burden conception indispensable to this finding or will the mere fact of disparate impact suffice? The answers may seem obvious but nonetheless choices have to be made about the premises and the positioning of the threshold for a finding of indirect discrimination and given, for example, that there is no ready dual burden analogy in the area of sex discrimination, it cannot be assumed that this threshold is susceptible to transplantation across spheres of law.

When we move outside of the area of natural persons to, in particular, legal persons, the distinction between direct and indirect discrimination acquires an additional layer of complexity. This is well illustrated by the Edwards article cited above. At this stage it is difficult to know how best to characterise the factor according to which the difference in treatment is based. This is particularly true in respect of a difference in treatment which is predicated upon the seat of the company. Edwards argued that this ought to be compared to a difference in treatment based on the residence of a natural person, and hence constitute indirect discrimination. The Court, more often but not always, characterizes it as comparable to the nationality of a natural person and hence as direct discrimination.

The thrust of the argument here is simply that discrimination, as a legal construct, is an artificial concept with no meaning apart from the manner in which it is applied. The manner in which it is applied depends upon the choice of premises selected to underpin it. In view of the artificiality of the concept and the difficulties associated with the concept of 'like', and with the distinction between direct and indirect discrimination, it may be thought that the limited scope of application of the mandatory requirements doctrine (applying only to measures which are applicable without distinction) rests upon a series of contingencies which come, as a result, to assume an centrality which is not warranted on normative grounds. These observations support the general conclusion put forward by de Búrca in her contribution to this volume.

It may be added that this discussion of the scope of application of mandatory requirements has assumed a renewed importance in the wake of the *Keck*
decision of the European Court. Pursuant to *Keck* selling arrangements within
the meaning of that and later judgments are contrary to Article 30 only where
these are such to discriminate either in law or in fact. As such the concept of discrimination once again comes to play a central role in the application of Article 28 EC. It is likely that in the future a selling arrangement found to fall within
Article 28 will be defended on grounds which are not included in Article 30 EC
(by good fortune the Swedish alcohol advertising ban was defended on grounds
of public health and not consumer protection[61]). As a result the issue of the susceptibility to justification of measures which are discriminatory—directly or
indirectly—will have to be more squarely addressed by the Court, as will its
relationship to the doctrine of objective justification.

THE WORLD TRADE ORGANIZATION

It is interesting in the light of the above to turn to consider the WTO experience.
It is notable at the outset that both GATT and GATS contain treaty based
exceptions to the free movement principle such that may be considered analogous with Articles 30, 39(3) and 46 EC. Whereas GATS Article XIV contains a
list of general exceptions, extending for example, to public morals, public order
and the protection of human, animal or plant life or health, Article XIV bis lays
down specific security exceptions. These relate to the essential security interests
of a State, including at times of war. The GATT is premised upon a similar
bifurcation with the general exceptions contained in Article XX, and the
security exceptions in Article XXI. It is significant that the general exceptions in
GATS and GATT are headed up by an identical 'chapeau' precluding application of measures in such a way as to constitute arbitrary or unjustified discrimination, or a disguised restriction on trade. Again this chapeau is resonant of
Article 30 EC and reminds us that the founders of the EC looked to the GATT
1947 in the formulation of the EC's free movement regime. Article XX GATT
has fallen, on a number of occasions, for interpretation by the WTO Appellate
Body. It has been strictly construed.

One of the most important agreements constituting the WTO package is the
Agreement on Technical Barriers to Trade (TBT Agreement). The concept of a
technical regulation is broadly defined in the following terms:

> Document which lays down product characteristics or their related processes and
> production methods, including the administrative provisions, with which compliance
> is mandatory. It may also include or deal exclusively with terminology, packaging,

---

[61] Case 123/00 *Konsumentombudsmannen (KO)* v *Gourmet International Products AB (GIP)* [2001]
ECR I-2795.

marking or labelling requirements as they apply to a product, process or production method.[62]

The significance of this Agreement lies in the manner in which it moves the WTO beyond a discrimination based approach to the free movement of goods. In this the TBT Agreement bears some comparison to *Cassis de Dijon*. Thus, Article 2:2 provides that 'Members shall ensure that technical regulations are not prepared, adopted or applied with a view to or with the effect of creating unnecessary obstacles to international trade'. Technical regulations, relating for example to the composition or packaging of a product, may be 'unnecessary' though applicable without distinction to domestic and imported goods. Whereas it may well be that there was a potential inherent in the text of the GATT itself to move beyond discrimination, the TBT Agreement represents a decisive and striking move in this direction.[63] It is, in the light of this, interesting to observe that this move beyond discrimination amounting to a substantial expansion of the basic rule is accompanied, as was *Cassis de Dijon*, by an expansion of the possibility for justification. Thus, Article 2:2 goes on to provide that:

> . . . technical regulations shall not be more trade-restrictive than necessary to fulfil a legitimate objective, taking account of the risks that non-fulfilment would create. Such legitimate objectives are, *inter alia*: national security requirements; the prevention of deceptive practices; protection of human health or safety, animal or plant life or health, or the environment. In assessing such risks, relevant elements of consideration are, *inter alia*: available scientific and technical information, related processing technology or intended end-uses of products.

A number of similarities with the concept of mandatory requirements are apparent on the basis of the text itself. Thus, the list of legitimate objectives laid down is clearly regarded as indicative rather than exhaustive, in the same way as is the *Cassis de Dijon* list. In this Article 2:2 contrasts with the Treaty exceptions in GATT and GATS. Further, application of the concept of legitimate objectives is underpinned by the language of necessity and least restrictive means; these constituting important elements of the proportionality principle, though arguably they do not exhaust its connotations. Inherent in the concept of mandatory requirements are the principles of necessity and least restrictive means, but these operate alongside a substantive conception of proportionality which is such that even a measure which is strictly necessary to achieve a given objective, and the least restrictive means of so doing, may be found to be unlawful as it is regarded as disproportionate having regard to the degree of

---

[62] Annex 1:1
[63] See Weiler, J.H.H, 'Epilogue: Towards a Common Law of International Trade' in Weiler, J.H.H., *The EU, the WTO and the NAFTA* (Oxford, OUP, 2000) who argues that the GATT never took Article XI seriously (prohibition on quantitative restrictions) and thus that it was rare to challenge non-discriminatory quantitative restrictions under the original GATT regime.

trade restriction implied. This is clearly apparent on the basis of the judgment
of the European Court in *Danish Bottles* whereby the extra degree of environmental protection achieved by the additional restrictions associated with the use
of approved containers, was deemed to be insufficient to justify the greatly
enhanced level of trade restriction which this implied.[64] In this sense though
necessity, proportionality and least restrictive means are closely related and
often regarded by the European Court as synonymous there is the occasional
case in which proportionality acquires a meaning distinct from necessity and
least restrictive means. It remains to be seen whether this substantive balancing
dimension may be deemed to be inherent in the concept of necessity as laid
down in Article 2:2. There are those who argue that the concept of proportionality is inherent in Article 2:2 by virtue of the language 'taking into account the
risks that non-fulfilment would create', an interpretation not shared by Howse
and Tuerk.[65]

Beyond this it is hard to pass comment upon the nature of the legitimate
objectives which underpin the TBT Agreement. While the AB of the WTO has
confirmed that this Agreement imposes obligations on Members which are different from, and additional to, the GATT 1994, there has been no report on this
subject on the part of either a panel or the AB. It was against this backdrop that
the AB in *Asbestos* declined to complete the legal analysis, notwithstanding its
reversal of the panel's finding that the TBT Agreement did not apply.[66]

Nonetheless in their recent paper on the *Asbestos* dispute Rob Howse and
Elizabeth Tuerk make some interesting observations on the TBT Agreement
which may be pertinent from our perspective here.

First, in the context of a complex argument about the relationship between
the TBT and the GATT, Howse and Tuerk argue that 'where a regulatory
scheme does not explicitly discriminate against imports, these claims will
normally be brought as TBT claims' and that 'if the regulatory process is in
conformity with TBT requirements, it is highly implausible that the non-
national-origin regulatory distinctions generated by that process could be
impugned under Article III [of the GATT]'.[67] Thus their argument implies that
as a matter of fact measures which are directly discriminatory on grounds of
nationality will fall for consideration under GATT Articles III/XX, whereas
with those measures which are facially origin neutral (though perhaps indirectly
discriminatory) it makes sense to address them from the perspective of the
discipline imposed by the TBT and in particular Article 2:2 thereof. According
to this argument the mandatory requirements style 'defence' laid down in

[64] Case 302/86 *Commission v. Denmark* [1998] ECR 4607.
[65] See discussion in R. Howse and E. Tuerk, in G. de Búrca and J. Scott (eds) *The EU and the WTO: Legal and Constitutional Issues* (Oxford, Hart Publishing, 2001).
[66] Paras. 59–83. This analysis gives a useful insight into the concept of a technical regulation as defined above.
[67] Above n. 65 at 312.

Article 2:2 will apply, in practice rather than in law, in the case of measures which are not directly discriminatory.

Second, the paper by Howse and Tuerk may be read as cautioning against a simple transposition of the mandatory requirements framework to the TBT Agreement. This is due to the manner in which they characterize the Agreement. They argue that Article 2:2 (and the TBT Agreement as a whole) must be seen in a fundamentally different light from GATT Articles III and XX. In relation to the latter 'the substance of the regulations must be justified by the defendant, because protection has already been determined to exist'[68]. However, as regards the TBT Agreement it 'does not set up a general presumption against such regulations as trade barriers, which must then be scrutinized to see if they fit within certain exceptions'. On the contrary they argue, having regard to the preamble of the TBT Agreement, regulatory measures are presumptively legitimate and hence do not require justification. Thus rather than viewing the Agreement in terms of a rule/exception construction, they see it as 'merely plac[ing] some conditions or qualifications on the exercise of that right [the right for Members to chose an appropriate level of protection].'[69] In this they present a picture which is distinct from that in the EU. While it is correct that formally mandatory requirements do not constitute an exception to the rule—because justification by virtue of mandatory requirements takes the measure outside the scope of the rule itself—in reality mandatory requirements represent a second source of exception to the rule which favours mutual recognition and creates presumption of equivalence. Thus whether justification proceeds by way of an explicit Treaty based exception or by way of mandatory requirements the burden of establishing necessity, proportionality and least restrictive means lies with the regulating state. In this, in rejecting the rule/exception paradigm, Howse and Tuerk may be highlighting an important difference in terms of burden of proof. If technical regulations which are non facially nationality discriminatory are presumptively legitimate under the TBT Agreement, then it is for the complaining party to demonstrate a prima facie case that the 'conditions' or 'qualifications' established by that Agreement have not been complied with. This, as Howse and Tuerk imply, may present some difficulties for the complainant, who will be required to demonstrate this on a balance of probabilities 'without the ability to compel disclosure of evidence by the defendant'.

It is not only in this respect that Howse and Tuerk aim to soften the de-regulatory blow struck by the TBT Agreement. They argue further that the TBT Agreement:

> Focuses largely on the regulatory process and its inputs, which involves necessarily *some* examination of the substantive regulatory choices of democratic politics, but avoids WTO tribunals sitting in *de novo* review of non-facially discriminatory

---

[68] Above n. 65 p 314.
[69] Above n. 65 p 314.

policies, against which there is no general presumption in WTO (unlike facially discriminatory trade restricting measures).[70]

While they go on to concede that 'Article 2:2 is perhaps the provision of the TBT Agreement that most clearly brings into the assessment of a Member's regulatory process an element of judgment or scrutiny of its substantive regulatory outcomes'[71], they claim equally that such are the qualifications on the substantive criterion in Article 2:2 that 'the substantive criterion is with a view, not so much to justifying the measures themselves . . . but to evaluating the regulatory process that has produced the measure.' What Howse and Tuerk appear to be doing—though this is a point which they do not follow through—is to seek to paint an empty TBT canvas with the symbols of procedural rather than substantive review. This reflects their own particular conception of how the balance between trade and social regulation should be struck. In this they are not operating in a legal vacuum. Notable in particular is the *Shrimp-Turtle* report of the WTO Appellate Body with its clear predilection for the 'proceduralization' of its assessment of legality. Thus in *Shrimp-Turtle* while the rule in question was found to be capable of falling within the GATT Article XX exception, the manner in which it had been applied was such to render it incompatible with the 'chapeau' to Article XX. Particularly significant in this respect was the failure of the US to engage in serious across-the-board negotiations with third countries with a view to concluding bilateral or multilateral agreements, the rigidity with which officials made certification decisions, and the existence of little or no flexibility in this respect, the failure of the US to respect standards of basic fairness and due process, and in particular the absence of any opportunity for the applicant to be heard or to respond to arguments, the failure to render a formal reasoned decision and to notify the party of it, and the absence of any procedure for appeal or review of the certification decision adopted, and the singularly informal and casual nature of the procedure, making it impossible for the applicants to know whether the law was being applied in a manner which was fair and just. While in some respects this is resonant of the language of the European Court in *GN INNO*,[72] few if any would seek to assert that an assessment of process has replaced substantive assessment in the application of mandatory requirements at the hands of the European Court.

---

[70] de Búrca and Scott, above n. 65, p 313.

[71] Above n. 65, p 313.

[72] The language here is somewhat resonant of that of the European Court in Case C-18/88 *GB INNO* [1991] ECR I-5941. Here the procedure for approval entailed delay and expense even where the importer satisfied the conditions. No opportunity is given to the subscriber or importer to establish that during the procedure for the granting of approval arbitrary or discriminatory action was taken, and no appeal lies against that decision. In the absence of such a possibility to challenge the decision, the authorities can adopt an attitude which was arbitrary or systematically unfavourable to imported equipment, and the likelihood of this is increased by the fact that the procedures laid down do not involve the hearing of any interested parties.

Third, Howse and Tuerk highlight the important question of to what extent economic reasons may be allowed under Article 2:2.[73] What is clear in the EU is that economic objectives can never justify trade restrictions either on the basis of the explicit Treaty based exceptions, or on the basis of mandatory requirements.[74] Significantly this appears to remain true even where it is argued that without the restriction, and the economic benefits which ensue, the underlying objective (for example, environmental) will not be realizable.[75] Equally in the EU there is no question of not favouring a less trade restrictive alternative due to its excessive economic cost. Within the GATT and GATS general and security exception economic objectives find no place.[76] Likewise in neither the preamble nor the TBT indicative list is any reference made to economic objectives. While the same is true of the SPS Agreement, in that economic objectives are not singled out as an autonomous ground for applying SPS measures to imports, that Agreement is distinct from the TBT Agreement in that

> a measure is not more trade-restrictive than required unless there is another measure, reasonably available taking into account technical and economic feasibility, that achieves the appropriate level of sanitary and phytosanitary protection and is significantly less restrictive of trade.[77]

No equivalent deference to economic feasibility is inscribed in the TBT Agreement, albeit that the list of 'relevant elements of consideration' in Article 2:2 is left deliberately open. While this is a question of interpretation, and

---

[73] Above n. 45 p. 316.

[74] See, for example, Case C-398/95 *Syndesmos ton en Elladi Touristikon kai Taxidiotikon Grafeion v. Ypourgos Ergasias* [1997] ECR I-3091. What is less clear is the scope of the concept of economic objectives in this setting. Thus, would regional policy objectives designed to promote the economic growth of less developed regions be recognized as a mandatory requirement? In Case C-21/88 *Du Pont de Nemours* [1990] ECR I-0889, for example, had the Italian government required all public companies to buy a proportion of their supplies from companies situated in 'Objective 1' regions, regardless of the Member State in which they were situated, the measure would then have applied without distinction and the Court would have to have considered the legitimacy of the regional policy defence. There is nothing in the wording of the judgment in that case to suggest that such a mandatory requirement would not be accepted.

[75] See, for example, *Dusseldorp*, above n. 11.

[76] See, by way of loose analogy, *India—Quantitative Restrictions on Imports of Agricultural, Textile and Industrial Products*. India had introduced quantitative restrictions on agricultural, textile and industrial products with the defense that they were justified by the balance-of-payments provisions in Article XVIII:B GATT. such restrictions must, according to Article XVIII:9 GATT, be necessary to prevent the threat of a serious decline of monetary reserves or to increase inadequate monetary reserves. In their reports, the Panel and the AB found that the contested measures taken by India were inconsistent with Article XI and XVIII:11 GATT and were not justified by Article XVIII:B GATT. Significant in this respect is the fact that the AB found that when reviewing the necessity (or proportionality) of such restrictions, macro-economic instruments must, as a general rule, also be taken into account as possible alternatives. See A. von Bogdandy in de Búrca & Scott, *The EU and the WTO* above n. 65.

[77] Footnote 3 to Article 5:6 SPS. See, however, the remarks of the Asbestos panel in the context of considering the necessity of the measure within the meaning of GATT Article XX(b). Here it accepted that economic and administrative feasibility concerns were relevant in assessing the availability of alternatives. The AB did not comment upon this element of the panel's findings.

remains open, what is clear is that it cannot be right that the least cost solution may be preferred regardless of the scale of additional costs associated with alternatives, and the extent to which the least cost solution is more restrictive of trade. Otherwise a ban would nearly always be the preferred solution, and the proviso that the measure be the least trade restrictive possible rendered meaningless. The most that Members can hope for is that economic feasibility be relevant to an assessment of whether there is an alternative less restrictive means which is regarded as available. One important issue arising here is the distribution of the costs associated with the regulation in question. The regulation may be regarded as economically feasible according to the preferences of the regulating state precisely because part or all of the costs of that regulation are externalised to other Members. It is where costs are internalised to the regulating state, through for example the costs of inspections and controlled use, that economic feasibility is perceived as an issue at all.

In discussing the issue of costs Howse and Tuerk bind it together with the issue of the effectiveness of alternative, less restrictive means, and the language of 'taking into account the risks non-fulfilment will create'. They allude to the degree of latitude enjoyed by Members in considering the adequacy of alternatives:

> Once interests of this kind of gravity are clearly seen to be at stake [life-threatening cancer on this occasion] a Member need not be required to adopt a less-restrictive policy instrument that provides less certain or perfect control of the risk, even by a small margin, despite the possibility that the less-restrictive alternative would be *hugely* less restrictive of trade—there is not place for balancing or proportionality analysis.[78]

That may indeed be so. But it is not clear that that implies in any way an entitlement to have regard to considerations of economic feasibility as opposed to considerations relating to the effectiveness of the measure in achieving the degree of risk regulation deemed appropriate by that Member.

If the TBT Agreement appears to conform to the EU model in that the expanding rule is accompanied by the expanding 'exception', it is worth noting that the same is not true for the SPS Agreement, also of crucial importance in moving the WTO beyond a discrimination based approach to free movement. Article 2:2 of this Agreement provides that SPS measures shall be applied only to the extent necessary to protect human, animal or plant life or health, are based on scientific principles and are not maintained without sufficient scientific evidence subject to the application of the precautionary principle in Article 7:5. Thus the concept of necessity takes the Agreement beyond discrimination and yet nonetheless a finite set of 'exceptions'relating to protection of human, animal or plant health apply. Thus we are confronted with an expanded rule and a constrained exception and an apparent break with the *Cassis*/TBT model. Such

---

[78] Above n. 45 p. 318.

a conclusion would, however, be misleading. The narrow and finite nature of the exceptions in the SPS Agreement is merely a reflection of the very concept of an SPS measure. This is defined in Annex A, and precisely in terms of the objective of the measure in protecting human, animal or plant life or health from certain risks including pests, diseases and additives etc. in foodstuffs.[79] Thus the restrictive nature of the 'exception' reflects a restriction inherent in the substantive scope of the Agreement by virtue of the definition of an SPS measure. In this sense the SPS Agreement does not serve to break the *Cassis*/TBT mould.

CONCLUSION

It is apparent from the above that the concept of mandatory requirements has served as a powerful and flexible instrument for balancing market integration and market regulation in the EU. It has evolved on a case by case basis, implying considerable authority for the European Court. The European Court, and the national courts in the application of the proportionality principle, have had to contend with difficult and sensitive questions, of an intensely political nature. This is particularly apparent in, but by no means confined to, the sphere of risk regulation. It is striking that the WTO appears, in many respects, to be borrowing from the EU market integration/market regulation bargain. Not only has the basic rule (taking us beyond discrimination) been extended, notably in the TBT Agreement, but the scope of the 'exceptions' to that rule have also been more flexibly drawn. As with the concept of mandatory requirements, these TBT 'exceptions' are barely defined, leaving the WTO panels and ultimately the Appellate Body with a monumental interpretative challenge, at a time when the legitimacy of the WTO as a whole is under the most intense public scrutiny.[80]

---

[79] In addition Annex 1(d) provides that any measure applied to prevent or limit other damage within the territory of the Member from the entry, establishment or spread of pests, would also constitute an SPS measure.

[80] For discussions of the legitimacy issue see R. Howse, 'Adjudicative Legitimacy and Treaty Interpretation in International Trade Law: The Early Years of WTO Jurisprudence' in Weiler (ed) above n. 63.

11

The Single Market, Movement of Persons and Borders

ELSPETH GUILD[1]

INTRODUCTION

THE PROGRAMME TO ACHIEVE the objective of the internal market as characterised by the absence of obstacles to the movement of goods, persons, services and capital has revealed substantial tensions among the Member States and the Community institutions. As Craig has argued in Chapter 1, the mechanisms for the achievement of the objective have been the main framework for the expression of this tension—the struggle between harmonisation and mutual recognition as the means for achieving the objective. In this chapter I will analyse the consequences of the choices of the EU and its Member States regarding the internal market in one area—people. The external dimension of this manifestation of the internal market is found in the changing definition of the European border and where it is for the movement of persons. My contention is that national political sensitivities around movement of persons, first expressed in respect of EC nationals moving among the Member States, became exacerbated by the prospect of movement of third country nationals[2] in particular after the fall of the Berlin Wall. When Europe's closest neighbours were no longer prevented from movement by their own governments, the issue of controlling their movement became central to the EU. The result was twofold: first, on the political decision making level, the UK flatly refused to co-operate with the intention of abolition of border controls on persons moving within the EU. Its reasoning was that the special position of the UK as an island gave it a better chance of controlling third country nationals than the others and this advantage must not be given up.[3] The other Member States

---

[1] This chapter is based on my inaugural lecture at the University of Nijmegen, 30 May 2001.
[2] I use this term to define nationals of any state which is not a Member State of the European Union or of the European Economic Area (whose nationals have rights virtually the same as Community nationals).
[3] This perception of an advantage has turned into something of an albatross around the UK government's neck as the camp at Sangatte of irregular migrants seeking to come to the UK has

(from a gradual start in the Schengen process) chose to pursue the objective of the abolition of borders for the movement of persons among themselves through a purely inter-governmental process—Schengen. This had the effect of cutting out the Community political actors for a period of over 15 years until the integration of the Schengen borders acquis into the EC Treaty in 1999. Secondly, on the level of content, within the internal market, the mode of achieving the result of free movement is through the creation of rights. Craig outlines clearly the judicial mechanisms which were deployed in this process. The debate over harmonisation or mutual recognition took place within a closed frame of rights which must be achieved. By moving the field of persons outside that EC framework of rights, the Member States also deprived it of the rationale of rights. The adoption of the mutual recognition approach within Schengen and beyond was detached from any need to give effect to rights to individuals and consequently the rights based approach was abandoned immediately. Instead the legislative programme was characterised by a move by interior ministries to seek to reclaim national discretion from the field of rights to individuals, reversing the trend of increasing judicialisation of immigration and asylum law which had taken place at the national level. The re-integration of the Schengen process into the EC Treaty in the Amsterdam Treaty and subsequent measures (with very little adjustment from the Nice Treaty) has created new tensions. How can a fully fledged mutual recognition system without a rights-based approach be incorporated into the EC Treaty? How can the EC's internal market swallow the flexible Schengen border? It is to these issues that this chapter is addressed.

PERSONS AND THE 1992 CHALLENGE

The task of the European Community is to achieve the common market, and an economic and monetary union. In order to do this, it is necessary to achieve 'the abolition as between Member States, of obstacles to the free movement of goods, persons, services and capital.'[4] The main obstacle to free movement of persons between the Member States are border controls on persons.

Part 3 Title III EC sets out the specific rights granted to individuals within the Community in order to give effect to the abolition of obstacles to their movement—the free movement of workers, the self employed ie establishment—and service providers and recipients, nationals of one Member States within the

shown. The French side of the Eurotunnel entrance has become virtually a militarised zone as the company seeks to prevent people from entering the tunnel to come to the UK. The reason why people seek to come to the UK is because they have been ordered to leave the area of the Member States other than those not participating in the open border regime (ie Denmark, Ireland and UK). The only country bordering France to which these persons can go is the UK.

[4] Article 3(c) EC; see also D. Wyatt & A. Dashwood, *European Community Law*, 3rd edn (London, Sweet & Maxwell, 1993).

territory of another. The rights of the individual in each case in the Treaty are circumscribed by the state's appreciation of the needs of public policy, security and health.[5] The transitional period for giving effect to these rights ended in 1968. So long as the European economy was flourishing, issues arising in the courts about free movement of persons were primarily limited to social security co-ordination matters. However, once the downturn took hold after 1973, Member States began seeking to expel migrant workers, including nationals of other Member States. Recourse to rights contained in Community law limiting the power to expel to grounds of public policy, security and health were the territory of disputes between the Member States and individuals. By a series of judgments from 1974 onwards the European Court of Justice found in favour of the right of the individual to free movement.[6] The subject of the dispute was the definition of public policy, security and health. The Court consolidated, through its decisions, a direct right of the individual to move and to defeat an effort by a Member State to prevent the movement or to expel the individual on the basis of Community law unless truly exceptional circumstances apply.[7] By narrowly limiting the scope of public policy as an exception to the free movement right, the Court privileged the individual over the Member State. The loss of power over individuals by the Member States particularly as regards control of the concept of security led to a high level of distrust of the Court which would manifest itself in a challenge to a Decision on immigration consultation issued by the Commission in 1985[8] before the Court itself.[9]

Economic challenges which began to crystalise in the early 1980s changed the debate. The renewed concerns about the competitiveness of the European market in comparison with the new Tiger economies of the far East led to a commitment to revitalise the common market project and the new appellation: the internal market. Although the objective of the common market remained consistent from the commencement of the Community in 1957, the approach to borders and their control changed. The preparatory work towards the new push for the Community led to the first major intergovernmental conference on re-negotiation of the Treaties between June 1985 and February 1986. The result was the Single European Act (SEA). Article 14[10], inserted into the Treaty by the

---

[5] Article 39 EC and Directive 64/221.

[6] 41/74 *Van Duyn* [1974] ECR 1337; 67/74 *Bonsignore* [1975] ECR 297; 36/75 *Rutili* [1975] ECR 1219; 48/75 *Royer* [1975] ECR 497; 118/75 *Watson & Belmann* [1976] ECR 1185; 8/77 *Sagulo* [1977] ECR 1495; 30/77 *Bouchereau* [1977] ECR 1999.

[7] Indeed, in the *Van Duyn* judgment the Court held for the first time that a Community Directive could have direct effect against a Member State (though not against a private individual). At the time this position was strongly criticised as weakening the power of the Member States to control the entry and residence of foreigners (see D. O'Keeffe 'Practical Difficulties in the Application of Article 48 of the EEC Treaty,' (1982) 19 *CMLRev* 35–60).

[8] OJ 1985 L 217/25.

[9] 281/85, 283-85/85, 287/85 *Germany & Ors v Commission* [1987] ECR 2625.

[10] This article started life as Article 8A then after the entry into force of the Maastricht Treaty became Article 7A. With the Amsterdam Treaty it became Article 14.

SEA, determined the internal market as 'an area without internal frontiers in which the free movement of goods, persons, services and capital is ensured' and became the flash point of the issue of Member States versus Community control of persons and in particular third country nationals.

The deadline for implementation was set for 31.12.92. It was not achieved. However, what is important is the principle: the borders were to move. The new area, comprised of the physical territory of the Member States combined, would have no internal frontiers. The manifestation of the lack of internal frontiers is free movement of various kinds: goods, persons, services and capital. This meant that internal border controls were to be abolished. As the end of the deadline for implementation approached, it was apparent that the objective was not nearing completion. The stumbling block however was not the free movement of goods, services or capital. It was exclusively as regards persons.[11] The UK's House of Lords Select Committee on the European Communities held an inquiry into the completion of the internal market. It received evidence from various officials who made it clear that an internal market without internal frontiers was fully possibly for goods, services and capital. The mechanism of the frontier for goods (customs controls) were capable of abolition and replacement by random checks. However, border controls on persons could not safely be abolished.[12] The reason: this would give rise to an increased security risk.

The Article 14 arrangement would give the EU one border—the external border between the Member States and third countries. Each Member State would share part of that border. Even Member States lacking physical contiguity with the others, such as Greece, would be part of the internal border as regards, for instance, direct flights and ships to and from other Member States. But as regards land borders they would have only an EU border. Even Member States surrounded by other Member States, such as Luxembourg, would participate in the external border through international flights, though otherwise they would lack a frontier at all.

This fundamental movement of the border was disputed on security grounds not only in the UK. In France there was substantial opposition to a regime which would have such important security implications.[13] The defeat of Article 14 between 1993 and 1997 can be attributable to this resistance by the interior ministries over the meaning of security for the movement of persons. The separation of the problem of borders for persons from borders for other purposes is, to no small extent, a result of the 1993 settlement of Article 14. Borders for

---

[11] European Commission, *Abolition of Border Controls: Communication to the Council and the Parliament* SEC(92) 877 final.
[12] House of Lords Select Committee on the European Communities: *1992: Border Controls on Persons*, Session 1988–9 22nd Report: 1992 (HL Paper 90).
[13] P. Masson & X. de Villepin, *Rapport de la Commission de contrôle du Sénat sur la mise en place et le foncionnement de la convention d'application de l'accord de Schengen du 14 Juin 1985* No 167, 26.06.91.

goods, services and capital become separated from borders for the purposes of the movement of persons. The interests of corporations doing business in the EU are accommodated by the achievement of a frontier free territory for the movement of these three commodities.[14] The internal market could be completed as regards the first three, the fourth remained highly disputed. After the implementation date of the internal market, individuals challenged the continued application of border controls on their movement within the Union. The answer, finally given in 1999 by the European Court of Justice, denied the individual's claim to rights in favour of the state's claim to security. There is no automatic legal effect to the provision for persons to cross intra-Member State borders.[15] The Court accepted that the lack of harmonisation of conditions for the crossing of external borders was fatal to the individual's claim: until the space is consistently controlled from external security risks, intra-Member State border controls on persons are lawful.

I would pause to consider further the judgment: control over where the border is as regards persons is an important power. The Commission and some Member States were in dispute about the position of that power. The EC Treaty, which is the framework for the struggle, provided, as a result of the SEA, power to the Commission only for the question of intra-Member State borders. If the borders for the movement of persons were to be moved to the external EU border, there was no provision for the Community to control that border. In 1987 the fields of immigration and asylum, ie the movement of third country nationals into the Community, remained fully within the jurisdiction of the Member States. Thus the interest of the Commission to seek abolition of the internal borders for persons is limited. Even after the Maastricht Treaty entered into force in November 1993, the Community's control over the external border remained extremely feeble as the subject was contained in the Third Pillar of the Treaty on European Union; the intergovernmental pillar. The Member States remained in the driving seat as regards the definition of the external frontier.[16]

The claim of the individual moving within the territory to the benefit of frontier free travel was opposed by those Member States which expressed a view. The Commission had only a weak interest in supporting the individual because it did not have clear competence over external borders. The result of the

---

[14] Of course issues regarding free movement of services, goods and capital would continue to arise before the Court of Justice: for instance *Alpine Investments*, regarding consumer protection in the face of uncontrolled movement of services; the meaning of obstacles in a frontier free Europe for goods in C-267/91 & 268/91 *Keck & Mithouard* [1993] ECR I-6097 and the treatment of capital for fiscal purposes. However, the principle of control of free movement is not challenged.
[15] C-378/97 *Wijsenbeek* [1999] ECR I-6207.
[16] It is thus ironic that it was exactly this failure to agree the contours of the external frontier that led to the Member States being unable to sign an intergovernmental agreement on borders (the External Frontiers Convention). The dispute between the UK and Spain over the status of the borders of Gibraltar would permanently prevent this convention being adopted. Instead a core of Member States proceeded intergovernmentally through the Schengen Agreement 1985, the subject of the next section.

acquisition of rights by the individual would not strengthen its position of power in relation to the Member States over the definition of borders. In fact, the Commission had failed to act at all to propose legislation on abolition of frontier controls until the European Parliament brought a case before the Court of Justice against it for failure to fulfil its Treaty obligations as a result.[17] Hence when the Court of Justice came to consider and reject the individual's claim, the outcome was not fundamental to the balance of power between the Community and the Member States as regards the articulation of the border for persons. Indeed, by the time the Court handed down its judgment the Community had once again been transformed as regards the balance of power in this field by the Treaty of Amsterdam. The cursory manner in which the Court dealt with the issue has been criticised on other grounds.[18] I would suggest that the failure of the individual's claim may also rest with the fact that he or she is not, in this case, critical to the settlement of power. It is when the individual holds the place of determinant of the legal battle that he or she is likely to be able successfully to claim rights. It is the individual's position as an intermediary in the settlement of powers between the Community and the Member States through the judicial system which may result in the acquisition of rights.

While the abolition of borders for goods, services and capital proceeded smoothly within the EC Treaty, subject to the control of the Commission, the Member States acted differently as regards persons. The newly separated borders for persons were not considered appropriate for Community regulation, notwithstanding the wording of Article 14 EC. Mistrust of the Commission on the part of Member State interior ministries and of the Court of Justice, dates back to their loss of control over the meaning of security for the purposes of movement of workers through the 1970s and early 1980s. The reaction was to oppose any move by the Commission to extend its control in the field of immigration. Although the Commission's White Paper on the internal market included an annex on immigration and asylum, the first step by the Commission to set up a system of exchange of information on legislation regarding immigration by third country nationals (in 1985) was the subject of an attack by five Member States. The fact that the Court of Justice found in favour of the Commission on virtually all aspects of its Decision did not endear the Court to the interior ministries.[19]

It is often suggested that the development of an intergovernmental framework for the abolition of border controls on persons between the Member States was the result of obstinacy of some Member States, such as the UK, to the principle. There must be some doubt as to whether this is the whole story. The decision to act intergovernmentally was taken between 1984, when

---

[17] The case was withdrawn when the Commission introduced measures in 1995, just as the case was progressing towards its hearing.

[18] H. Staples, 2000 *Nederlands Tijdschrift voor Europees Recht*, p 1–6.

[19] *Germany & Ors v Commission* above n 9.

President Mitterand and Chancellor Kohl announced at the Saarbrucken border that they would abolish border controls between the two countries in order to defuse industrial action by the transport industry over delays, and 1985, when the first Schengen Agreement was signed.[20] The Commission's White Paper on the internal market had not yet been published. Nor indeed had the Commission's Decision on information exchange which would so outrage interior ministries. While the Saarbrucken announcement was made in the context of a transport ministry initiative it was rapidly taken over by the interior ministries on grounds of the serious security consequences which abolition of border controls would have.[21]

The development from the Saarbrucken statement to the Schengen Agreement 1985 was characterised by a move from transport ministry control to interior ministry control and from two Member States to five: Belgium, France, Germany, Luxembourg and the Netherlands. Central to the first development was the issue of persons and security, to the second commercial interests—the transport industry in the Benelux feared the loss of markets if it were left out of the free movement territory. The balance of power between the Community and the Member States would find a rather symbolic expression in this field. Between the signing of the Schengen Agreement in 1985, its Implementing Agreement in 1990 and the TEU 1993, the competences as regards customs controls and goods of the Schengen Agreements were removed to Community law. Only people and security remained intergovernmental. The Member States got control over security and individuals, the Community got control over corporate interests including goods, services and capital.

WHERE ARE THE BORDERS? MOVING THE BORDERS OF SOVEREIGNTY AND THE BORDERS FOR PERSONS; THE SCHENGEN APPROACH

Schengen is a small town in Luxembourg but its name has become synonymous with the agreement which abolished border controls between five original parties[22] (Member States of the European Union) and established a system for common conditions of entry and exclusion of third country nationals into the combined territory. The Schengen *acquis*, the incorporation of which into EC law was made possible by the so-named protocol to the Amsterdam Treaty and now published in the Official Journal consists of:

---

[20] D. Bigo, *Polices en Reseaux* (Paris: Presses de Sciences-Po, 1996).
[21] Ibid.
[22] Belgium, France, Germany, Luxembourg and the Netherlands. Italy joined almost immediately thereafter.

1. The Agreement signed in Schengen on 14 June 1985, between the States of the Benelux Economic Union, the Federal Republic of Germany and the French Republic on the gradual abolition of checks at their common borders;

2. The Convention, signed in Schengen on 19 June 1990 between the Kingdom of Belgium, the Federal Republic of Germany, the French Republic, the Grand Duchy of Luxembourg and the Kingdom of the Netherlands, implementing the Agreement on the gradual abolition of checks at their common borders, signed in Schengen on 14 June 1985, with related Final Act and common declarations;

3. The Accession Protocols and Agreements to the 1985 Agreement and the 1990 Implementation Convention with Italy (signed in Paris on 27 November 1990), Spain and Portugal (signed in Bonn on 25 June 1991) and Denmark, Finland and Sweden (signed in Luxembourg on 19 December 1996), with related Final Acts and declarations;

4. Decisions and declarations adopted by the Executive Committee established by the 1990 Implementation Convention, as well as acts adopted for the implementation of the Convention by the organs upon which the Executive Committee has conferred decision making powers.

The initial Schengen Agreement of 14 June 1985 created a framework for the abolition of border controls on persons and goods between participating states. It was supplemented by the Schengen Implementing Agreement 1990 which set out the detailed provisions on the abolition of border controls between the participating states, the application of controls at the common external border of the participating states, provisions on division of responsibility in respect of asylum[23] and provisions on police co-operation.

The Implementing Agreement entered into force in September 1993 but was not applied for the purposes of abolishing border checks in any Schengen state until 26 March 1995. Even after that date France maintained border checks on persons moving between France and the other Schengen states. The abolition of border controls was achieved with Greece in March 2000 and the Nordic states in December 2000.

The title of the Implementing Agreement which covers free movement of persons contains seven chapters:

1. crossing internal borders (Article 2);

2. crossing external borders (Articles 3 – 8);

3. visas (Articles 9 – 17) and visas for long visits, (Article 18);

4. short term free movement of third country nationals (Articles 19 – 24);

[23] These provisions were superseded by the Convention determining the state responsible for examining applications for asylum lodged in one of the Member States of the European Communities (Dublin Convention) 14 June 1990 when it came into force in September 1997.

5. residence permits (Article 25);

6. organised travel (Articles 26–27);

7. responsibility for examining asylum applications (Articles 28 – 38 – superceded by the Dublin Convention when it entered into force in September 1997).

The legal basis of the Schengen Information System is found in Articles 92 – 119, creating a data base on objects and persons.

Over the next 12 years all other Member States of the European Union acceded to the Schengen instruments with the exception of the UK and Ireland. While the abolition of intra Member State border controls, *inter alia*, on persons was part of the internal market embodied in Article 14 EC, the priority of Community law was never officially used to impede the Schengen system. Rather it was given legitimacy through the use of the comparison with an 'avant garde' or experiment for the Community to adopt later. The argument was that the Schengen arrangement was legitimate, as it would enable the difficulties with the system to be dealt with in a controlled environment. It could then be used as the blueprint for the whole of the Community.[24] In fact the incorporation into Community law could hardly be messier or more difficult. The Commission has suggested that in its opinion all the so-called *acquis* must be replaced by Community legislation adopted in accordance with the Treaty rules in Title IV EC.[25]

The operation of Schengen was the responsibility of the Executive Committee established by the instruments. The Executive Committee was assisted by a small secretariat based at the Benelux Secretariat. Like the EU's Third Pillar, the Executive was aided by working groups on specific areas. Like the Third Pillar, the lack of a strong institutional structure meant there was only limited coordination on implementation and interpretation of the agreement.

The Amsterdam Treaty which came into force on 1 May 1999 attaches a Protocol on Schengen to the EC and EU Treaties which in effect provides for the insertion of the Schengen Agreement 1985, the Schengen Implementing Convention 1990 and the decisions of the Executive Committee made under the two agreements into the EC Treaty insofar as they involve borders and third country nationals. The same Protocol provides for moving into the Third Pillar of the Treaty on European Union those provisions of Schengen relating to policing and criminal judicial co-operation. The UK, Ireland and Denmark all negotiated protocols which permit them to remain outside of the new European

---

[24] C. Elsen, 'Schengen et la cooperation dans les domains de la justice et des affaires interiors. Besoins actuels et options futures' in M. den Boer (ed) *The Implementation of Schengen: First the Widening, Now the Deepening* (Maastricht: EIPA, 1997).
[25] European Commission Staff Working Paper: *Visa Policy Consequent upon the Treaty of Amsterdam and the Integration of the Schengen Acquis into the European Union* SEC (19999) 1213; Brussels 16.07.99.

Community rules on borders and third country nationals. Ireland and the UK may decide in each instance whether they wish to participate or not case by case in the new regime.[26]

By decisions, the Council allocated a legal base within the new EC Treaty as amended by the Amsterdam Treaty for the Schengen *acquis* as identified in its decision.[27] Accordingly, the European Community has inherited the Schengen border *acquis*, which has been transferred in a somewhat less than systematic manner into new Title IV of the EC Treaty: visas, asylum, immigration and other policies related to free movement of persons. The legal base for most of the Schengen border *acquis* which has been transferred into the EC Treaty is Articles 62(1)[28] Article 62(2)(a) and (b),[29] Article 62(3)[30] Article 63(3)[31] while having respect to Article 64(1) the internal security reserve of the Member States.[32]

As regards movement of persons, the Schengen system is based on three principles which are achieved through the deployment of four tools:

---

[26] See also, House of Lords, European Communities - 31st Report, Session 1997-98, *Incorporating the Schengen acquis into the European Union*, London 1998.

[27] Council Decision concerning the definition of the Schengen *acquis* for the purpose of determining, in conformity with the relevant provisions of the Treaty establishing the European Community and the Treaty on European Union, the legal base for each of the provisions or decisions which constitute the Schengen *acquis* OJ 1999 L176.

[28] 'The Council, acting in accordance with the procedure referred to in Article 67, shall, within a period of 5 years after the entry into force of the Treaty of Amsterdam, adopt: (1) measures with a view to ensuring, in compliance with Article 14, the absence of any controls on persons, be they citizens of the Union or nationals of third countries, when crossing internal borders;'

[29] 'The Council, acting in accordance with the procedure referred to in Article 67, shall, within a period of 5 years after the entry into force of the Treaty of Amsterdam, adopt: (2) measures on the crossing of the external borders of the Member States which shall establish: (a) standards and procedures to be followed by Member States in carrying out checks on persons at such borders;(b) rules on visas for intended stays of no more than 3 months, including: (i) the list of third countries whose nationals must be in possession of visas for crossing the external borders and those whose nationals are exempt from that requirement; (ii) the procedures and conditions which for issuing visas by Member States; paragraph (iii) a uniform format for visas; (iv) rules on a uniform visa;'

[30] 'The Council, acting in accordance with the procedure referred to in Article 67, shall, within a period of 5 years after the entry into force of the Treaty of Amsterdam, adopt: (3) measures setting out the conditions under which nationals of third countries shall have the freedom to travel within the territory of the Member States during a period of no more than 3 months.'

[31] The Council, acting in accordance with the procedure referred to in Article 67, shall, within a period of 5 years after the entry into force of the Treaty of Amsterdam, adopt:(3) measures on immigration policy within the following areas: (a) conditions on entry and residence, and standards on procedures with the issue by Member States of long term visas and residence permits, including those for the purpose of family reunion; (b) illegal immigration and illegal residence, including repatriation of legal residents;'

[32] 'This Title shall not affect the exercise of the responsibilities incumbent on the Member States with regard to the maintenance of law and order and the safeguarding of internal security.'

The Principles:

1. No third country national should gain access to the territory of the Schengen states (with or without a short stay visa) if he or she might constitute a security risk for any one of the states;

2. A presumption that entry across one Schengen external border constitutes admission to the whole territory and an assumption (not as high as a presumption in law) that a short stay visa issued by any participating state will be recognised for entry to the common territory for the purpose of admission (there are explicit exceptions justifying refusal specifically on security grounds);

3. once within the common territory, the person is entitled (subject again to security exceptions) to move within the whole of the territory for three months out of every six without a further control at the internal borders of the participating states.

The Tools

1. The Schengen Information System;

2. a common list of countries whose nationals require visas to come to the common territory for short stays (visits of up to three months); and a common list of those excluded from the requirement. The definitive black and white lists were achieved in December 1998.

3. a common format, rules on issue and meaning for a short stay visas;

4. common rules on crossing the external border and carrier sanctions.

The focus of the system is to ensure that persons who are or might be considered unwanted by any participating state are not permitted into the territory. Thus the rules focus on who must be excluded and provide little guidance on who should be admitted. Because the underlying principle of the system is cross recognition of national decisions rather than harmonisation, finding legal mechanisms to achieve this has unexpected implications. The lifting of border controls between the states means that positive decisions on admission of persons are likely to be respected by default—the parties have fewer identity checks on the crossing of borders.[33] The cross recognition of negative decisions requires more specific measures. When the concept of internal security, the primary reason for refusal of admission of an individual into the combined territory, is not harmonised any examination of the grounds for refusal of an individual by another state needs to be avoided. In the Netherlands the legal mechanism to achieve this is Article 109(4) and (5) Aliens Act 1999 which places

---

[33] But see K. Groenendijk's presentation on the maintenance of internal checks on persons after the entry into force of the Schengen Implementing Agreement 1990: Article 62 EC and EU Borders: Conference 11/12 May 2001, ILPA/Meijers Committee, London.

the Dutch border for the movement of persons at the extremities of the frontiers of all the Member States and incorporates the internal security of all Member States into Dutch internal security.

At the first level of exclusion are those persons on the common list of persons not to be admitted. The list is maintained electronically in the Schengen Information System and is made up of all persons signalled for the purpose by any of the Schengen states according to their national understanding of the criteria for inclusion and their national interpretation of public order and security.

The first step for determining access to the territory is whether a person has achieved sufficient personal notoriety in any one Member State to be included in the system. Persons whose behaviour justifies their exclusion from the territory are defined by Article 96 Schengen Implementing Agreement. The individual will normally have been within the territory of the Union for an Article 96 entry to have been made against him or her.[34] The definition of these persons for exclusion seems primarily based on what they did or represented while they were within the territory. It is here that the divergent conceptions of what constitutes a risk and what is security in the Member States becomes central. What is perceived as a security risk in one state is not necessarily the same in another. This difference of perception of risk as it relates to an individual's activities the last time he or she was within the Union will be the territory where national courts begin to question the legitimacy of the system.[35]

The second step relates to persons who have not yet been identified as an individual risk to any state but who might be one. The intention is to identify groups of persons more likely than others to include persons who might constitute a risk. This group then is the subject of an additional level of control over their potential access to the territory of the Union. The tool is the visa list which, on the basis of nationality, categorises persons as more or less likely to be a risk. For those persons who, on the basis of their nationality, are considered a potential security risk, a special control in the form of a visa requirement is imposed. This has the effect of moving the effective border for these persons to their own state. I have considered elsewhere in some depth the rules on the basis of which the Community defines which countries nationals are a sufficiently likely security risk to be on the list.[36] The system of justification reverses the relationship of the individual and the state. It is no longer the Community's relationship with the state which determines the treatment of its nationals. Rather it is the assessment of the individuals which determines the state's characterisation. The state's claim to sovereignty as the determiner of order

---

[34] It is possible to justify inclusion of someone who has never been in the EU but this is appears to be the exception to the rule from those cases which have come before the courts.

[35] E, Guild, 'Adjudicating Schengen: National Judicial Control in France' (1991) 1, *European Journal of Migration and Law*.

[36] E. Guild, *Moving the Borders of Europe* (Nijmegen, University of Nijmegen, 2001.)

internally within its territory, and thus of its relations with other states, is no longer relevant.

The enforcement mechanism is the involvement of carriers in the system through sanctions for their carrying persons who need visas but do not have them. The Member States distance themselves from the mechanisms of control abroad by devolving it to the private sector.[37]

The third step is identifying who, within the *prima facie* suspect group should get visas. A comparison may be made between the policing technique of profiling: anticipating who is likely to be a criminal (or become a criminal). The purpose of the mechanisms is to anticipate through a profile of risk, who is likely, if he or she were given a visa, to come to the EU territory to be a risk (which of course raises the important question of the definition of a risk and of security). In interviews with officials both at national and Community level,[38] it became apparent that a number of aids are provided to consular staff in consulates of the Member States abroad. First the formalisation of a system of consular cooperation facilitates the regular meeting of visa officers of the EU states (including Ireland and the UK) in capitals around the world.[39] Meetings take place normally at least once during each 6 month presidency of the Union. Within this context of cooperation, information is exchanged on persons who are considered 'bona fides'. This is reflected in the Common Consular Instructions which provide 'In order to assess the applicant's good faith, the mission or post shall check whether the applicant is recognised as a person of good faith within the framework of consular cooperation . . . '[40] It appears that in addition to the bona fides information exchanged, mala fides persons are also identified. As regards the identification of risk categories, the Common Consular Instructions provides 'it is necessary to be particularly vigilant when dealing with "risk categories" in other words unemployed persons, and those with no regular income etc.'[41] Thus the most precise categorisation on mala fides persons who

[37] V. Guiraudon, 'Logiques de l'Etat délégateur: les companies de transport dans le contrôle migratoire à distance' (2001) Cultures et Conflits.

[38] Interviews with French Foreign Affairs ministry officials carried out in the context of research on Schengen visas for the Institut des Hautes Etudes de Sécurité Intérieure, March 2001; with Community officials June 2000 and February 2001.

[39] The Council's Recommendation made in the Third Pillar on local consular co-operation regarding visas promotes 'local co-operation on visas, involving an exchange of information on the criteria for issuing visas and an exchange of information on risks to national security and public order or the risk of clandestine immigration' (Article 1 OJ 1996 C 80/1). Controls on the propriety of information are not included even though the Recommendation continues 'their consular services should exchange information to help determine the good faith of visa applicants and their reputation, it being understood that the fact that the applicant has obtained a visa for another Member State does not exempt the authorities from examining individually the visa application and performing the verification required for the purposes of security, public order and clandestine immigration control' (Article 6). The concepts of public order and clandestine immigration control are not defined.

[40] OJ 2000 L 238/332 point 1.5.

[41] OJ 2000 L 238/329 point V.

are profiled as a risk are the poor. These are the persons who will always threaten the Member States' security.

There is an extension of the bona fides/mala fides profile beyond the individual. In this extension the private sector is categorised as bona or mala fides and thus the individuals using their services are categorised by their choices as consumers. Travel agencies accept responsibility for submitting many visa applications for their customers. Indeed, in some countries, such as the Ukraine, I was told that the vast majority of applications for visas are submitted by travel agencies.[42] The success or failure of these applications is heavily dependent on the relationship of the agency with the consular officials. Information on agencies is exchanged within the framework of the common consular cooperation. The Common Consular Instructions refer to this practice as regards personal interviews: 'This requirement may be waived in cases where . . . a reputable and trustworthy body is able to vouch for the good faith of those persons concerned.'[43] It was indicated in interviews that there is some information that airline choice is also taken into account as an indicator of bona fides. If the individual has bought a ticket with the national carrier or the major carrier of a country, his or her bona fides are strengthened. I would add that the comments about this practice were negative. The officials considered this practice improper but they appeared to be aware of its existence. This means that the bona fides or mala fides of the individual may be the result of a disagreement with a visa officer in another consulate than the one where the application is directed. Further it may result from a poor consumer choice about which travel agency or airline to use.

Thus the SIS list of excluded persons as security risks is supplemented by information held in consulates on persons considered risky. This information is in turn supplemented by information about travel agencies which are risky and possibly even airlines. In such an atmosphere of extreme concern about security, even in the absence of apparently objective justification, what happens to the individual; what chance has he or she of reversing a negative decision? The Schengen system enjoyed a legal basis—the treaties, a rule making mechanism—the Executive Committee—but lacked a system for ensuring consistency of application and coherence. The problem began to manifest first through complaints of individuals entered in the SIS under Article 96. The inconsistencies of national interpretation of the criteria both by officials and courts would cause increasingly serious problems.

Following the insertion of the system into the European Community and Union, the framework of coherence has changed. By inserting an intergovernmental system into a highly legally structured supra-national framework a

---

[42] Interviews with French Foreign Affairs ministry officials carried out in the context of research on Schengen visas for the Institut des Hautes Etudes de Sécurité Intérieure, March 2001; with Community officials June 2000 and February 2001.
[43] OJ 2000 L 238/328.

number of consequences flow. First, the interstate regulation of duties no longer applies. While it is not yet clear exactly what the legal status of the Schengen *acquis* is in Community law, nonetheless it has been inserted into a system where rights for individuals is the field within which state versus Community tensions are frequently resolved. In this highly structured legal framework within which the individual plays a critical activating role, consistency is ultimately provided by the Court of Justice through its interpretation of the provisions of law and their effects.

In the insertion of the Schengen *acquis* special arrangements were made regarding the ECJ. First as regards all the border and visa related provisions, Article 68 EC limits the Court's jurisdiction by restricting to courts against whose decisions there is no judicial remedy under national law, the right to make references within the Title. This limitation will have the effect of slowing down the inevitable coherence as cases will have to pass through all levels of national appeals before arriving at a court competent to ask a question.[44] Secondly, as regards the SIS, no agreement could be reached on its inclusion in the First Pillar; thus by default it fell into the Third Pillar. The Third Pillar is subject to the ECJ's jurisdiction only in accordance with declarations made by the Member States (Article 35 TEU).

Within the Schengen system of mutual recognition of nationally constructed concepts of internal security threats has been created. The field in which it operates is sensitive—including issues of civil liberties such as data protection and access to information and human rights such as family life and asylum. The principle of recognition means that an individual will be excluded by all the states even when he or she only satisfies the exclusion criteria of one.[45] In the intergovernmental framework only national courts are competent to adjudicate the lawfulness of the security appreciation of the state. During the Schengen period, national courts varied increasingly as regards their assessment of the system. The insertion into the EC and EU Treaties of the Schengen system entails a common interpretation of the lawfulness of national appreciation of risk. The tension between civil liberties and human rights and a network of grounds of exclusion must now be supervised by the supra-national court: the ECJ. Over the shoulder of the ECJ, with ultimate responsibility for the protection of human rights, *inter alia* among the Member States, is the European Court of Human Rights which until now has tended to accept the special legal

---

[44] E. Guild and S. Peers, 'Deference or Defiance? The European Court of Justice's jurisdiction over immigration and asylum' in E. Guild & C. Harlow (eds) *Implementing Amsterdam: Immigration and Asylum Rights in EC Law* (Oxford, Hart, 2001).

[45] H. Staples referred to a celebrated case in the Netherlands where a New Zealand national, a Greenpeace activitist, was excluded from the Netherlands on the basis of an SIS entry against her by France. The legitimacy of the French appreciation of an internal security risk was not accepted by the Dutch public; presentation: *Judicial Control of the EU Border*: ILPA/Meijers Committee Conference: 11 & 12 May 2001, London.

regime of the Union, though it appears increasingly ready to assess its effectiveness in human rights protection.[46]

The reconstruction of borders in the Schengen system entailed a shift in the appreciation of individuals. The importance of identifying security risks, whether specifically defined in respect of individuals or collectively defined as regards all nationals of some states, took on increasing importance. Linking national assessments of security while protecting those assessments from examination was central to the Schengen system. However, with the communitarisation of the *acquis*, the role of the individual takes on a new importance. The highly structured legal regime of the Community encourages the use of judicial dispute mechanisms to resolve tensions over the position of power through the protection of individual rights. The insertion of a system based on a very loose assessment of security risk into this environment, itself liable to human rights compliance, is likely to change the relationship of states to borders, and of the Community and individuals.

---

[46] A special issue of the European Journal on Immigration and Law will be published in June 2001 on this issue with contributions inter alia by P. Cullen, T. Eicke and E. Steendijk.

12

Competition Policy and the shaping of the Single Market*

ALBERTINA ALBORS-LLORENS

INTRODUCTION

THE TRADITIONAL FUNCTION of competition law has been the stimulation of economic activity with a view to ensuring both an optimum allocation of resources and maximum consumer welfare. However, to confine the aims of competition policy to the achievement of these economic and consumer benefits would be an over-simplification. Competition law has other important objectives such as maintaining high levels of employment, protecting small firms against concentration of economic power or facilitating the restructuring of sectors in crisis. Competition policy is therefore, not only about the survival of the fittest but also about the protection of the weak and the pursuit of important social goals.

In addition to these general objectives, different systems of competition law protect idiosyncratic aims. Community competition law is not an exception, but rather a striking illustration of this rule. As the Commission has repeatedly emphasised, the competition provisions in the Treaty fulfil the additional function of contributing towards the achievement of the single market objective.[1] This objective is implicitly stated in Article 3(g) EC, which provides that one of the activities of the Community will be to put in place a system ensuring that 'competition in the internal market is not distorted'. The EC Treaty provisions on free movement of goods, persons and services are primarily concerned with the removal of barriers that Member States might put in place to compartmentalise the territory of the Common Market along national lines. The removal of these barriers, however, does not suffice to achieve a unified market. In particular,

* I am extremely grateful to Rosa Greaves, Elizabeth Freeman and Catherine Barnard for their comments on an earlier draft.
[1] See the Commission's IXth Report on Competition Policy (1979), pp. 9–11 and XXIXth Report on Competition Policy (1999), p. 19.

private parties could carry out anti-competitive practices[2] and Member States could give artificial competitive advantages to ailing national industries or prevent the liberalisation of markets traditionally subject to state monopolies. All these activities could effectively divide the Common Market. A system ensuring undistorted competition is, therefore, an essential piece in the single market jigsaw.

This chapter aims to examine the weight given by the Commission and by the European Court to the market integration objective of EC competition law in the interpretation and application of Articles 81 and 82 EC, the two key competition provisions in the Treaty.[3] It will also critically evaluate their approach.

ARTICLE 81 EC: ANTI-COMPETITIVE BEHAVIOUR RESULTING FROM COLLUSION BETWEEN UNDERTAKINGS

Article 81(1) EC lays down a prohibition on anti-competitive agreements, decisions by associations of undertakings and concerted practices, which have or may have an effect on intra-Community trade. Three elements need to be present for the prohibition to apply: a form of co-operation between undertakings, an anti-competitive object or effect and an effect on trade between Member States. In principle, any such agreements, decisions or practices are null and void, but they may, nevertheless, benefit from an exemption if they fulfil the conditions in Article 81(3) EC.

The promotion of the single market objective of the Treaty has been achieved through the interpretation of Article 81 in two ways. Firstly with the prohibition of agreements that may lead to the partitioning of the Common Market and, secondly, with the exemption of certain agreements that promote economic efficiency and cross-border trade. This approach pervades the treatment of horizontal and vertical agreements and concerted practices.

Horizontal agreements and concerted practices

Prohibited agreements and concerted practices

In deciding whether a horizontal agreement or concerted practice comes under the prohibition in Article 81(1) EC, the Commission and the Court have

---

[2] See Cases 56 and 58/64 *Consten and Grundig* [1966] ECR 299, [1966] CMLR 418, where the Court held 'an agreement between a producer and a distributor which might tend to restore the national division in trade between Member-States might be such as to thwart the most basic objectives of the Community. The Treaty, whose preamble and text aim to suppressing the barriers between States, and which in several provisions gives evidence of a stern attitude with regard to their reappearance, could not allow undertakings to reconstruct such barriers' (p. 340).

[3] For research already carried out in this field see Ehlermann, 'The Contribution of EC Competition Policy to the Single Market' (1992) 29 *CMLRev*, 257.

endorsed the single market objective in the application of the second and third limbs of Article 81(1) EC. The goal of market integration has therefore been relevant both in the assessment of the anti-competitive object or effect of an agreement or concerted practice and of its effect on intra-Community trade. These two aspects will be considered in turn.

There are three types of horizontal agreements or concerted practices traditionally labelled as having an anti-competitive object or effect, not only because of their undesirable economic and consumer effects but also because they threaten the unity of the Common Market. These are market sharing, price-fixing and collective exclusive dealing agreements.

The Commission and the Court have consistently and vigorously fought market sharing schemes.[4] The reason behind this approach is two-fold. First, they have an adverse effect on competition because they tend to be concluded to implement price fixing agreements, thus allowing undertakings to charge unchallenged high prices in their home markets. Second, because they contribute to the division of the Community markets.[5] In *Re Soda Ash*[6] the Commission found that Solvay and ICI, the two leading producers of soda-ash in the Community had agreed to confine their activities to their respective markets: Solvay to continental Europe and ICI to the United Kingdom and Ireland. The Commission took the view that the protection of national markets was 'in fundamental conflict with one of the basic objectives of the Treaty, namely the creation of a common market'.[7] More recently in *Re the pre-insulated pipe cartel*[8] and in *Re Seamless steel tubes*[9], the Commission strongly condemned market sharing on the same basis. Furthermore, it took into account the particular gravity of this practice by increasing the fines imposed on the relevant undertakings.[10]

Similarly, the Court has explained that price fixing agreements are repugnant to the single market ideal of the Treaty. Thus, in the *Dyestuffs* cases, where several producers of dyestuffs were found to have engaged in a concerted

---

[4] Article 81(1)(c) EC lists agreements to share markets or sources of supply as a form of anti-competitive agreements.

[5] In *Chemiefarma v. Commission* (Case 41/69 [1970] ECR 661), the Court took the view that a gentleman's agreement between quinine producers that aimed at protecting their respective domestic markets, and which was implemented by a system of quotas, had an anti-competitive object (at paragraphs 117 to 128 of the judgment).

[6] Decision 91/297/EEC, OJ [1991] L 152/1, [1994] 4 CMLR 454.

[7] *Ibid.*, at paragraph 60 of the decision.

[8] Commission decision of 21 October 1998 [1999] 4 CMLR 401.

[9] Commission decision of 8 December 1999, Bull. 12–1999.

[10] See the decision on the *Pre-insulated pipe cartel*, at paragraph 164 of the decision, and the Commission's summary of its decision on *Re Seamless steel tubes* in its XXIXth *Report on Competition Policy*, 1999 at points 48–52. See also the *Guidelines on the method of setting fines imposed pursuant to Article 15(2) of Regulation 17/62 and Article 65(5) ECSC*, (OJ [1998] C 9/3). The Guidelines list in the category of very serious infringements,—and therefore subject to the highest fines—price cartels, market sharing quotas or 'other practices which jeopardize the functioning of the single market'.

practice to fix prices, the Court explained that the function of price competition is to keep prices down to the lowest possible level and to encourage free movement of goods between Member States. Differences in rates encouraged 'the pursuit of one of the basic objectives of the Treaty, namely the inter-penetration of national markets'.[11] The Commission has also emphasised in its recent Reports on Competition Policy that price fixing agreements could imperil the achievement of a single economic and monetary union because their long-term effect is to push up inflation.[12]

Finally, the approach of the Commission to exclusive collective dealing is influenced by the important threat that such activities can pose to the single market. In the last few years, the Commission investigated the activities of three Dutch associations in the electrotechnical fittings market. The Commission found that by means of a gentleman's agreement, the Dutch association of importers of electrotechnical fittings (NAVEG) had agreed with the association of Dutch wholesalers (FEG) not to supply these products to wholesalers that were not members of FEG.[13] This arrangement, combined with the strict admission policy followed by FEG, made access to the Dutch market very difficult for newcomers. In deciding that the agreement distorted competition, the Commission made express reference to the fact that it made it 'considerably more difficult for foreign wholesalers to extend their field of operations to the Dutch wholesale market'.[14]

The requirement that an anti-competitive agreement or practice must have or be likely to have an effect on trade between the Member States in order to come under Article 81 EC,[15] has also proved to be an effective means of upholding the market integration aim. This requirement delimits the boundary between the areas covered by EC competition law and by national competition law[16] but its additional importance in strengthening the single market has been reflected in three ways.[17] First, the test to ascertain when this requirement is satisfied was

---

[11] See Case 48/69 *ICI v. Commission* [1972] ECR 619, [1972] CMLR 557, at paragraphs 115–116 of the judgment; Case 49/69 *BASF v. Commission* [1972] ECR 713, [1972] CMLR 557, at paragraph 33 of the judgment and Case 51/69 *Bayer v. Commission* [1972] ECR 745, [1972] CMLR 557, at paragraph 36 of the judgment.

[12] See the XXVIIIth Report on Competition Policy (1998) at point 63 and the XXIXth Report (1999) on Competition Policy at point 44.

[13] Commission Decision 2000/117/EC, OJ [2000] L 39/1.

[14] *Ibid.*, at paragraph 108 of the decision.

[15] This condition is also present in Article 82 EC (see below: The effect on Trade Between Member States), which requires that an abuse of dominant position by one or more undertakings should have or be likely to have an effect on trade between Member States.

[16] See *Consten and Grundig* (Cases 56 and 58/64, above n. 2), at p. 341.

[17] A particularly clear statement from the Court on the significance of this requirement is found in *Hugin v. Commission*, an Article 82 EC case (Case 22/78 [1979] ECR 1869, [1979] 3 CMLR 345). The Court held: 'The interpretation and application of the condition relating to effects on trade between Member States contained in Articles 85 [now 81] and 86 [now 82] of the Treaty must be based on the purpose of that condition which is to define, in the context of the law governing competition, the boundary between the areas covered by Community law and the law of the Member States. Thus, Community law covers any agreement or any practice which is capable of constituting a threat to

construed very widely in *STM* v. *Maschinenbau Ulm*.[18] In this case, the Court held that any effects, direct or indirect, actual or potential should be considered in deciding that an agreement has an effect on trade between Member States. This approach, reminiscent of the *Dassonville* test used to define measures having an equivalent effect to quantitative restrictions, is clearly based on the idea that free and undistorted trade should flow between the Member States and that any hindrance to such trade must be carefully monitored. Secondly, the Court has made it clear that even if an agreement is concluded at a purely national scale, it could still have such an effect on intra Community trade if it contributed to the isolation of the national market and made the penetration of imports more difficult. Thus, in *Cementhandelaren* v. *Commission*[19], an association of Dutch cement dealers enacted a series of decisions fixing target prices and preventing the sale of cement to traders other than members of the association or resellers approved by the association. Although this was a purely national cartel, the Court confirmed the view of the Commission that the decision had an effect on intra-EC trade because it contributed to the compartmentalisation of the national market and 'held up the economic inter-penetration that the Treaty is designed to bring about'.[20] Thirdly, the *Notice of the Commission on agreements of minor importance* states that the application of Article 81 EC to horizontal agreements that share markets or fix prices cannot be ruled out *even if* the market share of the participant undertakings falls below the established thresholds that would entitle an agreement to be treated as *de minimis*.[21] The same rule applies to vertical agreements that fix prices or attempt to secure territorial protection.[22] Although in the first instance it is left to national courts and authorities to take action in these cases, the Commission reserves the right to intervene in cases where there is a Community interest and 'in particular if the agreements impair the proper functioning of the internal market'.[23] This emphasises the degree of suspicion with which the Commission views such agreements.[24]

---

freedom of trade between member States *in a manner which might harm the attainment of the objectives of a single market between the Member States,* in particular by partitioning the national markets or by affecting the structure of competition within the Common Market [emphasis added]' (at paragraph 17 of the judgment).

[18] Case 56/65 [1966] ECR 234, [1966] CMLR 357. This case concerned a vertical agreement, but the same test has been applied to horizontal arrangements. See Joined Cases C-89/85, C-104/85, C-116–117/85 and C-125–129/85 *Woodpulp II*, [1993] ECR I-1307, [1993] 4 CMLR 407, at paragraph 143 of the judgment.

[19] Case 8/72 [1972] ECR 977, [1973] CMLR 7.

[20] *Ibid.*, at paragraph 29 of the judgment.

[21] See Commission Notice on *de minimis* agreements (OJ [1997] C 372/13), at paragraph 11.

[22] *Ibid.*

[23] *Ibid.*

[24] See also the new Draft Notice on *de minimis* agreements, published by the Commission in May 2001 (OJ [2001] C 149/28). The Draft Notice follows the practice of the current Notice and provides that horizontal and vertical agreements that have as their object the fixing or prices, the sharing of

Exempted agreements

The role of competition policy as a tool to consolidate market integration is also borne out, in the field of horizontal agreements, by the adoption of block exemption regulations on specialisation and research and development agreements.[25] Those regulations were adopted on the basis of Council Regulation 2871/71[26], whose preamble sets out two main reasons why such agreements, although potentially liable to distort competition, should be considered as beneficial overall. Firstly, because *they contribute to the creation of a common market* by encouraging undertakings to work more rationally and adapt their productivity to the demands of an enlarged market.[27] Secondly, because they are economically desirable: they increase efficiency by allowing undertakings to concentrate on the manufacture of certain products in the first case or by promoting technical progress in the second.[28]

The two current block exemptions on specialisation and research and development agreements follow the non-formalistic and economically-based approach pursued by the new umbrella block exemption on vertical restraints.[29] Thus, exemption is granted by function of the combined market power of the participant undertakings and there is only a list of hardcore restrictions, rather than lists of 'white', 'black' and 'grey' clauses as were present in the old system of block exemptions. The presence of one of these hardcore restrictions removes an agreement from the benefit of the block exemption. The list of prohibited clauses in both regulations also reflects the unwillingness of the Commission to exempt agreements that might have a market splitting effect. Thus, the Regulation on specialisation agreements prohibits allocation of markets and price fixing.[30] The Regulation on research and development agreements prohibits *inter alia*, restrictions on passive and active sales of the contract product in territories reserved to other parties, the requirement to refuse to meet demands from users or resellers who would market the products in other territories within the Common Market and the use of intellectual property rights to divide the markets of the Community along national lines.[31]

markets or include certain territorial and customer restrictions will not be treated as *de minimis*, even if the market shares of the participants fall below the established thresholds (see the Draft Notice at II. 12).

[25] See Commission Regulation 2658/2000 on specialisation (OJ [2000] L 304/3) and Commission Regulation 2659/2000 on research an development agreements (OJ [2000] L 304/7). These regulations have recemtly replaced the former block exemption regulations on specialisation (Regulation 417/85, OJ [1985] L 53/1) and research and development (Regulation 418/85 OJ [1985] L 53/5) agreements.
[26] OJ. En.Sp.Ed [1971] L 285/46.
[27] See recitals 3 and 4 of the preamble to Regulation 2822/71 and the preambles to Regulation 2658/2000 (above n. 25) and to Regulation 2659/2000 (above n. 25).
[28] See recital 5 to the Preamble to Regulation 2821/71.
[29] Regulation 2790/1999, (O.J. [1999] L 336/21, [2000] 4 CMLR 398).
[30] See Article 5 of Regulation 2658/2000.
[31] See Article 5 of Regulation 2659/2000.

Vertical agreements

Prohibited agreements and concerted practices

The Commission and the Court have mainly supported the single market objective by prohibiting some vertical agreements that include territorial and customer restrictions, limit the freedom of distributors to set resale prices, provide for the sharing of markets between participant undertakings or have the effect of isolating national markets. This has been achieved, as in the case of horizontal agreements, with the interpretation of the second and third limbs of Article 81(1) EC.

Vertical agreements that purport to grant *absolute* territorial protection are automatically caught by Article 81(1) EC. In its seminal decision in *Consten and Grundig*[32], the Court took the view that an exclusive distribution agreement that combined the imposition of export bans on a distributor and the use of intellectual property rights to prevent parallel imports had *per se* an anti-competitive object. The reasoning of the Court was based on the fact that the agreement aimed at isolating a national market and at artificially maintaining separate national markets in the Community.[33] The Court also held that such an agreement had an effect on trade between Member States because, by preventing the exports of goods between the Member States, it could harm 'the attainment of a single market between States'.[34] What is more striking about the judgment on this point is that the parties to the agreement had argued that the latter could actually *increase* the volume of trade between Member States. This point was also discussed by the Advocate General, who called for a more detailed examination of the actual effect of the agreement on trade between Member States.[35] The Court, however, chose to take a less analytical view and to give priority to the single market objective even if, from an economic point of view, it had not been proved that the agreement had an adverse effect on intra-Community trade.

Agreements that might partition the market, even if no absolute territorial protection is granted to the distributor, are also caught. Thus, in *Konica*[36], the Commission made it clear that an export ban on a distributor in itself is anti-competitive because 'it leads to artificial divisions in the Common Market and impedes the establishment of a single market between the member-States, which is the basic objective of the Treaty'.[37] The 1998 Commission's decision in the

---

[32] Joined Cases 56 and 58/64, above n. 2.
[33] *Ibid*. at p. 343 of the judgment. See also Case T-175/95 *BASF* v. *Commission* [1999] ECR II-1581, [2000] 4 CMLR 33, at paragraphs 133 to 135 of the judgment.
[34] *Ibid*., p. 341.
[35] See also the Opinion of Advocate General Roemer, pp. 360–361.
[36] Commission Decision 88/172/EEC, OJ [1988] L 78/34, [1988] 4 CMLR 848.
[37] *Ibid*., at paragraph 41 of the decision.

Volkswagen[38] case represents another powerful illustration of the particular attention that the Commission pays to market integration when it enforces competition law. In that case, Volkswagen imposed an export ban on its Italian distributors. Thus, the Italian dealers were prevented from selling cars to customers not resident in Italy. The system was enforced, *inter alia*, by means of penalties, by prohibiting cross-supplies with other authorised Volkswagen dealers in the Common Market and also by imposing on the Italian dealers an obligation to require their customers to agree in writing to restrictions in the use of the vehicles. In taking the view that the agreement had an anti-competitive object, the Commission placed the main emphasis on the fact that the effect of these measures was to partition the market. The Commission demonstrated that whether taken in combination or even in isolation, they had a market-partitioning and therefore a restrictive effect on competition.[39] Likewise, the Commission found that the measures affected trade between the Member States because they restricted cross-border trade by eliminating the Italian market as a source of imports and therefore allowed dealers in other Member States to charge much higher prices.[40]

The impact of *Consten and Grundig* is also highlighted by other decisions where agreements carrying an element of exclusivity, but not aiming to seal-off national markets, were held not to be *per se* subject to the prohibition in Article 81(1) EC. In *STM v. Maschinenbau Ulm*[41], the Court explained that an agreement conferring an exclusive right of sale was not *per se* contrary to Article 81(1) EC, as it might display overall pro-competitive effects, i.e facilitate the penetration of a new area by an undertaking.[42] Such an agreement was permitted provided that no measures were taken to curb parallel imports.[43] Similarly, in *Nungesser* v. *Commission*[44], the Court concluded that an open exclusive licence, i.e. one that does not affect the position of third parties such as parallel importers or other licensees, was not in itself incompatible with Article 81(1) EC.[45] However, an exclusive licence, the terms of which aim to prevent parallel imports would be caught.[46]

---

[38] Decision of the Commission of 28 January 1998 (Decision 98/273, OJ [1998] L 124/60; [1998] 5 CMLR 33).

[39] *Ibid.* at paragraphs 130 to 143 of the decision. See also the judgment of the Court of First Instance in that case (Case, T-62/98, *Volkswagen v. Commission*, judgment of 6 July 2000, not yet reported), which mostly upheld the Commission's decision, and, in particular, paragraphs 88–89 of the judgment

[40] *Ibid.*, at paragraph 149 of the decision.

[41] Case 56/65, above n. 18.

[42] The Court, however, was mindful to emphasise that such an agreement would come under Article 81(1) EC if it included clauses that are capable of distorting trade between Member States and of 'preventing the realisation of a single market' (*Ibid.*, p. 250).

[43] *Ibid.*, p. 250.

[44] Case 258/78 [1982] ECR 2015; [1983] 1 CMLR 278.

[45] *Ibid.* at paragraph 58 of the judgment.

[46] *Ibid.* at paragraph 61 of the judgment. See also the generous approach followed by the Technology Transfer block exemption regulation (Regulation 240/96 OJ [1996] L 31/2), below n. 70.

The recent decision of the Court of First Instance in *Bayer* v. *Commission*[47], however, sits uncomfortably with the consistently severe treatment given by the Community judicature to export restrictions. Bayer manufactured and marketed a drug intended to treat cardio-vascular disease whose price was, as a result of differences between national health authorities regulatory action, much lower in Spain and France than in the United Kingdom. This price difference caused Spanish and French wholesalers of the drug to export it in large quantities to the United Kingdom. Faced with this situation, Bayer changed its supply policy and successively reduced the amounts supplied to exporting Spanish and French wholesalers, only fulfilling their orders when these were placed at the level of their habitual needs. The Commission found that this practice came under Article 81(1) EC, as it constituted an agreement comprising an export ban.[48] The market integration aim was clearly at the very core of the Commission's decision.[49] The Court of First Instance however, struck down the Commission's decision on the grounds that the Commission had not proved the existence of an agreement between Bayer and its wholesalers. The Commission had relied on a longstanding line of case law to show that although Bayer seemed to have acted unilaterally, the wholesalers' conduct in implementing the export ban reflected an implicit acquiescence in the action. This proved the existence of co-operation between Bayer and its wholesalers for the purposes of the application of Article 81(1) EC.[50] The Court of First Instance took an uncharacteristically narrow and legalistic view. It held that the fact that the wholesalers did not interrupt their commercial relations with Bayer following the introduction of the latter's new policy, was not a sufficient ground to determine the existence of an agreement within the meaning of Article 81(1) EC.[51] The decision of the Court of First Instance, which is now on appeal to the European Court, seems therefore a retreat from the wide interpretation of Article 81(1) EC followed by the European Court in cases where export limitations are involved. The *Bayer* judgment, however, has not weakened the

The intention to prevent parallel imports is relevant even to agreements concluded outside the Community. In *Javico* (Case C-306/96 [1998] ECR I-1983; [1998] 5 CMLR 172) a prohibition on re-importation of products into the Community imposed on a distributor outside the Common market was held not to have an anti-competitive object if not intended to exclude parallel imports. The Court was nonetheless careful to underline that the effects of that prohibition on intra-EC trade should still be examined to determine whether or not Article 81 (1) EC would be applicable.

[47] Case T-41/96, [2000] ECR II-3383, [2001] 4 CMLR 126.
[48] The Commission emphasised that the arrangements had the effect 'of artificially partitioning the common market and of preventing the creation of a single market between the member States, the creation of such a single market being one of the fundamental objectives of the EC Treaty' (See the Commission's decision in *Bayer* (Decision 96/478 EC, OJ [1996] L 201/1), at paragraph 190).
[49] See the Commission's decision, at paragraphs 190 and 198.
[50] The Commission relied, amongst others on the decisions of the Court in Case C-2777/87 *Sandoz* v. *Commission* [1990] ECR I-45 and in Case C-279/87 *Tipp-EX* v. *Commission* [1990] ECR I-261.
[51] See the judgment of the Court of First Instance, at paragraphs 62 to 184.

commitment of the Commission to the promotion of parallel imports. Only a few months later, the decision of the Commission in *Glaxo Wellcome*[52], another case concerning medical products, supports as strongly as ever the single market objective of competition law. In this case, the Commission condemned Glaxo Wellcome's dual pricing system which required its Spanish wholesalers to pay a higher price for products intended for export to other Member States than the price paid for products intended for domestic consumption. The main objection of the Commission was that the system excluded or limited parallel trade from Spain to other Member States and therefore interfered 'with the Community's objective of integrating national markets'.[53]

Vertical agreements that aim to share markets between the participant undertakings have also been held to come under Article 81(1) EC. Thus, in *Pronuptia*[54], the juxtaposition of a clause whereby the franchisor undertook not to establish himself in the territories allocated to its franchisees and of one whereby franchisees undertook not to open a second shop was held to have an anti-competitive object. The underlying reason was that it led 'to a kind of market partitioning between the franchisor and the franchisees or among the franchisees'.[55] The Court also concluded that a clause with such market partitioning effect was *per se* capable of affecting trade between Member States.[56]

Furthermore, the Court has considered the cumulative effect of networks of agreements. It has held that, even if each agreement individually does not have an anti-competitive object, Article 81 EC may still apply. This is the case, in particular, where such networks result in the sealing off of a national market. In *Delimitis*[57], the Court considered an exclusive purchasing agreement between a small German publican and a German brewery. The German beer supply market was structured in a network of similar agreements. The Court, drawing on its judgment in *Brasserie de Haecht*[58], held that such an agreement would be prohibited if two conditions were satisfied. First, that the cumulative effect of all the exclusive purchasing agreements was to make it difficult for competitors to gain access to the market. Secondly, that the agreement in question contributed significantly to the sealing-off of the national market.[59] Some observations seem pertinent. In that case the Court considered simultaneously the second and third limb of Article 81(1) EC: the restriction of competition

---

[52] The Commission Decision in *Glaxo Wellcome* was enacted on 8 May 2001 and is yet to be published in the Official Journal (see the Commission's Press Release IP/01/661).
[53] *Ibid.*
[54] Case 161/84 [1986] ECR 353, [1986] 1 CMLR 414.
[55] *Ibid.*, at paragraph 24 of the judgment.
[56] *Ibid.*, at paragraph 26 of the judgment.
[57] Case C-234/89 [1991] ECR I-935, [1992] 5 CMLR 210.
[58] Case 23/67 [1967] ECR 407, [1968] CMLR 26.
[59] Case C-234/89, above n. 57, at paragraphs 14–27 of the judgment. See also Case T-25/99 *Roberts v. Commission*, judgment of the Court of First instance of 5 July 2001, not yet reported.

and the effect on trade.[60] In the consideration of both, the threat that such a network of agreements could pose to the unity of the market appeared to be the guiding principle. If such a threat did not exist, then even if the agreement restrained the economic freedom of the parties it would not come under Article 81(1) EC. This is evidenced by the same judgment, where the Court explained that a beer supply agreement that gave a reseller a real possibility to purchase beer from other Member States would be compatible with Article 81(1) EC.[61] Also, in its recent decision in *Markkinointi*[62], the Court has emphasised that the duration of the agreements is relevant in determining whether the cumulative effect of all of them is to foreclose the market. Thus, the Court held that exclusive purchasing agreements that may be terminated upon short notice are less likely to restrict market access than those concluded for a number of years.[63] These agreements may therefore escape the application of Article 81(1) EC, even if other exclusive purchasing contracts concluded by the same supplier would overall contribute significantly to the closing off the market and therefore be in breach of that provision.

Exempted agreements

The Commission was severely criticised for its treatment of vertical restraints.[64] In particular, critics argued that the Commission was too preoccupied in upholding the single market objective of the Treaty when striking down agreements that included territorial restrictions, even though these were perhaps necessary to minimise the economic risk undertaken by the participant undertakings or lead to an increase on trade. In other words, the market integration objective seemed always to prevail over the real impact of an agreement on trade. As a result of this wide application of Article 81(1) to vertical restraints, a set of block exemption regulations were enacted to provide some measure of legal certainty for Community undertakings.[65]

---

[60] See Case C-234/89, above n. 57, paragraph 14 of the judgment. The Court followed the approach of Advocate General Van Gerven. The Advocate General dealt with both criterion together as he thought they were very closely interconnected in the case of a network of agreements. This was because '[w]here such a network is extensive, it may restrict not only the competitive freedom of the contracting parties and third parties and reduce the number of supply and demand possibilities and thus compromise the competitive nature of the market structure, but also protect the national market from imports from other member States' (*Ibid.* at p. I–965).

[61] *Ibid.*, at paragraphs 28–32 of the judgment.

[62] Case C-214/99, judgment of 7 December 2000, not yet reported.

[63] *Ibid.*, at paragraph 33 of the judgment.

[64] See B. Hawk, 'System Failure: Vertical Restraints and EC Competition law' (1995) 32 CMLRev, 973 and Deacon 'Vertical Restraints under EU Competition law: new directions' [1995] *Fordham Corp.Law Inst.* 307.

[65] The Regulations were adopted on the basis of Council Regulation 19/65. The first Regulation enacted was Regulation 67/67 on exclusive dealing agreements (OJ Sp.Ed. [1967], p.11), which was replaced later by Regulation 1983/83 on exclusive distribution and its companion, Regulation 1984/83 on exclusive purchasing agreements (OJ [1983] L 173/1). Regulations on franchising

As the Commission recognised in its 1997 Green Paper on Vertical restraints, the 'ongoing integration process of the Single Market adds an extra dimension to the analysis of vertical restraints'.[66] Vertical agreements can be used either to promote or to hinder market integration.[67] On the one hand, they can promote integration because they increase efficiency and open up new markets. On the other, they may hinder it by dividing the territories of the Common Market with guarantees of exclusivity or by limiting the freedom of distributors or consumers to sell or purchase goods in other Member States.[68] Territorial and customer restrictions contribute in turn to the maintenance of price differences across the Member States, a result which is at variance with the Single Market programme. The Preamble to Regulation 2790/1999[69], the new umbrella block exemption regulation on vertical agreements, announces a less formalistic and more economically based approach to vertical restraints than the one followed by the old system of block exemption regulations. However it still removes from the scope of the exemption certain restrictions of competition such as the fixing of minimum resale prices or certain territorial restrictions irrespective of the market share of the participant undertakings. These obligations have been included in the list of hardcore restrictions in Article 4 of Regulation 2790/1999[70], with the result that the presence of only one of them in an

(Regulation 4087/88, OJ [1988] L 359/46), motor vehicle distribution and servicing (Regulation 1475/95 OJ [1995] L 145/25) and technology transfer (Regulation 240/96 OJ [1996] L 31/2) agreements followed. The regulations on exclusive distribution, purchasing and franchising agreements have been replaced by the new umbrella block exemption regulation (Regulation 2790/1999, above n. 29). The Preambles of these regulations illustrate the benefits that these agreements produce even if they can also restrict competition to a certain extent. For example, an exclusive distribution agreement improves distribution because the supplier is able to concentrate its sales activities and hence to overcome difficulties in international trade that result from linguistic and legal differences. It also makes it easier to promote the sales of a product and it is often the only way for a distributor to undertake the risk of selling a new product in a given market (see recitals 5 and 6 in the Preamble to Regulation 1983/83). Likewise, a franchising agreement gives a franchisor the possibility of establishing a uniform network with little investment, which assists the entry of new competitors in the market. At the same time, it allows independent undertakings to set up outlets more efficiently than without the benefit of the franchise(see recitals 7 and 8 to the Preamble to Regulation 4087/88) These agreements came under the scope of Article 81(3) EC provided that their terms coincided with the list of 'white clauses' in the relevant block exemption regulation and that no 'black clauses' were included. The list of 'black clauses' in these regulations often included those aiming to fix resale prices, to prevent parallel imports or to divide the Community market along national lines, a clear reflection of the importance of the single market objective (see, for example Article 3(c) and (d) of Regulation 1983/83 or Recital 12 to Regulation 4087/88 which explains the need that parallel imports should remain possible).

[66] See the Green Paper on Vertical restraints, [1997] 4 CMLR 519, at paragraph 70.
[67] *Ibid.*, at paragraphs 2 and 70–84.
[68] See the Guidelines on Vertical Restraints (OJ [2000] C 291/1, [2000] 5 CMLR 1074) at paragraphs 95 and 105–106. See also the Vth Report on Competition Policy [1975] at point 45.
[69] Above n. 29.
[70] The Regulation exempts a certain degree of territorial protection. For example, a distributor may be placed under an obligation to refrain from actively selling into the territory of other distributors, but no restrictions may be placed on passive sales (see Article 4(b) of the Regulation). The Technology transfer regulation (Regulation 240/96, *supra* n. 65) goes further than any of the other

agreement would bring the latter under the purview of Article 81(1) EC. The main reason behind this approach is the incompatibility of these restrictions with the market integration objective of the Treaty.

ARTICLE 82 EC: ABUSES OF DOMINANT POSITION BY ONE OR MORE UNDERTAKINGS

Article 82 EC prohibits abuses of dominant position by one or more undertakings. The aim of this provision is clear: to control the activities of firms whose economic strength makes them immune from the influence of competitive forces in the market. The prohibition in Article 82 EC includes three cumulative elements: firstly, an undertaking must hold a position of dominance within the Common market or in a substantial part of it; secondly, the undertaking must abuse that position of dominance. Thirdly, the abuse must have an effect on intra-Community trade. When interpreting Article 82 EC, the Commission and the Court have not only sought to protect the interests of small or medium sized undertakings, but also to support the single market objective of the Treaty. This has been achieved in the interpretation of the concept of abuse and of the requirement of an effect on trade between Member States.

The influence of the single market goal on the determination of abusive conducts under Article 82 EC

In its definition of abuse in *Hoffmann-La Roche*[71], the Court highlighted that abusive behaviour undermines or prevents competition. An additional and important dimension in that concept is the effect that such behaviour may have on the development of the single market. The Commission and the Court have examined certain forms of abuse through the lens of the market integration objective of the Treaty, although they have alluded to this goal less frequently than in Article 81 EC cases. This is evident in the case of discriminatory

---

regulations by exempting restrictions both on active and passive sales over a limited period of time, se Articles 1(1)(5), 1(1)(6) and 1(2) of Regulation 240/96. Parallel imports, however, should still be possible (see Article 3(3) of the Regulation)

[71] The Court defined abuse as 'The concept of abuse is an objective concept relating to the behaviour of an undertaking in a dominant position which is such as to influence the structure of a market where, as a result of the very presence of the undertaking in question, the degree of competition is weakened and which, through recourse to methods different from those which condition normal competition in products or services on the basis of the transactions of commercial operators, has the effect of hindering the maintenance of the degree of competition still existing in the market or the growth of that competition'. (Case 85/76 [1979] ECR 461, [1979] 3 CMLR 211, at paragraph 26 of the judgment).

practices and of imposition of imports or exports restrictions by dominant companies.

First, discriminatory treatment by a dominant undertaking on grounds of nationality will be abusive. In *GEMA*[72], the German music performing rights society was found by the Commission to be in breach of Article 82 EC *inter alia*, because the former discriminated against nationals of other Member States, who, in practice could not become members of the society. In another copyright case, *GVL v. Commission*[73], the Court upheld a Commission decision finding that the refusal of a German performers' rights collecting society to allow non-German artists not resident in Germany to benefit from rights of secondary exploitation constituted an abuse of dominant position.[74] In these cases, therefore, abuse was found because the behaviour of the dominant companies offended one of the premises of the Common Market: the principle of non-discrimination on grounds of nationality.[75]

Secondly, the Commission has staunchly, and controversially[76], targeted discriminatory pricing, which is expressly mentioned in Article 82(1)(c) EC as an example of abusive conduct, especially if accompanied by resale restrictions.[77] In *United Brands v. Commission*[78], the Commission and the Court took the view that United Brands, a leading world producer of bananas, had abused its position of dominance by charging different prices to its ripeners/distributors in the various Member States. The discriminatory prices were just one of several practices carried out by the dominant company. These included the imposition of a prohibition on the distributors on the resale of green bananas to foreign dealers, the effect of which was enhanced by the practice of United Brands to supply its distributors with lower quantities of bananas than those ordered.[79] The combination of these clauses seems to have influenced the consideration of the discriminatory prices as abusive. The Court explained that the difference in prices could not be objectively justified by variations in marketing conditions and intensity of competition in the markets of the

---

[72] Commission Decision 71/224/EEC, OJ [1971] L 134/15, [1971] CMLR D35.

[73] Case 7/82 [1983] ECR 483, [1983] 3 CMLR 645.

[74] *Ibid.*, at paragraph 56 of the judgment.

[75] More recently, in a highly publicised case, the Commission found that the CFO, one of the official ticket distributors for the 1998 Football World Cup had abused its position of dominance because it had implemented ticket-selling arrangements that were discriminatory against consumers not resident in France (see Commission Decision in *The Football World Cup 1998* [2000] 4 CMLR 963, at paragraphs 103–114 of the decision).

[76] See W. Bishop, 'Price discrimination under Article 86 EC: Political Economy in the European Court' [1981] 44 *MLR* 282.

[77] In the framework of Article 81 EC, agreements that result in the application of discriminatory prices have also met with strong opposition from the Commission and the Community judicature. See Article 81(1)(d) EC; Case 96/82 *IAZ v. Commission* [1983] ECR 3369; [1984] 3 CMLR 276 and the Decision of the Commission in *Re Pittsburg Corning Europe* (OJ [1972] L 272/35; [1973] CMLR D2).

[78] Case 27/76 [1978] ECR 207, [1978] 1 CMLR 429.

[79] *Ibid.*, at paragraphs 155–161 of the judgment.

Member States.[80] It then held that they constituted obstacles to the free movement of goods, especially in combination with the resale restrictions imposed by United Brands and created a rigid partitioning of national markets.[81] This approach was confirmed by the Court of First Instance in *Tetrapak II*[82] where the different prices charged by Tetrapak in the different Member States were held to be abusive, especially if considered cumulatively with the system of tied-sales imposed on Tetrapak's customers.[83]

The Community judicature was strongly criticised for its treatment of these cases. In particular, it was argued that its reasoning in *United Brands* was superficial and economically flawed and that the integration goal of EC competition law had once more prevailed over its economic and consumer welfare aims.[84] The Court's critics maintained that not only is price discrimination difficult to define but also that it has not been demonstrated from an economic perspective that it has a *per se* negative effect on competition.[85] Therefore, the underlying reason why discriminatory prices were held to be abusive in *United Brands* seemed to be the defence of the single market ideal.[86] Discrimination, whether on grounds of nationality, or geography, as in the present cases, will therefore breach Article 82 EC. The second type of discrimination will be saved only if objectively justified.[87] The same approach pervades the Court's treatment of the imposition of discriminatory trading conditions by a dominant company[88], of the discriminatory allocation of products during supply shortages,[89] and of loyalty rebates.[90]

The imposition of export or import bans by a dominant company or conduct intended to prevent parallel trade are also abusive, not only because they lead to a weakening of competition, but also because they are antagonistic to market integration. The reasoning followed by the Court runs in parallel to the one applied to market sharing or territorial restrictions under Article 81 EC.[91] Thus,

[80] *Ibid.*, at paragraphs 227–231 of the judgment.
[81] *Ibid.* at paragraphs 231 and 232 of the judgment.
[82] Case T-83/91 [1994] ECR II-755, [1997] 4 CMLR 726.
[83] *Ibid.*, at paragraphs 160 and 170 and 207–209 of the judgment.
[84] See Bishop, above n. 76, at p. 289 and 294.
[85] *Ibid.* See also Siragusa, 'The Application of Article 86 to the pricing policy of dominant companies: discriminatory and unfair prices' (1979) 16 *CMLRev* 179, pp. 180–185.
[86] See Bishop, above n. 76, p. 287. For a more balanced and less critical approach to the judgments, see Faull and Nikpay (eds) *The EC Law of Competition*, (Oxford, Clarendon Press, 1999) at paragraphs 3.322 to 3.327 and Bishop and Walker, *The Economics of EC Competition Law: Concepts, Application and Measurement*, (London, Sweet & Maxwell, 1999) at pp. 120–121.
[87] For recent examples of discriminatory pricing, see the judgments of the Court of First Instance in *Irish Sugar* v. *Commission* (Case T-222/97 [1999] ECR II-2969) and *Aéroports de Paris* v. *Commission* (Case T-128/98, [2001] ECR II-3929).
[88] See Case T-65/89 *BPB* v. *Commission* [1993] ECR II-389, [1993] 5 CMLR 32, at paragraphs 93–97 of the judgment.
[89] *Ibid.*, at paragraph 94 of the judgment.
[90] See Case 85/76, above n. 71.
[91] See above pp 312–315 and 317–321.

in *United Brands*[92], the clause prohibiting ripeners/distributors from exporting green bananas was held to be abusive. Likewise, in *Suiker Unie* v. *Commission*[93], export restrictions imposed on dealers came under Article 82 EC. In *General Motors*[94], the Court explained that the behaviour of a company holding a statutory monopoly in a national market that had the effect of curbing parallel imports would be abusive.[95]

The effect on trade between Member States

Support for the single market objective of the Treaty is also evidenced by the interpretation of the third limb of Article 82 EC. In particular, the Court and the Commission have emphasised that abusive behaviour has an effect on intra-EC trade when it leads to the partitioning of the Community markets and renders market access difficult or impossible for competitors.[96] The case law on exclusivity obligations and loyalty rebates, unfairly low pricing and refusals to supply represents a good example of this approach.

The imposition by dominant companies of obligations on their customers to obtain from them all or most of their requirements, with or without the incentive of a rebate has been consistently held to be abusive. In *Hoffmann-La Roche*[97], the Commission took the view that such obligations breached Article 82 EC first, because customers were restricted in their choice of sources of supply and secondly, because they had a discriminatory effect.[98] The Commission also found that they had an effect on trade between Member States because they restricted the trading opportunities of users and suppliers of bulk vitamins in the different Member States and therefore impeded the attainment of the objectives of a single market.[99] Likewise in its decision in *Solvay*[100], the Commission, after finding that the loyalty rebates and other inducements to exclusivity applied by Solvay were abusive, took the view that such practices affected trade between the Member States. It explained that they hindered access to the market by competing suppliers and had a market splitting effect 'and thus harmed or threatened to harm the attainment of the objective of a single market between Member States'.[101]

---

[92] Case 27/76, see above n. 78, at paragraphs 155–161 of the judgment.
[93] Cases 40–48/73, etc [1975] ECR 1663, [1976] 1 CMLR 295, at paragraph 398 of the judgment.
[94] Case 26/75 [1975] ECR 1367, [1976] 1 CMLR 95.
[95] *Ibid.*, at paragraphs 11–12 of the judgment.
[96] See Case 22/78 *Hugin* v. *Commission* (above n. 17), at paragraph 17 of the judgment.
[97] Commission Decision 76/642/EEC, OJ [1976] L 223/27, [1976] 2 CMLR D25.
[98] See paragraphs 63 and 66 of the decision. On discriminatory practices, see previous section.
[99] See paragraph 67 of the decision. See also the judgment of the Court in that case (Case 85/76, above n. 71, at paragraph 125), and in particular, the reference to the market-splitting effect of the 'English clauses' included by Hoffmann-la Roche in the contracts with its customers.
[100] Commission Decision 91/299/EC, OJ [1991] L 152/ 21, [1994] 4 CMLR 645.
[101] *Ibid.*, at paragraph 65 of the decision.

Other abusive practices, such as refusals to supply and unfairly low pricing can effectively drive competitors out of the market. If the behaviour of a dominant company results in the exclusion of a competitor from the market, the Court has taken the view that such behaviour will *per se* affect trade between Member States, without it being necessary to analyse the actual effect of the practice on trade.[102] Although there has been no express reference to the market integration goal, the latter clearly seems to infuse this line of cases, given that the total exclusion of competition will have as an effect market isolation and will encourage further abuse such as the imposition of unfairly high prices by the dominant company. In *Commercial Solvents* v. *Commission*[103], Commercial Solvents, refused to supply Zoja, a longstanding customer turned competitor, with the raw material necessary to manufacture a drug for the treatment of tuberculosis. The applicant argued that the refusal to supply, even if held to be abusive, would not come under the scope of Article 82 EC because the effect on intra-Community trade could not be made out. In particular, it argued that Zoja sold 90% of its production outside the Common Market and that even within it, Zoja's sales were reduced by reason of the patents held by other companies. In other words, it did not seem that the elimination of Zoja from the market would have a significant effect on imports or exports within the EC. The Court held that if the aim of a dominant company is to eliminate a competitor, it is irrelevant whether the conduct relates to the latter's exports or its trade within the Common Market.[104]

A similar approach can be seen in cases involving predatory pricing, where the aim of a dominant company is, by lowering its prices dramatically and temporarily, to force small competitors out of the market. In *AKZO*[105], even though there was a direct effect on the flow of trade between the Member States, the Commission referred primarily to the *Commercial Solvents* approach.[106] Similarly, in *Compagnie Maritime Belge*[107], the Court of First Instance held that such exclusionary practices are 'inherently capable of affecting the structure of competition in the market and thereby of affecting trade between Member States.'[108]

---

[102] See Faull and Nikpay, *supra* n. 86, at paragraph 3.333. This approach is reminiscent to the one, followed, in the framework of Article 81 EC in *Consten and Grundig* (see section above p 317).

[103] Cases 6 and 7/73 [1974] ECR 223, [1974] 1 CMLR 308.

[104] *Ibid.* at paragraph 33 of the judgment. See also *United Brands* (Case 26/77, above n. 78, at paragraph 201 of the judgment). See also the decision of the Court of First Instance in *RTE* v. *Commission* (Case T-69/89, [1991] ECR II-485, [1991] 4 CMLR 586, at paragraphs 76–77 of the judgment)

[105] Commission Decision 85/609 OJ [1985] L 374/1; [1986] 3 CMLR 273.

[106] *Ibid.*, at paragraph 88 of the decision.

[107] Joined Cases T-24/93, etc [1996] ECR II-1201, [1997] 4 CMLR 273.

[108] *Ibid.*, at paragraph 203 of the judgment.

CONCLUSIONS

The opening paragraph of the 1997 Green Paper on Vertical Restraints reads: 'the creation of a single market is one of the main objectives of the European Union's competition policy. Whilst great progress has been made, further efforts are still necessary if the full economic advantages of integration are to be realised'.[109] These two sentences underline not only the important contribution made by competition policy to the market integration goal of the Treaty but also the long road that lies ahead.

In the preceding pages, we have seen how the Commission and the Court have consistently interpreted Articles 81 and 82 EC with a view to upholding the single market ideal of the Treaty.[110] This has been achieved in two main ways. On the one hand, they have prohibited practices, whether collusive or unilateral, intended to divide the territories of the Common Market or that may substantially restrict access to a market. This runs in parallel with the case law concerning the four freedoms, where even non-discriminatory measures have been brought within the purview of the Treaty, if proven to have the potential to significantly hinder market access.[111] On the other, they have encouraged agreements that facilitate cross-border trade and market integration.[112]

The Commission, in particular, has come under intense scrutiny for its steadfast defence of that ideal at the expense, in the view of its critics, of proper economic analysis. Criticism has been levelled, *inter alia*, at its approach to the *per se* effect on trade of agreements granting absolute territorial protection and to vertical restraints in the context of Article 81 EC, or to discriminatory

---

[109] See Green Paper, above n. 66, at paragraph 1. The Green Paper also emphasises the vital role played by competition in order to obtain the economic gains from the single market (see paragraph 71)

[110] This article is focused on Commission decisions and decisions of the Community judicature in the framework of Articles 81 and 82 EC, but the single market goal of the Treaty has also presided over the interpretation of the whole system of competition rules in the Treaty. This is evidenced by the case law under Articles 86 and 87 to 89 EC, the provisions that apply to State intervention that may distort competition. The Court has ensured that public undertakings are subject to the Treaty rules on competition and in particular, to Article 82 EC (see Ehlermann, above n. 3, at p. 269). Furthermore, it has interpreted Article 86 EC teleologically to infer that if the position of exclusivity held by a public undertaking could *induce* the latter to behave abusively, then Article 82 EC would apply (See Case C-170/90 *Merci Convenzionali Porto di Genoa*, [1991] ECR I-5009, [1994] 4 CMLR 422 at paragraphs 20–26 of the judgment). Such a wide approach seems rooted in the fact that the absolute dominance granted by a monopoly is contrary to the principles of an open market economy and basically prevents market access. Likewise, in the framework of the provisions on State aids, the Commission has repeatedly emphasised that the provision of State aid is contrary to the Treaty not only because it distorts competition by granting an artificial competitive advantage to undertakings but also because it endangers the functioning of the Common Market (see the XXVIIIth Report of the Commission on Competition Policy (1998), at paragraph 197).

[111] See Case C-55/94 *Gebhard* [1995] ECR I-4165; Case C-384/93 *Alpine Investments* [1995] ECR I-1141, [1995] 2 CMLR 209. See further C. Barnard, 'Fitting the pieces into the goods and persons jigsaw?' (2001) 26 *ELRev*, 35.

[112] See the Commission's XVIIIth (1998) and XXIXth (1999) Reports on Competition Policy at pp. 35 and 30 respectively and above pp 316 and 321–323 on exempted agreements.

pricing in the framework of Article 82 EC. This criticism is firmly based on economic considerations. For example, the inclusion of certain territorial restrictions in a vertical agreement may, in some cases, improve economic efficiency and consumer welfare. This has been well demonstrated in US antitrust law, where vertical restraints other than resale price maintenance[113], are not *per se* illegal but subject to a rule of reason approach.[114] In *Continental TV Inc.* v. *GTE Sylvania Inc*, the Supreme Court considered an agreement whereby a television manufacturer had, in view of its declining market share, limited the number of franchises given for a certain area and required each franchisee to sell only from one location. It held that it was necessary to balance the positive effects of the agreement on interbrand competition with its negative effects on intrabrand competition in order to decide whether such an agreement was competitive or anti-competitive. [115] In other words, economic analysis should determine in each case which are the real effects on an agreement and therefore whether it should be prohibited or not.[116] In the framework of EC law, the Commission has viewed such territorial restrictions with suspicion, regardless of their actual economic impact, due to their damaging effects on the internal market. The new block exemption regulation on vertical agreements[117] has certainly heralded a more economically focused approach to vertical restraints, but it has also included a list of hard-core restrictions that are always presumed to be illegal. The prohibition of these restrictions is clearly based on the threat they pose to the single market ideal.[118] Similarly, it can be argued that although price discrimination or the granting of loyalty or target discounts by a dominant company have not been proved to be necessarily inefficient in economic terms, they have been rendered unlawful mainly because they are inimical to the common market principles.

The truth is, however, that the Commission was placed by Article 3(g) of the Treaty in the unenviable position of having to ensure that competition *in the internal market* was not distorted, a mandate which does not imbue the practice of competition law in other jurisdictions such as the United States. Very often, what is economically beneficial may conflict, at least temporarily, with

---

[113] And even the *per se* rule against resale price maintenance is subject to some narrowly defined exceptions (see Hovenkamp, *Antitrust*, 3rd ed., (St. Paul, Minn., West Group, 1999), pp. 181–184).

[114] *Continental TV Inc.* v. *GTE Sylvania Inc* (433 US 36, 97 S. Ct. 2549 (1977)). This decision overruled an earlier one in *US* v. *Arnold Schwinn & Co* (388 US 365, 87 S.Ct. 1856 (1967)), which had applied a *per se* rule to these restrictions.

[115] See, by way of comparison, the decision of the European Court in *Pronuptia* (see text at n. 54 above).

[116] See, by way of comparison, the reasoning of the Commission in its decision in *Re Distillers* (O.J. [1983] C 245/3; [1983] CMLR 173), a case involving export bans. This is considered to be a clear example of a decision taken solely to protect the market integration objective of EC Competition law and which neglected proper economic analysis. See the commentary on that decision by R. Whish, *Competition Law* 3rd edn., (London, Butterworths, 1993), pp. 565–566).

[117] Regulation 2790/99, above n. 29.

[118] See Article 4 of Regulation 2790/99 (above n. 29).

the internal market principles. The Commission and the Court were left to strike a balance between these two opposing forces and when they chose to give precedence to market integration, they were criticised for being legalistic and detached from economic reality. It is suggested that critics forget that Articles 81 and 82 EC cannot be taken in isolation but in the context of a Treaty, one of whose primary aims is to create a market without any national barriers. The removal of barriers erected by Member States would be a futile exercise if private parties were allowed to put in place similar territorial divisions in the Common Market or if concentrations of economic power could significantly restrict market access. It should not be forgotten that one of the main reasons why the Treaty included a set of provisions on competition was to contribute to the proper functioning of the internal market. Anti-competitive practices that contravene principles lying at the heart of the Common Market such as non-discrimination or removal of national barriers need therefore to be subject to the same strict treatment as national measures that hinder free movement of goods or persons.

Has the time come for the single market objective to play a less prominent role in the context of competition policy? After all, it could be argued the 31 December 1992 deadline has long expired and that competition policy should move into a more economically based terrain. This idea infused the debate on vertical restraints and culminated in the adoption of the new block exemption regulations on vertical and horizontal agreements.[119] In the context of that debate, some authors and the Commission itself have already argued that it might be too early to relax the importance of that goal given the price differences still subsisting between the Member States, the minimum impact of cross-border purchasing groups, and the prospective further enlargement of the Union.[120] Furthermore, two additional factors may have a decisive influence on the way the single market objective is deployed in the interpretation of Articles 81 and 82 EC. First, the fully decentralised system for the enforcement of these provisions envisaged by the Commission in its 1999 *White Paper* is likely to have an impact on this area.[121] While it is true that the Commission will continue to play a pivotal role in directing competition policy in the new system[122], it remains to be seen whether national competition authorities and national courts will be as motivated as the Commission is by the goal of market

---

[119] See above pp 317 and 322 See also the foreword to the Commission's XXXth Report on Competition Policy (2000), pp. 3 and 5, by Mario Monti, the Competition Commissioner.

[120] See Faull and Nikpay, above n. 86, at paragraphs 7.97 and 7.98 and the Commission's Green Paper on Vertical restraints (above n. 66), at paragraph 236.

[121] See the 1999 Commission's *White Paper on Modernisation of the rules implementing Articles 85* [now 81] *and 86* [now 82] *of the EC Treaty* (OJ [1999] C 132/1, [1999] 5 CMLR 208) and the ensuing proposal for a Council Regulation implementing Articles 81 and 82 EC, (27 September 2000), 5 CMLR [2000] 1148.

[122] See the Commission's White Paper (above n. 121) and Chapter Four of the proposal for a Council Regulation implementing Articles 81 and 82 EC (above n. 121).

integration. Second, the growing trend towards economic globalisation, which is progressively leading to the international integration of markets, may also have a diluting effect on the single market aim.

Once the internal market aims are fully achieved, EC competition law might become more independent from the other Treaty provisions and therefore less based on principles and more focused on economic analysis. A progressive and natural evolution seems, however, more advisable than any radical policy changes.

13

Free Movement of Capital: Learning Lessons or Slipping on Spilt Milk?

STEVE PEERS

INTRODUCTION

IF WE GOT TO 'do it all over again', would we do it any differently? Many of us, having made some mistakes and learned from experience, would probably do at least a few things differently. Normally it is pointless to 'cry over spilt milk', since we cannot change the past; but hopefully we can still use our experience to avoid making similar mistakes in future. The Community legislature, the Treaty drafters and then the European Court of Justice were presented with just such an opportunity, with the adoption of the legislation and Treaty rules governing the much-delayed completion of the free movement of capital, many years after the other internal market freedoms provided for in the EC Treaty were established. In the meantime, the Court has issued a considerable body of jurisprudence on the 'older' Treaty freedoms, which has been much criticised on a number of grounds, and the ambiguity and effect of the Treaty rules on those issues could well be regretted on a number of grounds. With the free movement of capital and payments, the drafters and the Court had the chance to start afresh and, with the benefit of relevant experience, avoid some of the problems that have led to such criticisms.

With the advent of substantial jurisprudence on the capital and payments provisions, it is an opportune time to assess these provisions and the jurisprudence, in particular from the perspective of how the 'innovations' as compared to other Treaty freedoms are working and whether problems have arisen that were 'avoidable' in light of prior internal market jurisprudence. To do this, this chapter examines in turn the primary and secondary rules governing free movement of capital and payments and then the jurisprudence on the topic, examining the latter in some detail given that most cases are recent. It then assesses the successes, problems and potential of the capital and payment rules to date. Unfortunately it emerges, that with great respect, to some extent the Court and the Treaty drafters have missed the opportunity which the capital rules offered to re-examine the past difficulties which have affected the internal market rules.

FREE MOVEMENT OF CAPITAL: AN OVERVIEW

Previous Treaty Rules

The Court of Justice recognised from the outset that the free movement of capital is 'one of the fundamental freedoms of the Community'.[1] However, prior to 1994 this freedom differed from the other freedoms in that the Treaty provisions concerning it were not directly effective.[2] Instead, it fell to the Council to adopt secondary legislation implementing free movement, and this legislation only allowed for limited liberalisation before a Directive requiring full liberalisation (subject only to limited derogations similar to those governing other Treaty freedoms) was adopted in 1988 ('the 1988 Directive').[3] Member States had to implement this Directive by 1 July 1990 (subject to certain derogations).

Initially, the Treaty distinguished between free movement of *capital* in Articles 67 to 73 EEC and free movement of *payments* in Article 106 EEC.[4] According to Article 106, payments had to be liberalised by Member States where payments were connected to free movement of goods, persons, capital or services which had been liberalised by the Treaty. 'Capital' and 'payments' could be distinguished in that the former concerned movements for an investment, while the latter concerned consideration for goods, services or capital.[5]

Current Treaty Rules

The Treaty rules on free movement of capital and payments were amended by the Treaty on European Union (TEU), with effect from 1 January 1994.[6] These

---

[1]   Para. 8 of the judgment in *Casati* (Case 203/80 [1981] ECR 2595).

[2]   Art 67 EEC; see *Casati, ibid*. For discussion, see J.-V. Louis, 'Free Movement of Capital in the Community: the Casati Judgment', (1982) 19 *CMLRev*. 443; M Petersen, 'Capital Movements and Payments Under the EEC Treaty after Casati', (1982) 7 *ELRev*. 167; P. Oliver, 'Free Movement of Capital Between Member States: Article 67(1) EEC and the Implementing Directives', (1984) 9 *ELRev*. 401.

[3]   Dir 88/361, OJ 1988 L 178/5.

[4]   For the case law prior to the 1988 Directive, see *Casati*, n. 2 above; Joined Cases 286/82 and 26/83 *Luisi and Carbone* [1984] ECR 377; Case 157/85 *Brugnoni* [1986] ECR 2013; Case 308/86 *Lambert* [1986] ECR 4369; Case 194/84 *Commission v Greece* [1987] ECR 4737; Case 143/86 *Margretts and Addenbrooke* [1988] ECR 625; and tangentially Case 95/81 *Commission v Italy* [1982] ECR 2187. See also analyses by P. Oliver and J.P. Bache, 'Free Movement of Capital Between the Member States: Recent Developments', (1989) 26 *CMLRev*. 61; J.-V. Louis, 'Free Movement of Tourists and Freedom to Provide Services in the Community: the Luisi-Carbone Judgment', (1984) 21 *CMLRev*. 625.

[5]   See *Luisi and Carbone*, n. 4 above.

[6]   Arts 73a to 73h EC (now Arts. 56 to 60 EC following renumbering by the Treaty of Amsterdam (ToA)). The ToA also deleted Arts 73a, 73e and 73h EC, which addressed transitional issues.

amendments have incorporated the main provisions of the 1988 Directive into the Treaty, although they have enhanced the Directive's provisions in certain respects. The present Treaty Articles are contained within Chapter 4 of Title III of Part Three of the EC Treaty. Article 56(1) first sets out the basic rule: 'all restrictions on movement of capital between Member States and between Member States and third countries shall be prohibited'. Article 56(2) sets out an identical rule as regards free movement of payments. Clearly, movement within the Community and between the Community and third states is, in principle, on the same footing. However, the subsequent Treaty provisions regarding movement to third countries are more complex than the provisions regarding movement within the EC.

Article 58(1) sets out two groups of possible exceptions which apply to free movement of capital and payments, regardless of whether they are moving internally or externally. First, Article 58(1)(a) allows Member States to apply their tax law which distinguishes between taxpayers who are not in the same situation as regards residence or 'with regard to the place where their capital is invested'.[7] A Treaty Declaration states that, as far as movement within the EC is concerned, this clause should only apply to measures which existed on 31 December 1993. Secondly, Article 58(1)(b), which partly resembles the exceptions clauses found in other Treaty free movement provisions, allows for three further exceptions: 'to prevent infringements of national law and regulations' (tax and prudential supervision are mentioned 'in particular'); to require declaration of capital movements for administrative or statistical purposes, or 'to take measures which are justified on grounds of public policy or public security'.[8] In addition, Article 58(2) provides that the capital chapter is without prejudice to restrictions which can be justified pursuant to the chapter on establishment. However, the first two paragraphs of Article 58 are subject to the proviso in Article 58(3) that such measures 'shall not constitute a means of arbitrary discrimination or a disguised restriction on the free movement of capital and payments'.

Over and above these possible restrictions, free movement of capital and payments to and from third countries is subject to four further potential restrictions. The first such restriction is *historic*: Article 57(1) EC 'grandfathers' any restrictions existing at 31 December 1993 on four types of free movement of capital (but not payments) pursuant to EC or national law.[9] The second restriction is *potential*: according to Article 57(2), the Council may adopt measures concerning the same four types of movement of capital to and from third countries. The third restriction concerns *balance of payments*. Article 59

---

[7] There is no equivalent clause in the 1988 Directive.
[8] The first two of these were listed in Art. 4 of the 1988 Directive, which set the condition that such national measures 'must not have the effect of impeding capital movements carried out in accordance with Community law'. However, the Directive has no 'public policy or security' clause.
[9] The four types are 'direct investment—including in real estate—establishment, the provisions of financial services or the admission of securities to capital markets'.

allows the Council to take safeguard measures concerning capital (but not payment) movement to and from third countries if monetary union faces 'serious difficulties', for a maximum period of six months, if this is 'strictly necessary'. This provision has not been used. The final provision is *political*: Article 60(1) allows the Council to adopt measures concerning capital or payments following a 'second pillar' (foreign policy) measure adopted pursuant to the TEU rules on such matters. In the absence of such a Council measure, a Member State can adopt unilateral restrictions on payments and capital 'for serious political reasons and on grounds of urgency', according to Article 60(2), although the Council can later override such restrictions.

The Court of Justice has now delivered sixteen judgments on the substance of the Treaty rules and the 1988 Directive.[10] In particular, the Court has addressed issues concerning taxation and home ownership on several occasions. In addition to these cases, the Court has on several occasions been asked to rule on the provisions concerning capital and payments, but has instead chosen to reply to questions on other Treaty free movement rights instead.[11] Also, the EFTA Court has issued one judgment on the equivalent provisions of the European Economic Area agreement.[12]

A number of judgments have clarified the meaning of 'capital' and 'payments'. In *Svensson and Gustaffson*, the Court simply asserted that a bank loan was an example of movement of capital.[13] So are banknotes and coins, according to *Bordessa*,[14] and direct foreign investments, according to *Eglise de Scientologie*.[15] In *Trummer and Mayer*, the Court explained that the nonexhaustive indicative Annex attached to the 1998 Directive could still be of use interpreting the concept of 'capital' set out in the Treaty. Applying this principle, liquidation of an investment in real property is a capital movement,[16] as is investment in real estate on the territory of a non-Member State by a

---

[10] Case C-148/91 *Veronica* [1993] ECR I-487; Case C-484/93 *Svensson and Gustaffson* [1995] ECR I-3955; Joined Cases C-358/93 and C-416/93 *Bordessa* [1995] ECR I-361; Joined Cases C-163, 165 and 250/94, *Sanz de Lera* [1995] ECR I-4821; Case C-222/97 *Trummer and Mayer* [1999] ECR I-1661; Case C-412/97 *ED* [1999] ECR I-3845; Case C-302/97 *Konle* [1999] ECR I-3099; Case C-355/97 *Beck* [1999] ECR I-4977; Case C-439/97 *Sandoz* [1999] ECR I-7041; Case C-54/99 *Eglise de Scientologie* [2000] ECR I-1335; C-58/99 *Commission v Italy* [2000] ECR I-3811; Case C-35/98 *Verkooijen* [2000] ECR I-4071; C-423/98 *Albore* [2000] ECR I-5965; Case C-478/98 *Commission v Belgium* [2000] ECR I-7587; Case C-464/98 *Stefan* [2001] ECR I-173; and Case C-178/99 *Salzmann-Greif* [2001] ECR I-4421. See also Advocates-Generals' Opinions of 3 July 2001 in Cases C-367/98, C-383/99 and C-503/99, *Commission v Portugal, Commission v France* and *Commission v Belgium*, and 4 October 2001 in C-279/00 *Commission v Italy* (cases pending).

[11] Case C-118/96 *Safir* [1998] ECR I-1897; Case C-410/96 *Ambry* [1998] ECR I-7875; Case C-200/98 *3 and Y* [1999] ECR I-8261; Case C-251/98 *Baars* [2000] ECR I-2787; Joined Cases C-397/98 and C-410/98 *Metallgesellschaft and Hoechst* [2001] ECR I-1727.

[12] Case E-1/00 *State Debt Management Agency*, judgment of 14 July 2000.

[13] Para. 10 (n. 10 above). See also paras. 18–22 of *State Debt Management Agency* (*ibid.*).

[14] Para. 13 (n. 10 above).

[15] Para. 14 (n. 10 above).

[16] *Trummer and Mayer*, paras. 19 to 21 (n. 10 above).

non-resident.[17] While receipt of dividends from a foreign country is not listed in the Annex, it is linked to a couple of measures listed therein, so falls within the scope of the Directive.[18] It was assumed by all parties to *Commission* v *Belgium* that the acquisition of securities constitutes movement of capital.[19]

As for free movement of payments, the Court indicated in *Sanz de Lera* that Article 56(2) would govern the movement of payments for particular goods and services, but that Article 56(1) was applicable in other cases where funds were being moved.[20] In *ED*, the Court ruled that the new Treaty provision had to be compared with the old Article 106 EEC, and concerned payments of sums of money 'in the context of a supply of goods or services'.[21]

Relationship with other Policies and Freedoms

First of all, securing free movement of capital was a necessary legal requirement before beginning the *second* stage of economic and monetary union (EMU), in which all Member States participated.[22] However, the *third* stage of EMU, the adoption of the common currency, is not formally connected to the free movement of capital. So the three Member States which have stayed out of EMU are still covered by the same free movement obligations as the twelve Member States in the euro-zone.[23] Having said that, the advent of EMU seems likely to encourage capital flows throughout the euro-zone, and it might be argued in future that the free movement rules should be interpreted in light of the existence of a common currency. Of course, such an intepretation could prove awkward as long as several Member States stay outside of the common currency.

The other freedoms guaranteed by the Treaty are obviously closely related to the rules on free movement of capital and payments. In particular, as acknowledged by Article 51 EC, capital movements are closely related to the free movement of financial services. Moreover, movement of funds across borders between subsidiaries of companies could potentially be described as an aspect of freedom of establishment, as well as free movement of capital. As for payments, they are obviously related directly to the movement of goods, services or indeed capital, as the former Article 106 EEC acknowledged.

There is little in the Treaty to govern the relationship between the free movement of capital and the other Treaty freedoms. The capital provisions state only first that Article 57(2), concerning EC competence to adopt measures governing

---

[17] *Konle*, para. 22, reaffirmed in *Albore*, para. 14 (both n. 10 above).
[18] Paras. 26 to 30 of *Verkooijen* (n. 10 above).
[19] N. 10 above.
[20] Paras. 16–18 (n. 10 above).
[21] Para. 17 (n. 10 above).
[22] Art. 116(2)(a) EC.
[23] See Art. 122(3) EC.

certain external capital movements, is 'without prejudice to the other Chapters of this Treaty'. Secondly, as mentioned above, the capital provisions provide that they are without prejudice to restrictions that might be justified pursuant to the rules on freedom of establishment.[24] In turn, setting up undertakings or pursuing activity as a self-employed person in accordance with the freedom of establishment is 'subject to' the capital chapter.[25] This is relevant because the Treaty rules on establishment derogations are different from those on capital derogations.

As for services, the relationship would appear to be governed by Articles 50 and 51(2). The former provides that the Treaty rules on 'services' are residual, applying only when the rules on goods, capital and persons do not. The latter provides that liberalisation of financial services 'shall be effected in step with the free movement of capital'.[26]

The Court's jurisprudence on the pre-1994 Treaty provisions concerning capital or payments provided some clarity. First of all, banknotes and coins fell under the capital or payments rules if they were legal tender, but under the goods provisions if they did not.[27] Secondly, the case law indicated that in certain respects property ownership is relevant to the application of other Treaty freedoms.[28] Thirdly, external payments are closely connected with the common commercial policy, and if a Member State blocks an external movement of goods by blocking a payment, it may be breaching the EC's commercial policy legislation.[29]

Despite the links between capital and the other freedoms prior to the 1988 Directive, the *Bachmann* judgment seemed to close off the prospect of using the capital rules where other Treaty rules did not apply. The Court concluded that the Treaty rules on free movement of capital do 'not prohibit restrictions which do not relate to the movement of capital but which result indirectly from restrictions on other fundamental freedoms'.[30]

In the case law on the 1988 Directive and the TEU provisions, the Court has not restated this principle from *Bachmann*, despite the arguments of

[24] Art. 58(2).

[25] Art 43, second indent.

[26] See Case C-222/95 *Parodi* [1997] ECR I-3899, para. 15: where a national restriction on financial services did not fall within the scope of a derogation exercised pursuant to the pre-1988 Directives, it had to be justified pursuant to Article 59 EEC.

[27] Case 7/78 *Thompson* [1978] ECR 2247.

[28] See Art. 9 of Reg. 1612/68 (OJ Spec. Ed. 1968, L 257/2, p. 475); Case 305/87 *Commission v Greece* [1989] ECR 1461 (ownership of property in 'border zones'); Case 197/84 *Steinhauser* [1985] ECR 1819 (leasing commercial property); Case 63/86 *Commission v Italy* [1988] ECR 29 (public housing); Case C-18/95 *Terhoeve* [1999] ECR I-345, paras. 48 to 53 (taxation of capital and other free movement). But see *Fearon* (Case 182/83 [1984] ECR 3677), in which the Court held that there was no discrimination within the meaning of Art 43 EC where a rule distinguished between residents and non-residents of a property, if that rule applied equally to citizens and non-citizens of the country alike.

[29] Case C-124/95 *Centro-com* [1997] ECR I-81.

[30] Case C-204/90 *Bachmann* [1992] ECR I-249.

Advocate-Generals on this point.[31] However, the Court has reaffirmed the link between payments and goods and services,[32] and the distinction between capital and goods where money can serve as a means of payment.[33]

As regards establishment and capital, the Court has ruled in two taxation cases that since the national measures in question violated establishment rules, there was no need to examine the capital rules.[34] However, in two other taxation cases, the Court took care to draw clear distinctions between the two freedoms. First, in *Baars*, it ruled that where a shareholder held enough of a foreign company's shares to give him or her 'definite influence' and to 'determine its activities', the Treaty rule at issue was freedom of establishment, rather than free movement of capital.[35] Conversely, in *Verkooijen* it ruled that the capital rules were applicable where the dispute concerned the cross-border movement of dividends due to an 'ordinary' shareholder.[36] In three pending cases concerning 'golden shares', the Advocate-General assumes that the establishment provisions are primarily applicable, without explaining why.[37]

As for establishment and property ownership, the Court has changed tack from its previous case law, as it has been inclined to examine the issue in light of capital rules. In *Konle* it found simply that since the national rules in question breached the free movement of capital, there was no need to examine the freedom of establishment,[38] while in *Albore* it confirmed this ruling, stating further that property purchase fell within capital rules '[w]hatever the reasons for it'.[39]

The situation is even more complex as regards the relationship between capital and services. In *Trummer and Mayer* and *Sandoz*, the Court assumed that the capital rules applied, apparently because the national court had only asked about such rules. The *Veronica* judgment simply analysed a national measure concerning broadcasting in light of the free movement of services and presumed that if was justified under the services rules, it did not infringe the capital rules.[40] In *Svensson and Gustaffson*, a case concerning public subsidies for home

---

[31] Paras. 8 to 11 of *Svensson and Gustavsson* Opinion (n. 10 above) and para. 40 of *Metallgesellschaft and Hoechst* Opinion (n. 11 above).

[32] *ED* (n. 10 above).

[33] *Bordessa* (n. 10 above), paras. 11–15.

[34] Para. 30 of *X and Y* and para. 75 of *Metallgesellschaft and Hoechst* (both n. 11 above).

[35] N. 11 above, paras. 18 to 22. For a detailed analysis of the cross-over between establishment and capital rules, see paras. 10–30 of the Opinion in this case.

[36] N. 10 above. In para. 63 of the judgment, the Court notes that in light of the violation of the free movement of capital, there is no need to examine the possible violation on the freedom of establishment.

[37] Para. 21 of Opinion in *Commission v Portugal, France and Belgium* (n. 10 above), pending. This interpretation could be explained in that most of the 'golden share' rules at issue concern large stakes in companies, but some of these relate to fairly small shareholdings and to control of management decisions that could also have an impact on small shareholdings.

[38] Para. 55 (n. 10 above); see the opposite approach followed by the Advocate-General's Opinion in this case (para. 22 of the Opinion).

[39] N. 10 above, para. 14.

[40] N. 10 above.

loans, the Court first found that the national law in question breached the free movement of capital as implemented in the 1988 directive, and then proceeded to examine its compatibility with Article 49 EC, without returning to examine whether it was a justified restriction on free movement of capital.[41] The Court did this because of the link between financial services and capital in Article 51(2) EC, although that Treaty Article requires financial services liberalisation to follow capital liberalisation, not the other way around. In *Safir*, the Court condemned national tax measures connected with insurance contracts in light of the services rules, and then found there was no need to examine questions relating to capital.[42] Finally, in *Ambry*, the Court ruled that it was unnecessary to examine the capital rules after finding a breach of the services rules; in contrast, the Advocate-General argued that the capital rules had not been breached on the facts.[43] However, the EFTA Court has concluded firmly that the services rules are clearly distinct from the capital rules in the EEA Agreement.[44]

LEARNING THE LESSONS?

The Court's case law on other aspects of free movement has particularly faced criticism regarding the wide and ambiguous scope of application of the free movement rules, followed by the unclear and uncertain retreat from them, particularly in the field of free movement of goods.[45] Also, since the classification of the different forms of restrictions on free movement has a differential effect on possible limitations on free movement, it is particularly important that the Court gives clear guidance as to whether 'indistinctly applicable' measures are permitted, which such measures may be permitted, and how they may be distinguished from discriminatory measures.

Threshold of application

The Court's jurisprudence has found that several categories of restrictions fall within the scope of the Treaty prohibition, but has not clearly set out principles

---

[41] Paras. 11 to 18, n. 10 above. See now the different approach followed by the Opinion in the pending *Commission* v *Italy* case (n. 10 above).

[42] N. 10 above, para. 35 of the judgment. See Advocate-General Tesauro's argument for a much more sophisticated approach (paras. 8 to 19 of the opinion).

[43] N. 11 above, para. 40 of the judgment and para. 10 of the Opinion.

[44] Paras. 30–34 of *State Debt Management Agency* (n. 12 above).

[45] See, from a huge literature, L. Gormley, 'Actually or Potentially, Directly or Indirectly? Obstacles to the Free Movement of Goods' (1989) 9 YBEL 197; K Mortelsman, 'Article 30 of the EEC Treaty and Legislation Relating to Market Circumstances: Time to Consider a New Definition?' (1991) 28 CMLRev. 115; S. Weatherill, 'After Keck: Some Thoughts on How to Clarify the Clarification', (1996) 33 CMLRev. 885.

distinguishing between discriminatory and non-discriminatory measures. Most obviously, an outright prohibition on the movement of capital falls within the scope of Article 56 EC.[46] Measures which are 'liable to dissuade' or 'liable to deter' residents from contacting foreign banks to obtain loans, making investments in other Member States, or denominating a debt in a foreign currency deprive persons of a right which is a 'component element' of the free movement of capital, and so constitute a 'restriction' or an 'obstacle' to the free movement of capital.[47] The Court has not ruled on what the threshold is for finding that a measure is 'liable' to have such effect.[48] Denying tax exemptions to foreign dividends both 'has the effect of dissuading' persons from investing in foreign companies and 'constitutes an obstacle' to those foreign companies raising capital abroad, so constitutes a 'restriction' on free movement.[49]

Similarly, the EFTA Court has ruled that imposing a higher guarantee fee for foreign loans as compared to domestic loans 'will render foreign loans more expensive than domestic ones', and so 'may dissuade borrowers from approaching lenders established in another EEA State'. Therefore such rules are a 'restriction' on free movement of capital. Unlike the Court of Justice, the EFTA Court has expressly ruled that the amount of such extra cost is irrelevant, by reasoning similar to *O'Flynn*: since the extra cost 'may dissuade borrowers from seeking loans in other EEA States. . . . [t]here is no requirement that an appreciable effect on the cross-border movement of capital be demonstrated'.[50]

Requirements of prior authorisation before a capital movement could also violate Article 56(1), although here the Court has distinguished between currency movements on the one hand, where prior authorisation is always apparently impermissible,[51] and authorisation in relation to immovable property or in the context of public policy and public security risks, which always still fall within the scope of the capital rules as 'restrictions' on capital movement, but which may be found permissible if justification is made out.[52] The rationale is that prior authorisation in the case of currency movement would subject such movement to administrative discretion and might render it illusory.[53] Prior authorisation is still problematic even if it is deemed to occur after a period of silence and if there is no penalty for movement without authorisation.[54]

---

[46] *Commission* v *Belgium* (n 10 above), para 19.
[47] *Svensson and Gustavsson*, para 10 ('obstacle'); *Trummer and Mayer*, para 26 ('component element' and 'restriction'); *Sandoz*, paras 19 and 20 ('obstacle') (all n. 10 above).
[48] Compare with Case C-237/94 *O'Flynn* [1996] ECR I-2617.
[49] Paras. 34 to 36 of *Verkooijen* (n. 10 above).
[50] Paras. 26 to 28 of *State Debt Management Agency* (n. 12 above).
[51] *Bordessa*, para. 24 and 25 and *Sanz de Lera*, para. 25 (both n. 10 above).
[52] *Konle*, para.39 and *Eglise de Scientologie*, paras. 14, 19 and 20 (both n. 10 above).
[53] In *Bordessa*, the Court also referred to the prospect of impeding movements of capital, but was apparently following the wording of the 1988 Directive, which it was called upon to interpret in this case.
[54] Para. 15 of *Eglise de Scientologie* (n. 10 above).

Direct discrimination on the basis of nationality as regards purchase of property is also caught by Article 56.[55] So is discrimination on the basis of where a loan is contracted, but here the Court also noted that such discrimination was 'likely to deter' contracting foreign loans, and was therefore a 'restriction' on free movement.[56] An Advocate-General has also argued that direct discrimination as regards purchase of shares violates Article 56 EC.[57] Finally, in *Commission v Italy*, concerning 'golden shares' in private companies held by the Italian government, there was no examination of how the capital rules applied, because Italy admitted that it was breaching the Treaty.[58]

Only once has the Court found that a measure falls outside the scope of the rules on free movement of capital and payments (in this case payments). In *ED*, it ruled that Article 56(2) EC did not apply to procedural rules governing creditors' pursuit of debtors.[59] It did not offer any explanation for reaching this conclusion. Advocate-General Cosmas' Opinion in this case had argued that in cases of *exports*, Article 56(2) is governed by the same conditions as Article 29 EC concerning the free movement of goods: for a national measure to fall foul of the rule, it must have the 'specific object or effect' of restricting exports of payments.[60]

Also, the Opinion in *ED* suggested borrowing a principle which applies in other free movement contexts: in the Advocate-General's view, the effect of the national rule at issue on free movement of payments was too 'uncertain and indirect' to justify application of the Treaty provision.[61] The Court did not comment on this suggestion.

In this area, the Court's case law is not at all clear. There is no overall rule comparable to *Dassonville*, as clarified by subsequent judgments, defining when the Treaty rules on capital will apply.[62] Instead, there is a selection of *ad hoc* judgments addressing individual situations, but the language in a number of these is very broad, encompassing the concept of 'obstacles' and measures 'liable to deter' or 'liable to dissuade' free movement. Discrimination is rarely mentioned. So far, the cases referred have largely been in the area of tax and property law, but even in those areas one could imagine an potentially limitless application of the capital rules unless the Court sets out some clearly defined

---

[55] *Konle*, paras. 23 and 24; *Albore*, para. 14 (both n. 10 above).

[56] *Sandoz*, para. 31 (n. 10 above).

[57] See paras. 22 to 30 in *Commission v Portugal, France and Belgium* (n. 10 above), pending.

[58] N. 10 above.

[59] Para. 17 (n. 10 above).

[60] Para. 58 of the Opinion (n. 10 above).

[61] *Ibid*. On this concept, see particularly Case C-69/88 *Krantz* [1990] ECR I-583, Case C-379/92 *Peralta* [1994] ECR I-3453, Case C-44/98 *BASF* [1999] ECR I-6269 and Case C-190/98 *Graf* [2000] ECR I-493.

[62] Case 8/74 [1974] ECR 837; see subsequently Case 120/78 *Rewe* (*Cassis de Dijon*) [1979] ECR 649 and Joined Cases C-267/91 and C-268/91 *Keck and Mithouard* [1993] ECR I-6097. On other free movement provisions, see Case C-55/94 *Gebhard* [1995] ECR I-4165 and Case C-415/93 *Bosman* [1995] ECR I-4921.

limitations on them. For example, in *Sandoz* the Court ruled that stamp duty was *per se* within the scope of the rules on free movement of capital. This suggests that any form of taxation of capital, including taxation of property, could fall within the scope of the rules and would therefore have to be defended.[63] The case law on property ownership as it presently stands could similarly give rise to potential challenges to any legislation which restricts the use of property in any way, including property legislation, landlord and tenant law and planning law, in the absence of any indication of a limit on the scope of the free movement rule.

Outside the areas of tax and property, the capital rules could logically extend to national measures which affect the cross-border movement of inheritances, maintenance payments and child support funds. More broadly, almost any form of national regulation which restricts corporate activity in any way could be described as a measure 'liable to dissuade' foreign investors. This would appear to be one potential reading of *Commission v Italy*, as a 'golden share' does not regulate the use of foreign capital as such. If the Court accepts the argument that non-discriminatory 'golden share' rules can be defended pursuant to Article 295 EC, the scope of the free movement of capital will not be relevant to such rules.[64] However, the issue will still be relevant to any other case.[65]

Could the Court have more clearly defined the threshold for application of the rules on free movement of capital? It is true that a wide variety of situations might be caught by the scope of the rules on free movement of capital, and that a single all-embracing test might be difficult to set out. One unsuitable candidate for a limitation was suggested by the Advocate-General's Opinion in *ED*, which argued for an extension of Article 29 EC to measures restricting capital exports.[66] On the facts, this is a perplexing argument, since the case appeared to concern a block upon the *import* of a payment. Moreover, a large number of the cases in this field have involved the 'export' of capital, where persons wanted to move, or had already moved, funds *out* of the Member State which was allegedly restricting their movement. In spite of this, the Court has not yet in any of these judgments suggested that there is any rule equivalent to Article 29 EC limiting the application of the Treaty in such circumstances. Nor should it, for the obvious reason that in comparison with other Treaty freedoms, Member States' nationalist economic interests generally lie in *encouraging* foreign investment (though ideally with as little foreign *control* as possible) and in encouraging their residents to keep

---

[63] Arguably a tax based solely on *residence* in a property as distinct from *ownership* of that property, like the UK council tax, would not be caught.

[64] See Opinion in *Commission v Portugal, France and Belgium* (n. 10 above), pending.

[65] The Opinion in in *Commission v Portugal, France and Belgium* (*ibid.*) expressly limits the application of any 'Article 295 defence' to rules concerning the control of undertakings, as distinct from rules concerning ownership of real property or non-controlling stakes in undertakings.

[66] N. 10 above.

their money *inside* the country, rather than export it elsewhere. An approach based on Article 29 EC would therefore simply be approaching the issue upside down.

There is no logical possibility of transposing to capital the much-criticised and rather tattered distinction between 'certain selling and marketing methods' and product characteristics, for the obvious reason that this distinction cannot easily be applied outside the sphere of free movement of goods. While there might be some possibility in theory of transposing this distinction between the context and content of transactions to the area of free movement of services (distinguishing between regulation of service content and regulation of the conditions in which services are provided), there are no clear comparable distinctions that one could apply to all movements of capital. Regulation of capital concerns not the content *or* the context of the capital, but rather the purposes for which it is used.

What about an approach based on forms of discrimination, prohibiting 'direct discrimination' at the core, with progressively less stringent bans on 'indirect discrimination', 'indistinctly applicable measures', and 'obstacles to free movement'? This would resemble the regime governing other aspects of free movement in broad outline, and some elements of such an approach can already be found in the case law in this area. However, an approach with a prohibition of 'discrimination' at its core would be difficult to apply, as there is no easy way to apply an anti-discrimination principle to most forms of capital movements in practice. With the advent of the single currency, it would not be logical to assimilate foreign currencies to foreign nationals, in the same way that the Court has assimilated company seats to nationality and non-residents to non-nationals;[67] even outside the single currency, it would not be convincing to argue that a UK national, whether resident inside *or* outside the UK, moving UK currency between the UK and other Member States (or third states) is outside the scope of the Treaty rules on free movement of capital.

Despite this, the Court's case law to date has applied a discrimination-based analysis concerning property ownership. It may be best to retain this traditional approach to this particular area since it appears more feasible to apply it. Moreover, this traditional approach could provide the basis for rejecting future arguments that *any* form of property regulation could potentially fall within the scope of capital rules and require justification. To do this, the Court will have to limit the application of the capital rules to those forms of regulation of property ownership which have, or are likely to have, a differential effect on property ownership by non-residents, non-nationals or holders of foreign currency.

What about a distinction based on 'access to the market', which can be identified as a significant element in the rules applying to other forms of free

---

[67] See in particular respectively Case 81/87 *Daily Mail* [1988] ECR 5483 and Case 152/73 *Sotgiu* [1974] ECR 153.

movement?[68] While there certainly are capital markets and property markets, the Treaty rules concern movement of capital as such, not just the use to which it is put. A 'market access' approach has at its heart a desire to ensure *equal conditions of competition*, but while would-be *recipients* of capital may compete to receive it, it would be a mistake to analyse *sources* of capital as if they were always in 'competition' with each other. While an investor certainly wishes to receive access to all investment possibilities and equality as regards return on investments, investors are ultimately concerned also with the ability to repatriate or otherwise transfer profits or some or all of the original capital. This situation is more closely analogous to the 'free movers' (or, more accurately, 'returnees') who are familiar from the field of free movement of persons,[69] but such forms of subsequent movement are even more likely in the field of free movement of capital. In any event, as noted already, the Treaty also protects the movement of capital *as such*, not just investment.

In light of these difficulties, the best test to adopt would be an 'adverse effect' test. Where it can be shown that a national rule is inherently likely to deter movements of capital from outside the country more than it would deter movements inside the country, then it should fall within the scope of the capital rules. Direct discrimination on grounds of nationality (including indirect discrimination based on residence), prohibitions and higher costs on cross-border movements as compared to national movements would fall within the scope of such a rule automatically. But regulation of corporate activity would be unaffected unless it could be shown that foreign investment would be adversely affected by such regulation.

Such a rule might require re-examination of some existing case law. On the one hand, leaving aside a possible 'Article 295 defence', it might be difficult to show that a 'golden shares' rule such as that in *Commission v Italy* falls within such a test, given that a non-discriminatory 'golden shares' rule would likely have an equal deterrent effect on local investors. On the other hand, this may mean a more robust attitude to distinctions based on residence, which in the context of other internal market freedoms, have been considered indirectly discriminatory. For example, the ambiguous judgment in *Fearon* should not be applied to the area of free movement of capital, if the Court was suggesting by that judgment that the restrictions in question fell outside the *scope* of the freedom of establishment. Since residence tests will always tend to discriminate in practice against foreigners, and will in particular affect persons with *multiple* property ownership (thus in a parallel situation to those who have 'double establishment' by means of professional practices in different Member States),

---

[68] See particularly *Keck* and *Graf* (n. 62 above) and discussion by C. Barnard, 'Fitting the Remaining Pieces into the Goods and Persons Jigsaw', (2001) 26 ELRev. 35, pp 52–59.
[69] See, for instance, Case C-370/90 *Surinder Singh* [1992] ECR I-4265 and Case C-19/92 *Kraus* [1993] ECR I-1663).

the Court should affirm that they fall within the scope of the Treaty rules on free movement of capital.[70]

Exceptions

Leaving aside the distinct provisions on *external* free movement and exceptions concerning the purchase of second homes, the Treaty sets out two sets of rules in Article 58(1), subject to Article 58(3).[71] The focus here is twofold. First, has the Court ensured coherence between the types of permitted exceptions and the types of prohibitions imposed? In other words, is the distinction between exceptions set out in the Treaty (which can only be applied in the case of discrimination) and additional 'imperative requirements' (which can also be applied in the case of 'indistinctly applicable measures') clearly maintained? The Court has had difficulty maintaining a coherent distinction between those two categories in other fields of free movement law, where it has on occasion either refused to categorise a measure as discriminatory in order to permit a Member State to impose an imperative requirement or has not clearly categorised a measure but permitted an imperative requirement anyway.[72] The second issue is the treatment of the entirely new exception for tax discrimination in Article 58(1)(a).

On the first issue, the Court has taken a wide view of the 'national law infringements' exception, confirming in *Commission* v *Belgium*, that tax evasion fell within the scope of the exception, and also ruling that 'fiscal supervision', a defence only available to non-discriminatory measures restricting the other Treaty freedoms, did also.[73] Starting with the *Trummer and Mayer* judgment, the Court has apparently recognised the admissibility of potential additional restrictions upon free movement of capital and payments *besides* those set out expressly in the Treaty. However, it has never expressly stated that such 'non-Treaty' exceptions exist.

First, in *Trummer and Mayer*, it accepted that Member States could take 'necessary' measures to ensure that the mortgage system sets out the rights of mortgagees as such and the rights of mortgagees compared to other creditors. It also noted that such rules are governed by the Member State in which the

---

[70] For instance, the potential effect on non-residents of the current UK rules which only allow leaseholders resident for three years to participate in compulsory purchase of the freehold is surely obvious.

[71] The Court has not yet had opportunity to consider Article 58(2), on the relationship between permitted establishment restrictions and permitted restrictions on capital and payment movement.

[72] See particularly Case C-2/90 *Commission* v *Belgium* [1992] ECR I-4431; Case C-275/92 *Schindler* [1994] ECR I-1039; Case C-379/98 *Preussen Elektra* [2001] ECR I-2099.

[73] Paras. 37 to 39 (n. 10 above); on fiscal supervision and the other freedoms, see *Cassis de Dijon* (n. 62 above) and Case C-250/95 *Futura Participations* [1997] ECR I-2471.

property is located.[74] The Court neither accepted nor rejected the Finnish government's argument that 'overriding factor[s] serving the public interest' could justify restrictions on free movement; nor did it assess whether the restrictions in question were discriminatory or not.[75] In *Konle*, the later Austrian rules at issue could, in the Court's view, be based on town and country planning objectives such as maintaining a permanent population and an economic activity separate from tourism.[76]

The obvious question is whether these derogations can only be used in the case of non-discriminatory rules, or whether they can also be used in cases of discrimination. In *Konle* and *Albore*, the Court stated expressly that where a national rule discriminated on the basis of nationality, then Member States could only justify that rule on the grounds set out in the Treaty.[77] However, there are more ambiguous rulings. When it examined the later national rules in *Konle*, the Court found that they could be permitted if they were non-discriminatory and if they were the least restrictive method available of achieving the permitted goal.[78] The former point appears to suggest that a Member State can only rely on exceptions outside the Treaty if they are non-discriminatory. However, the matter is confused because the Court then referred to the *Treaty* exception concerning infringements of national law.[79] In *Verkooijen*, the Court accepted that an 'overriding reason in the general interest' could be applied in conjunction with Article 58(1)(a).[80] In particular, it recognised an 'economic' argument, a 'fiscal cohesion' argument, and an argument that tax discrimination in one Member State was justified because of tax advantages available in other Member States, all by referring to case law governing the other freedoms.[81] Finally, in *Commission v Belgium*, the Court examined the 'fiscal cohesion' defence raised by Belgium, apparently not considering it as a defence based on the Treaty, without assessing whether it could only be used where a measure was genuinely non-discriminatory.

The Court's application of the exceptions to date is problematic. The lack of attention paid to the issue of discrimination in the sphere of free movement of capital may be justified, as discussed above. However, that still does not justify the Court's unclear rulings as to whether there are 'mandatory', 'imperative' or 'overriding' requirements besides the Treaty exceptions that can be used to

---

[74] Para. 31 (n. 10 above).
[75] The Advocate-General referred to 'overriding factors such as those mentioned in' Art. 58, also referring expressly to 'mandatory requirements' and to the 'public policy and public security' exception (paras. 13 and 16), but did not make clear which he thought applied.
[76] Para. 40 (n. 10 above).
[77] Respectively para. 24 and para. 17 (both n. 10 above).
[78] Para. 40 (n. 10 above).
[79] Para. 43 (n. 10 above).
[80] Para. 46 (n. 10 above).
[81] Paras. 46 to 62 (n. 10 above).

justify breaches of free movement of capital and as to what circumstances these further exceptions, if any, may be used.

There is a clear indication that a novel Treaty exception in this field has been inappropriately narrowly interpreted by the Court. This is Article 58(1)(a) EC, permitting tax discrimination within its scope. The Court has only examined this exception on one occasion, in the *Verkooijen* judgment. Its critical finding here was that although there is no equivalent in the 1988 Directive to Article 58(1)(a), permitting tax discrimination based on residence or place of investment, the Court ruled that such a exception applied nonetheless to the Directive, and that the exception in both the Directive and the Treaty corresponded to a principle which applied to the free movement of workers and services and freedom of establishment.[82]

The approach to Article 58(1)(a) in *Verkooijen* is remarkable. This subparagraph was placed in the Treaty following the first cases in what has proved to be a substantial line of cases about tax discrimination and the free movement of persons and services, applying to Articles 39,[83] 43[84] and 49 EC.[85] This case law makes clear that differential treatment of taxpayers based on their residence *does* violate the Treaty freedoms unless it can be argued that the situations of the taxpayers are wholly comparable or that the discriminatory tax treatment can be justified on grounds of 'fiscal cohesion'. Since the first few cases in this line of case law were decided before the 1991 negotiations on the Treaty of European Union,[86] it might be thought that the Treaty negotiators had included Article 58(1)(a) in an attempt to preclude the Court extending these principles to the sphere of free of movement of capital, and there is some evidence to this effect.[87] The Court has therefore interpreted the Treaty wording intended to

---

[82] Para. 43 (n. 10 above).

[83] Case C-175/88 *Biehl* [1990] ECR I-1779; *Bachmann* (n. 30 above); Case C-300/90 *Commission v Belgium* [1992] ECR I-305; Case C-279/93 *Schumacker* [1995] ECR I-225; Case C-151/94 *Commission v. Luxembourg* [1995] ECR I-3685; Case C-336/96 *Gilly* [1998] ECR I-2793; Case C-391/97 *Gschwind* [1999] ECR I-5451; Case C-87/99 *Zurstrassen* [2000] ECR I-3337.

[84] On Art 43 EC and taxation of natural persons, see Case C-80/94 *Wielockx* [1995] ECR I-2493 and Case C-107/94 *Asscher* [1996] ECR I-3089. On Art 43 EC and taxation of corporations, see Case 270/83 *Commission v France* [1986] ECR 273; *Daily Mail* (n. 67 above); Case C-330/91 *Commerzbank* [1993] ECR I-4017; Case C-1/93 *Halliburton Services* [1994] ECR I-1137; *Futura Participations* (n. 73 above); Case C-264/96 *ICI* [1998] ECR I-4695; Case C-311/97 *Royal Bank of Scotland* [1999] ECR I-2651; Case C-254/97 *Baxter* [1999] ECR I-4809; Case C-307/97 *Saint-Gobain* [1999] ECR I-6161; *3 and Y* (n. 11 above); *Baars* (n. 11 above); Case C-141/99 *AMID* [2000] ECR-11619; and *Metallgesellschaft and Hoechst* (n. 11 above).

[85] On Art 49 EC and taxation of natural persons, see *Safir* (n. 11 above) and Case C-55/98 *Vestergaard* [1999] ECR I-7641. Finally, on Art 49 EC and taxation of corporations, see Case C-294/97 *Eurowings* [1999] ECR I-7447.

[86] In contrast, only *Commission v. France* (n. 84 above) had been decided before the 1988 Directive was agreed.

[87] Note the stress in the *Safir* Opinion (n. 11 above) on the distinction between the exceptions governing the two freedoms, and the probable reasons underlying the Dutch government's argument in *Baars* (n. 11 above) that capital rules applied, rather than establishment rules.

protect tax discrimination in the sphere of free movement of capital to mean exactly the opposite.

While such an interpretation secures a uniform application of the Treaty freedoms as regards tax exceptions, it appears to flaunt the deliberate intentions of Treaty drafters. Thus the Court has achieved the goal of securing a coherent interpretation of the freedoms at the cost of ignoring the wording of the Treaty. As a result, any moves to adopt secondary legislation in this area will be undertaken under the shadow of the Court's jurisprudence on the primary Treaty rights, removing a great degree of discretion from national and Community legislators.

CONCLUSION

There is an inherent paradox in creating a (more or less) 'new' internal market right, perhaps akin to having a child some years after other children. On the one hand, there may be reasons to take a different approach in light of earlier experiences, but on the other hand, there might be a strong feeling that the new creation should be treated in the same way as the others, to make sure that it 'fits in'. Seen in this light, the internal coherence of the free movement of capital rules is potentially at odds with the overall coherence between capital and the other freedoms.

But surely the worst mistakes can at least be avoided, without creating inconsistencies which are impossible to reconcile. Hopefully if an older child once drove off in an articulated lorry as a toddler, parents will remember to hide the keys from the younger child at the same age. In that regard, the Treaty rules are welcome for their inclusion of third-country nationals and the extension of their territorial scope. Any inconsistency between the freedoms on these points could be avoided by maintaining a clear dividing line between them and clarifying whether they can apply simultaneously, but unfortunately the Court has not yet done this.

The Court has also not set out clear limits on the threshold for the capital rules to operate, or set out clear rules as to whether additional exceptions exist and how they should apply. It has also overreached itself in light of the wording of the Treaty as regards the 'tax discrimination' exception at least. One may question the wisdom of the Treaty drafters in allowing for discrimination in this area, but the underlying intention was clear.

The jurisprudence to date indicates that the capital and payments provisions are a useful but still flawed addition to the Treaty. The newest Treaty freedom could have a more positive role to play if the Court examines it with as much attention to the goal of avoiding copying the flaws in its other jurisprudence as it should do with the goal of avoiding inconsistency with them.

14

The External Dimension of the Single Market: Building (on) the Foundations

MARISE CREMONA

THIS CHAPTER WILL EXAMINE the legal foundations of the Union's external economic policy with a view to assessing what they are now, how they have developed and their rationale. It will also consider what the foundational principles of the Single Market's external policy might be: what might the external policy of a Single Market require—one that is based on the premises we are collectively examining in this book? In addressing this objective, it will look at the way in which some of the concepts discussed elsewhere in this volume, such as pre-emption, non-discrimination or flexibility, might apply to external economic policy. However, external economic policy has its own candidates as foundational principles: unity, exclusivity, liberalization, and reciprocity, for example.[1]

What do I mean by external economic policy? I have chosen this term to represent the external dimension of the core of the Single Market programme; it of course includes the traditional common commercial policy (CCP), but is also intended to cover what may be termed the 'new CCP': the external dimension of services and intellectual property that will be covered by the CCP under the Treaty of Nice amendments to Article 133 EC. In practice, the focus will be on goods and services. The movement of people, raising all the questions of immigration policy, is such a large subject in its own right that it could not be included here;[2] neither was there space for more than incidental references to capital movements and investment.

What then are the legal foundations of EU external economic policy? The only foundational Treaty-based statements of the content of the commercial policy are: that it should be based on uniform principles and that it should aim to contribute to trade liberalization (Articles 131 and 133 EC). These two

---

[1] For a discussion of non-discrimination in the EC's external economic policy, see M. Cremona, 'Neutrality or Discrimination? The WTO, the EU and External Trade' in de Búrca and Scott (eds.) *The EU and the WTO: Legal and Constitutional Issues* (Oxford, Hart Publishing 2001).
[2] See chapter 11 in this volume, by Elspeth Guild.

characteristics of the CCP reflect the focus of the drafters of the original Treaty of Rome: on the creation of the common market (now internal market) with its concomitant need to remove competitive distortions caused by divergent national trade policies; and on participation in the process of multilateral liberalization represented by the GATT (and now WTO). These two principles will therefore provide the structure around which to begin the process of building a conception of what the external dimension to the Single Market might look like.

The possible extension of the CCP to include other aspects of external economic policy raises questions as to the way in which these principles will apply to the 'new CCP', and indeed the extent to which a common group of foundational principles could or should apply across all aspects of the Single Market. The Commission argued for a global approach to external economic policy in the negotiations leading to both the Treaties of Maastricht and Amsterdam, and (at least in the field covered by the WTO) in *Opinion 1/94*.[3] It did not succeed. In fact, the Court, in *Opinion 1/94*, emphasised the differences between different aspects of the WTO as far as Community competence was concerned, basing itself on the differences in decision-making procedures internally and the special position that the movement of persons has within the Treaty. This last point in itself means that it is highly unlikely that a common approach could ever be adopted towards the external dimension of all aspects of the Single Market.[4]

As a result of this very diverse and patchy picture, with a heavy consequent reliance on implied powers, multiple legal bases will often be required for international agreements in the internal market field. For example, the Council Decision concluding the WTO negotiations on financial services in December 1998 was based on EC Treaty Articles 44, 47, 52, 55, 56 to 59, 93, 94, 95 and 133, as well as Article 300.[5] The amendments to Article 133 EC envisaged by the Treaty of Nice may simplify this patchwork of legal bases but will not introduce any real convergence of external powers. Not only does it not cover all aspects of the Single Market (it excludes capital, investment, competition policy and some aspects of IP to name a few), in those areas that are included, the provision will only apply to the conclusion of agreements, not to the adoption of autonomous measures. And, of course, it creates differential decision-making

---

[3] For further discussion, see M. Cremona, 'EC External Commercial Policy after Amsterdam: Authority and Interpretation within Interconnected Legal Orders' in J. Weiler (ed.) *Towards a Common Law of International Trade?: The EU, the WTO and the NAFTA* Collected Courses of the Academy of European Law 1999 (Oxford, Oxford University Press, 2000).

[4] In fact of course even within the internal market, the removal of border controls has proved to be a very different matter for persons, as opposed to goods.

[5] Council Decision 1999/61/EC of 14 December 1998 concerning the conclusion on behalf of the European Community, as regards matters within its competence, of the results of the World Trade Organisation negotiations on financial services OJ 1999 L20/38. In the text I have cited the Treaty Articles using new numbering.

procedures and preserves the non-exclusivity of Community competence. Most importantly, neither the new Article 133 nor the existing Treaty provisions on the four freedoms, with the exception of Articles 56 and 57 EC on capital movements, establish any real substantive principles on which the external dimension of the Single Market might be based. As far as policies are concerned, the different objectives of the CCP, development cooperation, competition policy and agriculture are far from a common external policy. The challenge is rather to ensure compatibility of policy mechanisms.

This chapter attempts to trace an evolutionary process in the objectives and needs of the Community's external policy. In this process we can see a move from an essentially instrumentalist view—of the CCP in particular—a view that is based on the needs of the internal market and which sees the external dimension as an expression of ultimately 'internal' objectives, towards a growing sense of the Single Market as having distinctively external interests and objectives. In terms of trade, the Community interest is increasingly perceived in terms of international competitiveness and opportunities in third country markets; the need to preserve (and create) the unity of the Single Market is still important, but the emphasis is less on formally uniform rules which protect the internal market from competitive distortions. In this way, the flexibility which has emerged in the development of the internal market,[6] and the balance struck between market integration and national regulatory autonomy is reflected too in EC external policy.

We can see a parallel change in the way that the Court approaches the CCP. The shift in approach, from the early judgments of the 1970s to the WTO Opinion of 1994, is not just a move from expansionism to caution. In the 1970s the Court bases itself on the functional and instrumental character of the CCP. By 1994, it was concerned to emphasise the importance of preserving the integrity of the internal division of power and competence structures within the Community. The CCP (or Article 133) must not be used as a way of evading the 'internal constraints' imposed on the institutions when adopting measures at the internal level.[7] The Court is here asserting its credentials as a constitutional court concerned to ensure that 'the law is observed'. This reaction is consistent with a sense that the original concepts of commercial policy are no longer sufficient. They are being replaced (or at least added to) by the need to define a Community position in external policy-making fora, and to further the interests of the Community on world markets. We see a developing 'Community interest' in a number of other policy dimensions—environmental, developmental, foreign policies among others—which interact with external economic policy and the Community's commitment to trade liberalization in a variety of ways. The external dimension

---

[6] See G. de Búrca, 'Differentiation within the Core: The Case of the Common Market' in de G. Búrca and J. Scott (eds.) *Constitutional Change in the EU: From Uniformity to Flexibility?* (Oxford, Hart Publishing 2000).

[7] *Opinion 1/94* [1994] ECR I-5267 at para 60.

of a mature Single Market will reflect not only the internal 'freedoms' but also the place of market regulation in increasingly liberalized world markets as the Community, as a Single Market, looks beyond its internal borders and contributes to the global debate. These policies are not so readily extrapolated from internal legislation and it is not surprising that the Court stresses internal, procedural constraints and Treaty structure rather than the content of the policies as such, or whether there is any inherent concept of commercial policy.

In what follows, these themes are explored through two principles—unity and liberalization—which have provided a foundation for the Community's commercial policy. In examining their rationale, their evolution and changing function, we will also appreciate the profound connections between the internal market and its external identity.

THE PRINCIPLE OF UNITY

Unity and uniform principles within the CCP

The core of the Single Market, historically at least, is the customs union and it is the needs of the union as a single customs territory that have formed the basis for its most powerful foundational principle. This concept of unity is behind the idea of a *common* commercial policy, based on *uniform* principles (Article 131(1)EC). The definition of a customs union, for example in Article XXIV:8(a) GATT 1994, involving the substitution of a single customs territory for two more such territories, creates a link between the internal abolition of duties and other 'restrictive regulations of commerce' and the application of 'substantially the same' duties and regulations to trade with other, non-Member, States. For a customs union of this type, full uniformity may not be required as long as restrictions on external trade are substantially the same: the WTO's Appellate Body has held, in fact, that Article XXIV may not provide protection for a more complete alignment of restrictions if this cannot be justified as necessary to the customs union.[8] However, the greater the economic integration within the internal market—the closer it becomes to a Single Market—the greater the need for common rules in relation to external trade. Hence the realisation that the completion of the internal market would require—in addition to the common customs tariff—the completion of the common commercial policy: the removal of differential national policies on non-tariff barriers which might justify internal frontier controls, to be replaced where necessary by Community-level restrictions.[9]

---

[8]   Turkey—Restrictions on Imports of Textile and Clothing Products, Appellate Body Report WT/DS34/AB/R, 22 October 1999.
[9]   M. Cremona, 'The Completion of the Internal Market and the Incomplete Commercial Policy of the European Community' (1990) 9 *ELRev.* 283.

Even the early post-transitional period case law of the 1970s recognised that the Treaty objectives, those of undistorted competition as well as free movement, would require a liberal interpretation of the Community's commercial policy powers. Although the Treaty provisions on the common customs tariff and CCP did not contain specific reference to common rules on customs valuation and nomenclature, for example, these have been found to be essential for the proper operation of a common tariff, and therefore within the scope of Community competence in this field. In *Massey-Ferguson* the Court held that

> The proper functioning of the customs union justifies a wide interpretation of Articles 9, 27, 28, 111 and 113 of the Treaty and of the powers which these provisions confer on the institutions to allow them thoroughly to control external trade by measures taken both independently and by agreement.[10]

Similarly, although the EC Treaty chapter on the establishment of the customs union makes no mention of charges of equivalent effect to customs duties, it would have been incompatible with the 'equalization' of customs charges at the Community's external borders to have permitted the unilateral introduction of new charges by Member States; such a prohibition could therefore be implied from the Treaty and the Regulation establishing the common external tariff.[11] The Court based itself both on the internal market need to avoid 'distortion of free internal circulation or of competitive conditions', and on the reference to 'uniform principles' in Article 113 (now 133), which involves the 'elimination of national disparities'.[12]

In *Opinion 1/78* the link between the needs of the internal market (intra-Community trade) and external policy is made clear. In discussing the fact that the agreement under discussion in this case, the UNCTAD-based commodity agreement on natural rubber, 'stands apart from ordinary commercial and tariff agreements which are based primarily on the operation of customs duties and quantitative restrictions' in seeking to establish a form of world-wide market organisation, the Court said:

> The question of external trade must be governed from a wide point of view and not only having regard to the administration of precise systems such as customs and

---

[10] Case 8/73 *Massey-Ferguson* (1973) ECR 897 at para 4. The Court of Justice held that there was nevertheless 'no reason why' the Court could not legitimately use Article 235 (now 308) as a legal base for the Regulation on customs valuation; however this conclusion flowed from the Court's attitude at the time towards Article 235 rather than its view of the proper scope of the Treaty rules on customs and commercial policy. In a later case, the Court confirmed its view of the necessary scope of these specific provisions, and concluded that Article 235 should therefore *not* form part of the legal base for a Council Decision concluding the International Convention on Nomenclature: Case 165/87 *Commission v. Council (Harmonised Nomenclature Convention)* [1988] ECR 5545. In addition, these two cases illustrate the use of both autonomous and contractual commercial policy instruments.
[11] Joined cases 37 & 38–73 *Sociaal Fonds voor de Diamantarbeiders v. NV Indiamex et Association de fait De Belder* [1973] ECR 1609, at paras 9–18.
[12] Ibid. at paras 9 and 16.

quantitative restrictions. . . . a restrictive interpretation of the concept of common commercial policy would risk causing disturbances in intra-community trade by reason of the disparities which would then exist in certain sectors of economic relations with non-member countries.[13]

As is well known, the Court concluded that the list of matters to be covered by the 'uniform principles' of Article 113 (now 133) was not exhaustive and 'must not, as such, close the door to the application in a Community context of any other process intended to regulate external trade.'[14]

This case illustrates a further point, fundamental to this particular discussion. The focus of the GATT exception for customs unions, and of the early Community instruments, is on *measures which restrict trade* (through either tariff or non-tariff barriers), whether they concern the imposition or the removal of restrictions. However it was soon recognised that the Community's common commercial policy would need to go beyond measures essentially concerned with the volume or flow of trade,[15] and encompass the alignment of trade policy more generally. A few years earlier, in 1975, the Court had significantly described commercial policy as a 'concept having the same content whether it is applied in the context of the international action of a State or to that of the Community',[16] thus inevitably including all aspects of export policy. In *Opinion 1/78* this is taken further, as not only was the type of agreement envisaged not explicitly mentioned in the Treaty provision, it was indeed an example of a trade policy instrument being used to further purposes which go beyond commercial policy in a narrow sense, including development policy and general economic policy objectives. The rationale given is in part based on the argument already mentioned: that problems in intra-Community trade would be caused by divergencies in trade policy in a broad sense. But it goes further than that; the Community must be able to respond, as a unified entity, to developments in trade policy at a global level:

> Following the impulse given by UNCTAD to the development of this type of control it seems that it would no longer be possible to carry on any worthwhile common commercial policy if the Community were not in a position to avail itself also of more elaborate means devised with a view to furthering the development of international trade. It is therefore not possible to lay down, for Article 113 of the EEC Treaty, an interpretation the effect of which would be to restrict the common commercial policy to the use of instruments intended to have an effect only on the traditional aspects of external trade to the exclusion of more highly developed mechanisms such as appear in the agreement envisaged. A 'commercial policy' understood in that sense would be destined to become nugatory in the course of time.[17]

---

[13] *Opinion 1/78* (re International Agreement on Natural Rubber) [1979] ECR 2871 at para 45.
[14] Ibid.
[15] See the arguments of the Council cited in *Opinion 1/78*, above note 13, at para 39.
[16] *Opinion 1/75* (re OECD Understanding on a local cost standard) [1975] ECR 1355.
[17] *Opinion 1/78*, above note 13, at para 44.

We will, later in this chapter, explore the implications of and the limitations to this dynamic interpretation of Article 133 (former 113). At this point, I wish to emphasise the recognition that commercial policy will need to develop, that it will include new, non-traditional mechanisms, and that the Community's 'uniform principles' must include these regulatory approaches to commercial policy.

Unity and exclusivity

The corollary of uniformity is exclusivity. A common, or single, external tariff precludes the Member States from setting their own external tariffs and from legislating in areas which affect its operation, such as classification of goods,[18] or the imposition of charges of equivalent effect.[19] During the mid-1970s the principle of exclusivity was recognised as applying both to the conclusion of international agreements (*Opinion 1/75*[20]) and the adoption of autonomous measures (*Donckerwolcke and Schou*[21]). Two points are worth noting here.

First, the rationale for exclusivity is based on the distortions that would result to the *internal* market were Member States permitted to adopt unilateral trade measures.[22] Thus, in *Donckerwolcke*, the emphasis is on the need for goods in free circulation to be 'assimilated' to Community-origin goods in order to achieve full free movement of goods within the customs union. In *Opinion 1/75* distortions of competition between Community undertakings may result from divergent national policies.

In *Opinion 1/75*, however, another rationale for exclusivity is put forward: the need to preserve the unity of the Community position with respect to third States, and to defend the 'common interests' of the Community.

> The common commercial policy . . . is conceived in that Article [113] in the context of the operation of the common market, for the defence of the common interests of the Community, within which the particular interests of the Member States must endeavour to adapt to each other. . . .
> The provisions of articles 113 and 114 . . . show clearly that the exercise of concurrent powers by the Member States and the Community in this matter is impossible. To

---

[18] Case 40–69 *Hauptzollamt Hamburg-Oberelbe* v *Firma Paul G. Bollmann* [1970] ECR 69 at paras 4 and 9.

[19] Joined cases 37 & 38–73 *Sociaal Fonds voor de Diamantarbeiders* v. *NV Indiamex et Association de fait De Belder* [1973] ECR 1609, at para 13: 'Although that Regulation [950/68/EEC] does not expressly allow for the elimination or equalization of charges other than customs duties as such, it is nevertheless clear from its objective that under it Member States are prohibited from amending, by means of charges supplementing such duties, the level of protection as defined by the common customs tariff.'

[20] *Opinion 1/75*, above note 16.

[21] Case 41/76 *Donckerwolcke and Schou* (1976) ECR 1921.

[22] See *Opinion 1/75*, above note 16 at sect.B.2; Case 41/76 *Donckerwolcke and Schou*, above note 21, at paras 26–32.

accept that the contrary were true would amount to recognizing that, in relations with third countries, Member States may adopt positions which differ from those which the Community intends to adopt, and would thereby distort the institutional framework, call into question the mutual trust within the Community and prevent the latter from fulfilling its task in the defence of the common interest.[23]

This rationale for exclusivity will need to be reconsidered in the light of the Court's approach to shared competence within the context of the WTO agreements, and the changes to Article 133 agreed at Nice in December 2000.[24]

Second, in both cases, exclusivity applied even where there had not yet been any internal Community legislation dealing with the matter in issue; in other words, exclusivity does not depend on the completion of the common commercial policy. In *Opinion 1/75* the Court describes how (exclusive) competence to enter into an international agreement on credit guarantees does not depend on the pre-existence of a detailed body of Community rules on the matter.

> The common commercial policy is above all the outcome of a progressive development based upon specific measures which may refer without distinction to 'autonomous' and external aspects of that policy and which do not necessarily presuppose, by the fact that they are linked to the field of the common commercial policy, the existence of a large body of rules, but combine gradually to form that body.[25]

In *Donckerwolcke* the Court confirmed that although full freedom of movement for goods in free circulation would depend on the completion of the CCP, which had not yet taken place, any restriction necessitated by Member States' commercial policies required specific Community authorisation:

> As full responsibility in the matter of commercial policy was transferred to the Community by means of Article 113(1), measures of commercial policy of a national character are only permissible after the end of the transitional period by virtue of specific authorization by the Community.[26]

The decision thus accepts that until there is a complete CCP adopted at Community level, Member States will need to adopt national measures; however, Member States no longer have full autonomy, they may act only with Community authorisation.[27]

---

[23] See *Opinion 1/75*, above note 16 at sect.B.2.

[24] See p 374 below

[25] *Opinion 1/75*, above note 16 at sect.B.1.

[26] Case 41/76 *Donckerwolcke and Schou*, above note 21 at para 32.

[27] See also Joined cases 37 & 38–73 *Sociaal Fonds voor de Diamantarbeiders* v *NV Indiamex et Association de fait De Belder* [1973] ECR 1609, in which the Court held that the adjustment (equalization or elimination) of national charges of equivalent effect to customs duties which predated the introduction of the common external tariff fell within the exclusive jurisdiction of the Community institutions.

THE LIMITS OF UNIFORMITY: HOW 'COMMON' IS THE CCP?

These are early cases, but we should not assume that the 'completion' of the internal market during the 1990s has entailed a consequent 'completion' of external commercial policy resulting in a fully unified system of common rules. In fact, there are still a number of ways in which commercial policy is not fully common, either because harmonisation has in fact not taken place internally, or because new approach harmonisation does not completely pre-empt Member State regulatory choice. If, as we have seen, the logic behind the uniformity of the CCP in external trade policy is driven by the desire to create an *internal* market, an 'area without internal frontiers', we should not be surprised to find that where there are gaps in the uniformity, or harmonisation, of policy internally, there are also gaps in the CCP's uniform principles. Expressed slightly differently, we may ask: where there is room for flexibility internally, to what extent is uniformity possible, necessary or desirable at the external level?

The example of indirect taxation

The indirect taxation of goods provides an example of the limits to uniformity in relation to external trade, in contrast to the common external tariff. As far as internal trade between the EU Member States is concerned, the harmonisation of indirect taxation is envisaged 'to the extent that such harmonisation is necessary to ensure the establishment and functioning of the internal market' (Article 93 EC). Some harmonisation has been achieved, notably in relation to VAT, but there is still, for example, wide variation in indirect tax rates across the EU. What of imports from non-Member States? There is no provision in the EC Treaty requiring either uniformity of Member States' policies on the taxation of goods from third countries, or even non-discrimination in relation to third country goods on initial entry onto the Community market. Article 90 EC, which prohibits discriminatory internal taxation, refers to 'products of other Member States'. This has been interpreted by the Court of Justice to include goods from third countries in free circulation within the Member States, although the Treaty provisions on the customs union and free circulation (Articles 23 and 24 EC) make no reference to internal taxation.[28] The rationale for this interpretation is based on the need to ensure freedom of movement of goods within the internal market itself, with Article 90 acting 'to fill in any breaches which a fiscal measure might open in the prohibitions [of customs duties and charges] laid down.' This rationale does not however apply to third country goods on their initial import into the Community. In *Simba*

---

[28] Case 193/85 *Cooperativa Co-Frutta (bananas)* [1987] ECR 2085 at para 24–29.

SpA—which concerned an Italian consumption tax on fresh bananas—Article 90 was held not to prohibit discrimination against third country bananas which were not in free circulation.[29] The Court also held that Article 133 did not of itself prohibit such discrimination:

> The Treaty provisions concerning the common commercial policy, and in particular Article 113 [now 133], do not of themselves prohibit a Member State from levying on products imported directly from a non-member country a duty such as the national tax on consumption. . . . [F]or trade with non-member countries, and as far as internal taxation is concerned, the Treaty itself does not include any rule similar to that laid down in Article 95 [now 90].[30]

Further, although discriminatory taxation may be prohibited where the Community has entered into an international agreement containing non-discrimination rules relating to the goods in question,[31] such an agreement will not in itself create uniformity between the Member States in relation to taxation of imported goods. The imports will be taxed at the same rate as domestic goods in the importing Member State; however to the extent that there is no harmonisation of tax rates across the European Community, this tax rate may vary according to the particular State of importation. The position therefore is this: goods imported into the EU from a non-Member State will be subject to uniform rates of customs duty; we have also seen that the requirement of uniformity may be extended to charges of equivalent effect to customs duties. However the lack of uniformity and potential distortions of competition between Member States resulting from differential rates of indirect taxation imposed on imported goods still persist, as they do within the single market itself.

Common rules for imports

In 1994 a substantial step was taken in establishing a system of common rules for imports. The Regulation currently in force was adopted in December 1994, in order to bring the Community's rules on safeguard measures into line with the WTO agreements (concluded by the Community on the same day).[32] This replaced a Regulation adopted earlier in 1994, whose purpose was to establish a Community-level system for all quotas and safeguard measures. Regulation 518/94/EC was by no means the first to establish common rules for imports;

---

[29] Case C-228/90 *Simba SpA (bananas)* [1992] ECR I-3713 at para 14–15.
[30] Case C-228/90 *Simba SpA (bananas)* above note 29 at para 17–18. See also case C-130/92 *OTO SpA* [1994] ECR I-3281.
[31] See for example case 104/81 *Hauptzollampt Mainz* v. *Kupferberg* [1982] ECR 3641, in the context of the free trade agreement with Portugal (then not a Member State).
[32] Council Regulation 3285/94/EC of 22 December 1994 on the common rules for imports and repealing Regulation 518/94/EC, OJ 1994 L 349/53.

however, earlier legislation (most recently, Regulation 288/82/EEC) had allowed a number of national quotas to subsist.[33] As the 1994 Preamble stated, the completion of the internal market required the removal of these national differences:

> Whereas completion of the common commercial policy as it pertains to rules for imports is a necessary complement to the completion of the internal market and is the only means of ensuring that the rules applying to the Community's trade with third countries correctly reflect the integration of the markets;

> Whereas in order to achieve greater uniformity in the rules for imports it is necessary to eliminate the exceptions and derogations resulting from the remaining national commercial policy measures and in particular the quantitative restrictions maintained by Member States under Regulation (EEC) No 288/82 . . .

The current Import Regulation (as it may be termed) covers imports from all countries except a group of non-market economy (and non-WTO Member) countries,[34] and all products except for textiles insofar as these have not yet been integrated into GATT 1994 disciplines.[35] It establishes a Community regime, based on the removal of all quotas, but subject to the possibility of GATT-compatible safeguard measures. Surveillance and safeguard measures are adopted by the Community legislature, albeit that Member States may initiate the preliminary consultation procedure. The regimes established for those countries and products which are still outside the scope of the Import Regulation differ in terms of their commitment to liberalization of imports (removal of quotas) but, like that Regulation, have as their objective the operation of Community-wide rules.

The picture is thus of a regime that will operate uniformly across the Community market. However, in two respects, the regime established by the Import Regulation may leave room for national variations.

In the first place, the Commission may, exceptionally, decide to impose either surveillance or safeguard measures with respect to imports into 'one or more

---

[33] See Regulation 288/82/EEC of 5 February 1982 on common rules for imports, OJ 1982 L35/1; this Regulation, repealed by Reg.518/94, allowed the continuation of national import measures in respect of certain products from certain countries. Note that in accordance with Case 41/76 *Donckerwolcke and Schou*, above note 21, these national measures were subject to Community authorisation.

[34] Imports from these countries are covered by Council Regulation 519/94/EC on common rules for imports from certain third countries OJ 1994 L 67/89.

[35] Textiles not yet integrated into GATT 1994 are covered by Council Regulation 517/94/EC of 7 March 1994 on common rules for imports of textile products from certain third countries not covered by bilateral agreements, protocols or other arrangements, or by other specific Community import rules OJ 1994 L 67/1. In practice, a number of countries have bilateral textile agreements with the Community; see e.g. Council Decision of 4 December 2000 on the conclusion of Agreements on trade in textile products with certain third countries (Republic of Belarus, Kingdom of Nepal, Former Yugoslav Republic of Macedonia, Armenia, Azerbaijan, Georgia, Kazakhstan, Moldova, Tajikistan, Turkmenistan, Uzbekistan, People's Republic of China, Ukraine, Arab Republic of Egypt) OJ 2000 L 326/63.

regions of the Community' if measures applied at this level would be 'more appropriate' than measures applied throughout the Community.[36] Although these regional measures must be temporary and must 'disrupt the operation of the internal market as little as possible', if deployed they would clearly threaten the uniformity of the common import regime. They are not autonomous Member State measures (they do not threaten the exclusivity principle) as they are to be adopted by the Community itself, much as national sub-quotas were.[37] It is a moot point whether such regionally-based measures could justify the use of Article 134 [ex Article 115] EC to give them full effect, as they are not 'measures of commercial policy taken . . . by any Member State' as envisaged in that provision.[38] Regional safeguard (or even surveillance) measures have not, at any rate, been adopted since the 1994 Regulation came into force.[39]

The second provision leaves scope for the application of more truly national policies. Article 24(2) of the Import Regulation provides:

(a) Without prejudice to other Community provisions, this Regulation shall not preclude the adoption or application by Member States:

(i) of prohibitions, quantitative restrictions or surveillance measures on grounds of public morality, public policy or public security; the protection of health and life of humans, animals or plants, the protection of national treasures possessing artistic, historic or archaeological value, or the protection of industrial and commercial property;

(ii) of special formalities concerning foreign exchange;

(iii) of formalities introduced pursuant to international agreements in accordance with the Treaty.

(b) The Member States shall inform the Commission of the measures or formalities they intend to introduce or amend in accordance with this paragraph. In the event of extreme urgency, the national measures or formalities in question shall be communicated to the Commission immediately upon their adoption.

This provision (which existed in the earlier pre-1994 versions of the Import Regulation) is undoubtedly intended to carry over into import policy the discretion preserved to the Member States under Article 30 EC. The parallel approach to the interpretation of the equivalent to Article 24 in the common Export Regulation, adopted in the *Werner* and *Leifer* cases, seems to support

---

[36] Regulation 3285/94/EC, OJ 1994 L 349/53, Art.18.
[37] See for example, Case 218/82 *Commission* v. *Council* (rum imports from ACP) [1983] ECR 4063.
[38] Case 59/84 *Tezi-Textiel* [1986] ECR 887.
[39] For a recent example of Community-wide surveillance of imports, see Commission Regulation 2727/1999/EC of 20 December 1999 introducing prior Community surveillance of imports of certain iron and steel products covered by the ECSC and EC Treaties originating in certain third countries OJ 1999 L 328/17, which applies to imports originating in all non-member countries other than products originating in EFTA countries, in countries which are parties to the Agreement on the European Economic Area (EEA), and in Turkey: Art 1(1).

this view.[40] There are two aspects to this Member State discretion. On the one hand these provisions[41] authorise an exception to the principle of liberalization set out in the Regulations; this aspect will be considered further later in this chapter. In addition, they authorise the Member States to act in an area (external trade) within the exclusive legislative competence of the Community, and thus provide a basis for the application of divergent national policies to external trade. In both senses, the authorisation, and Member State discretion, is subject to the parameters established by the Court, and in *Werner* and *Leifer* the Court refers to the criteria developed in the application of Article 30 EC, in particular the principle of proportionality: the measure must be necessary and appropriate to achieve the relevant objectives, and it must also be considered whether or not those objectives could have been attained by less restrictive measures.[42]

The impact of Community legislative intervention

Article 24 of the Import Regulation, and Article 11 of the Export Regulation, also operate 'without prejudice to other Community provisions'. Community legislation may circumscribe, to a greater or lesser extent, Member State policy choices. In *Centro-Com*, the Court said:

> However, a Member State's recourse to Article 11 of the Export Regulation ceases to be justified if Community rules provide for the necessary measures to ensure protection of the interests enumerated in that article.[43]

To illustrate the effect of Community harmonisation on national policy choices, we can compare two cases on exhaustion of IP rights, *EMI v CBS* in 1976 and *Silhouette* in 1998. Both cases concerned so-called 'international' exhaustion of IP rights; in other words whether or not a right holder could use those rights to prevent the marketing within the Community of a product initially put on the market outside the Community. In such cases, the single market justification for exhaustion of rights does not apply as the initial marketing is outside the single market.[44] In *EMI v CBS* the Court held that Community law did not restrict the exercise of trademark rights in such circumstances. The 'unity of the common

---

[40] Case C-70/94 *Fritz Werner Industrie-Ausrustungen GmbH* v. *Germany* [1995] ECR I-3189, and Case C-83/94 *Criminal proceedings against Leifer, Krauskopf and Holzer* [1995] ECR I-3231, on the interpretation of Reg.2603/69, Art.11.

[41] Reg.3285/94, Art.24(2) and Reg.2603/69, Art.11.

[42] Case C-83/94 *Criminal proceedings against Leifer, Krauskopf and Holzer*, above note 40, at para 34.

[43] Case C-124/95 *The Queen, ex parte Centro-Com Srl* v. *HM Treasury and Bank of England* [1997] ECR I-81 at para 46.

[44] For exhaustion of rights within the single market, see e.g. case 78/70 *Deutsche Grammophon* v. *Metro* [1971] ECR 487; case 15/74 *Centrafarm* v. *Sterling* [1974] ECR 1147.

market' was not jeopardized[45] and the common commercial policy, in the absence of a specific bilateral treaty obligation, did not extend the prohibition of measures of equivalent effect to quantitative restrictions (MEQR) to trade with third countries. It is of some interest that the Court bases its judgment here, not on the equivalent to Article 24 in the Import Regulation of the time,[46] but rather on a finding that the general prohibition of quantitative restrictions on imports in Article 1 of that Regulation did not cover MEQR. While that reading of the 1974 Regulation may perhaps be justified, given its much more limited liberalization of imports, it is not possible to apply it to the current import or export Regulations. In *Leifer* the Court expressly rejected this argument, holding that:

> A regulation based on Article 113 of the Treaty, whose objective is to implement the principle of free exportation at the Community level, as stated in Article 1 of the Export Regulation, cannot exclude from its scope measures adopted by the Member States whose effect is equivalent to a quantitative restriction where their application may lead, as in the present case, to an export prohibition.[47]

It would be difficult, given the wording and objectives of Article 1 of the 1994 Import Regulation, to justify a different interpretation. Thus, justification for a measure of equivalent effect maintained by a Member State would now have to be sought in Article 24, or, possibly, within the scope of accepted 'mandatory requirements'.

What, though, if there has been harmonisation at Community level? We are familiar with the idea that, in the context of the internal market, the existence of Community legislation may preclude a Member State's reliance on Article 30.[48] How does this principle operate in the context of external trade? In *Silhouette*, decided in 1998, the Court returned to the issue of international exhaustion of trademark rights.[49] In the intervening years since *EMI v CBS* the Trade Marks Directive had been adopted, and this Directive provides for exhaustion of rights where a product has been put on the market in the Community (and in the EEA since the EEA Agreement entered into force) by the proprietor or with his consent.[50] It was clear that the Directive does not

---

[45] Case 51-75 *EMI Records Limited v. CBS United Kingdom Limited* [1976] ECR 811, para 11.
[46] Regulation 1439/74 of 4 June 1974 OJ 1974 L 159/1.
[47] Case C-83/94 *Criminal proceedings against Leifer, Krauskopf and Holzer*, above note 40, at para 23.
[48] See for example, case C-5/94 *R v. MAFF ex parte Hedley Lomas* [1996] ECR I-2553. In the passage from the judgment in case C-124/95 *Centro-Com* cited above at note 43, the Court refers expressly to this aspect of Article 36 (now 30) EC as interpreted in case 72/83 *Campus Oil and Others v. Minister for Industry and Energy* [1984] ECR 2727, at para 27.
[49] Case C-255/96 *Silhouette International Schmied GmbH & Co. KG v Hartlauer Handelsgesellschaft mbH* [1998] ECR I-4799.
[50] First Council Directive 89/104/EEC of 21 December 1988 to approximate the laws of the Member States relating to trade marks OJ 1989 L 40/1, as amended by the Agreement on the European Economic Area of 2 May 1992 OJ 1994 L 1/3, Art.7.

itself provide for the full 'international' exhaustion of trademark rights (taking effect irrespective of where the goods were first put on the market, provided that it was by the proprietor or with his consent). The question was, rather, whether the Directive left the issue open for the Member States to determine according to their own national law. The Court held that although the Directive does not harmonise the whole of trademark law, this was one aspect of that law which it does harmonise, thereby precluding further Member State discretion:

> the Directive cannot be interpreted as leaving it open to the Member States to provide in their domestic law for exhaustion of the rights conferred by a trade mark in respect of products put on the market in non-member countries [i.e. international exhaustion].[51]

Tellingly, this interpretation was based on the need to 'safeguard the functioning of the internal market' and the threat posed by (potential) diversity of national policy:

> A situation in which some Member States could provide for international exhaustion while others provided for Community exhaustion only would inevitably give rise to barriers to the free movement of goods and the freedom to provide services.[52]

Again, therefore, the need for uniformity in external policy arises out of the need to harmonise within the internal market.

This reading of the balance between Member State discretion under Article 24 of the Import Regulation and compliance with 'other Community provisions' is supported by the legislation on technical standards adopted in 1980 following the conclusion of the Tokyo Round and the Agreement on Technical Barriers to Trade, designed to ensure national treatment for third country imports in relation to technical standards.[53] The Council Decision also deals with the possibility of mutual recognition of both standards and conformity assessment procedures, mutual recognition being closely connected with national treatment in both the Community and the WTO regimes.[54] The Decision makes a critical distinction between those standards harmonised at Community level, and those which are not. Where standards have been harmonised, these Community standards will apply:

> The technical regulations, standards and certification and verification procedures laid down in the Directives for the removal of technical barriers to intra-Community

---

[51] Case C-255/96 *Silhouette International Schmied GmbH & Co. KG v Hartlauer Handelsgesellschaft mbH*, above note 49, at para 26.
[52] Ibid. at para 27.
[53] Council Decision 80/45/EEC of 15 January 1980 laying down provisions on the introduction and implementation of technical regulations and standards OJ 1980 L 14/36.
[54] Effective non-discrimination may require a willingness to recognise the equivalence of different standards.

trade shall apply . . . to all products on the Community market irrespective of their origin . . . [55]

Where there are no Community harmonised standards, Member States are to apply their *national* technical regulations, standards and certification and verification procedures on a non-discriminatory basis:

> The Member States shall take all appropriate action within their power to ensure that the technical regulations, standards and certification and verification procedures which are not harmonized at Community level, but are applied in these Member States and drawn up by official authorities or non-governmental bodies, are applied under any special conditions which may be laid down in the national texts to all products on the markets in question, irrespective of their origin . . .[56]

Again, therefore, while the secondary legislation provides for national treatment in relation to technical standards, as required by the TBT Agreement, it does not of itself provide for uniformity of standards between the Member States. Such uniformity will only operate to the extent that standards have been harmonised within the single market. As the Court of Justice pointed out in *Opinion 1/94*, the TBT Agreement is not concerned with the harmonisation of standards.[57] Where standards have not yet been harmonised, varying national standards will be applied. However, in requiring national treatment in the application of those national standards the Decision also evidences the competence of the Community to circumscribe Member State discretion as far as import policy is concerned (measures of equivalent effect as well as customs duties and quotas).[58]

Minimum harmonisation and uniformity

The 1980 Decision makes a simple distinction between which standards are—and are not—'harmonized at Community level'. However, in the two decades since then, the techniques of harmonisation have become more complex. Where a New Approach directive sets minimum standards Member States are constrained in their implementation by the fundamental Treaty rules on (inter alia)

---

[55] Council Decision 80/45/EEC, Art 1(1). For an example of the application of harmonised rules to third country imports, see Regulation 339/93/EC on product safety checks on goods from third countries OJ 1993 L40/1.

[56] Council Decision 80/45/EEC, Art 1(2).

[57] *Opinion 1/94 (re WTO Agreement)* [1994] ECR I-5267 at para 33.

[58] A similar approach is evidenced in the Regulation setting out a procedure to be followed by national authorities in checking the safety of imported products: Council Regulation 339/93/EEC on checks for conformity with the rules on product safety in the case of products imported from third countries OJ 1993 L40/1. The Regulation does not itself harmonise standards as far as product safety is concerned; the detailed standards applied by the Member States will be either national or Community based, e.g. under Council Directive 92/59 on Product Safety OJ 1992 L 228.

freedom of movement.[59] The directive itself may contain a 'market access' clause guaranteeing market access for products (or services) complying with the directive-set minimum standards.[60] In such a case, under what obligation is a Member State with respect to direct imports (not goods in free circulation) from third countries?

Let us take as an example the Tobacco Labelling Directive.[61] This directive allows a certain amount of discretion to Member States in its implementation, for example in relation to the size of health warnings on cigarette packets. However, under Article 8(1), Member States 'may not, for reasons of labelling, prohibit or restrict the sale of products which comply with this Directive.' Although, therefore, the directive imposes a minimum standard as far as the size of health warnings are concerned, a Member State choosing to impose the stricter requirement of a larger warning on its own tobacco manufacturers must nevertheless allow the marketing on its territory of tobacco products imported from other Member States which comply with the (minimum) standards set by the directive.[62] It is clear that 'products which comply with this Directive' in Article 8 includes all products coming from other Member States (whether originating there, or in free circulation there). Does it include products imported *directly* from third countries? Would a Member State imposing a stricter standard be entitled to apply that standard to imports from non-Member States as well as to its own production? Or does the directive require that it is the minimum standard which must apply to third country imports? The directive, both in Article 8 and elsewhere, is worded in general terms; the Court of Justice, in *Gallaher*, assumed that the market access clause in Article 8 applies to products imported from other Member States:

> Member States which have made use of the powers conferred by the provisions containing minimum requirements cannot, according to Article 8 of the directive, prohibit or restrict the sale within their territory of products imported from other Member States which comply with the directive.[63]

The United Kingdom, whose implementation was at issue in *Gallaher*, also applies the market access clause only to imports from other Member States. In a clause headed 'Products imported from other member States', imports *from*

---

[59] Case 382/87 *Buet and Educational Business Services Sarl* v. *Ministere Public* [1989] ECR 1235.

[60] Indeed, Case C-376/98 *Germany* v. *Parliament and Council* [2000] ECR I-8419 suggests that a market access clause, protecting and advancing free movement, is a necessary element of a harmonisation measure based on Article 95 EC; see paras 99–104, and Weatherill chapter 2 in this volume.

[61] Council Directive 89/622/EEC of 13 November 1989 on the approximation of the laws, regulations and administrative provisions of the Member States concerning the labelling of tobacco products OJ 1989 L359/1, as amended by Council Directive 92/41/EEC of 15 May 1992 OJ 1992 L 158/30.

[62] Case C-11/92 *The Queen* v. *Secretary of State for Health, ex parte Gallaher Ltd, Imperial Tobacco Ltd. and Rothmans International Tobacco (UK) Ltd.* [1993] ECR I-3545.

[63] Ibid. at para 16.

another Member State 'shall be regarded . . . as complying with the requirements' of the UK implementing regulations if they comply with the exporting Member State's requirements pursuant to the directive.[64] There is no mention of products imported from third countries. However, the implementing regulations apply to all 'producers', defined in terms of those manufacturing or importing the product 'with a view to the product being supplied for consumption in the United Kingdom',[65] and there is thus no doubt that under these regulations the UK's stricter labelling standards will apply to producers (including importers) from non-Member States, as well as to the UK's home producers.

The Court in *Gallaher* implies that this result is compatible with its reading of the directive (although the issue was not relevant to the case and will not have been argued as such). Is this result compatible with the 1980 Decision on standards? If the degree of discretion allowed to Member States by the directive is taken to mean that on this point the standard has not been 'harmonised at Community level' then there is no difficulty with a Member State applying its own domestic standards on a non-discriminatory basis to third country imports; indeed this is what the Decision requires. However, it is surely correct to view tobacco health warnings as having been harmonised at Community level, albeit in such as way as to allow Member States some discretion. In this case, Member States are required to apply the 'standards . . . laid down in the Directive'.[66] So we return to the Directive. These standards, as we have seen, allow some Member State discretion as to the size of the health warnings. There is no reason why this discretion should not operate in relation to imports from non-Member States, subject to the national treatment rule which would require Member States to impose on those imports the same standards as are applied to its own producers—unless, contrary to the implication of the Court in *Gallaher*, the market access clause is held to apply. The market access clause reflects one of the objectives of the Directive: to remove obstacles to trade between Member States.[67] It is an expression of the free movement obligation, with which Member States must comply in their implementation of Directives; a free movement obligation which applies only to goods of Community origin and those in free circulation.[68] As we shall see, no overriding market access, or

---

[64] Tobacco Products Labelling (Safety) Regulations 1991, SI 1991 No.1530, regulation 8. This is not exactly the same as compliance with the directive, to which Article 8 refers, but this point was not raised by the Court in *Gallagher*.

[65] Ibid. Reg.2(1).

[66] Council Decision 80/45/EEC, Art 1(1).

[67] The Preamble to Directive 89/622/EEC states, 'Whereas there are differences between the laws, regulations and administrative provisions of the Member States on the labelling of tobacco products; whereas these differences are likely to constitute barriers to trade and to impede the establishment and operation of the internal market; Whereas these possible barriers should be eliminated and whereas, to that end, the marketing and free movement of tobacco products should be made subject to common rules concerning labelling'.

[68] Article 23(2) EC.

free movement, obligation with respect to third country imports can be derived from the Treaty itself. Applying the logic of the *Silhouette* judgement, the market access clause in the Directive ensures the freedom of movement of goods in free circulation; the internal market will not be obstructed by the application of the same higher standards both to domestic production and to third country imports. And as the Court put it in *Gallaher*, any 'inequalities in conditions of competition' which might result 'are attributable to the degree of harmonization sought by the provisions in question, which lay down minimum requirements'.[69]

These conclusions are consistent with the approach to different types of harmonisation, and their impact on Member State external competence (in the context of contractual relations) taken by the Court of Justice in *Opinion 2/91*.[70] Where internal Community legislation (or the Treaty rules themselves) allow Member States to adopt more stringent standards, then Member States will be able to enter into contractual obligations with respect to third countries which require stricter standards than those imposed to-date at Community level, without 'affecting' the Community rules.

Our conclusion here is thus that in considering the application of measures of equivalent effect to third country imports, the existence and type of Community harmonisation measure is crucial. Where there has been complete harmonisation, there will be little or no room for Member State policy discretion (*Silhouette*) as it has been displaced by a Community level rule. In cases of minimum harmonisation, however, that discretion may be preserved; it will be subject to the limitations imposed by the specific directive, but where these include a market access clause, that clause will not apply to direct imports from non-Member States. In such cases, therefore, the primary Community-law based constraint will be the obligation of national treatment imposed by Decision 80/45/EEC, as opposed to any objective of uniformity.[71]

Our conclusion at this point is that the common commercial policy cannot, in itself, create a completely uniform market for imported goods. This depends on more than the creation of a common external tariff, and common rules for safeguard measures and quotas. In the end, as the needs of the single market have provided the rationale for the principle of uniformity, its application is

[69] Case C-11/92 *The Queen v. Secretary of State for Health, ex parte Gallaher Ltd, Imperial Tobacco Ltd. and Rothmans International Tobacco (UK) Ltd.*, above note 62, at para 22.
[70] *Opinion 2/91* (re Convention N° 170 of the International Labour Organization concerning safety in the use of chemicals at work) [1993] ECR I-1061.
[71] Note however that, insofar as the imported product is covered by the Import Regulation, any higher national standards would also have to comply with Article 24(2) of the Regulation, discussed further below at note 131, and in particular with the requirement of proportionality. Note, too that we are here concerned with the constraints imposed by the Community's external commercial policy on Member State autonomy in imposing regulatory standards on imports; we are not addressing directly the impact (on either the Member States or Community policy) of contractual obligation with third countries, notably within the WTO framework, although Community policy and legislation, including Decision 80/45/EEC, has been formulated in the light of these obligations.

dependent on the full realisation of that single market. And to the extent that flexibility and lack of uniformity have become accepted as a feature of the internal market landscape, so complete uniformity may not after all be essential in external trade policy.

UNITY AND UNIFORMITY WITHIN THE 'NEW CCP'

So far, the focus of this chapter has been on trade in goods, the traditional CCP. To what extent can we apply the conclusions reached above to the Community's external economic policy more generally, and in particular to trade in services and commercial aspects of intellectual property (IP), what we might call the 'new CCP', following the Treaty of Nice amendments to Article 133?

Under the amended Article 133(5):

> Paragraphs 1 to 4 shall also apply to the negotiation and conclusion of agreements in the fields of trade in services and the commercial aspects of intellectual property, insofar as those agreements are not covered by the said paragraphs and without prejudice to paragraph 6.

The paragraphs 1 to 4 referred to include the concept of uniform principles, provisions on decision-making for the negotiation and conclusion of agreements, and (by virtue of Court of Justice case law) the principle of exclusivity. As we shall see, both the existing CCP decision-making process and the exclusivity of Community competence in these new areas are heavily qualified by the remainder of paragraph 5 and paragraph 6. However, the principle of uniformity appears to remain intact. What might it mean in this context? To what extent does the principle of uniformity already operate within these areas?

There are no specific rules in the EC Treaty dealing with the initial establishment of third country nationals. Such rules as exist are found in the secondary legislation and in international treaty commitments (OECD-based Decisions, the GATS, and the Europe Agreements, for example) as well as in a third pillar Council Recommendation.[72] Foreign-owned subsidiaries are treated as Community companies for the purposes of Article 48 EC. However Article 48 requires formation in accordance with the law of a Member State, and Community law does not prevent a Member State from attaching nationality (or other equivalent) conditions to the formation of companies engaging in particular types of business as long as these are limited to third country nationals: *Factortame II*[73] does not apply to third country nationals. Likewise, Member States may impose their own national conditions upon the operation of

---

[72] Council Resolution of 30 November 1994 relating to the limitations on the admission of third-country nationals to the territory of the Member States for the purpose of pursuing activities as self-employed persons OJ 1996 C 274, 19.9.1996, p. 7.

[73] Case C-221/89 *Factortame II* [1991] ECR I-3905.

branches of companies whose head office is outside the Community (known as 'direct branches').

Article 49(2) EC gives the Council the power to enact legislation extending the Treaty provisions on services to 'nationals of a third country who provide services and who are established within the Community.' This power, which has not yet been used,[74] is closely connected with the operation of the internal market; it would not affect the initial establishment of the third country national, nor the direct provision of services from outside the Community without a prior Community establishment.

As things stand at present, there is thus no Treaty-based regime, or common import or export Regulation for trade in services.[75] Nor is there general Community legislation imposing a national treatment obligation in relation to third country service suppliers, although such obligations have been entered into within the context of bilateral and multilateral treaty commitments.[76] As a result, we need to look at the legislation regulating specific services, and as an example with a well-developed internal legislative framework, we will take the financial services sector (specifically, banking).

The Preamble to the consolidated Banking Directive sets out the Community position in relation to branches and subsidiaries of third country banks:

> The rules governing branches of credit institutions having their head office outside the Community should be analogous in all Member States. It is important at the present time to provide that such rules may not be more favourable than those for branches of institutions from another Member State. It should be specified that the Community may conclude agreements with third countries providing for the application of rules which accord such branches the same treatment throughout its territory, account being taken of the principle of reciprocity. The branches of credit institutions authorised in third countries do not enjoy the freedom to provide services under the second paragraph of Article 49 of the Treaty or the freedom of establishment in Member States other than those in which they are established. However, requests for the authorisation of subsidiaries or of the acquisition of holdings made by undertakings governed by the laws of third countries are subject to a procedure intended to ensure that Community credit institutions receive reciprocal treatment in the third countries in question.[77]

---

[74] The Commission has, however, published a draft Directive: Proposal for a Council directive extending the freedom to provide cross-border services to third-country nationals established within the Community COM(99)3, amended proposal COM(2000)271 final. In its explanatory memorandum the Commission stated, 'this initiative does not affect the competence of the Member States to determine which third-country nationals are admitted in order to establish themselves and exercise an independent economic activity on a permanent basis.'

[75] It should be noted that the Treaty provisions on capital movements (Articles 56–60 EC) do cover capital movements between the EC Member States and third countries, and will thus relate to some aspects of the provision of services and establishment, such as direct investment. These provisions are further discussed below p 389.

[76] For examples, see below note 80.

[77] Directive 2000/12/EC of the European Parliament and of the Council of 20 March 2000 relating to the taking up and pursuit of the business of credit institutions OJ 2000 L 126/1, Preamble at para 19.

As will be seen from this summary of Community policy, a major distinction is drawn between branches and subsidiaries, which reflects that distinction as it operates within the internal market. Subsidiaries, as separate legal entities, are Community companies, within the meaning of Article 48 EC, even where the parent company is governed by the law of a third country. They require to be authorised by their 'home' Member State, and then this authorisation will entitle the subsidiary to establish branches and offer services in other Member States.[78] The Banking Directive does however establish a system for the authorisation of these foreign-owned banks which is designed to encourage reciprocity of treatment; this includes the requirement to notify the Commission of such authorisations and to inform the Commission of 'any general difficulties encountered by their credit institutions in establishing themselves or carrying on banking activities in a third country'.[79]

Branches of credit institutions having their head office outside the Community are in a different position. Each branch will require authorisation by its Member State of establishment; and unlike a subsidiary it will not, once authorised, enjoy rights of establishment or provision of services in other Member States. Conditions for authorisation have been harmonised by the banking directives and, like the tobacco labelling directive, these are minimum standards accompanied by a market access provision. A Member State adopting more stringent conditions for the authorisation of its own banks will therefore apply those conditions to branches of third country banks (i.e. branches of banks which have their head office outside the Community; sometimes referred to as 'direct branching'). A Member State is, in addition, not prevented by the Banking Directive from imposing even more stringent conditions on such 'direct branches' than on its own banks (although this would be contrary to national treatment obligations that may be found in bilateral treaties and also in OECD and GATS commitments[80]). However, the Banking Directive does prevent Member States from applying to 'direct branches' *more favourable* conditions

---

[78] Ibid. Arts 4–17 (on conditions of authorisation), and 18–22 (on rights of establishment and provision of services).

[79] Ibid. Art.23. The Directive then makes provision for negotiation where it appears that a third country is not granting *effective market access* to Community credit institutions, comparable to that granted by the EC to credit institutions from that third country, with a view to obtaining comparable competitive opportunities for Community credit institutions. Where a third country does not offer *national treatment* to Community credit institutions, there is again provision for negotiation, with the possibility of suspension of authorisations of banks from that third country pending a satisfactory outcome.

[80] This chapter will not discuss such contractual constraints on Community (and Member State) policy, but for an example of bilateral agreements containing a national treatment obligation, see the Europe Association Agreements (e.g. the Agreement with Poland, OJ 1993 L 348/2, Art.44); for an example of a multilateral agreement, see the OECD Revised Declaration of 21 June 1976 on International Investment and Multinational Enterprises and the Third Decision on national treatment annexed thereto (the Third Decision, a binding instrument, was concluded jointly by the EC and its Member States); see also GATS Art.XVII, the Understanding on Commitments in Financial Services and the Fifth Protocol on Financial Services (OJ 1999 L 20/38).

than are applied to branches of Community banks.[81] Thus, although Community law does not currently impose uniform treatment of direct branches, there are constraints on Member State regulatory policy-making, in that the minimum standards imposed by the Directive will apply to all banks authorised by a Member State, including 'direct branches'. This degree of flexibility is reflected in the Directive Preamble, which states that 'the rules governing branches of credit institutions having their head office outside the Community should be *analogous* in all Member States'.[82] The Directive itself does however provide more specifically for the possibility of negotiating Community level agreements with third countries that would achieve *uniform conditions* of operation for direct branches:

> . . . the Community may, through agreements concluded in accordance with the Treaty with one or more third countries, agree to apply provisions which, on the basis of the principle of reciprocity, accord to branches of a credit institution having its head office outside the Community identical treatment throughout the territory of the Community.[83]

The rationale for this possible development is unstated, but hinted at in the reference to reciprocity. The nature of the financial services regime established by the Banking Directive is such that differential national conditions imposed on direct branches do not pose a threat to the internal market in terms of deflection of trade or competitive distortions. A branch does not benefit from the 'single licence' principle, and a direct branch of a third country bank will thus not benefit from rights of establishment or provision of services available to Community companies under Article 48 EC. Its activities can therefore (in theory) be confined to the territory of its home Member State, which limits the possible deflection of trade caused by regulatory competition.[84] On that market, it will be competing with banks from other Member States, but the Directive requires that it must not be treated more favourably. There appears to be no need, from the perspective of the current requirements of the internal market, for a greater degree of uniformity (any more than complete uniformity of authorisation conditions is required). This provision of the Directive envisages uniformity, rather, as part of a bargain to be struck with third countries, a bargain that includes the principle of reciprocity. In other words, uniformity becomes a useful mechanism for negotiating the best possible deal for access to third country markets for Community branches. The principle of uniformity is—significantly in the light of what follows—showing signs of moving from an instrument of the

---

[81] Directive 2000/12/EC, above note 77, Art.24(1).
[82] Emphasis added.
[83] Directive 2000/12/EC, above note 77, Art.24(3).
[84] In practice, it would be very hard to control so-called 'mode 1' (cross-border) services offered outside the home Member State.

unity of the internal market, to becoming an instrument of the unity of the Community as it acts to maximise its competitive position on world markets.[85]

This brief example confirms that when we move beyond the customs union, into other regions of the internal market, uniformity is no longer a critical imperative. The extent to which it will be required will depend on the extent to which uniformity of regulation is a feature of the Community's legislative approach internally. In the fields of establishment and services, at least, mutual recognition and minimum harmonisation techniques have generally prevailed, leaving scope for flexibility and limited regulatory autonomy (and regulatory competition[86]) on the part of Member States. In addition, important areas of relevant legislation (aspects of company law, for example, or taxation) have not been harmonised. We have seen that within the traditional CCP, the absence of pre-existing Community legislation was no barrier to the demand either for uniformity or for exclusivity of Community competence. However, in the fields now covered by the 'new CCP', as the Banking Directive illustrates, even where internal Community legislation exists, an absence of regulatory uniformity will not necessarily threaten the Community interest. It is notable, however, that the Directive precludes individual Member State negotiation with third countries; any such agreement will be negotiated by the Community alone and will thus be able to promise uniformity of treatment to direct branches.[87]

Here again we see the link between uniformity and exclusivity. Let us now turn to examine the principle (or doctrine) of exclusivity as it applies within the 'new CCP'.

EXCLUSIVITY AND PRE-EMPTION IN THE 'NEW CCP'

One of the most characteristic features of the CCP has been its exclusivity. The Court itself has accepted that the inclusion of a particular aspect of trade within the CCP carried with it the consequence of exclusivity.[88] As we have seen, the rationale for this has been closely linked to the need for uniformity in trading relations with third countries.

---

[85] In the area of financial services, for example, the Community has listed a number of market access restrictions imposed by both developed and developing countries: 'ceilings on foreign shareholdings; economic needs tests to allow new market entry; limitations on the form of commercial presence (e.g. only through a subsidiary, or via a branch); restrictions on geographical expansion; discrimination as to the types of activities that can be carried out in different geographical areas; quota systems, or even a prohibition on new entries'; GATS 2000: Financial Services Proposal from the EC and their Member States, December 2000.

[86] N. Reich, 'Competition Between Legal Orders—A New Paradigm of EC Law?' (1992) 29 *CMLRev* 861.

[87] Note that in *Opinion 1/94* (re World Trade Organisation Agreements) [1994]ECR I-5267, at para 95, the Court held that exclusive external competence would arise where Community legislation expressly confers upon Community institutions the power to negotiate with third countries.

[88] *Opinion 1/94* (re World Trade Organisation Agreements) [1994]ECR I-5267, at para 55.

Exclusivity was, of course, the central point at issue in the legal debate over the conclusion of the WTO Agreements, and the Court famously concluded that not only were aspects of the GATS and TRIPS Agreements outside the (exclusive) CCP, but that the implied power to conclude them, based on other Treaty provisions, was not exclusive to the Community but was shared with the Member States. The amendment to Article 133 agreed in the Treaty of Amsterdam, which envisaged the possible extension of the CCP to cover international agreements relating to services and IP, left open the question as to whether, were this option to be exercised, exclusivity would follow.[89] The Treaty of Nice, in amending Article 133, for the first time clearly separates the CCP from the doctrine of exclusivity. The new CCP fields will be subject to varying types of shared competence. These differences are themselves interesting.

We have first a distinction between different types of Community instrument. The new CCP provisions only cover the negotiation and conclusion of agreements; autonomous measures have not been affected and will continue to fall under the respective internal Treaty provisions, even where trade with third countries is involved. The Banking Directive considered above, for example, is based on Article 47(2) EC, and would continue to be so, in spite of the inclusion of provisions on third country banks. This reflects the desire for a simplified legal base and clear negotiating procedure for international agreements, particularly in the services sector. As a result, however, exclusivity will operate differently in respect of international agreements and autonomous measures.

Then we have the category of services and IP agreements that were held to be covered by the traditional CCP in *Opinion 1/94*. These include agreements concerning cross-border ('mode 1') services and agreements concerning aspects of IP that affect trade in goods directly, such as measures at border crossing points intended to enforce intellectual property rights.[90] As part of the original CCP, the implication is that exclusivity applies to them in the same way as it does to agreements on trade in goods. This position is preserved, albeit rather clumsily, by the new Article 133(5) which applies to 'agreements in the fields of trade in services and the commercial aspects of intellectual property, insofar as those agreements are not covered by the said paragraphs [1 to 4]'.

This brings us to the question of the scope of 'trade in services' and 'the commercial aspects of intellectual property', which are to be brought under the CCP regime. The term 'commercial aspects of intellectual property' is not defined; it must cover at least those aspects included in the TRIPS Agreement, and other aspects of IP may be included in the paragraph 1 to 4 regime by future unanimous decision of the Council.[91] The concept of services presents a particular problem: the term 'services', as it is used elsewhere within the EC Treaty, has a specific meaning; it is regarded as a residual concept, one which applies

---

[89] See further M. Cremona, above note 3.
[90] *Opinion 1/94* (re World Trade Organisation Agreements) [1994] ECR I-5267, at para 55.
[91] Article 133(7) EC, as amended by the Treaty of Nice.

insofar as the activities (normally provided for remuneration) are not covered by the other Treaty freedoms (goods, capital and persons).[92] More specifically, within EC internal market law, services are distinguished from establishment, largely on the basis of the inherently temporary nature of the provision of services.[93] Within world trade law, on the other hand, services is a broader concept, encompassing aspects of establishment and indeed capital movements. Under Article I(2) of the GATS, four different modes of supply are identified: cross-border supply (with no movement of persons or commercial presence), supply within one State to a consumer from another State, the commercial presence of one State's service supplier in another State, and supply through the presence of a natural person of one State within another State. How should 'trade in services' in Article 133(5) EC be interpreted? Should it be defined by reference to the meaning of services elsewhere in the same Treaty? This would be the obvious solution, in terms of normal drafting practice, but for a number of reasons is probably not what was intended by the drafters of this provision. We have already seen that, according to the Court of Justice, 'mode 1' services are already covered by Article 133(1) and the wording of Article 133(5) preserves this position. Thus, the precedent set by the Court in *Opinion 1/94*, in adopting the GATS approach to services, has been followed by the Treaty drafters. As we have seen, Article 133(5) only applies to the negotiation and conclusion of international agreements: in this context it would be strange if the term were not used in the sense in which it is used internationally. Much of the point of the amendment would be lost if the new negotiating procedures and legal base were only available for those (limited) aspects of 'services' which fall within Article 50 of the EC Treaty. In addition the term 'trade in services' used in Article 133(5) reflects exactly the phrasing used in Article I of GATS, and could be distinguished from the 'freedom to provide services' and 'liberalization of services' used in Articles 49–55 EC.

If this reading is correct, the 'new CCP' will cover establishment as well as traditional services, and the commercial aspects of IP.[94] Under Article 133(5) these fields will come under the regime of paragraphs 1 to 4, but with significant inroads into the paragraph 4 provision for qualified majority voting.[95] In addition, exclusivity is ruled out. The last subparagraph of paragraph 5 states:

---

[92] Article 50 EC.

[93] See the discussion of the distinction in cases 205/84 *Commission v. Germany* (insurance services) [1986] ECR 3753; C-221/89 *Factortame No2* [1991] ECR I-3905; C-55/94 *Gebhard* [1995] ECR I-4165.

[94] The Treaty already contains a clear legal base in Article 57(2) EC for Community legislation on the movement of capital to and from third countries; it is however possible that Article 133(5) could be used for international agreements on trade in services which involved commitments relating to capital movements (such as direct investment or financial services).

[95] Under Article 133(5), the Council shall act unanimously when negotiating and concluding an agreement that includes provisions for which unanimity is required for the adoption of internal rules or where it relates to a field in which the Community has not yet exercised the powers conferred upon

This paragraph shall not affect the right of the Member States to maintain and conclude agreements with third countries or international organisations insofar as such agreements comply with Community law and other relevant international agreements.

Community competence is established, but this does not preclude the continuation of Member State competence in these fields. The wording is similar to that used in the context of development cooperation, for example.[96]

The fourth distinction covers a category of agreements on services where a specific form of shared competence is to continue. This is not a question of preserving a residual competence for Member States while granting the Community competence to negotiate alone. Rather, the Treaty insists on shared competence in the sense of the joint negotiation and conclusion of agreements by Community and Member States in certain areas:

> ... by way of derogation from the first subparagraph of paragraph 5, agreements relating to trade in cultural and audiovisual services, educational services, and social and human health services, shall fall within the shared competence of the Community and its Member States. Consequently, in addition to a Community decision taken in accordance with the relevant provisions of Article 300, the negotiation of such agreements shall require the common accord of the Member States. Agreements thus negotiated shall be concluded jointly by the Community and the Member States.

These (apart from social and audiovisual services) are areas where the internal Treaty provisions require the Community and Member States to 'foster cooperation' with third countries and international organisations, without granting express treaty-making powers.[97] The Treaty provisions on social policy and services generally (which include audiovisual services[98]) do not refer expressly to external action. The new provision therefore removes uncertainty as to treaty-making competence in these areas, but requires the joint conclusion of international agreements: the Community alone will not be able to conclude agreements in these sectors.

The picture that emerges, therefore, is inevitably more complex than before. Without entering into the debate about whether or not it has promoted clarity to complicate Article 133 competence in this way, the questions remain: to what

it by the Treaty by adopting internal rules. This provision reflects the position under Art. 300(2) EC, and the concern of the Court over decision-making procedures evidenced in *Opinion 1/94*.

[96] Article 181 EC.
[97] See Art.149(3) EC on education; Art.150(3) EC on vocational training; Art.151(3) EC on culture; Art.152(3) EC on public health. As Dashwood points out, however, it 'must surely be intended' that such cooperation may be pursued within the framework of international agreements; A. Dashwood, 'The attribution of external relations competence' in A. Dashwood and C. Hillion (eds.) *The General Law of EC External Relations* (London, Sweet & Maxwell 2000), 115 at 138.
[98] See, inter alia, case 52/79 *Debauve* [1980]ECR 33; case C-23/93 *TV10* v *Commissariat voor de Media* [1994] ECR I-4795.

extent will this change affect the development of external economic policy? And, how does it affect the principle of uniformity?

One answer to the first question is that it will change very little. The Member States have attempted, in their amendment to Article 133, to reflect the existing position as far as possible, while clarifying some points of competence. The extension of Article 133 does not entail the extension of QMV to cases where it did not exist before:

> ... the Council shall act unanimously when negotiating and concluding an agreement in [the fields of trade in services and the commercial aspects of intellectual property], where that agreement includes provisions for which unanimity is required for the adoption of internal rules or where it relates to a field in which the Community has not yet exercised the powers conferred upon it by this Treaty by adopting internal rules.

Nor are the amendments intended to extend the scope of the Community's powers by allowing the Community to conclude (under the CCP umbrella) agreements that it would not have been able to conclude before, under the implied powers doctrine, on the basis of internal competence:

> An agreement may not be concluded by the Council if it includes provisions which would go beyond the Community's internal powers, in particular by leading to harmonisation of the laws or regulations of the Member States in an area for which this Treaty rules out such harmonisation.[99]

Thus the new Article 133 cannot be used as a means to outflank explicit restrictions on the Community's attributed (internal) powers, again a result which conforms to the approach of the Court of Justice in *Opinion 1/94*.

But as far as exclusivity is concerned, the preservation of the *status quo* reflected in Article 133(5) and (6) has consequences for the future. Where external competence is implied, the scope of exclusive powers may change, as Community competence is exercised in new fields. In *Opinion 1/94* the Court held that exclusive implied powers in the field of services might arise, either where legislation gives a specific competence to negotiate with third countries (as for example under Articles 23 and 24 of the Banking Directive considered above), or where internal harmonisation is 'complete':

> The same [exclusive competence] applies, in any event, even in the absence of any express provision authorizing its institutions to negotiate with non-member countries, where the Community has achieved complete harmonisation of the rules governing access to a self-employed activity, because the common rules thus adopted could be affected within the meaning of the *AETR* judgement if the Member States retained freedom to negotiate with non-member countries. That is not the case in all service

---

[99] Article 133(6) subpara 1 (as amended by the Treaty of Nice); for example, an agreement which would entail harmonisation in the field of protection or improvement of human health: see Art.152(4)(c) EC.

sectors, however, as the Commission has itself acknowledged. It follows that competence to conclude GATS is shared between the Community and the Member States.[100]

The implication here is that the situation might change: either a new piece of secondary legislation would grant the Community (exclusive) competence to negotiate in a particular field, or the harmonisation may be 'completed'. The *AETR* principle[101] is essentially dynamic. In contrast, the new Article 133(5) will preserve Member State competence (to conclude agreements) whatever actions are taken at Community level, internally or externally.[102] The solution adopted is to require that Member State agreements 'comply with Community law and other relevant international agreements'.[103] Instead of an expansion of exclusive competence, then, we have the preservation of shared competence, together with a rule designed to avoid conflict.

This extension of the CCP will thus create a 'built-in' obstacle to full uniformity in external economic policy. If exclusivity is necessary to uniformity, then the indefinite preservation of non-exclusivity must, at least potentially, compromise uniformity. In practice, the change may be more apparent than real; as we have seen, even where legislation is adopted at Community level, minimum harmonisation techniques may leave scope for Member States to adopt external commitments which do not 'affect' the common rules. Compliance with Community law will require that the Member States do not endanger, by means of the unilateral exercise of their treaty-making competence, the unity of the single market. The existence of shared competence implies a constraint upon the exercise of national competence as far as is necessary to avoid undermining the Community interest.

The obligation to respect Community law found in the new Article 133(5) EC reflects the obligation articulated many years previously by the Court in *Kramer* and is based on Article 10 EC.[104] It is one aspect of what has become known as the duty of cooperation in cases of shared competence:

---

[100] *Opinion 1/94 (re WTO Agreements)* [1994]ECR I-5267, paras 96–98; see also paras 102–103 for similar reasoning in relation to TRIPS. For a fuller discussion of exclusivity in relation to implied powers, see M. Cremona, 'External Relations And External Competence: The Emergence Of An Integrated External Policy For The European Union' in P. Craig and G de Búrca (eds) *EU Law: An Evolutionary Perspective* (Oxford, Oxford University Press 1999).

[101] Case 22/70 *Commission* v. *Council (AETR)* [1971] ECR 263.

[102] In contrast, the addition of new express legal bases for external action in the TEU with respect to exchange rate policy, environmental policy and development cooperation was accompanied by a Declaration that these provisions 'do not affect the principles resulting from the judgement handed down by the Court of Justice in the *AETR* case' (Declaration 10 attached to the TEU).

[103] Relevant international agreements would include those to which the Community is a party and which bind the Member States by virtue of Article 300(7); this provision is intended to avoid a conflict of norms between Community agreements and Member State agreements, which might give rise to Community responsibility. The term 'comply with Community law' appeared as 'respect Community law' in earlier texts of the Nice Treaty.

[104] Joined cases 3, 4 and 6–76 *Cornelis Kramer and others* [1976] ECR 1279, at paras 42–43.

... where it is apparent that the subject-matter of an agreement or convention falls in part within the competence of the Community and in part within that of the Member States, it is essential to ensure close cooperation between the Member States and the Community institutions, both in the process of negotiation and conclusion and in the fulfillment of the commitments entered into. That obligation to cooperate flows from the requirement of unity in the international representation of the Community.[105]

Our conclusion thus far is that the acceptance of non-exclusive competence in the 'new CCP' is likely to reinforce the already-present tendency to move away from the insistence on uniformity which characterised the formation of the traditional CCP. However, if uniformity may be losing its position of centrality as a feature of external economic policy, we can see moving to centre stage the principle of unity. This principle emphasises the need to establish common positions with respect to external negotiations, the complementarity of Community and Member State activity, the avoidance of conflict, and the presentation of the Community and its Member States as a unified entity, a Single Market, in external policy. The flexibility implied by focusing on unity rather than uniformity is essential to the development of an external economic policy encompassing such diverse fields as industrial goods, banking, telecommunications and trademarks. In fact, uniformity (whether in the form of common rules or their interpretation) has never been an end in itself; it has been justified as necessary in order to protect the unity of the single market, seen in particular as a need to avoid the distortions of competition that would follow from a diversity of approaches to external trade. In other words, Community policy was designed to avoid national external trade regimes becoming an instrument of competition between the Member States. As the concept of external trade policy enlarges beyond the customs union to encompass the regulatory dimensions to market integration, and new forms of trade in services, the focus on uniformity also shifts. A shift of focus which also signifies a movement, away from an essentially defensive position as regards competition from outside the Community market, and towards an emphasis on the need to maximise opportunities in third country markets, through unilateral, bilateral and multilateral initiatives.[106]

THE PRINCIPLE OF LIBERALIZATION

This shift, or movement, carries implications for the second major principle we will discuss in this chapter: the principle of liberalization. Uniformity, seen as a defensive mechanism of the customs union, and the increasingly perceived need

---

[105] *Opinion 1/94 (re WTO Agreements)* [1994] ECR I-5267, at para 108.
[106] P. Van Dijck and G. Faber, 'The EU in the World Economy' in P. Van Dijck and G. Faber (eds.) *The External Economic Dimension of the European Union* (The Hague/London/Boston Kluwer Law International, 2000).

for unity in the promotion of the interests of the Community's single market, pose different challenges to the Community as it seeks to make good the stated aim of its founders to contribute to progressive liberalization of world trade. Liberalization, as an important objective of Community external—and internal—economic policy, also raises questions as to the relation between external economic policy and other Community (and Union) policies and the compatibility of their objectives. Trade policy, and external economic policy more generally, may be connected to—in particular—agricultural, competition, development, environmental and foreign policies, and these policy objectives will of course impact on liberalization as an element of trade policy.

In what follows we will examine these different aspects of liberalization. Our starting point has to be Article 131 EC:

> By establishing a customs union between themselves Member States aim to contribute, in the common interest, to the harmonious development of world trade, the progressive abolition of restrictions on international trade and the lowering of customs barriers.

This statement of objectives, written into the original Treaty of Rome, placed the new EEC and emergent common market in the context of the Member States' pre-existent commitment to trade liberalization within the framework of GATT 1947.[107] Unlike the obligation to create a common commercial policy based on uniform principles, the abolition of trade restrictions is expressed as an aim; a reflection of the fact that under GATT the lowering of trade barriers was to be accomplished through reciprocal and staged negotiations. The Community does not, in Article 131, promise to liberalize unilaterally; effectively, it undertakes to engage in constructive negotiation. The provision can also be seen as an expression of the expectation evidenced in Article XXIV GATT that the formation of regional free trade areas and customs unions would further the general GATT objective of an overall reduction in trade barriers. As such, it contains an implied undertaking to comply with the GATT conditions for the establishment of customs unions, including the requirement that 'duties and other regulations of commerce' applied by the customs union to third countries' imports 'shall not on the whole be higher or more restrictive' than the duties and regulations previously applicable in the constituent territories.[108] However, and crucially, it does not impose an obligation to mirror internal trade liberalization at the external level:

> the provisions of the Treaty on commercial policy do not , in Article 110 et seq.[now Article 131], lay down any obligation on the part of the Member States to extend to trade with third countries the binding principles governing the free movement of

---

[107] Joined cases 21 & 24/72 *International Fruit Company NV and others* v *Produktschap voor Groenten en Fruit* [1972] ECR 1219.
[108] Article XXIV:5(a) GATT 1994.

goods between Member States and in particular the prohibition of measures having an effect equivalent to quantitative restrictions.[109]

The fact that Article 131 is expressed in terms of 'aims' rather than absolute obligation, affects not only the Community's direct obligations towards third countries, but also the level of constraint imposed upon internal policy-making. It cannot, in other words, be used to override the exercise of executive discretion in the ongoing formulation of commercial policy. This point is best illustrated through two cases arising out of the process of formulating a common import policy out of disparate national policies.[110] As part of its establishment of a common policy towards imports of goods from third countries, the Council enacted a Regulation in 1994 dealing with imports from non-market economy countries.[111] Although, according to the Regulation's Preamble, 'the liberalization of imports, namely the absence of any quantitative restrictions, must . . . form the starting point for the Community rules', certain imports from these countries (not members of the WTO) were potentially subject to quotas, and quotas were imposed *inter alia* on toys from China. In the first case the UK, supported by Germany, objected to the quota for toys on the ground that it replaced national quotas with a Community-wide quota, thereby imposing new restrictions in respect of those Member States which had previously operated without quantitative restrictions in this trade (and at the time of its enactment Spain was the only Member State restricting imports of toys from China). In the second case, Spain objected to a subsequent increase in the quota intended to ease the transition to the common import system. Neither challenge was successful. The Court recognised the breadth of executive discretion in formulating the EU's commercial policy:

> . . . the Court has consistently held that the Community institutions enjoy a margin of discretion in their choice of the means needed to achieve the common commercial policy . . . In a situation of that kind, which involves an appraisal of complex economic situations, judicial review must be limited to verifying whether the relevant procedural rules have been complied with, whether the facts on which the contested choice is based have been accurately stated, and whether there has been a manifest error in the appraisal of those facts or a misuse of powers . . . [112]

---

[109] Case 51–75 *EMI Records Limited v CBS United Kingdom Limited* [1976] ECR 811, at para 17.

[110] Case C-150/94 *UK v Council* (import quotas for toys from China) [1998] ECR I-7235; Case C-284/94 *Spain v Council* (import quotas for toys from China) [1998] ECR I-7309. The pre-1994 national import quotas were enshrined in Community legislation: Council Regulation 1766/82/EEC on common rules for imports from the People's Republic of China OJ 1982 L 195, p. 21; Council Regulation 3420/83/EEC on import arrangements for products originating in State-trading countries not liberalised at Community level OJ 1983 L 346, p. 1.

[111] Council Regulation 519/94/EC of 7 March 1994 on common rules for imports from certain third countries, OJ 1994 L 67/89. Under the fourth recital in the preamble, 'in order to achieve greater uniformity in the rules for imports, it is necessary to eliminate the exceptions and derogations resulting from the remaining national commercial policy measures, and in particular the quantitative restrictions maintained by Member States under Regulation (EEC) No 3420/83.'

[112] Case C-150/94 *UK v Council (import quotas for toys from China)* [1998] ECR I-7235, at paras 53–54.

The UK, supported by Germany, sought to rely on the commitment to trade liberalization found in Article 131 EC. The Court replies that this provision establishes an objective rather than imposing a binding obligation:

> that provision [Article 131 EC] cannot be interpreted as prohibiting the Community from enacting any measure liable to affect trade with non-member countries . . . its objective of contributing to the progressive abolition of restrictions on international trade *cannot compel the institutions to liberalise imports from non-member countries* where to do so would be contrary to the interests of the Community.[113]

Consequently, even where the Community institutions themselves decide to make trade liberalization the basis of the EU's commercial policy, as in the case of this Regulation, this is an exercise of executive discretion which may be subject to exceptions and which does not have 'rule of law' status:

> although the introduction of the contested quotas constitutes an exception to the liberalization of imports which, according to the fifth recital in the preamble to the Regulation, must form the starting point for the Community rules, it should be noted that the abolition of all quantitative restrictions for imports from non-member countries *is not a rule of law which the Council is required in principle to observe*, but the result of a decision made by that institution in the exercise of its discretion.[114]

The reference to the Community interest in the *Chinese toys* case quoted above suggests that the aim of trade liberalization may have to give way in the face of competing Community policies. This indeed has been the result in the context of the common agricultural policy. In *Durbeck*, a German importer challenged the legality of a Commission Regulation suspending the release into free circulation of apples from Chile, a protective measure taken in the context of the common organisation of the market in fruit and vegetables. The applicant sought to rely, inter alia, on infringement of Article 131 (then Article 110) EC and the GATT. The underlying Regulation establishing the common market organisation stated that the Regulation 'shall be so applied that appropriate account is taken, at the same time, of the objectives set out in Articles 39 and 110 of the Treaty'.[115] According to the Court,

> That reference to the two Articles shows that the Regulation is intended to maintain a reasonable balance between the objectives of the common agricultural policy and the interests of world trade to which reference is made in Article 110.[116]

The Court goes on to say that maintaining this 'balance' precludes an interpretation of Article 131 which would over-ride other Community interests, in this case, those of the Community's domestic apple producers:

[113] Ibid., at para 67 (emphasis added).
[114] Ibid. at para 34 (emphasis added).
[115] Council Regulation 1035/72/EEC of 18 May 1972 OJ English Special Edition 1972 (II), p.437, Art.37. Article 39 (now Article 33) EC sets out the objectives of the common agricultural policy.
[116] Case 112/80 *Firma Anton Dürbeck v Hauptzollamt Frankfurt am Main-Flughafen* [1981] ECR 1095, at para 43.

Article 110 of the Treaty [now Article 131] . . . cannot be interpreted as prohibiting the Community from enacting, upon pain of committing an infringement of the Treaty, any measure liable to affect trade with non-member countries even where the adoption of such a measure is required, as in this case, by the risk of a serious disturbance which might endanger the objectives set out in Article 39 of the Treaty and where the measure is legally justified by the provisions of Community law.[117]

Trade policy may thus pursue objectives other than liberalization. We have here a classic expression of the use of trade policy to defend the interests of the internal market, and in particular its agricultural policy, at the expense of liberalization. Thus, although the Common Import Regulation makes the absence of any quantitative restrictions on imports the starting point of Community policy, it does not have the same over-riding and Treaty-based status as the removal of quantitative restrictions in internal Community trade. Not only, as we have seen, are public interest exceptions possible; the Regulation also envisages the possibility of safeguard measures in cases of serious injury, or threat of injury, to Community producers.[118] At this point it is worth recalling that we are here concerned with trade liberalization as an objective of the Community's commercial policy, independently of any externally-derived obligations. Of course, the extent to which other Community interests may be allowed to take precedence over free trade depends ultimately on an assessment of these obligations: the extent to which specific products are covered by GATT disciplines, whether the country of export is a WTO member, and the effect of any other bilateral obligation. Thus, the provisions on safeguard measures in the Import Regulation have been designed to comply with the WTO Agreement on Safeguards. The absence of GATT-based restraint in the cases of *Chinese toys* (China not being a WTO member) and apparent GATT-compliance in *Durbeck*[119] allow us to assess the internal constraints on Community policy, and their limits.

It is of interest that in the *Durbeck* scenario, Chile was singled out for the application of protective measures because the other relevant exporting countries (South Africa, Argentina, Australia and New Zealand) had entered into voluntary export restraint agreements (VERs), whereas a voluntary export quota could not be agreed with Chile. The extensive use until recently by the Community of VERs as an instrument of trade policy called into question not only the relationship between trade policy and trade liberalization but also that between trade policy and competition policy. The Commission would actively seek, on a state-to-state basis, undertakings to restrict exports, which—if in the form of agreements between private undertakings—would have been

---

[117] Ibid. at para 44.
[118] Regulation 3285/94/EC, OJ 1994 L 349/53; see also text above at note 36.
[119] Case 112/80 *Firma Anton Dürbeck* v *Hauptzollamt Frankfurt am Main-Flughafen* [1981] ECR 1095, at paras 45–46.

condemned under Article 81(1) EC.[120] The connection is recognised in Article 11 of the WTO Agreement on Safeguards, which prohibits VERs and requires WTO Members not to encourage or support the adoption by undertakings of non-governmental measures equivalent in effect to VERs. We can see this continuing tension in comparing price fixing agreements prohibited under Article 81(1) and price undertakings which still form an important part of the Community's anti-dumping regime.[121] The close links between EC competition policy and the creation of the single market are well known.[122] The tension between EC competition policy and trade policy illustrated here is a further indication that market integration does not have the same foundational status in the Community's external economic policy as it does for the internal market.

The need for the CCP to look beyond trade liberalization has been recognised since the Court considered the UNCTAD commodity agreements in 1978, rejecting the Council argument that the CCP was limited to measures whose aim was to influence the volume or flow of trade:

> Although it may be thought that at the time when the Treaty was drafted liberalization of trade was the dominant idea, the Treaty nevertheless does not form a barrier to the possibility of the Community's developing a commercial policy aiming at a regulation of the world market for certain products rather than at a mere liberalization of trade.[123]

The regulation of the world commodity market that was the objective of the UNCTAD agreements had development as well as market stabilization purposes. In both *Opinion 1/78* and later in the context of the GSP (the generalized system of preferences, applying preferential tariffs to imports of certain products from developing countries), the Court of Justice has accepted that trade instruments may be used for development purposes:

> The Community system of generalized preferences ... reflects a new concept of international trade relations in which development aims play a major role. ... The existence of a link with development problems does not cause a measure to be

---

[120] For an example of a Commission Decision finding an infringement of Art.81 (then Art.85) EC in the case of an agreement between Taiwanese exporters and French producers of preserved mushrooms, see Commission Decision 75/77/EEC of 8 January 1975 relating to a proceeding under Article 85 of the EEC Treaty (IV/27.039—preserved mushrooms) OJ 1975 L29/26. Although the Commission has frequently resorted to protective measures against imported preserved mushrooms, and was prepared to accept that a serious disturbance of the market might be threatened, in its view this did not justify the private undertakings in taking the initiative.

[121] Compare Commission Decision 74/634/EEC of 29 November 1974 relating to proceedings under Article 85 of the Treaty establishing the EEC (IV/27.095—Franco-Japanese ball-bearings agreement) OJ 1974 L 343/19 (informal agreement by Japanese ball-bearing manufacturers with French counterparts to raise prices found to be a breach of Art.85) with Council Regulation 1778/77/EEC OJ 1977 L196/1 (application of anti-dumping duty on ball-bearings originating in Japan).

[122] For a full discussion, see A. Albors-Llorens, 'Competition Policy and the Shaping of the Single Market', in this volume.

[123] *Opinion 1/78 (re International Agreement on Natural Rubber)* [1979] ECR 2871, at para 44.

excluded from the sphere of the common commercial policy as defined by the Treaty.[124]

Reciprocal trade preferences within bilateral agreements are also justified by the Community in development terms, as bringing the developmental benefits of open markets to the partner States, as well as to the Community. If development operates alongside liberalization (or rather, perhaps, if liberalization is seen as an instrument of development rather than an end in itself), then exceptions to a fully liberalized regime may be easier to justify; for example, the 'infant industry' clauses in recent free trade agreements,[125] or an 'asymmetric' timetable for liberalization. Other aspects of external economic policy may also have a development dimension; for example, the provisions on establishment, investment and competition policy in the agreements with the ACP countries or the emerging economies of the former Soviet Union.

At the time of the GSP case cited above, the EC Treaty did not contain specific provisions on development policy. Although the EC Treaty does now include specific provisions on development cooperation, which provide a legal basis for both autonomous measures and international agreements, these do not preclude the use of other treaty provisions, and especially CCP provisions, in furthering development policy. Indeed, the Treaty provides that the Community is to 'take account' of development policy objectives (as set out in Article 177 EC) in implementing its other policies which are 'likely to affect' developing countries.[126] The GSP Regulation continues to be based on Article 133 EC, and the Cooperation Agreement with India on Partnership and Development was concluded by the EC on the joint basis of Articles 133 and 181 EC.

Similarly, the addition of a specific legal basis for environmental policy has not excluded the use of commercial policy instruments to support environmental objectives. The Regulation on leg-hold traps of 1991, for example, was based on Articles 113 as well as 130s EC (now Articles 133 and 175 EC), as it concerns the import of pelts and other goods from third countries.[127] Whereas development objectives (as least as formulated by the Community) will, as we have seen, tend to support trade liberalization, this example illustrates that environmental policy may well lead to import restrictions.

Most recently of course, we have seen external economic policy used as an instrument for achieving common foreign and security policy (CFSP) objectives. In the imposition of economic sanctions, trade liberalization objectives give

---

[124] Case 45/86 *Commission v. Council* (Generalized tariff preferences) [1987] ECR 1493, at paras 18–20.

[125] For example, the Euro-Mediterranean Agreement with Tunisia OJ 1998 L 97/2, Art.14.

[126] Article 178 EC.

[127] Council Regulation 3254/91/EEC prohibiting the use of leg-hold traps in the Community and the introduction into the Community of pelts and manufactured goods of certain wild animal species originating in countries which catch them by means of leg-hold traps or trapping methods which do not meet international humane trapping standards, OJ 1991 L 308/1.

way before the political demands of wider external policy objectives. In the use of trade preferences as an incentive, liberalization operates within a policy of conditionality.[128] In both these cases a Community policy is being used in order to achieve objectives which are outside Community competence, albeit now within the scope of European Union policy and action. Before the TEU, the use of Community powers (in particular, what was then Article 113) to achieve objectives which were not only outside trade policy but also beyond Community competence was controversial.[129] Difficulties also arose where sanctions covered matters, in particular transport services, which arguably fell outside the scope of Article 113.[130] Since the TEU amendments, specific legal bases (now Articles 60 and 301 EC) have been available for the imposition of economic sanctions, under a procedure which requires a supporting common position or joint action under the TEU provisions on the CFSP. The existence of this specific provision does not, however, alter the fact that Community external economic policy is being used to support CFSP objectives, and as such the (commercial, or economic) objective of trade liberalization will be subservient to the political objectives pursued by the Union.

More could be said of each of these examples. For the purpose of this chapter, however, they serve to illustrate two fundamental points. First, within trade policy itself liberalization is a contingent objective, subject both to the progress of reciprocal negotiations internationally and to the 'Community interest' which may lie elsewhere (for example, the protection of domestic traders, or the desire to privilege certain trading partners by granting trade preferences). Second, the interaction between external economic policy and other Community and Union policies will impact on the priority given to trade liberalization, as well as the uses to which it is put.

---

[128] See for example Council Conclusions of 29 April 1997 on the Application of Conditionality with a view to developing a coherent EU strategy for relations with certain countries of southeast Europe. Bull. EU 4–1997, p. 132; see further M. Cremona, 'Creating the New Europe: The Stability Pact for South-Eastern Europe in the Context of EU-SEE Relations' *Cambridge Yearbook of European Legal Studies Volume II 1999* (Oxford, Hart Publishing 2000), p 463.

[129] The pre-TEU practice was for the Member States to agree the imposition of sanctions within European Political Cooperation, for the economic sanctions to be implemented via a Regulation adopted under (what was then) Article 113 EC; for an example, see Council Regulation 1432/92 prohibiting trade between the Community and Serbia and Montenegro OJ 1992 L151/4. Aspects of agreed sanctions falling outside exclusive Community competence, such as an arms embargo, or freezing of financial and other assets, were implemented by Member States individually.

[130] The advantage of Article 113 for the imposition of sanctions lay in its potentially fast procedure, requiring only a qualified majority vote by the Council, and no formal involvement of the European Parliament. As a result, the sanctions against Iraq, for example, including measures on transport services, were adopted under Article 113 as a sole legal base: see Council Regulation 3155/90/EEC of 29 October 1990 extending and amending Regulation 2340/90/EEC preventing trade by the Community as regards Iraq and Kuwait OJ 1990 L304/1. This was not regarded by the Court, in *Opinion 1/94*, as a relevant precedent for the application of Article 113 to services generally. See further I. Macleod, K. Hendry and S. Hyett, *The External Relations of the European Communities* (Oxford, Clarendon Press, Oxford 1996), pp 352–366.

Let us take this a little further. As we have already seen, the principle of liberalization articulated as a general principle of Community external trade policy in its Common Import and Export Regulations,[131] is subject to the imposition of restrictive measures by Member States on public interest grounds.[132] This exercise of Member State discretion is subject to the application of the justificatory principles developed by the Court of Justice in the context of Article 30 EC.[133] In *Leifer*, the Court said that to interpret the elements of the public interest exception more restrictively in the context of the Export Regulation than in the context of Article 30 and intra-Community trade 'would be tantamount to authorizing the Member States to restrict the movement of goods within the internal market more than movement between themselves and non-member countries'.[134] The same logic would suggest that Member States should also be able to rely on mandatory requirements (such as environmental protection) in order to justify restrictions that would otherwise be contrary to the Import or Export Regulations. As within the Internal Market, then, the Member States have a certain margin of manoeuvre, or a degree of regulatory autonomy, subject to the need to justify their unilateral measures. However, we need to be careful not to push this parallel too far. When considering Article 30 EC, the primary focus is essentially on whether a justified national restriction outweighs the interest of the Community in free trade and the single market. In the context of import (and export) policy, although the balance between regulatory restrictions and free trade is clearly relevant, the primary focus is rather on the balance of competence between the Community and the Member States and the impact this has on the unity of the market. Within the internal market, the regulatory autonomy of the Member States is limited both by the Treaty-based obligations of free movement and by secondary legislation which, while itself engaging in market regulation, does so with the primary aim of facilitating free movement.[135] Both in applying the Treaty rules, and in formulating secondary legislation, the balance between liberalization and regulation is reflected in a balance between home state and host state control.[136] Within the framework of external economic policy on the other

---

[131] Regulation 3285/94/EC, OJ 1994 L 349/53, Art 1(2); Regulation 2603/69/EEC OJ 1969 L324/25, Art.1.

[132] Regulation 3285/94/EC, OJ 1994 L 349/53, Art 24(2); Regulation 2603/69/EEC OJ 1969 L324/25, Art.11.

[133] Case C-70/94 *Fritz Werner Industrie-Ausrustungen GmbH* v. *Germany* [1995] ECR I-3189, and case C-83/94 *Criminal proceedings against Leifer, Krauskopf and Holzer* [1995] ECR I-3231, on the interpretation of Reg.2603/69, Art.11.

[134] Case C-83/94 *Criminal proceedings against Leifer, Krauskopf and Holzer*, above note 133, at para 26.

[135] Cases C-376/98 *Germany* v. *Council and European Parliament* and C-74/99 *The Queen* v. *Secretary of State for Health and Others, ex parte: Imperial Tobacco Ltd and Others* (tobacco advertising) [2000] ECR I-8419 at paras 95–105.

[136] C.f. S. Weatherill, 'Pre-Emption, Harmonisation and the Distribution of Competence to Regulate the Internal Market' in this volume.

hand, as we have seen, free trade may be a starting point but it does not possess the same fundamental status; the need to exercise control over national regulatory autonomy is more closely linked to the need for unity as a single market. The home state—host state balance does not translate easily into the external sphere, where rather a balance between the Community's own liberalization and regulatory objectives must be found.

This being so, we may now have a clearer view of the relationship between external trade policy and other Community policies, especially those (such as environmental, public health, competition and agricultural policies) which have a strong regulatory dimension. The traditional internal market rationale for regulatory intervention at Community level, based on the need to remove market barriers and distortions created by a multiplicity of national rules, does not operate in the same way in the case of external trade. From the point of view of the unity of the single market, what is important is that the rules that are applied to imports do not impede free movement *internally*; their effect on free trade externally is of secondary importance. Hence the tensions (in the international trade context) caused by, for example, the introduction of the Community's regime for the banana market, or the leg-hold trap Regulation. The challenge for the unified Community market, and the Community's own external economic policy, is in presenting and justifying to its trading partners its own regulatory policy choices, whether these are development-based preferences or environmental or public health priorities.[137] The additional element, which we are not specifically addressing here, is that this process is carried out against a background, not only of existing bilateral and regional treaty obligations, but also in the context of a developing world trading system which is itself exploring methods for reconciling these potentially conflicting goals.

The discussion so far has centred on trade policy, and in particular the existing CCP under Articles 131–133 EC. We should now briefly turn to other aspects of external economic policy in order to assess the extent to which these conclusions may be applied more widely.

The Treaty provisions on capital movements contain a full set of provisions on movements of capital between the EC and third countries. Unlike the movement of goods, the liberalization of capital movements between the Member States and third countries is stated as a fundamental objective (albeit subject to certain defined exceptions); more than this, it is treated alongside 'internal' liberalization, as part of the same process: '. . . all restrictions on the movement of capital between Member States and between Member States and third countries

---

[137] I do not here wish to imply that liberalization and regulation are inevitably opposed; the EC experience is evidence enough that (re)regulation is often a mechanism for liberalization. Rather, that as the tobacco advertising case shows, a tension may exist between liberalization and other regulatory objectives, and that a regulatory measure adopted primarily for the purpose of liberalization may display different policy choices from a regulation with an alternative primary purpose (public health or environmental protection, for example).

shall be prohibited.'[138] Against the background of this general prohibition of restrictions, the Council may adopt safeguard measures where capital movements to and from third countries cause or threaten to cause 'serious difficulties' for the operation of EMU.[139] In addition, certain restrictions on the movement of capital to and from third countries in existence on 31 December 1993 may be maintained.[140] The Council may legislate in this area with the 'objective of free movement of capital between Member States and third countries to the greatest extent possible', and these measures may involve direct investment, establishment, the provision of financial services and the admission of securities to capital markets.[141] The provision for decision by unanimity in cases where the measure in question constitutes a 'step back' as regards liberalization of capital movements, emphasises the underlying principle of liberalization. Competence to legislate on external policy with respect to capital thus clearly lies with the Community institutions. Although Member States are entitled to maintain some existing restrictions (and have not therefore lost all competence in this field) new restrictions and removal of existing restrictions must be determined by the Council.[142] Agreements on monetary or foreign exchange regime matters with third countries or international organisations may be negotiated by the Community; as the Community does not have formal status within some of the international financial organisations, arrangements for the negotiation and conclusion of these agreements are to be determined ad hoc by the Council, in such a way as to 'ensure that the Community expresses a single position'.[143]

From this it will be clear that the Treaty provisions on capital provide at least a partial basis for the liberalization of external trade in services of the type included within the revised Article 133(5) EC. Indeed, Articles 56–59 EC were included among a number of legal bases for the Council decision approving the adoption of the GATS Fifth Protocol on financial services.[144] The very close links between capital movements, establishment and services,[145] especially but

---

[138] Article 56(1) EC; an identical provision in Article 56(2) refers to restrictions on payments.

[139] Article 59 EC. The Council is to act after consulting the European Central Bank (ECB), and measures must be 'strictly necessary' and may not be maintained for more than six months.

[140] Articles 56 and 57(1) EC; these permitted restrictions are those involving direct investment, including real estate, establishment, the provision of financial services and the admission of securities to capital markets.

[141] Article 57(2) EC.

[142] Subject to Member States' continued ability to take measures justified on grounds *inter alia* of public policy, public security, prudential supervision of financial institutions and national tax laws: Article 58 EC.

[143] Article 111(3) EC.

[144] Council Decision 1999/61/EC of 14 December 1998 concerning the conclusion on behalf of the European Community, as regards matters within its competence, of the results of the World Trade Organisation negotiations on financial services OJ 1999 L20/38.

[145] It will be recalled that, within the internal market, 'the liberalization of banking and insurance services connected with movements of capital shall be effected in step with the liberalization of capital': Article 51(2) EC.

not only in the financial services sector, suggest that the commitment to liberalization found in respect of capital will be extended to services more broadly. This is supported by the Treaty of Nice amendment: although Article 133(5) only refers to the application of paragraphs 1–4 of that Article, the inclusion of trade in services within Article 133 EC implies at least the influence of the aims set out in Article 131.

In fact, access to the Community market *per se* has not been of primary concern in relation to services. The EC has been concerned rather with the ability to assert regulatory control over third country service suppliers, with establishing a regulatory regime to underpin internal market liberalization, and with securing adequate market access for its own suppliers on third country markets. Thus, to revert to our earlier sectoral example, financial services legislation imposes the same authorization conditions, including the principle of 'home country control', on subsidiaries owned by third country undertakings, while including reciprocity clauses designed to ensure market access for Community undertakings.[146] The market is thus in principle open, but subject to an element of conditionality. Liberalization—offering access to the Community market—is seen as instrumental in furthering Community interests on third country markets, a process we have already identified in connection with the unity of Community external policy.[147] Reciprocal liberalization of financial services is also—the Community argues—beneficial for economic development in promoting regulatory maturity and encouraging capital flows.[148] In the broader services context, the EC position in relation to GATS negotiations emphasises the interrelation between liberalisation and regulation: 'the need for regulatory disciplines to underpin market access and national treatment commitments appears increasingly important, and also includes the question of pro-competitive principles.'[149]

What conclusions can we draw from this discussion of the role of liberalization as a principle of EC external economic policy? First, we have identified the contingent nature of liberalization as an objective of trade policy. Second, we have examined trade liberalization as it is affected by the interaction between external economic policy and other Community and Union policies; in particular we can see that the relationship between liberalization—or market integration—and regulatory policy that has emerged in the course of building of the internal market operates differently as the Community's single market seeks to promote more liberal trade while furthering its own policy priorities in the wider global community. Third, we can conclude that liberalization is an objective, not just of trade policy within the traditional scope of the CCP, but

---

[146] Consolidated Banking Directive OJ 2000 L 126/1, Article 23; see further note 79 above.
[147] See text at note 85 above.
[148] See for example the Proposal from the EC and its Member States on GATS 2000: Financial Services, December 2000.
[149] European Commission, 'The EC Approach to Services', March 2001.

is to be found underpinning other elements of external economic policy, including capital movements and services; an objective likely to reinforced by the Treaty of Nice amendments to Article 133. Finally, we return to the increased emphasis on the promotion of Community interests on external markets, and in external fora. In the context of reciprocity, liberalization is an important mechanism for achieving this objective, particularly in the 'new CCP', accompanied by developing attention to the external dimension of Community regulatory policies.

FROM CUSTOMS UNION TO SINGLE MARKET

We cannot expect the two first principles of the CCP, the principles of uniformity and of liberalization, to apply automatically or easily to the other dimensions of the Single Market. They grew out of the needs of the customs union, and its place within the GATT-based regime of world trade liberalization. In this chapter we have seen that even within the traditional CCP, neither of these principles is absolute. There are many gaps to uniformity, and a degree of flexibility emerging which reflects the flexibility of the internal market project itself. Liberalization has never been a 'rule of law', trumping other policy objectives, and 'the Community interest' is given precedence. Within the broader context of external economic policy, uniformity and liberalization are likewise present, but not as over-riding principles, and the Community interest has to be formulated in the light of the growing range and scope of other Community and Union policies. In particular, the entrenchment of non-exclusive competence in relation to services and IP will require a re-thinking of what uniform principles might mean. Unity of purpose, implying consistency and cooperation, may be more important than formally uniform rules.

   This shift reflects another development, which is harder to conceptualize. In the Community's early years as the customs union was being established, and also at the time of the 1992 programme for the completion of the internal market, the emphasis of external policy was on the needs of the common, and then the internal, market: the nature of external rules was determined by the need to achieve the removal of *internal* barriers to trade. The result was what we might call an instrumentalist view of the common commercial policy exemplified by the quotation from *Massey-Ferguson* cited at page 355. Its purposes (and therefore the justification for the interpretation of its provisions) were tied to the purposes of the customs union and the internal market. The result was also a policy which emphasised the need to protect that market: common rules on trade protection, on anti-dumping, on import restrictions and quotas, on product safety, on technical standards. In this sense external economic policy could almost be seen as one aspect of internal policy.

So what has changed? Gradually the Community is assuming an active role as a Single Market. Its concern is as much with export markets as with imports.[150] It is developing a sense of its autonomy, which derives from its identity as a Single Market, and which enables it to play a part in developing trade (and wider) policies at a global level. The major role played by the EC within the WTO is one part of this. The principles which govern its external economic policy need to reflect this: reciprocity, for example, becomes important, as does conditionality, and the trade and environment interface. Other examples could be added: the shift of emphasis, for example, in the international dimension of the Community's competition policy from a jurisdictional doctrine based on the effects of anticompetitive acts on the Community market,[151] to the current stance in favour of a multilateral agreement on competition which would, inter alia, promote fair competitive conditions on external markets.[152] The concept of defence of the Community interest is still very much present; what has expanded is the sense of what that interest might entail. The needs of the internal market (though still there) are no longer the only real source of policy making.

One effect of this development can be seen in the way in which external trade policy is used, as we have seen, in order to achieve non-trade, and even non-economic, objectives. The Union's foreign and security policy uses the whole of the Community's external policy as a source of potential instruments, including the CCP and external economic policy more generally. In one sense this has always been true. But as other policies become more defined and more active, the effect is greater. Just as we can no longer look only at the traditional CCP of trade in goods, but need to expand our concept of external economic policy, so it is no longer possible to see that policy in isolation from other Community, and Union, objectives. If the Community is to project its international identity, further its own priorities, and contribute effectively to the debates surrounding trade and regulatory policy, it needs to formulate external policies which do not solely reflect its own domestic interests, nor which merely project onto a larger stage its own experience of market integration, but which are based on a coherent and outward-looking view of the Single Market. In this sense the foundational principles underlying the Single Market, examined in the other chapters of this volume, are critical to the maturing of the Community as an international actor.

---

[150] P.Van Dijk and G.Faber, 'The EU in the World Economy: New Policies and Partnerships' in P.Van Dijk and G.Faber (eds) *The External Economic Dimension of the European Union* (The Hague, London, Boston Kluwer Law International 2000).
[151] Joined cases 89, 104, 114, 116, 117 and 125 to 129/85 A. *Ahlström Osakeyhtiö and others* v *Commission* [1988] ECR 5193.
[152] Commission Communication of 17 June 1996, 'Towards an International Framework of Competition Rules', COM(96) 284; see further, M. Cremona, 'Multilateral and Bilateral Approaches to the Internationalization of Competition Law: An EU Perspective' in M. Cremona, I. Fletcher and L. Mistelis (eds.) *Foundations and Perspectives of International Trade Law* (London, Sweet & Maxwell 2001).

Index